FREDERICK JACKSON TURNER

Frederick Jackson Turner in 1910, when he was president of the American Historical Association.

Frederick Jackson Turner

HISTORIAN, SCHOLAR, TEACHER

Ray Allen Billington

NEW YORK   OXFORD UNIVERSITY PRESS
1973

PREFACE

HOW DOES ONE write a biography of such a man as Frederick Jackson Turner? I debated that question a good many times during the half-dozen years that this book has been under way. Turner is known today (to the few who know him at all) as the proponent of two historical concepts that have altered our understanding of the nation's past —the frontier and sectional interpretations. Should a biographer attempt an intellectual portrait, focusing on those two theories and ignoring the irrelevant details of Turner's career? Should he settle for a scintillating little essay of 150 pages describing the genesis, history, and significance of those two hypotheses? If not, how could he justify the pages needed to detail the everyday life and modest accomplishments of a very ordinary college teacher who lived a very commonplace existence? Who today could possibly be interested in the thoughts and aspirations of a man who was scarcely known to all but a handful of his countrymen during his lifetime, who made no dramatic impact on his turn-of-the-century generation, and who has been forgotten by all but American historians today?

Those were the questions I asked myself without finding a satisfactory answer. Satisfactory to myself, that is, for I *wanted* to tell *all* about Frederick Jackson Turner. By this time I had fallen under his spell, as must anyone who reads his letters, and nothing would do but a full-length portrait of the man and his ideas. But how to justify such an extravagance with words? I posed that problem a year or so ago at a session on biography staged by the Southern California Chapter of the

American Studies Association. Professor Leon Howard of the English Department of the University of California at Los Angeles was on his feet with the answer. "Why not," he suggested, "write a biography of a college professor. We have had biographies of statesmen and politicians and athletes and rogues and preachers. Why not, just once, a realistic life of a classroom teacher?"

This, then, is the biography of a college professor. Frederick Jackson Turner was not a typical professor; he did have two original ideas, which is two more than most. Yet his way of life, his ambitions, his hopes and frustrations, were those of the thousands of teachers who labored in the classrooms of his day, and of today. His dream, and the dream of most of his descendants in modern universities, was to broaden man's knowledge by dedicated research and publication. Turner did shed light on America's past with his bold generalizations concerning frontier and section, but these were only fragments of the historical edifice that he wanted to erect. He, and his contemporaries and successors, found instead that their lot was one of repeated interruptions, frustrating demands upon their time, and a disheartening failure to reap the harvest that they expected to nourish the intellects of those about them.

The college professor must be understood not as an ivory-towered recluse, spinning out his fine threads of learning in splendid isolation from the mundane world of affairs, but as a hard-working citizen responding constantly to the demands of the community. Turner was such a man. Hours, days, years of his time went into the trivia of university administration—department meetings, faculty meetings, committee meetings, meetings of every sort that could be devised to torment their victims. More time was dedicated to his students, with an endless routine of classroom preparation, teaching, conferences, thesis and bluebook reading. Like most professors, he succumbed too often to the pressure of town on gown, speaking to women's clubs, service clubs, church clubs, teachers' clubs—all manner of clubs that acted on the theory that the college teacher had nothing better to do than address their membership—without fee. Like most, too, Turner could not resist trying to improve the world, and he occupied himself for months on end battling alumni who sought to professionalize university football or insurgents who fought to wrest control of the American Historical

Association from the Establishment. He, with the rest of his breed, found life a constant battle of the bills as he strove to finance the high standard of living expected of professors with the low salaries that all were paid, at the same time preferring to broaden knowledge with learned articles for non-paying professional journals rather than succumbing to the blandishments of textbook publishers who promised him affluence and a comfortable old age. Frederick Jackson Turner may have been more imaginative than most professors, but his life serves as a case study for the entire profession.

That is the story that I have tried to tell in this book. Too often, perhaps, I have strayed far from the intellectual contributions for which he is justly known to describe his manifold activities as a good citizen and better teacher. My theme, if I have one, is that Turner's desperate desire to write—to popularize the historical concepts and fresh interpretations that crowded his mind—was frustrated by the pressures that have afflicted the academic world from time immemorial, and that afflict it today. When I have discussed his intellectual contributions I have done so in terms of his letters and unpublished essays, acting on the theory that his published works are either well known or readily available.

My effort to depict the many-sided Frederick Jackson Turner accounts for several unorthodox features of this book. Most biographers skip hurriedly over their subject's formative years, to concentrate on his later and more productive life; I have reversed this formula and paid perhaps undue attention to his background in rural Wisconsin, his education at the University of Wisconsin and the Johns Hopkins University, and his baptism into teaching. This has been a deliberate choice, for those formative years not only equipped Turner for his professorial career but were a principal influence in shaping the historical concepts that revolutionized the study of our past. I have also devoted a good deal of space to the routine events of his adult life—the extracurricular concerns that monopolized so much of his time—his passion for fishing and wilderness vacations; his love of "Darling Little Mae" and Dorothy, his lovely daughter; his political beliefs and activities; his devotion to reading and music; his uncanny ability to devise time-wasting pleasures rather than buckle down to the books that he wanted to write. Insignificant aspects in the life of a man whose sole contributions were intellectual, perhaps, but important if we are to understand the whole man, and that has been my purpose.

Turner's magnetic charm, inescapable even to those reading his letters, has made the writing of this book a pleasant task. That pleasure has been heightened by the many friends, associates, and librarians who have given me a helping hand along the way. Their help began more than a decade ago, when the Huntington Library, in January 1960, opened its vast collection of Frederick Jackson Turner papers to scholarly use. I was there, on leave from my teaching post at Northwestern University; so was Professor Wilbur R. Jacobs of the University of California at Santa Barbara, and so was Miss Norma B. Cuthbert, the skilled manuscripts cataloguer on the Library's staff. What thrilling months lay ahead as we read those thousands of pages of letters and unpublished speeches and essays, calling for help now and then with an undecipherable phrase, summoning the others to glory over a particularly important find. My purpose then was to learn something of Turner's views on his frontier thesis for a volume that appeared in 1966 as *America's Frontier Heritage*, but before we finished our labors that fall I was Turner's slave. I had to attempt his biography, even though others were far better equipped for the task.

Other commitments to publishers had to be satisfied first, but when in 1963 the Huntington Library's able director, Dr. John E. Pomfret, offered me a permanent post on the staff as Senior Research Associate I leaped at the opportunity to be closer to sources that would be more and more used in the future. Since that time I have had the joyful experience of almost total immersion in the Frederick Jackson Turner papers; I have also been blessed with release from teaching and academic obligations, and all my time has been free for research and writing. That happy combination has made the Huntington Library an academic heaven, a Valhalla of scholarship beyond compare. So I am particularly grateful to Dr. Pomfret and the Library's trustees for inviting me into paradise, and to Miss Norma B. Cuthbert and her capable successors as custodians of the Turner collections for easing the problems that inevitably arise in using any voluminous assemblage of manuscripts such as those left by a prolific writer. My gratitude extends to Dr. James Thorpe, Dr. Pomfret's successor as Director of the Huntington Library, whose warm friendship and generous aid have brightened my life during his tenure, and to the very capable staff who can now be counted among my most treasured friends.

Their reward should have been release from the barrage of questions that they have answered so cheerfully, now that this book is completed, but I must inflict still more upon them. The first draft of my manuscript, running to some 2000 pages and with from 300 to 400 footnotes to the chapter, has been deposited in the Library for the benefit of those seeking more detailed information than provided by the scant documentation on the pages that follow. I am sure that the Huntington's staff will answer questions concerning this compendium of information about Frederick Jackson Turner as capably as they have my own.

Indispensable as are the Huntington Library's Turner collections, I have traveled a good many miles to supplement them from other depositories. In the many libraries that I have visited—libraries identified in the bibliography of this book—I have been universally welcomed warmly and treated admirably by thoroughly helpful librarians. A few whose aid went well beyond the call of duty deserve special mention. Dr. J. E. Boell, Director of the Archives of the University of Wisconsin, not only guided me through the complexities of the rich collection that he administers, but on my several visits favored me with a desk amidst his treasures where I could sample and copy with a minimum of wasted effort. Miss Josephine L. Harper, Curator of Manuscripts at the State Historical Society of Wisconsin, allowed me equal freedom with the fine collections over which she presides so efficiently. Since my over-long visits to their institutions, both Miss Harper and Dr. Boell have responded cheerfully to my many letters of inquiry—letters usually necessitated by my own deficiencies as note taker. Dr. Clifford K. Shipton, former Custodian, and Mr. Kimball C. Elkins, Senior Assistant, at the Harvard University Archives, gave invaluable aid during a summer spent in research on the papers of the Harvard Commission on Western History, and during subsequent visits called my attention to important materials that might otherwise have eluded me. Dr. L. W. Towner and his capable assistants made the hours that I spent at Chicago's Newberry Library, where much of the preliminary work on this volume was done, as delightful as they were profitable. Shorter periods in the Manuscripts Division of the Library of Congress, the Firestone Library of Princeton University, the Clements Library of the University of Michigan, the Bancroft Library of the University of California at Berkeley, and the Beinecke Library of Yale University were rendered pleasant by the cheerful cooperation of the staffs of those fine institutions.

To all I am grateful; without their help this book could not have been written. Nor would my acknowledgments be complete without particular tribute to one fellow historian who has helped shape my life and thought more than he will ever know. Merle Curti, Frederick Jackson Turner Emeritus Professor of the University of Wisconsin, has been a treasured friend for more decades than either of us cares to remember. During those years he has heightened my enthusiasm for historical studies by his faith in the significance of the past, buoyed my ambition by the energy with which he has pursued his own studies, broadened my vistas by the breadth of his own vision, and provided encouragement and wise counsel by his generous appraisals of much that I have written. More than any man I know Merle Curti personifies the passionate belief in the usefulness of history, the breadth of interdisciplinary imagination, and the freshness of vision that made his teacher, Frederick Jackson Turner, worthy of his mantle among the nation's greatest historians. To him I gratefully dedicate this book.

San Marino, Calif.   R.A.B.
October 1972

CONTENTS

TO MERLE CURTI

whose scholarly attainments and breadth
of historical vision do honor to his teacher,
Frederick Jackson Turner, this book is
gratefully dedicated.

FREDERICK JACKSON TURNER

I

From Boyhood to Manhood

1861-1884

D URING his waning years, Frederick Jackson Turner wasted a
sizable amount of time poring over genealogical tables and drawing charts of his family tree—not because he had succumbed to the cult
of ancestor worship, but because he had found that his forebears had
been pioneers, who had shifted westward with the frontier, founding
new towns as they did so. This was an exciting discovery to the high
priest of the "frontier school," that group of historians which by the
1920s dominated the interpretation of American history. Heredity was
less important than environment in Turner's explanation of the nation's
past—he spent his life proving that the unique physical and social conditions in pioneer communities helped shape the character and institutions of the people—but he recognized that hereditary factors played
their role and must not be neglected. Particularly when the ancestors
proved to be as colorful a lot as his own.

They were, Turner found to his satisfaction, Puritan to the core.
Humphrey Turner, first of the line to reach America, migrated from
England to Massachusetts in 1634, and settled in Scituate. There he
lived out his life, as did his son after him, but his grandson John Turner
succumbed to the lure of westering and moved on to Guilford, Connecticut. There the Turners tarried for two generations. Then Samuel
Turner, born in 1721, took to the road, first to Salisbury, Connecticut,
then more northward, still with the New England frontier, to Tin-
mouth, Vermont. There Samuel prospered, siring six children and adding to the family glory by serving under General Washington at the

Battle of White Plains. The third of his children, Abel Turner, succumbed to the West's magnetism and, with his ten offspring, migrated
to Schuyler Falls, in upstate New York. The eighth-born of that
numerous brood, also named Abel Turner, was Frederick Jackson
Turner's grandfather. The young Abel Turner fought at Plattsburg in
the War of 1812. After the war he returned to Schuyler Falls, and in
1818 he married. Abel and his wife had twelve children. One of these,
born on September 24, 1832, was named Andrew Jackson Turner, in
honor of the President elected that year. Thus did Turner's father
come into the world.[1]

Jack Turner, as he chose to be called, was reared in a pioneer community where hard work rather than formal education was the way of
life. He learned to fell trees and handle a plow; he later remembered
how his arms ached and his fingers bled. Only on rainy days was he
happy, for then he could escape to the shop of a printer who let him set
type and operate the tiny press. Thus Jack Turner equipped himself for
his life's work. He also gave himself opportunity to escape farm drudg-
ery: itinerant printers could always pick up a job in those days and
were free to wander where they chose. Jack did wander, first to western Michigan and then to Wisconsin. He arrived at the hamlet of Portage in September 1858 with only ten cents in his pocket. There he spent
the winter, setting type on the weekly *Portage Independent.*

Of his several journeys—to Madison and other nearby communities—
the most important was to Friendship, in Adams County, a spanking
new town built in New England style by a group of speculators under
"Squire" Samuel Hanford. There Jack Turner first saw the Squire's
daughter, Mary Olivia Hanford, a petite beauty with rich auburn hair
who served as the local schoolmarm. "I'm going to marry that red-
headed girl," he told a friend, and he did, although it took two years to
persuade her. In the spring of 1860 they settled into a modest home in
Portage where he divided his time between setting type for the *Portage
Record* and serving as clerk of the circuit court. Mary Hanford was to
remain at her husband's side until his death in 1905.[2]

Mary's ancestry was as deeply rooted in Puritan New England as her
husband's was. The first of her forebears to reach America, the Reverend Thomas Hanford, arrived in 1642. He settled in the frontier community of Norwalk, Connecticut, where he served as pastor for forty
years—despite near-dismissal when faulty false teeth led his congrega-

tion to believe he had called them "Injun devils" instead of "individuals." The Hanfords were as infected with wanderlust as the Turners; over the next years Thomas Hanford's descendants shifted westward with each generation, through the Delaware Water Gap, first to Delaware County in New York, then on to found the village of Friendship in the northern reaches of the colony. They also, like the Turners, fought the Indians in King Philip's War and the British in the Revolution. And, like the Turners, they sired numerous descendants, including Mary Hanford, who was born at Walton, New York, on April 27, 1838. This was the young lady who with her parents came to Friendship, Wisconsin, where twenty years later she met and married Andrew Jackson Turner. Frederick Jackson Turner, their first child, was born on November 14, 1861.

When, in his later years, Turner speculated on the influences that inclined him toward the study of the frontier, he gave considerable weight to the preachers and pioneers among his ancestors. "Is it strange," he once asked, "that I preached of the frontier?" Perhaps not, but in his franker moments he freely confessed that he knew nothing of his forebears until long after his historial interpretations were commonly accepted. Turner also believed that his New England and New York background made him less provincial, and inclined to a "more dominantly American view."[3] Again, he may have been right, yet during frontier days the most provincial provincials were the products of decades of migration. Proud though he may have been of his heritage, Turner's views owed more to the environment in which he was reared than to remote family connections.

Young Fred was born in November 1861, at a time when the village of Portage was just emerging from its pioneer past and was richer in history and prospects than in achievement. Near the settlement, the crumbling ruins of old Fort Winnebago, built in 1828 to guard the portage between the Fox and Wisconsin rivers that gave the town its name, recalled the not-too-distant day when Marquette and Jolliet passed on their way to the Mississippi and French *voyageurs* sang as they carried packs of Indian trading goods across the two-mile passageway. This meant little to Fred at the time; he testified later that instruction in history was so sparse in the Portage schools that he did not hear of Marquette and Jolliet until many years later. Far more impressive to the lad was the beauty of Columbia County's countryside—rolling hills where forest and prairie mingled and where tiny lakes and sparkling streams beckoned the angler. This was good country and it was filling rapidly; in the fifteen years before 1860 the county's population sky-rocketed from 1969 to 24,421.[4] Central Wisconsin was in its first boom period of pioneer growth.

So was Portage, where 2879 persons lived in 1860, two-thirds of them native-born, and one-third from abroad. All were newcomers; not until 1851 were the last Indian land cessions completed, and not until 1857 was a rail connection established with Milwaukee. Business flocked in then: a four-story flour mill, an iron works, a planing mill on Canal Street, a towering grain elevator near the LaCrosse and Milwaukee Railroad station, two breweries whose output challenged the capacity of the town's citizenry. Portage was a bustling frontier community, bursting with optimism and cockily confident of the future. Everywhere were signs of progress: a three-story court house of cream-colored brick, built in 1863; an ordinance banning hogs from the streets, adopted in 1864; six oil lamps set out in 1868 to illuminate the main thoroughfares.[5]

Andrew Jackson Turner, who was prospering with the times, believed in the town's future. So much so, indeed, that in April 1861 he purchased the small newspaper for which he worked, the *Portage Record*, combined it with a struggling rival, and emerged as principal editor of the weekly *Wisconsin State Register*, a lively journal that he continued to own and publish until 1878. In it, seven months later, he chronicled the birth of his first son: "He cannot talk—he has never been known to coo—his eyes do not work perfectly as a pair, but each on its own hook sometimes, so that we have caught him looking both ways at once in evident wonder and distraction. . . . He hasn't advanced far enough yet to discover that night is the time for sleep; (nurse thinks that is one of his worst failings)—and we lack the proof (and rest assured, my dear friends, we have vainly sought for it) that he could tell his father from 'any other man' to save his life."[6] Thus was Frederick Jackson Turner introduced to the little community where he was to grow to manhood.

And what a peaceful little hamlet it was. Fall was in the air that November day, with merchants urging sweet cider and choice apples on their customers; L. Funkenstein's emporium advertising winter clothing unequaled for "Fit, Cheapness, and Quality"; the local hardware store boasting "the largest and best assortment of STOVES ever brought to Wisconsin"; the partners Wood, Loomis, and Osborn promising shoppers dry goods "cheaper than can be bought west of New York"; A. A. Kenyon's Livery Stable was eager to show its assortment of harnesses, bridles, and whips, "and perhaps sell a few of them"; and the Portage Brewery urged the thirsty to taste its freshly brewed lager beer. Yet there was little peace beyond the borders of Portage. The first issue of the *Portage Record,* published by Jack Turner on April 17, 1861, described the outbreak of hostilities at Charleston, and by the time Fred Turner was born the Civil War was a grim reality. The *Register* was as uncompromisingly Republican as its owner, trumpeting each northern victory, glorifying John C. Frémont as its favorite hero, and urging "the complete *subjugation* of the rebels; there is no other possible *cure*."

Of all of this turmoil young Fred was happily unaware. He was a healthy baby, gaining weight so astoundingly that in the first ten weeks of his life he grew from eight to thirteen pounds, and even at that age he was able to shake a rattle and "play considerably." His not unprejudiced parents thought him a beautiful baby, with a nicely shaped head, round face, handsome mouth, and "bright blue eyes bright as 'sixpences.'" His lusty appetite for "vituals" persisted; when he was a year old he was still a "great fat baby" who loved life. Young Freddie, as he was called, was probably spoiled by his doting mother and father; a family story describes how, at the age of three, he waited impatiently while a visitor, who could play the accordion and mouth organ at the same time, went through three encores, then pushed his way to the center of the room and sang at the top of his lungs "There'll Be Something in Heaven for Children To Do."[7]

As Fred advanced from babyhood, the larger world of Portage opened before him. The Turners lived in the Fifth Ward, in a modest wooden house on a lot famed for a two-ton boulder that graced the front yard, having been imported from northern Wisconsin at considerable expense. There young Fred spent his boyhood; not until 1882, when he was at college, did they move to a larger brick home on Franklin Street in the Fourth Ward. Despite his father's prominence as editor and publisher of the town's leading newspaper, they were not numbered among the affluent of Portage; Andrew Jackson Turner's name never appeared on the published tax lists of those paying fifty dollars or more, and as late as 1893 their property was appraised at only $1850. Yet they lived comfortably, and even added irregularly to the family circle. Rockwell Lafayette Turner, born in August 1864, soon abandoned his pretentious array of given names for the more prosaic "Will" that he used for the rest of his life. Eight years later, on November 1, 1872, a daughter was born. Ellen Breese Turner, or "Breese" as she was always known, remained through her lifetime one of her older brother's closest companions.

There was much to keep a small boy busy in a town such as Portage, where each season offered fresh attractions. Winter might hold few pleasures for the aging—temperatures regularly skidded to thirty or forty below zero and during one memorable month in 1875 the average reading at sunrise was 7.5 below—but for children the wood-burning stove in parlor and kitchen was a warm spot for games and reading, while milder days provided unparalleled skating and sledding. Spring arrived in late March or early April when the ice "went out" of the Wisconsin River, an event always watched by the citizenry and reported in the local press. With warmer water, the swimming season was at hand; that meant excursions to the "Second White Bridge" over the Fox River or to near-by Silver Lake. "Professor" Clark's Portage Cornet Band began its regular weekly concerts in the village park now. The Fourth of July always meant a parade finishing at the court house lawn, where there was singing by the Portage Liederkranz Society, band music, the reading of the Declaration of Independence, speeches, and in the evening a grand ball at Pettibone Hall with dancing to Schultze's Band. This inaugurated the town's strawberry-and-ice-cream festival season, with every church and most of the charitable societies vying in offering the fattest berries and the richest cream to the customers. The crisp nights of autumn heralded the coming of the Columbia County Fair, with its tents of home-canned goods and splendid floral displays, and its gay carnival atmosphere; then came Halloween, when the boys of the town indulged in their "fantasies," from upsetting privies to suspending a cabbage over a doorway and ringing the bell.

Nor did Portagites have to provide all their own entertainment, for spring, summer, and fall witnessed a constant parade of professional talent. City dwellers who mourned the dullness of the lives of their country cousins would have been astounded at the fare offered in a typical two-week period in 1869: Miller's Athenaeum for five nights, a traveling acting troupe that closed its brief season with a performance of *The Hidden Hand*, Orton's Old Badger Circus for a one-night stand, a demonstration of a patent fire extinguisher by an agent who triumphantly doused a pile of lighted kerosene barrels, a performance by "Blind Tom," a talented piano player.[8] Entertainment might have been unsophisticated in rural America, but Fred Turner and his friends had plenty to keep them busy.

As they grew older, their activities widened. Spelling bees occupied some of their time; in one at the Presbyterian Church between teams of boys and girls young Fred failed on the word "satellite"—a less common word then than today. On a less serious plane, he was one of the younger set who organized a series of "Young Fogy" parties in 1873 —inspired by their elders, who held dances as the "Old Fogies"—to meet fortnightly at Pettibone Hall, where the Virginia reel was performed with the aid of Clark & O'Keefe's band. Parents took pride in watching as their children "waltzed, and swung, and 'hoed 'er down,' in all the exuberance of youthful joy and vigor."[9] They were equally delighted when Fred and his friends decided to enhance the elaborate celebration planned for the Centennial Fourth of July in 1876 by organizing a military company called the "Guppey Guards," so named to honor a civic leader named Joshua J. Guppey. After only a month of preparation they led the grand parade from the Court House to Loomis's Grove for the inevitable speeches. This success assured the Guppey Guards a degree of permanence, particularly after their command passed to the elder Turner, who not only supervised their drills but secured them Springfield rifles and uniforms: gray cloth trimmed with gold lace and dark facings, a black sash with gold edging, and gray caps topped with black and decorated with gilt. This splendid array made the Guppey Guards so attractive to the opposite sex that their annual ball became *the* social event of Portage; young Fred Turner may not have enjoyed the regular drills that won them prizes in state competitions at Madison, but he stayed a member until he left for college.[10]

Growing up in Portage meant not only fun and games, but a surprising number of cultural opportunities. By the time Fred was fourteen he was interesting himself in the oratorical activities that won him modest fame in later years, serving first as a messenger for the Young Men's Lyceum, where debates were held regularly, then when he was only fifteen, delivering one of the "declamations" that honored the Civil

War dead on Memorial Day. At the same time he was reading widely in a variety of books quite unusual for a quasi-frontier town of two or three thousand. The elder Turner owned a respectable library (on one occasion he asked borrowers to return such volumes as *The American Conflict, Don Quixote, The Federalist,* and Napoleon's *History of Caesar*), which could be supplemented from a permanent circulating library and a traveling library of four hundred works that went on display at John Graham's Drug Store each Saturday. That young Turner used these collections is clear. Starting in 1876, when he was fifteen, he kept a scrapbook in which he pasted items that interested him; these included voluminous extracts from Ralph Waldo Emerson (his favorite author) and from every important literary figure, as well as speeches that would interest a budding orator. A short time later he began contributing a regular "Pencil and Scissors Department" to his father's newspaper, filled with quotations and extracts that he found noteworthy. In the two months the column appeared he quoted extensively from Emerson (most frequently), Goethe, Disraeli, Harriet Beecher Stowe, Robert G. Ingersoll, Victor Hugo, Charles Lamb, Sydney Smith, Daniel Webster, Fielding, Rousseau, Thomas Carlyle, Schuyler Colfax, and a score more.[11] Even as a boy, Fred Turner displayed the unusual talent and catholicity of reading interest of a scholar.

He also excelled in school. He first attended the Franklin Street Primary School, briefly; then he went on to the Intermediate School, under Miss K. C. Wright. Fred was apparently a model student; the one yearly record preserved shows that in 1873 when he was twelve he missed only six of the 49 school days in the spring term—an attendance record bettered by only one other pupil—and earned a top rating of ten in conduct. He next attended Portage's single high school, where he spent the years between 1874 and 1878. This was hardly a lavish institution; built ten years before of the yellow brick for which the city was famous, the building was showing the signs of wear. It had an inconvenient recitation room, poor ventilation, inadequate blackboards, and a furnace that not only smoked and gave little heat but blocked the fire exit route. These physical deficiencies were offset by a rigid curriculum: English grammar, geography, arithmetic, reading, spelling, and map-making the first year; more doses of these subjects plus Latin grammar and United States history in the second; algebra, physical geography, history, botany, German, and Latin through Caesar and Virgil in the third; and, in the senior year, algebra, geometry, astronomy, rhetoric, philosophy, psychology, and German or French.

Fred Turner stood this diet well. During his first term he was one of nineteen on the top honor roll; a year later he tied with his friend Arthur C. Cole at the head of the class with 100 per cent attendance, 100 per cent punctuality, 96 per cent in scholarship, and an over-all average of 99 per cent. These astronomical heights were impossible to maintain consistently; on one marking he fell to a 93 per cent scholastic average and on another to 85 per cent in deportment, but he was almost always first or second in his class. This was no mean achievement; many years later a classmate remembered that "you were the despair of our entire class, because, no matter how diligently we worked, we could never equal the examination marks that you had."[12]

Such a record meant that Fred Turner would receive special distinction when graduation rolled around on the afternoon of Friday, June 28, 1878. The exercises were held in the Court House, specially decorated for the occasion. Flowers decked the speakers' stand, and a banner, bearing the words "Class of 1878" was stretched across the windows. There was standing-room only when Dr. A. C. Kellogg, superintendent of schools, opened the ceremonies, led the audience in singing the class song, and called on the eighteen graduates to deliver the orations that were the final requirement. Fred Turner came fourth, speaking on "The Power of the Press." The local reporter was pleased; "his thought was original, his style clear and forcible, and his manner self-possessed and very earnest." So was his father as he listened to the flow of words: the press was "a necessary adjunct of every free government. . . . the people will make known their power through it, and will resist all tendency toward oppression. . . . as Freedom of the Press increases, so does the freedom of the people. . . . a want of education among the lower classes of the nation is shown by the rise in our midst of Communism, that fell child of ignorance and crime. . . . with the aid of the press, however, that great and long wished for reform—the education of the masses—becomes not only a possibility, but even a probability." These stirring words were more than the three judges could resist. Young Turner proudly carried from the hall not only his diploma, but a set of Macauley's *History of England*, awarded as the first prize.[13]

When, many years later, the historian Frederick Jackson Turner looked back on his boyhood days and tried to isolate the influences that shaped his career, he singled out two that were particularly important: his family and the quasi-frontier atmosphere of Central Wisconsin. When he recalled his family relationships he had surprisingly little to say about his mother. She was apparently a capable housewife, able to enter into the regular discussions about the dining-room table, and wise enough to let her son grow to manhood without any of the oedipal problems common in modern society. Turner's father was of a different stripe. A cockily aggressive runt of a man, so small that he was the constant butt of jokes among his fellow-journalists (one reported seeing him approach two twelve-year-olds, and of hearing one say to the other, "Carry in that hoe or may be that boy that's coming will steal it"),[14] Andrew Jackson Turner was always popular, always sought after, always in the limelight. In public he was gay and outgoing, at his best when bantering with countless friends or haranguing a Republican audience for the Grand Old Party's standard bearer. Yet toward his family, and toward his first-born son, he was shy, almost aloof. Turner remembered him as "the best of fathers to me; undemonstrative, often taciturn, but always kind and full of that deep affection that does not show itself on the surface so much—but which abides."[15] If he learned from his father—and he learned much—it was by example and not by forced feeding.

The example was there, and proved admirable for a future historian. Jack Turner was a newspaper owner and editor by profession, but a politician by instinct, so dedicated to the success of the Republican party that he saw the Credit Mobilier scandal as a Confederate plot and the corruption-ridden Grant administration as "so patriotic, so wise, so beneficent, and so thoroughly American in all its distinguishing features, as to command the admiration of the patriotic men of this country."[16] This proved a handicap to his own office-holding ambitions in strongly Democratic Portage, but Jack Turner's personal popularity won him election after election: as clerk of the circuit court, as a four-term member of the state legislative assembly, as delegate to state and national conventions, as a perennial official of the county Board of Supervisors. His reward came in 1878 when he was named to the Wisconsin Railroad Commission by the Republican governor, a post with such ample financial rewards and speculative opportunities that he sold his interest in the *Wisconsin State Register* to devote full time to his business ventures. Jack Turner could no more abandon publishing and politics than he could vote Democratic; when a rival editor a dozen years later charged that Jack had written nearly every editorial in the *Register* for two decades, he was guilty of exaggeration rather than prevarication, and when the party urged Turner as mayor of Portage in 1881, he was not only elected but performed so effectively that he served for four terms, two of them as the unanimous choice of the voters.[17]

Jack Turner did not set the world afire as either politician or business-man, even though he was a walking encyclopedia of facts and statistics needed in planning any campaign and boasted a gregarious nature that made him a personal friend of every man, woman, child, and dog in Columbia County. In politics he lacked the vision to plan boldly or to place the state and national interest above petty local bickering; in the business world his vision was too broad, his optimism too unquenchable, to succeed. He did prosper in modest ventures, such as a contract to pave a Portage street with cedar blocks at $1.22 a square yard, but when he helped organize the Portage and San Juan Mining Company to develop gold mines in Colorado, or invested heavily in pine lands of northern Wisconsin, or formed the Portage and Superior Railroad Company to build from his home town to Stevens Point and Bayfield on Lake Superior, he did more to help his friends and community than he did himself. He worked hard through a long lifetime, and again and again seemed certain of turning a speculation into a fortune, but he died a relatively poor man, even though he provided comfortably for his family as long as he lived.[18]

In the long run, Andrew Jackson Turner's most significant legacy was his son. Frederick Jackson Turner learned three things from his father that stood him in good stead through his lifetime. One was to appreciate the importance of local history: the elder Turner helped form the local "Old Settlers' Club" to record the impressions of early inhabitants and prepared a number of newspaper articles and pamphlets on the pioneer history of Portage and old Fort Winnebago.[19] More important was the lesson in practical politics that Jack Turner taught his son. Young Fred spent his youthful years in the office of the *Register*, learning to set type and chronicle local news, but learning far more about the community, and about the wire-pulling that went on as politicians vied for office. Lessons continued at the dinner table in the evening, as his father told of the means he had used to harmonize conflicting ethnic groups, or to bring peace to warring religious factions, or to influence the legislature through pressure on this committee or that. Fred was taught much about the formation of the "composite American nationality" of which he would write.[20]

He was taught more as he watched his father pull the strings that elected Republicans to office. Once, when the two were riding among the Baraboo Bluffs, they happened on a country blacksmith shop, covered with pictures advertising Barnum's Circus, where a dozen farmers were gathered for a local caucus. Young Turner watched with admiration as his father leaned against the anvil and spoke persuasively of the candidates he recommended for the next election. "It was so picturesque," he wrote that night, "and so characteristic of our institutions."[21] Here for the future historian to see was the practical working of frontier democracy, and he never forgot the experience. "I understand party politics very much better," he recorded some years later, "from having seen, at close range and from the inside, his own interests in that subject and his skill in shepherding the many nationalities that lived in Columbia County."[22]

If young Fred learned something of local history and politics from his father, he learned far more about the art of fishing—and this was knowledge more essential to his future well-being than the most valuable classroom instruction. Jack Turner was completely irrational in his passion for the out-of-doors and for the three sports that absorbed much of his time: curling in the winter, fishing in the spring and summer, and hunting in the fall. "You know," he warned his son, "it is a cardinal principle with me to never allow anything to interfere with my shooting, fishing, or curling."[23] And nothing did interfere. Every clear winter day found Jack Turner on the rinks of the Portage Curling Club, serving as "skip" with a vigor that overawed his opponents, then leading the competing teams to the famed Haertel's saloon and brewery to drink to success or drown the sorrow of defeat. In the autumn he was as often as not playing hookey from his newspaper office to escape to the headquarters of the Puckaway Club on Puckaway Lake, there to bag his quota of wild ducks and geese; Jack Turner estimated that he spent from ten to twenty days behind a gun each fall, often with his son Fred tagging behind him.

These were satisfactory pursuits, but they paled when the fishing season opened each spring. Jack Turner was a master fisherman, a devoted fisherman, a slightly mad fisherman, who judged his friends by their competence with a rod and who would neglect the most promising business deal for a half-hour on a trout stream. His junior editor reported sadly in the spring of 1867 that Jack had fished but little, having made only four trips to the Tunnel, eight to Briggsville, five to Swan Lake, six to Silver Lake, and thirteen to the "Big Slough," and that he had caught only two thousand trout and a dozen barrels of pickerel. Jack Turner endowed his son with a share of his own piscatorial enthusiasm. When Fred was only five years old, his father sent word that he wanted his "sprouts" brought up properly, "and by all means learned to fish."[24] The boy was "learned to fish," so effectively that his love of lakes and trout streams rivaled that of his father. They made trip after trip together, sometimes to a neighboring stream for an hour's casting, sometimes for weeks on end as they sounded lakes in more distant counties.[25] This apprenticeship left Fred Turner a devoted fisherman, and he remained one through his lifetime.

The stamp of Jack Turner's influence remained on Frederick Jackson Turner throughout his life, but so did the memory of the quasi-frontier environment in which he spent his boyhood. Portage was just emerging from its pioneer past during his impressionable years; in 1870, when he was nine years old, it had no more than 4000 inhabitants, and in 1880 only 4346. All about were reminders of frontier days certain to make their imprint on a small boy. Through the dusty streets each summer lumbered prairie schooners loaded with "emigrants" bound for the free government lands of northern Wisconsin or the Dakotas. Almost every issue of the local newspaper told of Indian outbreaks in the West, flavored with the editor's damnation of the "savages" who began the Modoc War or wiped out Custer's command on the Little Big Horn. Occasionally, events at home reminded him that civilization was in its swaddling clothes: a hunting party was formed to track down a wolf-pack, vigilantes were recruited to help the sheriff capture an over-ambitious horse thief. The wilderness was not quite subdued, and young Turner felt its influence.

Now and then frontier lawlessness touched close to home. Twice in 1869, when he was seven years old, vigilantes turned Portage into a wild-west town—once in September when two hot-headed Irishmen shot it out on the main street (the winner was promptly hanged to a tree by a mob), again a week later, when a notorious troublemaker was arrested after bludgeoning a drinking companion to death (he was dragged from the jail and strung naked from a branch, where his body was found the next morning).[26] These were events that the boy would never forget. Nor did he forget the great lumber rafts that passed the city almost daily during the summer months, bound from the "pineries" of northern Wisconsin to the prairies of Illinois and Iowa, or the journeys that he made with his father to that virgin northern country where the train ran through a narrow aisle cut in the towering forests, or through clearings where homesteaders were building their cabins.[27] The frontier was near and meaningful to Fred Turner.

It was brought even nearer when he mingled with the Indians who clung to their ancestral homes near Portage. Both the Winnebago and the Menomonee had long since been forced to cede their tribal lands, but many refused to move to the Nebraska reservation assigned the tribes, and they continued to hunt along the Baraboo and Wisconsin rivers. There Fred visited their villages on his frequent fishing trips; he saw Indians often in Portage when they came to trade or beg, or to drink themselves into trouble with the authorities. He probably shared the town's satisfaction when troops arrived in 1873 to drive the red men westward, and that December he probably watched as the remnants of the proud tribesmen were marched through the city, herded onto railroad cars, and started toward Nebraska.[28] Certainly he realized that many drifted back, for their villages were common sights even through the 1880s; Fred Turner was often among them, "hearing the squaws in their village on the high bank talk their low treble to the bass of our Indian polesman" as he fished the river, "feeling that I belonged to it all."[29]

He was close to the frontier then, and he was closer as he watched the newcomers to that near-wilderness area merge into the composite nationality that he was later to describe. Roughly one-third the inhabitants of Portage were foreign-born, and the percentage was even higher in the small farm communities that he regularly visited on his fishing trips; in Caledonia, Scots, Welsh, and Germans far outnumbered the few natives, and Lewiston's 234 settlers included 95 Germans, 33 Scandinavians, 35 Irishmen, and 53 American-born. As a boy, Fred Turner was unaware of the census statistics that described this mixing bowl, nor did he realize that, when he was eleven years old, the Portage city council included one native of Ireland, one of Baden, one of Prince Edward Island, one of Prussia, one of Wurthenberg, one of Holland, one of Wales, one of Massachusetts, and one of New York—a mixture to be found only in an emerging community on the fringes of settlement. But he did know that he daily rubbed elbows with men of all hues and backgrounds who were merging into the American society. "It was a town with a real collection of types from all the world," he remembered some years later, "Yankees from Maine and Vermont, New York Yankees, Dutchmen from the Mohawk, braw curlers from the Highlands, Southerners—all kinds. They mixed, too, and respected and fought each other."[30]

These were indelible impressions, and they were still fresh in Turner's mind when he began speculating on the nature of American society. They were part of him, not something he learned from books. They altered his perspective in two significant ways. First, he knew himself to be the product of a social order whose life-patterns and values differed from those of established communities. "I am," he wrote in 1887, "placed in a *new* society that is just beginning to realize that it has made a place for itself by mastering the wilderness and peopling the prairie, and is now ready to take its great course in universal history."[31] Clearly, Turner sensed the differences between the pioneer West and the stabilized East long before he began the studies that led to the frontier hypothesis. Second, his close contact with nature planted in him an almost Emersonian sensitivity to the wilderness; he was doubly aware of the impact of the frontier's closing because he resented civilization's assault on the primitivism that he had enjoyed as a boy. He tended to glorify nature as a generative force, playing a larger role than it actually did in creating new societies. Had Turner been city born and bred he would almost certainly not have evolved his frontier thesis.

Fred had learned much during his Portage years, but now a wider world beckoned. His outstanding high school record meant that he was destined for college, and to central Wisconsin, college meant the University of Wisconsin in near-by Madison. This was a radical step in a day when higher education was for the few, but his father readily agreed, with one strict admonition: "If I supposed you were going to learn to be a loafer, as some boys I know of have done, I should say to you that you *can* be learned at home, at less expense. But that is not what my boy is going for."[32] Nor was it. Young Turner had already shown his mettle by adding a special preparatory "Greek Course" to his heavy senior schedule in high school, mastering Xenophon's *Anabasis*, beginning Homer's *Iliad*, and suffering stiff doses of Greek grammar to meet the university's requirements for its "Ancient Classical Course." He did well, too, with marks ranging from 86 to 95 per cent in what was actually a college-level subject.

In September 1878, Fred Turner entered a strange new world when the train deposited him and five of his classmates at the busy Madison depot the day before classes began. The university was hardly large by modern standards—449 students divided into three colleges—but it was a bit terrifying to one accustomed to Portage's small-town atmosphere. So this newest freshman wandered about in awe. He found a room with board at the usual price of three dollars a week, walked up State Street to the "Hill," and officially enrolled as a "sub-freshman"—a designation alloted to students so poorly trained in small high schools that they entered with less-than-adequate preparation. There were few frills in the courses that busied him that year—Greek and Latin reading and composition, for the most part, with concentration on Cicero, Livy, Homer, and Lysias; solid geometry and trigonometry; general botany; and a touch of oratorical training in the required "rhetoricals." His over-all average, 90.8 per cent, was thoroughly respectable for one with his training; more importantly, he received a baptism in classics that stood him in good stead through his lifetime, endowing him with a sense of the nicety of literary expression, a vigorous prose style, and a storehouse of classical allusions that he used in his own writing.[33]

Fred J. Turner (as he now signed himself) seemed destined for an uneventful four years in college, but the situation abruptly changed during the summer of 1879, when he accompanied his mother and aunt to Omaha, where his father's brother, Charles Turner, lay dangerously ill. Uncle Charlie recovered in due time, but in mid-August Fred was stricken with a mysterious malady. For a time death seemed certain—his father and brother hurried to his bedside, where they stayed until mid-September, when the crisis was passed. Not until October could the boy be returned to Madison, where a Chicago physician diagnosed his ailment as spinal meningitis in its most acute form. His momentary improvement was deceptive, for in November the disease struck with full force again; once more his life was despaired as he grew weaker and weaker. Then, in February 1880, he began to improve. By May Fred was able to ride about the town in a carriage, and by summer he was fully recovered, yet so weakened by the months of pain that a return to college was impossible.[34]

That autumn and winter Turner apparently stayed at home, doing a little tutoring in Greek at the request of the principal of the high school, and gradually regaining his strength. This was an important interlude in his life, for there was little to do but read, which he did—constantly, widely, intelligently. Early in 1881 he jotted down the names of the books he had devoured in the preceding year. The list represented a respectable library: Milton's *Paradise Lost*, eight of Charles Dickens's novels, Taine's *History of English Literature*, Byron's *Don Juan*, Swift's *Gulliver's Travels*, Thackery's *Pendennis*, Hawthorne's *Scarlet Letter*, George Eliot's *Adam Bede*, Irving's *Alhambra* and *Sketch Book*, and scores more. This was solid fare, but far less solid than his more serious self-imposed intellectual diet. The "Commonplace Book" that he kept at the time—an ordinary paper-bound notebook in which he jotted quotations, passing thoughts, and observations on his reading—was filled with translations from the Latin, all carefully signed with "Translated by FJT." Mingled with these were his own random thoughts, largely on literature and the books he was reading, and quotations that pleased him. "Too great zeal in acquiring other's thoughts," he wrote in one moment of near-rebellion, "may . . . lead us to neglect our own and become imitators and not originators."[35] He was to be an originator in the future, but now he was stocking his mind with invaluable learning, sharpening his wits, and perfecting a writing style that was to become his trademark. Turner's forced months of leisure were probably more valuable to him than any number of classes at the university would have been.

He had to finish his education, however, and by the spring of 1881 he was back in Madison for the final term of the college year, taking the usual courses, helping unite two defunct literary societies into the Adelphia Society with such success that he emerged as secretary of the new organization, and delivering Marc Anthony's "Address to the Romans" in the College Rhetoricals so effectively that it was judged "the finest declamation and the best rendered that has yet been heard from the Assembly Hall stage."[36] All this despite bothersome remnants of his illness; twice during the academic year he was forced to return home to nurse himself back to health, and once his father was sufficiently concerned that he warned the professors that his son required special consideration. Yet Fred Turner was on the road to a normal life once more, prepared to resume a full program of studies that fall.

When he enrolled again, on September 6, 1881, the university was little changed; 38 professors were prepared to welcome 401 students, 52 of them in Fred's sophomore class, and the only visible signs of progress were the new paths that led up the Hill to University Hall. The University of Wisconsin, in common with its sister educational institutions, was woefully out of step with the modern world. Theorists in those days held that mental faculties could not be trusted to mature without proper guidance; strict mental and moral discipline was needed to develop the mind. This, rather than the acquisition of knowledge, was the purpose of schooling. Students were not to question or even to reason; learning was by rote, and the classroom a means of testing their ability to recite the set body of material they had memorized. They were never to doubt the rigid prescriptions imposed by their elders. When President John Bascom, one of the nation's ablest and most progressive educators, greeted Fred Turner's sophomore class that fall of 1881, he talked not of the world scene or intellectual values, but of the need to have their food well-cooked but not burned, of the dangers of eating between meals, of the value of healthful exercise, of the virtues of eating slowly, and of the evils of intemperance.[37]

Wisconsin's physical setting was as archaic as its intellectual life. Situated on "The Hill" above beautiful Lake Mendota, it was dominated by University Hall, where most of Turner's classes were held. This venerable building had no central heating until 1883; until that time students sat muffled in overcoats and mittens in classrooms where wood-burning stoves provided more smoke than comfort in temperatures that dipped to twenty or thirty degrees below zero. Hallways had no heat at all; students wrapped themselves in coats and scarfs as they hurried between classes. Such lighting as there was on dark winter days came from flickering gas jets that only seemed to deepen the blackness. Conditions in the university library were even worse. A fee of two dollars combined with the pitifully small collection to discourage student use; in Turner's sophomore year only 39 of some 400 students had "joined" by mid-November, while 180 had enrolled at the free city library.[38]

Yet if Madison offered neither intellectual excitement nor physical comfort, it did provide temptations to which young Turner gleefully succumbed. The local and Milwaukee theaters offered a constant parade of the lowly and near-great, ranging from Buffalo Bill and a full company of Sioux chiefs in *The Prairie Waifs*, through *Uncle Tom's Cabin*, to Edwin Booth in *Hamlet*. During his college years he witnessed Thomas Keene and McCulloch in *Richard III*, Barrett and Booth in *Hamlet*, Fanny Davenport in *As You Like It*, Signor Salvini in *Othello*, Frank Mayo in *The Virginian*, Joseph Jefferson in *Rip Van Winkle*, and a dozen more. Turner could also listen to excellent lecturers, including Bayard Taylor, Henry Ward Beecher, Robert Ingersoll, John Fiske, Edwin Meade, and Matthew Arnold, all within a year.[39]

On a less elevated plane were the student activities that captured the time of the undergraduates. Athletics played a lesser role in those days; an attempt to form a football team in the autumn of Fred's sophomore year ended when someone kicked a hole in the football, but the university did manage to launch a baseball team that suffered ignominious defeats at the hands of the "Racines" and the "Ann Arbors." Things were better the next year, due partly to Turner himself. He was elected to the Athletic Association in September 1882, not because he was passionate about sports, but because this least-prominent of all student activities gave him a chance to serve his college. The Association had much to do; it was an unofficial body entrusted with managing the school's intercollegiate program and, particularly, with exciting enough student interest to field a team to meet Beloit, Racine, and Northwestern, the members of the Western College Baseball League. Turner, acting as vice-president, did his work well, raising enough money to buy uniforms for the team (consisting of nine men and a substitute), arranging adequate time for practice, helping arrange schedules, and even inspiring some interest in a football eleven. College spirit rose during his term on the Association, even to the point where the first college yell—the now-familiar "U Rah Rah Wis-con-sin"—became part of the student vocabulary.[40]

Young Turner was drawn more closely into the vortex of college life when he joined a social fraternity, Phi Kappa Psi, shortly after his

arrival in Madison. He was an enthusiastic fraternity man, even to the
degree of writing a singularly unoriginal song for the brethren:

> Not Phi Delta nor Chi Psi, drink her down
> Not Beta Theta Pi, drink her down!
> But old Phi Kappa Psi, is the shout we send on high
> Drink her down, drink her down, drink her down, down, down.[41]

Any contribution of this significance deserved recognition, and
Turner's came when he was chosen to respond to the toast "Madison"
at the annual fraternity "Symposium" at the Park Hotel in November
1882. Despite its name, this was a gala affair with wine, women, and
dancing—"the most *recherché*" ever witnessed in university circles,
according to the local reporter—and it gave Fred a chance to display
some of his most lush oratory: "Although to most of us she is only a
foster mother, and on this Thanksgiving night our own household fires
are burning in distant places, yet, like the ancient Greeks, we, too, may
meet around a common hearth and offer our praises to Madison, the
beautiful queen of Wisconsin, throned on the hills, gilded with gleaming lakes and clothed in the robe of rich sunsets."[42]

Fred Turner found his true niche in two other extra-curricular activities that were more to his talents. One, quite naturally, was student
journalism. His arrival in Madison coincided with the founding of a
weekly campus newspaper, *The Campus*, soon to be renamed *The
Badger*, whose second issue, published in October 1881, announced that
Fred J. Turner would be one of two exchange editors. From this post
he rose to become secretary-treasurer of the Badger Association in his
junior year, and president in his senior. This was tantamount to the
editorship, and he performed his duties well; *The Badger*'s awareness of
the problems that faced students throughout the nation, its crusades to
elevate the academic standards of the university, and its professional
tone all indicated that Turner was a cut above the usual student journalist of his day.[43]

Even more important than his editorial duties in shaping his future
career was Fred Turner's activity as a public speaker. He could not
have selected a field better suited to his talents; oratory was the surest
road to popularity on the campuses of that day, when the prize speaker
was far more acclaimed than the superior athlete. The heart of all social
life lay in the "literary societies," whose elected members enjoyed a
prestige denied lesser souls, and who in return had to engage in rhe-

torical exercises, debates, and inter-society oratorical competitions. "They are," wrote one student editor, "the strongholds of a college course, and are, if not quite, almost as important as the college course itself."[44] For some reason Turner was passed by the two prestigious societies at Wisconsin, the Athenean Society and the Hesperian Society, and helped form the Adelphia Society, a poor relation of its more distinguished counterparts. Adelphia had to be content with rented clubrooms in downtown Madison until 1883, when it was assigned a room in Science Hall, and in Fred's senior year it could boast only twenty-three members.[45]

Such fame as Fred Turner won as an orator was not due to his literary society. His supreme moment came at the end of his junior year, when he captured the most coveted of all honors, the "Burrows Prize" (a wretched steel engraving that would grace the walls of the triumphant literary society for a year), in the Junior Exhibition. Five orators vied for this honor yearly, one from each of the literary societies (three for men, two for women), with each nominating its best orator. When Fred Turner was named to represent Adelphia in the spring of 1883, he was assured the most difficult competition of his young speaking career.

Over the next months he filled his Commonplace Book with jottings as his composition took shape. His theme was a happy one—"The Poet of the Future"—for in it he would contrast the sterility of despotism with the cultural opportunities under democracy. "Our poems," he wrote, "live in the grand meter and rhythm of our armies marching to the rescue of the shackled slave and the grandest lyric that ever fell from pen was the Proclamation of Emancipation." This was the message that he brought to the "cultured audience" that packed the University Assembly Hall on the night of May 18, 1883. Turner spoke first, and the knowing realized that the competition was over then and there. "The well rounded figures of his oration," said the local reporter, "the striking metaphors, the graceful gestures, the perfect enunciation, taken in connection with his perfect self-possession placed him far beyond the reach of his competitors." Other speakers followed, but the decision was foreordained. To the audience, Turner's oration was the superior one of the evening in all qualities, and the verdict of the judges was greeted with cheers.[46]

"The Poet of the Future" was a remarkable oration that revealed many of the qualities that were to shape Turner's views during his professional life. Its theme was the twin forces that had remade modern civilization, science and democracy. Science had given man new beauty blessed with utilitarianism; democracy had allowed all mankind to share in benefits reserved for the kings of former ages. Now democracy was waiting for its poet, a poet who would find his inspiration in popular rule and the scientific achievements that rule made possible. "In his lap science will pour her glorious jewels and bid him give to them the setting of his song. In his ear humanity will whisper deep, inspiring words, and bid him give them voice."[47] Turner's oratorical flourishes have little appeal to a modern reader, and his youthful enthusiasm was untempered with realism. But in "The Poet of the Future" he voiced his deep-seated faith in democracy, a faith never to be shaken, and in it he proclaimed his belief in the inevitability of progress. Turner was certain in 1883 that the ordinary people, working through democracy, would eventually achieve a perfect society.

He triumphed in the Junior Exhibition not only because his extracurricular activities included literary society activities and student editorships, but also because he was spending a great deal of time reading. Whatever the press of other duties, he read constantly, widely, appreciatively. The paper-bound Commonplace Books that he kept through college mirror his changing tastes in authors, and they show, too, how deep his understanding and how thoughtful his speculations were. His tastes embraced the classics—Shakespeare he read daily, with samplings of Carlyle (a perennial favorite), Hawthorne, De Quincey, Goethe, Longfellow, and J. A. Symonds—but he also developed a marked fondness for Herbert Spencer's *Education*, Green's *History of the English People*, and, particularly, the essays of Ralph Waldo Emerson. Emerson was perennially exciting, and through the 1881 and 1882 Commonplace Books are sprinkled quotations from his essays and comments on his ideas. Turner was tuned especially to the Emersonian form of democracy; he heartily agreed with the Sage of Concord that "the artistic idea of our age *is* that of the practical as applied to the people." Here was the germ of the concept that he developed in his "The Poet of the Future," and here was fuel for thought that required more investigation. "Read up on Evolution and apply to this thesis,"[48] he reminded himself.

The formal education prescribed by the rigid requirements of the

Ancient Classical Course that he elected was somewhat less broadening than his own reading. Until the end of his junior year he was classed as a "special student," an inferior designation shared by undergraduates who came from small high schools with inadequate programs in the classics.[49] This did not lighten his burdens; with his classmates he spent the sophomore year reading Horace in Latin, Demosthenes in Greek, Anglo-Saxon texts, and lyric poetry, along with a course in rhetoric, one in oratory, and one in mathematical mechanics. Turner did well, too, ending the year with an average grade of 90.5 per cent, and he would have done even better save for an inability to master mathematical mechanics. According to local legend he was scheduled to fail that course completely, but was given a passing grade when the instructor confused him with another student.[50] In any event, he entered his junior year well equipped in Latin and Greek.

This was just as well, for no sooner did Fred Turner return to Madison as a junior in the fall of 1882 than he discovered a new interest that made the classics seem dull and archaic. He found history, through a remarkable teacher named William Francis Allen. From the time he entered Professor Allen's class, Fred was a lost soul, so absorbed with this exciting new field of learning that all other studies seemed unimportant. He often testified in later life that no other person so greatly influenced his future. "Allen," he wrote in 1920, "has always looked over my shoulder and stirred my historical conscience."[51] This was only a slight exaggeration. That wise and good man shaped his young student into a first-rate historian, equipped him with the tools of the trade, broadened his perspectives, and kindled the enthusiasms that sustained him for the rest of his life.

A transplanted New Englander, a classicist by training and a medievalist by choice, Professor Allen brought to the classroom the rigorous "scientific" techniques he had learned at Harvard and Göttingen, techniques which were then revolutionizing historical studies in the United States. His courses were strictly conventional—in the junior year the students undertook a three-term study of "Dynastic and Territorial History" that surveyed political events from classical times onward, a two-term sequence in ancient institutions, mythology, and art, and the required one-term introduction to American history; in the senior year they worked on a three-term combination of medieval institutions, the English constitution, and the history of civilizations. But whatever the subject, Professor Allen's students entered a world far removed from the usual rote-learning and recital technique then universally employed. In some of his courses Allen lectured, but in most he used the "topical" method, sending undergraduates to the sources to investigate assigned topics, prepare fifteen-minute papers, and present their findings to the class with the aid of a syllabus, charts, and maps.[52] Fred Turner learned history by research in the sources, spiced with the excitement of exploration and the thrill of discovery. Had Professor Allen followed the usual practice of giving textbook quizzes, his prize pupil might have continued the journalistic career that he intended. Instead he found in history an intellectual excitement provided by no other discipline.

The content of Allen's courses was as important to Turner's conversion as the methodology. Professor Allen saw history not as a chronicle of wars and politics, but as a search for the subsurface social and economic forces that shaped political behavior, a concept that was revolutionary in that day. This quest led him into comparative studies, in which he contrasted institutions in ancient, medieval, and modern times for clues to their origin and operation; it also inclined him to a genetic approach that sought to discover *why* and *how* institutional growth occurred. To him, history was an exercise in cause and effect; the historian's duty was not simply to record an event, but to understand the causal forces behind it. "No historical fact has any value," he told his students, "except so far as it helps us to understand human nature and the working of historical forces."[53] These were invaluable lessons for Turner; they not only underlay his whole concept of the nature of history, but inspired him to search for the subterranean currents that explained the American past, thus leading him directly to his frontier and sectional hypotheses.

Professor Allen's research techniques were also progressive for his time. He preached the heretical doctrine that scholars should use every possible tool in their quest for the truth; to him the study of the past required a thorough knowledge of metaphysics, theology, military science, political economy, and jurisprudence.[54] When Turner, in later years, urged historians to use economics, political science, sociology, and anthropology to solve their problems, he was echoing his master. He echoed him again when he used maps to illuminate the nation's expansion and its division into sections. Allen was a pioneer in this technique both in the classroom and research, and he indoctrinated his students in its value. His own studies on the expansion of ancient Rome were based on a series of carefully drawn maps, while the catalogue descriptions of his courses regularly noted that "historical charts and maps are constantly used."[55] Turner later testified that his own passion for mapping all data was inspired by Allen's courses.

The most important lesson learned by young Turner was that the historical process was one of constant growth and relationship. Societies, Allen taught, changed constantly, just as did the biological organisms then being popularized by Charles Darwin and his follow evolutionists. Allen viewed the great breakthroughs in man's progress—the invention of the bow and arrow, the domestication of animals, the smelting of iron ore, the development of the alphabet—as steps in the "evolution of society," each triggering a series of radical changes in the social structure. To him the shift from community to private land ownership was the final step in "the evolution of barbarism into civilization."[56] Allen's course on medieval institutions, which Turner took in his senior year, was largely a study of institutional response to social and economic change. From it Turner emerged with two basic concepts. He saw society as a living, dynamic organism, constantly changing in response to forces governing its evolution. He saw, too, that the pace of change could best be measured by using comparative techniques—the social pressures shaping medieval land tenure, for example, became clearer when contrasted with those governing the land system in a primitive New England or Illinois town.[57] These were essential in Turner's beliefs; his understanding of society as an evolving organism underlay his whole approach to the past, and his application of medieval examples to the American West led him closer to his frontier thesis.

Despite his later, half-joking remarks that he learned so little American history in college that he could approach the subject from a fresh perspective, Turner benefited a great deal from Allen's one-term course on that subject. There he received a surprisingly modern over-all interpretation that even recognized the significance of frontier expansion. Allen viewed the age of colonization as a final phase of the expansion of Europe, and an end-product of the rise of national states, the ferment of the Reformation, and the intellectual explosion of the Renaissance. He pictured the spread of settlement across the continent as a continuation of European expansion, saw the Louisiana Purchase as a watershed in the early history of the Republic, and interpreted even the slavery conflict as a by-product of the westward march. "It must be noted," he told his class, "that it was the *extension* of slavery that thus became the leading issue. The *existence* of slavery in the states was wholly a different question, and one which under our political system could never be more than a moral issue."[58] Allen also recognized that expansion increased the powers of the central government, especially as the demand grew for federal control of slavery in the territories. When his pupil wrote, as he did in 1893, that "loose construction increased as the nation marched westward," he was parroting his master's wisdom.

The books assigned in Allen's courses added to Turner's growing store of knowledge. Most were dreary chronicles; students in the 1880s endured the boredom of the chronological monstrosities that passed as textbooks—one by Alexander Johnson on the *History of American Politics* (1879) was almost universally used—or were sent to pasture in the multivolume works of George Bancroft, John Schouler, Richard Hildreth, and Hermann von Holst. Yet Turner may have found a few volumes more to his liking on Allen's reading lists: the books of Francis Parkman on the French and Indian wars; J. G. Shea's *Discovery and Exploration of the Mississippi River*, which was judged "indispensable to the student of western history"; and Consul W. Butterfield's *Washington-Irving Correspondence*, which was listed as "an important work on the history of the Northwest." These volumes may have stirred Turner's interest in the West, but he learned far more from a less pretentious *History of the United States*, by a young Englishman named John A. Doyle, which was published in 1876.[59]

Doyle's textbook was largely traditional, but he did defy orthodoxy in two ways. He included in the book four colored maps drawn by Francis A. Walker of Yale's Sheffield Scientific School, one showing the territorial expansion of the United States, the other three picturing the westward movement by four-color gradations between the frontier (less than six persons to the square mile) and the fully occupied areas (more than forty-five). Here was a graphic presentation of the expansion process. Doyle also discussed expansion. The story of America would be incomplete, he wrote, without "the history of a movement from the coast towards the west," made by "new settlers, or those born in America who wanted land, gradually moving westward without losing their connection with the original settlements."[60]

No less suggestive were Doyle's speculations on the results of expansion. The westward movement, he wrote, was responsible for "many of the features which distinguish America from the Old World." Because of a frontier, men in America always had the chance to better themselves by moving westward. "Moreover the great demand for labour has given them a free choice of occupation, and thus led to rapid changes. The ease too with which money can be made has led men to concentrate their energies in business, and thus the luxuries and refinement of life has been to a great extent neglected." When free lands were exhausted, all this would change, and the United States become another Europe. These were remarkable statements for that time; in them Doyle isolated many of the characteristics that Turner was to trace to the frontier: the mobility of the people, the greater opportunity for self-advancement, the tendency toward materialism. When Allen recommended Doyle's book as "an excellent English work," he was pointing his student in the right direction.

Allen moved Turner still nearer his future career by directing him into a fascinating research project. This originated in a request from Professor Herbert Baxter Adams of the Johns Hopkins University; could Allen provide information on early land holdings in Wisconsin that would illuminate Adams's study of the origins of New England towns? Allen could; he had six capable students who would be asked to investigate land tenure among the original French settlers. "One of them," he told Adams, "is going to examine the records of Portage where is an old French grant (Grignon)."[61] Turner set to work with enthusiasm, bothering his father and his father's friends with questions, poring over volumes of the *Annals of Congress* and the *American State Papers*, reading reminiscences of old settlers in the State Historical Society library, and combing documents in the Columbia County courthouse.[62] Here was his first chance to apply the techniques he had learned from Allen, and he found the venture exciting.

The result was hardly a historical masterpiece, but it did display the author's skill as an investigator. Turner described the land claim purchased by Augustin Grignon from John Lecuyer, the dispute over ownership that forced Grignon to appeal to a congressional land commission in 1823, the reaction of Lecuyer's heirs, the patent issued by President Andrew Jackson on the commission's recommendation, and the history of the tract from that time on. Little interpretation livened the narrative, nor was interpretation necessary, for the facts spoke for themselves. But the thoroughness of the research, the expertness of the critical evaluations, and the logic of the presentation testified to the fact that Turner has learned his lessons well. Even as a junior in college, he was a capable investigator, viewing history as a record of social growth, and able to picture the evolution of Portage in two generations from an Indian camp site to a settled community.

Turner's study of the Grignon Tract was principally important because it set him to thinking about the differences between land tenure in the United States and that in Europe. Why, he asked himself, was the area about Portage one of small farms, or "peasant proprietorship," instead of great estates? He speculated a great deal on that problem, and he recorded some of his thoughts in his Commonplace Book for 1883. "Investigate land holding peasantry about Madison," he wrote, "(e.g.) just as one would from the remains of ancient land systems (census—Ag[ricultural] Reports—Talks) etc. How many acres average. What kind of houses live in? Food? Manners—sports etc. Need of village system. Significance of Eng." He noted that "if our lands in the west had not been opened to and filled with foreign emigrants it is not unlikely that they would have fallen into the hands of capitalists and have been made into great estates." This, Fred Turner reasoned, would have reversed the democratic trend, "the revolution going on which is to raise *man* from his low estate to his proper dignity." Instead, "such institutions as peasant proprietors" served as a democratizing force, "all the stronger that it works quietly."[63] These were giant steps forward in his thinking: he was relating America's unique institutions to the existence of an area of cheap land, which discouraged aristocratic tendencies.

No less indicative of Turner's future contributions was his discovery of the evolutionary hypothesis and its application to his historical concepts. Society, he saw, was an organism evolving in response to various internal and environmental pressures, just as did the biological organisms described by Charles Darwin and Herbert Spencer. "They have given us a new world," he wrote in his Commonplace Book. Their ideas, if applied to history, would reveal what he called "the persistence of historical forces"; all the past must be restudied "in the light of the development hypothesis."

An intellectual understanding of the past by this key would give so many generalizations that the proper completion of such a work would inaugurate a new era. Science has of late years revolutionized Zoology, Biology, etc. It must now take up recorded History and do the same by it. This I would like to do my little to aid.[64]

These were not unusual beliefs—most of the nation's historians were applying Darwinian techniques in their investigations—but they were hardly to be expected from a college junior in a backwater university. Allen taught him well, and, more than any other teacher, he launched him on the road to his own original interpretations. Turner spoke the truth when he wrote some years later: "I have never, in Johns Hopkins or elsewhere, seen his equal as a scholar."[65]

The stiff doses of history inflicted on Fred Turner during his junior and senior years absorbed most of his time, but there were other courses to be mastered, orations to be prepared, a student paper to be edited, and a modest social life to be enjoyed. The courses could not be neglected—as a junior, he took a sequence in physics, chemistry, and zoology, two courses in English literature, one on the Latin poets, and one in constitutional law; as a senior, the study of political economy, logic and aesthetics, astronomy, and the inspiring lectures by President John Bascom on "Mental and Moral Philosophy." These last he especially enjoyed; President Bascom was a premature Progressive, who glorified democracy and preached that property was usually acquired by happy accident and belonged less to the holder than to society—strong words for that day, and words that vastly influenced young Turner.[66] There were also required courses in public speaking and declamation, where Turner's oratorical skills were further developed. In all he did well; his one undistinguished grade was an 80 in chemistry. All the rest save two were in the 90s, with his marks in Allen's classes usually 97 or 98, and he always was ranked at the top of the class.[67]

There was no question of Fred Turner's graduation with distinction as the spring of 1884 brought his commencement near. With it came the usual round of study, the usual class picnic with its "elegant repast," the usual bickerings that delayed the election of class officers until just before graduation. The senior album described Fred J. Turner as twenty-two years old, five feet eight inches tall, 130 pounds, a liberal in religion and an independent in politics. He was to receive his degree with "Honors of the Second Grade"; only two of the 86 graduating students had earned first honors.[68]

Ceremonies began on Sunday, June 15, when President Bascom preached the baccalaureate sermon on "The New Theology"; continued through Monday, when seniors read their honors theses to a sparse audience; and reached the first climax on Tuesday, "Class Day," when a room full of sweating parents heard the class prophecy read. One verse appealed especially to the visitors from Portage:

> *Turner*, "in cloisters immured and to painful study devoting
> Day and night, his patient and innocent life exhausting."
> *Turner*, than whom no senior with loftier intellect gifted,
> Nor with a finer soul, nor in virtue absolute ever.

Then the class valedictorian spoke, the class song was sung, and the parents filed from the hall, with only one more ceremony to be endured.

Commencement day, on Wednesday, was dark and dismal, but Assembly Hall was overflowing when President Bascom, the regents, the governor, and the faculty filed onto the platform. There was traditional music first, then a prayer, and presentation of flowers to the feminine graduates until "the hall was redolent with their perfumes." Orations, eighteen in all, followed. Turner was the second to last speaker, but he brought the dozing audience to life with his rich voice, his forceful gestures, his lush prose. "Architecture through Oppression" was his theme; the beauty of the past had been created by the toil of the many for the enjoyment of the few—"millions groaning that one might laugh, servile tillers of the soil, sweating that others might dream." Now the age of oppression had passed. "Now the world begins to see that true progress, true enlightenment, means the progress, the enlightenment of all. . . . When the greatest happiness of the greatest number shall have become something like reality, when life's tragedy shall cease to clash with life's romance, and the squalor of the hovel shall no longer mar the cathedral's beauty, then again may music 'freeze into marble' and forests blossom into stone." This flood tide won its just reward; the three judges announced that the "Lewis Prize" of twenty dollars had been awarded to Fred J. Turner of Portage. Fred Turner walked from the platform, diploma in hand, knowing that he had won the two most coveted oratorical awards of the university.[69]

Turner left Madison that spring well endowed with learning. He had acquired a thorough grounding in Latin and Greek, and an excellent training in literature; his future writing was to benefit in its crisp style, its colorful metaphors, its freshness of allusion. He had learned something of the natural sciences, and especially of biology; these lessons he was to apply in his total concept of society as an evolving organism, in his belief in the continuity of historical events, and in his unshakable faith in progress. Most important of all, he had been equipped by Professor Allen with a thorough knowledge of historical methodology, an understanding of comparative techniques, and an unquenchable enthusiasm for research into the past. Fred Turner did not know his own future when he boarded the train for Portage that spring day, but it was foreordained. He would be a historian.

II

The Making of a Historian:

WISCONSIN

1884-1888

IN 1884, when Fred Turner graduated from the University of Wisconsin, he was well into his twenty-second year. He had no set plans for the future. History, true, was his passion, but no sensible person would consider a career in a subject that could lead only to boredom or the poorhouse: boredom if he elected high school teaching and was doomed to a lifetime of listening to disinterested students recite memorized passages from a wretched textbook; the poorhouse if he had the audacity to seek a college professorship. There were few opportunities for the historian in those days; not until 1881 did any university establish a professorship in American history, and in 1884 only fifteen professors and five assistant professors of history could be counted throughout the nation. President Eliot of Harvard was not far wrong when he warned two young men that year that to consider history teaching as a livelihood would be "extreme imprudence on their part."[1] Nor was improvement likely. Established professors in respectable disciplines saw history as an auxiliary subject, so unrelated to the main body of classical knowledge that it could be taught by any hack—if taught at all. This was no field for an enterprising young man, if that young man planned to eat regularly.

So Turner reluctantly turned his back on his new love, and instead he weighed two possible careers. One was to capitalize on his fame as a college orator and become an instructor in rhetoric; he was sorely tempted when the regents of the University of Wisconsin offered him an assistant instructorship in rhetoric and elocution that summer, at a salary of $600 a year. But after a few weeks of soul-searching he decided that such a career was not for him. The other was to join with Reuben Gold Thwaites, editor of the *Wisconsin State Journal*, in a glamorous venture. Thwaites, eight years Turner's senior and an experienced newspaperman, had long dreamed of starting his own paper in Colorado or New Mexico, where he could "grow up with the country," and he tried to persuade his young friend to go along as his assistant. Turner listened to tales of the cattle country and the profits to be made from advertising cattle brands, but in the end he decided that the risk was too great.[2] Madison was too attractive to leave, even for the Wild West.

Journalism, however, was an obvious career for a young man whose second home had been a newspaper office. Even before his graduation he had been offered a part-time post as Madison correspondent for the *Milwaukee Sentinel,* and he had accepted with alacrity. That was a busy summer for Fred as he bustled between university and state capitol and city hall to gather news for his dispatches—dispatches not notable for their brevity, as he was paid at space rates. He proved himself an extremely capable reporter, with a nose for news and a willingness to reveal the truth whatever the consequences. In June 1884 he unearthed a plot to unseat John Bascom as president of the university, and in a series of biting articles he showed the flimsiness of the evidence and the prejudiced nature of the charges. Again that fall his snooping revealed a Democratic plan to use the Madison state fair for political purposes, so angering many politicians that they slammed their doors in his face from that time on.[3]

As a reward for his efforts he was dismissed from his post in January 1885, when the state legislature reassembled and a more experienced correspondent was sent from Milwaukee to report its doings. Turner used his father's influence to land a political plum as transcribing clerk of the state senate, then convinced the *Chicago Inter-Ocean* and the *Wisconsin State Register* that he should report Madison's news for their columns. Once more he distinguished himself with his crisp dispatches, his bold denunciation of corruption, and his tenacity in ferreting out information.[4] His reputation was growing, and a career as a newspaperman seemed certain.

Then, overnight, his whole future course was changed. His beloved Professor William Francis Allen was responsible. Long overburdened with an excessive teaching load, and increasingly frail in health, Professor Allen finally won from President Bascom a term's leave of absence that would allow him to renew his acquaintance with Europe's classical antiquities. A substitute had to be found for the spring term, and Allen's prize pupil, who was conveniently at hand, was offered the post. Turner was ready; he had been reading history in every moment of his spare time ("his favorite theme in literature," one of his fellow reporters noted), and was eager to preach what he had been practicing. When the Allens sailed for Italy, in April 1885, Fred Turner was ready to trudge up the Hill once more, this time to face his first class as "instructor in history." "That he will make a success of the branch in which his whole soul is enlisted," wrote one of his friends, "goes without saying."[5]

Turner's weeks in the classroom that spring convinced him that he had found his true vocation, even though he had to labor endlessly to teach classes in dynastic history and medieval institutions in a manner worthy of his mentor. By fall, when Professor Allen returned, Fred Turner was willing to make any sacrifice to continue his studies. There was no opportunity in the history department, where Professor Allen handled all the instruction, but an assistant was needed for Professor David B. Frankenburger in rhetoric and oratory, and even that was preferable to a return to newspaper work. The prospect was hardly alluring. His assignment was to conduct the courses in elocution required of all freshmen and to supervise the "rhetoricals"; this chore meant not only heavy class hours, but listening to the six essays and six declamations required of all freshmen and sophomores each term, and coaching the most talented for roles in the three "rhetorical exercises" where the entire student body assembled to applaud the most successful lower-class orators. "Private rehearsals precede public declamation" read the college catalogue, "and each student has personal criticism passed upon his essay."[6] Turner had to provide hours of individual instruction for more than half of the 416 students enrolled that spring, in addition to teaching a larger-than-normal class load. His "assistantship" had blossomed into a full-time job—and more.

He plunged into this academic maelstrom in September 1885, after finding comfortable quarters in a rooming house at 772 Langdon Street, kept by the kindly Mrs. Bross. The year that followed was one that he would gladly have erased from his memory—no history, little time for pleasure, only the endless monotony of coaching inept pupils in speaking skills ill-suited to their inclinations. Even so, the freshman declamatory contests that ended the school year, in May 1886, showed he had done his distasteful job well. One by one his pupils mounted the stage and spoke: a young lady whose voice broke occasionally as she recited "The Creed of the Bells," a lusty youth who deafened the audience with "The Storming of Mission Ridge," a pretty girl who charmed her hearers with "The Sioux Chief's Daughter," and many more. "The whole programme," reported the local scribe, "spoke well for the efforts of Mr. Fred J. Turner, instructor in elocution."[7] Turner was delighted, of course, but he was also exhausted. When he fled to Portage that summer no history books weighted his suitcases; he was content to escape to the northern lake country, where bass lurked under every lily pad and the trout streams were so overflowing that Fred, his father, and his brother landed as many as 160 a day, some of them well over a pound. This was the life he loved. "Blessed be the woods," he wrote feelingly, "Wish I might never see a city again." Especially when that city was Madison, where classrooms of students had to be taught elocution. "How I dread returning to my work at the University," he confessed as autumn approached. "Yes, I know I ought to be ashamed to say so, but I do."[8]

Fate, in the form of a sudden increase in student enrollment, changed his life for the better. With the freshman class almost doubled, Professor Allen's dynastic history course attracted such a large audience that nearly half were forced to sit on the floor. His complaints, added to those of the students, forced the Board of Regents to divide dynastic history into two sections. Allen, in turn, surrendered the American history courses to Turner, who was relieved of about half his instruction in elocution. This program was preferable to a steady diet of rhetoric and oratory, but Fred Turner soon found that he had not relieved his work load. Fifty-three juniors crowded his upper division history course, and 32 freshmen comfortably filled the room for his lower division offering; in addition, he taught four classes in oratory, each ranging from 31 to 41 pupils. Twelve hours a week in the classroom, 229 students to be taught and examined, eight hours a week in rehearsals for his oratorical students, special coaching for those scheduled in declamation contests—this was the schedule that kept Turner hard at work during the fall term that year.[9]

This baptism into the academic world hardened him for still more rigorous tasks ahead. During the winter and spring terms his teaching load was increased from twelve to fourteen hours—two sections of territorial and dynastic history were substituted for his American history courses—and he held five hours of daily rehearsals for the declamation contests required of all students in oratory. To add to his burdens, Professor Allen fell ill in January, and again in May, forcing Turner to assume his classes and to take on the burden of managing the department for two or three weeks at a time. Yet so eager was Turner to study and teach American history that he responded to a student request that he offer a special advanced course on the Civil War. Twenty students were admitted, though a larger number applied, and sessions were held twice weekly in the rooms of the State Historical Society of Wisconsin, then housed in the state capitol building.[10]

If this were not enough, that academic year 1886-87 added one more burden to his already overflowing schedule. By this time his future was decided: he would be a history teacher, whatever the cost and however poor the rewards. To fit himself for that career advanced work was in order, for a master of arts degree was a necessity and a doctorate in philosophy desirable. The University of Wisconsin could provide the first—it awarded its first master's degree in 1886—and Allen would be a superb director of his master's program. That year Fred J. Turner was listed in the catalogue as a candidate for the degree of Master of Arts, and as spring approached he finally stirred himself into making some progress toward that degree. The sole requirement was an acceptable thesis; with his usual unrealistic optimism he was certain that would be finished by fall, even if part of his vacation had to be sacrificed.[11]

The subject was already decided upon. While poking about in the State Historical Society library, preparing his paper on the Grignon Tract, he had stumbled on bundles of letters from French fur traders in the area, water-stained, tied with leather thongs, and written in what Turner described as execrable French. Here was a glamorous page from the past that had never been turned. Why not write a thesis on the early fur trade of Wisconsin? Such an ambition had been in the back of his mind since 1885, when he had toyed with the idea of a book on the trading activities at Green Bay.[12] Allen gave his blessing, and, in May 1887, Turner began his exploratory investigations. These proved discouraging. He was innocent of any knowledge of French, and even if he had been a master of that tongue the letters were so badly written, and couched in such eccentric grammar, that progress would have been slow. This he discovered when he pressed Therese S. Favill, an attendant at the library who used French expertly, into service. "With my guessing I could get along faster than she could," he reported ruefully.[13] He made some progress over the next weeks, but with the temptations of Lake Mendota in the spring, the pressure of the end-of-year class work, and a natural inclination to avoid unpleasant tasks until the last moment, the work moved very slowly. By summer he found that he had scarcely scratched the surface of the material, and his prospects for a degree were no brighter than they had been a year before.

Two related events that summer of 1887 gave Fred Turner the direction he lacked before. Both had to do with a charming young lady named Caroline Mae Sherwood. The two had met a year before—in late June, 1886—when Mae (as he always called her) visited Madison with her mother to enroll a younger sister in the university. Turner, who knew Mrs. Lucinda Sherwood vaguely, through his parents, gallantly suggested that they put up at Mrs. Bross's boardinghouse, where he was living. That was the happiest suggestion of his life. Madison sweltered in a heat wave, with temperatures in the high eighties and dust ankle-deep everywhere after a two-month drought, but Fred and Mae spent two happy days walking the tree-lined lanes near the city, talking of books and the mysteries of life. Scarcely had she returned to Chicago when she was followed by the first of the hundreds of letters Fred was to write her; "Dear Miss Sherwood," it began, and went on to complain that the days just past had been so enjoyable that the rest of the summer "will be like a plum pudding when all the plums were at the top."[14]

Turner was hopelessly lost at the first sight of Mae. His letters, stiff and formal at first, as befitting that Victorian generation, warmed rapidly, and the "Dear Miss Sherwood" gave way to "Darling Little Mae." There were visits to Chicago, too, at Christmas and Thanksgiving and during the Easter holidays, with walks about the streets of the Kenwood section where she lived, and with them protestations of love. By mid-winter Turner was filling his Commonplace Book with love songs instead of historical jottings:

While thy dear head nestles close to my shoulder
While thy soft bosom is swelling in mine
Ever my thoughts grow bolder and bolder
Closer my face unto thee doth incline.

The next step was inevitable. Fred proposed to Mae on one of their Christmas walks, soberly pointing out that he was a poor risk because his health might fail and his profession was highly unlucrative; Mae was properly Victorian when with a "dark little face" she said a soft "Yes." He went back to Madison the next day and poured out his love in a letter that she always treasured: "I love you as I fancy in the old mediaeval days a Catholic loved the pure face of the Madonna. . . . You seem to me a bit of God's best work. . . . I feel something within me say that I will justify that love if God will let me."[15] They kept their engagement a secret at first, telling only their parents, but by April the news was out and the congratulations were pouring in. Fred Turner was committed to marry Mae as soon as he was able to provide for her.

This gave Turner a new purpose, but such was his love for Mae that he could not resist one last fling before settling into his career. She suffered badly from hay fever and spent part of each summer in the Massachusetts Berkshires; why not forget the labors of the past year and spend an idyllic holiday together? Too, Professor Allen planned to attend the 1887 commencement ceremonies at Harvard that spring, and he urged his young disciple to come along. So the plans were laid: Turner would do his sightseeing at Cambridge and Boston, then join Mae and her mother at Chatham on Cape Cod, where he had found an economical rooming house. After a week or so there they would journey together to Conway, in western Massachusetts, for a few more weeks of pleasure before he returned to work. He would bring along a volume of Tennyson and one of Whittier to read as they walked the New England lanes, and a volume on Tennessee that he had agreed to review. He would also have a French grammar tucked in his suitcase. "I propose to know lots of French before the few weeks of summer life are over," Fred warned, "and you will have to study how to instruct a pupil—dull exceedingly, and very prone to tell his 'Je t'aime' with wordless lips and forget the book in looking at the teacher."[16]

There was little French learned that summer. Fred Turner boarded the train for Chicago as soon as commencement was over, stopped to gape in awe at Niagara Falls, enjoyed the lazy look of the Mohawk Valley, and watched fascinated from the speeding car's windows as the Hudson fell behind and the Berkshires loomed before him. "The hills wrote their rugged autographs against the skyline," he wrote, "the people began to say na-ou, the farms were little patches of stone and daisies turned up slantingly on the hillsides—and I knew I was near New England." Boston was a "veritable Aladdin's palace," and he savored it all —the Common, Faneuil Hall, Old South Church, Bunker Hill, Trinity Cathedral. Harvard's commencement ceremonies were fascinating to one unaccustomed to pageantry; so were the student orations phrased in terse Anglo-Saxon "with none of the bombast that is found in our western college commencements." He loved every moment; "I could gladly pitch my tent on Boston Common for the rest of my days." But Chatham beckoned, and there Turner journeyed on July 1 to join Mae in a succession of heavenly days—dips in the chilly Atlantic, moonlit walks on the beach, gargantuan meals of clams and lobsters, a day with the fishing fleet, where he caught a few cod before succumbing to seasickness. Then the train ride to the northern Connecticut Valley, where a carryall waited to take their little party to the hill town of Conway and Mr. Lyon's boardinghouse, presided over by an eighty-seven-year-old patriarch who inflicted such lengthy prayers on the guests that Turner learned more of the Scriptures than he had in years. The young lovers spent hours strolling down stone-walled lanes, reading Tennyson while they perched on hilltops, stealing an occasional kiss on moonlight walks, visiting historic Deerfield, near by. Never had Fred suffered as when they said their last farewells; even a fishing trip to northern Wisconsin with his father failed to erase the pangs of separation. By August 21 he was back in Madison, sad that "the play time of the happiest summer of my life" was past.[17]

Fred Turner did not realize that he stood on the threshold of a new life. For two years he had dawdled away his time—fishing, talking with friends, playing whist, reading aimlessly—as he followed his daily teaching rounds with little thought of tomorrow. Even now, safely installed in Mrs. Bross's new rooming house at 620 State Street, he found buckling down to his thesis difficult; "I don't accomplish as much as I wish to," he confessed, "for I am sure to come across someone to talk to every hour or so, and besides my work is puzzling."[18] Yet there was no room for laziness in Turner's new life, and the mood soon passed. Suddenly, unaccountably, he found himself moved by a compelling ambition. His eastern trip was responsible; it had shaken him from his comfortable routine and had forced him to take a fresh look at his purpose in life. "I understand myself better since I went to New England," he told Mae. He had been growing provincial, overly ascetic, lazily contented. He had patterned his routine on the monotony of the Midwest countryside. "There were no wide sweeps of water horizontally, no lofty hills, no deep valleys. It was *commonplace*."[19] Now all was changed; that eastern journey had broadened his horizons and stretched his imagination. It had offered him new goals and stirred the ambition that was needed to achieve them. "I have learned the lesson of the struggle that there is in life. . . . I am sure I can make the future my own. If determination will do this for me, it will be done."[20]

Here was a new Turner speaking, one capable of conquering giants. His first task was clear: he must win a permanent teaching post at a reputable university (Wisconsin, if at all possible). This could be achieved only by earning his degree and beginning the publication program that would make him known to the academic world. There was a practical reason for this now, for his good friend and sponsor, President John Bascom, retired that summer of 1887. Bascom's successor, Professor Thomas C. Chamberlin, a locally well-known geologist from Beloit College, was a friend of Fred Turner's father, and received Fred warmly when he called—even listening to a request for a salary increase. Chamberlin listened, but he did nothing. This was discouraging, for Turner's youthful optimism had led him to believe that the new president might make him a professor and head of a new department of American history. Rightly or wrongly, he believed his future to be less secure now than it had been under President Bascom. He felt he had to prove himself to win a permanent spot on the faculty. "Just now," he wrote, "my vision embraces only one object—a *reputation* sufficient as a basis for demands upon the university."[21]

That urgent need taught Turner an important lesson: he could produce books or articles or lectures only under pressure. If something *had* to be done, he did it well and on time. If not, he squandered his working hours on play or makeshift tasks until a deadline loomed. This was to be the pattern of his life, and it was the pattern of that 1887-88 academic year. His daily routine was rigid: rise at 6:45, breakfast an hour later, classes from 9 to 1, an hour for dinner, classes from 2 to 4, the library for an hour, a walk and tea from 5 to 7, study from 7 until 11, bed at 11:30.[22] Gone from his letters now were accounts of long walks, of games of billiards, of hours in his canoe on Lake Mendota, of leisurely evenings with friends; they were filled instead with comments on books read, papers prepared, and progress on his thesis. What an amazing amount this regime accomplished. During that academic year Turner not only revised his courses to make them more challenging, but published a number of book reviews and his first small pamphlet on American history, prepared two major historical papers for club meetings, wrote an extended article for the *Encyclopaedia Britannica*, and completed his dissertation.

Teaching came first, for he had to prove himself in the classroom to assure a permanent post on the Wisconsin faculty. Turner was fortunate here, for he was no longer a temporary substitute for Professor Allen, but a full-fledged instructor with two courses of his own in American history: "Subcourse IV," an introductory class that met twice weekly in the fall and winter terms, and "Subcourse V," an advanced offering in which the subject was studied "more largely from the genetic viewpoint than the preceding, developed by topics." Added to these were the usual "Rhetorical Exercises" for freshmen, which took an undue portion of his time. More work was added during the winter quarter, when Professor Allen succumbed to pneumonia, brought on by sub-zero temperatures (the classrooms stood at 45° and students sat wrapped in scarves and overcoats). Once more Turner was asked to take over Allen's courses, in return for some relief from his own rhetorical work. That term he taught his own two American history courses, with 103 students enrolled, Allen's two classes in dynastic history, with 74, and four freshman classes in oratory, with 158—a total of 334 students and sixteen hours of instruction, some of it in medieval history, in which he was ill-prepared. "It was like floundering in deep water," he confessed.[23] Allen recovered in time to resume teaching in the spring term, but Turner again added to his own burdens by offering a course in the Civil War, this time limited to fifteen pupils who met for two hours weekly. This was a back-breaking load, but Turner did not mind—so long as he could study and teach the subject he loved. "I have had delightful work this month," he wrote Mae in October, "—no elocutionary classes until this week so I have been able to devote my time largely to history."[24]

Such burdens might have justified Turner in parroting a textbook or repeating the lectures he had given the year before, but his materials for each class were specially prepared, usually after extensive reading, and always with fresh interpretations that mirrored his maturing thought. "It demands a year to get fully into the spirit of the thing," he complained, after spending a whole morning and evening preparing a one-hour lecture on the Spanish explorers, "and a lifetime to be an expert on the subject."[25] These efforts were demanded especially for the advanced course, in which the subject was treated from "the genetic viewpoint"; there Turner had his first chance to venture along untrod paths of interpretation. His instructional methods were strictly conventional; he used Alexander Johnston's *History of American Politics* (1879) as his basic textbook (a dull chronicle that devoted a chapter to each presidential administration and piled fact on fact with little concern for causal forces), and required reading in orthodox sources that ranged from George Bancroft and Francis Parkman to current magazine articles. Turner made his own contribution in his lectures and discussion, for there he opened vistas on the past that would not seem out of place in a classroom of today.

He began with some sound words on the nature of history. "Society," the students were told, "is an organism developing upon certain *lands*, with changes at certain *times*. History takes account of these changes and their causes, and needs geography and chronology." To understand the evolution of that organism, the historian must know what it received from the past, how it was affected by surrounding organisms, and the physical conditions in which it developed. Once these were understood, the organism could be studied in four ways: vertically (inheritance), horizontally (interaction of neighboring organisms), physically (the impact of the environment), and sympathetically (understanding the peculiar conditions of the time).[26] Perhaps Turner revealed his immaturity by his pretentious imitation of biological terms, but he was preaching Darwinian doctrine to his students long before the evolutionary theory had altered the viewpoint of many better known historians. He was also showing them that human society was infinitely complex, and could be comprehended only by awareness of the multiple forces operating to cause change.

His fresh interpretations explained the reasons for America's unique course. He saw the nation's history unfolding in a series of chronological stages: *exploration* in the fifteenth and sixteenth centuries, *colonization* by France and England in the seventeenth, *possession* as England ousted France in the eighteenth, *revolution* as independence was won, *federation* as local and national interests were reconciled between 1789 and 1820, *economic growth* as natural resources were utilized in the quarter-century before 1845, *separatism* as the slavery conflict checked the trend toward centralization from 1845 to 1869, and *expansion* between 1869 and 1886 as the West was peopled. Modern scholars might quarrel with the neatness of Turner's categories, but they made far more sense than the division into presidential administrations which was common in his day. So also did the basic theme through which he sought to explain the distinctiveness of America's history. The nation's story, he believed, had to be told in terms of the occupation of the continent, and of the ideas and institutions resulting from that occupation. Chief among these were the concept of democracy and the principle of federation. Turner saw the distinctive "form" of the American past to be "territory growth," the distinctive "idea" to be the relationship between local self-government and the federal authority. The interaction of these forces underlay the federal system of government and, in turn, influenced the conduct of foreign affairs, the slavery controversy, and "western growth." He viewed "land—homesteads—railroads" as instruments of that growth, and worthy of study. These were unusual concepts in a day when every historical work available to Turner viewed the history of the United States from the vantage point of New England and scarcely mentioned the westward expansion of the American people, let alone the impact of the West on the nation.

Sprinkled through Turner's lectures were occasional references that indicated his growing conviction that the frontier had played a part in shaping the past. The Salem witchcraft outbreak resulted from the impact of "the wilderness behind [the] settlements on [the] minds of people from populous England of somber temperament and rigid adherence to [the] Jewish code"; the English, Germans, and Scots-Irish who settled interior Pennsylvania formed a "frontier mixture"; in the lands ceded by the states national sovereignty was elevated above the "historic spirit of State Sov[ereignty]," and served as a strong nationalizing force. These were but a few straws in the wind, significant (if at all) only because of his later theories. Turner's basic views were orthodox, and he gave little attention to social and economic forces, but more than most young scholars of his day he was searching for the causal forces influencing the social organism he was studying.

If he was less bold than he might have been in his teaching, Turner's private speculations on the historical process were more unrestrained. These he jotted as he read. More and more now his home was the library of the State Historical Society, housed in the south wing of the state capitol building, where it overflowed the second floor. Lyman C. Draper, the dedicated wisp of a man who presided over the library's riches from 1854 to 1886, had built its collections from less than fifty volumes to more than 110,000, and he had stocked its shelves with an unrivaled collection of manuscript materials on the early history of Kentucky and Tennessee, newspaper files, government documents, and miscellaneous sources on the older West. His successor, Reuben Gold Thwaites, who took office on January 1, 1887, rivaled his predecessor in energy and in eagerness to aid scholarly investigators. Nowhere could Turner have found more ideal working conditions. Here was a scholar's heaven. "The books," he wrote Mae that year, "stand on their long lines of shelves like great armies; armies made up of the wisest men who ever lived. . . . To sit down on a stool and see the unexplored riches about one, riches that he couldn't begin to dig into in a lifetime, makes him very aware of his *littleness*, too."[27]

Turner's digging was thorough that year, and the more he dug the more he found history irresistible. The more, too, he realized that one aspect of the past fascinated him more than any other. "The more I dip into American history," he told Mae that fall, "the more I can see what a great field there is here for a life study. One must even specialize here. I think I shall spend my study chiefly upon the Northwest and more generally on the Mississippi Valley. The history of this great country remains to be written."[28] A few months later he was still boiling with enthusiasm. "I do not talk anything now but Western history. . . . I have taken a fever of enthusiasm about the possibilities of the study of the great west and of the magnificent scope of United States history in general."[29]

When came this decision? Turner never answered that question satisfactorily, and no one else could even approximate an explanation. His boyhood in Portage's quasi-frontier atmosphere, his awareness of his pioneer ancestors, the jolting realization during his trip to New England that the West was unique, the sectional pride that resented the neglect of his region by New England historians, his belief that the comparative techniques he had learned from Professor Allen could be used to unlock secrets about the American past—all these, perhaps, contributed to Turner's determination to study the West at a time when such an interest was unheard of. He understood the boldness of his decision. "I have," he wrote at the time, "started in a line that is not well travelled and I can see a way of treating it that is out of the usual line."[30]

Did he even then vaguely visualize the theory that was to make him famous? We will never know, but we do know that as he read, new ideas, new interpretations, new plans for research projects, crowded into his mind. We know, too, that a surprising number of these had to do with the role of the West as a formative force. The Commonplace Books he kept that year are filled with notes that mirrored his interests.[31] Some suggested topics worthy of investigation: collate the date of each permanent settlement in Wisconsin with the causes influencing migration; collect the treaties and state papers bearing on the West Florida controversy and show its relation to expansion into Louisiana, Texas, and Oregon; investigate the effect on American nationalism of the Georgia Indian controversy, Daniel Webster's speeches on nullification, the Civil War, and migration into new western states; study the connections between the boundary question, the weakness of the general government, and John Jay's attitude toward the Burr Conspiracy; investigate railroad construction as a consolidating force for the nation and show how railroads introduced groups of foreigners into the United States; explain why the North was so ready to coerce the South in 1860 in terms of Mississippi Valley commerce and the desire to possess the West. These might seem traditional subjects today, promising few riches for the prospector, but in 1887 they were revolutionary.

So were his interests in the formation and structure of western society, and in the role played by immigrant groups in community organization. These stemmed from observations made on his regular fishing trips into backwoods Wisconsin, where he saw recent German

arrivals "dispossessing whole townships of Americans and introducing
the customs and farming methods of the fatherland."[32] Sights such as
these suggested new fields for investigation. How were societies formed
in the West? "Need of study of foreign groups," he wrote in his Commonplace Book. "Anthropology, political economy, sociology, politics.
Votes by districts. Why are Nor[wegians] Rep[ublican]. Irish Dem-
[ocrats]?" A short time later he added another observation: "Our composite nationality. Glances through a microscope in the historical laboratory. Biological methods applied to the study of a typical group of
immigrants. The Pomeranian settlement at Portage. Evolution." The
notations suggest Turner's line of thought. What would be the results, he was asking, as Europeans crowded Yankees from their lands,
adjusted to American conditions, and adapted their imported techniques to the differing environment? Would the resulting civilization
differ from that of their homelands? If so, what features of the new
environment would cause alterations? These were exciting questions.
"If I fill my letters with speculations about the evolution of American
society from diverse elements of European origin," he warned Mae,
"—don't think I am insane or that I love you the less; it will simply be
an experiment in enthusiasm."[33] Turner reached no conclusions and was
still a vast distance from his frontier hypothesis when he made those
observations, but he was groping in that direction.

He was also beginning to build a reputation beyond the borders of
Madison. Turner's first ventures into the world of publishing was probably arranged by his mentor; Professor Allen was a tireless book reviewer, and he saw no objection to sharing some of his spoils with his
disciple. The reviews gave Turner little chance to expound his own
interpretations; he was asked to appraise two volumes on Benjamin
Franklin by Edward Everett Hale—*Franklin in France* and *Franklin
the Peacemaker*—for *The Dial*, a well-known literary magazine. Thirty
pages of notes on the reading done for those reviews attest to the thoroughness of Turner's preparation. This bore sturdy fruit; his judgments were sophisticated, judicious, and properly critical, particularly
in pointing out the specific contributions made by each volume.[34] The
editor of *The Dial* was delighted, calling it "an excellent article," and
Professor Allen was sufficiently impressed to recommend Turner to
his friends on the staff of *The Nation*. More reviews followed, most

of them short notices that were published unsigned in that worthy journal. One that he particularly enjoyed was a review of James R. Gilmore's *John Sevier*, a book that he found good because it showed that "the valley of the Mississippi is a too much neglected branch of the history of the country," and bad because it stressed boldness of characterization and smoothness of narrative rather than "the accuracy and cautiousness of statement that should mark historical composition."[35] These sound judgments pleased the editor of *The Nation*, who sent on a whole bundle of books for review, as well as Lyman C. Draper, who praised them highly and made cautious suggestions that Turner aid him in editing some of the manuscripts he had gathered, and Reuben G. Thwaites, who thought that his young colleague might join him in writing a history of the state.

Kudos bred kudos, and Turner did not wait long before more came his way. President Chamberlin was the instigator; he had been invited to prepare the article on Wisconsin for the *Encyclopaedia Britannica*, and while he felt competent to do the sections on physiography and geology, he was less certain that he could deal with the history of the state. Would Turner be interested? Turner was interested, even though he was burdened with the excessive teaching load of the winter term and a thesis that demanded attention. He put himself to the task at once, combing census returns and government reports for statistics, digging into the capitol archives, and wringing information from his friends in the legislature. For three weeks he worked steadily until well after midnight; "I feel as though I had been through a threshing machine," he reported to Mae when it was done at last.[36] The result was worthy of the effort. In remarkably few words he sketched the evolution of the state's complex economic and political system from its primitive beginnings, tracing the stages of growth, describing the transition from lead mining to lumbering to agriculture, and showing the effect of the Civil War on the emergence of an industrial-urban civilization.[37] In the article Turner again demonstrated his concept of history as genetic growth, and of society as an evolving organism constantly altered by internal and external forces. One has only to contrast Turner's treatment of Wisconsin with the antiquarian histories of other states in the ninth edition of the *Encyclopaedia Britannica* to realize the extent of his contribution.

More to Turner's liking was his third publication to be completed that busy year, even though the pressure of other duties forced him to delay this until the summer of 1888. Once more Professor Allen was responsible. He had been asked to compile an outline and reading list on the history of the West to be distributed through the National Bureau of Unity Clubs as a guide for women's groups, but was too ill to do a proper job. Turner was delighted to accept an assignment so congenial to his tastes, even though the deadline was only a few weeks away. He soon discovered that he had taken on a major task; only the best books on each subject could be mentioned, but all books had to be read to select those to be included. Yet the work was done on time, and in a manner that won Professor Allen's verdict of "very good."[38]

Outline Studies in the History of the Northwest was hardly a precedent-smashing contribution to western historical studies, but it was the first booklet to bear Turner's name, and it was typically Turnerian in its genetic approach, its stress on geography as a necessary backdrop for historic events, and its emphasis on the stages of growth common to emerging societies. Its fifteen topics (that being the number specified as fitting best into the club year) began with "The Land of the Aborigines" and progressed through "French Exploration," "French Occupation," "French and Indian Wars," "English and Spanish Dominance," "The Northwest in the Revolution," "The Ordinance of 1787," "The Northwest Territory," "The Louisiana Purchase," "Slavery in the Northwest," "The Exploration and Occupation of the Northwest Coast," "The Struggle for Oregon," "The Great American Desert," and "The Alaska Purchase," to "The Northwest of Today." Under each heading the best books were listed and described, a bibliographical exercise that revealed its author to be far better versed in the history of the Old Northwest than of the far western states.[39] Whatever its merits, Turner had produced the first published outline of frontier history. The hundreds that were to follow, from Turner's pen and from the pens of his followers, were to make many improvements but add little to the basic structure.

If Fred J. Turner was gaining his first slight national reputation, his local fame was growing far more spectacularly, and with good cause. He had an irresistible combination of virtues as a public speaker; his melodious voice and training in oratory allowed him to captivate any audience, while his knowledge of western history provided him glamorous subject matter that few Wisconsinites could resist. So it was that he found himself pushed into the limelight on two occasions during that overcrowded academic year, both with exciting results and both adding to his reputation as a student of the West.

The first grew from his activities in the Madison Unitarian Church—strangely enough, for he was a scoffer who had been turned from religion by the "nonsense" preached by his first Sunday School teacher, and he now felt that theology was "about as substantial as an ice to a man who hasn't eaten anything for a month."[40] But Professor Allen was a pillar of Unitarianism, and the minister, the Reverend Dr. J. H. Crooker, was a rationalist whose staunch defense of the University had won him the loyalty of its faculty. When Allen urged his young colleague to join the two young people's clubs sponsored by the church, he readily did so. One, the Channing Club, was devoted to religious discussions and had little appeal to Turner, although he did become a member and participated in at least two lively meetings, one on New England's church history, the other on Benjamin Franklin's religious views.[41] The other, the Contemporary Club, was more to his taste; this was divided into five groups that met fortnightly to hear papers on contemporary history, current literature, social science, modern art, or the latest scientific discoveries. The contemporary history group was made to Turner's inclinations, and he entered into its activities with such enthusiasm that he became the club's president during the 1887-88 year—an office foisted on him, he told Mae, because he dozed off during a long discussion of Rider Haggard's novels and was elected before he could protest.[42]

Turner learned a great deal at the Contemporary Club, and he gave a great deal to it in return. Twice he engaged in discussions that provided background for his later theories—one an analysis of Hermann von Holst's *Constitutional History of the United States,* which he was to recall when, a few years later, he berated that eminent historian for failure to reckon the frontier's significance, another on a lecture delivered in 1887 by Henry George, who spoke on "Land and Labor." Turner paid less attention to that land reformer's views than he should —his thoughts drifted to Mae and how pleasant it would be to be a landowner in a shady part of Mendota's shore—but something of the single tax lodged in his mind, to be unearthed when he pondered the effect of free land on the settlement process.[43]

He was also preparing himself for his major contribution to the Contemporary Club's program. The suggestion came from Professor Allen: why not give a series of lectures on the history of the Old Northwest? Boston's Old South Church was attracting national attention with its scholarly lectures, pleasingly presented; shouldn't some be given at Madison? Then, too, such a series would popularize American history as a field of study, correcting the imbalance that made European history so popular. Turner rose to the bait at once, drafting the surprisingly rich local talent—Consul W. Butterfield, Reuben Gold Thwaites, Allen himself—scheduling dates between January and April 1888, and preparing a syllabus that would guide the audience. These preparations proved so effective that the Unitarian Church was packed to overflowing for the first lecture and even more crowded for the second.[44]

All this acclaim made his own task more difficult. His assignment was the third lecture on "The Ordinance of 1787," a subject not unduly difficult to prepare. Or so he thought as he began writing during the Christmas holiday, well in advance of his March 5, 1888, delivery date; he would have the whole thing done in two days. Two weeks later, as the vacation was drawing to a close, he had "just begun to write a little," and found it "uphill work." Another month and a first draft was ready, but it was a rough first draft with much yet to be done. At that point Turner made a near-fatal mistake: he showed his paper to Allen and Thwaites. "Allen thought I had not prepared the lecture sufficiently; Thwaites thought it was too long. Allen said read your documents in full; Thwaites said cut 'em out and generalize." Caught between this conflicting advice, he followed his own path by trying to "lighten it up" and shorten it a bit. This took time. Two days before that March 5 delivery date he was still at work, fortifying himself with a daily glass of sherry as "a good thing to use for a 'spurt.'"[45]

These heroic sacrifices bore fruit, for he was ready by March 5 to face the audience-jammed church with a completed manuscript before him. Judged by modern historical standards, the result hardly justified the effort. His views were thoroughly orthodox; his oratory embarrassingly ornate. "On the side of Wolfe fought the English language, democracy, and local self-government"; the Revolution was won by "men of the Anglo-Saxon race" who "against the divine right of the King, set the divine right of *man*"; George Rogers Clark was a holy crusader who won the West for the new Republic; the American peace negotiators were "a trio of Americans [who] beat the crafty ministers of France and Spain at their own game"; the unselfishness of "plucky Maryland" forced greedy Virginia to cede its western lands; the Ordinance of 1787 was a "charter of liberty" that struck a death blow at slavery.[46] Turner was treading no new paths when he laid those platitudes before his audience, but they loved it. For an hour and a half they listened enraptured as he read his way through sixty-seven pages of manuscript; then they rocked the hall with their applause. "He is," judged the local critic, "thoroughly conversant with his subject and handled it in a scholarly manner, evincing great enthusiasm and historical research."[47]

Here was glory, and Turner loved it. More was to come over the next days as tributes poured in—from his students, from other lecturers in the series, from Thwaites, who thought he had "made a ten strike." He was in seventh heaven. "I am," he confessed to Mae, "surprised at my love of praise. It is like wine to me."[48] More was to come as the series moved to its triumphant conclusion with a lecture by Professor Allen on "The Position of the Northwest in General History"—a lecture marred by the fact that Allen was ill and asked Turner to read his paper for him. There was no gainsaying that Madison was well pleased with the program; even more gratifying was the fact that it attracted national attention. A number of newspapers noted its success, educators and historians voiced their approval, and the influential *New England Journal of Education* described it as worthy of imitation elsewhere.[49]

There was no time for Turner to bask in his glory; spring was at hand and he still had his master's thesis to complete. He had made precious little progress that academic year, partly because he was juggling a half-dozen assignments in addition to his teaching, partly because the French language required more time for mastery than he could allot. He tried, but there were too many temptations. "If I can possibly find opportunity this term I mean to take up some French studying," he confided to Mae as the school year began. "I need that language especially." A month later he could report some progress: "Last evening I read French—half a dozen pages. It was easy French of course, and I guessed at some things." That spurt did not carry him far. December found him still floundering, and in April, with the thesis deadline only weeks away, he was almost ready to give up. "I must," he told Mae, "learn to read French fluently this summer."[50] No prophet was needed to predict that Turner's dilly-dallying would delay his degree well beyond the 1888 commencement, and perhaps forever.

It might have done so, but for one saving factor. Like many compulsive non-finishers, he could work under the lash; given a deadline and enough pressure, and Turner would respond. This came in the form of an invitation from Professor Allen to read a paper on the Wisconsin fur trade to the prestigious Madison Literary Club, a gathering of the cultural elite of town and gown. Here was a summons that could not be refused; from the day in October when he accepted, Turner knew he *had* to have a paper ready by mid-May of 1888. "I shall," he admitted, "have to do some lively scratching if I don't get picked all to pieces. It will be good exercise for me."[51] All that fall and winter he worked only haphazardly, picking his way slowly through the water-stained pages of trading records, painfully deciphering badly scrawled letters, building a pile of notes so slowly that the end seemed nowhere in sight. Cheerfully optimistic, as usual, Turner was not in the least alarmed—not, that is, until May Day awakened him to the unpleasant fact that his paper had to be delivered in only two weeks and that scarcely a line had been written.

These were the conditions under which he worked best. For the next fortnight Fred Turner lived, breathed, thought, the Wisconsin fur trade. "My room is rustling like a forest with leaves on the price of beaver skins and whiskey, bread and bullets, brass ear knobs and tobacco. . . . The gay chant of the Canadian voyageur rings out . . . in my nightly dreams and I murmur fantastic French in my sleep"—"At present when anyone says 'dear' I think of deer, mention of Martin Luther makes me say 'yes a martin was worth $1.00,' . . . I have hobnobbed with the midnight stars regularly and allowed lessons to care for themselves." Those were the words of a young man who was very hard at work indeed. By the end of those two weeks Turner was in disgrace with his family, his friends, and even with Mae, "and all because I have been trying to get some style and spice and connection into a long row of facts and figures."[52]

His dilemma was as old as Herodotus: should he be dully realistic or imaginatively glamorous as he told his story? Fred Turner knew what he wanted to do. He wrote to Mae:

I am trying to tell how the forest which was to the Englishman a gloomy, repellent, witch haunted realm, lying in its darkness behind his doors, tenanted with lurking foes—not to be entered except with defiant conquering spirit—was to the Frenchman a gay, witching, inviting thing. If it wasn't too flowery I should also like to say that the St. Lawrence flushed an irresistible invitation down its watery course, and whispered to the Frenchman of the Great Lakes from which it came—that the wilderness sang to him in the melody of its waterfalls, thrilled him by the solemn music of its pines, dashed him with the spray of cataracts, awed him by the mystery of its dark glades, and brought him its untutored children to wonder at his goods and call him master—even as Caliban lay at the feet of Trinculo and the potent bottle on Prospero's enchanted island.[53]

He could not do so, of course; one can almost hear him sigh as he went on to say that he had to stick by his facts. Yet the struggle took time. Two days before the paper was due the final draft was only half written; not until minutes before it was to be delivered were the last flourishes added. "I feel," he confessed, "like a Freshman who is coming on with an essay and must write it at twelve o'clock the night before."[54]

Miraculously, Turner was ready when he arrived at the door of Burr W. Jones's Langdon Street home, to find an unusually large audience awaiting him. The next two hours were something less than pleasant to Turner. He spoke well, and the critics named by the Literary Club to comment were extravagant in their praise. So was the local press when it reported the event the next day. He had prepared a "capital" paper that was both "interesting and instructive"; he had "re-peopled the dark forests of early Wisconsin with the now forgotten *couriers des bois;* revived the old Canadian boat songs which were wont in olden times to echo through the gloomy and bluff-girt valleys"; "presented a vivid picture of life at those outposts of civilization."[55] But Turner knew better. "I am not proud over its success," he confessed; in his own mind he had made a reputation "as a digger in fields uninteresting" and had proven that the dry subject could never captivate a popular audience.[56]

Whether he was right or wrong, the Literary Club appearance had forced him to complete his thesis. He read the entire document to Professor Allen a short time later and was duly praised; Allen thought it good enough to be published by the State Historical Society. Allen was right, for despite its overemphasis on detail and its underemphasis on interpretation, "The Character and Influence of the Fur Trade in Wisconsin" was a pioneering work that revealed many of the virtues of Turner the mature historian. His concern was not only with the "what" but with the "why"; his careful study of the state's geographic features allowed him to show that trading routes not only determined the early economic growth of the region, but played their role in international diplomacy. Even more significant was the evolutionary approach he adopted; brushing aside George Bancroft and Francis Parkman, who viewed the fur trade as an insignificant phenomenon, he pictured the trader as a herald of progress and an essential ingredient in the emergence of civilization. "The Indian village," he wrote, "became the trading post, the trading post became the city. The trails became our early roads. The portages marked out locations for canals. . . . In a word, the fur trade closed its mission by becoming the path finder for agricultural and manufacturing civilization."[57] This was state history at its best, unmarred by the antiquarianism so universal in that day, and linking the local events that Turner was studying with the national scene.

It was also the last step in his progress toward the coveted (and in those days, rare) master of arts degree. Fred J. Turner was graduated on a stifling hot day in June of 1888, together with five others who had completed their graduate work, then vanished into the north woods with his father, to enjoy the healing balm of trout fishing. He needed such an interlude, for his future had already been determined—much to his dissatisfaction. He was to continue his graduate work and earn a doctor of philosophy degree, not in his beloved Madison, with Mae in near-by Chicago, but at the awesome Johns Hopkins University, in distant Baltimore. And he was to begin that painful ordeal that autumn.

This thoroughly disagreeable prospect was forced on Turner by President Chamberlin. An able administrator with high ambitions for his little university, Chamberlin recognized the potential skills of his young friend and saw in him a chance to add to the faculty a degree-holder from the nation's outstanding history department. Turner had other ideas. He wanted the doctorate eventually, and he recognized the preeminence of Johns Hopkins, but he also wanted assurance that he could return to Wisconsin as a professor as soon as he had earned his degree.

Or, if this proved unacceptable to the president (as it did), he would stay on as instructor for one more year, but as the head of his own American history department, then accept a leave of absence for study at Hopkins in 1889-90. He was confident that he would succeed. "I have," he wrote Mae, "a line of work mapped out in Western history which is untouched and which I think will prove worth my study and a basis for securing position in some institution if not here [*sic*]."[58]

Turner had rosy dreams, but it was President Chamberlin who had the power of decision, and, in April 1888, he laid down the law. Turner would spend the 1888-89 academic year on his doctorate; he would not be assured a professorship or even a post until he had proven himself; if he did well in competition with the cream of the nation's historians in the East, he *might* be welcomed back as an instructor at a considerably higher salary than he had been earning. Turner had no alternative but to accept this ruling with good grace. He asked only that his leave of absence be kept secret until a substitute could be found who was not sufficiently talented to get a foothold in the department. By June all arrangements were made, and the Board of Regents publicly announced that Turner had been granted leave "to enable him to perfect himself in his specialty at Johns Hopkins University."[59] "It is hoped," wrote the local editor, "that at the end of his course at Johns Hopkins he may return to Madison and again take up his work as instructor of oratory and history, for which he is so well fitted."[60]

Fred Turner must have shuddered as he read those remarks, for he had no intention of suffering through more instruction in oratory, and he was determined to return to nothing less than a professorship. Yet the decision had been made. He would be a university teacher, he hoped at the University of Wisconsin, if not there, then at some other institution. Twice that summer he refused lucrative offers of high school posts—one paying $1400 and the other $1500—even though the temptation was strong to settle into a comfortable existence with Mae at his side.[61] He had to prepare himself for a career in teaching and research, and Johns Hopkins was the ideal training ground. Turner chose wisely, for that year in Baltimore was to be one of the most pleasant, and probably the most significant, of his whole career.

III

The Making of a Historian:

JOHNS HOPKINS

1888-1889

FRED J. TURNER arrived in Baltimore on September 25, 1888, thoroughly dissatisfied with himself and dismally unhappy. He was gloomily aware that he had wasted most of the summer. True, he had completed the syllabus on *Outline Studies of the History of the Northwest*, which was soon to be published, but he had scarcely touched his French studies and had done little of the reading needed to prepare himself for the awesome Johns Hopkins courses. Instead he had squandered weeks on the trout streams of northern Wisconsin and had spent an idyllic fortnight with Mae in the cool forests of northern Michigan, near Marquette. Those were happy experiences, but his conscience burdened him now as he thought of the responsibilities ahead. "I am ashamed of myself at the end of every summer," he confessed, "when I think how very little I have worked. It is a bad habit I have gotten into."[1] He would have to pay for his sins now, and the price would be high.

To add to his woes he was nursing a miserable cold, apprehensive of the new world that he must conquer, and desperately lonesome for Mae. They had parted in New York, she to settle into her hay-fever sanctuary at Conway, he to take "the cars" southward. "You must be with me or I am the most miserable man in the world," he wrote.[2] Sad at heart, he checked into the Carrollton Hotel, reported his presence to the registrar of the university, and spent twelve unhappy hours tramping the streets in search of a room. Never had he seen such run-down, bad-looking, vile-smelling boardinghouses in all his life. All were the same: the haircloth chair on which he was seated while the servant sought out the mistress, the gilt-framed pier glass and sepulchral fireplace, the engravings of Robert E. Lee and "Stonewall" Jackson, the relics of the late departed husband, the mysterious odors that blended garlic, dust, and antiquity. The mistresses were all the same too, drab and yellow in appearance, gushing that they only took in boarders because they were lonely and loved young men, eager to show the cells that they called rooms, and the beds that were perfect racks, built on slabs with a husk mattress covered with quilts that might have covered the limbs of Noah, save that neither flood nor washing had ever touched them. "So I have wandered from street to street all day with almost exactly the same experience."[3]

When he finally came upon the boardinghouse kept by Mary Jane and Hannah Ashton, at 909 McCulloch Street, Turner knew he had found his haven. Mary Jane, who managed affairs, was an "old maid" of some thirty summers, but she was perennially young in her understanding of youth, able to regale them with lively conversation, and sympathetic when they rebelled against long hours of study with pranks and high jinks. His room was comfortable—"the most elegant room for sleeping I have ever found," he reported to his mother—and the meals bountiful—deviled crab, beefsteaks, toasted crackers, rolls, corn cakes, sweet and Irish potatoes, pears and grapes, for breakfast; roast, vegetables, hot breads, and sweets for the noonday dinner; cold ham, tongue, bologna, a box of sardines, and crackers for tea; fish or meat with hot breads for the light supper. Best of all was the companionship. For a half-dozen years Miss Ashton's ample care had attracted history students—Woodrow Wilson, Charles Howard Shinn, Albert Shaw, Charles H. Levermore, and a host more—all of whom made a point of returning to her establishment when visiting Baltimore; Woodrow Wilson was to spend the spring term there, to Turner's lasting benefit. The present company was almost as distinguished: Charles Homer Haskins, the brilliant young medievalist, and Robert K. Aikman of New York University, whose passion for photography sometimes overbalanced his scholarly interests, boarded at Miss Ashton's. Only two old maid spinsters who occupied one of the rooms cast a pall over this lively crew.[4]

His physical needs satisfied, Turner sought out the Johns Hopkins professors who would be his guides. There he experienced a major disappointment. J. Franklin Jameson, who taught most of the American history courses, was to be on leave that year, dooming him once more to heavy doses in two areas outside his major interest: medieval and European history under Herbert Baxter Adams, and political economy under Richard T. Ely. The program that they helped him arrange was memorable both for quantity and variety: the "History of Politics," "Church History," and "International Law" under Adams; "The History of Political Economy," "Elements of Political Economy," and "Special Economic Questions," with Ely; a study of "Social Science" taught by visiting lecturers, and, for some inexplicable reason, a freshman survey of "Advanced Algebra, Analytical Geometry, and Calculus." Capping this strange smorgasbord was the famed history seminar, which met each Friday night from eight to ten, and was taught by the entire department.[5]

Whatever his courses, Turner could learn much, for Johns Hopkins was then an oasis in the intellectual desert of American education. Still in its lusty infancy, it centered within itself the renaissance that was revitalizing the quest for learning in the United States. All was turbulent, all was new, all was exciting, as students and faculty united to push back the borders of knowledge, unhindered by the tradition and lethargy that made such older institutions as Harvard "as solidified as the bones of the Mammoth," in Herbert Baxter Adams's phrase. Hopkins, Turner later remembered, lured students from all the nation and let them form the university; Harvard attracted nationally but forced its undergraduates into the matrix of New England culture.[6] This was not far wrong, for in those days Johns Hopkins approached the ideal of the national university of which George Washington had dreamed. Graduates of ninety-six colleges were enrolled in the graduate school in 1888-89, merging their sectional enthusiasms into a common purpose, and generating a yeasty atmosphere that encouraged adventuring along untrodden intellectual trails.

These were many, for in the 1880s, the whole world of the mind, in both Europe and America, was in ferment, stirred by Charles Darwin's evolutionary hypothesis. As this gained credence, scholars in every discipline reappraised their subjects by applying biological concepts: geologists talked now of the earth as an "organism," economists applied the same term to institutions, and historians applied it to human societies. These were pictured as constantly changing, constantly evolving, for this was the law of the universe. All past knowledge was out-moded; man must restudy every branch of learning for evidence of the growth that was now recognized as the basic fact of life, whether of biological or social organisms. Scholarship was on the threshold of a vast adventure that would reveal the truth for the first time, and in America Johns Hopkins University was the nucleus of that search.

All faculty members and students were aware of this distinction, and all were determined that the university should wear its badge proudly. This meant constant, furious, dedicated work. When Charles McLean Andrews, a contemporary of Turner's, observed that there was "almost a religious fervor among the younger scholars," he was telling only half the truth; that same fanaticism toward learning infected the faculty and drove them to heroic effort. There was competition among the students to excell; there was competition between faculty members; there was competition between students and faculty. Professors—and there was one for every nine pupils—goaded the students to work ever harder, then worked ever harder themselves to keep abreast of the students. "Johns Hopkins," Turner reported after he had been there a few months, "keeps a man at work from morning till after mid-night. . . . Here it is a constant race between the professors and the students to see who can do the most work."[7]

The marketplace where they displayed the fruits of their learning was not the classroom (Turner was disturbed to find that lectures—and very dull lectures, at that—were the normal method of instruction, rather than the "topical" approach used so successfully at Wisconsin), but the famed "Seminary" under Professors Adams and Ely. This, the catalogue declared, is not a class but "an association of instructors with the fellows and other graduate students in this department for the prosecution of original studies in American history, institutional, social and economic." Its purpose was not to teach history but to learn history; its students would become master historians by working with master historians, then they would apply the research techniques they learned to problems of their own. Herbert Baxter Adams saw the semi-nar as a meeting place for scholars who would work cooperatively to unlock the secrets of the past, exchanging views, sharing discoveries, and gaining knowledge by their joint efforts. Here the entire history of the United States—and of the world—would be rewritten.

The seminar's setting was worthy of its objectives. Stretching down the middle of a third-floor room in the university library was a red-topped table strewn with the latest journals and pamphlets, with seats for twenty-four students, each of whom had a drawer for his writing materials. Eight thousand books, arranged in alcoves by subjects, lined the walls; above them were hung portraits of the giants of the historical world—Edward A. Freeman, Lord Bryce, George Bancroft, Hermann von Holst—and interspersed among these were plaster busts of Jared Sparks, Francis Lieber, Alexander Hamilton, and John C. Calhoun. Emblazoned above a bulletin board, in large letters, was the theme of the seminar: Edward A. Freeman's dictum that "History is Past Politics, and Politics Present History." Opening from the main room were offices for instructors; two lecture rooms; a newspaper "bureau," where copies of the latest journals were displayed; and "a geographical and statistical bureau."

Fred Turner found fascinating new interests in every corner of the seminar room, but the "geographical and statistical bureau" excited him most. Here were the raw tools that he was to use through a lifetime devoted to mapping data on political demography and applying statistical techniques to cartography. The room was the creation of the able president of Johns Hopkins, Daniel Coit Gilman, himself a statistically oriented geographer; at his insistence it was equipped with maps, charts, diagrams, atlases, and a series of wall maps that could be used to illustrate the physiographic basis for the history of any nation. Professor Adams heartily agreed with this emphasis; "In the Johns Hopkins University," he wrote, "physical and historical geography are made the basis of instruction in historical and political science."[8] This approach was not completely new to Turner; Professor Allen had relied heavily on the use of maps, and he had infected his prize pupil with his interests. But for the first time Turner could realize the variety of the tools available to the historian interested in the graphic presentation of data. His lifetime use of statistical and cartographic techniques was certainly shaped by his Hopkins experience.

If Turner gained much from Hopkins's "geographical and statistical bureau," he gained far more from the exciting new world of historical studies that awaited him. Professor Allen, gifted though he was, and alert to changing intellectual tides, was too isolated to stay abreast of the latest developments along the eastern seaboard or to be fully aware of progress in allied fields that influenced historical thought. At Madison, Turner had been in a cultural backwash, better supplied than most, but still distant from the populous East, where the winds of change blew most strongly. In Baltimore he was in the center of the academic world, surrounded by the half-dozen historians and political economists who were primarily responsible for these changes. He entered that mainstream, moreover, just at a time when historical scholarship was in the midst of the twofold transformation that ushered in its modern age. On the one hand, it was shedding its "amateur" status and becoming professionalized; on the other, it was shifting from a "romantic" to a "scientific" methodology. Turner was cast into the middle of this revolution, to his lasting benefit.

Professionalism was a natural outgrowth of the multiplication of universities during the late nineteenth century, and of the utilitarian assault on the traditional classical curriculum that followed. With education reaching an ever-widening segment of the population, and with preparation for life rather than for the clergy its objective, historical studies assumed new importance as essential to training for citizenship. For that reason, history courses proliferated; between 1884 and 1894 the number of full-time teachers of history skyrocketed, from twenty to more than a hundred. The reluctant classicist or philosopher who had been sufficient for such instruction in the past would no longer do; departments of history began to appear in the burgeoning graduate programs that were remaking American universities; by the time Johns Hopkins was founded, in 1876, twenty-five institutions awarded the doctoral degree, and more were to come. The trademark of these universities was the historical seminar, introduced into Michigan, Harvard, and Johns Hopkins during the 1870s to train the research-oriented young professors who would staff the growing number of history departments. These scholars, all thoroughly impressed with the quality of their own education, felt vastly superior to the "literary" historians who had long dominated the field—the George Bancrofts, the Francis Parkmans, the William H. Prescotts, the John L. Motleys—and demanded a professional society that would recognize their elevated status. This was formed in 1884, when Herbert Baxter Adams summoned forty-one eminent historical scholars to Saratoga Springs, New York, to draft a constitution for the American Historical Association. By 1890 the association had more than six hundred members, many of them amateurs, but all dedicated to the dual purpose of indoctrinating their countrymen in history and serving as guardians of the nation's cultural heritage.[9] The craft had its guild, and was proudly conscious of its professionalism.

Even more important to Turner was the rise of "scientific" history. This began to emerge in the early 1880s, fostered by a rebellion against the traditional romanticism that had characterized historical studies for generations. America's scientific historians found their inspiration in the theories of two individuals. One was Leopold von Ranke, whose school of German historiography was then in full flower; practitioners of this cult made objectivity their idol and sought to reveal exactly what happened in the past, unmarred by interpretation or evaluation. The other was Charles Darwin, who, along with his fellow biologists was then in the public eye. From the evolutionists, scientific historians adopted a methodology based on experimentation and inductive reasoning, and a concept of society as a continuously evolving organism responding to changing pressures, just as did animal organisms.

Objectivity was the first essential, and to achieve this they had to re-study critically the primary sources that recorded mankind's history, extracting from them exact facts, just as a paleontologist would use fossil remains to reconstruct the precise truth about a phase of animal evolution. These facts should speak for themselves, unmarred by the prejudices or opinions of the investigator. Hypotheses and interpretation were outlawed, lest they distort the objectivity of the interpreter. The sole duty of the historian was to accumulate masses of facts, arrange them in proper order, and allow a synthesis to emerge. Scientific historians saw history as the purest of all disciplines, for it alone was built on inductive reasoning and banned all conjecture.

The evolutionary hypothesis was just as essential to the new methodology. Scholars had to re-examine the past not only to achieve objectivity, but to record the growth of institutions as they responded to internal and external pressures. Historians could reveal the continuous, connected, chain of events through which social organisms evolved from their genesis to the present day. This was a noble ambition, but they soon found it unattainable; nature provided biologists with the succession of fossil remains needed to show the evolution of a species, but man's written records were too few and too recent to allow institutions to be traced to their remote beginnings. The ingenious solution to this dilemma was to adopt the "comparative" technique of the philologists. Linguists taught that similarities in word forms revealed their common origin; why not assume that institutions could be studied in the same way? The scientific historian could compare a modern institution—such as a New England town—with an ancient institution—the medieval German *tun*—and if he found similarities, conclude that the one evolved from the other. This was the twisted logic that fostered the "Teutonic" or "germ" school of history in the 1870s and 1880s. Its members held that the Aryo-Teutonic peoples who had occupied the Black Forest of Germany in the days of Tacitus had developed the democratic institutions later to be shared by Great Britain, Germany, and the United States. The task of the historian was to compare American institutions with those of the ancient Teutons, and when the comparison proved exact, proclaim that he had discovered the "germ" of that institution.[10]

The holy temple of the Teutonists was Johns Hopkins University, and its high priest was Herbert Baxter Adams. Adams's own contribution to the succession of absurdities that they produced was to link select New England towns with the tribal councils of Germanic tribes. There Teutons brandished spears to show their assent, or muttered their dissent. This proved they practiced democracy. So did New England towns. Therefore New England towns were "survivals" of the tribal councils, the flowering of a "germ" that had lain fallow in Anglo-Saxons for a thousand years. So Adams wrote in his *Germanic Origins of New England Towns*. He also added an unbelievable amount of nonsense. The ancient Teutons developed in their *moots* "the seeds of parliamentary or self-government, of Commons and Congresses," the concept of a single head of state, the use of a small council, and the delegation of authority to "a general assembly of the whole people." In these practices "lay the germs of religious reformation and popular revolutions, the ideas which have formed Germany and Holland, England and New England, the *United States*." "It is," wrote Adams, "just as improbable that free local institutions should spring up without a germ along American shores as that English wheat should have grown there without planting."[11] These were the views, weird delusions though they were, that formed the mainstream of American historical thought when Turner entered Johns Hopkins. He was to sit for a year at the feet of the man who had done more to professionalize history, and to popularize

the then-accepted Teutonic germ theory, than any other scholar in the
nation.

This was the thrilling new world that waited Turner as he settled
into the routine of the Hopkins graduate school. His schedule was
filled with a constant round of lectures, work at the library, endless
reading in the assigned textbooks, and (the brightest spot of all) the
seminar. From the first, on October 5, he found those Friday night
meetings the most exciting event of the week. Across from him were
the older graduate students, sitting in awesome array: Charles L. Smith,
who had studied in Germany; Charles McLean Andrews, one of the
two university "Fellows," strikingly handsome, with "a dark expression,
and finely moulded face"; Charles Homer Haskins, "very young, but a
strong man"; others whose names he had not yet learned. Beside him
was a fellow-westerner, Frank W. Blackmar of the University of California. Dr. Adams, seated at the head of the table, explained the methods
and purpose of the seminar, called on Frank Blackmar to read a paper
on "Relation of the State to Higher Education," joined with Dr. Ely in
comments that showed how much he knew about higher education, then
talked until ten o'clock about his own experiences in adult education at
the summer Chautauqua assembly. "A wonderfully energetic man,"
Turner described him when he wrote to Mae that night, "able to get
work out of a crowd."[12]

Evenings such as that, with a dozen men as sharp as himself, were
glorious experiences to a young man of Turner's inclinations, and his
letters glowed with enthusiasm. "I was," he reported to his mother,
"likely to drift into superficial work when I left Madison—now I have
caught a little of the spirit of genuine scholarship—and it is rejuve-
nating." To Mae he was more outspoken: "I am in the full swing of
university life and I *like* it! I am becoming to feel like a boy let out of
school,—and I really wish to jump and shout aloud in the new freedom
and happiness of having pleasant work and *only* pleasant work. I am
growing like a plant in the sunshine."[13] When Adams and Ely assured
him that he could complete his doctorate in one year—if he learned
enough French and German to pass the reading tests—his happiness
overflowed. Johns Hopkins was an academic heaven, and all was right
with the world.

This exultant mood soon dimmed; as the first excitement died away, he felt a little lost in the impersonal vastness of Baltimore. He was strictly on his own, with no Professor Allen at his elbow to give advice and encouragement, and this heightened his sense of loneliness. Then, too, the excessive number of courses that he had elected proved an impossible burden, and he was daily falling behind in his work. A period of soul-searching and some good counsel from Professor Allen solved his problem; he decided to focus his reading on work for the seminar, the course on the nineteenth century under Adams, and Professor Ely's courses in political economy, in the process dropping church history, and listening to the lectures on Roman history and international law without attempting to do the assignments. This sensible adjustment made life easier, but Turner was still unhappy that his enthusiasm for the West found few sympathizers; only two fellow-students showed a spark of interest, one studying the Spanish missions of California and the other willing to consider a dissertation topic suggested by Turner on the frontier land companies of the post-Revolutionary era.[14] Madison was a happier hunting ground for one of Turner's inclinations.

These dissatisfactions were minor, and they were soon forgotten as he immersed himself in his studies or sought relaxation in Baltimore's abundant culture. Long hours of work, when his brain felt so thoroughly saturated that it would shed any additional information, were balanced with walks about the Maryland countryside, or vigorous daily exercise in the college gymnasium, or musical performances that stirred him to tears of joy; after hearing *Il Trovatore* he felt that he should pawn all his books and become an artist, and he realized after attending a series of six symphony concerts that he had never properly lived before. He spent his Sundays visiting the churches of the city, one by one—Catholic, Protestant, and, most frequently, Quaker—to be overwhelmed by the music and pagentry but untouched by the spiritual appeals. The Quaker services were his favorites, but their drab monotony soon palled; "I don't like colorless things too long," he explained to Mae. "There must be some novelty, some spice about things, or I am in danger of getting ennui."[15] Turner did not know it, but he was admitting one trait that would make it impossible for him to write books that parroted well-known facts of the past.

The Christmas holidays offered fresh diversions, for his flattened pocketbook decreed that he could not go to Chicago to see Mae. Instead, a very lonesome Turner dined that Christmas day at the home of

Dr. Ely, forgot his troubles by immersing himself in Edward Bellamy's *Looking Backward*, and spent a memorable three days at the annual convention of the American Historical Association, in near-by Washington. The papers that he heard intrigued him not at all—they were too detailed and their "facts were not *illuminated*"—but he did enjoy rubbing elbows with the greats of the profession, and he did enjoy giving a paper himself. This was a favor for Professor Allen, who was unable to attend and asked Turner to present the essay that he had previously read to the Contemporary Club on "The Place of the Northwest in General History." Turner did so so effectively that the association's secretary wrote glowingly of the manner in which he had described "that march across the continent which really constitutes America."[16]

He was to perform again during the next weeks, and on no less than three occasions. The first took place without his presence; on January 2 in distant Madison his master's thesis on the Wisconsin fur trade, revised into suitable form, was read to the State Historical Society of Wisconsin by its secretary, Reuben Gold Thwaites. This was an important step in Turner's career, for his thesis could now be published by the society, and he could follow his soon-to-be-usual practice of ordering a hundred copies to be distributed wholesale throughout the profession. Some responded with less enthusiasm than he would have liked —Francis Parkman could unbend only to the extent of finding it "interesting"—but Turner was pleased with the "complimentary letters" that came his way and eager to get on with a publication that "will really justify praise."[17]

His second assignment was more to his liking. The seminar was progressing in its usual confusing way—Turner listened that winter with varying degrees of interest to papers on the statistical techniques of the Interstate Commerce Commission, congressional legislation in Indiana, the relation of the Continental Congress to the colonies, and the history of Greek coinage—but his turn was to come. Two turns, in fact, first with a review of William Barrows, *The Indian Side of the Indian Question*, then, on February 15, with his own paper on "The Influence of the Fur Trade in the North West from the Particular Standpoint of Wisconsin." This was carefully moulded to Johns Hopkins' "scientific" atmosphere; larded with statistics on the quantities of goods sold, and bursting with factual information on the nature of the tribes and traders, it shunned even such interpretation as enlivened his master's thesis. Yet such was the nature of the seminar that his audience found it a lively antidote to constant doses of the "germ" theory. "This," one of the instructors told him, "is the kind of atmosphere in which we can breathe." Those words he never forgot; they encouraged him to generalize and to seek bolder interpretations.[18]

Turner found even greater satisfaction in an extracurricular task given him by Professor Adams. Adams had returned from his graduate study in Germany as an ardent admirer of the German state-administered educational system, which offered a high level of instruction from the primary grades to adult classes. This was beyond the reach of the United States, but when he lectured at the Chautauqua Institute in upstate New York during the summer of 1888, he thought he had discovered an adequate substitute. He would make Johns Hopkins the hub of a nationwide program of adult education, with printed study programs, books specially written for such an audience, lecturers recruited from the graduate students, and examinations set and graded by the university. Eventually this network would be extended through the nation, with all universities participating under Hopkins's direction, and the whole population would be instantly converted into college graduates. "Adams," Turner reported, "found in the Chautauqua school an evolution from the camp-meeting, which in turn came from the hunters' outdoor life, and he insists that the Chautauqua assembly is only another form of the Folk-Moot."[19] With these "germs" it was a laudable institution, deserving support from the graduate students. If Adams had his way, Johns Hopkins would be converted into "a veritable school of peripatetic historians," traveling about the country spreading instant culture.

When Turner offered these wry comments he did not realize that he was to be the principal victim of Adams's enthusiasm. His summons came not long afterward; would he take over as an extension instructor with a modest compensation, sending out lessons to subscribers, reading their papers, and grading their examinations? His first assignment would be to prepare three syllabi on primitive, Chaldean, and Egyptian history. Thus Turner, unable to refuse such a request, added paper-reading and examination-grading to his overcrowded schedule. Nor was this the end, for Adams had still another favor to ask. He had agreed to give a "Teachers' Course of Lectures on American History" to forty or fifty

Washington schoolteachers, but found himself too busy to meet the class regularly. Would Turner give the March lecture on "The Conquest and Organization of the Northwest Territory?" This royal command was less burdensome; Turner had only to polish the lecture on the Northwest Ordinance that he had delivered before the Contemporary Club a year before, but he was terrified when he learned that the audience had swelled to ten times its projected size. "I shiver at the thought of seeing 800 eye glasses all leveled at me," he confessed to Mae. His fears were groundless; his training on elocution stood him in good stead as he led his listeners through the story of the upper Mississippi Valley, from the fall of Quebec in 1759 to the settlement of Marietta in 1788. There was still no hint in his orthodox narrative of the influence of frontiering on men or institutions, but his audience was more than satisfied. "I came, I saw, and I talked the regulation time," he reported, "—and got more than regulation applause."[20]

Recognition such as this—by Adams in selecting his young student to teach extension courses or lecture to such an audience, by Ely in asking Turner to take over his introductory political economy class when he was out of the city—was wonderous balm for the ego. Gone now were the doubts that burdened Turner in September; as the school year progressed he grew more sure of himself, more relaxed, more willing to enjoy the companionship of his fellows. Miss Ashton's boardinghouse offered abundant opportunity. Robert Aikman moved out in February, but Charles Homer Haskins remained, and Woodrow Wilson—on leave from his post at Wesleyan University to give a course on "Administration"—offered an exciting new friendship. "Dr. Wilson is here," Turner reported to Mae in early February, "homely, solemn, young, glum, but with the fire in his face and eye that means that its possessor is not of the common crowd."[21] From that time on, his letters were filled with tales of stimulating conversation over cider and doughnuts, of Wilsonian anecdotes that sent them into gales of laughter, of discussions of a chapter of Wilson's latest book that lasted far into the night, of carefree exchanges of wit and learning. "You would never recognize him as the grave author of a book that has called out the admiration of the ablest statesmen and historians of the world."[22] These were ever-to-be-remembered days—and nights—as the two men matched fine minds and deepened their friendship. They made a perfect pair: Wilson brilliant, inclined to leap to conclusions, an astute political philosopher;

Turner slower of mind but more accurate, exceptionally logical, a social philosopher. The bonds they formed over Miss Ashton's table were to last until Wilson's death, and to give both men intense satisfaction.

Yet all was not scholarly conversation at Miss Ashton's. That winter two of her pretty nieces, Miss Maud and Miss Cora, took up residence there, and on many an evening they inspired high jinks in place of learned discourse. On one memorable occasion, Haskins and Turner, making their regular raid on the kitchen for cider and cake, found the two girls in possession and baptized them with a liberal allowance of flour—to their ill-concealed delight. On another, Mary Jane Ashton treated her boarders to a tempting dish of caramels—heavily laced with red pepper. All were delighted when Miss Cora and Haskins began a gay flirtation, "making large eyes at each other" as he pretended to study. "You would," Turner wrote Mae, "hardly care to hear of my lectures, or . . . of how Haskins and I found Miss Hannah making waffles the other evening, and took possession of the kitchen until it looked like a battlefield, and how Miss Maud threw water over both of us—and all that sort of stuff. It does rest one's brain after a hard study over political economy."[23]

For Turner was studying, and studying harder than ever before. His courses for the second term varied little from those he had elected in September—"History of Politics," "International Law," "Social Science," "Elements of Political Economy," "History of Political Economy," "Special Economic Questions," "American Constitutional Law," elementary mathematics—with an additional twenty-five lectures on "Administration" given by Woodrow Wilson.[24] Even though Turner was auditing some courses and concentrating on those that satisfied his needs, his burden was still great, and it was intensified now by the need to complete all the requirements for the doctoral degree that June. His thesis had to be written; for a time he toyed with a history of government legislation concerning Indians, but common sense prevailed, and, rather than beginning a new topic he settled on revising his study of the Wisconsin fur trade to conform to Johns Hopkins standards. He also had to pass the reading tests in French and German and prepare for searching five-hour written examinations over the fields of his major interest as well as the dread oral examination, which would cover the entire scope of history. Add to these chores reading for his regular courses, grading examinations for extension students in Egyptian or Chaldean history, and keeping abreast of the seminar, and Turner was doomed to some of the busiest months of his life. He survived only by following a rigid schedule: rise at 8:44 each morning, breakfast at 8:45, classes from 9 to 2, dinner and chat with friends at Miss Ashton's from 2 to 3:30, study from 3:30 to 5:30, exercise at the gymnasium from 5:30 to 6:30, supper and talk from 6:30 to 8, and study from 8 to 11:45.[25]

Turner's dreams of a June doctorate, which inspired that Spartan regime, were unrealistic; he might master history and political economy, but French was a major stumbling block, and he had to pass a sight-reading test to qualify for his degree. He simply could not drive himself to study grammar or plod through dull translations when the reading matter of his courses was so enticing. He did make a try that March, but with disastrous results. "The Hopkins instructor," he reported to Mae, "had hard work to keep a sober face when I read some French aloud at his request." Turner did manage to salvage something from this debacle when Professor Ely consented to his taking the examinations in political economy before satisfying the language requirements. This meant he had an added work load, but the reward was worth the effort; with one-third of his examinations completed, he could master French and German while teaching, then return in the spring of 1890 to face the remainder. He would also win the favor of Professor Adams by his industry—an important consideration, for Adams was talking about a textbook in American history and hinted that he might ask Turner to write the section on the Old Northwest. This was necessary to a young man anxious to make western history his domain; "I cannot," he wrote, "let anybody else do my own ground."[26] A bit of slavery was justified to win such a prize. "A Baltimore spring coupled with study necessary to get off my work in Political Economy is not a good thing to grow fat on."[27]

Especially when the preparation of his dissertation was added to his other burdens. This was not a major task; he had only to re-write his master's thesis in terms suitable to the "scientific" tone of Johns Hopkins instruction. The principal shift in emphasis was the association of the trading post as an institution with its "germs" in primitive times. "The trading post," he began, "is an old and influential institution," then he traced its development from the days of the Phoenicians to modern times, showing that early traders pioneered the trails over which Europe was peopled. "The routes of the Migration of the Peoples were to a considerable extent the routes of Roman trade, and it is well worth inquiry whether this commerce did not leave more traces upon Teutonic society than we have hitherto considered."[28] Thus did Turner make his bows to Professor Adams and his "germ" theories—not to cater favors, but because he had to conform to the institutional interpretations so favored at Hopkins, and because he was genuinely interested in the evolution of nongovernmental institutions.

In two other ways Turner's dissertation mirrored the course of his historical thinking while at Johns Hopkins. In his thesis the genetic approach was even more strongly emphasized than in his earlier version; he saw trading posts as "the pioneers of many settlements," furnishing supplies for the miners, lumbermen, and farmers who carried civilization in their knapsacks; he pictured the trappers' trails as "slender lines of Eastern influence, stretched throughout all our vast and intricate water system" over which were to flow agricultural and manufacturing cultures. No less indicative of Turner's altered views was his emphasis on the stages of social growth that occurred along frontiers. Civilization, he believed, progressed in a series of well-defined steps, each building on the one before. Each frontier, he wrote, offered a "prototype" of the frontiers that were to follow, as well as furnishing "an exemplification of all the stages of economic development existing contemporaneously." Traders and hunters were first on the scene, then the cattle-raisers, then the "cultivators of the soil." "The manufacturing era belongs to our own time." The borderlands where "a primitive people comes in contact with a more advanced people," deserved careful study. "As a factor in breaking the 'cake of custom' the meeting of two such societies is of great importance."[29] Turner could never have written these words without his Johns Hopkins training.

If Fred J. Turner had paused to take stock as his Baltimore year ran its course, he would have recognized that he had grown substantially in knowledge, reasoning power, and self-assurance. No longer was he fearful that he might not measure up to the standards of the profession; he had successfully stood the test given by America's greatest historians in America's greatest university. Of this he was fully aware.

"One is at the heart of university life in America here," he wrote
that spring, "and very close to German thought, too."[30] Turner realized, too, that he owed his fresh learning and new self-confidence to
the four instructors who played a major role in guiding his studies:
Herbert Baxter Adams, Albion W. Small, Woodrow Wilson, and
Richard T. Ely.

Herbert Baxter Adam's contribution to Turner's emerging beliefs
must remain an enigma. That Adams respected Turner highly was made
abundantly clear by the posts he offered Turner and by the prospect
(which never materialized) of seeking Turner's collaboration in preparing a textbook; that Turner reciprocated this regard was shown by the
repeated favorable references he made to Adams in his letters. Never,
he testified, had he met a teacher who could inspire his students with
such enthusiasm for serious historical work, or demonstrate so successfully the relation between past and present.[31] Yet, in his later years,
Turner repeatedly stated that his rebellion against Adams's teaching
drove him to develop the frontier thesis. He was particularly irked, he
remembered, by his teacher's insistence that further research in American history was unnecessary, as every institution had been traced to its
"germ" in medieval Germany; students should turn to European topics
instead. If Adams ever told his seminar this (and the records do not
reveal such a remark), he had no intention of being taken seriously. In
his eyes every town in America housed institutions whose origins could
be traced; there were enough subjects crying for investigation to keep
students busy for a century. "Institutional history," he wrote in 1884,
"was as untouched as were once the forests of America."[32] Nor did
Adams turn his back on the West, as Turner later recalled; in 1885 and
1886 he directed the seminar into studies of land legislation, and he repeatedly called attention to the relationship between land and the free-
silver question. This was Turner's brand of history.

What Turner remembered as dislike of Adams was probably resentment of the smug self-satisfaction of all eastern historians of that day.
New Englanders particularly, and Middle State men to a lesser degree,
were indifferent to events beyond the Hudson, and they were inclined
to view the seaboard states as the nation's heartland. This bruised
Turner's strong sense of local pride. "Not a man that I know here," he
wrote Professor Allen, "is either studying, or is hardly aware of the
country behind the Alleghenies."[33] When he testified, as he did in

later years, that "my essay on the 'Frontier' was a protest against the tendencies of the eastern historians at the time it was written," he was nearer the truth than when he laid his resentment at Adams's doorstep.[34] Adams taught him a great deal, even though his teachings did little to bolster Turner's knowledge of the West.

Turner learned slightly more from Albion W. Small. Later a famed sociologist, Small was at this time an advanced graduate student who had been drafted to give a course on "The Growth of American Nationality" to a small group of Turner's contemporaries. This was admirably suited to Turner's needs; each member of the class was required to search source documents to show how and when sovereign power was transferred from colonies to states, and from states to nation. This gave excellent training in documentary research, but it also required a great deal of thought on the nature of nationalism.[35] The emphasis that Turner later placed on the frontier as a source of a nationalistic spirit in the United States owed something to the strict training he received in Albion Small's course.

Woodrow Wilson taught him far more. Wilson's lectures on "Administration" proved an exciting antidote to some of Adams's Teutonism, partly because they opened new vistas on state-federal relations, partly because they reflected a mild spirit of rebellion against the dominant "germ" theory. Wilson was still a Teutonist; he saw the New England town as "a spontaneous reproduction of the ancient Germanic Mark." But he also told his class that environment altered imported institutions, to the degree that the colonies, "without losing their English character, gained an American form and flavor," because each "borrowed what was best suited to its own situation."[36] Institutions, to Wilson, were not frozen monoliths, but dynamic organisms that responded to external and internal pressures. This was a concept that Turner learned from Professor Allen, but it was strengthened by Wilson's lectures.

Turner benefited even more from his hours of conversation with Wilson, as the two men took long walks about Baltimore or bantered away their evenings at Miss Ashton's boardinghouse. Wilson was an unreconstructed southerner, Turner a loyal westerner; both resented the disrespect shown their sections by easterners. As they sputtered their indignation, they agreed that each had to rewrite the history of the country in a way that would pay proper tribute to his homeland. They also talked a great deal about the nature of nationalism, a subject always of interest to Wilson and very much on Turner's mind now that he was under Albion Small's influence. One important point emerged; both agreed that the role of the West as a nationalizing force had been neglected by historians. If that were the case, had the West—and the process of expansion—influenced the nation's development in other ways? Should not that section's role be investigated in search of truths ignored by eastern-oriented scholars? These were key questions, and their impact on Turner cannot be overestimated. Throughout his lifetime he remained grateful to Wilson for planting many of the ideas that helped shape his frontier thesis.[37]

He was equally grateful to Richard T. Ely, and with somewhat more justification. This eminent economist hardly seemed suited to mould disciples. Overweight, short, with a low squeaky voice and a habit of swinging his glasses on a black cord as he paced about the platform, Ely was far from a sensational lecturer. Yet his ideas were so fresh, so invigorating, that he opened a new world to his students, and particularly to Turner. He was, those students knew, the leader of a group of young economists who were rebelling against the prevailing Ricardian view that man's behavior was governed by immutable natural laws. Man, they held, could better himself by bettering his environment. The duty of the political economist was to point the way by surveying the history of mankind's progress and directing it toward greater reform.[38] These were heretical doctrines for those days—Ely was subjected to periodic witch-hunts as a radical—but they helped reinforce Turner's growing belief that the social order was changeable.

They also led him into a solid diet of political economy, from which he emerged with a number of ideas that he was to weld into his frontier thesis. Ely's technique was to assign books that upheld both the classical and modern viewpoint—for example, John Stuart Mill's *Principles of Political Economy* and Francis A. Walker's *Land and Its Rent* —to supplement these with such varied viewpoints as those in John B. Clark's *Capital and Its Earning* and Henry George's *Progress and Poverty*, and to weave the opposing theories together in his lectures so skillfully that the students scarcely realized they were being converted to the modernist viewpoint. In the more advanced courses Ely's concern was largely with theories of rent; there his students grappled with the obtuse phrasing of Simon H. Patten's *Premises of Political Economy* and listened to their professor compound their confusion as he sought to reduce a complex subject to understandable terms. From this indoctrination Turner emerged with two concepts that vastly influenced his future thought: the understanding that societies evolved in well-defined stages, and that land "rents," or values, were determined by a variety of factors, including the concentration of settlement.

The stages of social evolution had been recognized by political economists since the 1850s, when the German scholar Friedrich List, in his *National System of Political Economy*, distinguished between savage, pastoral, agricultural, agricultural-manufacturing, and manufacturing-commercial states. Ely, in his books and lectures, adopted and refined these classifications; he saw civilization emerging through five well-defined steps: hunting and fishing, pastoral, agricultural, trading and commerce, and industrial. Each of these he explained in detail.[39] Turner recognized their significance to American society at once. "Apply in discussing stages of econ. life," he wrote in the margin of his textbook. "Instance of Indians and fur traders."[40] Later he was to describe the march of settlement across the continent in almost identical terms, with hunters and trappers leading the way, then herdsmen, miners, pioneer farmers, equipped farmers, and urban dwellers following. We know today that his classification was oversimplified; men seldom followed the well-ordered schedules that political economists postulated. But Turner had been introduced to a concept that he could use to advantage.

Ely also led Turner into the study of the theory of rent. "Rent," as the term was then used, meant simply the return on land; land that returned nothing to society, and hence was of no immediate value, was "free" land. Land was "free" in unsettled or sparsely settled areas; as population thickened and markets emerged, the land's rent increased in the form of higher returns and market value. Political economists quarreled over what determined these increases, or the amount of rent the land yielded. The classical economists, personified by John Stuart Mill, argued that land values were set solely by population pressures; the greater the pressure the higher the return. They bolstered their argument by giving as an example the situation in United States. There the lands were poorly cultivated and yielded less than their capacity because land was so plentiful and labor so dear that intensive agriculture was uneconomical. An abundance of land, combined with a scarcity of population and markets, lowered the profit, or rent, that could be

taken, and hence lowered the value of the land. Classicists recognized
that there was no completely "free" land in America, but that much
was relatively "free" because its value in terms of rent was less than in
populated areas.[41]

Arrayed against these theories were those of the "modernists," led
by Francis A. Walker, Simon H. Patten, and, particularly, Richard T.
Ely. Turner was thoroughly indoctrinated in their views; he carefully
read the books of Patten and Walker, and listened with equal care to
Ely's lectures. Basic to the modernist interpretation was the belief that
land values, or rents, were determined by social as well as physical
factors; they held that popular tastes, changing market conditions, in-
equities in distribution, and the living standards of cultivators affected
the quantity of production and consumption, and, hence, determined
the rent chargeable to land. Applying these theories to the United
States, they recognized that the "marginal lands" on the edge of the
cultivated areas provided their owners only a return on capital and
labor expended, and hence paid no rent, at least not when compared
with lands in thickly settled regions, which did more than "just pay"
for their use. The difference between the yield on heavily settled land
and the yield on land on the "margin of cultivation" was the amount
of rent. When a country was new, thinly settled, and distant from
markets, land of high fertility would yield no rent and would be
classed as poor, even though that same land, when settled, would be
judged "very good" and would return a high rent. In the first stage,
when land paid little or no rent, the political economists called it "free
land."[42]

From this formidable dose of economic theory Turner distilled a
number of concepts essential to his frontier thesis. He learned that
returns, or rents, on farm lands were determined by a variety of social
and physical factors, including soil fertility, transportation facilities,
nearness to markets, and relationship to cheaper lands. He recognized
that "free land" in the traditional sense was nonexistent, but that some
lands produced such a low rent that they could not advantageously be
cultivated. These lands would no longer be free, but would return a
steadily increased rent as markets emerged with a growing population.
These were essential lessons for Turner in understanding the settlement process in the United States. They are equally important to a
modern reader who would understand his frontier theories. When he

spoke of "free land" in the West, as he often did, he meant not lands that were actually free, but that paid a lesser return than lands more favorably endowed or situated. He recognized, too, that free lands disappeared as the coming of settlers and markets allowed them to command an ever-increasing rent. These definitions underlay Turner's later thinking, and stood him in good stead as he developed his understanding of American history.

That he had learned them well is shown by a remarkable letter he wrote to Professor Allen that year. "Wisconsin," he told his old mentor, "is like a palimpsest. The mound builders wrote their record and passed away. The state was occupied . . . by the most various peoples of the Indian race. Then came the French. Then a wave of Northern New York and Vermont fur traders—those who lived near the Lake Champlain route or the Great Lakes caught that fur trading spirit. At nearly this time came the miners from the South. Then the emigration from the *New York parallel* again to the farm lands. Now begins the State's policy of attracting immigration," and the coming of Germans in large numbers. Their lower living standards allowed them to displace the Yankees who had settled before them. "I do not," he went on, "regard the movement as entirely to be feared. I think peasant proprietorship is not being weakened by these German settlers. The quick settlement of lands in small farms has, I judge, prevented the absorption of such territory into great estates."[43]

Turner was now aware that society in the newer West was an evolving organism, responding to the repeated intrusion of newcomers from the East or Europe. He recognized that the relative ease with which "free land" could be acquired there served as a democratizing force, checking the growth of "great estates." Most important of all, he had learned that by applying theories learned in the classroom to his native Wisconsin, he could test historical concepts just as a biologist might test a new substance in a test tube. Turner had located the laboratory he was to use through his lifetime. His year at Johns Hopkins, which gave him a new perspective as well as a great deal of learning, made that discovery possible.

Valuable though that year was, Turner was impatient to leave Baltimore that spring of 1889, and to see his darling Mae after what seemed an eternity of separation. Two tasks remained before he could depart.

One—securing a teaching post—had occupied him through much of the spring. Turner knew what he wanted—a professorship in American history at Wisconsin—and he held three aces in his hand when he began his negotiations with President Chamberlin: a solid offer of an instructorship at Ohio State University for one year only, a chance to stay on at Johns Hopkins as Ely's assistant, and a vague hint from Professor Adams that there might be a position open on the Johns Hopkins faculty. He played these cards well, suggesting to his friends in Madison that they might "frighten the authorities" with news of the Ohio State prospect, and allowing his newspaper friends to raise the alarm in the press.[44] "We certainly hope," wrote one editor, "that Wisconsin may not lose the services of so bright a young historical specialist as Mr. Turner, who gives promise of making a decided mark for himself in the early future."[45]

President Chamberlin was no amateur at bargaining, and he refused to be panicked into a decision. He wanted Turner back, but on his own terms: as an assistant professor, who would do some work in elocution. Turner refused to accept; even Ohio State would be preferable to those endless sessions of coaching would-be orators. The negotiations went on until Chamberlin made a compromise proposal: would Turner return as an assistant professor of history with a salary of $1500 a year and the understanding that in a few years he would be elevated to a professorship in charge of the work in American history? Turner accepted, and in due time the formal invitation arrived with the rank and salary assured in return for seven or eight "exercises in history weekly," in addition to some work in civics. That letter was hurried off to Mae in Chicago with a note penned across the top: "Dearest One—" this "settles one of the problems of my life."[46] Fred Turner would return to his Valhalla with his course set. "Now again," he wrote, "I have a goal and a far away one—and I am nearly ready to shoulder my knapsack."[47]

Nearly, but not quite, for one task remained. He had to pass the examination in political economy that would assure completion of his doctorate a year later. Turner studied with assurance as he prepared for that ordeal, but with apprehension, too, for he realized that his whole future depended on the outcome. He was well prepared when he seated himself with the other candidates on June 10 in an empty recitation room, accepted the ten questions from the examiner, and settled down to five hours of strenuous composition. Midway through the morning a boy served them coffee and they talked and gossiped a while, eating sandwiches, and carefully refraining from mentioning political economy, as was the John Hopkins custom. Then it was over, there was a long wait for the result, for Ely was busy as usual. Two weeks later the word arrived: "It can scarcely be necessary for me to let you know that you have passed."[48] Turner had ended his John Hopkins year with a major success. Wisconsin and Johns Hopkins had fashioned a young historian of great promise; now he had to go back to Madison, to prove himself as teacher and scholar.

IV

Teaching—and the
Emerging Frontier Thesis

1889-1892

HEN Fred J. Turner left Baltimore that June of 1889, he was heavily freighted with both learning and ambition. He had to justify his assistant professorship by completing his doctoral degree, winning his spurs as a teacher, and proving himself as a scholar, all within the year. Only then could he persuade President Chamberlin to elevate him to a permanent professorship with a salary that would allow him to marry Mae. Gone now was the lethargy that had slowed his early progress toward his master's degree. "I discover," he wrote, "that my year away has had the effect to stir up the most inordinate amount of ambition in my nature."[1] That was true. The next three years were to be among the most productive—and rewarding—of his life.

In other years Turner would have used the summer to recuperate from his grueling Johns Hopkins ordeal by haunting the lakes of Wisconsin, but Portage seemed dull after the excitement of Baltimore. "You cannot understand how quiet and uninteresting my summer is," he complained.[2] By mid-July he was back in Madison, prepared to buckle down to his tasks, but even that charmed city was less attractive than he remembered it. Mrs. Bross's boardinghouse was so filled with teachers attending summer school that he had to live in a fraternity lodge; most of his old friends were provincial and uninteresting, with only Professor Allen and Reuben Gold Thwaites reflecting the "university atmosphere" to which he was accustomed; and Mae was far away. Never robust, she had tried to build her strength that spring at a health resort in upstate New York that fed its patients codfish and onions; when this medication failed, her mother decided to take her on an extended European tour. They left in May and were not to return until mid-October. Fred Turner was very lonely as he went about his tasks that summer. He spent mornings at the State Historical Society, afternoons studying French and teaching himself typing (with only moderate success), late afternoons on Lake Mendota or exercising in the college gymnasium, evenings at concerts or lectures at the annual Monona Lake Assembly.[3] Always thoughts of Mae haunted him; he spent more time than he should have pressing his married friends for information on the cost of living (a couple could get along on $1000 a year) or calculating the daily income from a salary of $1500 (365 into $1500 = $4.10).[4]

He also thought a great deal about the role of the West in American history, with impressive results. These appeared in a lengthy review of the first two volumes of Theodore Roosevelt's *Winning of the West*, which was published by *The Dial* that August. Turner could not resist displaying some of the nonsense learned from Adams; he wrote approvingly of Roosevelt's descriptions of the "forted villages" of the Kentuckians in which "reappeared the old Germanic 'tun,' their popular meetings, 'folk-moots,' and their representative assemblies, 'witenagemots.'" But he also made some sound observations on the West's influence on the nation's development. There, not in New England, lay the "center of gravity" of the United States. This must be recognized by the younger generation of historians. Once they did so, they would find that beyond the Appalachians "a new composite nationality is being produced, a distinct American people, speaking the English language, but not English." They were forming self-governing communities that were "growing into states of the federal union." In the West, economists would discover forces altering the economy of the nation and of Europe; students of migration would reveal mass movements of people comparable to the *Völkerwanderung* of the Middle Ages.[5] The West had to be understood if American history was to be understood. Here was Turner's challenge to the Wise Men of the East who viewed the United States from the perspective of New England. It was also a watershed in Turner's own development; he remembered later that preparing that review brought home to him "the need of a history of the continuous progress of civilization across the continent."[6] His ambition to study the history of the West was taking a practical direction.

This study had to wait, for the autumn term was at hand, and Turner must return to the academic world. "I feel," he confessed, "much like a man about to plunge into cold water."[7] In fact, he was to experience something like total immersion in a very icy bath. Few students of that day were interested in bettering their minds; they wanted only a college degree that would elevate their social and economic status. To them a "C" grade was just as acceptable as an "A," and much easier to secure; fraternities and clubs ranked far above the classroom in their value scales; and a good time was more desirable than good marks. The handful who showed serious interest were scorned as "grinds" who did not really fit into the lighthearted atmosphere of a university. To make matters worse, there were more students than had been anticipated, for Wisconsin was expanding rapidly; eight hundred crowded the campus that fall, swamping the fifty-six faculty members and overcrowding the boardinghouses—although Turner did manage to arrange a comfortable room at Mrs. Bross's.[8]

These numbers posed problems for Turner and the history department. He had worked out an admirable teaching program. He would offer, in addition to some required sections in Territorial and Dynastic history, a freshman survey in American history, a brand new course in the "Constitutional and Political History of the United States" (which would eventually alternate with another new course in American economic history), and a seminar on the economic development of the Old Northwest.[9] Alas for his well-laid plans! So many students demanded his freshman courses in Dynastic and American history that each course had to be divided into two sections. In the end he taught these four uninspiring classes with sixty uninspired underclassmen in each, the course in constitutional history with seventeen, and the seminar, which attracted only six.[10]

Turner was instantly popular as a teacher. He was nearing his twenty-eighth year at this time, but looked far younger; a persistent Madison legend holds that sophomores mistook him for a freshman that autumn and tossed him into Lake Mendota. He was a strikingly attractive man, of slight build and medium height, with flashing blue eyes, fair hair, a well-trimmed moustache, and a face that glowed with ruddy health. All who knew him commented on his personal magnetism and the deep, vibrant, melodious voice that commanded attention from his classes and charmed his friends. They remembered, too, the quickness of his mind, and the vastness of his knowledge.

Turner's first hint of success as a teacher cemented a resolution in his mind; with a decently paid post and a measure of security, why delay the marriage that he and Mae both wanted? No sooner did she return from Europe that October than he suggested that they marry immediately. She was agreeable; they would live in a large upper room at Mrs. Bross's boardinghouse, with an alcove where Fred could study, and a fireplace to offer cheer. And they would be married in just a month. That arranged, both plunged into the countless tasks required: three hundred invitations to be mailed, a decision to be made about the gloves for the ushers, furniture to be carted from the freight station, wedding presents unpacked, the license to be obtained. Turner hurried through these chores in a haze of happiness. "Everybody looks at me very smiling and cheerful," he reported.[11]

Finally on November 16, 1889, they were married, in a formal ceremony at the Kenwood Evangelical Church. There was a brief wedding supper at the bride's home on Madison Avenue, enlivened by the arrival of a telegram from Turner's class in American history, extending hearty congratulations to their late sovereign and hoping that they could return to their former alliance with him "if no dangerous or hostile alliance be contracted by him during the interregnum."[12] The Turners went on a brief honeymoon in Milwaukee, then attended another reception at the Turner home in Portage, an "uncommonly brilliant" affair, marred by the fact that the groom failed to appear until it was well under way, having been detained in Madison to teach the course of a colleague who was ill. When he did arrive, at nine in the evening, the bridal couple led the way to the dining room, where "a most *recherché* lunch was served in the most dainty manner."[13]

Fred and Mae were married now, but there were problems ahead. Only a few days after their return to Madison he took to his bed with a bad case of measles, and she fled to her mother's home in Chicago, letting her husband know that boardinghouse life was not for her. When he recovered, he went house-hunting, finally finding one at 21 West Gilman Street, at a rental they could afford. This must be properly prepared before Turner could ask Mae to join him; there was a stove to buy, a full-time maid to be hired, the floors stained a color that would please her. Fred Turner was desperately lonely as he went about these tasks, but by the end of January all was ready, and the Turners were able to set up housekeeping in their own home.[14]

Just before they did so an event occurred that changed the pattern of Fred's life. On December 9, Professor Allen, who had taken to his bed with a miserable cold, suddenly died. His passing plunged the university into mourning; classes were canceled, the massive pillars at the entrance to the campus were draped in black, and all social events were put off until after the funeral, three days later. Few wept over Allen's death as much as Turner did, and few were as deeply affected. He had to honor his mentor's memory by seeing to the publication of a book on which Allen had labored for some time, *A Short History of the Roman People,* then in proof form, but with final arrangements still to be made and an introduction prepared. Turner worked feverishly on this task during the next weeks, with satisfactory results. His prefatory remarks were admirably phrased to stress the contributions made by Allen: the blending of political, economic, literary, and religious history into a unified whole; the "policy and process by which the Roman dominion was secured and organized"; and "the social and economic causes of the failure of self-government among the Romans."[15] The study of society as a whole, the importance of expansion, the underlying forces that determined the rise and fall of democratic institutions—there were Allen's themes, and they were the themes that were to occupy his disciple through his lifetime. Turner's tribute mirrored his own historical interests while revealing his debt to his teacher.

Allen's death was tragedy, but it was also opportunity. If Turner could cheerfully cooperate with President Chamberlin by teaching extra courses, and at the same time complete his doctoral work at Johns Hopkins, he might win the professorship that was his goal. The courses were burdensome, even though a graduate student was imported from Harvard to teach some of the elementary work; Turner taught not only his own subjects but sections of the courses on Dynastic and Territorial history, the French Revolution, Nineteenth-Century Europe, a new course on the "History of Society," and the seminar, the latter his own now rather than shared with Professor Allen. This was a killing schedule for those winter and spring terms, compounded by the fact that he was giving his own courses for the first time, and they required extensive preparation. "My courses," he wrote, "are all so nearly new, that I am finding my hands full."[16]

To add labor to labor, he had to win his doctorate that spring or be pushed aside for a more experienced teacher. So he worked furiously on French and German and slaved over the mountains of books that he was expected to know by heart. By the end of May he was ready. Canceling his classes, he set out alone for Baltimore, put up at Miss Ashton's boardinghouse, satisfied his language requirements, and, at four o'clock in the afternoon of the fatal day presented himself to his inquisitors in College Hall. There the entire historical and literary faculty awaited him, seated about a long table, and looking very formidable indeed. Turner was placed at one end; Professor Basil L. Gildersleeve at the other. The written examinations and thesis were satisfactory; would Professor Adams begin the questioning? This went on for three-quarters of an hour, then Ely followed for half an hour and the remaining faculty displayed their intellectual plumage by asking the usual questions to show the depth of their learning. When it was all over Turner left the room, waited those agonizing minutes in the hall, and heard the good news as Professor Adams emerged with his hand extended in congratulations.[17]

Frederick J. Turner (as he now began to sign himself) was a doctor of philosophy, but he was by no means happy with his performance. Later he assured a student who did badly that his examination "could have been no worse than my own experience," taking solace in the thought that his failure "was a spur that sent me further than if I had distinguished myself."[18] Recriminations were for the future, however; he had passed and could return to Madison in triumph. He went home, carrying a box of Maryland crabs to share with Mae, and so excited that he forgot to deposit Miss Ashton's key and left behind his umbrella and glasses. There was still the technical requirement of a published thesis, but this proved easy, for Professor Adams was so pleased with the dissertation completed during Turner's year of residence that he arranged its publication in the prestigious *Johns Hopkins University Studies in Historical and Political Science*. It appeared in December 1891 under the pretentious title, "The Character and Influence of the Indian Trade in Wisconsin, A Study of the Trading Post as an Institution."[19] Turner—the unshakable perfectionist—was not happy with his own words when he saw them in print, but the reviewers were kind, commenting especially on the flowing style that made the book "a popular as well as a scholarly production."[20]

With those coveted letters, "Ph.D.," after his name, he was at last in a position to press President Chamberlin for the professorship that was his goal. This was by no means assured; Chamberlin quite naturally wanted to replace Allen with a teacher of comparable reputation and even asked Turner to recommend a distinguished scholar who would measure up to these standards. Fortunately, Turner's friends rose to the occasion, spurred on by Reuben Gold Thwaites, who broadcast word that Turner might be sacrificed unless the president could be convinced of his future; Woodrow Wilson and Herbert Baxter Adams wrote so glowingly that no administrator could remain unmoved. Of this Turner knew nothing, living through the spring under the pressure of uncertainty, and "growing weary of having to keep one eye off his work to keep his head from the axeman's block."[21] His first glimmer of hope came when the president followed his advice by naming his Hopkins friend, Charles Homer Haskins, to an instructorship in European history. Turner was kept waiting for another year before his goal was achieved, but in the spring of 1891 he was elevated to a professorship, given the chairmanship of the department, and paid a magnificent salary of $2000 a year. At the same time Haskins was granted an assistant professorship. Chamberlin had elected to gamble on the future reputation of these two young men, rather than to recruit an eminent elder statesman. Seldom had a university president chosen so wisely.

With security, an expanding reputation, and an income that would stretch within sight of covering his needs, Turner could face the future with a degree of assurance. Now he could settle to the task of justifying President Chamberlin's faith by devoting himself to teaching and scholarship. His wife was happy to cooperate; Mae was never strong, and she was content to avoid the gay social life of Madison's elite—a wise decision when society's vogue in 1891 was "progressive tiddley winks" and, a year later, "progressive cinch." The Turner's name seldom graced the social columns of the local press; when it did appear, it was usually in a report that Mae was visiting her mother in Chicago. Yet family life was bound to absorb hours that Turner needed for his research—much to his delight. There were luncheons to be given for

Teaching—and the Emerging Frontier Thesis

89

visiting dignitaries, dinner parties for colleagues, stag gatherings where the living room at 21 West Gilman was filled with friends, talk, and tobacco smoke, and the guests stuffed themselves on grapes, pears, rye bread, mustard, caviar, sardines, marmalade, olives, Edam cheese, and salted almonds, all washed down with beer.[22]

Then the babies came. Dorothy Kinsley Turner was born promptly at noon on September 1, 1890. All went well. "Having babies," the doctor told the proud father, "is Mrs. Turner's vocation." Dorothy grew briskly until she was six months old when near-tragedy struck. A mild cold burgeoned overnight into a severe case of the "grippe" that soon laid not only Dorothy but the maid and the mother low. Turner, aided by his own mother, watched over the baby's bed as she grew steadily worse. Twice during the night of March 24, she seemed on the point of death; each time Turner ran coatless through the night to the doctor's home, overheating himself so badly that he succumbed to the disease the next day. Not until March 28 did the child take a turn for the better, allowing the worn-out father to take to his own bed; not until mid-April was he strong enough to meet his classes. No such disaster marred the arrival of the second child, Jackson Allen Turner, on June 26, 1892. Jack was a husky youngster, and he was the apple of his parents' eye. Happily, his parents could not recognize the prophetic accuracy of his grandmother's proud remark that he was "too angelic to live."[23]

At the same time there were the endless rounds of duties expected of every professor—in the 1890s, as today—at the sacrifice of his own research and leisure. The university called on him to serve on all sorts of committees—to arrange a lecture series, revitalize the student newspaper, aid the literary societies in planning their programs—and to address the students at their weekly convocations, all tasks that consumed an alarming amount of time. The State Historical Society pressed him into service as a "curator" and asked him to serve with a committee on historical monuments. Clubs took their toll: the Madison Lawn Tennis Club, which he joined in 1891; the Channing Club, which he rejoined when he returned to Wisconsin and enlightened with discussions on such unlikely subjects as "Ingersollism," "Religion in Revolutionary Times," and "The Social Life and Religion of Turkey"; the Contemporary Club, which made him its vice-president in 1891 and enlisted him for papers or discussions on "The Chilean Affair,"

"The Political Situation in Europe" ("a profound study," according to the local reporter); "Australian Federation," "The Relations of Portugal and England," "The Pan-American Congress," and "Turkish Control of the Bosphorus."[24]

Turner's earlier successful lecture series on the Old Northwest was so pleasantly remembered that he was prevailed on to stage another for the Contemporary Club on "Crossing the Alleghenies," this time with a charge of ten cents a head. Once more crowds turned out in droves, this time to hear of Daniel Boone, George Rogers Clark, the Kentucky pioneers, and the Battle of King's Mountain; once more Turner was the star of the show when he spoke on March 4, 1890, on "The Land and the People." The "panorama of brilliant word pictures" that enraptured his audience contained little new; he told of the coming of the French to the Mississippi Valley, the invasion of British traders, the advance of Yankee and Scots-Irish settlers down the Great Valley. But a new note was apparent. Now his stress was less on the trader and more on the pioneer farmer. "Indian with his painted face and eagle feathers, voyageur with his turban handkerchief, his beaded moccasins and his birch canoe, trader with his peltry-laden pack horse, all are doomed. For the backwoodsman is in sight; clad in hunting shirt, axe and rifle in hand, attended by wife and children, he bears with him the promise of the clearing and the farm, the promise of local self-government." He was the one who would win the West.[25] Turner was beginning to focus on those who conquered the wilderness, not those who succumbed to its savagery. Realism was pushing aside romance, as it had to before he could realize that the frontier helped mould the American social order.

These extracurricular duties absorbed a fair amount of Turner's time, but far more went into building a respectable history department for the university. The time was ripe for expansion. Wisconsin was growing rapidly, with some two hundred students added to its population each year and the demand for classrooms so great that the regents launched a crash building program during the 1890-91 academic year. Additional faculty was also needed, and Turner wanted to make sure his department received its share. President Chamberlin was a willing ally, for he realized that the university's greatness would be measured not by its buildings, but by the quality of its instructional staff. He knew, too, that unless he could attract eminent scholars, the newly founded University of Chicago, aided by John D. Rockefeller's millions and led by an aggressive president, William Raney Harper, would skim the cream from the prospective graduate enrollment of the Midwest. If the University of Wisconsin was to escape becoming a commonplace undergraduate college, sending its best students to Chicago for their advanced degrees, it must look to its laurels. He and Turner saw eye to eye on the needs of the history department.

They differed on how to meet those needs. Turner wanted two instructors to take over the lower division classes, leaving Haskins and himself to handle the advanced courses. Chamberlin hoped for a mature scholar who would add luster to the university. As they sparred gently, word reached Turner of one man who would more than live up to Chamberlin's expectations, and, at the same time, bring an unbelievable amount of prestige to the department. Richard T. Ely, the nation's foremost economist, was available! The academic grapevine told why. He and Herbert Baxter Adams, both empire-builders, had struggled for years over control of the Johns Hopkins history department. Their battle broke into the open during the 1890-91 school year, when both were offered attractive professorships at the University of Chicago. Each hoped the other would go, for neither wanted to work under President Harper. Ely tried to force Johns Hopkins's hand by resigning, hoping the president would meet his terms and drive Adams to Chicago. Instead, his resignation was accepted, and Adams was elevated to a professorship. Ely had no choice but to eat crow and retract his resignation, but his life was now intolerable at Baltimore. Hearing that Wisconsin sought a prestigious professor, he did not hesitate to tell his former student that he was available.

Turner responded at once, even though such an appointment would deny the department the instructors it needed and doom him to continued lower-level instruction. President Chamberlin was equally interested, but the $3500 salary demanded by Ely was far above Wisconsin's professorial level. Why not, Turner suggested, form a new "School of Economics, Political Science, and History," with Ely as its head? This would justify a dean's salary, and allow Wisconsin to build a graduate program in the social sciences more prestigious than Chicago's. "It will be," he wrote enthusiastically, "the center of postgraduate work for the Northwest."[26] In February 1891, when the Board of Regents gave its stamp of approval, President Chamberlin journeyed eastward, and when he returned, Wisconsin had its new professor. All concerned were delighted, but Ely most of all. With abundant enthusiasm, and little knowledge of midwestern university budgets, he was sure that more instructors and graduate fellows could be added at once to lift some of the teaching burdens from Turner's shoulders. If the legislature would not provide, he would raise the money himself among the region's businessmen, who would be eager to support such a school.

Turner's letters now bubbled with enthusiasm; he wanted to introduce two new courses, one on the "Social and Economic History of the United States," with special emphasis on the progress of western settlement, immigration, internal improvements, land legislation, and labor; the other on "Colonization." "This would be a new course in American colleges, so far as I know, and I think I have some new ideas in regard to the subject."[27] Alas for such grandiose plans! Ely managed to persuade one New Yorker to donate $500, but there the money-raising campaign ended. In the end the changes made were minimal. One assistant professor of economics was added to the staff, Turner became "Professor of American History," and Haskins "Professor of Institutional History."[28] Yet Turner's optimism was unquenched. It was expressed in an article describing the new school which he prepared for the student newspaper. Here a generation of experts would be trained to grapple with the complex political and economic problems arising from the nation's expansion into the world arena. No one discipline would suffice. "The relation of economics to politics and to history, is plain. We cannot hope to understand either the industrial life, or the political life, of a people, while the two are studied apart; each modifies and conditions the other, and both are intimately related to the welfare of the state."[29] Those were sound judgments, and Turner showed the breadth of his vision in making them.

He showed that breadth again when school began in the fall of 1892. Why not, he suggested, enlist the aid of Madison's economic elite by founding a town-gown "Historical and Political Science Association"? Some 150 leading citizens responded to his invitation to meet at the Opera House on the night of November 15, there to adopt the constitution that he had drafted, to listen to an address from Dr. Albert Shaw, editor of the *Review of Reviews*, on "The West as a Field for Economic Study," and to hear Turner himself talk for some time on the importance of the West in history. This was not a trial run for the famed paper that he was to read a year later; instead he argued that the political history of the Mississippi Valley could be understood only against the patterns of trade on the Great Lakes and river systems which determined the course of settlement and urban growth.[30] Turner's every activity during those years was broadening his knowledge and heightening his interest in the West.

So was his teaching. He was not, in this phase of his career, a popular spellbinder; his "History of Society" normally attracted from ten to fifteen students, and his "Constitutional and Political History of the United States" an even smaller number, especially after 1892, when he divided it into two courses, with a solid year on the period to 1815 and another on the years from 1815 to the 1870s. Even his lower division courses were but sparsely attended, with from ten to twenty-five or thirty in each. One term, when he taught only advanced classes, his total enrollment for twelve hours of instruction was sixty-three. His seminar varied from three to nine, all but one or two enlisted from the senior class.[31] This was not the record of a student idol, but the better equipped and more interested recognized that they were listening to a master instructor. The student yearbook for 1891 was still a bit skeptical when it judged that

> Turner, too, was sure to suit
> If "budding state's omnipotence"
> Agrees with your aesthetic sense

but two years later the yearbook's writer made a more mature evaluation: "A man with wonderful energy and power of application, who sees and uses his opportunities, with youth and hope to aid him in the struggle of life, he is certain of success in his undertakings. Though but a few years the senior of the students he teaches, yet he exercises over them a strong and beneficial influence, and commands alike, their confidence and respect."[32]

Certainly those who ventured into his classes were offered a rich intellectual fare. Two of his courses, "Constitutional History" and the "Nineteenth Century," were singled out for special attention. "Constitutional History" he taught as he would a seminar, assigning stiff doses of reading and asking each student to prepare a report that was presented to the class, searchingly criticized, and extensively debated.

Students emerged with a knowledge of the constitutional and political growth of the nation that was not only thorough but up-to-date. To Turner the Constitution was no sacred document, handed down by a benevolent deity, but the product of social and economic forces operating through the colonial era. "The constitutional convention of 1787," he told his class, "was only one stage, not an abrupt unconnected beginning." Nor had its evolution ended with its adoption. "It was still played upon by all the vital forces of American growth and adapted itself to them," particularly to "the needs of the wonderful expansion which is the dominant fact of American history."[33] These were heretical views; little wonder that one student judged his law-school course in constitutional history an anticlimax, after Turner's instruction.

If Turner revealed his unquenchable interest in the evolution of institutions by stressing growth in his "Constitutional and Political History," his course on the "Nineteenth Century" showed his equal concern with the usability of the past. He began with the French Revolution, then only one hundred years in the past, and in lectures and class reports he thoroughly analyzed European diplomatic and commercial interrelationships for the remainder of the century, spending the last weeks on current problems that carried the class down almost to their own day. The second term was devoted to reports. Each student was assigned one nation of Europe and instructed to show how its political, social, and commercial history made understandable its behavior during the preceding decade. This was an intriguing assignment—students talked of forming a "Nineteenth-Century Club," and several eastern colleges imitated Turner's methods—but it also told something of his faith in history as a guide to contemporary conduct.[34] To Turner, historical studies were essential not only for cultural, but also for practical enlightenment; no man was properly educated unless he was sufficiently familiar with the past to apply its lessons to the present. Hence the duty of the teacher was to spark student interest; if this could be done better by studying the nineteenth century than the ninth, so be it. Any history was better than none.

Some history, however, was particularly fascinating, and none more so than the investigation of social and economic forces that underlay political behavior. Turner launched himself into that field in the autumn of 1892, when he added a completely new offering to his list, "The Economic and Social History of the United States." The cata-

logue announcement read: "The subject is studied . . . with reference to the origin and development of the social and economic characteristics of the country." Among the topics to be treated would be
the relationship between physiographic features and political behavior,
changes in thought patterns, the material development of the nation,
and "the process of settlement across the continent." Here, for the
first time in any catalogue, was an announcement that the westward
expansion of the American people would be investigated. A year later
this aspect received even greater stress: "Particular attention will be
paid to the spread of settlement across the continent and to the economic and social causes of sectional and national sentiment."

We have no way of knowing how extensively the westward movement was treated in these early courses, but one or two fragments of
information suggest that it bulked large. One note, which Turner
scribbled as he was outlining his subject matter, shows the nature of
his thinking: "Soc & Ec U.S. Divide up into a series of *studies. Land.*
History of land tenure. Am. problems. Comparative & historical study.
Agriculture. Agrar. politik. Movement of population. Study historically."[35] We know, too, that each student was assigned a broad topic—
immigration, migration, banking, finance, land, internal improvements,
slavery, religion, literature—for special study, then required to present
a report on one aspect of this to the class. At the end of the term all
of the students prepared correlation papers relating the subjects discussed, with Turner serving as listener and interpreter as he knit them
together to show how they supplemented or corrected existing histories.[36] This was exciting; even the uninterested students felt that
they were contributing to knowledge and pioneering a new subject
matter. "History can no longer be studied according to the old
method," wrote a reporter, after listening to some of the reports.
Turner was infecting his followers with his own belief that the enig-
mas of the past could only be unlocked by investigating the subterranean social and economic forces that governed mankind's behavior.

Turner's seminar offered an even more unusual intellectual fare. The
course met weekly in the library of the State Historical Society, still
housed in the state capitol in downtown Madison, and Turner taught it
jointly with Professor Allen until his death, then with Haskins. First
there was a series of lectures on "scientific" history, in which the in-

structors parroted their Johns Hopkins mentors (but with some sensible correctives added), then there were talks on the sources of United States history, then student reports. It was Turner's ambition to study successive periods of the American past, beginning with colonial days, but this proved impossible; the varied interests of his students and his own changing enthusiasms directed investigations into a helter-skelter of topics, often only slightly related. His first seminar, offered in 1890-91, was grandiosely proclaimed as a course on the "Old Northwest," but it was actually on Wisconsin history, and largely on German migration to the state, a subject much on the public conscience as debate went on over the Bennett law, which would require all instruction in the public schools to be in English.[37] A year later Turner made a vain effort to direct attention to the 1830-40 decade, "with particular reference to the reciprocal influences between East and West at that time," but once more student interests and his own universal curiosity about the past generated a variety of papers that defied classification.[38] In 1892-93, the topics were again so diverse that he was hard put to find a central theme when he summarized their contents at the end of the year.

Yet these seminar reports, scattered over time and subject as they were, did mirror Turner's growing passion for the study of the West. Virtually all related in some fashion with expansion, or with the impact of expansion on the nation. Their content varied—"The Migration of German Lutherans to Wisconsin," "The Westward Spread of Population across New York State, 1750-1810," "Iowa's Federal Relations," "The Influence of the Erie Canal on the Economy of New England," "The Relation of the Land System to the Panic of 1837," "The Interpretation of the Ordinance of 1787"—yet an interest in migration, or in the influence of migration, underlay each.[39] Such a list would have been unthinkable in any other seminar in the United States.

The few graduate students attracted to Wisconsin during the early 1890s helped Turner whet his own appetite for studying the frontier. These were not many; there was little about this small backwater college to lure doctoral candidates from the prestigious universities of the East, especially when its regents did not vote to grant that degree until 1893. Emory R. Johnson was Turner's first advanced candidate; he prepared a master's thesis on "River and Harbor Bills" before moving on to a doctorate and, eventually, a professorship at the University of Pennsylvania. On his heels came Kate A. Everest, who earned her master of arts diploma in 1892 and her doctor of philosophy a year later with studies of German immigration into Wisconsin. Turner was delighted with her thesis—it was built on questions and methods uniquely Turnerian. Miss Everest began with a question—why did Wisconsin have a higher proportion of German-born inhabitants than any other state? Then she sought the answer in church and governmental records, printed sources, census returns, and personal interviews. Turner worked along with her, questioning old German settlers and gathering all the information that he could about them.[40] Miss Everest was not destined to make the scholarly reputation of some of the students he trained in later years, but she shared with them an enthusiasm for history that was traceable to her master. The secret of Turner's success in graduate instruction was that he enlisted the student as a co-worker in an exciting quest for truth, glowing with him over each new discovery, talking over the results, and applauding every valid conclusion. Nothing could be more flattering than such intimate attention and such genuine interest. Turner, even in his first assignments as a teacher, showed the qualities that in later years would attract to his seminar the cream of the nation's would-be historians.

Strangely, however, his own thinking about the American past was stimulated less by his pupils during those years than by a troublesome academic chore, forced upon him by the heady idealism of the social reformers who were blueprinting the re-design of society during the 1890s. One of their ideals was instant education for the people; if universities installed adult extension courses, added summer schools to their schedules, and sent their best faculty members into the countryside to spread culture among the common folk, poverty would be wiped out, the success of democratic institutions assured, and morality enshrined. Fred Turner had heard that message preached at Johns Hopkins by Richard T. Ely and Herbert Baxter Adams, and he was ready to help wholeheartedly when Wisconsin turned toward an extension program.

This began in 1859, when "Farmers' Institutes" and "Teachers' Institutes" were inaugurated on the campus, and when the first regular "Teachers' Summer School" began its sessions—a summer school in which Turner taught regularly over the next years. This was only the beginning; the university would not be completely committed until it adopted an "English type" extension program that sent its faculty members in the humanities and social sciences traveling about the state, conducting regular lecture courses and awarding degrees to farmers and townsmen who completed their requirements. Turner was an enthusiastic advocate of such a program, cooperating cheerfully when the president asked him to report on the subjects the history department could offer, and doing what he could to convince Chamberlin to take the plunge.[41] He made a major contribution early in 1891, when he persuaded Herbert Baxter Adams to speak in Madison on "The Higher Education of the People," an address that converted a number of leading citizens to the belief that total education for all the people would make the world a better place to live in.[42]

Something more than the endorsement of an outside educator was necessary to convince university authorities that extension lectures would pay for themselves. Turner saw an opportunity to drive that message home, at least for his own subject, when he was invited to address the Southwestern Wisconsin Teachers' Association, which met in Madison during the late summer of 1890. Here was a chance to show this influential group that history was no archaic exercise in rote memory, preserved in the mothballs of antiquarianism, but a living discipline, spiced with new interpretations and dealing with a subject matter thoroughly relevant to the present. If he could infect the state's teachers with the excitement of research, they would become local ambassadors for the extension lectures that would soon be given throughout the state. This was Turner's hope when he addressed the schoolteachers on a hot August night in 1890 on "The Significance of History," and this was his hope as he improved his remarks for publication in the October and November 1891 issues of the *Wisconsin Journal of Education*.[43] He could not realize as he did so that his masterly essay would one day be seen as a charter of the Progressive school of historiography, and one of the most remarkable articles published in that generation.

Turner's thesis was that the common people were important. Their motives and actions could be understood only if historians focused on economic and social data; all the past must be re-surveyed to show how they lived and worked and played. History could no longer be viewed as past politics; "history is past literature, it is past politics, it is past religion, it is past economics." All were elements in "society's endeavor to understand itself by understanding the past." Modern conditions of industrial growth made this investigation imperative. "Each age writes the history of the past anew with reference to the conditions uppermost in its own times." Thus, history was "ever *becoming*, never completed." American history could be understood only as a continuation of European history, evolving under the impact of New World conditions. It also had to be viewed as part of world history, for the two were too intimately linked to be separated. National history was as outdated as tribal history—"our present life is interlocked with the events of all the world"—and could never be fully understood until global migration patterns and the world-wide impact of American trade and ideals were understood. This could only be accomplished by borrowing from many disciplines, for the source materials that revealed the life of the common people were infinite in number and variety. The task was difficult, but the rewards great. "The priceless service of history" was to show man the richness of his cultural inheritance, to better his life, and to reveal the grandeur of the present.

Had "The Significance of History" been written by a prominent eastern historian and published in a national journal, it might have been hailed at the time, as it has been since, as a blueprint of the "New History" that was to sweep the profession during the next quarter-century. In it Turner advanced most of the concepts that were to be popularized later: "relativism," with its recognition that each age studied the past in the light of its own experiences; "presentism," with its understanding that the principal importance of yesterday was to explain today; "socialism" (as Turner would have phrased it), with its creed that all facets of human behavior should be studied; and "globalism," with its belief that modern trade and communications linked all the world so tightly that no one part could be studied in isolation. These were doctrines destined for general acceptance a generation later. By voicing them in 1890 and 1891 Turner showed himself to be far in advance of his time.

These doctrines had the immediate effect of bringing university extension to Wisconsin—and with it new burdens and challenges. Turner gave his first two extension courses—at Stoughton and Columbus—during the 1890-91 academic year, but not until the fall of 1891, when a full-scale program was inaugurated did he plunge in completely. He offered three lecture series: "The Colonization of North America," "American Development, 1789-1829," and "American Politics, 1789-1840." Hardly lively topics, but Turner was an immense success overnight. Such was the demand that his first lecture in Madison had to be scheduled in the assembly chamber of the state capitol; 500 attended. When he spoke at the Plymouth Church of Milwaukee under the "espionage" (to quote the local scribe) of the Chautauqua Circle, the hall was jammed, and many were turned away. In all, Turner gave courses of six lectures in seven communities that year, with audiences of about 175 persons each. At Poynette, 200 of the town's 600 inhabitants were enrolled. Most simply listened, but the dozens who sought credit proved so numerous that Turner tried to discourage any additions to avoid the paper work that took hours of his time.[44]

This was only one of the hardships of extension lecturing. The pay was little enough—$10 a lecture plus expenses—but for this he was expected to visit seven widely separated communities once each week for six weeks, traveling in cold trains through the sub-zero Wisconsin nights, sleeping in drafty hotel rooms, or with a family in towns too small to boast hotels, talking to large audiences that kept him far beyond his allotted time with questions, dining with prominent townspeople, then catching the train for the long ride home or to the next assignment. This grueling schedule left Turner little time for anything else. "I must," he told a friend that year, "have some time for *intension.*"[45] Yet such was his crusading zeal, and such the monetary demands of his growing family, that he followed the circuit until the spring of 1896, although not always at the same furious pace as in 1891-92.

This was fortunate, for his fees were far overbalanced by his rewards. These he gathered as he prepared and revised his lectures on "The Colonization of North America." These lectures spanned several centuries, from the pre-Columbian voyages through the occupation of New England and the conquest of New France, and they required a vast amount of reading in widely scattered books, ranging from Herman Merivale's *Lectures on Colonization and Colonies* (1861) to John A. Doyle's *English Colonies in America* (1887). As he read, Turner more and more directed his attention to the questions of *where* people moved, and *why*. There were clues scattered along the way, and as he digested them he jotted notes that revealed the direction of his thinking. When he learned, from Merivale's *Lectures on Colonization,* that overcrowding drove people to move, Turner listed a series of motives for migration: overcrowding, love of adventure, fear of military service, hope of social and economic betterment, a desire for a more congenial religious climate. When he read, in Doyle's *English Colonies in America,* that physical barriers helped determine the direction of migratory peoples, he picked up his pen and observed that population movements followed the path of least resistance, whether along the lower Danube or the Hudson.[46] Turner was thinking about migration, and storing away tidbits that would be useful in shaping his frontier thesis.

He was also learning another very important lesson. Life in the colonies differed markedly from life in England and Europe. Why? John A. Doyle's *English Colonies in America* suggested that the environment might be partly responsible. In England, primitive societies were formed that evolved over the course of years into full-grown communities, differing from the communities from which they sprang. "We can," Doyle wrote, "trace their life and institutions from the very fountain-head. In their cases we can see those stages of growth going on under our very eyes which elsewhere can be traced only imperfectly and obscurely."[47] Here in America, Turner may have reasoned, was a chance to study universal history in a local laboratory; the evolution of all society could be observed in microcosm in the emergence of a pioneer community. But why did this evolution produce a product so different from its English ancestor? Merivale suggested one answer in his *Lectures on Colonization;* the abundance of cheap land, he pointed out, encouraged farmers to move to fresh fields rather than to manure their worn-out lands. If cheap land encouraged this change in habit, did it encourage others? So Turner must have speculated as he copied out his notes or phrased the sentences that he would someday use in his essays. "Beneath the constitutional forms and ideas," he wrote one night, when marooned in the Atherton Hotel in Oshkosh, "beneath political issues, run the great ocean currents of economic and social life, shaping and reshaping political forms to the changes of this great sea, which changes continuously."[48] This concept, improved in metaphor and syntax, was to become one of the best-known sentences in his essay on the significance of the frontier.

His current thinking found expression in several ways. The syllabi
that he prepared for his extension courses mirrored the progress of his
ideas. The first, apparently written in 1891, was a highly factual mimeographed production that listed fifteen topics for study, ranging from
the geography of North America to "The Colonial Governments," but
the second, printed a year later, was more enlightening. "The History
of American Colonization," he wrote, "shows how European life entered America and how America modified that life." It could be understood only by recognizing that American colonization was part of the
great historic movement known as the Aryan migrations, and that
Europe was as profoundly affected as the United States was.[49] Turner,
as he read and pondered, was moving toward belief in environmentalism; when he judged that America modified the life and institutions
of Europeans he had reached the threshold of his frontier theory.

The lectures that Turner prepared for his extension audiences were
designed to cater to their tastes, with a maximum of rhetoric and a
minimum of interpretation; the Norsemen were "dwellers of the
North," and the "grandeur of the gloomy fjords, . . . the rugged
cliffs and lofty mountains stamped their impress on the race"; New
Englanders were surrounded by "fogs and snow, and snarling break-
ers" that "invited no easy life as did the Spanish southland, and no
broad plantations stretching along the slow flowing rivers as did the
Virginia region."[50] But when Turner paused to think about the colonization process, a very important truth dawned. Colonization, he realized, did not stop with the coast but continued inland as "colonizers"
overran the continent. The peopling of America was part of his story.

He voiced these views in a paper on "American Colonization" which
he delivered before the Madison Literary Club in February 1891, a
paper that anticipated most of the concepts made famous by his 1893
essay on the significance of the frontier. "American history," he told
his audience, "is the account of how the environment was occupied by
a new organization. It is the history of the application of men and
ideas to the physical conditions." Because this was the case, "colonization" must be re-defined to include the migration of any considerable
body of people of the same nationality into unoccupied territory.
"Taking this liberal use of the term, we may call much of the European settlement of the West, colonization." This deserved investigation.

"We can never understand our country until we know the materials out of which our western states have been constructed." Historians must no longer waste their time on Pocahontas or the name of the first child born in Brown County; they should study "where and by what means the characteristics and the population of western states like Kansas and California and Wisconsin were produced." They should also recognize that colonization from abroad did not end with the Puritans and Cavaliers, but continued through the nineteenth century, as immigrants flooded the seaboard and pushed westward. "They have brought us not merely so much bone and sinew, not merely so much money, not merely so much manual skill; they have brought with them deeply inrooted customs and ideas. They are important factors in the political and economic life of the nation. The story of the peopling of America has not yet been written. We do not understand ourselves."

Such an understanding was imperative, for the "colonizing era" in the nation's history was drawing to a close, and "colonization" was the key to an understanding of that history. "As the occupation of the New World transformed Europe, so the occupation of the Great West has determined the flow of American energies, been the underlying explanation of American political history, and has had profound reactive effects upon the social and economic life of the East." American history would never be understood until the nation's expansion westward had been traced and its impact on the East and Europe appraised. "What first the Mediterranean sea and later the New World were to the Aryan peoples, breaking the bonds of custom, and creating new activities to meet new conditions, that the undeveloped West has been to the American descendants of those Aryans." Yet expansion was too rooted in the nation's character to end. "We have a national self-consciousness, a self-sufficient industrial organization. Will not this organization bud as did the trans-Allegheny organism?" Turner thought that it would, and that American commerce would move outward to dominate markets in Latin America and the Pacific.[51]

When Turner prepared that paper in January 1891, he moved well along the road toward the hypothesis he was to announce two years later. He saw interior settlements as "colonies" of the seaboard, advancing civilization westward just as the English colonizers had in the seventeenth century. He recognized that these new civilizations differed from those that gave them birth, and that these differences were due in part to the influence of different environments. He realized that one period in the nation's history—the period of "colonization"—was ending, and that readjustments had to be made in the social, economic, and political structure. These were basic concepts in Turner's frontier thesis, yet more had to be added before that thesis was completed. He had yet to use the word "frontier," or to understand the process through which expansion went on. He had still to appreciate the alterations in the national character and institutions stemming from three centuries of westering. These next steps would follow easily; he had only to flesh out the skeleton to reach the point where his hypothesis could be pronounced.

His next step came naturally. In the autumn of 1891 the undergraduate newspaper, *The Aegis,* announced a series of articles by faculty members on their research, including one by Turner on "New Aspects of the Early History of Wisconsin."[52] Fortunately, he procrastinated, as usual; by the time his contribution was due he was so deeply immersed in his colonization studies that the essay on Wisconsin no longer excited him. Why not write instead on the reinterpretations that were revising his understanding of American history? This would popularize his department's offerings by demonstrating that the subject provided intellectual attractions without parallel, that its study was an exciting adventure in creative thinking. His was a happy inspiration, for the result was his "Problems in American History," published in *The Aegis* on November 4, 1892, and destined to take its place among the most important contributions made by Turner to the understanding of the past.[53]

Past historians, he charged, had erred in ignoring "the fundamental, dominating fact in United States history," the expansion of population from sea to sea. "In a sense American history up to our own day has been colonial history, the colonization of the Great West. The ever retreating frontier of free land is the key to American development." To investigate the impact of this would be to shed new light on every facet of the nation's past. Politics would take on a new dimension, for "behind institutions, behind constitutional forms, lie the vital forces that call these organs into life and shape them to meet changing conditions. The peculiarity of American institutions is the fact that they are compelled to adapt themselves to the changes of a remarkably developing, expanding people." These changes influenced Europe no less than the United States. "We have to observe how European life entered the continent, and how America modified that life and reacted on Europe." We must appraise the effect on the Old World of free land in the New; we must measure the changes wrought in Europe by American freedom of speech, democracy, and economic progress. These were the "problems in American history" that were crying for a solution.

These problems could be solved only if historians added new tools to their kitbags; those of geologists, mineralogists, biologists, and geographers were essential to understanding the impact of physiographic forces on the settlement process. Only by using such tools could the ebb and flow of expansion be understood, the course of migration plotted, and the extent of regional influences on the social and economic behavior of the people be appreciated. This last was especially important, for the moving frontier left behind a succession of "sections" formed when intruding stocks interacted with the natural environment. These differed one from the other in economic enterprise, governmental practices, and cultural interests. Their continuous pressure on the national government tended, on the one hand, to divide the United States into quarreling factions, each seeking congressional legislation beneficial to its own interests, and, on the other, to unify the nation as people of divergent backgrounds blended into one social order. "State sovereignty is lost in the West, where appears a checkerboard division of states which recruit their population from all parts of the Union."

Sectionalism in all its aspects could be understood only after all manner of subsidiary problems were solved by historians. They must investigate immigration, for the newer arrivals brought habits, ideals, and customs which reacted with the native culture. "We shall not understand the contemporary history of the United States without studying immigration historically." Scholars must study the disposal of the public domain, the building of the transportation network, interstate migration. They must determine the role of free land as a democratizing agent. But, most essential of all, they must view all the past anew from the vantage point of the West. This was the neglected key to American history, and until it unlocked the story of the nation that story would be misunderstood. "What the Mediterranean Sea was to the Greeks," Turner concluded, "breaking the bond of custom, offering new experiences, calling out new institutions and activities, that the ever retreating Great West has been to the United States directly, and to the nations of Europe more remotely."

"Problems in American History" must be ranked with "The Significance of History" as a landmark in Frederick J. Turner's intellectual growth. In that essay he identified the two basic forces—frontier and section—that he believed responsible for much of the distinctiveness of American civilization. Perhaps even more important, he isolated material causes stemming from expansion as basic in the alteration process, rather than mysterious hereditary forces. This was a giant leap forward. So was his insistence that the tools of social and physical scientists be added to the kits of historians, for it was a pioneer insistence on interdisciplinary research. These bold suggestions show Turner as original in thought, rebellious of convention, and inventive in both the concepts and methods of historical investigation. He was not far wrong when he wrote a quarter-century later that, in that one essay, "I said pretty nearly everything I have said since."[54]

His own generation viewed matters differently. Copies of *The Aegis* containing his "Problems" paper were broadcast wholesale among scholars, but with disheartening results; Turner's views were too advanced to be appreciated by most of his contemporaries. Professor Simon N. Patten felt that it provided "a very helpful way of looking at our social problems" (which it did not); Professor Francis N. Thorpe termed it a good outline that would have been improved by the use of some of his own studies on constitution-making; Professor Emory R. Johnson was impressed with the improvement in *The Aegis* since he was a student at Wisconsin under Turner; and Professor Charles M. Andrews was not sure that the profession was ready to write the history of expansion until his own colonial period had been properly investigated. This faint praise, however, was more than offset by a glowing tribute from Herbert Baxter Adams. Adams was not only much interested, and so impressed that he would call its "suggestive views" to the attention of the Hopkins seminar, but he believed its author worthy of a place on the program of the American Historical Association at its next meeting. Would Turner be willing to prepare a paper for the sessions scheduled for Chicago in July 1893?[55] Thus, ironically, the invitation that led to "The Significance of the Frontier in

American History" came from the man whose views Turner later judged so archaic that his frontier thesis was a rebellion against them!

At the time Turner accepted the invitation, he had laid the foundations of his hypothesis, but he had built only a speculative structure. Now he had to add bricks and mortar, in the form of proof, and alter the framework as further study demanded architectural refinements. He had to spend the next months poring over census statistics, maps, and the few books that described western life with any degree of accuracy. He had to probe the works of political scientists, economists, geographers, publicists, and biologists, in search of theoretical justification for his conclusions. Busy times lay ahead.

V

The Genesis of
the Frontier Thesis

1892-1893

MERICANS for generations had been aware that a frontier existed, and that it had altered their lives and institutions.[1] From the days of Benjamin Franklin and Thomas Jefferson they had talked of a "safety valve" in the West that attracted surplus laborers from eastern factories, thus discouraging radical protest. They had linked cheap lands with democracy and had speculated on the uniquely American traits—mobility, inventiveness, individualism, optimism, impatience with authority—traceable to the frontiering experience. One publicist, E. L. Godkin, in an essay on "Aristocratic Opinions of Democracy," published in 1865, anticipated much of what Turner was to say thirty years later. Godkin had held that three centuries of pioneering had bred into Americans a faith in democracy, an individualistic contempt for social authority, "a self-confidence that rises into conceit," "a devotion to material pursuits," "a lack of taste in art and literature," "a prodigious contempt for experience and for theory," and a respect for the practical that made them distrustful of "book-learned" politicians.[2] Yet Godkin, and dozens who preached his message, went unheeded. Why did Turner succeed where they failed?

One answer can be found in the changed social atmosphere of the 1890s. Americans were gradually coming to realize that the frontier was closing, and the era of cheap western lands near its end. How could the nation adjust itself to a closed-space existence? Thinking men believed that for three centuries American prosperity had rested on the exploitation of virgin natural resources, and democratic values had rested on the equality of opportunity provided by the public domain. Would poverty and despotism be the lot of the United States now? Some thought it would, and in the crumbling social order about them they found evidence to bolster their beliefs. A depression gripped the country between 1873 and 1896, a depression that bore every mark of permanence. It forced a new mood on the nation. Past depressions had been endured because renewed expansion would inevitably rejuvenate the economy, but now that hope was glimmering and social critics sang a new tune. Publicists—such as Henry George or Thorstein Veblen—preached the inequity of a system that created profits for the few instead of benefits for the many; newspaper headlines told of crippling strikes, the Haymarket Riot, the shrill demands of the Knights of Labor and the People's party for a more equitable distribution of wealth. To many Americans these were disturbing portents of a future in a frontierless land. Class conflict and revolutionary demands threatened to transform the United States into another Europe.

Actually the frontier did not close abruptly at the end of the nineteenth century, nor did diminishing opportunity there underlie the social turmoil of those decades. The "Commercial Revolution" was responsible for the social upheaval; the mechanization of commercial interchange brought into the world marketplace agricultural goods from every corner of the globe to compete with those of traditional producers, driving prices downward and disrupting trade patterns. But in the minds of many Americans the exhaustion of cheap lands and the depression were inseparably linked. Prophets of doom held that overproduction had driven prices downward, an overproduction fostered by "a practically unlimited area of fertile land, free as the air we breathe." They also held that, while prices might recover, prosperity was a thing of the past, never to be enjoyed again. That prosperity, and "the comparative freedom from the social and economic problems long confronting Europe," they laid at the door of "an almost unlimited area of fertile land to which the unemployed could freely resort." Some saw the nation's future as one plagued by "social disturbances of grave significance," a peon-like caste system, and a giant standing army that would provide work for those who could no longer escape to the frontier.[3]

All of this clamor—and the popular magazines were studded with articles sounding the alarm—focused attention on the frontier and its passing. So did others, with less lofty designs, who sought to stir national sentiment against continued immigration. The real objective of these zealots was to close the gates against the "New Immigration" from southern and eastern Europe—Italians, Hungarians, and Jews—but they dared not resort to racist tactics and so seized on the closing of the frontier to justify laws against all newcomers. Why share the few remaining lands with the "depraved dregs of European civilization?" "There are no more new worlds," wrote Josiah Strong, a leading spokesman for this view. "The unoccupied arable lands of the earth are limited, and will soon be taken."[4] These were the views not only of bigoted crackpots, but of informed citizens, as well. Francis A. Walker, an educator and statistician, whose works Turner greatly admired, used his presidential address before the American Economics Association to warn that "alien breeds" menaced the nation, since free lands could no longer absorb them. Albert Shaw, a Johns Hopkins friend of Turner's, saw to it that each issue of the *Review of Reviews* that he edited contained at least one article tub-thumping for exclusion.[5] These propagandists symbolized, and encouraged, a groundswell of anti-immigration sentiment that climaxed with the founding of the "Immigration Restriction League" in 1894, just months after Turner read his essay on the frontier.

We can never know the degree to which Turner was influenced by publicists who connected immigration restriction and the depression of the 1890s with the closing of the frontier, but we do know that he clipped articles from Chicago papers by leaders of the exclusion movement, that he included a "free land" period in a section of his economic and social history course that dealt with immigration, and that he directed an undergraduate honors thesis on "The Effect of the Settlement of the Public Domain on Immigration."[6] Certainly any young historian of his sensitivity and interests would have read anything that came his way on the frontier. Whether he did so or not, however, is less important than the fact that this outburst of polemic writings indicated a wave of interest in expansion that had not existed even a decade before. People were ready to ask the questions that Turner was prepared to answer. They would listen when he told them that three centuries of westering had influenced the nation no less than the end of westering was affecting it now. The social atmosphere of the 1890s encouraged Turner's investigations, and assured him a body of readers who would welcome his views.

This was his good fortune. He was fortunate, too, to reach his maturity at exactly the time when the intellectual world was ready to welcome his hypothesis, and when the various disciplines on which he had to lean—history, geography, biology, and statistical cartography—could provide him with the tools he needed in his research. He was equipped, as earlier scholars had not been, to translate his speculations into scientifically based theories backed by impeccable authority.

The revolutionary changes that transformed historical studies during the 1890s benefited him particularly. By this time a group of young professionals were challenging the fantasies of the Teutonists' "germ" theory. Historians who produced learned monographs on the relationship between Saxon tithingmen and New England constables, on the Germanic basis for life in Salem, and on the Kentucky Chautauqua as a survival of the medieval *folkmoot*, could no longer be taken seriously by anyone but themselves. So the attack began, led by Edward Channing and Charles MacLean Andrews, who leveled their lances against the naïve assumption that a modern institution had evolved from a Teutonic "germ" because they resembled each other. As well insist that New England towns descended from Masai villages in Africa as from German *tuns* because both of the earlier models were surrounded by defensive walls. So Channing argued in his *Genesis of the Massachusetts Town*, published in 1891, and Andrews backed his judgment by pointing out that the Connecticut towns he studied were by no means identical to their Germanic ancestors, having been altered by geographic, economic, and ethnic pressures. Their common-sense message deeply impressed the oncoming generation of historians. So did the insistence of other scholars, particularly in England, that politics was not the only clue to understanding human behavior, and that social and economic pressures upon society must also be investigated. When, in his essay on "The Significance of History," Turner quoted approvingly from a book by James E. T. Rogers, *The Economic Interpretation of History*, published in 1889, he was simply moving with the tides.[7]

Turner benefited, too, from the emerging rebellion of midwestern writers against eastern domination. This was long overdue; decades of truckling to New England as the cultural fountainhead of the nation had stifled the growth of native expression in literature and the arts, no less than in history. Hamlin Garland spoke for his section in his *Crumbling Idols*, published in 1894, when he urged his fellow midwesterners to further the coming American democracy by ceasing to worship the "crumbling idols" of the past, to create rather than imitate, and to tap the rich literary resources waiting exploitation in the Mississippi Valley.[8] Turner was to speak for his section when he dedicated himself to showing that the Midwest played an essential role in the emergence of the nation, and that its contribution to national greatness was no less than that of the eastern seaboard. He was responding to an impulse that formed part of the intellectual climate of his region, just as he was responding to the climate of his day. He recognized this. "The ideas underlying my 'Significance of the Frontier,'" he wrote some time later, "would have been expressed in some form or other in any case. They were part of the growing American consciousness of itself."[9]

Historians could rebel against traditionalism, but, to be accepted, their new interpretations had to be bolstered by scientific evidence. Turner's hypothesis, which he developed gradually as he prepared his colonization lectures and his course on economic and social history, was that the frontiering process altered man and man's institutions. This seemed clear to Turner as he read the works of travelers who described the behavior of westerners—a behavior clearly different from that of easterners, who lived in compact communities. But *how* did life on the frontier reshape the pioneers and their institutions?

Turner found his answer in the geographic theory of the day. Since the time of Hippocrates, mankind had believed that the physical environment shaped human behavior, and that variations in climate, topography, and soils determined the nature of the differing civilizations that dotted the globe. This venerable theory—glorified in Turner's day as "environmental determinism"—gained new importance during the controversy over evolution in the 1880s and 1890s. Darwinians, seeking to account for the wide variety of species that had evolved, agreed that these many life forms had been moulded by the equally wide variety of physical environments in which they had existed. This was a common-sense viewpoint, endorsed by Charles Darwin himself. Nor did they stop there. If animal organisms could be so altered by natural forces, so could the supreme animal organism: man. To Turner this meant one thing: the unique social and physical environment of the frontier endowed the pioneers with the distinguishing traits noted by travelers.

That view had the backing of the highest world authority. The crown prince of the environmentalists was the German geographer, Friedrich Ratzel, whose system of "Anthropo-Geographie" was set forth in two fat volumes, published in 1882 and 1891. Man, Ratzel preached, was shaped by the physical world about him, and he succeeded only to the extent that he adapted to his environment. Differences between modern nations were the outcome of earlier migrations into differing regions, each isolated from the others by seas, deserts, or mountains, and each developing differently due to differing physical conditions. These doctrines were universally accepted by American geographers, who parroted them in their books and publications. "That man," declared one in 1889, "has been influenced in his development by his physical, climatic and social surroundings is well nigh indisputable."[10] Textbooks mirrored the universal belief in environmentalism. James A. Dana, revising his well-known *Manual of Geology*, went on record that "favoring conditions in environment" produced "superior races"; a more modern textbook proclaimed that physical forces "determined the pursuits, character, and total life of the people."[11] With geographers standing shoulder to shoulder in this belief, historians had no choice but to follow. They did, almost to a man. "I would not say," wrote Justin Winsor in his *The Mississippi Basin*, "that there are no other compelling influences, but no other control is so steady." When a manual on *How To Study and Teach History*, published in 1893, held that physical conditions created civilizations, shaped their development, and caused their downfall, it simply mirrored the viewpoint of the entire profession.[12] The wonder was not that Turner believed in environment as a moulding force, but that he did not succumb more completely to that belief; he stated repeatedly, and truthfully, through his lifetime that he was not an environmental determinist.

He was on equally sure ground when he accepted the prevailing view that the characteristics and behavioral patterns that the pioneers developed because of their frontier environment were handed down from generation to generation to influence present-day American life. Biologists were not as united behind a belief in the inheritability of acquired characteristics as geographers were in holding to environmental determinism, but Turner had sound scientific backing when he accepted that viewpoint as essential to his hypothesis. His principal authorities were in the ranks of biologists, then much in the public eye as they proclaimed the virtues of Charles Darwin's evolutionary hypothesis. Disciples of Darwin's theory built their case on two "proven" assumptions: that, as species evolved, a process of "natural selection" operated to perpetuate those best adapted to the environment, and that new species broke off from old by a process of "mutation," which was not clearly understood but had been demonstrated by experimental means.

These generally accepted theories were challenged in the 1880s by German scientists, whose experiments suggested that acquired traits were not inheritable; rather, that all characteristics were present in each organism's germ plasm and were passed on from generation to generation without being altered by the environment. These "New Darwinians," enlisted largely from among the younger biologists, went beyond all reason in denying environmental influences, holding that all traits were present in the germ cell at conception, and could never be changed. This overstatement stirred such resentment that opponents of the theory closed ranks; calling themselves the "Neo-Lamarckians," they swung to the view that *all* traits were acquired and passed on to later generations. Environments changed organisms, they insisted, and these changes were passed on to the progeny. This was the view of nine-tenths of the scientists in America and Europe when Turner was formulating his theories. Wrote one: "If there is any principle in inheritance which has appeared self-evident and not requiring any demonstration at all, it is that acquired characteristics *are* inherited."[13] If ever two scientific principles were widely accepted on the basis of unimpeachable scientific support, they were that organisms responded to environmental pressures and that characteristics thus acquired were bequeathed to subsequent generations. This was the state of scientific knowledge when Turner prepared his 1893 essay.

That he was familiar with these developments seems certain. During the months when he was formulating his thesis, he was in almost daily contact with his good friend Charles R. Van Hise, a geologist of repute whose broad interests brought him in touch with the conflicts raging among geographers and biologists over the Darwinian thesis. As a member of the Wisconsin Academy of Sciences, Arts and Letters, Turner heard numerous papers by Van Hise and his fellow geologist, President T. C. Chamberlin, all couched in evolutionary terms, and all extolling environmentalism. There, too, he listened to discussions in which "New Darwinians" and "Neo-Lamarckians" threshed out their differences or struck sparks with their arguments. He was certainly aware of the battle between these opposing schools, for heated articles upholding one viewpoint or the other filled English journals and spilled over into American magazines, many of which he read regularly.[14] His own language suggests his familiarity with this scientific literature, bristling as it did with biological metaphors such as "organism," "plastic," and "adaptation."

We know today that the biologists and geographers led Turner astray, and that the doctrines they preached were false, or not suitable to application to social organisms. By 1910 the scientific world had come to agree that acquired characteristics could not be inherited, and not long thereafter geographers and geologists concluded that the physical environment played a lesser role in altering behavioral patterns than they had formerly believed. These later findings should not cloud the fact that when Turner voiced his thesis he had the best of scientific backing for two of the foundation stones on which it rested.

If he was fortunate enough to voice his views at the exact time they would be most hospitably received, he was doubly fortunate in the progress in statistical cartography that allowed him to illustrate them graphically. Without the efforts of a generation of statisticians and map-makers he could never have visualized the nation's expansion accurately, and without that visual image before him he might never have arrived at his hypothesis. His study of census reports, atlases, and statistical tables allowed him to picture the march of population westward, and to theorize from that picture as his thesis took shape.

German map-makers pioneered the techniques that were to revolutionize their subject in the 1870s and 1880s, but the American who did most to hurry the revolution was Francis A. Walker, eminent educator, statistician, and director of the censuses of 1870 and 1880. Walker sensed the possibilities of the German methods and insisted that they be incorporated in *The Statistical Atlas of the United States Based on the Results of the Ninth Census, 1870*, published in 1874. This bulky volume, which was pivotal in stimulating Turner's interest in the West, contained two features that were particularly useful to him. One was a series of maps showing population density for each decade from 1790 to 1870, shaded to indicate five degrees of concentration between two and six inhabitants to the square mile at the edge of settlement and ninety to the square mile in the populated East. This graphically depicted the westward movement. "The movement of population," judged one reviewer, "seems to take place under our very eyes."[15] Equally important to Turner was an essay on "The Progress of the Nation, 1790-1870," which was based on the maps and which described "the line of continuous settlement" or the "frontier line." There he learned that expansion progressed in set stages, with cattle-raising and other occupations suitable to a sparse population at the outer edge, primitive and technologically advanced farming next in order, and finally an industrialized and urbanized civilization.[16] Here were the "stages of society" that Turner had studied under Richard T. Ely in his political economy courses at Johns Hopkins.

This was enough to excite Turner; he jotted down notes as he read, and he thought well enough of the volume to assign it to his students.[17] His excitement mounted as he read other articles from Walker's pen that traced the westward movement more exactly and noted that it was proceeding at the rate of from seventy to seventy-five feet a day in a direction generally west but slightly north, usually following latitudinal lines.[18] The bulky official report of the 1880 census appealed especially, for its population-density maps were more sophisticated than those of a decade before, and its essay on "The Progress of the Nation" was more emphatic in its description of the westward movement than that in the 1870 census. An article by Henry Gannett, a census bureau geographer, that appeared in the *International Review*, was also useful. "An arbitrary line," Gannett wrote, "must be drawn somewhere beyond which the country must be considered as unsettled, although it may not be absolutely without inhabitants." This, he suggested, might follow the zone occupied by from two to six persons to the square mile.[19] Here was a definition tailored to Turner's needs; he could now visualize a "frontier line" with an exact meaning.

All of these works added something to his knowledge, but none so much as the *Scribner's Statistical Atlas of the United States*, prepared by Gannett and Fletcher W. Hewes, and issued in 1885. This was a key work in the evolution of his thought; he urged it on his students, parroted it in his writings, and almost certainly had it at his elbow when he prepared his 1893 essay. The maps intrigued him especially —maps that vividly pictured in striking color the physical features of the continent, the advance of settlement, the immigration intrusion, the racial composition of the nation. So did the essays: one, on the progress of the nation, spoke of the "westward movement" and the "frontier line"; another, probably by Gannett, described the sequential pattern followed in expansion, with stress on the evolution of pioneer communities from a primitive to a developed economy.[20] Turner's hours of poring over *Scribner's Atlas* taught him a great deal about the nature of the frontier process.

They also alerted him to the value of census bulletins and converted him into a regular reader of their less-than-sparkling prose. This was fortunate, for no one but an avid enthusiast could have been attracted to a four-page pamphlet that reached his desk sometime during the 1892-93 academic year, atrociously printed, and bearing a title designed to repel all but the most dedicated census buffs: *Extra Census Bulletin No. 2. Distribution of Population According to Density: 1890.* Turner turned those pages, and was richly rewarded. He found a colored map showing the population of the United States in 1890 in six degrees of density. And he found also a striking statement: "Up to and including 1890 the country had a frontier of settlement, but at present the unsettled area has been so broken into by isolated bodies of settlement that there can hardly be said to be a frontier line."[21]

We can never know Turner's thoughts as he read those lines. We know what he did; he wrote his name on the first page, labeled the pamphlet "Density," underlined a few passages—but not, strangely enough, the sentence he was to quote later—and filed it away among his notes. Did he realize then that the westward movement was now history, and could be subjected to sociological analysis to reveal its significance? Did he recognize that the American experience capsulized the entire story of society's evolution, and that the lessons he had learned in his Portage upbringing offered clues to the whole nature of civilization? Probably not. Certainly he had the frontier hypothesis well in mind before that census bulletin reached his desk; it had been stated in skeleton form in his February 1891 lecture on colonization, and more completely in his essay on "Problems in American History," which may have been prepared before he saw the announcement of the frontier's closing. More probably, Turner, as a good journalist, saw that announcement as an eye-catching phrase to introduce the essay that was already taking shape in his mind. If so, he was ready now to plunge into the investigations that would add substance to his theories and allow him to present a full-blown hypothesis to the profession.

Turner haunted the State Historical Society library during the next several months. One would like to imagine that he went about his task systematically, reading travel accounts, guide books, western newspapers and magazines, frontier writers, and contemporary observers to find out *how* expansion altered traits and institutions of the pioneers, then studying the works of theorists to understand *why*. It is far more likely that Turner read in a haphazard fashion, mingling contemporary and modern authors, westerners and easterners, travelers and commentators. Certainly he was already familiar with some of the books on which he leaned most heavily, and he had only to dredge their message from his memory. Still, this was no light task. He had to absorb a vast amount of information, assimilate it, sort it, arrange it in an orderly pattern, and interpret it in terms of the national experience. We can appreciate his accomplishment if we recast the evidence that he gathered into the pattern that it assumed in his mind, rather than in the helter-skelter disorder in which he accumulated it.

Observers of pioneer life in early America taught him a great deal. From them he learned that travelers generally noted differences between easterners and westerners, and that western traits exaggerated the national characteristics that Europeans labeled "American." Nationalism was one: frontiersmen, "wholly freed from that local attachment which arises from habit and long residence," demanded services—protection, lands, roads—and there was no power that could provide them "except the general agent of all the states, at Washington."[22] Hence allegiance shifted from the state to the national government. Their mobility accentuated this nationalizing tendency; pioneers were constantly on the move, shifting from territory to territory, and forming no attachment to place.

Most writers agreed that the West also fostered democratic practices; the problems facing pioneers were unique, and required solutions easterners could not understand. So "every new settlement is already a republic *in embryo*." Social democracy was also rooted in the West, for class distinctions seemed meaningless in a land where the turn of a shovel or a fortunate land speculation could transform a pauper into a millionaire. "A pleasing feature of Western life," Turner read in an 1850 issue of *The American Whig Review*, "is the perfect social equality. . . . Strong arms and stout hearts their only wealth; all classes at last salute each other as brothers."[23] Westerners, he learned, were unusually individualistic, marked by an "independence of thought and action"; they were also infected with "a spirit of adventurous enterprise," free to venture into new lands or adopt new ideas, with little respect for tradition. "More new tools, implements, and machines . . . have been invented in this new world," wrote one westerner, "than were ever yet invented in the old."[24] When Turner added inventiveness to his catalogue of western traits he had an imposing list: nationalism, individualism, social and political democracy, mobility, independence, adventurous spirit, and inventiveness. Here was evidence that West did differ from East. Here also was the gallery of frontier traits that he would name in his 1893 essay.

He still had to determine *why* these differences emerged, and the quest for that answer led him into a strange variety of reading matter. Two French theorists whose work Turner read carefully had helpful ideas about western democracy. Emile Boutmy, whose *Studies in Constitutional Law: France-England-United States* appeared in English translation in 1891, argued that in overcrowded Europe strict authority was needed to maintain order, but in America "the vast tracts of land which were without owners" spread the population thinly, rendering force unnecessary. Those newer regions had no aristocratic establishments to be overthrown, and hence turned naturally to democratic practices; democracy would persist so long as men could become owners of the soil by moving a few miles westward. Behind this political democracy was a social democracy that undermined all caste systems and created a unique equality. So argued another French observer, André Churillon, in an article that appeared in the spring 1892 issue of the *Review of Reviews*. This was because opportunity was so abundant on the frontier that class lines could never be drawn; society was fluid, with no "fixity of professions" such as plagued older nations. When all men were potentially equal they were more inclined to treat each other as equals.[25]

Henry George was another theorist on whom Turner leaned. Turner read *Progress and Poverty* first as a graduate student at Wisconsin, studied it more intensely in Professor Ely's courses at Johns Hopkins, and perhaps reviewed it now as he was exploring the nature of the frontier; one note he recorded at this time was a reminder to transcribe a passage from page 349 of his own copy. This passage contained several helpful ideas. In it George reiterated his stout faith in the importance of the environment as a moulding force, and ascribed to "unfenced land" the nation's "general comfort, the active invention, the power of adaptation and assimilation, the free independent spirit, the energy and hopefulness."[26] These were sweeping generalizations, but they bolstered Turner's realization that a connection existed between free land and the frontier characteristics he was isolating.

He gained far more from the volume on *Physics and Politics* by the English political economist, Walter Bagehot. Turner's copy of this work, probably purchased in 1888 or 1889 at the suggestion of Herbert Baxter Adams, is badly worn, tattered from frequent use, and heavily underlined and annotated. It is obviously a book on which he relied heavily. Bagehot believed that the American character was shaped by the centuries-long struggle against the wilderness; those who led the assault became the nation's folk heroes, and their traits, acquired in their conquest, became the traits of all. "The eager restlessness," he wrote, "the high-strung nervous organization, are useful in continual struggle, and also are prompted by it." When Turner finished reading that passage, he reached for his note pad and recorded an idea it suggested to him: "West. Infl[uence] on U.S.—Custom. It stood to East as the sea to Phoenicia, to Egypt, to Greece."[27] Here, in very rough form, was the phrase that he would use in all his basic essays on the frontier.

The characteristics that Bagehot saw emerging in the West he ascribed not only to "colonial" conditions, but also to the mingling of peoples there, creating a fluid social order and lessening the strength of traditionalism. Turner had only to substitute "frontier" for "colonial" to realize that frontiering fostered new traits through intercultural borrowings as well as through environmental pressures. He thought that over and wrote at the bottom of the page: "Influence of West. It was the attractive force to immigration." Bagehot also believed that the newness of the West encouraged alterations in the social structure; in older "arrested civilizations," institutions and habits were too firmly implanted to be changed. The problem, as he saw it, was not to create a new society, but to escape an old one; not of "cementing a cake of custom, but of breaking the cake of custom." That observation inspired another of Turner's notes: "West. Influence on Am[erica]. Breaker of *custom*. The Leavening power in U.S. hist[ory]. Always at the edge of civ[ilization] creating new needs, conditions, opportunities."[28] Here were bits of substance for his theories, dovetailing nicely.

Francis A. Walker added more pieces to his jigsaw puzzle. This eminent political economist and statistician stood high on Turner's list of favorite authors, so he paid attention when he came across a Phi Beta Kappa address on "The Growth of the Nation" delivered by Walker at Brown University in 1889. "The extraordinary progress of the population westward over new lands," Walker believed, was responsible for many of the distinguishing features of the American character. An inventive ability was one; living in a thinly peopled land with few tools and no division of labor, the pioneers had to "make do" by providing for their own needs. "To save time, to diminish labor, to cut corners and break down barriers in reaching an object, to force one tool to serve three or four purposes, and to compel refractory or inappropriate material to answer urgent needs; this was the daily occupation of our ancestors." Pioneer conditions also fostered the extreme nationalism that had become a national characteristic. "No one can doubt that both the increase of our population and its expansion over a continually wider territory, have been the chief causes of the remarkable development among us of that public spirit which we call patriotism." Only when settlers from the "Old Thirteen" met and mingled in the Ohio Valley did this emerge, for only when a people had no history of their own, no local pride, no dependence on a single state's authority, could the nation command their primary affection.[29] Turner borrowed many of his views on frontier nationalism directly from Walker's address.

He borrowed even more from a germinal volume by an Italian political economist, Achille Loria, whose *Analisa della Proprietà Capitalista* was published in Turin in 1889. An economic determinist, Loria believed that human behavior was governed by the relationship between man and the quantity of "free land" available to him. To prove his theories he focused attention on the "colonial" countries, for he shared the common belief that emerging cultures repeated in exact sequential order the steps by which civilizations in older countries had evolved

over the centuries. Loria saw industrialism as the final stage in this
social evolution, unattainable so long as "free lands" allowed a laborer to
change into a proprietor without expenditure of capital. The United
States offered a splendid example. He described the dispersal of population westward, the depletion of the soil's fertility by wasteful farming methods common where land was abundant, the importation of
indentured servants and slaves in an attempt to offset declining yields,
and the final evolutionary stage in which efficiency was heightened by
forming great estates, releasing laborers from farms to factories, and
inaugurating the industrial era. Loria predicted that the exhaustion of
"free land" would lead the United States into a period of social evils
such as those plaguing Europe, where economic freedom and democracy were threatened by the plutocrats who controlled farming and
manufacturing.[30]

That this was grist for Turner's mill, but grist not easily come by. He had
no knowledge of Italian, nor was this the sort of book that would normally come to his attention—or to the shelves of the State Historical
Society library. In all probability Richard T. Ely brought Loria's book
to Turner. Ely was familiar with the *Analisa* when he joined the Wisconsin faculty in the fall of 1892; he was then revising his *An Introduction to Political Economy* to incorporate the system of land economics
that Loria set forth. Then, too, Harry H. Powers, a graduate student
who was aiding Ely in the revision, had studied in Italy, knew the language well, and was preparing the chapters based on Loria's theories.
Turner probably first learned of the Italian economist when he read
those chapters in manuscript at Ely's request. He would certainly have
recognized the importance of Loria's theories concerning land; in passage after passage Turner read that "free land," rather than protective
tariffs, assured high wages for the United States; that "free land" tempered the impact of the class struggle; that the exhaustion of "free land"
would alter the nation's economic and political structure.[31] This was
valuable information, but clearly incomplete. Nothing would do but
that he read the *Analisa* itself.

That he did so, in whole or in part, is certain, for he borrowed not
only ideas but phrases and metaphors, from Loria's work. It is very
likely that Powers was pressed into service to read the book aloud, translating as he did so, as Turner listened, summarizing on a scratch pad the
sections that interested him most. In all probability this took place in

September and October of 1892, for Professor Ely did not arrive in Madison with his pupil until that September, and Turner was familiar with the *Analisa* when he published his "Problems in American History" on November 4 of that year. As he listened, Turner jotted notes applying Loria's theories to his own hypothesis. Loria's description of cheating and speculating during the early colonial period inspired this: "Work up one part on colonial law. Frontier in 1765 regulators etc." Reference to the common law started a new chain of thought: "Too great stress has been laid on the democratic character of the immigrants to America. Free land is the explanation at bottom." Again, when Turner considered Loria's argument on the value of slavery to primitive societies, he added: "The dissolution of a wage society by free land. Anti social tendency. Creation of economic inertia. Satisfaction in small agric[ultural] holdings. Lack of intellectual stimulus arising from contact."[32]

To emphasize these fragments of information garnered from Loria's *Analisa* is to obscure its major contribution to the frontier hypothesis. By the time he encountered that work, Turner understood why men moved West, he was familiar with the routes they followed and their methods of travel, and he had identified certain enduring traits as resulting from the frontier experience. Not until he encountered Loria, however, did he fully comprehend *how* expansion altered the character and institutions of pioneers. Free land was responsible. The abundance of opportunity in the form of readily obtainable natural resources determined the pace of society's evolution, recast British law and custom into an American mould, underlay colonial prosperity, and decided the nature of the labor system. Free land was the synonym for self-advancement on the frontier, and the relatively great opportunity there for economic and social betterment was responsible for the social changes that Turner had observed. This was the arch-stone of his hypothesis, and while others stressed the significance of "free land," none brought the lesson home as forcefully as Loria.

To assign Loria major credit, however, is to deny the indisputable fact that the frontier thesis blended many ideas from many sources. Emil Boutmy, André Churillon, Henry George, Walter Bagehot, Francis A. Walker, and Achille Loria all made their contributions, just as had the dozens of guidebook authors, magazine writers, newspaper editors, and foreign travelers whose works Turner combed for information. None, however, did more than stimulate Turner's imagination and provide him with the facts needed to illuminate his theories. He had arrived at most of his basic conclusions by January 1891, when he prepared his talk on "American Colonization" for the Madison Literary Club, long before he read Loria or many of the other writers who supposedly influenced him most. His reading during 1892-93 was not in quest of a new interpretation, but a search for collaborative evidence to bolster an interpretation he had already arrived at. He studied western travelers and guidebooks, not to learn that westerners differed from easterners, but to discover *how* they differed. He consulted Bagehot and Loria and Walker, not to find a new theory, but to explain how his own theory operated. In essence, the frontier hypothesis was a product of Turner's creative ability. This alone allowed him to provide unity and meaning to speculation about the pioneering past, and to fashion a tentative hypothesis that was worth laying before the profession in the form of a paper on "The Significance of the Frontier in American History."

Turner would have written his essay eventually, for he was too intrigued by his speculations not to share them with the world. But the fact that it was ready for delivery by July 1893 can be blamed on Christopher Columbus. That worthy's landfall was to be celebrated with a World's Columbian Exposition in Chicago, and the Chicagoans would only be satisfied with a world's fair that would outshine any in history. Determined that the fair would not be all amusements and whoopla, they wanted a whole galaxy of cultural attractions, to show that the prairies of mid-America could produce something more than corn and Populists. They must have a series of "Auxilliary Congresses" on literature and the arts, each packed with glittering stars of world renown. One would be a "World's Congress of Historians and Historical Students," arranged by local talent, but enlisting the aid of the American Historical Association, which was invited to hold a special meeting in the city during July. William F. Poole, librarian of the Newberry Library, would prepare a program, aided by a committee from the association led by its perennial secretary, Herbert Baxter Adams.[33]

This proved a near-fatal arrangement, for Adams had a nose-in-air disdain for the outlanders with whom he must work, and he was determined to run his own show, lest the Congress become "a pandemonium or an exhibit of cranks." "Every Chicago man," he complained, "wants the earth and proposes to dump everything into his lakeside show."[34] His solution was to ignore Poole and the Chicagoans completely, arranging for the historians to meet in some quiet spot far from the Exposition's turmoil. Not until President James B. Angell of the University of Michigan, himself a distinguished historian, made a special trip to Chicago was a compromise arranged. Dr. Poole and his local committee would retain their titles, but the program would be drafted by Adams and his fellow association members. "In this way," Adams wrote with obvious satisfaction, "we can capture the historical congress."[35]

All this squabbling took time, and not until late February and early March of 1893 did the first invitations go out, just four months before the sessions were to begin. Adams saw the list of proposed speakers and thought well of it, but he was still skeptical. Few eastern notables would risk their lives by venturing as far west as Chicago, nor would the greats of the profession be appreciated by the motley crew attracted by an overgrown carnival. "I fancy," he sniffed, "people at the World's Fair will not care much about hearing historical papers."[36] One invitation Adams could approve. This was to Turner, who replied on February 23 that he would gladly read a paper on "The Significance of the Frontier in American History."[37]

Other historians were less willing to accept. By March 20 Poole was assured of only four participants, and he had been refused by such notables as Edward Eggleston, Henry Cabot Lodge, Hermann von Holst, and Albion W. Small. This was hardly an impressive beginning; Justin Winsor thought it a "pitiful show," and predicted that the quality of the performers was so low that the committee was unjustified "in asking any reputable writer to take part in the Congress to the extent of reading a paper."[38] Despite these forebodings, the list grew, and it sparkled with a few names acceptable even to that crotchety Bostonian: Moses Coit Tyler, Edward Everett Hale, Ephriam Emerton, Frederic Bancroft, and the Honorable William Wirt Henry. By June twenty-seven scholars had accepted, and Herbert Baxter Adams reluctantly admitted that "we have a large number of good papers and the literary success of the Congress is assured."[39]

Adams could not know as he penned those words that the program was threatened by the loss of the one paper that was to give it lasting significance. On April 23 Turner wrote Poole that he had two fine students—Orin Grant Libby, whose thesis was on the "Geographical Distribution of the Vote on the Ratification of the Constitution of the United States," and Albert Hart Sandford, who had written on "The Judicial Interpretations of the Ordinance of 1787"—who deserved a place. Could their excellent papers be included? Poole was doubtful. This so disappointed Turner that he was willing to make the supreme sacrifice. On May 10 he suggested that were there any question of including Libby's study, "kindly put it in place of my own paper on 'The Significance of the Frontier in American History.' "[40] Fortunately, Turner's academic prestige was sufficiently low that Poole could ignore his request, preferring to sprinkle his program with professors rather than graduate students.

So it was that Turner was among the performers when the historical congress first assembled, on July 10. He and Mae arrived several days before, traveling by train from Madison with their friends, the Reuben Gold Thwaites, the C. L. Hendricksons, and Charles Homer Haskins, and putting up at a University of Chicago dormitory near the fair.[41] Once unpacked, the party joined the throngs gaping at the wonders of the Exposition—all, that is, but Turner. He shut himself in his room to do what he should have done long before: finish the essay that was to be read two days later. "I am," he wrote a friend, "in the final agonies of getting out a belated paper."[42] He interrupted his labors to attend the opening sessions at Chicago's new Art Institute at the foot of Adams Street; there he presumably made his formal bows to the "Committee on Historical Literature," which had assembled in Room 24; lingered only briefly in the Hall of Columbus, where Dr. Poole and a harp soloist held forth; and hurried back to the university dormitory to add the final touches to his paper.

The Historical Congress opened its sessions the next morning, when the members went through the formalities of electing agreed-upon officers, listened to an address by the newly elected president, and settled back to endure the round of papers scheduled for presentation during the next three days. Morning and evening sessions were planned, with from three to five learned papers at each, and only the afternoons free for recovery and glimpses of the Exposition. "It will be seen," wrote the official chronicler of the Congress, "that amateur historians and sensational theorists had no place on the programme."[43] Professionals, their systems inured to such a heavy diet, were numerous enough to provide audiences of from one to two hundred persons for each meeting.

Turner's turn came on the evening of Wednesday, July 12. The day was intolerably hot, but a lake breeze in the late afternoon cooled the air for the thousands milling about the fair grounds, some jamming the lakefront to watch the arrival of the replica of a Viking ship from Norway, more standing in silence as firemen raked through the ashes of a giant storage plant that had burned two nights before. Turner was not among them; he even resisted an invitation extended to the historians to attend a showing of Buffalo Bill's Wild West Show that afternoon. Those last precious hours were needed to put the finishing touches on his paper. So he was ready when the usual audience of scholars and curiosity seekers gathered at the Art Institute that night.

They were a hardy lot, but even their endurance must have been tested by the procession of scholarly papers: Dr. George Kriehn on "English Popular Uprisings in the Middle Ages," Dr. George P. Fisher on "The Social Compact and Mr. Jefferson's Adoption of It," Professor Jesse Macy on "The Relation of History to Politics," Dr. Reuben Gold Thwaites on "Early Lead Mining in Illinois and Wisconsin." Only then did Turner's turn come, with an audience so deadened by this display of learning that he doubtless read only a portion of the lengthy essay he had prepared.[44] For those able to free themselves from the prejudices of that day, even this was enough to show that he was issuing a declaration of independence for American historiography.

Taking his cue from the census bureau's announcement that there "can hardly be said to be a frontier line" remaining, Turner proclaimed his text: "the existence of an area of free land, its continuous recession, and the advance of American settlement westward explain American development." The frontier was one of several vital forces lying behind constitutional forms "that call these organs into life and shape them to meet changing conditions." The nation's institutions owed their originality to the fact that they had been "compelled to adapt themselves to the changes of an expanding people—to the changes involved in crossing a continent, in winning a wilderness, and in developing at each area of this progress, out of the primitive economic and political conditions of the frontier, the complexity of city life." This perennial rebirth of civilization made the frontier—"the meeting point between savagery

and civilization"—the area of the "most rapid and effective Americanization." Here new traits, new institutions, were born.[45]

One by one Turner chronicled these traits. In the crucible of the
frontier newcomers were Americanized and fused into a mixed race,
"English in neither nationality nor characteristics." The result was "the
formation of a composite nationality for the American people." The
nationalizing tendency was accentuated as the central government
broadened its powers to care for its burgeoning settlements. "Loose
construction increased as the nation marched westward," transforming
the republicanism of Jefferson into the national republicanism of Monroe and the democracy of Andrew Jackson. Then, too, a principal
function of the frontier "has been in the promotion of democracy here
and in Europe." This frontier democracy, "born of free land," was
"strong in selfishness and individualism, intolerant of administrative experience and education, and pressing individual liberty beyond its
proper bounds"; it encouraged lawlessness, lax business honor, and
harmful currency policies. This in turn alarmed the less democratic
East whose efforts to control the West helped explain the political
history of the nineteenth century.

Finally, Turner saw the frontier as a spawning ground for many of
the social and intellectual traits that distinguish Americans from Europeans. "To the frontier the American intellect owes its striking characteristics:" coarseness and strength combined with acuteness and
inquisitiveness; a practical, inventive turn of mind, quick to find ex-
pedients; a masterful grasp of material things but lacking in the artistic;
a restless, nervous energy; a dominant individualism working for good
and evil; and, above all, the buoyancy and exuberance that came with
freedom. These were the traits bred into Americans by three centuries
of westering.

What would happen to the United States now that the frontier was
closing? Turner saw a major shift in the national psychology. Never
again would nature yield its gifts so generously. Never again would a
stubborn environment help break the bonds of custom and summon
mankind to accept its conditions. No longer would frontiering "furnish
a new field of opportunity, a gate of escape from the bondage of the
past." Now Americans must learn to adjust their economy, their politics, their daily lives to life in a closed-space world. "What the Mediterranean Sea was to the Greeks," Turner concluded, with a final ver-

sion of his often-used metaphor, "breaking the bond of custom, offering new experiences, calling out new institutions and activities, that, and more, the ever retreating frontier has been to the United States directly, and to the nations of Europe more remotely." Now the frontier was gone, and with its closing had ended the first period of the nation's history.

Turner's essay was to stir controversy for generations to come, but it probably had little impact on the audience that remained as that interminable session came to a close. Those who had not departed or been lulled into indifference by listening to five lengthy addresses were so tuned to the belief that the "germs" of American institutions were generated in the forests of medieval Germany that they simply could not comprehend a doctrine that flew in the face of all tradition and "common sense." One young historian who was present remembered that the audience reacted with the bored indifference normally shown a young instructor from a backwater college reading his first professional paper; he recalled, too, that discussion was totally lacking.[46] Turner must have returned to his dormitory room that night burdened with a heavy sense of failure.

Nor was he heartened by the reaction that followed. Only one Chicago newspaper bothered to mention his address—in a small paragraph on page three. Dr. Poole, who prepared the official report for *The Dial* and *The Independent*, found Reuben Gold Thwaites's dull chronicle of lead mining a valuable contribution and praised another speaker so highly that she gushed her thanks, but he had no place for even a word about the significance of the frontier.[47] Even President Charles Kendall Adams, who was almost certainly in the audience, did not deem the paper worth mentioning when, five days later, he summed up Turner's historical qualifications for the editor of an encyclopedia. Nor did Turner's father: he reported to the home folk that Fred was an admirable guide to the fair—but did not feel that his contribution to history merited even a sentence. Three months later Wisconsin's newspaper revealed the same deplorable judgment. It published a pretentious article on the effects of the Columbian Exposition on historical writing, without mentioning Turner's contribution.[48]

This less-than-enthusiastic reaction portended the fate of the essay when it appeared in printed form, issued first by the State Historical Society of Wisconsin, where it was read a second time in December

1893. Edward Everett Hale acknowledged "your curious and interesting paper," while Theodore Roosevelt congratulated Turner on "striking some first class ideas" and putting "into shape a good deal of thought that has been floating around rather loosely." Frances A. Walker judged "the mere title is a success in itself," but apparently read no further. To Charles M. Andrews it was "extremely interesting," but he envied the "elements of romance" in Turner's materials in contrast with the dry bones of his own colonial period. Even those who stooped to faint praise did so because they saw his ideas as projections of their own: B. A. Hinsdale agreed that easterners needed to learn more about the West; K. C. Lamprecht found in the American experience "a strong similarity in many respects with our colonizing pioneers"; and Achille Loria applauded the publication of a "learned substantiating piece" for his own theories.[49]

Turner, who enjoyed praise rather more than the next man, could find little solace in these offerings, but others gave him genuine satisfaction. John Fiske lauded his "excellent, *admirable* essay," then cast a dash of cold water by adding that for some time he had been "working along toward the same *perspective*." Friedrich Ratzel found it "a very important work," and "an instructive example of the view of the state and its geographic origins." Of all who passed judgment, however, only Talcott Williams, a Philadelphia editorial writer, wrote prophetically that "it seems to me the most informative and illuminating contribution to American history that I have read in several years."[50] Williams was virtually alone in his perception. More typical was the remark of an easterner, that "Turner must be a very provincial type of historian."

This reaction was predictable. New ideas displace old ideas only slowly; man is a conservative creature and changes his mind—and living patterns—reluctantly. Nor had Turner offered the tangible evidence needed to make his thesis convincing. This was not his purpose; he intended only, as he put it, "to call attention to the frontier as a fertile field for investigation," and to "suggest some of the problems which arise in connection with it." Most fatal of all, his youthful enthusiasm had misled him into claiming far too much from what scant evidence he did use. His examples were drawn from one small segment of the frontier—the eastern upper Mississippi Valley that he knew so well—yet he deduced from them a social process that "formed a huge page in the history of society" and luminously revealed "the course of universal history." He was equally at fault when he exaggerated the role of the frontier in American development; to say that the existence and recession of an area of free land *explained* the nation's past was to fly in the face of common sense and known historical knowledge. Turner's generalizations were too sweeping, his assertions too positive, to convince historians who considered themselves exact scientists. Nor did he aid his cause by his imprecise definitions and faulty logic. A writer who spoke of the "frontier" as a line, a region, a place, and a process, or who ascribed to its influence idealism and materialism, nationalism and sectionalism, cooperative enterprise and individualism, would find little following among tough-minded scholars of any generation. Only if a reader looked beyond the exaggerations and loose terminology would he realize the true significance of "The Significance of the Frontier in American History."

In the long run, Turner's faults played only a minor role in the total impress of his hypothesis on the historical profession—save during the period of negative reaction of the 1930s and 1940s, when they provided ammunition for his critics. True, he had solved few problems, but he had asked a number of very pertinent questions. His purpose was not to close, but to open a chapter in American historiography. He offered the profession not a completed historical structure, but a blueprint from which to build one, and he told his fellow craftsmen that, if they built along the lines he suggested, they would understand a great deal more about the *why* and the *how* of their country's past. The true significance of his essay was that it laid down a challenge that was to occupy scholars for generations to come. Few historians have done more—or as much.

VI

The Busy World of the Professor

1893-1903

REDERICK J. TURNER had written his ticket to fame in his paper on the significance of the frontier, but he had to do a great deal more before the academic world would be ready to award him his due. He had to popularize his theories, and he turned to this task with enthusiasm. He also had to win converts, some from among fellow history teachers, more from the young zealots trained in his seminars. Turner, to find his place in the sun, had to sharpen his teaching skills, win his spurs as a graduate instructor, attract to his classrooms the cream of the Midwest's college crop, and send them forth as missionaries to convert the profession to a belief that the frontier was a basic moulding force in American history. This was no mean assignment.

That Turner succeeded, and succeeded within a remarkably short time, was due to the spectacular development of the University of Wisconsin, no less than to his own talents. Its president, Charles Kendall Adams, who took office in 1892 when President Chamberlin resigned, was as able as his predecessor, and as dedicated to the success of the School of Economics, Political Science and History. During President Adams's ten-year regime the university's student body grew from 1200 to 2000, its faculty from 70 to nearly 200; at the same time he charmed enough money from a responsive legislature to change the campus skyline with a half-dozen imposing new buildings, including a badly needed library. Adams's prime concern was with undergraduate education, and he was tolerant of the social life and athletic contests that increasingly absorbed student attention, but he also stood solidly behind the research activities of his faculty and did his best to staff it with able scholars. The university was a pleasant haven during his years in office.

So was the town of Madison, now earning the designation of city as its population skyrocketed from 13,000 to 19,000 in the decade of the 1890s. All about were signs of progress: the first "horseless carriage" appeared in 1896 (an electric wonder that ran for fifty miles on a single battery charge); an "Edison Parlor" was opened later that year, and there a nickel investment bought a view of a cockfight or a carmencita dance while four phonographs played banjo tunes; the police force got blue uniforms, complete with three-quarter-length coats with brass buttons; a paid fire company with a chemical pumper, was formed; and the city built a sewage disposal plant to save Lake Mendota from pollution. Of all the city's daring innovations, Turner benefited most from the paving of Frances Street, in 1901, for there he had built the house that he occupied for the rest of his teaching days in Madison.

He took this plunge in 1894, buying a lakefront lot at 629 Frances Street for $2000, with the encouragement of a builder who promised him a suitable house for less than $4000. That figure proved as unrealistic as the estimates of most builders; when the Turners moved to their new home that fall their investment was $7906.40, and their mortgage a healthy $6000—a sizable sum for a man with a family and a $2500 salary. The Turners had to go on a regime of skimping and budgeting and overdrawn bank accounts, but they managed to live well: they spent $800 a year for food, fuel, light, and the two servants demanded by academic standards in that genteel age; $500 for taxes and interest; $250 for life insurance payments; $200 for clothing; $100 for doctors and medicine; and a paltry $150 for "sundries," which included trips, pleasure, entertainment, and the books that Turner could not resist buying. Turner hoped to gross an additional $1000 from lecture fees, summer school teaching, and other odd jobs to retire the principal on his mortgage, but that hope was seldom realized.[1]

So the Turner's lived quietly, by inclination as well as by necessity, allowing themselves only such extravagances as membership in the Madison Literary Club, annual visits to Portage, fishing expeditions on Lake Mendota, a camera that earned Fred a considerable local reputation for his "clever work," and, for Mae, membership in the town's Audubon Society and regular bird-watching hikes into the wilds that surrounded the city.[2] This was enough, for their children were a source of never-ending joy. The youngest, Mae Sherwood Turner, born on April 27, 1894, was only a baby, but lively and lovable. Jackson Allen Turner, three years old in 1895, had already proclaimed his intention to be a "foot-ball boy" instead of a professor; his sister, Dorothy, aged five in 1895, leaned in the other direction and could repeat on demand a phrase from one of Dr. Ely's books that "political economy is the housekeeping of the state"—much to her father's delight.[3] Turner was happy with his children and Mae, and needed no other companionship. They were always together, save when Mae visited her family in Chicago or Fred journeyed to the Library of Congress in Washington, as he did in the summer of 1899. They sat by the fireside in the evening, reading, pedaled about Madison's outskirts on their tandem bicycle each morning that the weather allowed, and found happiness in each other.[4]

This was fortunate, for, if Turner was to build the department that he hoped and prove himself as a teacher, there could be little time for play. Building the department was essential; President Adams had encouraged a revision of the curriculum to supplement "required" courses with a series of junior-senior "electives" in each "major" subject. If these were to be properly staffed—and the introductory courses adequately taught—the two-man history department would have to have some help. President Adams was willing, and the money was available. Charles Homer Haskins found his assistant in European history in the capable person of Victor Coffin, a Canadian with German experience and an 1893 degree from Cornell University. He was added to the faculty that year as an assistant professor with responsibility for the freshman and sophomore work in the non-American subjects. Turner preferred to wait for a man who shared his own concepts of history, and such men were rare indeed in that day of Teutonism and the "germ" theory.

They were so rare that in the end he chose one of his own students, Orin G. Libby. Young Libby was ideally suited for his role. An 1892 graduate of the university, his doctoral dissertation, "The Geographic Distribution of the Vote of the Thirteen States on the Federal Constitution, 1787-1788," was so brilliantly conceived and executed that Turner felt it belonged on the program of the 1893 meeting of the American Historical Association. It would, indeed, have been a fit companion for Turner's own essay on the significance of the frontier. Libby, using revolutionary mapping methods, had plotted the vote on ratification by geographic areas, showing how soil patterns and environmental forces shaped opinion on the Constitution just as did economic status. That Turner, rather than Libby, had devised that technique, and would continue to use it in his later seminars, was unimportant.[5] Libby had performed well, and deserved the instructorship that was offered to him in 1895. Turner was shamelessly proud as his protégé continued to pioneer the novel techniques that he suggested, reading a paper before the American Historical Association in 1896 on the need of mapping congressional votes to reveal the sectional foundations for political behavior, and, a year later, introducing a new course at Wisconsin on "American Sectionalism."[6] Libby was following well in his master's footsteps by exploring new methods to show the socioeconomic basis of political decision-making in the United States.

Libby's appointment allowed Turner to broaden his own teaching program—with one significant result. Until 1895 he had had no choice but to offer his traditional subjects: the freshman survey course, his "Economic and Social History" and his "Constitutional and Political History" on alternate years, and two sections of the seminar, one for graduate students, the other for undergraduates, both taught jointly with Haskins. With Libby to shoulder some of the underclass instruction, Turner was free for the first time to specialize in subject matter dear to his own heart. The college catalogue that fall proclaimed a revolution. The "Constitutional and Political History" was abandoned, never to be revived. The "Economic and Social History" was broken into two year-long courses, dividing at 1789. A "Seminary in American History" was introduced, to be taught by Turner without Haskins's aid, and with the announced purpose of studying the political history of the nation by concentrating on successive periods, the first for the 1895-96 academic year to be the era between 1815 and 1820. Turner and Haskins would cooperate in a special course on the teaching of history in the public schools, and would together conduct a "historical conference" for graduate students, who would meet fortnightly to read papers, review books, and discuss current historical literature. The catalogue also announced a completely new course: "History 7. The History of the West," which would meet at noon three times weekly throughout the year. Particular attention would be paid to "the advance of settlement across the continent, and to the results of this movement."[7]

Here was innovation, indeed—this was the first course on the history of the frontier to be offered anywhere—and the local press glowed with pride that Wisconsin's own Turner, "one of the chief exponents of the momentous influence that westward expansion exercised on the course of events in the United States," should be responsible.[8] The introduction of this course did not mean that Turner was succumbing to provincialism or surrendering to sectional pride. His subject matter was to deal not with the "West," but with a succession of "Wests," as the frontier was traced from coast to coast. Too, Turner's investigations increasingly convinced him that the American nationality was a product of the interplay and interaction between the regions of the nation, and that each section had to be understood before their total pattern would become clear. His own decision to explain the "West" to his students coincided with the coming of Professor William P. Trent of the University of the South to offer a one-term course on "Southern Statesmen of the Old Regime."[9] Given the emphasis on regionalism of that day, this was a sensible program.

All of these new and revised courses took a deal of preparation time, but the end was not yet. The Turner budget could be balanced only by adding extra income to his $2100 salary, and this meant work in summer school and extension lecturing. Turner returned to the extension circuit, reluctantly, in the fall of 1893, with his familiar series on "The Colonization of North America" and "United States Politics, 1789-1840," and, in 1895, with a third series, "Western State Making in the Revolution"—the subject of his current research. These seemed sufficiently archaic to discourage any popular audience, but such was his fame that he spent hours during the next years traveling to such unlikely spots as Eau Claire, Wausau, La Crosse, Necedah, and Augusta. Lecturing monopolized far too much of his time during those years, but more had to be spent reading papers, correcting examinations, and drafting the syllabi that were expected in every course. These syllabi appeared regularly—on colonization in 1893, 1894, and 1897; on *American Development, 1789-1829* in 1895—each with up-to-date reading lists, and outlines that revealed Turner's expanding interests. "One cannot understand the history of any people without comprehending their physiographic environment," read one; "The West, a nationalizing force," proclaimed another, and added: "The history of America is the development of democracy in connection with free land."[10] These exercises helped sharpen his knowledge of frontiering, but they took too heavy a toll in his time and energy. The 1896-97 academic year began with the announcement that three of the series' most popular lecturers—including Turner—had withdrawn from the extension staff.

Summer school was not so easily forsaken, even though it meant back-breaking work for modest rewards; he normally taught three courses, which met five or six times weekly for six weeks, for a salary of $300. If Turner had been content to dole out segments of his regular courses, as he did now and then—"American Growth from 1789 to 1829," or "The Beginnings of the West"—he would have more than earned his keep. But that was not his way. These were schoolteachers he was instructing, and he had to equip them to make history live for their students. So he labored over new courses or altered old ones to meet the special needs of his audience. One, on "The Study of History," began with standard lectures on the meaning of history and proper methods of study and teaching, then for four weeks examined intently one segment of European history selected by the class. The purpose was laudable—to illustrate the procedures needed to instruct a class about an era that was not the teacher's specialty—but those eras were not Turner's specialties either, and he had to work with his pupils to offer them a proper model.[11] Equally valuable to the teachers was a course on "The Elements of American History," introduced in 1896, which explored the causal forces shaping the development of the nation, and another, added two years later, on "The History of the West," which capsulized his year-long treatment of the subject into the six weeks of the summer session. These were no light assignments that Turner took on, and because of them he sold his soul to the classroom summer after summer, instead of pursuing research. Nor was that $300 salary, important though it was, solely responsible. Knowledge of history was the torch that would lead mankind from the darkness of ignorance, and Turner's duty was to light that torch for secondary-school teachers no less than for his graduate students.

This same zeal condemned Turner to constant experimentation, as he revised and re-revised his offerings year after year in a perpetual quest for a teaching technique that would make his students realize the importance of historical studies. He gave no set lectures, carefully prepared and written in full, as he had when he first began his career; that method, he told a student, "takes time from more engaging occupations, and . . . is apt to commit you to a settled body of doctrine."[12] Now he began preparation for each class by pulling from his files all the materials that he had gathered on the topic to be surveyed—reading notes, newspaper clippings, chapters torn from books, magazine articles —and reading through the mass of information, sensing new interpretations or fresh organizational possibilities as he did so. These he scrawled on full or half-sheets of paper, together with an outline that he intended to follow—but seldom did. Armed with this material he entered the classroom, spread the outline on the desk with the notes and quotations to be used for illustrations around it, and was ready to begin his lecture. His materials were always fresh, always supplemented with information garnered from recent reading, and always so exciting to Turner that he was able to transmit something of his own enthusiasm to his students.[13] This was a never-ending process, for Turner was a perfectionist, and he constantly reminded himself to make this change or that to improve his instruction. "Change my course in Soc. and Ec. Hist. US into a study of Economic and Social Problems," he wrote one year.[14] In doing this, he sacrificed the writing that would mean his own self-advancement for the benefit of his pupils.

Turner also varied his teaching methods from year to year, as he sought the ideal means of capturing student interest. The "topics" technique, which he had inherited from Professor Allen—each student reporting to the class on a topic he had investigated—he abandoned about the mid-1890s as less suited to testing ability than written term papers based on investigation of the underlying forces that were Turner's principal concern. So his pupils labored over such topics as "Effect of the Revolution on Manufactures," "Literature in the Revolution," "The Threatened Secession of the West," and "Economic Influences on Ratification," all unique for that day, and all designed to test the student's interpretative abilities no less than his industry. So were the examination questions that Turner inflicted on his charges: "Outline the history of the State of Franklin and point out the physiographic factors involved," "What industrial conditions are revealed by the Tariff of 1789?" and "Discuss the relations between the history and physiography of the Blue Grass Country." These were searching inquiries, designed to separate the gifted from the dullards. One student remembered with amusement that after an intense study of the pre-Civil War period the class was asked only one question on an hour examination: "Tell all you know about Kansas."[15]

These examinations—and the total content of Turner's courses—mirrored his objectives as a teacher. He was shaping his students to ask not only the *what*, but the *why* of the past, not only to add a random stone to the mosaic of history, but to understand that stone's relationship to the entire pattern. They had to develop a critical sense first of all; this he instilled by having them read such traditional authors as Hermann von Holst and James Schouler, to discover not only the biases and distortions of the writers, but their failure to describe the "whole life" of the people. Then the students had to grasp the universality of the topic they were studying, no matter how minute. One of Turner's favorite remarks, borrowed from Achille Loria, was that the United States, which was thought to have no history, revealed the hidden, intricate forces that moulded all of mankind's past. "In no other course," one of his students testified, "did I ever get a clearer view of the forces that produce history and of the immense importance of the common impulses of the common man."[16] Turner's concern was never with the period under observation, or even with the total sweep of American history, but with the universal history of mankind.

This was weighty stuff, designed for the serious student and deliberately pitched above the heads of the drones who sought amusement rather than knowledge in the classroom. Turner's purpose was not to entertain but to enlighten, not simply to instruct but to infect his charges with his own fiery enthusiasm for historical studies. Those who succumbed became his disciples, spreading word of his greatness throughout the land, and creating an image of their master as the nation's finest teacher. Some left their impressions behind, Carl Becker in singing prose, Joseph Schafer and Louise P. Kellogg in essays of worshipful adulation, still others in comments less extended but no less adoring.[17] These are the word pictures that have given later generations their impression of Turner as a master teacher beyond parallel.

They are utterly accurate—in the eyes of their creators. They portray a superb lecturer who captivated his students and left them his slaves. His voice was not deep, but it was full, rich, vibrant, musically cadenced. He spoke informally, in conversational tones, always serious but seldom solemn, and never giving the impression of reciting well-prepared remarks. Time and again he paused to illustrate a point on one of the many maps hung about the room, or to search through the stacks of manila folders and sheafs of notes piled on his desk for the apt quotation or the exact statistic needed to illuminate a statement. His lectures were studded with bibliographical information, usually a casual mention that such-and-such a recent book was the best work on the subject. "It gave me the feeling," one student recalled, "that I had to read most of the University library." They abounded in informal stories or bits of verse, and sparkled with references to modern-day problems comparable to those under discussion. His brilliance attracted not the indifferent mass, but the cream of the student body.

Most of all, Turner won his disciples by what he said, not by how he said it. He laid down no unassailable "truths," no dogmatic solutions to historical quandries. He gave his pupils no ordered body of information, weighted with the authority of his own knowledge. Instead, they felt that Turner was not teaching at all; he was himself studying history before their eyes. They shared with him exciting discoveries, and delighted with him when he referred them to their textbook only to point out its errors. Turner taught few facts (indeed, he gave the impression that facts were unimportant), but he taught the students how to select from the infinite variety of facts that composed history the few that had meaning and significance. He showed them that history was no agreed-upon convention, to be learned by rote, but the complex story of interrelating men and events leading to the achievement of noble objectives. He made them realize that the past concealed more questions than answers, that it was something to be delved into, thought about, written about; that it was an exciting world demanding exploration. This was a stirring discovery. "Until then," wrote Carl Becker, "I had never been interested in history; since then, I have never ceased to be so."[18]

Carl Becker and others who testified to Turner's greatness succumbed to his intellectual charm because they were to be historians. His appeal to future lawyers and engineers and bookkeepers was less irresistible. To them the minutes Turner spent in pawing through piles of notes for a usable quotation were not titillating pauses in the quest for learning, but embarrassing interludes. To them the constant bibliographical suggestions were not challenges, but assignments that would discourage the most dedicated student. Turner offered little of the methodical, orderly information desired by unthinking undergraduates; the students left his lectures not with a neatly arranged array of facts that could be memorized at examination time, but with information that had to be digested and questions that had to be answered. He required his students, even his most elementary students, to think, to interpret, to understand the past. This was a difficult assignment, and one from which most of them shied. They were proud that the university boasted a scholar who commanded national attention and published in national journals, but the mass of the students, who had no particular concern for history, showed little inclination to shoulder the heavy burdens required in his courses. Turner, even at the height of his popularity, was no spellbinder who packed his lecture hall and hypnotized his audience with the brilliance of his rhetoric.[19]

That this was Turner's image during the 1890s, at a time when his teaching skills and enthusiasms were at their height, is indicated by both the smallness of his classes and his relative obscurity. Only his required survey course in American history attracted between 50 and 100 students regularly; his "Social and Economic History" began with 41, dwindled the next term to 32, and never again lured more than 30; his "Constitutional and Political History" only once boasted more than 20 (21 enrolled in the fall term of 1895). Even his much-publicized "History of the West" was offered to only 41 students when it was first presented in 1895; this fell to 35 a term later, and it usually attracted less than 30 thereafter.[20] Nor did Turner fare well when judged by another gauge of popularity: mention in the undergraduate publications. His name appeared only infrequently in the yearbook, *The Badger*, and the humor magazine, *The Sphynx*, and then usually as the author of a sufficiently unhumorous remark to suggest that laughter seldom swept his classroom. Thus: from a student asked why Virginia was so named, "After the Virgin Mary"; from one requesting to be excused from an absence, "Because I was sick to my stomach from Professor Turner's class May 20"; from one asked, during a discussion of topics, whether she were the only one who had religion, "Yes, sir, I am afraid I am." The 1896 *Badger* could find nothing more inspirational to say about Turner than:

> It's Dr. Turner who turned o'er the pages
> Which bear written on them the work of ages

He was clearly not a popularizer who bartered intellectual standards for student approval.[21] Turner's later reputation as a master teacher was well-earned, but only among the few who found in history the same stimulus that inspired his own passions.

For those students the rewards were great, for instruction under Turner seemed a talisman to a distinguished career in historical studies. During the 1890s a fair number entered his undergraduate seminar or prepared the "honor's thesis" required for graduation with distinction under his direction. Each student received special attention, yet none was moulded into a replica of the master. Turner's own interest in the frontier was sublimated to allow every student to select a thesis topic that would inspire his best effort, and the variety was infinite: "The National Nominating Power," "The Claims of Georgia to State Sovereignty," "The Pan-American Policy of James G. Blaine," "An Economic Interpretation of the Lead Region of Illinois."[22] Given that free rein, they blossomed, each with an interest in his own historical domain that sent him on to graduate work, and many to leadership in the profession. What other teacher of that day could boast of training such historical giants as Carl Becker, Joseph Schafer, Herbert Eugene Bolton, William J. Hocking, Louise P. Kellogg, Guy Stanton Ford, and William S. Robertson? All of those scholars launched their careers under Turner in the 1890s.

Even more remarkable was the number and quality of graduate students attracted to Madison by his presence. Turner was still a relative unknown during the 1890s, the author of one paper that was only gradually attracting attention within the profession, and a minor faculty member in a backwater college that was overshadowed by the great eastern universities. Yet such was the efficiency of the academic grapevine that by the mid-1890s capable students from throughout the Midwest were journeying to Madison to sit at his feet, and by the end of the century he was luring a few from the East and the Far West. In all, Turner trained or played a major role in training eight doctors of philosophy in history during the decade, and eighteen master's candidates. This was the more remarkable because the doctorate was a little-known degree at Wisconsin, recently introduced and awarded infrequently. Not until 1897 was the history department allowed the fellowships usually needed to attract better students, and then the two allotted it were hardly passports to easy living; for the $400 yearly they paid, the Fellows were expected to spend several hours weekly instructing in the introductory courses. Those who came to Madison under these circumstances were drawn by tales of Turner's excellence, not by the promise of an academic bed of roses.

These tales were persuasive, for his seminar was one of the most remarkable workshops then enlivening the world of historical studies. It met weekly in the library of the State Historical Society, housed in the south wing of the state capitol building, where a long table was set aside for their two-hour sessions, and where the students were surrounded by row on row of books that could be readily consulted. There were not many seminar students—four or five each year before 1895, ten to eighteen thereafter as Turner's fame spread—but they were a well-chosen lot, eager to work at a pace equaling that of their master. He saw to it that each did so, not by force, but by persuasion. The subject matter varied from year to year, changing with Turner's own research interests, but members were allowed to select topics that would interest them within this framework. If a student chose a subject not to his liking he had only himself to blame, and this seldom happened.

So they worked with a will, each digging into the source materials that Turner insisted they use, each reporting his results for general discussion. This was a common practice in other universities; where Turner differed was in his relations with his students. To them he was simply a fellow-researcher, sharing in their excitement when they unearthed an important document, pouncing on each fresh interpretation with an enthusiasm matching their own, suffering their disappointment when their data failed to substantiate their conclusions. Turner did this deliberately, but he was no play actor; he *was* a student, as eager to applaud a find by one of his followers as to cheer one of his own. "Our method," he explained, "is to take the student into the workshop where the chips are flying and where he can see the workman cut his finger and jam his thumb as often as the occasion arises."[23] All were on common ground in that seminar, driven by one common passion—to discover the truth about the past. Turner's function was to provide guidance, to stimulate greater effort by words of praise, to blunt the too-harsh criticism that sometimes greeted a report, and, at the end, to award the able with his blessing or chastise the laggards with mild reproof. Never was there complete rejection. Turner was not interested in punishing the fallen, but in salvaging them for the historical tasks that lay ahead.

These were the techniques that allowed Turner to train more capable graduate students during his first decade in the classroom than many instructors produced in a lifetime. Kate A. Everest was the first of his doctoral candidates, in 1892; then came Orin G. Libby and George H. Alden in 1895, John B. Sanborn and Balthasar H. Meyer in 1897, Paul S. Reinsch in 1898, and Louise P. Kellogg and Charles McCarthy in 1901. All became useful, and some distinguished, citizens, Kate Everest, George Alden, and Orin Libby as teaching historians, John Sanborn and Balthasar Meyer as economists, Paul Reinsch as a teacher and international lawyer, Miss Kellogg and Charles McCarthy as librarians. Turner could justly pride himself on their accomplishments—and did so.

To survey the subjects chosen for investigation by these would-be scholars, or to thumb the theses produced by the eighteen masters trained by Turner during his baptismal years as a teacher, is to recognize both his selflessness and the breadth of his intellectual enthusiasms. He was deeply immersed in his frontier studies at this time, yet not once did the word "frontier" appear in the title of a dissertation he directed, while most were only remotely connected with the West. Instead, they ranged over all American history: "Diplomatic Relations between the United States and Mexico, 1850-1857," "The Attitude of the American Colonies to the English Common Law," "The Origin of the System of Land Grants in Aid of Education," "Congressional Grants of Land in Aid of Railways," "Massachusetts Federalism," "The Colonial Charter," "The Anti-Masonic Party"—the list could be extended, but the point would be the same.[24] Turner's tastes were too catholic to fit into any mould. By giving his students free rein, and by learning with them as they explored the byways of the past, he was broadening his own knowledge of history, and this was one purpose in his life.

All of this took a great deal of time, for he had to keep abreast of the varied topics his students selected, just as he had to spend hours poring over their papers, blue pencil in hand. As Turner waded deeper into the academic stream, however, he discovered that the demands of teaching were as nothing compared to the energy-sapping tasks daily inflicted on professors by their university and community. Outsiders might envy Turner his twelve-hour weekly teaching load, but they knew nothing of the advice he had to give, the lectures he had to deliver, the clubs he had to address, the faculty meetings he had to attend, the committee assignments he had to perform, the departmental duties he had to discharge. All this in addition to the research and writing that he had to do for his own and the university's advancement. Turner, like other instructors from that day to this, found himself increasingly enmeshed in a network of duties that covered the spectrum of the educational process, and went well beyond.

Some of this stemmed from his interest in secondary education. This was genuine; Turner sincerely believed that history instruction on the lower levels had to be improved, and he was willing to labor to that end. So he accepted, even welcomed, a post as one of the university's high school inspectors, who were charged with traveling about the state urging educators to improve their standards. Each school had to be visited yearly, its teaching investigated, its library appraised, and its offerings judged—to determine whether it was worthy of accreditation. This was a time-squandering task; Turner was frequently on the road for a week at a time, traveling from town to town, lodging in inferior hotels or rooming houses, spending hours talking with teachers and principals, and finally getting back to Madison just in time to rush to an eight o'clock class of his own.[25] What he saw on these journeys convinced him that reform was overdue. During the late 1890s he willingly accepted membership on a state committee to standardize instruction in history in the schools, and he used every excuse to preach the need of instilling the normal schools with what he called the "university spirit." Good teachers could never be trained, he believed, until the normal schools were brought into the university's orbit; they should be transformed into respectable academic institutions where would-be schoolteachers would be taught academic subjects, where historians and economists and other academicians would replace professional educators, and where students would be equipped to enter the university for their final training.[26] Turner's recipe for the training of teachers was that of the twentieth century, when normal schools were transformed into state colleges, and finally into universities in their own right.

This concern for secondary education might not have endeared him to the educationalists, but it did enmesh him in the professional teach-

ers' associations and force him to spend too much time at their meetings. He spoke regularly at such gatherings as those of the State Educational Association and the South Side Educational Association of
Milwaukee, usually on historical topics that reflected his current interests, but sometimes on broader subjects, such as "Some Relations between the History and Physiography of the United States." He urged
on his audiences the virtues of analytical as opposed to narrative history, and the necessity of explaining to their charges the social and
economic forces that underlay human behavior.[27] Turner's one-man
crusade gave some high school teachers, at least, a chance to hear some
very good advice as well as to take some solid doses of history.

It also brought him to the attention of principals, with the inevitable
result that he found himself in demand as a commencement speaker at
high school ceremonies. This meant more squandered time, for Turner
was not one to undertake such tasks lightly, and he prepared each address carefully, sometimes after wide reading in areas not close to his
own interests. Two were particularly burdensome: one an address to
the Madison High School in the spring of 1895, on "The High School
and the City," the other, the dedication of a new high school in Portage, in January 1896. In both he made post-frontier America his
theme. The fifty graduates of the Madison school and their parents
were told that Americans would develop a social conscience when
they could no longer escape society's problems by fleeing to frontiers;
then the lakes of Wisconsin would again sparkle unpolluted; no longer
would "the central part of our city be overhung with smoke and the
air choked with its odors."[28] In that frontierless land, cooperation would
supercede individuality, and men would learn to live together in peace.
In Portage he again harped on his closed-frontier theme, urging support for higher education to train the scientists and agricultural experts
needed for survival in a non-expanding world, diplomats to solve problems created by the international contests for the globe's dwindling
resources, social scientists to devise the controls needed in a society
where a frontier no longer existed as a "safety valve for social danger,
a bank account on which they might continually draw to meet losses."[29]
Turner spent a great deal of his energy on those two addresses, and in
them he said a good many things that he was to fit into his whole historical framework in the future.

He learned less from another chore demanded by his educational interests. This stemmed from the Wisconsin Free Library Association's decision to equip a number of mobile libraries to travel from town to town throughout the state. In that day of horse-drawn vehicles, heavy books could not be moved. Instead, the commission would prepare fifty-five paperbound volumes dealing with the colonial and revolutionary periods of American history, all small and easily transported. Turner was naturally called into service as a consultant, and he was assigned the tasks of planning the Revolutionary series and of preparing an introduction for the first book, a bibliographical pamphlet of fourteen pages.[30] He did so with no reward, save the satisfaction of knowing that the Wisconsin townsfolk would be subjected to some sound history. To Turner that was enough.

More to his liking, although just as destructive of his research time, were the duties that he owed to (or assumed for) the university. These ran the gamut, from weekly faculty meetings—each lasting two hours or more, and debating every issue from an unexcused student absence to a curriculum revision—through innumerable committee obligations, to preparation of a column on "Progress of the University" for the alumni magazine. Of these none was more disturbing than the need to defend one of his colleagues against the attack of a minor politician. Richard T. Ely was the intended victim; in the summer of 1894 a newly elected state superintendent of public education accused that distinguished professor of favoring strikes, aiding strikers, and advocating "utopian, impractical and pernicious doctrines" in his books and classroom. When the Board of Regents took these charges seriously and named a committee to investigate, Turner rightly feared a witch-hunt that would not only crucify Ely but damage the university. He could meet this danger only by showing the charges to be false. Much of that summer went into writing a lengthy report that not only vindicated Ely, but revealed his accuser as an unprincipled officeholder whose accusations should not be taken seriously. Turner's testimony before the investigative committee helped carry the day; Ely emerged as a brilliant scholar whose views were untainted by socialistic doctrine and who, rather than indoctrinating his students, encouraged them to "look and see things" for themselves. So impressed were the regents that they not only exonerated Ely, but adopted a classic statement on academic rights that has served as a beacon light for freedom of expression since that day.[31]

Turner took satisfaction in Ely's triumph, but he must have been plagued by the realization that some of the unspectacular duties he performed for education were less useful than his own research. Such must have been his frame of mind when he inserted a notice in the student newspaper begging college and high school debaters to stop using him as an information bureau for material needed in their speeches, or when he represented the university at the inauguration of presidents of other institutions, or when he traveled far and wide to speak to alumni groups that cared more about football than learning,[32] or when he opened his home to high school teachers of history and political science seeking to form a state-wide society to encourage research, or to the "Historical and Economic Club" of Wisconsin that lured to Madison history and economics teachers from the normal schools.[33] These were services beyond the call of duty, but Turner was interested in furthering education, and he could no more refuse than could his successors of a later day. Nor could he fail to give endless hours to the committees that made faculty life a burden. He served on a succession of time-consuming bodies that grappled with such diverse problems as the reorganization of the college faculty and the type of degree to be offered by the school of commerce.

These services were irksome to one eager to establish his reputation as a scholar, but no more so than the inevitable invitations to speak before this university society or that. They were many, and all required careful preparation, whether he was addressing a student convocation on "Washington and the West," or a "New Orleans Day" ceremony on Andrew Jackson, or a "Lafayette Memorial Meeting," or the History and Political Science Association on "The Relation between the Physiography and History of the Middle West." Turner gave far too many speeches for his own good, but his time was not completely wasted. As he went through the agony of preparation, his views on the nature of history were sharpened, and his understanding of the frontier deepened.

Turner's interpretation of the past, his lectures showed, was constantly broadening, and his impatience with historians whose focus was narrower than his own was steadily increasing. His most biting invective was reserved for Hermann von Holst of the University of Chicago, and it was unleashed in an extensive review of that distinguished author's *Constitutional and Political History of the United States*, a review delivered before the University of Wisconsin's Historical and Political Science Association in January 1894. Turner spent a vast amount of time on that task, reading all eight volumes carefully, consulting reviews, and laboring long to produce a forty-seven page manuscript that showed how deeply he was committed to a frontier interpretation.[34] Von Holst was wrong, Turner charged, because he totally misunderstood the elements that contributed to American democracy: the evolution of a composite nationality through immigration, freedom from European influences, the spread of settlement westward, the evolution of an industrial society, the emergence of sectionalism, and changing interpretations of the Constitution. Of these omissions, the most fatal was von Holst's failure to understand the "effect of free land in promoting democracy." For *American* democracy differed completely from the European democracy known to that German-born scholar. "It was born from conditions that can never be possible in Europe. It was a democracy that came not from the political theorist's dreams of the primitive German forest. It came stark and strong and full of life from the American forest." Von Holst had written a distorted treatise on slavery; he had not written a constitutional history of the United States.

Turner was perfectly right when he launched those barbs, but he was treading on dangerous ground, for von Holst was one of the nation's most respected historians and a power in the American Historical Association. Turner very much wanted to publish his views, but he was also wise enough to realize the consequences of an assault by a brash young man on the dean of the profession. His doubts were heightened when friends at the University of Chicago told him that von Holst was impatient of anything but praise, and that even a brief newspaper notice of Turner's remarks had created a mild furor on the Chicago campus. So he held firm when the editor of a respectable journal sought publication rights. His views on von Holst remained unpublished during Turner's lifetime.[35]

This was Turner's last foray into personal attack, but he never wavered in his view that the past was far too complex to be explained by a single force (as von Holst had attempted to do in assigning the slavery issue the major role in the evolution of the United States), and that one to be taken into account must be the expansion of the frontier. Historians, he charged in one of his speeches, had almost always erred in refusing to recognize that complexity. "Nothing is so difficult as to discover every motive of a man in any given action and yet nothing is so common even among historians as offhand judgments of events." Those who failed to emphasize this were violating a basic principle of their profession, for if history taught any lesson, it was that "society cannot be explained by a single theory or successfully modified by a single stroke."[36] Historians should realize that expansion was a force to be reckoned with in illuminating the American past. Even modern-day problems were understandable only against that background. The nation's principal need in the twentieth century was to conserve and adapt the early frontier-bred ideals to the changed conditions of contemporary society. The universities must play a major part in solving that problem, and the lead must be taken by western universities, where the social stratification that was already deadening eastern institutions was less advanced.[37] Turner saw America as changing, but he also saw that its direction was—and should be—governed partly by the traits and institutions that had emerged during its pioneering era. This was a theme that he was to stress more and more in the future, as he speculated about the post-frontier world in which he lived.

Less tuned to his own interests were the tasks forced upon him by the community. The State Historical Society demanded a healthy share of his time; he served as curator, arranged a program for the 1899 meeting at Green Bay, and shouldered more than he should of the burden of planning the magnificent new building that was opened on the lower campus in 1900. He was also in demand by the state government when any historic occasion had to be recognized. He was drafted to serve on the committee that planned the celebration of Wisconsin's fiftieth year of statehood in 1898. Turner must have enjoyed naming his father to a speaker's role on the elaborate program held that June, but he paid for that pleasure by being conscripted for the committee that edited the commemorative volume published on the occasion.[38] Turner never complained about these duties, and in some instances he took considerable pleasure in his accomplishments—he judged the State Historical Society's library building as "perfect" and "a delight to the eye and soul," for example—yet now and then he wished that the ivory tower in which he supposedly lived was more impregnable.

This was especially true when the women's and social clubs—those supreme enemies of all academicians—took to his trail. The Contemporary Club, which he had served so well as a graduate student, apparently viewed him as a universal scholar, capable of shedding light on the most obscure subject; he was called upon to speak on such improbable subjects as "Charles Sumner," "The Place of History in Modern Education," and "Drawing in the Public Schools," the last a topic on which he displayed a surprising degree of knowledge. His assignments for the Madison Literary Club were directed toward his own interests, but they still required impressive preparation: "The Louisiana Purchase," "The Origins of Andrew Jackson," "Aspects of Civilization in the Old Northwest," and so on.[39] Whatever the subject, and no matter how alien it was to his own specialties, Turner was able to offer fresh insights and to link his topic with the broader stream of history that he considered important.

This doomed him as a performer before women's clubs, much to his delight. His perfectionism and sound scholarship rebelled against the glamorous popularizations they wanted, as two incidents in which he was involved admirably demonstrate. In 1896, when he addressed the Madison Women's Club on "The Spaniards in North America," Turner made no mention of the romantic *conquistadores,* discoursing instead on the impact of native cultures on Latin America's social structure and the inflationary effect of New World gold on Spain's finances.[40] On another occasion, when he was invited by the Milwaukee Colonial Dames to speak on the "Colonization of the James," he ignored John Smith and other heroes so dear to the hearts of his audience and read a forty-eight page manuscript that explained "the process of actual colonization, the forming of communities, and the social and political life along the lower James." Painstakingly, Turner analyzed the successive waves of settlement in the four river valleys of Virginia in the seventeenth century, and the differing cultures that emerged as man and nature interacted.[41] The excessive amount of research that went into that paper—even to paying $40 for copies of documents that would shed light on the problem—resulted in an essay that could have graced any historical journal, but it must have been received with little enthusiasm by his audience. He received few invitations to address women's groups thereafter.

The kaleidoscope of activities in which Turner was involved during the 1890s did not enshrine him as a hero on the local lecture circuit, but they did bring him his first national recognition—with important results. His fame was beginning to spread—as a scholar whose germinal paper on the frontier was attracting increasing attention, as a teacher whose students sang his praises in a growing number of universities—and with this fame came opportunities to leave Madison for greener pastures. Not unnaturally, the first offer came from Woodrow Wilson, an unabashed convert to the frontier thesis, who was then head of the history department at Princeton. Wilson approached Turner in the fall of 1896: would Turner fill a soon-to-be-created chair in American history, at a salary of $3400? Turner was interested, as anyone earning $2500 was bound to be, but his heart was in Madison and he was too good a bargainer to show any enthusiasm. His cautious response aroused Wilson to his persuasive best, and Turner cast himself in an inquisitorial role as he asked question after question about the library, the living costs, the quality of students (generally considered to be too frivolous at Princeton), the relative advantages of East and West. Wilson parried with skill; the Princeton library was inferior to that of the State Historical Society in Wisconsin, but Turner could have a special fund to buy books; living costs were only slightly higher (houses $500 a year, servants $12 to $16 a month, groceries about the same); he could add another $1500 to his salary by lecturing (Wilson had earned $4000 the year before); the students might be frivolous, but some were serious, and the teaching load would be light.[42]

Turner had to decide between the West, with its "atmosphere of creative activity" and the superb resources of his beloved library, on the one hand, and the admitted prestige of an eastern professorship, on the other. Fortunately, he was spared that decision, for in December 1896, Wilson wrote that the trustees had failed to create the chair in history he had been promised, using lack of funds as an excuse to conceal their real objection to Turner: he was a dangerous religious radical—a Unitarian. Wilson was horrified, and confessed that he would happily leave Princeton if he could. "I am," he wrote, "probably at this writing the most chagrined fellow on the Continent."[43] Turner stayed at Wisconsin, but only after he had used the near-offer as a club over the administration; he asked nothing for himself, but he did request two graduate fellowships to provide readers in his and Haskins's lower-division courses, and $500 a year for books in European history.[44] These minor concessions cost the university little and made a great deal of difference to Turner. His roots were sinking ever deeper in Madison's soil.

This was well, for only a few weeks passed before he was tempted again. The University of Pennsylvania was creating a chair in American Constitutional and Institutional History. Would Turner come East and talk matters over? He did, to such mutual satisfaction that a letter followed him home with a definite offer of a professorship at $3000. But such interest as he had had vanished when Wisconsin agreed to match that salary. Turner had obviously not been tempted seriously, nor was he later that year when asked what terms might lure him to Cleveland's Western Reserve University.[45] He was too happy at Madison to be tempted by any but the offer of the most prestigious post elsewhere.

Such an offer might come soon, but in the meantime Turner had every reason to feel self-satisfied. He was still short of forty years old, yet he was the holder of a professorship in a rapidly growing university at a respectable salary. His articles and reviews were attracting sufficient attention to win him offers from first-rate institutions. The graduate students trained in his seminars were appearing on excellent faculties and spreading his fame as a teacher, resulting in a steadily increasing flow of new and better students into his graduate classes. He lived in a community that was something more than a town but not quite a city, and this he found much to his liking. His home at 629 Frances Street was attracting congenial neighbors who could be counted as intimate friends. His health was sound, and he was able to enjoy canoe trips on Lake Mendota, summer fishing expeditions into northern Wisconsin, and regular exercise on his bicycle or tennis court. He adored Mae and their three growing children. Turner, it seemed, was a man who had everything.

Then tragedy struck. February of 1899 was an unusually cold month even for Madison, with the thermometer dipping to 29 degrees below zero, and sickness rampant. Early in the month the Turner's youngest child, five-year-old Mae Sherwood Turner, contracted diphtheria, a dread killer in those days of scant medical knowledge. The doctors did what they could, but on February 11 little Mae Sherwood died. For two weeks Turner mourned, a broken and disheartened man. Yet more was to come. That October his only son, Jackson Allen Turner, seven years old, complained of intense stomach pains. By the time these were diagnosed as symptoms of appendicitis the appendix had ruptured and inflammation had set in. A doctor came from Chicago to operate, but by this time it was too late. Day after day the lad weakened as doctors did what they could and his father maintained a twenty-four hour vigil at the bedside. The end finally came on the afternoon of Sunday, October 22, 1899.[46] Within a few months the Turners had been reduced from a happy group of five to a bereaved family of three, with only nine-year-old Dorothy Kinsey Turner to comfort her stricken parents.

For weeks Turner remained in seclusion; "I have not done anything, and have not the heart to do anything," he wrote.[47] When he finally returned to his classroom, he was only a walking shadow, his spirit gone. "I would like to go up and shake him by the hand," one of his students recorded. "I guess we all feel the same."[48] Months passed, but friends noted that the sparkle was gone from his eyes, the bounce from his step. Overnight he had been transformed into an older man, haunted by memories that could never be erased. His pride and stamina forced him to continue the routine of life, but Mae succumbed so completely to her grief that she was taken to a sanatarium in Chicago to recover. "Her poor little body could not stand so heavy a load," Turner explained.[49] Not until June 1900 was she able to return home. Turner's last act before she arrived was to erase from the living room wall the marks that recorded the growth of their three children, leaving to the end the most tragic of all: "J A T Jan. 1898. 3 feet 8½ inches."[50]

Marks could be erased, but memories could not. So Turner, living in lonely mourning that spring of 1900 with only Dorothy to comfort him, probably welcomed a situation that required him to make one of his most difficult decisions. This was forced upon him by the master-persuader of the academic world, President William Rainey Harper of the University of Chicago. He had been in touch with Turner in the past, luring him to the campus for a six-weeks summer school assignment in 1898, and a year later for a weekly seminar as a replacement for the ailing Professor Hermann von Holst. These not only allowed Turner to demonstrate his teaching skills, but placed him near at hand when President Harper was ready to make his move. On March 10, 1900, over what was probably an excellent meal at the Quadrangle Club, Harper stated his case: would Turner become head of the Chicago history department at a salary of $4000 and a half-time teaching load for two years, and a full-time salary of $5000 thereafter? Here was an offer to turn the head of any academician, but Turner was not swept away by it. This was a chance to wring favors from the University of Wisconsin, not for himself, but for his students and the history department. He would, he told Harper, make his decision by April 1, but only after consulting his friends in Madison.[51]

Those next weeks witnessed bargaining on both sides that would have done credit to a Near Eastern camel trader. Turner, after consulting his good friends Charles Homer Haskins, Richard T. Ely, and Charles R. Van Hise, told President Charles K. Adams that he would consider staying only if the university guaranteed four things: a full-scale graduate program, the creation of a separate School of History under his directorship, a salary of $3500 commensurate with that post, and a year's leave of absence to allow the Turners to recover from the loss of their children. These terms were approved by the university regents on March 22, after being assured by President Adams that Turner's going would "be regarded as a misfortune, scarcely less than a calamity."[52] With his victim wavering, President Harper swung into action once more. The big guns on the Chicago campus were urged to fire their barrages in the form of letters extolling the virtues of Chicago, and such influential personages as John Dewey, Albion W. Small, and T. C. Chamberlin responded with a will. At the same time Harper multiplied the attractions: a special $30,000 fund to buy American history books for the library, with annual appropriations of $5000 to $10,000 thereafter; a professorship at $3000 for Charles Homer Haskins; a history department expanded to four professors, an associate professor, four assistant professors, and an array of instructors and assistants. "I am hoping," Harper added wistfully, "that you are beginning to see more clearly that the path of duty leads in the direction of Chicago."[53]

Each move on Chicago's part gave Turner a new card to play in his game with President Adams, and he played them well. The welfare of the department, he told the president, required the use of seminar rooms in the State Historical Society library, the publication of a history series in the university bulletin, two additional fellowships, a new assistant professor in American history and an instructor in European history, and that crowning appointment that was the ambition of every professor: a stenographer of his own. If these could be assured, he would agree to stay in Madison. President Adams responded so favorably that five days after Turner laid down his terms, President Harper's assistant wrote coldly: "I beg to congratulate you on your success with the Board of Regents."[54]

Turner's decision was hailed as a major triumph for the University of Wisconsin. His classes greeted his first appearance with "spontaneous and prolonged applause," while the student paper editorialized that "an institution of learning is known much by the members of its faculty," and congratulated the university on holding one of its brightest stars.[55] Turner was delighted with this acclaim, although deep in his heart he realized that he had elected to remain at Wisconsin not because of loyalty, but because his historical ambitions could be better satisfied there than at Chicago. The State Historical Society library offered attractions that could not be duplicated elsewhere; then, too, he feared that administering a large department would take time and energy better spent on research.[56] His commitment now, and for the future, was to historical writing, not to administration.

These feverish negotiations were a godsend, for while they continued there was little time to brood over the loss of his children. With the decision made, and with Mae's return home in June 1900, his problems crowded upon him once more, compounded now with the realization that she needed a change of scene to recover her health. What better way to provide this than a year in Europe? His assured leave of absence for 1900-1901 made this possible. Having made up his mind, Turner threw himself into preparations with the same intensity that had marked his dealings with President Harper. He filled a paper notebook with information on how to transpose miles into kilometers and Fahrenheit temperatures into Centigrade, lists of old masters to buy in reproductions, travel books to be consulted, and notations on the virtues of Pape Roach Seasick Drops. He solicited from the governor a formal document, complete with ribbons and seals, proclaiming Frederick Jackson Turner to be a "gentleman of good character and standing in the community," worthy of attention from American ministers and consuls. He rented the house at 629 Frances Street and made arrangements with two Madison banks to receive the rental money and pay the taxes and insurance.[57]

All was in readiness, but the departure had to be delayed until fall, for the Turners planned to spend $250 a month on the trip and could accumulate that sum only if he taught summer school. This over, they sailed from New York on August 18, accompanied by the array of trunks usual in that day of leisurely travel. They even took Turner's bicycle, which he planned to pedal about Europe. The Atlantic transport *Mesaba* carried cattle as well as passengers, and the odors reminded him more of a farm than the ocean, but he found happiness in the "silvery chasing of the wonderful blue of the waves" and the vastness of the sea. They stayed first in London for a few days, then went on to the Low Countries and took the traditional barge journey up the Rhine before making a short stop-over at Lake Luzerne, where Turner climbed Mount Pilatus. Eventually the family settled into modest lodgings above a wine shop in the village of Wengen, not far from Interlaken, where they could view the splendid whiteness of the Jungfrau at a cost of $3.40 a day for board and room. There they spent the summer, taking long walks into the mountains, visiting Swiss chalets, and listening to the music of the streams and cow bells as Mae recovered her health. But memories faded slowly. "You know what we all felt of heart pain," he wrote his parents, "to be in such a beautiful world without our two children to whom this kind of beauty belonged."[58]

With autumn they moved on, traveling by rail along the Rhone Valley, climbing the Grimsel Pass in a carriage, and finally settling in Bern. There Turner retrieved his bicycle, which had been delayed at customs, and set out by himself to explore the Rhone Valley, where vineyards and orchards and brown-stained houses colored the countryside, and where he could climb to Zermatt to marvel at the Matterhorn. He returned to Bern to find Dorothy and Mae rebelling against the steady rainfall, so they moved on again, to the village of Vevy on the shores of Lake Geneva, for a month of good Swiss food for Mae, tutoring for Dorothy, and extended bicycle trips for Turner into high mountain pastures where each mile was more picturesque than the last. Again they were driven southward when snows mantled the Alps, through the Gothard Tunnel into Italy, with stops at Lugano and Milan. They settled in Florence, where they stayed until February 1901. Mae and Dorothy made a valiant effort to master Italian—so they could start an organ and peanut business in Madison, Turner reported—but he himself turned to his travels again and pedaled through the rich countryside, even as far as Pisa, fifty-five miles away.

It was a pleasant life, but by the end of February the Turners were growing restless and suffering pangs of homesickness. Their funds were so far exhausted that they had to borrow $200 from the elder Turner; this financed several weeks in Rome, Sorrento, and Naples before they finally sailed for home at the end of March. By this time their financial plight was such that Turner had to leave Mae and Dorothy with Mae's sister in Massachusetts, borrow ten dollars from his brother-in-law and five from a friend to pay his way to Portage, then borrow another eighty to transport his wife and daughter to Chicago. By April 20 he was back in Madison, happy to be amidst familiar surroundings, but saddened at the memories they conjured. His first mission was a pilgrimage to Forest Hills Cemetery with a tribute of Easter lilies to place on the children's graves. "How much the little place means to us," he wrote Mae that night. "But Jackson and Tita are not here."[59]

Turner returned to his native land with a new perspective and altered interests. He had deliberately elected to spend most of his European year in Switzerland and Italy, feeling that they contrasted most violently with the United States, and hoping that these contrasts would sharpen his awareness of the distinctive features of American life. Three differences struck him particularly. One was the compactness of the European countryside; distances there were so short and the landscape so varied that the sense of uniformity bred by America's broad vistas was lacking, with each tiny community sensing its independence from all others. Another was the strong role played by European tradition, which decreed that fixed social customs and crafts should be perpetuated virtually unchanged from the sixteenth century, and that the easy democratic practices of his own country would be lacking. Finally, Turner was impressed with the aesthetic appreciation of Europeans, and Italians particularly, who supported—and patronized—art galleries and museums and libraries as the Americans never would. This he also ascribed to the strength of tradition; the people of Florence and Rome were inheritors of an artistic heritage that would not develop in the United States for centuries.

Realizing these things, Turner found that his impression of America had altered radically. Some of his reaction was unfavorable; he was shocked by the newness of everything, annoyed by the crassness of the people, and suddenly aware of the overstress on materialism. The nation, he felt, had much to learn from Europe. It had also much to teach. Turner felt his spirit expand when he left the cramped European cities and returned to the vast open spaces of the United States. He was invigorated by the newness of American life, the detachment of the people from tradition, the tendency to look toward the future rather than the past. Here was opportunity, and opportunity not for the few, but for the many.[60] Here, in other words, was a land made different by a frontier that spread the bounties of nature before all the people and invited them to partake of its riches.

Turner turned his back on the most tragic year of his life—a year that saw two of his most treasured possessions snatched from him and his family able to survive only by months of escape in a distant countryside. He returned ready to renew life, but that life would never be the same that he had known. To his friends he was a different man, quieter, more sedate, less inclined to gay remarks or spontaneous bursts of laughter. Some of the sparkle had gone from his eyes, some of the rich timbre from his voice, some of the sprightliness from his walk. This new Turner was more serious, more mature, inclined to view his nation's history from the broader perspective made possible by his year in Europe. He was ready to settle into hard work, for in hard work there was escape from memory, and by hard work he could share his fresh views on the nation's past with the scholarly world to which he was committed.

VII

Broadening Historical Horizons

1893-1910

EACHING, graduate students, departmental building, responding to the endless demands of town and gown—these were only half the burden assumed by any aspiring instructor who entered the academic world in the 1890s. The other was the professional writing that would enlighten the specialists in his field while also enhancing his own reputation in academic life. This came easily to Frederick Jackson Turner. He believed that history was mankind's savior—and he recognized the fact that his understanding of the past was different from, and slightly superior to, that of most of his contemporaries. Research was his passion, and during these early years, at least, he was able to translate his findings into the articles and reviews on which his reputation ultimately rested.

If he had been a practical young man, governed only by self-interest, he would have directed his efforts toward proving the frontier thesis that he had announced so boldly in 1893, but he was not that kind of man. His mind could never be stirred by warmed-over ideas; he was happy only when probing the past for fresh information that would support still newer interpretations. Then, too, Turner's interests were too catholic to be confined within one historical pasture; even this early in his life he saw himself not as a frontier historian or an economic historian, but as an American historian, whose concern was the broad scope of the nation's experience. He was equally excited about *all* the past, not just one compartment. "I don't quite care," he wrote at the time, "to figure in leggins and breech clout all the time."[1] So, instead of buckling down to his frontier studies during these formative years, Turner plunged into research on western state-making, the diplomacy of the early Republic, immigration, and a dozen other topics, all seemingly unrelated, and all only remotely linked with frontiering. To be worthy of his attention they needed only one qualification: they must shed light on the social and economic forces that underlay social evolution.

His breadth of interest and his natural inclination to recognize that a variety of causal forces explained each historical event were bolstered by his encounter with a new theory that the historical profession was to borrow from geology. In 1889, T. C. Chamberlin, friend of Turner and president of the university during his early teaching years, presented his paper on "The Method of Multiple Working Hypotheses," which was later printed in *Science* and, in revised form, in the *Journal of Geology* in 1897.[2] Chamberlin's purpose was to describe a research technique that would allow "the dangers of parental affection for a favorite theory" to be circumvented. He pointed out that if an investigator began his studies with a single hypothesis—that the frontier, let us say, shaped the American character—his mind would happily accept the facts that supported his theory and automatically reject those that did not. This could be avoided only by postulating every single explanation possible for the phenomenon under investigation, then testing each in turn. "The investigator thus becomes the parent of a family of hypotheses; and by his parental relations to all is morally forbidden to fasten his affections upon any one." In fact, he would probably find that an adequate explanation required the coordination of several causal forces operating together to produce a single event.

Here was a methodology made to order for Turner's purposes. He came across Chamberlin's paper soon after it was written, and he cited it frequently thereafter as a testament to which he completely subscribed. Human nature, he insisted, could be understood only by weighing the dozens of forces operating upon it in any given situation. The problem of the scholar was to determine the degree of weight that must be assigned to each, and to do so impartially. Thus one causal force, or several, might be more persuasive than a group of others, but all must be considered: economic, social, cultural, and political. If Turner did not always practice what he preached, and was inclined to allot the frontier a larger role in American history than it deserved, he did so only because he felt that the frontier had been too much ignored in the past. He was aware, as were few of his contemporaries, that not only expansion, but immigration, sectionalism, class conflicts, industrialization, religion, and a host of other forces operated to shape the nation's history.

Turner's thinking at this stage of his intellectual development was nowhere better shown than in the speculations he made on the origins of New England towns as he prepared his course lectures during the middle 1890s. To a modern historian, no subject could be more archaic or insignificant; to Turner's generation, none was more lively or challenging. At stake was the validity of the dominant "germ" theory; Herbert Baxter Adams had built his whole historical structure on his study of *The Germanic Origins of New England Towns*, while his antagonists, such as Edward Channing and Charles McLean Andrews, used these same institutions to launch assaults on the teachings of the Teutonic school. Turner, characteristically, refused to accept the findings of any of the controversialists, reading them first, then plunging into an intensive study of colonial documents so he could draw his own conclusions.

He first analyzed all existing theories: that the New England town was a transplanted Germanic *tun*, that it was modeled on the English parish, that it originated by a process of "constitutional retrogression" when long-forgotten features of medieval German communities were revived amidst comparably primitive conditions, that it duplicated English towns but in an earlier form than they existed in the seventeenth century. None seemed satisfactory to Turner. Surely, he wrote, their origins could be explained by some "simpler and less occult method than by the hypothesis of reversion," then so popular at Johns Hopkins. Were they not, indeed, only the natural product of social evolution under the distinctive environmental conditions of frontier America?

Turner thought that they were. His studies convinced him that one of the characteristics of New England institutions was their adaptability. The settlers, finding themselves in a wilderness environment similar to that of their Teutonic ancestors, adopted many practices that had been suitable in medieval Germany, not because there was a conscious "retrogression," but because they sought practical means of living in a primitive environment. This accounted for many of the similarities that historians had noted: the common ownership of land, a division of tillable fields and pasturage among the villagers, a tendency to deny membership in the community to strangers. These were the products of an abundance of land and a need for defense that existed in both ancient Germany and New England.

To substantiate this belief, Turner examined a number of specific practices of the New Englanders, then found counterparts in the contemporary English scene which they could have borrowed for their own use, or a tendency in human nature that would explain their action. The award of village grants to a group of proprietors, he discovered, was consistent with contemporary practice in the homeland, and was merely applied to the new situation. The practice of restricting community membership was based on the Puritan desire to maintain ecclesiastical purity among true believers. The hard line drawn between town proprietors and newcomers who wanted to share their land mirrored the selfishness of human nature, and not a "reversion" to the custom of the *Märker* and *Ausmärker*. The separation of groups from established villages to found their own communities was not a return to the *dörfer* concept of the past, but was caused by the lure of free land and the bitterness of religious conflicts within the older society. Each practice, Turner noted, was "a case of similar causes leading to similar results."[3] New England towns were not patent-office duplicates of either the English parish or the German *tun*, but the product of accepted practices applied in a distinctive environment. This was common sense, but it was also a bold exercise in historical ingenuity for his day.

Turner chose never to publish his speculations on the genesis of New England towns, and he might have gone on garnering knowledge for its own sake had not two unrelated circumstances forced him to take up his pen once more. One was the opening to scholars in 1896 of the splendid "Draper Collection" by the State Historical Society of Wisconsin. This was a treasure trove—four hundred fat volumes of manuscripts accumulated by Lyman C. Draper during a lifetime of collecting, and willed to the society on his death in 1891: letters, documents, reminiscences, interviews, reports, deeds—all the raw materials for the study of the early trans-Appalachian West, and all unused and waiting exploitation! Here were historical riches to occupy Turner for his lifetime. At the same time, he was assured an opportunity to publish what he found under the most auspicious circumstances. In the spring of 1895 a group of the rising new generation of professional historians, distressed that they had no outlet for their scholarly articles save semi-popular magazines, launched the *American Historical Review*, with J. Franklin Jameson of Brown University as editor. An article published in such a journal would be the best way to present Turner's new findings.

The opportunity to do so came knocking at his door. Jameson had never met Turner, but he had heard about him and lost no time in inviting him to submit a contribution for the first issue, preferably in western history. Turner was delighted; here was a chance to use the Draper documents to test his assumptions on the frontier's influence by examining a specific topic in depth. This, he decided, must lie in the late eighteenth century, for by then the coastal colonies were giving birth to new colonies in the interior which were sufficiently free of England's influence that they could respond to environmental forces. There, "the interaction of *American* institutions and political ideas, with free land" could be studied. Hence, he told Jameson, he would explore "State Making in the West, 1772-1789," to determine the extent to which free land altered the colonizing process and shaped the emerging settlements.[4]

This was a larger assignment than Turner knew, and the more deeply he dug into the Draper manuscripts the more he realized that he could neither meet the August 1, 1895, deadline nor tell his story in the sixteen pages alloted him. (His agonized efforts to wheedle more time and space from Jameson were to be repeated with little variation whenever he undertook a writing assignment from that day to his death.) Could he have until August 14? Was there room for an unknown letter of Patrick Henry, and a map? Jameson reluctantly parted with four more pages and promised that August 15 would not be too late, knowing full well that the article would never be finished by that time. Nor was it. The map went off on August 16, half the paper on August 19, another quarter the next day, and the last on August 21— with Turner rushing to the Madison railroad station each night to catch the last mail train. "I undertook a bigger task than I anticipated when I began," he confessed, "and there is some uncanny spell about those Scotch-Irish manuscripts." Optimistically, he had estimated that his manuscript would fill twenty pages. Jameson, more realistic, judged it would reach thirty-five pages in print and crowd out some worthy article—unless it was published in two installments. Turner fought for a time, fearful lest someone steal his ideas and materials before the second part appeared, but he backed down gracefully, muttering that he could not yet understand how his few words could fill thirty-five pages—which they did.[5]

Jameson, still a neophyte in the editorial chair, may have felt relieved when that over-long manuscript went off to the printers, but if he did he sighed too soon. Turner, ever the perfectionist, dawdled so long over each set of proofs that only urgent reminders extracted them from him, again after nightly dashes to the railroad station. Nor did this satisfy him. He had to see the page proof to make sure that he had caught every mistake and to assure himself that the mountain ranges were properly placed on his map; a map without mountains was like Hamlet without the Prince of Denmark. Jameson protested that there was no time. He protested in vain; in the end the proofs were returned, only to prove Turner correct: his mountains were not there. And there were more delays. Only when everything was completed to Turner's satisfaction could the first issue of the *American Historical Review* go to press, its final article (so placed because it came in last) "Western State-Making in the Revolutionary Era" complete with a colored fold-out map—with no mountains.[6]

Turner was still happy with the result, and well he might be; it provided, *The Nation* observed, the "main feast" in an excellent new journal. His story was as fresh in 1895 as it is familiar today—that the new states created by settlers during the Revolutionary era—Vandalia, Wautauga, Nashville, Westsylvania, Franklin, and the rest—demonstrated the significant role played by pioneers in shaping their own governments, the consistency of the trend toward self-determination on frontiers, and the willingness of frontiersmen to accept congressional control as soon as it could be exerted. Turner also proved, to his own satisfaction at least, that westerners, whether from Northeast or Southeast, adopted the same solutions for their common problems, resented the authority of unsympathetic eastern states, and served as a nationalizing force by demanding a place in the central government. These were not insignificant findings, but the article's principal importance was in its demonstration of the fact that solid research in western sources produced both worthwhile results and support for the hypothesis that Turner had presented. Turner had opened a new avenue for historical investigators, and he invited them to share the adventures to which it led.

His next explorations failed to live up to his own promises, for by this time he was so intrigued with the riches in the Draper collections that he was unable to resist burrowing further, whatever the significance of his findings to frontier theory. Fortunately he could do so with some purpose, and without the agonies of composition, for once more J. Franklin Jameson provided him with exactly the task that he most enjoyed. For some time that gadfly of the profession had been urging his colleagues to publish the basic documents of American history, a one-man campaign that bore fruit in 1895, when the National Historical Manuscripts Commission was established. Jameson was chairman, Turner was a member, and modest funds were available for a publications program. They agreed on procedures at their first meeting in New York in June 1896—they would compile a list of manuscripts in public and private depositories, select some of the more significant to be printed in an annual report, and publish only complete documents, rather than summaries. They decided, too, that their first publication would contain documentary materials illustrating the history of Canada, England, New England, the Middle States, the South, and the West. Turner's task, of course, was to compile the section on the West, from the resources of the Draper collection.[7]

Here was an assignment tailored to his interests, and he fell to work with a will, neglecting his friends, his family, and even his classes to spend long hours in the State Historical Society library, joyfully reading document after document and making discovery after discovery that altered the traditional history of the post-Revolutionary era.[8] The whole story, he knew, could not be told within the space assigned him; hence, he settled on the intrigue between Citizen Genêt and George Rogers Clark, as they plotted a campaign against Spain's Mississippi Valley colonies in 1793 and 1794. This was an unknown episode, and the evidence available was astoundingly rich—letters of George Rogers Clark, of Charles De Pauw, of Jonathan Clark, government documents galore, dispatches copied from the Spanish Archives. The French side of the story had to be supplied; Turner spent many hours directing a copyist toward materials in the Archives du Ministère des Affairs Étrangères, then translating and annotating the results. He worked very hard that winter of 1896-97, and before it was over he sent off to Jameson a fat bundle of ably edited manuscripts, ponderously entitled "Selections from the Draper Collection of the State Historical Society of Wisconsin, to Elucidate the Proposed French Expedition under George Rogers Clark Against Louisiana in the Years 1793-94." The manuscripts filled two hundred pages of the *Annual Report of the American Historical Association for 1896.*

Turner's editorial labors added a chapter to the history of the West, but they also wrought a major change in his own scholarly interests. Why bother with proving the frontier hypothesis when the diplomacy of the early Republic offered such a fascinating field for investigation? Here was an unexplored byway paved with unsolved problems, and any unsolved problem was irresistible. Then, too, documents from the French copyist continued to arrive long after the Clark-Genêt correspondence had been sent to the publishers, and these told a story far too important to be discarded. This was the combination of attractions that converted Turner from a frontier to a diplomatic historian, and kept him on that course for the next half-dozen years.[9]

What joy he knew as he read each document from France, hunted down the appropriate supporting information in the Draper collections, added his documentation and introduction, and hurried the result off to the *American Historical Review* or the National Historical Manuscripts Commission! He accomplished little else during 1897 and 1898, but the results were impressive: a long letter from Baron Carondelet on the defense of Louisiana in 1794; the extensive correspondence of the French consul at Charleston, concerning Citizen Genêt's proposed attack on the Floridas in 1793-94; a revealing letter from Thomas Jefferson to George Rogers Clark; a series of documents on the Nootka Sound controversy of 1790, copied from the British Public Record Office, which for the first time satisfactorily explained the shift in the Pacific balance of naval power from Spain to England.[10]

His publications, adding steadily to his reputation, also prepared him for his major task as a diplomatic historian. This came about through a happy accident. As was his habit, Turner sent an offprint of his article on the Nootka Sound documents to the distinguished historian and editor, Worthington C. Ford, and, as usual, he received a guarded acknowledgment, but this time with a difference. Ford had once been interested in publishing all correspondence relating to the three ministers representing France in the United States during the years from 1791 to 1797—Genêt, Fauchet, and Adet—and had secured copies from the French archives. Would Turner be interested in seeing any of the letters? He surely would. He would even be willing to edit the entire collection—350,000 manuscript pages—if Ford would consent. Ford was agreeable, and so was the Historical Manuscripts Commission, when Turner, with his remarkable inability to estimate either space or time, promised that they would fill only one hundred pages, and would be ready for publication in the next annual report.[11]

With all obstacles hurdled, and the vast bundle of manuscripts safely in his hands, Turner was ready to begin his editorial chores by the end of 1902. These proved formidable. Some documents were missing, others had to be recopied, more had to be added. Turner wanted the work done in Madison, where he had a capable copyist, a student named Homer C. Hockett; the Commission insisted that it be done in Washington, where their copyist charged only 35¢ for a thousand words. All of this took a heavy toll in money, patience, and even-temperedness, as well as unbelievably hard work, until Turner was forced to flee to Maine for a vacation during the summer of 1903, or risk a collapse. This meant that deadlines were being missed, and that tensions were mounting. At long last, however, the massive job was done and the bulky manuscript shipped to Washington. Controversy flared again when he demanded the services of Homer Hockett to aid him with the mountains of galley proof, even threatening to hire him with his own funds if the Commission was too niggardly to pay. Once more the Commission backed down; Hockett was hired and the proofs were returned more or less on time to be fitted into the annual report for 1903—which, fortunately, did not appear until late in 1904.[12] There they filled no less than 1,100 pages, forming an enduring monument to Turner's industry, no less than to his passion for diplomatic history.

This was Turner's last editorial venture—save for a modest collection of documents on the Blount Conspiracy of 1795-97, which he gathered from Paris, London, and New York, and which appeared in the April 1905 issue of the *American Historical Review*—but he would gladly have gone on had funds been available. His plans were as ambitious as they were unrealistic: he would edit all correspondence of French ministers to the United States through the Monroe administration, throwing in additional dispatches from the British and French archives, and, for good measure, adding all Russian and Spanish documents that shed light on the Monroe Doctrine.[13] Fortunately for Turner, the Manuscripts Commission failed to catch his enthusiasm; had it done so he might have spent the rest of his days editing documents in diplomatic history.

Even though his editorial plans were dampened, he could continue to write learned articles in the field. These appeared at regular intervals, paralleling his editing assignments. His first, quite naturally, was a thoroughly researched, admirably written, essay on Citizen Genêt's intrigue in the Mississippi Valley, published in the *American Historical Review* in July 1898. He then turned to a subject that occupied him for several years: the diplomatic background of the Louisiana Purchase—a topic of particular appeal in view of the coming centennial celebration. Turner's purpose was laudable—to link the Genêt episode with Napoleon's decision to acquire and sell the territory, thus demonstrating the continuity of events and the significance of the historical antecedents to the purchase—but the complexity of the problem, and the quantities of additional documentary evidence that the French copyist had to provide, involved him in a far longer effort than he had intended. He hoped to reveal his findings to the American Historical Association at its December 1901 meeting, but the paper he prepared for that occasion was so inadequate that he declined to deliver it, trying it out instead on the Madison Literary Club a month later and on the North Central History Teacher's Association in March.[14]

Two more years of research and writing were necessary before Turner was ready to display his brainchild in public. It first appeared as a popular article in the *Review of Reviews* for May 1903, as "The Significance of the Louisiana Purchase." A few months later, and in vastly more sophisticated form, it was presented as a paper on "The Relation of Spain, England, and France in the Mississippi Valley, 1789-1800," before the American Historical Association. It was then published in the *Atlantic Monthly*, where it was printed in the May and June issues in 1904 as "The Diplomatic Contest for the Mississippi Valley." Again, it was recast as a dinner speech when Turner was invited to address a St. Louis celebration of the centennial on "The Historical Significance of the Louisiana Purchase." This time he added oratorical touches that greatly pleased his hearers: "Napoleon gave to the United

States a spacious, a vast way of looking at our destiny, which has yet to work out its full result (Great applause)."[15] Still Turner sought a wider audience, this time among his peers, when his findings were presented in their most sophisticated form in the January 1905 issue of the *American Historical Review* as "The Policy of France toward the Mississippi Valley in the Period of Washington and Adams."

"Now," he wrote a friend, "I am giving up the diplomacy of that period." Then, knowing his own weaknesses, he added, "I hope."[16] He retired to his other interests with a reputation as a master interpreter of American diplomatic history, for his studies added a new dimension as well as fresh interpretations. He demonstrated that European archives held riches essential to the understanding of the nation's foreign relations, that local episodes, such as the Genêt incident, assumed international significance when fitted into the mainstream of events, and that happenings in the back country were often more important to early diplomats than better-known occurrences in national capitals. Here, as in all his investigations, Turner was peering below the surface to find the subcurrents that shaped national action. In bringing this lesson home to craftsmen in the field, he stamped himself as a major contributor to the study of diplomacy.

This is not the reputation that Turner enjoys today, even among specialists in the field; indeed, his diplomatic studies are almost forgotten. Their own excellence doomed them to this fate. Turner's findings were so significant, and his presentations so correct, that they were immediately absorbed into textbooks as part of the acknowledged pattern of history. We view his essays on diplomacy as hackneyed; they are not worth reading because they say nothing new. But they said a great deal that was new to his own generation, which ranked him among the foremost experts in the field. He was so highly regarded that he was invited to deliver two lectures on "The Diplomatic Struggle for the Mississippi Valley" before the Naval War College in Newport, and was twice—in 1906 and 1907—selected as the prestigious Albert Shaw Lecturer in Diplomatic History by the Johns Hopkins University.[17] On a lesser scale, Turner was viewed locally as an expert who could explain such complex issues as the Russo-Japanese War, a reputation built not only on his published works, but on the fact that in 1901 he introduced a course in diplomatic history, the first at Wisconsin and one of the first to be offered at any university in the United States.[18] In his own day, and in both Madison and the wider academic world, Turner was rated a first-rank student of foreign policy.

His contributions in another area, one far distant from frontier history, were less laudable in either motive or result, but they also stamp him as a pioneer in a field not often associated with his name. Turner's venture into immigration history was inspired by a letter that reached him in July 1901, shortly after his return from Europe. Would he prepare a series of articles on the coming of the Italians, Germans, Jews, and French-Canadians to the United States for the *Chicago Record-Herald*? The pay was suitable, and the essays, 2500 to 3000 words each, would not be due for several weeks. Turner, eager to rebuild his bank account after the European venture, accepted, and he immediately plunged into the more-than-necessary research that he expended on all projects, however trivial. For the next weeks he worked long and hard, often until two in the morning, gathering notes, writing drafts, compiling statistics, and even drawing a map correlating German communities in Pennsylvania with the limestone soil areas there—apparently the first of the hundreds of such maps that Turner was to prepare during his lifetime.[19]

He wrought no miracle in the articles that resulted, but they were so vastly superior to most writing on immigration at the time—and for a good many years thereafter—that he must be ranked as a constructive pioneer in this area, no less than in diplomatic history. The clichés and stereotypes of his generation were there—Germans were a "conservative, thrifty and religious folk," Italians were "quick-witted and supple in morals," because they had been taught "self-preservation by deception," Jews were "thrifty to disgracefulness" and their "ability to drive a bargain amounts to genius," the "New Immigration" from eastern and southern Europe brought "a lowering of the standard of comfort," sweatshops, congestion, political corruption, and pauperism—but overbalancing these hostile judgments were words of praise for the recent arrivals that could hardly be duplicated in that day. Turner saw two things about the immigrants that escaped other scholars: that they were the victims of social forces which were responsible for the poverty and crime usually associated with newcomers, and that their material and cultural contributions to American life far outweighed the problems they created during their period of adjustment.[20]

This did not mean that his viewpoint was that of today or that he saw the immigrant as an unalloyed blessing. Wedded as he was to the belief that American virtues were rooted in the rural past, Turner deplored the tendency of newcomers to crowd into cities and live in squalor. But he also realized that immigrants contributed much to America's adjustment to its post-frontier era. They stimulated appreciation of music and the arts. They introduced a Sabbath far more suitable to modern conditions than that of the Puritans. They offered an example in temperance by their adherence to beer and wine. Even the traits of Italians and Jews that were most resented in the United States would soon be abandoned; they were the products of centuries of oppression, and would vanish in the free atmosphere of the New World. Turner did close his eyes to some of the virtues of the newcomers, but he still believed that periodic transfusions from Europe enriched American civilization and should be encouraged rather than prohibited.

His essays not only preached a message alien to that day, but taught his fellow scholars a great deal about the techniques of proper immigration history. Better than any historian of his time, he recognized that the study of immigration must begin in Europe, that there was a significant interaction between geographic and ethnic factors, and that the impact of migration was almost as great on the country of origin as on the country of destination. Turner's description of the coming of the Palatine Germans in the eighteenth century might have been written today, so rich was it in understanding of the political, social, and religious conditions in Germany that underlay the exodus. His explanation of the mass migrations of the 1830s and 1840s laid far more stress on the failure of the potato crop than on the 1848 revolutions, a judgment that is acceptable to modern scholars. He also recognized that artificial inducements—steamship agents, land and immigrant companies, land-grant railroads, and factory owners in search of cheap labor—helped shape migration patterns.

Turner's venture into immigration history wrought no revolution in scholarship; buried as they were in a local newspaper, his articles had no impact on other historians. They are significant only because they reveal the degree to which Turner could generate new ideas on every aspect of the past. He was writing rather good immigration history, and underlining the cultural contributions made by the newcomers, at a time when historians ignored the subject completely, and when the sociologists and publicists who did profess some interest agreed that immigrants carried with them poverty, slums, crime, and immorality, and that this "degenerative breeding stock" was undermining the fiber of the Republic. Turner had an unusual ability to escape the straitjacket of his times, no matter how unique the area into which he ventured.

Those of his fellow craftsmen who refused to follow, and who had the misfortune to write a book that fell into Turner's hands for review, were certain to be reminded of their sins in language more sharp than charitable. Turner was a prolific and highly critical reviewer, for both professional and popular journals, during his early teaching years. Unlike most critics, though he was ruthless, he was also impartial in his judgments; his bludgeon could fall on his closest friend, or a godlike leader of the historical guild, just as it could on an unimportant unknown. All were exactly weighed, and if found wanting in areas that he deemed essential—sound scholarship, careful documentation, recognition of the subsurface economic and social forces shaping human behavior, belief in multiple causation—their errors were paraded and roundly condemned. Turner's book reviews shed light on his historical beliefs, and reveal his convictions, no less than do his other writings of the time.

His particular ire was reserved for those who ignored basic causal forces, and particularly for writers who failed to mention the frontier. "We are now," he wrote in a long review article in the *Atlantic Monthly* in 1896, "coming to recognize the vital forces in American society whose interaction and transformation have called political institutions into life and moulded them to suit changing conditions. Our history is that of the rise and expansion of a huge democracy in an area unoccupied by civilization, and thus affording free play to the factors of physiography, race, and custom."[21] Using these standards, Turner found such eminent scholars as James Ford Rhodes and John W. Burgess sadly wanting. Rhodes, in overemphasizing the slavery controversy, ignored the intimate relationship between the political struggles he described and the subsurface pressures creating those conflicts; Burgess, by concentrating too much on the politics of the middle period, had neglected "the vast social transformations by immigration, interstate migration, industrial development, revolution of the transportation system, and all the tremendous forces of change involved in the Westward expansion of settlement." Both were blind to the multiple forces that created the pre-Civil War social order, forces that operated particularly during the 1850s. "This," Turner reminded Rhodes, "was a decade of American expansion and material growth, a period of the transformation of the social organism by immigration and industrial change, of the reorganization of sectional relations by railroad-building, by the revolution of commercial connections, and by interstate migration." Only the historians who had the power and the insight to analyze and interpret the economic and social evolution of American society could understand that complex period.[22] Rhodes and Burgess, Turner strongly implied, did not.

Authors who were slipshod in scholarship or antiquarian in method were just as firmly reprimanded, whatever their status in the profession. Justin Winsor's *Westward Movement* was dismissed as an ill-digested mass of facts that resembled more a thesaurus than history; Elliott Coues was soundly castigated for careless editing and faulty transcription when preparing his collected works of Lewis and Clark; Alexander Brown was condemned for a multitude of sins—including a lack of objectivity—in his *English Politics in Early Virginia History*. This did not mean that Turner was scornful of editors who compiled documents, or local historians who squandered pages on minute aspects of the past. Good editing and good local history inspired sincere praise. Turner found Reuben Gold Thwaites's multi-volume *Early Western Travels* laudable, partly because it was meticulously edited, partly because it would allow scholars to probe social and economic development on successive frontiers.[23] He had only commendation for studies that linked minor episodes with the broader stream of history. "The humblest locality," he wrote in a review of a town history, "has in it the possibility of revealing in its history, rightly told, wide reaching historical events." One of Turner's basic principles was that historians must study the states if they were to understand the nation.[24] Authors who met those objectives were rightly praised; but antiquarianism was a sin he never forgave.

These highly critical standards met their test when Turner was asked to review the collected works of Francis Parkman. Parkman was a subjective historian, rarely aware of underlying social forces, and sadly deficient in scientific research techniques. But he had been an idol of Turner's since graduate-school days. Even so, Turner did not flinch. Parkman, he decided, was faulty in his refusal to recognize social development, the economic relationships between *voyageurs* and merchants, the depressed living conditions in the French parishes, and the class struggle that accounted for so much of French-Canadian history. The charm of his narrative hid the stark grimness of the life he was depicting. Yet all this could be forgiven by a reader swept along by Parkman's style. "He was the greatest painter of historical pictures that this country—perhaps it is not too much to say, that any country—has produced." Parkman might fail to meet the standards of scientific history, but his work would live forever because he was greater as an artist than as a historian.[25] Turner, sensitive to the language as he was, could forgive any author whose words sang as Parkman's did, no matter what his offenses to the canons of objectivity.

Yet he was frank in revealing his hero's weaknesses, just as he had been in condemning Rhodes and Burgess and Coues for their transgressions. This was a practice that made enemies—and friends. James Ford Rhodes apparently forgave Turner his criticisms; the two saw much of each other after Turner moved to Harvard in 1910. Woodrow Wilson proved just as understanding. He had been an admirer of Turner's since their Johns Hopkins days together, and the sentiment was returned with interest; Turner considered Wilson's *Division and Reunion* one of the masterpieces of historical interpretation, and he looked forward to Wilson's next venture—a five-volume history of the United States—as a work that would be "*the* American history of our time."[26] Hence he welcomed the opportunity when the *American Historical Review* asked him to prepare a critical evaluation of the *History of the American People* in 1903. His disappointment mounted as he read. Some features deserved praise; the sentences flowed "so gracefully and buoyantly that the reader easily overlooks the burden which they bear"; no other author had produced "so sustained and vital a view of the whole first cycle of the nation's history." But these virtues were offset by two serious defects. Wilson was "more at home in characterizing political leaders and the trend of events than in dealing with the deeper undercurrents of economic and social change." He was also wrong when he stated that state sovereignty had not changed since the drafting of the Constitution; Turner pointed out that southern views had altered greatly since the 1780s, and that these alterations were traceable to the elasticity written into the Constitution by the framers. He was right, but these were damaging criticisms, for Wilson's concept of state sovereignty was the foundation on which his whole argument rested.[27]

In later years Turner remembered Woodrow Wilson's offense at these judgments, and his own chagrin at having hurt one of his closest friends. He resolved then and there, he recalled, to write no more reviews—a resolution from which he turned on only a few occasions.[28] Yet there is no hint in the contemporary records that Wilson was offended or that he voiced his discontent. He was well aware that his *History of the American People* was a commercial venture, prepared for the popular market, and sadly lacking the refinements expected by his professional colleagues. Wilson visited Madison in April 1903, spent hours with Turner, and departed feeling that their friendship was as intimate as ever—even though Turner, frank as always, almost certainly used the occasion to read his soon-to-be-published review to his visitor.[29] Actually, Turner's decision to review no more books probably followed his meeting with James Schouler at the American Historical Association, after he had castigated that venerable scholar's latest volume as "essentially commonplace." He was, he told a friend, shocked to think of the effect of his harsh judgment on "such a nice old man."[30] Perhaps the memory of this episode flooded back now as he thought of Wilson's reaction to his criticisms. Reviewers, he insisted from that time on, should temper their judgments with praise and always end on a note of commendation rather than faultfinding;[31] better still, they should leave the weighing of their colleagues' scholarship to others.

If frankness threatened to sever Turner's friendship with one future President of the United States, it had the opposite effect with another. His reviews of the third and fourth volumes of Theodore Roosevelt's *Winning of the West* spared no punches; the books were hastily prepared, contained many minor errors, failed to mention the intrigues that divided the western country in the Revolutionary era, and ignored the "land politics" that played such an important role in Congress and at the Constitutional Convention. Roosevelt was also at fault in charging Jefferson with active participation in the Genêt conspiracy; such a rash accusation should not be made unless supported by documents in the Paris archives. Yet there were words of praise as well. Roosevelt had used his authorities "with the skill of a practised historian," and had produced a work of literary merit that added new meaning to a period essential to understanding the truly national history of the United States.

These mixed judgments gave no offense; instead they inspired Roosevelt to ask *The Nation* (where the first review appeared) for the name of its author and to launch an amiable correspondence with him. Their letters reveal something of the political philosophy of both men. Roosevelt cheerfully admitted his neglect of land companies and "land politics"; his purpose was to tell who the frontiersmen were and what they did, leaving to Turner the broader implications of expansion: the interaction of West and East, and the institutional modification that occurred as the westward movement went on. He was also ready to back down in his charges against Thomas Jefferson; he was, he agreed, thoroughly prejudiced in his opinion about the third President, linking him as he did with William Jennings Bryan and the Populist radicals who were threatening to ruin the country.[32] Theodore Roosevelt might retreat, but he retreated gracefully and in good spirit. Turner remained his friend and staunch admirer—and was to be his ardent supporter in the presidential campaigns that followed.

Such was not the case of Edward Channing, another victim of Turner's outspoken reviewing. That bristly New Englander, holder of a Harvard professorship and a rising power in the historical profession, was little inclined to accept criticism from a backlander from remote Wisconsin, yet Turner was no more inclined to respect the demigods of the East than he was his own associates in the West. Less so, in fact, if they failed to recognize the significance of the frontier. This was Channing's sin in his *A Student's History of the United States,* published in 1898. Turner, as usual, found features deserving praise; here was a text that presented history as a discipline of the mind rather than an exercise in rote memory, and it was particularly valuable for the training that it gave on decision-making on political and industrial questions. But these virtues were overbalanced by its complete failure to recognize the significance of the West and South in the nation's history. This was a fatal error; Channing's statements on these important sections were so completely inadequate "as to be misleading, if not entirely incorrect."[33] These were harsh words, and Channing never for-

gave them. The rift that developed between the two men when colleagues at Harvard—a rift for which Channing was solely responsible
—originated in Turner's brutal, but absolutely correct, appraisal of a
textbook that was destined to monopolize the market, whatever its
merits.

If Turner's outspoken reviews revealed his maturing ideas on the
nature and function of history, so did the lectures that he gave during
these years, the letters to his friends, and the occasional notes that his
reading inspired. To Turner, historical studies were things of beauty,
no less than of practicality. "There is," he told an audience in 1908, "a
charm in restoring the past, in compelling the procession of leaders
of human thought and action again to traverse the stage of human consciousness, in rescuing from oblivion what is worth the memory of the
present day. The events of past years, the institutions that have passed
away, the life and manner of societies that are gone are a precious
heritage, not to be wantonly ignored in the heat and bustle of the
day." The scholar who brought that past to life was no idle chronicler.
His function was to enlighten those around him, and to help shape the
future "as he presents the acquisitions of the past to the consciousness
of the men of today."[34]

But history's role was neither to entertain nor to enrich mankind.
Turner saw the study of the past as a searchlight into the future, a guide
for the public conscience. He was fond of quoting the German historian Johann Gustav Droysen, whose books he read often, that "history is the self-consciousness of humanity." "It is," he told one audience, "humanity's effort to understand itself by understanding its
origins, by taking stock of the forces that have made a nation what it
is."[35] Hence, while society changed and re-changed with the passing
generations, the historian provided the balance wheel that kept men
and institutions on an even keel. Men could never break completely
with their past; the past was a stubborn force that compelled mankind
toward traditionalism, even as they changed with the times.[36]

The importance of history placed momentous responsibilities on the
historian. The fragments of the past were so numerous that he could
reconstruct falsely if he strayed from objectivity. Turner saw the materials of history as a great heap of tiny pebbles that had to be fashioned
into a mosaic. The supreme test of the historical scholar was to find the

essential, the really typical and vital, in the mass of evidence that lay before him. If he sought to enforce a creed, a philosophy, a political dogma, or a pet theory, the past had material at hand, "ready for the artful combination and presentation." Nor was the historian a free agent as he went about this task of selection and arrangement. He was a man, a human, affected by his own ideals and experiences, and influenced by the age in which he lived, his class, and his nationality, no matter how he tried to resist.[37] He could minimize these handicaps only by constantly striving for objectivity, however difficult or impossible the quest. This was made especially difficult with the broadening scope of historical studies. Now the narrative was outmoded; scholars must trace each of the interests of society, studying the many activities of the common people that influenced the evolution of the nation. With this new focus, Turner pointed out, all the old materials had to be restudied, archives, monuments and remains re-examined, and new collections made to permit understanding of the nation's growth. Therein lay the joy of investigation. "There are always new harvests to be reaped."[38]

Therein, too, lay the realization that there could be no simple explanation of the past, no single key to the understanding of human behavior, no universal laws of history. In the past, writers had thought they had found the key to the nation's progress in the struggle between Puritan and Cavalier, in the conflict over slavery, in the contest between states and nation, in the rise of democracy. "In truth there is no single key to American history. In history, as in science, we are learning that a complex result is the outcome of the interplay of many forces. Simple explanations fail to meet the case." Turner had no patience with those who sought to formulate laws of human behavior. "The human soul is too complex," he wrote, "human society is too full of vital energy and incessant change, to enable us to pluck out the heart of its mystery —to reduce it to an exact science or to state human development in terms of an equation."[39] Man was a complex animal, fascinating to study, and worthy of the most intense investigation, for nothing was more interesting than human behavior. Individuals were insignificant in this story, and the narrative of events unimportant. Society, ever-changing, restless, mobile, swept by subterranean currents and ruffled by the winds of popular emotion, was the challenge that historians must accept. For in America society had shaped the men. This was Turner's creed.

He stated his beliefs with particular clarity in two papers on "Problems in American History" prepared during these years, one in 1901 for a university function, the other three years later, when he was invited to address a historical congress at the World's Exposition held at St. Louis in 1904, celebrating the centennial of the Louisiana Purchase. Turner was delighted with this latter assignment, partly because he stood to pocket a fee of $150 as soon as his paper was delivered, partly because the similarity between this opportunity and one offered by the Chicago World's Fair of 1893 was too obvious to be ignored.[40] Here was Turner's chance to make another major revelation to the profession. This required careful preparation, even though he would repeat some of the ideas—and even words—he had used in his "Problems in American History" in *The Aegis* in 1892, and restated in a 1901 address to a Wisconsin audience on the same theme.[41] Turner, as usual, arrived in St. Louis with his task still to be completed. He stayed at the Inside Inn (which he renamed the "Thinside Inn" because its walls were so flimsy he could hear every conversation in the room next door), and settled to work while his roommate, Charles Homer Haskins, enjoyed the sights. As usual, too, his essay was ready by 9:30 on the morning of September 25, the day it was to be presented. Promptly at ten Turner entered the hall, to face an audience kept sparse by a driving rainstorm. The quality was high if the numbers were low; he counted the eminent German historian, Karl Lamprecht, among his listeners, and he was well-satisfied that his words would have a decided impact on interdisciplinary studies even beyond national borders.[42]

They did not. Turner was almost as far in advance of his generation in discussing the nature of history as he had been when he had expounded his frontier hypothesis a decade before. His paper, however, offers insights into his beliefs, particularly as they had changed since his original essay on the subject in 1892 and its revision in 1901. Much that he said was familiar. He echoed Achille Loria in proposing that the nation's history capsulized the social and industrial stages that had taken centuries in Europe, and that it offered insights into the evolution of all societies. It should be viewed, Turner thought, not as a narrative or chronicle, but as the record of social transformation to ever higher cultural levels. Loria, however, had ignored the fact that in America there were repeated colonial experiences as new "colonies" were established with every move westward, and that each was modified by the differing physiographic environment in which it grew, and by the character and intensity of the industrial life of its parent society. The study of American history was the study of these transformations, of the expansion and formation of societies, of the interaction of differing peoples, their institutions, their economic activities, their fundamental assumptions. This was the basic problem facing all investigators.[43]

They must also grapple with a whole series of subordinate problems. When Turner wrote his 1901 essay, he pictured these as largely related to expansion. The profession's principal need was a shift of emphasis from New England's internal history to the economic, social, and religious forces that drove that region's multitudes into a Greater New England that formed in the West. Historians should investigate that exodus, which was as important as the coming of the Puritans, and determine its effect on the nation, and on New England. They should pay equal attention to the history of the South, studying the settlement of the upland and the conflicts that developed between that region and the seaboard areas—a subject untouched by scholars. The economy of the southern states was also crying for investigation; the plantation system had to be appraised, the relationship between cotton and slave prices established, and the impact of economic tides on political change studied. Nor should the other sections—the Lake Plains, the Prairie Plains, and the Pacific Coast—be ignored. All should be subjected to the same analysis, from early contacts between Indians and whites through the occupation of the public lands. These, Turner believed in 1901, were the major problems in American history deserving study.

Three years later, his understanding of sections was far more sophisticated. He no longer thought of traditional physiographic provinces, but of interrelated regions forming a "nation of sections," some of them as large as the largest of the European nations, and all rising through successive stages to achieve cultural identity. Sectionalism was a basic fact of American history, no less than expansion, and equally important. Until historians understood how each region was colonized, the contributions made to it by incoming stocks, its industrial evolution, the leaders it had produced, the psychological traits of its people, and its relations with other sections, the history of the United States could not be understood.

This was the fundamental problem as Turner saw it in 1904, but others bulked large. Students must investigate the formation of the

American character for the light it would shed on the evolution of society. They should study the forces operating to create a composite nationality. They should seek to understand the relationships between literature and the other arts, the social and economic conditions that influenced cultural expression, and political action. "We need to give a social and economic interpretation to the history of political parties in this country." This would be possible only if a complex of subordinate problems were solved: the effect of the public domain on legislation, immigration and the European conditions that underlay each wave of migration, the contributions of the Indian and Negro to the nation's civilization, the role of labor in industry and politics. Legal and religious forces still awaited investigation, while the study of the transfer of political power to the common people had only begun. Students should investigate comparative frontiers in Canada, Australia, Russia, and medieval Germany to appraise the uniqueness of the American experience. Whole eras of the past had been neglected: the eighteenth century and "the wonderful development of the nation since the Reconstruction period" were particularly flagrant examples. Similarly, vast areas had been ignored; virtually nothing was known of the history of the region between the Mississippi and the Rocky Mountains. New England had been over-studied, Turner was saying. Now let us broaden our scope and see how the nation took shape.

Because history was no longer past politics, but a study designed to enable a people to understand itself by understanding its origins and development in all the main features of human activity, the past could be understood only by calling into cooperation sciences and methods hitherto little used. Data drawn from literature, art, economics, politics, sociology, psychology, biology, and physiography were grist for the historians' mill, just as were statistics and the techniques of critical evaluation of evidence. "There has been too little cooperation of these sciences and the result is that great fields have been neglected." Too many fertile areas that lay between disciplines had been left uncultivated, too many problems had been studied with inadequate apparatus. Only by the use of all the social and allied sciences could the nation's development be understood.

Here was Turner's concept of history and its problems as he reached the climax of his career. He was still naïve in some of his judgments, still too inclined to accept stereotyped concepts—he had, for example, yet to appreciate the complexity of social evolution, and he pictured progress in the well-defined stages he had learned from Richard T. Ely. But Turner's thought had undergone a remarkable transformation since he had written his "Problems in American History" in 1892. Then the basic, the one essential, problem was to understand the nature of westward expansion. Now he saw expansion as only one element in the equation, important, to be sure, but no more so than sectionalism or cultural influences or economic forces. When Turner admonished his fellow craftsmen to focus on the history of labor, cultural progress, immigration, and social development, he was preaching a doctrine tuned to the twentieth century rather than to the nineteenth. His pleas for an interdisciplinary approach and for the study of comparative history have a more familiar ring in the 1970s than they did in the 1900s. Turner, more than any historian of his day, recognized the complexity of the past, and the need to trace each of the dozens of forces that governed human behavior before that past could be understood.

That he was to spend the rest of his life largely in the study of two of those forces—the frontier and section—did not mean that he was indifferent to the others. During his earlier years he had shown lively interest in immigration, diplomacy, and recent industrialism; for a time he toyed with the idea of dedicating himself to diplomatic history. He was fascinated by every aspect of history, but in the end one captivated him above all others. This was not the frontier; the more deeply he delved into the history of expansion the more convinced he became that its significance was somewhat different than he had first supposed. The primary importance of the westward movement was that it had left behind a series of sections, each differing from the others in racial composition, physiographic conditions, and the psychology of the people. To Turner the formation and interplay of these sections was the real bedrock on which the story of the past rested. Thus, early in his life, he made sectionalism his primary interest. Yet he was too wedded to the frontier concept, and too well known as the father of a theory that was increasingly altering historical studies, to divorce himself entirely from his first love. From this time on, Turner's intellectual life was dedicated to proving the significance of sectionalism, while his public life was dedicated to demonstrating the importance of the frontier.

VIII

Popularizing the Frontier Thesis

1893-1910

WHEN Frederick Jackson Turner first pronounced his frontier hypothesis, in July of 1893, his message fell on deaf ears. To historians in his audience he was an audacious young man from a back-water college whose theories were either incomprehensible or so alien to long-accepted interpretations that they deserved no respect. To the larger public, Turner was a complete unknown, not worthy of mention in the press or even in the more intellectual magazines of the day. In the three years after he announced his theory, neither he nor his frontier thesis was mentioned in the five leading American journals, including the *Review of Reviews*, which abstracted forty others, save in three brief items written by one of his friends.[1] Here was a theory—and its author—that seemed on the way to oblivion.

Then, slowly, the tide turned, as, first, historians, then the reading public, began to realize that Turner's thesis offered reason and hope in an era sadly in need of both. His theories, the nation discovered, not only explained what was happening to the United States in the 1890s and 1900s, but promised that the best of the American past would persist into the twentieth century. This was what the people wanted to hear. A prophet who preached such doctrines, and the disciples who spread his message, was sure to be heard. Turner's theories began to gain support in the late 1890s, and continued to win converts for a quarter-century thereafter, because they fit the public mood so well.

Certainly the American people were ripe for explanations. The world they knew—the comfortable world of the nineteenth century—was

184

crumbling away. The hard times that had persisted since the Panic of 1873 were deepening into a major depression during the 1890s. On the western plains, wild-eyed Populists were demanding cheap money and government meddling in the sacred temples of private enterprise. In the cities, slums were spreading and class divisions deepening, bolstering the growing realization that the United States no longer offered equal opportunity to all. In Washington, reformers were preaching the heretical doctrine that big business must be controlled for the common good. Overseas, American war vessels were beating Spain to its knees and carving out empires amidst the clamor of debate between imperialists and anti-imperialists. These were happenings alien to the nation's experience. The United States was entering a new era at the turn of the century, and the people wanted to know why, and what lay ahead.

The frontier thesis offered them no panaceas, but it did provide an understandable explanation and a great deal of hope. For those who predicted that empire-building beyond the seas would plunge the United States into the maelstrom of world politics, the Turnerians answered that expansion underlay both the strength and liberties of the nation, and that the newly won empires would nurture democracy and gird the United States against European meddling. For those who feared the central government's growing power, they replied that three centuries of pioneering had engrained a belief in individualism so deeply into the national character that it could never be destroyed. For those who pictured the deepening gulf between rich and poor as a threat to democracy, they countered that the frontier faith in equality was too firmly planted ever to be threatened. Jacob Riis and his fellow reformers might shock the well-to-do with revelations of poverty in a land of plenty, Charles Graham Sumner and his fellow publicists might offend the masses by arguing that the social inequalities of the new industrialism were inevitable and must be endured, but Turner provided hope that frontiering had made all people equal and that the injustices of the day would soon disappear.

The outstanding feature of the frontier thesis was its optimism. The frontier was disappearing, but the pioneer experience had bred into Americans not only value judgments and beliefs that elevated them above lesser peoples, but a hardihood and an aggressive spirit that would allow them to protect their way of life and thought against hostile forces. Turner had pictured a Promethean struggle between man and the wilderness, with man emerging triumphant. By his victory he had liberated himself from pettiness, embraced the loftiest of ideals, and absorbed power and resolution beyond compare. Whatever the results of the closing of the frontier, Americans had been so endowed by their triumph over the wilderness that they could fashion a new civilization, embodying the best of their pioneer days, but benefiting from the new industrialism. Turner's theories were acceptable—and accepted—because they gave substance to folk myths that satisfied the need of Americans for a rose-tinted view of the future.

They were also appealing because the masses of Americans, living increasingly in crowded cities rather than on farms, were developing a new attitude toward the wilderness at the turn of the century. No longer was the forest the "enemy," as it had been in pioneer days; now it was a haven for peace and relaxation for those seeking escape from the tensions of urban life. This was the change of mood that gave rise to a "wilderness cult" in the United States during the 1890s and 1900s. When Theodore Roosevelt and his fellow conservationists urged the creation of national parks and wilderness areas, they were only recognizing popular demand. So were the leaders of the Boy Scout movement that swept the country in the early twentieth century, and so were "nature writers," such as John Burroughs, John Muir, and Jack London, who glorified the primitive for ever-widening audiences. The back-to-nature movement helped create a ready-made interest in the frontier, endowing the nation's rural past with a halo of romance that it never possessed in reality.[2]

The changing conditions that altered the national viewpoint at the turn of the century created a receptive audience for the frontier hypothesis, but that thesis could not be known until Turner recruited an army of proselytizers to preach his doctrines. This proved easy, for younger historians were eager to embrace an interpretation of American history less absurd than the now-discredited "germ" theory of Herbert Baxter Adams, and broader in scope than the "slavery" thesis argued by Hermann von Holst and James Ford Rhodes. Turner's explanation answered their needs to perfection. It was "scientific" in stressing demonstrable cause and effect. It meshed with the current vogue of Darwinism by emphasizing the development of social organisms, yet it substituted for biological determinism a more reasonable environmentalism. It set forth a hypothesis that demanded testing, thus assuring aspiring scholars subjects for investigation that would occupy them for years to come. It gave scholarly respectability to research into one of the most romantic phases of the national past. And, most important of all, it provided a more rational explanation of the national experience than those current at the time. Little wonder that historians who read Turner's essay were not only converted, but transformed into disciples, eager to spread his doctrines.

Most who did so—whether his students or others who came under his spell—were neophytes in the profession, whose voices were not to be heard until well into the 1900s. For immediate publicists, Turner had to rely on the few established scholars who were swayed by his arguments. Of these none was more important than Woodrow Wilson. Wilson felt a proprietary interest in the frontier thesis; he and Turner had talked of the significance of the West during their hours together at Johns Hopkins, and he had read with enthusiasm the early statement of the theory in the 1892 issue of *The Aegis* that Turner sent him. His chance to parade his new faith came when he was asked to review a traditional history of the United States by Goldwin Smith. Smith was absolutely wrong, wrote Wilson, in viewing American history through New England spectacles. The truly "American" part of America in colonial times was not New England, but the Middle Colonies; during the nineteenth century it shifted beyond the Appalachians, where "not only new settlements, but a new nation sprang up." There the people took on a unique character, and it was this transformation that was the key to understanding the nation's development. "That part of our history, therefore, which is most national is the history of the West."[3]

Turner was delighted, even though Wilson's statement of his thesis, published in *The Forum* in December 1893, appeared before his own paper on the significance of the frontier. He found it "very gratifying," and certain to encourage a more rational understanding of the past.[4] He had reason to be gratified soon again, for Woodrow Wilson was a prolific writer in the popular journals and from that time on used every opportunity to trumpet his young friend's views. His "Calendar of Great Americans," which appeared in *The Forum* a year later, did not include such notables as Alexander Hamilton, John Adams, and John C. Calhoun, because they had never imbibed the "true American spirit" by contact with the wilderness. Later in the decade, when Wilson was invited to address the New Jersey Historical Society on "The Course of

American History," and when he prepared an article for *The Forum* on "The Proper Perspective in American History," he did little more than summarize Turner's views and spice them with rhetorical embellishments that made them more palatable, if less accurate, than they were in their original form. Expansion was "the central and determining fact in our national history," breeding into the pioneers "a new temper, a new spirit of adventure, a new impatience of restraint, a new license of life." In the West, "social distinctions were stripped off, shown to be the mere cloaks and masks they were"; there all men were reduced to equality by the compelling powers of the wilderness.[5] Wilson was so dedicated a convert that he was willing to out-Turner Turner in preaching the frontier interpretation.

His was a lonely crusade at first, for not until after the turn of the century did the younger historians who had been converted to Turner's view begin to make their influence felt—and then largely in professional journals. To capture the public mind, the thesis had to have help from Turner himself, even though he was off on fresh scents and scattering his historical energies into documentary editing, diplomatic history, immigration history, and speculations on the nature of the historical process. This he recognized, and he was never reluctant to take up the cudgels in behalf of his own theories—whenever he could be attracted from his other investigations by a firm invitation with a monetary inducement attached. His writings on the frontier, which originated often as addresses or articles for popular magazines, did little to prove his concepts or add a firm foundation to his beliefs, but they did popularize the hypothesis as the efforts of no other propagandist did.

Reprintings of "The Significance of the Frontier in American History" helped. So long as that germinal essay was buried in the *Annual Report of the American Historical Association* and the *Proceedings of the State Historical Society of Wisconsin* it was available to few readers, but as interest in the theory quickened, so did the interest of other editors in giving Turner's essay wider circulation. Particularly pleasing to Turner was its appearance in 1899 in the *Fifth Yearbook of the Hebart Society*, a publication read by a sizable portion of the nation's schoolteachers. This required special attention; the original essay was refurbished with "Suggestions to Teachers" and a good deal of sound advice on how to approach American history from its "western side." "The spread of settled society into these continental wastelands," the schoolteachers were told, "and the free development of a democracy in relation to unoccupied lands, constitute the peculiar features of our national life."[6] Less to Turner's liking, but more to his amusement, was a request from A. M. Simmons, editor of the *International Socialist Review*, that he be allowed to share the essay with his readers. It was, Simmons assured him, "the first contribution of any significance to the industrial evolutionary treatment of American History." Turner was not sure that he should be used to further views with which he had little sympathy, but he gave his consent, and in 1905 the article appeared, accompanied by a laudatory note proclaiming it "the greatest contribution yet made in the application of the materialistic interpretation of history to American conditions."[7] Two years later it appeared again, this time in a highly respectable book of readings edited by the eminent economist Jesse C. Bullock.[8] This was only the first of a series of reprintings in academic source books that made "The Significance of the Frontier" a familiar phrase among historians, economists, geographers, and sociologists for a generation to come.

Reprintings were well enough, and welcome, but Turner was also concerned with broadening the appeal of his hypothesis among his fellow craftsmen. He found an ally in Henry Morse Stephens of Cornell, a pillar of the profession who had heard so much of Turner's ability that he made a special visit to Madison in 1895 to make sure that the rumors were sound. They were, he found; Turner was going to be heard from, and the sooner the better. Stephens had his chance a year later, when he helped to arrange the program for the meeting of the American Historical Association scheduled for December 1896. Would Turner read a paper reflecting his current research interests? Turner tried to step from the limelight in favor of Theodore Roosevelt or some other authority on the West, but Stephens stood his ground, and by the appointed time Turner had a paper ready on "The West as a Field for Historical Study." Having found it satisfactory in a trial run before the Wisconsin State Historical Society on December 10, he turned it over to Reuben Gold Thwaites for presentation in New York, being unable to afford the journey east himself.[9]

He submitted the paper with genuine apprehension, for he recognized that his subject was alien to the interests of the eastern historical establishment. "I hope," he wrote Morse Stephens, "you can manage to get up a discussion, to prevent the matter from falling with a dull thud."[10]

Turner might have spared himself his fears. A sizable audience listened attentively as his points were made: the role of the West in the election of 1896 proved that the nation's history could not be understood without "extended and earnest historical inquiry into the development of Western society"; this should center on the region between the Mississippi and the Rockies, where a new society was forming; it would be untainted by provincialism, for the West was only a laboratory where the emergence of new societies could be studied in microcosm, revealing truths pertinent to the total evolution of mankind. "The wilderness," Turner wrote, "has been the melting pot and the mold for American institutions; it has been a field for a new species of social life." It deserved study, and was a virgin field for investigators.

Such was the changing atmosphere of the times that this message, far less stirring than that delivered in 1893, was welcomed with enthusiasm. True, the praise of the commentators was directed more toward Turner than toward his ideas: Justin Winsor believed him the one person who had at last grasped the inner meaning of western history; Andrew C. McLaughlin urged the entire profession to accept his challenge and begin research on the story of the West; Woodrow Wilson hailed him as one of the few men in the profession who could combine breadth of comprehension with attention to minute details, who was not afraid of hard work, and who could illuminate his findings by fitting them into the general pattern of history. "Such men," Wilson insisted, "ought to be not only appreciated, but they ought to be loved and supported."[11] Turner was clearly making an impact on his colleagues, and, by doing so, he was widening interest in his frontier theory.

His opportunity to waken the broader public was not long in coming. The first chance was provided by Charles Kendall Adams, who served not only as president of the University of Wisconsin, but also as consultant for *Johnson's Universal Encyclopedia*. When Adams was called upon by the editors to recommend writers in American history, he passed over the shining lights in the field—Justin Winsor, John Bach McMaster, Albert Bushnell Hart—as too busy or too worn with work to lend their talents. Why not try a young man on his faculty named Turner—"a very successful teacher, precise in his methods, and comprehensive in his judgment"? Someone in the editorial office had the good sense to accept this sound advice, and Turner was invited to write an essay on "The Frontier." This was an admirable choice. Turner's article restated his thesis without the rhetorical embellishments and vague metaphors that had marred his original paper; it omitted, too, the extravagant claims for the frontier's influence. He began, as he should have begun his 1893 essay, with a definition of the "frontier"—"a belt of territory sparsely occupied by Indian traders, hunters, miners, ranchmen, backwoodsmen, and adventurers of all sorts"—then traced its movement westward. His estimate of its role in altering the American character was modest; the hardships of frontiering, he concluded, "conduced to an energetic and self-reliant spirit among the pioneers," underlay lawlessness in border communities, and played no small share in developing the practical ability and inventiveness of the American people.[12] This was a fair statement of the frontier theory with which few of Turner's later critics could quarrel.

Encyclopedia articles were well enough, but the emerging response to his ideas convinced Turner that they deserved a wider audience. Why not aim at the very top, and find a place in the columns of the *Atlantic Monthly*, then without peer in its influence on American intellectuals? This meant bringing his theories up to date and applying them to the current scene. Turner spent a good many months at the task, poring over books and articles and census returns to form a picture in his mind of the modern West—its ethnic composition, its industrial potential, its cultural aims. The notes that he jotted mirrored his interests: "West is a region of formation: as an area in US it is like the period of the Middle Ages in Europe," or "Western NY, Penn gave birth to Old Northwest. Old Northwest gave birth to prairie West." Eventually Turner merged the notes into a satisfactory essay that finally reached the desk of a subeditor of the *Atlantic Monthly*. The answer was couched in flattering terms, but firmly rejected the article as not sufficiently timely for the magazine's audience.[13] Turner had suffered his first (and one of his last) setbacks as an author.

He did not have to nurse his bruised ego long. Walter Hines Page, the distinguished editor of the *Atlantic Monthly*, knew of Turner and had read his 1893 essay (Turner had seen to that by sending him a copy). Why not direct this talented historian's writing skills into an article suited to his magazine's readers? Page thought first of an analysis of the contrast between traits of easterners and westerners, and Turner was willing to tackle the assignment, but the nomination of William

Jennings Bryan by the Democratic party in July 1896 changed the situation. Could Turner explain why a major party had embraced Populism, and how the nation should react to its present dilemma? This was a task made to order for Turner's interests, and he went to it with such enthusiasm that by July 29 he could telegraph that the article was on its way to Boston. "Your telegram is a pleasant western breeze indeed," Page assured him.[14] The September 1896 issue of the *Atlantic Monthly* appeared on schedule, with "The Problem of the West" in the place of honor.

The essay was as timely as Page desired, yet it scarcely mentioned Populism and attempted no analysis of current politics. "The problem of the West," Turner began, "is nothing less than the problem of American development." This was his springboard into a thorough discussion of the frontier's influence on traits and institutions: free lands bred into westerners boundless energy, faith in social equality, impatience of restraint, materialistic attitudes, belief in progress. The westerner differed from the easterner; he was "less conservative and less provincial, more adaptable and approachable, less a man of culture, more a man of action." These differences underlay the nation's current problems. The energy bred of expansion could not be stifled with the passing of the frontier. Turner saw demands for a vigorous foreign policy as the inevitable aftermath of the peopling of the continent; these would continue to project the nation's business into overseas markets and the nation's sovereignty over possessions throughout the Pacific. He foresaw equally important changes in domestic policy. By this time Turner realized, as he had not in 1893, that agrarian discontent transcended the demands of a few hotheads for cheap money; it portended a vast social revolution as the country adjusted to a closed-space existence. The outcome would be an extension of government authority in behalf of both the depressed farmers and the workers who could no longer escape to free land. Turner anticipated an era of storm and turbulence as the social revolution ran its course, but eventual benefits to all with the working out of improved social ideals and practices.

If Turner, and Walter Hines Page, had intended to subject public opinion to a form of shock treatment, they succeeded admirably. Only a few days after it appeared, Page wrote to Turner gleefully, "the newspapers here are at once taking up your article for discussion—very favorable."[15] Extracts and summaries dotted the press; the widely read magazine *Public Opinion* reprinted much of the essay, and others reproduced shorter extracts. Editorial writers approved or disapproved as their sectional prejudices dictated. To the *Chicago Tribune*, Turner's essay was a "profound and striking" vindication of the paper's contention that the half-dozen states that it defined as "Chicagoland" would lead the nation into its new era; to the *Boston Herald* and other New England papers, it was a terrifying warning that the center of gravity was shifting westward and that the wild-eyed radicals of the prairies could no longer be ignored.[16] Thanks to the nation's concern over Populism, Turner had won a wider audience for his theories than he could have done with a dozen historical articles.

He had also mightily pleased Walter Hines Page, who now wanted a whole series of articles to shake the national consciousness. For some time Page had been toying with a plan for discussions of the sectional characteristics of the Northeast, South, and Midwest; Turner was surely an ideal analyst for the Midwest. Would he do two or three articles that would explain that region to non-midwesterners? Turner wanted to, but he was filled with doubts. He laid them before Page in a twenty-one page letter. What was the Midwest? What elements should enter into its definition? Geographic? economic? psychological? Probably the best definition would combine physiographic analysis, groupings revealed by congressional votes, crop areas, literary output, and immigration statistics. To pursue this properly would require far more time than Page had suggested. If Page had been a realist, he would have dropped the matter at that point; an author who took twenty-one pages to define his subject—without success—would never be able to appraise the civilization of such a complex area as the Midwest. But Page was persistent. He did not want a complete painting, only a charcoal sketch. Why not simply write about the Old Northwest plus Minnesota? Turner was agreeable. Page was so sure of his man now that he advertised a series of articles by Turner, W. P. Trent, and A. F. Sanborn, to begin in the winter of 1897, articles that would explain the nation to itself as none had in the past.[17]

That was a false hope. Turner wrote one article—"Dominant Forces in Western Life"—which appeared in the April 1897 issue of the *Atlantic Monthly*, but this was hardly an earth-shaking contribution. It was obviously designed as the first of a series; Turner traced migration patterns into the Old Northwest, analyzed the contributions of migrants from the older sections and Europe, and showed their importance in economic development down to the present. These migration patterns he linked with Populism; the older types of farmers who led the way westward were turned back now by arid lands into an industrial society they neither understood nor liked. They could see, as could few others, the sharp contrast between frontier America as a land of equal opportunity, and non-frontier America where class stratification spelled an end to the equalitarian tradition. This, Turner held, was the basis of the revolt that nurtured Populism.

Once more editorial and reader reaction convinced Page that Turner was one of the most valuable assets in his stable of authors, and that he must be encouraged to complete the series that he had promised. Turner was agreeable, promising to have the next article in Boston by June 15, 1897, to appear in the August *Atlantic Monthly*. That date came and went, but no article arrived. A reminder from Page brought no assurance, only a confession that progress was slow, and that writing was a painful process to be avoided if possible. That was the last the *Atlantic Monthly* heard from Turner. Page sent him a "gentle reminder from a hungry editor" a few months later, but there was no response.[18] Turner wanted to publicize his frontier theory, and he was not averse to accepting the modest sums paid to contributors, but he was too much a perfectionist to do a slipshod survey of a complex subject.

A major analysis of the social evolution of one frontier area proved too much of a challenge, but Turner had sensed the national interest in his theories, and he was perfectly willing to seek more acclaim with less ambitious topics. He produced a spate of publications for respectable journals over the next years: "The Middle West" in the December 1901 *International Monthly*, "Contributions of the West to American Democracy" in the January 1903 *Atlantic Monthly*, "The Democratic Education of the Middle West" in the August 1903 *World's Work*. All were gracefully written, all preached the frontier thesis, and all developed aspects of the thesis that particularly interested Turner. They also, it must be confessed, drew heavily on his earlier essays, cataloguing over and over again the traits and institutions that stemmed from the pioneering experience, stressing the significance of free lands as a moulding influence, and striving for current interest by emphasizing that Populism resulted from the exhaustion "of the further free lands to which the ruined pioneer could turn."[19]

The influence of the frontier on American democracy interested Turner particularly, partly because it lent itself to popular treatment at a time when democratic traditions seemed threatened by the rise of big business and big government, partly because he could embroider that theme with a minimum amount of research and a maximum amount of speculation. The very existence of a haven of opportunity in the West, he wrote, prompted economic equality and opportunity, for men would not accept permanent subordination when a promised land of freedom was theirs for the taking. Free lands meant free opportunity, and this distinguished American democracy from the democracies that had preceded it. Its most distinctive feature was the social equality that it fostered; the freedom of the individual to rise in society outlawed European class distinctions and placed all men on a common plane. This conception had vitalized American democracy and brought it into sharp contrast with the democracies of Europe. The passing of free lands would force the United States to readjust its values, but would not doom its faith in human equality. A perennial optimist, Turner predicted that the West would work out a new organization of society that would conserve the democratic ideals of the nation; the western state universities were already pointing the way by substituting for free lands universal education as the key to individual progress. "Let us," he advised, "see to it that the ideals of the pioneer in his log cabin shall enlarge into the spiritual life of a democracy where civil power shall dominate and utilize individual achievement for the common good."[20] This was the democratic gospel according to Turner as his views on the impact of the frontier solidified.

There can be no question that Turner's enthusiasm and an urge to satisfy popular taste led him into exaggerations that he would have avoided if he had confined his writing to scholarly journals. He was even more inclined to cater to the public taste—and bend the truth in doing so—when he took to the lecture platform to explain the frontier thesis. His tendency to employ inexact words and indulge in extravagant metaphors became almost uncontrollable when he was charming an audience or infecting them with his own enthusiasm. He was at his best then, oratorically speaking, and few could resist. "To sit in quiet rapture under the spell of words as harmonious as poetry," exulted one hearer, "falling on the ear in clear and resonant tones, and then to feel,

as the moments go by, the heart glow, the mind expand, the fires of
aspiration burn because there is added to the beauty of form and expression, thoughts pulsating with life and strength and practical wisdom
and moral earnestness—this was the experience of many and the privilege
of all who sat in that favored audience."[21] Turner cast a spell; he also
fell under that spell himself now and then, and was tempted into extravagances that he would have shunned in a less euphoric situation.

Unfortunately, he was offered ample opportunity to lecture. His
fame as a speaker spread rapidly, prompting a series of invitations from
universities, teachers' groups, ladies' clubs, and social gatherings; if
Turner had been greedy enough to accept all of them, he could have
added a healthy sum to his income with commencement and Phi Beta
Kappa addresses alone. To catalogue his public appearances during these
years would be tedious, but a sampling can indicate the diversity of his
audiences: five lectures before the summer school of the University of
Pennsylvania in 1894, one at a Lake Forest College ceremony the following April, addresses to the University Club of Chicago, the Northwestern Association of Johns Hopkins Alumni, and the Geographical
Society of Chicago in 1897 and 1898, a mounting number of Phi Beta
Kappa banquets beginning with one at Minnesota in 1900, talks before
such patriotic groups as the Loyal Legion of Milwaukee (which heard
a stirring lecture on "The Frontier Soldier") and the Sons of the
American Revolution, others to enlighten the Collegiate Alumni Association of Milwaukee or to raise funds for the Portage public library, still
more before such diversified teachers' groups as the Janesville public
school instructors and the Milwaukee Teachers Historical Club, a number to neighboring colleges and local historical societies, and lectures
galore to the students of his own university, where he was in perennial
demand as an adornment for celebrations of the birthdays of George
Washington and Abraham Lincoln. Lecturing was a profitable business
—Turner's fees varied between $50 and $150 for a single performance
and up to $500 for a university series—but it also offered an admirable
opportunity to propagandize his views. Whatever the announced subject, the frontier could be—and was—glorified as a principal influence in
American history, often with the same arguments and sometimes in the
same language used in his 1893 essay; when pressed for time Turner was
not above borrowing whole paragraphs from that essay, acting on the

probably correct assumption that they would be unknown to his audience.[22]

His ability to extract excessive mileage from one theme was admirably illustrated when he was invited to deliver the Phi Beta Kappa address at the University of Kansas on June 7, 1909, for the modest fee of $50—he to pay his own travel expenses. Turner's subject—"Pioneer Ideals and the State University"—proved so acceptable to his audience that he used the same speech on a similar occasion at Iowa a week later, substituting a few sentences on the local scene for earlier remarks on popular sovereignty in Kansas. When called back to the lecture circuit in the spring of 1910, he pulled his manuscript from the files, polished a few phrases, and was ready to deliver it once more, as a Phi Beta Kappa address at the University of Michigan on May 14, as the baccalaureate address at the University of Wisconsin on June 21, and as the commencement address at Indiana University a day later.[23]

Unfortunately for his later reputation, this attempt to satisfy the popular taste did not generate his soundest historical thought. His "Pioneer Ideals and the State University" is a case in point. The theme was a familiar one: the role of the state university in adjusting pioneer traits to a frontierless society. Two traits particularly required alteration. The frontiersman's triumph over the wilderness made him impatient of any governmental restriction on his individual right to control his own economic affairs. With individualism went faith in domocracy, stemming from the abundance of opportunity in the West. "He had a passionate hatred for aristocracy, monopoly and social privilege; he believed in simplicity, economy and in the rule of the people." Now, as the frontier era ended, the West was increasingly dependent on the East; the westerner was surrendering his economic independence to captains of industry, who alone could provide the farm machinery, the transportation, and the agricultural techniques needed for survival. He must find a way of preserving individualism and democracy "without the former safety valve of abundant resources open to him who would take." This must be through governmental legislation. But governmental legislation depended on intelligent legislators and administrators; they must represent all the people rather than the "capitalistic classes" or the "proletariat"; they must be capable of dulling conflicts between classes and convincing the masses that pioneer ideals should be retained in the post-frontier world. These leaders could be educated only in the state universities, for there alone education was dedicated to social needs rather than the training of an elite.[24]

That lecture typified the many public speeches that he gave and the many popular essays he wrote during the years that his frontier thesis was gaining acceptance. In it he said little that was new; he had stressed democracy and individualism as frontier beliefs in 1893 and had pondered the effect of the frontier's closing at least as early as 1896. This lack of originality might be excused on the ground that his audience preferred challenging ideas to fresh interpretations, but Turner was more at fault when he pronounced unsubstantiated theories as indisputable facts. At the very beginning and end of his career he carefully avoided labeling the frontier as a "safety valve" for displaced eastern workers, even though that doctrine had been generally accepted for more than a century. Now, however, he wrote boldly of the West as a "safety valve of abundant resources." This was typical of the overstatement that marked his writing during these years of popularization. Throughout his essays and speeches were evidences of exaggeration, and a willingness to sacrifice historical accuracy for rhetorical effect.

The nature of Turner's scholarly interests made this inevitable, though regrettable. Had he possessed a less mercurial mind, he would have been content to spend his years testing aspects of his frontier thesis and presenting the results in learned papers and monographs. Instead, his inquisitiveness about *all* the past led him into a series of only faintly related quests: western state-making, the diplomacy of the post-Revolutionary period, immigration, and the regional studies that he was soon to publish on the Old West and colonial New England. While thus involved, he was besieged with invitations to write and speak about the frontier. These could not be refused, partly because he was eager to popularize his theories, partly because the monetary rewards were too tempting; a publisher's check for $150 or a fee of $100 for a commencement speech meant a great deal at a time when academic salaries seldom exceeded $3500 a year. Turner found himself in a position where he had to speak or write, but had nothing new to say.

Thus tempted, he could do one of two things. He could abandon his research to supply proof for his frontier thesis—the subject demanded by editors and college administrators—or he could expand and amplify the theories that he had already advanced, basing his expansion on speculation rather than investigation, and building an increasingly shaky structure on an untested foundation. Turner's temperament dictated that he follow the latter course. Rather than forsake his research, he chose to magnify some of the more popular themes mentioned in his 1893 essay—particularly the impact of pioneering on individualism, democracy, and nationalism—using logic and imagination rather than factual evidence to do so. Most of his writing during this period demonstrated how the frontier *should* have shaped the American character and American ideals, not how it *did* shape them, for he advanced not a shred of evidence to substantiate his statements. Unfortunately, Turner's frontiersmen did not always behave as he reasoned they should behave. Modern scholarship has demonstrated that social stratification did exist on frontiers, that racial disharmony in the West rivaled that in the East, that free land was seldom a sufficient magnet to draw displaced workers westward, and that political democracy was lacking in many communities. This Turner recognized or felt instinctively, as the reading notes he kept at the time indicated, but he realized also that his audiences wanted simplicity of statement rather than the carefully qualified admonitions of the professional historian.

That this was a deliberate choice was shown by the contrast between his popular and his professional writing during these years. The latter was of two sorts. On several occasions he was invited to address university audiences—he gave five lectures at the University of Michigan in 1903 on "The Beginnings of the West," two on "Western Society" and "Western Politics" at the University of Chicago in 1909, five on "Western Influences in American History" at the University of Pennsylvania in 1910. These were conventionally phrased, thoroughly unsensational, and distressingly factual, lacking completely the high-flown phrases and imaginative speculations of his public performances. They were also something less than appealing even to university audiences. He found the listeners at the University of Michigan momentarily terrified when he spread his mountain of notes on the table, but reported that they recovered and "stood it nobly." His hearers at Chicago sat patiently as he explained the role of the West in early state-making and politics, but they were hardly enthusiastic. At the University of Pennsylvania the small audience did not dwindle after the first lecture, as he feared it might, but even grew slightly—largely, Turner believed, because of the hostile reaction in the press to his statement that George

Washington was a western land-grabber. Yet the audience was tiny, at best, and made up largely of graduate students from the Midwest and his own friends or former students.[25] Turner was disappointed that he had not appealed to the native Philadelphians, but he had made it clear that he would not cheapen the quality of his scholarship when provided with the right audience.

He made this even clearer when he spoke before two professional organizations, addressing the Ohio Valley Historical Association in 1909 on "The Ohio Valley in the Making of the Nation," and the Mississippi Valley Historical Association a year later on "The Significance of the Mississippi Valley in American History." Both addresses rested on the theme that physiographic conditions altered intruding civilizations; these alterations Turner examined with care, basing his statements on a thorough understanding of the geography of both regions. Both addresses also transcended local history by demonstrating that political and diplomatic events originating in the interior river valleys influenced national politics and diplomacy. And both served as vehicles to reveal the transformations wrought in the American character by the influence of free land. "There has been," Turner told his Ohio audience, "no single element more influential in shaping American democracy and its ideals"; to his fellow craftsmen of the Mississippi Valley Historical Association he added that the true significance of the Mississippi Valley was the development there "by growth among free opportunities, of the conception of a vast democracy made up of mobile ascending individuals."[26] He might have exaggerated the influence of "free land" in the growth of American democracy, but with such restrained statements he was on far safer ground than he was in his public addresses.

Had Turner maintained scholarly standards in popularizing his frontier thesis as he did when speaking to professional colleagues, he would have escaped much of the abuse heaped on him by later critics. He was unquestionably at fault when he succumbed to extravagant rhetoric and unsubstantiated generalizations in magazine articles and public speeches, but so were his later attackers when they accepted these fantasies as his true beliefs. The true Turner could be found only in the *professional* articles and papers that were his major interest. These reveal a scholar well known to fellow historians of his own generation, but scarcely recognizable today—a Turner respected for his meticulous scholarship, the cautiousness of his generalizations, the depths of his

research, and the freshness of his interpretations. These were the attrib-
utes that won him the respect of his peers, not the popular article in the
Atlantic Monthly or the audience-gripping commencement address.

They also brought Frederick Jackson Turner to the attention of
book publishers, and plunged him into a maelstrom of negotiations that
burdened his conscience for years to come. These began when the energetic firm of Henry Holt & Company launched an "American Historical
Series," under the direction of Charles Homer Haskins, to produce a
series of textbooks stressing social and economic developments. Turner,
Haskins told his employers, would be the ideal man for the volume on
American history, and they were wise enough to act at once. They had,
they assured him, discovered from his publications that he might be the
coming man to write the needed college history of the United States.
Turner was interested, but his cautious reply suggested that the book
would be long a-borning. Writing another narrative history did not
appeal to him, and the pathmaker's task was not to be taken lightly.
How long a volume was wanted? One that resembled Green's *Short
History of England*, or one like Gardiner's *Student History of England*?
When must the manuscript be submitted? He had just turned down a
similar proposal from the Chautauqua people because they would allow
him only eight months. The publishers reassured him: Gardiner rather
than Green should serve as the model, no definite deadline was necessary, and the book should contain a liberal supply of facts as well as
generalizations. Could he "throw into shape the material for a chapter
or two" to let them see what he planned?[27]

This exchange took place in the early spring of 1895. Nine months
later a Holt representative who called on Turner was told that the
sample chapters were well under way and would be submitted within
a few weeks. More months fled by before another polite inquiry
brought a less optimistic response. Turner was working on the outline
and had a chapter or so under way, but his research was pressing, and
he was beginning to wonder if he should not make his reputation as a
scholar in a limited field before attempting such a broad treatment. The
publisher replied that his position in the profession was already "pretty
satisfactorily made," but this flattery had little effect. The more Turner
pursued his studies, the more he realized that he was not ready for such
a major task. "The subject is growing *as a whole*," he confessed, "and
is just now in so formative a condition in my mind that I find it im-

possible to crystallize any particular portion." Not until he had re-explored all American history in the light of his frontier studies would he feel competent to begin writing. If Holt had another author in mind, they should forget that Turner existed.[28]

These modest disclaimers reveal Turner's perfectionism, but conceal the fact that another publisher was tempting him with a more attractive project. This was the brain-child of Professor W. P. Trent of the University of the South, a friend of Turner, a highly respected author in his day, and a consultant for the Macmillan Company. He suggested to Macmillan that they should enlist Turner, J. Franklin Jameson, Andrew C. McLaughlin, and other young scholars of the rising generation to prepare a series of books on the regions of the United States. Turner was the ideal candidate for the volume on the "Old West"—the area straddled by the Applachian Mountains. Trent had one word of caution that proved prophetic: "His university work and the pleasures of his delightful family life seem to me to interfere somewhat with his concentrating his energies in some one piece of work."[29] George P. Brett, the energetic president of the Macmillan Company, was undeterred. His invitation to Turner went off at once, and brought a predictable response. The subject was a fascinating one, crying for investigation, for the region did have unity and its history would reveal the evolution of the forces in American history to which the term "western" was applied. But a great deal of research was necessary, and Turner could devote his full time to the project only if sufficient inducements were offered. Brett was too canny a publisher to rise to this bait, but he did indicate that a contract would be forthcoming as soon as a portion of the manuscript was submitted. Turner was less than happy with this arrangement, but he promised that Macmillan would have the book within a year or eighteen months.[30]

Assuming this back-breaking task did not deter Turner from listening to the siren call of other publishers. He did decline an invitation, from G. P. Putnam's Sons, to write a two-volume history of the United States for their "Story of the Nations" series, but an editor from Macmillan's juvenile department, Kate Stephens, was more successful. She wanted a book of lively "pen stories" on the Lewis and Clark expedition, running to only 60,000 words, and carrying with it a $250 advance and royalties of 15 per cent after the first 1500 copies. Turner pricked up his ears when he heard those terms, for he knew the subject well and could have a manuscript in Miss Stephens's hands in less than two years.[31]

Rumors that their prospective author was straying from the fold stirred Henry Holt & Company into activity. If, their agent told Turner, he found the entire history of the United States too time-consuming, why not prepare the book in three sections which could eventually be merged into one? This was a suggestion tailored to Turner's temperament. He would be teaching the colonial and revolutionary periods next year, and could simply condense his lectures into the first section. His would be no narrative textbook; it would deal with the development of economic, political, and social institutions, and would show how these emerged from European conditions and were modified by the American environment. "If I am not wrong," he assured the publishers, "it is in this idea of unity and grasp of the essential phases of development, that most of our textbooks are defective." He would have the first section completed in eighteen months, the second a year later, and the third a year after that. What "inducements" did Holt offer to make the work pleasurable? Their terms were generous for that day: the usual royalty of 10 per cent and an advance of $500 delivered in three installments, one at the completion of each section of the book. Turner had a few more questions, but when these were answered, the contract was ready to be signed.[32]

Before Turner could seal the bargain, fate intervened in the person of George Brett of the Macmillan Company. In one of his periodic letters of inquiry on the progress of the book on the "Old West," Brett had the misfortune to mention a rumor that Turner was preparing a textbook; was this true, and if so, could Macmillan be the publisher? Turner, deep in his negotiations with Henry Holt & Company, was interested. Brett might have the volume if terms were satisfactory. What would Macmillan offer? The response was eye-opening: 10 per cent on the first 1000 copies, 12.5 per cent on the next 1500, and 15 per cent thereafter. Turner could also write the book in three installments if he wished, and might condense it into a grammar school textbook that would pay handsome royalties for very little effort.[33]

This was just the ammunition that Turner needed when Edward N. Bristol, Henry Holt's representative, called on him in Madison on October 18, 1897. He would prefer to publish with Macmillan, but would be governed by his prior commitment to Holt if they met Macmillan's terms. Poor Bristol had no choice. The contract, which Turner signed on November 9, provided for the same generous royalties offered by Macmillan, an advance of $1500 paid in three installments on delivery of the three parts of the manuscript, permission to publish a grammar school textbook and other works with other houses, and a commitment by Holt to print a high school textbook that Turner would distill from his larger work. "We want to go on record," the publishers wrote with feeling, "that we have never before risked as high terms on any educational work whatever, and unless there is a revolution in business methods, we do not expect to risk them again." In due course the contract for the high school text was signed, with royalties of 10 per cent on the first 2500 copies and 12.5 per cent thereafter.[34] The Holt editors, despite their complaints, were delighted, as well they might be. The only loser was George Brett. "It seems to us," he wrote bitterly, "that we have been somewhat unfairly treated in the matter of the publication of your College History, in that you have allowed another publisher to revise his offer for the publication of your book . . . without giving us a similar opportunity."[35]

Turner had proven himself a hard bargainer, and he was soon to exercise his skills again, for by the turn of the century he was recognized as the brightest rising star of the profession and fair game for all publishers. Ginn & Company offered him a contract for the grammar school textbook that he had discussed with Holt. A short time later A. C. McClurg Company proposed that Turner edit the works of a western traveler for a series they were planning; he was not interested, but he would like to write a book for them on "Western State-Making." They were agreeable, and another contract was signed, with the manuscript to be delivered within a year.[36] Houghton, Mifflin and Company fell into line next, for one of their editors was Walter Hines Page of the *Atlantic Monthly*, who was an admirer of Turner and determined to add him to that company's stable of authors. Page suggested several subjects—"The Conquest of the Continent," "The Disappearance of the Frontier," "The Extension of the Frontier"—but Turner warmed to none of them, despite Page's repeated assurance that such volumes could be dashed off in a few months from materials already at hand, and that they would assuredly be "the most popular and most influential books ever written in America." A whole generation of eager readers awaited the right book on the frontier, and Turner alone could write it. "The audience you have. They stand ready to give thanks, applause, and gate money." Turner could not resist such honeyed praise. He would prepare a volume, not on one of the suggested topics, but on "The Retreat of the Frontier," and have it ready for delivery within a year.[37]

During these negotiations Turner made the mistake of mentioning his growing interest in George Rogers Clark. Houghton, Mifflin just happened to have an ideal medium for a book on that frontier hero; their Riverside Biographical Series, made up of 25,000-word volumes designed for children, would welcome such a manuscript and pay suitable royalties. Turner not only agreed, he announced still another work well under way: a volume of essays, some published before, but all dealing with aspects of frontier expansion. Would Houghton, Mifflin be interested? They were, only mildly—but they would be happy to publish anything he wrote. So another bargain was sealed. The "Retreat of the Frontier" would be ready within a short time, the book of essays was almost completed, and the George Rogers Clark biography would be in their hands before the year was out.[38]

Turner had, in the five years before the end of the century, established a near world's record for contract signing. He had promised a grammar school textbook for Ginn & Company, high school and college textbooks for Henry Holt & Company, volumes on "The Old West" and the Lewis and Clark expedition for the Macmillan Company, a volume on "Western State-Making" for A. C. McClurg and Company, and a collection of essays on the frontier and books on "The Retreat of the Frontier" and George Rogers Clark for Houghton, Mifflin and Company. Neither the author nor the publishers realized that those contracts were to provide them all with years of embarrassment and discomfort.[39]

The publishers learned their lesson first. They began with reminders that the several manuscripts promised "within the year" were slightly overdue; Ginn & Company inquired politely about progress on the grammar school textbook in December 1901 and suggested that Turner no doubt found himself busier than expected; A. C. McClurg and Company used the same gentlemanly tone in pointing out that they had to have the outline and contents of the book on "Western State-Making" to prepare their 1902 catalogue. Houghton, Mifflin and Company was less gentle, insisting that the George Rogers Clark manuscript must be in their hands by February 1902 if it was to appear that year, and that they hoped to print the other two promised volumes a year later. That February deadline came and went, but no Clark biography arrived at the office of Houghton, Mifflin. Instead, the publisher's letters became increasingly insistent. Turner countered as best he could. "I am so much occupied by my various university duties that I cannot promise the book with certainty as early as you wish it, but I shall do my best to get it into your hands early in the spring," he assured the publishers in January 1902, "—probably in the first part of March or possibly the last of February."[40]

That was as unrealistic as all of Turner's promises. Once more a year passed, and once more the perennially optimistic Houghton, Mifflin editors made their regular inquiries. They very much hoped that the forthcoming volumes could be listed for 1903 publication. Turner was not sure that he could meet the January 1, 1903, deadline that they suggested, but the Clark biography would be in their hands by late February or early March, and the other two manuscripts would follow shortly. By June the editors were growing impatient; they were assured that the whole summer would be devoted to the volumes and that they would be told within a month when each would be completed. Apparently Turner wasted that summer on other tasks, for in October he reported that he was about to start work on both manuscripts, and would submit the Clark biography by the close of the semester. That was his last promise. By the spring of 1904 the Riverside Biographical Series, for which the book was intended, had been abandoned, and with it the last hope that Turner would write a life of George Rogers Clark.[41] Among his papers was a large file drawer packed with notes—hundreds and hundreds of them, drawn largely from manuscript sources—carrying the story of Clark's life only to 1783. Here was a monument to Turner's perfectionism no less than to his impracticality; he had labored endless hours gathering material for a 25,000-word book designed for children.[42]

There was still a spark of life in Houghton, Mifflin's ambitions. The projected volume of essays they were happy to forget, but Turner owed them "The Retreat of the Frontier," as they reminded him periodically. In November 1904, and again in the spring of 1905, they made the usual inquiries, to be told that he had been busy with other writing but would soon turn to the task. That was his last word of encouragement. Three years later Turner was reminded that when last he wrote them, the book was "in the last stages of composition," and asked whether those final pages had been written. There matters rested until 1924, when his retirement from teaching prompted a sly letter from the publishers, who hoped that his new leisure time would allow him to complete the volumes he had promised.[43]

Turner's unhappy relations with Houghton, Mifflin were duplicated with every publisher who cajoled him into a contract. In each instance the story was the same—increasingly demanding letters on the one hand, unrealistic promises on the other, and, finally, silence. Only Holt, lured by the prospect of two lucrative textbooks, continued to make life unpleasant for him—a story that belongs later in this volume. The result was tragedy not only for the publishers, but for Turner. As the months and years slipped by with promises unfulfilled, his mood varied from exuberant optimism to dark pessimism. Sometimes he was confident that he would find the leisure to finish—or even begin—the many books that he desperately wanted to write; then he would fill his letters with happy phrases about manuscripts "nearly finished" or promises that "sometime in the course of the year, I hope to get out a book on the subject."[44] At other times he would sink into despair as he realized that those books would never be written. In those dark periods he brooded long over letters from friends urging him to publish his views, lest others usurp them. Max Farrand warned him in 1905, "You are not getting sufficient credit for your ideas because you delay so long in publication. For goodness sake, hurry up and get out some of those western history books."[45]

This was salt in the wounds, but Turner simply could not respond. He was inclined, during these years, to blame his failure to write on the pressure of university duties; "it is not," he confessed, "an easy task to bring books to fruition when you are running a history department at the same time." His dream was a private income that would free him of all obligations save writing. "As my incomplete books—*unwritten* would be more to the point, loom up before my imaginative vision," wrote Turner to a friend, "I grow more and more covetous of the freedom from University work needed to bring them about." His solution was a best-selling "kindergarten history in words of one syllable, phonetically spelled!" that would shower him with riches.[46]

Actually Turner was as incapable of writing such a primer as he was the textbooks promised to Ginn and Holt. He was a perfectionist by nature and a dawdler by inclination, unable to endure the sustained effort needed to produce a major volume and unwilling to place on record the imperfect account demanded by any broad subject. Not a sentence could be written until every statement it contained had been tested, and repeatedly tested, by reference to the sources. Turner was a glutton for detail and a champion of accuracy, and no man of such temperament could ever complete a textbook. While pleading lack of time to finish his biography of George Rogers Clark, he was writing a whole series of articles reinterpreting the diplomatic history of the Mississippi Valley; while begging for a few hours to work on his textbooks, he was devoting months of patient research to his editorial tasks for the National Historical Manuscripts Commission. Turner's problem was not lack of time, but lack of inclination to undertake a task that he could not complete to perfection.

This doomed any chances that his publishing contracts would be fulfilled, but the death blow to the hopes of the publishers was a new historical interest that obsessed Turner during the opening years of the century. Through his frontier and diplomatic studies he gradually became aware of the fact that the United States was not one nation during its early years, but a complex of regional groupings, or "sections." Sectionalism, no less than expansion, held the key to understanding the nation's past. Once Turner awakened to this realization, he was a lost man. He had found a new subject, one of infinite complexity, that would require a lifetime of investigation for complete understanding. From the day that he awakened to the significance of the section, the frontier was of secondary importance in his hierarchy of enthusiasms. Turner was off to blaze a new trail, one that was to monopolize his attention and affection for the rest of his days.

IX

The Genesis of the
Sectional Concept

1893-1910

REDERICK JACKSON TURNER rode to fame—and the publishing contracts that plagued his remaining years—on the coattails of
the frontier thesis, but even before that controversial theory gained full
acceptance he had moved on to a new interest. This was a typical
about-face. Others might find satisfaction in tracing migration patterns
into the Old Northwest or studying the evolution of democracy in the
constitutions of western states, but not Turner. Such investigations,
essential though they were to the proof of his hypothesis, posed few
intellectual problems. He required new challenges, new interpretations
of the American past, new excitements to stir the mind. And he found
them all in the study of sectionalism.

His frontier theories led him naturally into this fascinating topic.
Westward migration, he knew, spread population across a series of
differing physiographic provinces. In each, a distinctive social order
emerged; no expert knowledge was needed to realize that New England
differed from the South Atlantic states, or the Old Northwest from the
lower Mississippi Valley. What caused these differences? Did soils, climate, topography, and precipitation shape the economic, social, and
cultural behavior that gave the region its unique character? Or were
environmental pressures modified by the ethnic blendings that differed
so markedly from section to section? How did the unique combination
of natural and human forces that evolved in each section alter political
attitudes and cultural expression? Most important of all, how could
these sections, each comparable to a European nation, cooperate to

achieve national harmony when their differences were so obvious? These were challenging questions indeed. If Turner could determine how sectional compromises shaped the nation's legislative history, how sectional pressures acted as counterweights to excessive nationalism, how internal conflicts were converted from a class to a regional basis, he would have a better understanding of American history. He was on the scent of a subject that made even the frontier seem insignificant.

Nor was it a subject that Turner could possibly ignore. Through his lifetime his concern was not with one facet of American history, but with *all* American history. "I was," he later recalled as he remembered this period of his life, "trying to see it as a whole—on its institutional, social, economic and political side." The frontier was only a part of the past, but the interplay of the sections held clues that would illuminate every aspect, and this was Turner's primary concern. Then, too, he saw history as a spotlight on the present, principally useful for guiding mankind along the road to the future. Sectional forces, he believed, were shaping national policy at the turn of the century (and who could believe otherwise, as rural discontent, urban unrest, and free silver divided the United States into battling regions?); those forces could be understood and modern problems solved only by understanding their role in the past. To Turner the whole national spirit—"Uncle Sam's psychology," he called it—was a product of a federation of sections, and could be diagnosed only by an analysis of how sections were formed and how they interacted.[1] This was an irresistible challenge. "I was," he wrote simply, "forced to undertake a survey of the Regions in American history."[2]

Turner's intellectual curiosity had much to do with exciting his interest in sectionalism, but so did another influence of which he was totally unaware. New ideas, new concepts, new approaches, always rest on a foundation of fact and theory produced by prior investigators, and they emerge because the intellectual atmosphere is favorable to their appearance. Turner lived at a time when scholars throughout the western world were awakening to the significance of regional studies, and when statistical and cartographic techniques had become sufficiently developed to allow them to be pursued scientifically.

Stress on regionalism came naturally to early twentieth-century geographers, who viewed the environment as all-powerful. Sectional studies originated in Europe, where the influence of Friedrich Ratzel, the high priest of environmentalism, was especially strong, particularly after 1897, when he published his influential book, *Political Geography*. This was an eye-opening volume, advancing detailed evidence to show that the growth and character of political units was determined by their position on the earth's surface, their size, the nature of their boundaries, and their distance from oceans.[3] Politics, Ratzel claimed, could be explained only by an analysis of the geographic factors that shaped the attitudes and desires of the people of any natural region. This was an extreme statement, and one to which Turner never subscribed, but it does show the extent to which regional forces were recognized by intelligent men of that day.

Nor was Ratzel alone, for everywhere geographers were focusing on the regions of the world, seeking in them keys to man's economic, social, and political behavior. In France the dominant figure in geographic circles was Vidal de la Blache, whose classic work, *Tableu de la Géographie de la France* (1903), analyzed the regions into which the nation was divided and showed how soils and water supply determined the behavior of each. In England, scholars conducted germinal studies of geographic provinces, or wrote learned articles, such as one on "The Major Natural Regions of the World," by A. J. Herbertson. In the United States, the pioneer investigator of geographic sectionalism was William Morris Davis of Harvard University, who argued so effectively for regional analysis that by the close of the 1890s the American Geographical Society was filling its publications with physiographic data rather than accounts of Arctic exploration.[4] When Turner began his sectional investigations, he was only responding to a climate of opinion that was affecting all scholarship.

Turner was also benefitting from progress in statistical and cartographic techniques that made such investigations possible. Just at this time, soil geography was emerging as a respected discipline; E. W. Hilgard, its pioneer, published his "A Report on the Relation of Soil to Climate" in a bulletin of the Department of Agriculture in 1892. This study was so revealing that two years later the department began a long-term project of mapping the soils of the entire United States. Here were data galore for the sectional historians, for differences in soils and vegetation would explain regional differences in agricultural production.[5] When Turner, in his later studies, equated cultural progress with limestone soil belts, he was building on knowledge supplied him by soil geographers.

He was equally indebted to the statistical cartographers, who taught him how to correlate regional data in graphic form. In this the high water mark was the publication in 1883 of *Scribner's Statistical Atlas of the United States*, ably edited by Fletcher W. Hewes and Henry Gannett. Turner found in this remarkable volume not only the vivid population maps that brought home to him the course of westward expansion, but a number of others that showed county-by county variations in social, economic, and political behavior. One series illustrated the percentage strength of the leading candidate in all presidential elections; another, that of every candidate, by county, in the election of 1880. Turner had only to compare these with soil maps to recognize that a correlation did exist between better soils and political conservatism. Nor did he have to depend on *Scribner's Atlas* alone, for its example was followed in a number of other studies. *Appleton's Annual Cyclopedia* for 1888 printed a map showing the leading presidential candidate's plurality in each county for the period 1872-88; the 1896 edition performed the same service for the McKinley-Bryan contest.[6] When Turner began his sectional studies, the tools needed to translate complex relationships between political, economic, and social behavior into understandable graphic form were at hand.

Census experts came to Turner's aid in still another way. Since the late eighteenth century, when Jedidiah Morse wrote of the "Grand Divisions of the United States" in his pioneering *American Geography*, scholars had recognized that regions, or sections, divided the nation, but those sections had never been exactly defined, nor had their significance been appraised. Not until the publication of *Scribner's Statistical Atlas* were the sections subjected to serious analysis; in a suggestive essay in that volume, "The Natural Grouping of the States," Henry Gannett proposed five divisions: North Atlantic, South Atlantic, North Central, South Central, and West. Each, he found, had distinctive characteristics: thus, the North Atlantic and North Central regions contained 85 per cent of the foreign-born and most of the urban units, the South Atlantic and South Central 90.5 per cent of all Negroes. Gannett's groupings were unsophisticated and his findings unspectacular, but, in a day when the nation conceived of sectionalism in terms of

"North" and "South" alone, he had taken a long step forward. The theoretical foundation was laid on which Turner was to build.

He began the speculations that were to merge into his sectional studies early in his academic career. As an undergraduate he had awakened to the importance of regional forces when Professor William Francis Allen's *History Topics for the Use of High Schools and Colleges* taught him something of the differences between New England and the Old Northwest. As a graduate student at Johns Hopkins, living in a southern environment heightened his awareness of regional differences, while his conversations with Woodrow Wilson deepened his understanding of regional problems. "My studies of sectionalism," he told a friend a few years later, "in the sense of Western, Middle, Southern and New England, rather than of North and South alone, began in that same time."[7] Turner was sufficiently enthralled to prepare a six-page memorandum on "Sectionalization and Nationalization," which he planned to read to Wilson, then use as the basis for one or two articles. All American history, he reasoned, was a struggle between two tendencies—sectionalizing and nationalizing—with the latter gradually prevailing as unifying forces triumphed over those of division. Turner listed those forces: immigration, the navy, free trade agitation, arbitration, growth of commerce, world's fairs, and travel.[8] The projected article was never written, but he was even at this tender academic age thinking of sectionalism as something more than the North-South division that climaxed in the Civil War.

Turner's concern with regional problems in his days as a student produced no tradition-shattering results, but they did spark an interest that he continued to nurture during his early teaching career. He listened intently when one of Allen's students, Humphrey Desmond, addressed the Wisconsin Academy of Sciences, Arts and Letters on "The Sectional Feature in American Politics," then read, annotated, and heavily underlined the published version of the talk, especially the part that advanced the heretical doctrine that the federal Constitution was "a treaty of alliance between two great sections."[9] He copied into his notes occasional phrases that struck his fancy: one, from a volume on *American Constitutional Law*, brought home the fact that "the states had for the most part no boundaries."[10] He eagerly read the essay by

John W. Powell on "Physiographic Regions of the United States" when it appeared in 1896 in a publication of the National Geographic Society. As he did so, Turner recognized its importance, for Powell's analysis was far more sophisticated than any he had read. Powell drew no rigid boundaries, recognizing that regions merged with slow gradations one into the other, but he did distinguish sectional groupings that were more sophisticated than those of earlier geographers, ranging from the "Atlantic Plain," "Piedmont Plateau," and "Appalachian Ranges" on the east to the "Columbia Plateau," and "Basin Ranges," and "Pacific Mountains" on the west.[11] Although excessively detailed, Powell's divisions lent themselves to the type of analysis that Turner was to undertake, and he added them to his vocabulary at once.

But he did this only with variations, for he was far from satisfied. The problem, as he saw it, was to define the "*natural* economic-social-political groups" that formed each section. Such a definition must ignore state lines, but it must also recognize the wide variety of forces that underlay regional psychology. Geographic influences were important, but by no means determinative. Also to be considered were economic activities; congressional votes, which would show how representatives grouped themselves; political behavior, as revealed in state elections; newspaper attitudes; literary output; ethnic composition; and the historical background. Turner was too aware of the nature of sectional divisions in the West of the 1890s to be seduced by a purely geographic explanation. Geographers might merge the area between the Mississippi and the Rockies into the "Plains," but farmers in western Kansas and Nebraska behaved differently from farmers in eastern Kansas and Nebraska. The western farmers raised "more hell than corn," and would continue to do so until a social structure was devised that was suited to an arid climate where irrigation was the way of life and frontier individualism was sublimated to the needs of society.[12] No single mode of analysis would explain western behavior—or the regional conflicts of the past. Sections must be defined in geographic, economic, political, cultural, and psychological terms.

This was a major assignment. Simply to define the regions whose interaction explained the past required years of patient research and analysis. It also demanded recognition of the complexity of forces shaping sectional attitudes, for Turner realized that environmental and ethnic influences blended to create the unique characteristics of each region, and that these characteristics manifested themselves not only in political and economic behavior, but in literature and the arts, education, and every facet of social life. Many years later Turner recalled the problems that he faced in 1895 and 1896, when he began his studies: "I had to have some knowledge of American physiography; I had to know something of demography as well; and I had to recognize that these changes and interrelations affected American social life and characteristics in general: its literature, art, religion, ideals."[13] He had to accomplish all this, moreover, when his energy was directed into the diplomatic studies that were his principal concern, and when sectionalism was more a hobby than a vocation.

Yet it was a hobby that was too fascinating to be shelved, and during the late 1890s Turner launched a systematic program to prepare himself for the investigations he was already considering. This took two forms. One was self-education; he read as widely as he could (though there were few publications on sectionalism), taking notes, analyzing one region after another in his search for the features that distinguished each, learning a great deal about the ice sheets that had transformed North America during the glacial era, and phrasing definitions that approached the exactness he sought. One that impressed him particularly was borrowed from a Phi Beta Kappa address on "Provincialism," given by Josiah Royce: "any one part of a national domain which is, geographically and socially, sufficiently unified to have a true consciousness of its own unity, to feel a pride in its own ideals and customs, and to possess a sense of its distinction from other parts of the country."[14] These were valuable tidbits, but haphazard reading was not enough for Turner. In the fall of 1898 he enrolled in a seminar on physiography given by his colleague Charles R. Van Hise, and he attended regularly through the term as that eminent geologist described the "Atlantic Coastal Plain," the "Piedmont Upland," the "Gulf Plains," and other provinces in intimate detail.[15]

At the same time, Turner was enlisting allies among his students and fellow historians. As early as the spring of 1895 he directed his senior seminar into the study of regionalism, assigning such topics as sectional groupings in colonial times, sectionalism in the Revolutionary period, and evidence of sectionalism in votes on the tariff, internal improvements, and other major issues.[16] Seniors were also encouraged to prepare honors theses on regional topics, or to study voting behavior in presidential elections in terms of sectional influences. One capable undergraduate analyzed members of the Wisconsin state legislature in 1850, 1860, and 1870 according to place of birth, occupation, wealth, and party, then classified the legislators by their voting records on important issues. These pioneer ventures into statistical techniques that were needed to comprehend regional voting patterns—the study of "Demagogics," Turner called it—were ground-breaking studies which cast more light on the principles and methods of political leadership than did any others then under way.[17] Yet they were peripheral to his principal interest in diplomatic history, generated by intellectual curiosity rather than any practical objective.

The only immediate impact of Turner's mounting interest in sectionalism was on the course offerings of his department. In 1896 he encouraged his colleague, Orin G. Libby, to launch a new offering on "American Sectionalism," which dealt with "the geographical distribution of political parties, with special reference to votes in Congress and in the state legislatures." At the same time, Turner's own lectures in his "History of the West" took on more and more of a regional tint. A detailed physiographic map was his most essential tool as he carefully explained each detail. "Notice this map of southeastern Pennsylvania," he told his students. "You see the Susquehanna River and the pink portion, which is the limestone flooring of the Great Valley. . . . Now notice beyond the Great Valley those canoe-shaped regions which constitute the coves or inter-montane valleys beyond. See how the mountains spread in thickly, and how inaccessible to settlement they are."[18] He repeated this stiff dose of geography for each section, as he traced settlement westward. The United States, he told his students over and over again, was nothing more than a "congeries of geographic regions," each as large as a European nation, and American history the story of "the outcome of the interaction of the various sections."[19] Here was a neglected key to understanding the nation's past, and the more Turner read and speculated, the more he became convinced that it alone would unlock secrets that had remained hidden from earlier scholars.

His mounting conviction was shown when he was asked to revise his essay on "The Significance of the Frontier in American History" for publication by the National Hebart Society in 1899. The westward movement was still the all-important fact of American history, but

Turner saw it now as a means of occupying successive physiographic areas, "economically and socially comparable to nations of the old world." "We must," he wrote, "observe how these areas affected the life of the immigrants from the older sections and from Europe." Viewed from this perspective, the study of the frontier became "the fascinating examination of the successive evolution of peculiar economic and social countries, or provinces, each with its own contributions, and individuality."[20] By the turn of the century Turner was convinced that the history of the United States had to be rewritten to reveal the role of sections. He was too absorbed in his diplomatic studies to turn to the task at once, but only an excuse was needed to set him off on the new scent.

This was provided by an ambitious scheme launched by the American Historical Association in 1899. The time was ripe, that body decided, for a multivolume collaborative history of the United States, built on the findings of the "Scientific School" then in vogue. Turner found himself involved as the sole western member of the committee named to plan the series, even though he was determined not to commit himself as an author; he had a work of his own on the stocks—or at least the lumber for one—as well as an abundance of contracts to fulfill, and would never add another.[21] In this laudable determination he reckoned without Albert Bushnell Hart, chairman of the planning committee and eventual editor of the series. Hart wanted Turner on his list, and would move mountains to have him. The stage was set for a battle of wills that could have only one outcome.

One by one Hart played his trump cards. Harper & Brothers had been signed as publishers; that prestigious firm would add glory to the series. A committee of the State Historical Society of Wisconsin was asked to advise on the proper treatment of the West—with Turner a member and principal consultant. The official invitation, mailed on January 2, 1902, was properly baited with flattery: "Yours was one of the first names to occur to my mind as fundamental in any scheme of cooperative scholarship in American history." Would Turner agree to produce a volume—any volume that he wanted to write—for a fee of $1500, half to be paid on delivery of the manuscript? Turner disliked the terms and preferred a royalty arrangement; he also had to consult his other publishers, long-suffering already, but he was interested.[22] This was enough to bring Hart to Madison, to press his case personally with Turner and with Reuben Gold Thwaites, whom he also wanted. He pleaded his cause well; no other historian was so well equipped to reveal the impact of the frontier on American life and to demonstrate the significance of sectional interplay. Turner had only to pick the period best suited to his purpose. This was too tempting to be dismissed. "I am," Turner wrote the next day, "praying not to be led into temptation, and yet there is one field which he proposes to me which may possibly lead to my participation."23

Hart had all but landed his victim, and had only to hit upon the right formula to bring him into the net. He found it soon after his return to Cambridge. The larger projects that Turner had undertaken—books that would fit his frontier theory into the broad framework of American history—would take years to complete. Why not interrupt his labors for the brief time needed to dash off a volume applying his concepts to a short span of history? "What I should like from you," Hart wrote, "is not a resumé of the whole result of your studies on western history, but one ship in my squadron, which shall fairly represent your ship yard." A book on the period from 1819 to 1829 would serve as a case study of the importance of expansion and sectionalism; it would also reveal the rise of the western spirit culminating in the election of Andrew Jackson. This combination of temptations was more than Turner could resist. He agreed to add one more contract to the formidable list already signed. He would use the volume to work out his ideas "with respect to the importance of treating American history from the point of view of the existence of great provinces, irrespective of state lines, which have served to determine the development of American conditions."24

To describe such a book was one thing; to accomplish the mountains of research and writing necessary was quite another. Turner was sufficiently aware of his own weaknesses to realize that he could stick to his task only by using his classroom as a workshop, where daily assignments would have to be performed. Beginning with the fall of 1903, his "History of the West" took on a new complexion; it was concerned not only with expansion, but also with the "economic, political and social aspects of the occupation of the various physiographic provinces," while his seminar dealt with the administration of James Monroe. A year later, when still deep in research, Turner went so far as to offer a year-long course on the United States from 1816 to 1837, repeating it the year following. Even within this narrow time span, he spent so much time discussing the Missouri Compromise, the election of 1820, the foreign relations of the administrations of Monroe and John Quincy Adams, and the conflict over tariffs and internal improvements before 1829, that he was half way through the second semester before he reached the presidency of Andrew Jackson.[25] Here was concentration with a vengeance, but a concentration that forced Turner to keep his nose to the grindstone.

And the noses of others as well. His students were willing victims, particularly those in his seminars who were forced to sublimate their own interests to study details of the Monroe era, or analyze roll-call votes in Congress for sectional groupings, or list the greats and near-greats of the 1819-29 period with biographical information that Turner might find useful. Select graduate students were pressed into service, several to prepare model tables of contents for a "Proposed History of the United States, 1819-1829," others to produce theses on such topics as "Internal Improvements in the United States during Monroe's Administrations," and "Some Political Aspects of the Press between 1816 and 1830." Solon J. Buck, later to become a prominent historian, was assigned the unenviable task of listing all iron manufacturing plants in Pennsylvania for the decade of the 1820s, as a basis for testing regional opinion on the tariff—a chore only slightly less challenging than those of students made to prepare biographical sketches of all congressmen for the period.[26] During the three years Turner's book was under way, his graduate students received a baptism of fire they never forgot.

Turner's own efforts dwarfed theirs. He spent every spare hour in the State Historical Society library, supervising copyists who transcribed hundreds of items from congressional speeches, newspapers, and *Niles' Register*, or filling sheet after sheet of five-by-eight notepaper with information on internal improvements, the tariff, land policy, foreign affairs, roll-call votes—everything that bore on the sectional alignments of the 1820s. Occasionally Turner tried to bring order to this chaos by using a trial outline: one, which he made in October 1904, listed seventeen chapters and included such topics as "Survey of the Decade in Terms of Literature, Reform, Education, Labor, and American Ideas"; another, done a year later, discarded such peripheral topics to concentrate on the sectional problem in manageable form.[27] Occasionally, too, he was forced to compress portions of his findings into rough drafts, as he did when he delivered five lectures at the University of Michigan that spring on "American Development in the Decade 1820-1830."[28]

If Turner had followed his own inclinations, he would have gone on forever with the research that he loved, but Albert Bushnell Hart had other ideas. His first warning was issued in the fall of 1904; the twenty-odd volumes of the *American Nation* series were being printed in lots of five, and Turner's was in the lot to be published in the autumn of 1905. That meant his maps had to be submitted at once for proper preparation. "At once" to Turner meant six months later, and then only after a wordy exchange over the number to be included; he wanted fifteen, the publishers allowed only nine, and eleven were finally agreed upon. The manuscript proved harder to extract. By July 1905, not a line had reached Cambridge, and Hart was growing desperate. He had to have it by August, he warned; "your volume is becoming the needle's eye for the series." Twice the delivery date had been extended, but that was the end. Turner, tense and overwrought, struck back blindly, accusing Hart of responsibility for the delay, much to that innocent victim's amazement. His assurances smoothed the troubled waters, but he saw that Turner was near the breaking point and had to have some relief. If the chapters already completed could be sent at once, the remainder need not arrive until the end of September. This would mean no vacation, "but I do not see why young fellows like you need vacations."[29]

This was the incentive Turner needed, and all that late summer and fall he worked furiously, rising with the sun, taking a brief dip in Lake Mendota, fishing for pickerel between five and six o'clock, then ascending to the attic study at 629 Frances Street to begin work. There his secretary, a capable student named Merrill H. Crissey, awaited him, and dictation began. Turner paced the floor as he talked, often chewing an unlighted cigar and pausing now and then to consult his notes. When tensions grew too great, or the apt phrase escaped him, or a difficult problem in interpretation proved unsolvable, he would leave the room to pace along the shores of the lake, smoking furiously.[30] So the writing went on, as page followed page and the pile of completed manuscript grew larger. "I am 'pegging away' at my volume for the Hart series," he wrote a friend, "and have a profound respect for a man who has a volume behind him."[31]

By mid-August the introduction and three chapters were on their way to Cambridge, leaving Turner so exhausted that he pleaded with Hart for a little time off to recuperate. This was grudgingly granted; "I hope that you will take the rest, and that the remainder of the book will go the quicker for it." Hart's concern was genuine, for one look at the completed chapters convinced him that he was midwifing a masterpiece. Paragraphs were too long, quotations over-abundant, and the whole so bulky that it far exceeded the publisher's space limitations, but these were minor faults when contrasted with the excellence of the product. "No volume which has so far gone through my hands," he assured Turner, "will do more to set in people's minds right notions of how things actually came about."[32] Another chapter, that on the "Far West," which reached him in early September, only confirmed these impressions. Turner's words were worth waiting for.

But not for too long. By early October Hart was cracking the whip once more. All other volumes for the third set of five books were completed; unless Turner's was added in time to go to press by December the publishers stood to lose a healthy sum. These threats produced three more chapters by the end of October and the promise of the remainder by mid-November, a date that Hart reluctantly accepted. Mid-November came, and still no book. "I have been looking out of the window for a week hoping to see the expressman," he wrote on November 21. He did not have to wait much longer. On December 7, 1905, Turner wrote exultantly to his wife: "Finished my rough draft of the last chapter today. Ecco! Selah! Voila! Whoopla! I may drink up the last bottle of Nucleus Club's champagne when I revise the chapter and actually post it." That drink was soon forthcoming, for on December 11 the entire manuscript was in Hart's hands.[33]

If Turner drank that champagne, the celebration was premature, for both his labors and Hart's were far from over. His manuscript was grossly oversized. "I see nothing for it," Hart wrote as he viewed the vast pile of pages on his table, "but to reduce the manuscript to procrustean dimensions." Nor was size the only problem. The whole book had to be reviewed to avoid repetition and bring events into consecutive order, two chapters lacked point and needed sharpening, dates had to be added throughout to orient the reader, footnotes were too many and too long, the maps were hopelessly overdetailed, transitions had to be supplied and choppy sentences combined. All of this had to be accomplished within two weeks, for January 1, 1906, was the absolute deadline. Thus Hart laid down the law, then tempered his judgment with the words of praise that would inspire Turner to take up his blue pencil: "This piece of work will enhance the large reputation which you enjoy for scholarship and for insight. It is a suggestive, revealing kind of book."[34]

Turner glowed, and accepted the criticism with good grace. He set to work at once, with two stenographers at his side, and, miraculously, completed the revisions on time. Hart was delighted; the manuscript was still too long, but it was publishable if the bibliographical essay could be kept to 3000 words. On January 16 it was shipped to the publishers, and three days later the first payment of $750 reached Madison. If Hart assumed that he was shifting responsibility to Harper & Brothers when he mailed them the manuscript, he was badly mistaken. Galley proofs began to arrive within a few days, and when Turner saw them he was inspired to a new burst of perfectionism. Here was a chance to make all the changes he had longed to make in his manuscript! By February 8 Hart was inquiring anxiously when the first galleys would be returned, pointing out that the whole printing schedule hung in the balance, but not until more than a month later did Turner reluctantly relinquish the last. This taught Hart a lesson. When Turner submitted a bibliographical essay of 6000 words, just double the space allotted him, Hart made the needed deletions himself and did not even send the proofs to the author.[35]

The product was worth the ordeal, and both men were highly pleased. Each recognized the debt owed the other. "One thing I do owe to Hart," Turner confessed to Max Farrand, "and that is the steadfast way he has worked the reel and finally landed the MS. It is a poor sucker instead of a trout, but it fought like the devil against coming to the landing net." Hart, on his part, took pardonable pride in extracting the manuscript from its perfectionist author. "It ought to be carved on my tombstone," he wrote many years later, "that I was the only man in the world that secured what might be classed an adequate volume from Turner."[36] So he had, and revealed himself as a model editor by doing so. No other succeeded, and while Hart did not rely on the technique that rumor ascribed to him—sending so many collect telegrams that Turner was forced to finish the book to avoid bankruptcy—he did display skills in angling that any might envy.

Well might both be proud, for the *Rise of the New West, 1819–1829* was a remarkable volume for its day. Turner's thesis was radically new: beneath the surface calm of the "Era of Good Feeling" were arising disruptive issues and party formations stemming from sectional divisions that were to effect basic changes in the structure of society. To reveal these, he first analyzed the economic and social life of the major sections—New England, the Middle States, the South, the West, and the Far West—in a series of chapters that were unique in their day and have lost little of their charm since. Having set the stage, he described the principal events of the decade, ranging from the Panic of 1819 and the Missouri Compromise through the nullification controversy that signaled the surfacing of the sectional conflict. Yet he wrote no narrative history in the traditional sense. Each episode was analyzed in terms of regional forces, each individual viewed as a symbol of his own section, each congressional act appraised against the sectional divisions that accounted for its success or failure. "I have," Turner wrote, "kept before myself the importance of regarding American development as the outcome of economic and social as well as political forces."[37] This was his purpose, and he succeeded so admirably that the *Rise of the New West* was destined to be read long after most of the volumes in the *American Nation* series were forgotten.

Fortunately, that generation agreed with posterity's judgment. Professional journals were universal in their praise; some few reviewers even understood Turner's purpose, and they pointed out that the history of the nation would have to be rewritten to incorporate the sectional theme. Popular magazines and newspapers echoed this endorsement. "No more profound study of any period of American history has been written," declared *The Independent*, a sentiment that was repeated in *The Nation*, *The Literary Digest*, and every major opinion-making journal.[38] Friends and even distant acquaintances joined in the chorus of approval; the months of agonizing labor must have seemed worth while to Turner as he read James Ford Rhodes's judgment, that the book was "a right grand piece of work," or harkened to his good friend Charles R. Van Hise, who predicted that now other books would follow explaining "the great forces which have moulded the nation, and which will still further mould it in the future."[39]

The publishing world was Turner's now, and the future one of financial security. He had proven himself as an author; now he would complete the college and high school textbooks for Henry Holt & Company, and the grammar school text for Ginn & Company, all within the next year or two. Those volumes would reward him so handsomely that he could abandon teaching for the scholarly researches that were his true passion. So Turner dreamed that spring of 1905 as he labored to complete his *Rise of the New West*.

If those dreams were to come true, he had to have both assistance and leisure, and what was more logical than that this be provided by the publishers who would benefit from his labors? Letters of inquiry to Holt and Ginn brought encouraging responses. Holt felt that he should concentrate on the high school textbook first of all, but had no objections if he worked on the grammar school volume at the same time. They were even willing to discuss a cash advance "to free you from the financial cares that interrupt." Thus encouraged, Turner was ready with his proposition. Would Holt and Ginn together advance him $2000 yearly against royalties for the next two years, with the assurance that both books would be finished well within that time? This was something more of an investment than either publisher had contemplated. Authorities at Ginn made cautious remarks about a mutual agreement on a lesser figure, but Holt was more specific; they would give him $1000 as an advance by installments on *completion* of each section of the manuscript.[40]

This was hardly the cornucopia envisaged by Turner—he wanted his cash before, not after, the writing was completed—but a crumb was better than no cake at all. He would be ready to start work on the high school textbook in October 1905, and would be willing to devote his full time—even delaying the grammar school text—if the publishers would allow him $500 for assistance. This was a sum worth betting for a Turner book, and Holt agreed. "Luck to us," they wrote, as arrangements were made and the check sent in October 1905. They needed luck, for if anything was necessary to show Turner's complete divorcement from reality it was this exchange. He opened negotiations with Holt in May 1905, just when Hart was applying pressure for completion of the *Rise of the New West*, and in August, with that pressure still mounting, he assured the publishers that he could begin work on the textbook in October. That was the month when he accepted the Holt check, with the volume for Hart still six months from completion; as he did so, he blithely wrote a friend that he was "looking over the ground for the book," and would devote all his time to it when the other manuscript was completed, "which will be in a few weeks."[41] This unrealistic self-confidence so misled the publishers that by the beginning of 1906 they were briefing their salesmen on the gem that was to come their way, and beginning their advertising campaign.[42]

He was just as unrealistic when he began planning the volume, even with the book for Hart still far from finished. His notes to himself written during these weeks show the type of textbook he hoped to write; "Clothe these factors," he wrote at one time, "and disguise them but keep steadily in mind: Physiography, Economic basis, Political and social and religious ideals and parties"; or "Men—make the *leading characters* in each era and period *live*." This was a large assignment, and so was the time schedule that he prepared early in 1906: the chapters on Spanish colonization would be completed by November, those on the French and early English colonies in December and January, the story of developments between 1660 and 1688 written in February and March, the period from 1688 to 1763 covered between April and June, and the rest of the volume finished that summer.[43] Here was pipe-dreaming, indeed!

Sometime that year Turner did begin work, but the result fell far below his expectations: a four-page introduction, a thirty-four-page chapter on the geography of North America, part of a chapter on the Indian inhabitants, and less than half a chapter on Spanish colonization, all in rough draft with frequent marginal notations suggesting changes. These samples, pitifully few though they were, suggest that the book, if written, would have gained the popularity envisaged by author and publisher. His thesis, set forth in his introduction, was tuned to the times; the spread of civilization westward, he wrote, had been accompanied by the adjustment of peoples to diverse sections. "The evolution, interaction and consolidation of these sections, had made an American nation with a composite people; with institutions mainly derived from Europe and deeply modified to meet American conditions; and with an American spirit and democratic ideals differing from Europe, and fundamentally due to the experience of the people in occupying a new continent."[44] Turner's theme—based on expansion and sectionalism—was to dominate the interpretation of the American past for the next quarter-century. Had his book been completed, it would probably have swept the field and enriched him with the royalties he so desperately wanted.

But that book was never completed. His friends did what they could over the next years, showering him with appeals to bring it on the market for use in their classes, inquiring about the publication date, and pointing out that if he did not produce soon, others less competent would fill the gap.[45] Embarrassing as these inquiries were, they were less humiliating than the recurring reminders from Holt & Company. The company's officials did their best, pointing out the profits that only a book by F. J. Turner could assure, urging him to keep the $500 advance as a gift, promising him the $1500 advance as soon as the whole manuscript was in their hands. "The completed book," they assured him, "would provide a source of revenue for both of us—one likely to last for years."[46] Their pleas were in vain, for not a scrap of manuscript did they see. "Lunched with Bristol of Holt & Co.," Turner wrote his wife in 1908, "—who is a gentleman and didn't worry me." Seven years later he again reported that a Holt representative had called, "to my discomfort."[47]

His pangs of remorse caused him few sleepless nights, however, for by this time he was off on a new quest—one that made textbook writing dull by comparison. This followed naturally on his studies of the Monroe and Adams administrations in his *Rise of the New West*. If the decade of the 1820s yielded so bountifully to analysis in terms of sectional forces, what could be expected of the years between 1830 and the 1850s? That was an era when sectionalism was at its height, yet scholars had been so long blinded by their study of a North-South division that they had completely neglected the more important and more complex alignments that held the key to a true understanding of the period. Here was a virgin field for the investigator. If he could demonstrate that the abrasive issues of the Jacksonian era—the tariff, land policy, finance, internal improvements, expansion—exerted a divisive influence comparable to that of slavery, he would not only advance a logical interpretation of a misunderstood era but prove to his fellow historians that sectionalism was a force to be reckoned with in all ages. Turner was ready to launch a new crusade, and one that promised intellectual pleasures that textbook-writing sadly lacked.

His opportunity came when he was granted leave of absence for the second semester of the 1906-7 academic year. A practical man would have used those months to finish the textbooks. Not Turner. Financial security was nothing when compared with the excitement of research;

he headed for Washington, installed his wife at the Marlborough Hotel, where an excellent cafe provided meals, and established himself in the Library of Congress amidst the books, newspapers, and manuscripts that he loved. There he spent the next months, save for necessary interruptions—a four-day vacation in Virginia with his friend Charles Homer Haskins, a journey to New York to address the annual dinner of the Wisconsin Club, where the audience included "railroad presidents to burn, and all kinds of heavy ordnance," a visit to Johns Hopkins to show his wife and daughter his university and to address the seminar on "American Sectionalism."[48] But work was the order of the day, from nine until six daily, as Turner devoured manuscript collection after manuscript collection, or leafed happily through yellowing newspapers for tidbits on sectional attitudes in the days of Andrew Jackson and Martin Van Buren.

Those were happy weeks for Turner—morning and afternoon spent watching his pile of notes grow steadily, lunch at the "Round Table," where distinguished visitors were invited to meet with the Librarian of Congress, evenings of reading or talk with Mae and Dorothy. Mae's health and the damp Washington weather proved so irreconcilable that she departed for Madison on May 3, leaving Turner even more time for his investigations; he breakfasted heartily at the Marlborough, went without lunch, returned to his rooms for crackers and cheese at supper time, then worked again until ten, when he dined on oysters at Harvey's Restaurant. Even this rigorous schedule left room for homesickness. The treasures of the library, he decided, were too vast to be conquered all at once.[49] Within a few weeks of Mae's departure, he was on his way to Madison, bulging with information and with a bundle of notes that would keep him busy for weeks to come.

Turner's intense study bore important fruit, for it convinced him that no historian, no matter how broad his interests, could understand the complexities of sectional interplay without calling on his fellow social scientists for aid. Geographers were particularly essential for their knowledge of the earth's physical features and climate, but so were sociologists, who could share their understanding of the social order and of the forces underlying social change. Reading in the expanding literature of these two infant disciplines would help, and Turner read every pertinent item that came his way, but progress would be speeded if historians and geographers and sociologists could be brought together to share their knowledge. They might even be persuaded to launch an interdisciplinary investigation into American sectionalism. This was Turner's ideal, and this was the dream that inspired two significant ventures that he undertook during the autumn of 1907.

One was a special session that he arranged for the meeting of the American Historical Association, scheduled for Madison that December. He hoped to attract a handful of eminent geographers to share their findings on the role of physiography in historical causation, but those he wanted proved impossible to recruit, and in the end he was forced to settle for only one. Ellen Churchill Semple, a disciple of Friedrich Ratzel, whose *American History and Its Geographic Conditions* was then in the academic limelight, agreed to present a paper on "Location as a Factor in History." To fill the remaining spot, Turner was forced to turn to his own colleague, Orin G. Libby, who promised to speak on "Physiography as a Factor in Community Life." This was hardly the tradition-shattering session that Turner had hoped for, but he took solace in the belief that the discussion would spark such interest that his fellow craftsmen would join him in appraising the role of sections in the nation's history.[50]

He was to be sadly disappointed. The papers were received with only a modicum of enthusiasm. Miss Semple indulged in overlong generalizations on geographic influences in history drawn largely from her own book, while Libby ascribed the superior culture of the Mandan Sioux to their dwelling place. The discussion that followed was even more disastrous. Professor George Lincoln Burr of Cornell University, its leader, had warned Turner that he would protest against the "misunderstanding or over rating of what calls itself 'the influence of geography on history,' " and he did so vehemently. Human action or causation, he insisted, could not be ascribed to inert objects; when historians gave nature credit for mankind's behavior they were guilty of a fallacy that injured the whole cause of history. Geographic forces might play some causal role, but this was minor; people, not physiography, determined the location of settlements in the United States. Burr's arguments were strongly backed by Henry Morse Stephens, another of Turner's close friends, and even the president of the Geographical Association refused to join the environmentalist cause, confining his remarks to pious words on interdisciplinary cooperation. There was little in that discussion to comfort Turner, let alone provide the tools and comrades needed for his assault on the secrets of sectionalism.[51] He confessed to a friend, "I haven't quite gotten sure of what I think myself on the degree of *control* of geographic factors."[52]

Nor did his second effort—aimed at enlisting the sociologists in his campaign—prove more successful. By a happy coincidence, the American Sociological Society also met in Madison that December of 1907, and Turner readily found a place on its program for a paper entitled, "Is Sectionalism in American Dying Away?" He prepared this carefully, drawing illustrations from the mountain of notes he had gathered in Washington, and incorporating the findings of a fellow historian, Allen Johnson, who had recently sent him an article on "The Nationalizing Influence of the Party."[53] Turner began, quite properly, with definitions; he identified a section as an area that resisted national uniformity, whether by formal protest or unity of opinion or combining votes in Congress; a section was also marked by "manifestations of economic and social separateness involved in the existence in a given region of a set of fundamental assumptions, a mental and emotional attitude which segregates a section from other sections or from the nation as a whole." Having thoroughly confused his listeners, Turner traced the history of sectionalism in America to illustrate the counterbalance between regionalizing and nationalizing forces. Of the latter he isolated two as particularly important—political parties, which served as bonds of union, and small subsections within the larger sections, which tended to make the large sections less stable. These forces had been bolstered in recent years by the unifying influence of industry, communications media, labor organizations, and professional associations, but despite their importance, Turner refused to concede that sectionalism was declining. Instead he saw the nation reaching a state of equilibrium, with a stabilized population pressing on the means of existence; in this condition, sectionalizing forces could operate more effectively than they did during the frontier era, when men were migratory. "National action," he warned, "will be forced to recognize and adjust itself to these conflicting sectional interests."[54]

His audience could not have disagreed with him more. In the spirited discussion that followed, sociologist after sociologist argued that sectional lines would be wiped out eventually by the same nationalizing forces that were even then destroying state lines. "My sociological

critics," Turner confessed, "pointed to tendencies toward national consolidation, to the welding together of agencies of communication,
credit, and business, and thought they found evidence that sectionalism
was doomed and that nationalism, with possible class struggles, would
replace the importance of the section."[55] This was a fair appraisal of the
reaction. Sociologists, like historians, simply were not convinced that
the section was enduring, or that it had played the role in American
history that Turner believed it had.

Turner could bow before his critics, or he could try to convince
them that they were wrong. He was far too good a scholar to doubt his
own findings; the section was important, and the historical profession
had to be awakened to its significance. This was to be his personal crusade for the remainder of his days. His duty—to his conscience and his
craft—was to produce solid research studies that would convince even the
skeptics that American history was actually the story of regional interplay.

His first opportunity came when he was invited to address the State
Historical Society of Wisconsin at its autumn meeting in 1908. The
paper that he produced for this occasion—"The Old West," he called
it—was designed as a case study of one region during the eighteenth
century. Turner saw the "Old West"—the Piedmont highlands, the Appalachian Mountain system, the interior valleys, and the New England
upland—as a single region, separated from the coastal lowlands by the
"fall line" of the rivers, and subjecting newcomers to the full impact of
a wilderness environment. His purpose was to show the manner in
which these newcomers responded to natural conditions; New Englanders and, particularly, Germans, he proved, changed little, continuing their life patterns and farming techniques in the new setting, while
southerners and the Scots-Irish adapted far more rapidly. Yet all were
altered to some degree; Palatine Germans might model their barns after
those in the old country, but they enlarged their holdings and adjusted
to large-scale agriculture; New Englanders might cling to village settlements, but the availability of cheap land bred a speculative spirit among
them no less than among southerners. Turner saw self-government and
individualism as popularized by frontier opportunity, but he saw also
that racial stocks differed in the degree to which they democratized
their institutions.

Despite the varying response of ethnic groups to the environment, the "Old West" in Turner's eyes was a distinct section, thoroughly aware of its uniqueness. This was natural; physical conditions there created a different mode of life than that of the coastal lowlands—different agricultural techniques, different governmental patterns, different religious concepts, different social pursuits. Yet Tidewater and Piedmont were united in each colony, with the Tidewater elements dominating the legislative assemblies. Here was a recipe for conflict, as the "Old West" rebelled against Tidewater control in colony after colony. Turner described these clashes in colorful prose, emphasizing especially the Regulators of the Carolinas, who took up arms against an unjust legal and tax system. The "Old West," he was saying, illustrated the whole history of American sectionalism and proved that the subject could not be ignored.[56]

His was an effective argument, for his solid research—in contrast to the unsubstantiated generalizations that marred his lectures on the significance of sections—was convincing to his fellow historians. Their praise was unstinted. Charles M. Andrews considered it one of the most suggestive papers he had ever read, opening a whole new field for interpretation and showing the insufficiency of current understanding of colonial history. "Your monograph on the Old West," wrote Albion W. Small, "makes me feel like thirty cents of which twenty-five are a lead quarter." Carl Becker confessed that his whole viewpoint on early American history was changed by reading the paper, and Max Farrand intended to build an entirely new course on its theme. "The rest of us," he assured Turner, "can potter around and contribute our mites, but you are the man to round up the whole subject." Only crotchety Edward Channing of Harvard failed to join the chorus; he noted that one of his maps of the Carolina settlements had been branded "rather conservative" and wondered testily if Turner had ever tried to draw a similar map.[57]

The essay on the "Old West" climaxed the first period of Turner's investigations into sectionalism, and foreordained his future scholarly career. Historians—and sociologists—had failed to be convinced by his generalizations, but they had warmed to his case study of one section. Hence he must adopt a different approach than the one he had used in presenting his frontier thesis. Instead of arguing for "The Significance of the Section in American History" he must prove his case by analyzing section after section, to demonstrate that the "Old West" was not unique. He must apply what he learned by investigating the inter-action of these sections throughout American history, taking up the story first where his *Rise of the New West* ended. This was the plan that shaped his research interests for the rest of his life; his detailed studies of early New England, the Mississippi Valley, and the Ohio Valley were attempts to duplicate his analysis of the "Old West," while his life-long labors on the sectional problem in the period from 1830 to 1850 were made to confound his critics by rewriting the history of an era in sectional terms. Not until 1925 did he feel that the foundation was firm enough to risk an essay on "The Significance of the Section in American History," and even this was premature. Turner's future as a scholar was firmly committed by 1910.

X

Teacher and Administrator

1901-1910

TO SURVEY the contributions made to historical studies by Frederick Jackson Turner during his years at the University of Wisconsin—the pages of well-edited documents, the procession of learned articles on diplomacy, the *Rise of the New West*, the ground-breaking investigations of sectionalism—is to conjure up a vision of a dedicated scholar, withdrawn from the practical world and closeted amidst his documents at the State Historical Society. Such was far from his fate. Like all professors, he was forced to snatch rare moments for research from the mundane duties that busied his days—and, often, his nights. Most of his time and energy went not into the investigations that he loved, but into teaching small armies of undergraduates, ministering to the needs of an ever-increasing following of graduate students, caring for the details of departmental administration, and shouldering the countless duties demanded by his position in the university.

He had little time for social activity, save that demanded by his professorship; the Turners entertained seldom unless a visiting dignitary required recognition, or the arrival or departure of a colleague called for a modest dinner party. They lived quietly in their lakefront home at 629 Frances Street, bicycling together when the weather was suitable, paddling about Lake Mendota in the canoe that was always stored on their front porch, reading before the fire in the "front room," with Turner sitting in his favorite Morris chair, puffing at his pipe or cigar.[1] Now and then Turner sought more active companionship than fragile Mae could provide; he helped organize a curling club (its members were pledged to appear on the Lake Mendota rink two afternoons a week), was a founder of a tennis club, and played an occasional game of golf.[2] Now and then, too, he and Mae spent an evening with their neighbors on Frances Street: the Charles R. Van Hises, the Moses S. Slaughters, the Charles Sumner Slichters. They made a happy company—a historian, a geologist, a Latin scholar, a mathematician—all of an age, all distinguished in their fields, all as passionately fond of camping trips and trout streams as Turner was.

They also lived well, as they strictly upheld the standards demanded of their profession—on a salary woefully inadequate to maintain those standards. Turner was relatively well paid for his day: a salary of $3500 to 1905 and $4000 thereafter, an additional $300 to $500 earned by summer-school teaching, an occasional lecture fee of $50 or $100. But costs were high, and rising. At least one maid was a necessity, both because of Mae's delicate health and because no self-respecting professor could be without servants. Their debts were a constant burden; the $5000 mortgage on their home increased rather than diminished as more borrowing went on. By 1909, Turner's indebtedness reached $10,000 and absorbed $600 yearly in interest charges. In addition, Turner had to pay premiums on life-insurance policies totaling $7000.[3] He could meet his debts only by periodic borrowing, usually a few hundred dollars backed by an insurance policy to replenish an overdrawn bank account. Mae was repeatedly warned to pay cash for nothing that could be charged, and to write no checks until the next installment of salary was deposited. "I paid lots of bills including Oppels $133+," he wrote in 1908. "We shall have the satisfaction of being poor but honest."[4]

Despite their constant flirtation with insolvency, the Turners denied themselves few pleasures that would satisfy their modest desires. Mae's expenditures for clothing inspired occasional mild admonitions, but Turner was inordinately proud of his wife and wanted her to appear at her best. She viewed his reckless purchase of books with the same mixture of disapproval and pride. So their money vanished, but there was always enough to meet some of the bills and occasionally enough to finance a wild extravagance. Such was Turner's purchase in 1908 of a Weber pianola, for the astronomical sum of $950—$150 raised by selling their old Chickering, $100 borrowed from their daughter, the rest to be paid in $25 monthly installments at 6 per cent interest. Turner forgot the belt-tightening needed to meet these payments when he fed a roll into the mechanical monster and annoyed his friends with "The First Heart Throbs" or "Life is a See Saw."[5]

They knew sadness as well as happiness. In the late spring of 1905 Turner's father, Andrew Jackson Turner, contracted pneumonia, rallied, then, on June 10, died suddenly of heart failure. All Portage, and much of the state, mourned his passing, for he was a well-loved man, but Turner mourned him most of all. He had leaned heavily on his father, for friendship and companionship on their fishing expeditions, for sound advice, for the understanding needed in time of doubt or stress. Andrew Jackson Turner's death removed a prop that his son badly needed. Less than a year later, on February 11, 1906, his mother died suddenly of heart failure, at the home of her daughter in Evanston. Only six months were to pass before Mae's mother, Lucinda Allen Sherwood, succumbed on October 22, 1906, after a brief illness.

The Turners received no substantial inheritance from any of their parents. Mae did inherit from her mother some $7000 in Madison real estate and $2340 in insurance, but Turner insisted that she use the income for her own pleasures, and not to lessen pressure on the family budget. His own father's estate amounted to only $15,400, which was divided among the three children. After persuading his younger brother Will not to invest the whole amount in get-rich-quick mining stock, Turner used his share to pay some of his debts, then borrowed his sister's $5000 to retire his mortgage, contracting to repay her in monthly installments of $75.[6]

All this took a heavy toll. Turner appeared in the best of health—he was a robust man in his forties, deeply tanned, bouncy in step—but already the succession of illnesses that were to plague his remaining years were slowing his progress. An appendectomy in 1903, performed in a Chicago hospital with enough nurses in attendance to staff a girl's boarding school (or so he reported to Dorothy), was successful, but months passed before he regained his strength. This, and the passing years, weakened his system so drastically that any sustained period of overwork caused trouble. "I have," he reported to Max Farrand in the fall of 1907, "been hard pressed to do anything but the daily routine of lectures and departmental matters, owing to a condition of half- (or quarter-) health this semester. My thinker has been in a state of mushy inactivity."[7] To make matters worse, his hearing began to fail, even to the point where he considered a hearing aid. Doctor bills were becoming sizable for the Turners, especially since Mae's hay fever showed no improvement and required expensive travel to flee from the Midwest in the late summer and autumn. There was only one remedy, and that was escape into the northern woods, fishing rod in hand. The summers of 1907 and 1908 found the three Turners and the four Van Hises traveling together to the wilds of Canada, renting canoes, hiring guides (one of them "strong as the propeller of an ocean liner") and casting forth from civilization for a blissful interlude. Turner was never happier, as he slept in the open (often in drenching rain), portaged hundred-pound packs from stream to stream, fought his way across wind-whipped lakes or through rock-strewn rapids, or pulled his canoe up a swift-running stream, surrounded by a cloud of mosquitoes.[8] One twenty-pound pickerel landed with a light rod was worth any discomfort. Those summers gave him a transfusion of energy that let him return to his labors in fighting trim.

Summer vacations, no less than bouts of illness or the luxury of a mechanical pianola, cost money, however, and Turner spent his last years in Madison ever-alert to lucrative opportunities. Fortunately, his fame as a historian was soaring, and with it a chance to supplement his regular income with lectures and summer-school teaching in a variety of institutions with salary scales superior to Wisconsin's. Why not capitalize on his prestige to spend summers in mountain areas, where his hours in the classroom would pay for even more hours of camping and trout fishing? This decision led the Turners to a roving life that they thoroughly enjoyed and that paid dividends in health, if not in dollars.

His first opportunity came in the summer of 1902. Would he be willing to give a series of lectures at the Garden of the Gods Assembly and Summer School at Colorado Springs that August? The pay would be minimal—only $100 and transportation—but it would finance a vacation in the Rocky Mountains and remove Mae from the pollen-infested Midwest during the hay fever season. This proved an unhappy bargain. The school's authorities insisted that the Turners journey westward by one rail route rather than another because the discount was greater, pressed a public lecture on Turner in addition to the eighteen he had agreed to give on "The Influence of the West upon the Nation" and "Methods of Teaching History," and then paid him only $50 of the $100 agreed upon.[9] These indignities were forgotten when Turner led Mae and Dorothy into the Rockies, there to marvel at the sight of Pike's Peak and Cripple Creek, to test his skill in swift-running trout streams near Wagon Wheel Gap, and to ride a "cow pony" deep into the wilderness for a week of sleeping beneath the stars.[10]

These pleasures meant that Turner was ready to accept any summer-school assignment that promised equal delights. No comparable offer came his way in 1903—only Cornell sought his services, and even Ithaca seemed unattractive when his friends the Slaughters offered the use of their cabin at Hancock Point, an isolated spot on the Maine coast where forest and sea met. Thence the Turner family departed that June, to spend the next months in loafing and sailing and mountain climbing— but not in writing.[11] The only untoward incident of the summer occurred in Madison, where their house tenants managed to set fire to a waste basket, starting a blaze that made some headway when the fire engines were delayed by an unpaved street.[12] Damage was slight, however. The Turners returned to Madison that fall with renewed energy.

They were soon on their way east again, this time for a longer and more significant stay. Harvard University was their destination. Negotiations that led to this appointment began in the winter of 1902, when President Charles W. Eliot inquired whether Turner would be interested in a one-semester appointment as replacement for an absent faculty member. Turner decided he would be, when assured that the "modern history" mentioned by President Eliot could be American history, and that he could offer the "History of the West." Negotiations almost broke down when a salary of $1500 was mentioned; Turner pointed out that he was earning more than this at Madison and must have at least $2000 to offset travel costs. This was agreed upon, but only with the understanding that Turner help Albert Bushnell Hart teach a seminar on "American History and Institutions." He would also offer a course on "Selected Topics in the Historical Development of American Institutions"—a high-flown title designed to lure a few advanced undergraduates into study of the politics of Monroe's presidency.[13] These details settled, the contract was signed; Turner would teach the two courses agreed upon and aid in Hart's seminar for the second semester of the 1903-4 academic year with a salary of $2000.[14]

The Turners left for Cambridge early in February 1904, happy to be leaving behind them one of the coldest Madison winters in years. They settled comfortably into a rented house at 5 Craigie Street, only a short distance from Harvard Yard. He was welcomed royally, with a round of luncheons and dinners climaxed by a banquet given by James Ford Rhodes at the Examinar Club, "with wine in all kinds of glasses." An extraordinary dinner it was, with Cotuit oysters served with a Chablis, clear green turtle soup with an Amontillado, soft-shelled crabs in horse radish sauce with a Chateau Yquem, cutlets of spring lamb á la Maison Dorèe with a Corte Blauche, frozen Tom and Jerry, roast larded squabs with a Pommard champagne, bombe glacée, fruit, Camembert and Roquefort cheese, ripe olives, and coffee.[15] Madison offered nothing like this.

If this extravagant reception could not turn Turner's head, neither could the modest response to his course offerings. His "Wild West Show," as his friends called it, was smaller than he had expected, while only a handful were attracted by his other classes. Those who did elect his "History of the West" were treated to precious little about the "West"; not until April 13 did he arrive at the end of the eighteenth century in his lectures, and not until May 2 did he close the War of 1812 and begin a discussion of sectional problems that lasted to the end of the month, leaving him only three days to settle the trans-Mississippi West.[16] Undergraduates who expected a glamorous dose of "cowboys and Indians" were disappointed, but they did receive a generous lesson on early expansion and a healthy amount of frontier theory.

Turner embraced Cambridge that spring with somewhat less enthusiasm than Cambridge embraced him. He never felt quite at home there; "I am in the midst of a little too much Harvard to be really homelike," he confessed.[17] He enjoyed the companionship: a May weekend with Albert Bushnell Hart at his New Hampshire summer home, where the two climbed Mount Monadnock; faculty dinners; a doctoral examination in the rooms of Professor Roger B. Merriman, where cold tea was served and the examiners passed a mediocre candidate because they could not bear to think of tears in his pretty wife's eyes. Turner was proud of an invitation to address the Graduate History Club and delighted that "they were polite enough to seem pleased with my account of French *designs*." He was satisfied with the chorus of farewells when time for departure arrived, a chorus joined by the entire history faculty save Edward Channing, who could say nothing more flattering than, "We remember your stay in Cambridge with interest."[18] Yet Turner was not sorry to board the train for Madison that June, "Harvard," he reported to a friend, "has behaved with the discretion and reticence of a New England maiden of two and a half centuries."[19] Boston's chilling social atmosphere was no substitute for the enthusiasm and get-up-and-go spirit that he knew in the Midwest.

Nor did he find the West Coast completely satisfying when he first went there. He had agreed to teach a six-week session at the University of California at Berkeley in the summer of 1904, offering two courses on "The Beginnings of the West" and "The Teaching of American History" plus a seminar on the diplomacy of Monroe's administrations, for a salary of $750. His students may have been disappointed when they found that the West began at Jamestown rather than the Pecos River, and Turner himself was depressed by the condescending attitude of faculty members to the Midwest (Californians recognized only Asia, Boston, and San Francisco, he found, and would send their students to Harvard or Yale but never Wisconsin), but he and Mae and Dorothy thoroughly enjoyed themselves. Best of all was the pack trip into the High Sierra as soon as the last class was over, there to cast for trout in the icy streams near Lake Tahoe and to camp for weeks in the shadow of the snow-clad peaks.[20] That summer Turner began a love affair with the Sierra Nevadas that lasted the rest of his life.

So it was that when Berkeley beckoned again, Turner responded—this time in the summer of 1906—agreeing to offer two courses on "The Advance of the Frontier" and "The Presidencies of Monroe and John Quincy Adams" for a $750 salary and the chance to renew his romance with the high mountain country. This time he and his family journeyed westward by the southern route, stopping to view the wonders of the Grand Canyon ("We saw the world made at sunrise yesterday," he reported), mixing teaching with visits to the experimental farm where Luther Burbank was performing his miracles with hybrid plants, attending the famed "High Jinks" of San Francisco's Bohemian Club in its grove of giant redwoods near the city. Once more the Turners disappeared into the High Sierra as soon as summer school was over, establishing themselves in the Lake Tahoe country, where Turner experienced one of his greatest thrills when he landed a Loch Levin trout fifteen inches long.[21] By September 22 he was back in Madison, after a stopover with relatives in Omaha. "I am now," he reported, "making exploratory casts with the fountain pen but there isn't a good ripple in the ink."[22]

These were happy interludes as well as needed restoratives for Turner's health, but they were only pauses in the busy academic life that began with classes each fall. Most of his time from that moment forward was already spoken for by the demands of the classroom and departmental administration, for there was little opportunity for play in the schedule of a truly dedicated college teacher. Nine-tenths of Turner's waking hours went not into research or trout fishing, but into instruction and efforts to improve the University of Wisconsin and its educational standards. This was his duty; Turner was emerging as his university's best-known and most influential professor. He had to use his position to assure Wisconsin the leadership it deserved, to build a strong history department, and to train the graduate students who would preach his doctrines. These were objectives no less important than popularizing the sectional concept.

His opportunity to secure strong leadership for the university came in October 1901, when President Charles Kendall Adams resigned because of poor health. Adams's logical successor was Dean Edward A. Birge of the College of Letters and Science, a respected zoologist, a brilliant teacher, and a capable administrator who had proven himself by running the university well during President Adams's illness. Moreover, Birge made no secret of his desire to be elected, and most of the faculty accepted his nomination as a matter of course. Not so Turner and a handful of his friends. They liked Birge but were fearful that he was too unimaginative to build in the traditions of John Bascom, T. C. Chamberlin, and Charles K. Adams, too immersed in petty details to provide the bold leadership necessary to create a really great university. Birge could be defeated, Turner realized, only if a rival candidate entered the field. He was not willing to offer himself, although he was proposed as a candidate;[23] his own choice was his Frances Street neighbor, Charles R. Van Hise. Turner's role, as he saw it, was to serve as campaign manager for Van Hise, converting the faculty, button-holing regents, and swaying popular opinion to his choice. His two assistant managers were readily enlisted—Moses S. Slaughter, his next-door neighbor, and Charles S. Slichter, whose home was directly across the street from his and next to that of Van Hise.[24]

The "Frances Street Cabal," as they were called, worked effectively, marshalling their forces during the months that the regents canvassed the national scene in a quest for an outsider worthy of the post. Turner carried the major burden. He worked first with Emil Baensch of Milwaukee, president of the Wisconsin Press Association and a major power in Progressive Republican circles, who could influence the state's editors and serve as a pipeline to Governor Robert M. La Follette, then with two of his friends on the regents' selections committee, James C. Kerwin and Arthur J. Puls. Kerwin was particularly cooperative, meeting with Turner in clandestine sessions where he was briefed on arguments needed to convert his fellow committeemen: that choosing a professor from outside the state would be to admit that Wisconsin had none of equal merit; that selecting a president from another university would be unwise, for none of proper excellence would leave his own school; that naming a business leader or a politician would inflict on Wisconsin a man who lacked the university point of view. Nor would Birge do; under his leadership, Turner warned, "we are drifting with the current, taking whatever direction the wind blows, and we are losing ground in competition with other universities. We take second-hand ideas and simply live from hand to mouth."[25] Van Hise alone would provide the imaginative leadership needed.

The majority of the regents were still not convinced, but Van Hise's strength mounted so steadily that by July 1902 the field had narrowed to two men: Van Hise or Henry S. Pritchett, president of the Massachusetts Institute of Technology. A month later Van Hise's selection seemed so certain that a Milwaukee newspaper announced his election. This proved premature; the regents' committee was so hopelessly divided that in April 1903 it reported that no decision could be reached. Instead of naming a new committee, the board took matters into its own hands. A motion to elect Van Hise was made, briefly debated, and voted upon, with ten in favor, three opposed, and one abstaining.[26] Turner had played his role of "King Maker" to its climax.

He must have taken satisfaction that night when he watched from the windows of his home as two thousand students paraded to the Van Hise home, listened to their new president speak briefly on the responsibilities of his post, and heard him saluted by what must be ranked as the most unusual college yell ever to honor a college head:

> Hematite, Biotite, Sis Boom Bah
> C. R. Van Hise Rah Rah Rah

Turner could well be proud, for Van Hise was to earn a place among the greatest university presidents. A top-ranking geologist, he was also a humanist with an awareness of social problems that made him both a center of controversy and a powerful force for good. He saw the university as an arm of the state, to be used to achieve justice for all, extend learning, and conserve natural resources against the inroads of corporate wealth or private monopoly. These were views that hardly endeared him to the large business interests represented within the Stalwart wing of the Republican party, but they won him the support of Progressive Republicans and of most of the faculty.

Turner had indoctrinated the new president with many of his social opinions, and he underlined them again when he spoke at Van Hise's inauguration. The university, Turner declared, existed by the bounty of the state to serve all its people in an atmosphere of learning; it could best do so by training young men and women "to aid in the work of giving intellectual and moral power and high ideals to this vast industrial democracy." Van Hise responded to this challenge magnificently. His inaugural address was a plea for pure research in the humanities and social sciences. A professor could perform no more valuable service for mankind than "his own creative work and the production of new scholars in the laboratory and seminary." "Practical" considerations should be ignored, for no one knew what would be practical in the future; "there is no investigation of matter or force of mind today in progress, but tomorrow may become of inestimable practical value."[27] These were heretical views in a state that saw farmers and engineers as the most useful products of its university, but Turner and his faculty friends were jubilant.

Now the way was clear to build a notable university and a distinguished history department. Turner's advantageous offer from the University of Chicago in 1900 authorized him to establish a School of History independent of the School of Economics, Political Science and History; he was also empowered to select a new assistant professor of American history to supplement the work given by Orin G. Libby and himself, and to hire an instructor in European history to aid Charles H. Haskins and Victor Coffin. George C. Sellery, then completing his doctoral work at the University of Chicago, was chosen for the latter post, but searching out a young man in American history demanded greater effort. Turner spent hours seeking advice from leading authorities before compiling a list of candidates. On it were many of the future shining lights of the profession: Arthur Lyon Cross, Carl Russell Fish, Charles E. Merriam, Carl Becker, and others of only slightly less stature. In the end he chose Fish, then a teaching assistant at Harvard, largely because of enthusiastic recommendations from both Albert Bushnell Hart and J. Franklin Jameson, who had taught the young man as an undergraduate at Brown University. Fish was, Jameson promised, "a really brilliant young man" who saw the West "with the eyes of Hart rather than with the eyes of Channing." This was enough to prompt an offer of an instructorship at $1000 a year, which Fish accepted.[28] The history department, reported the student humor magazine, promised sumptuous repasts with Fish and Sellery for the beginning courses.[29]

Turner had assembled a galaxy of greats and near-greats in his first effort at department-building, but he was to find that the more talented the appointee, the more attractive he was to other institutions. He learned this lesson first from his closest friend, Charles Homer Haskins, when Harvard beckoned with a professorship at $3000 and the promise of $3500 three years hence. Cambridge offered one thing that Madison did not—a good library in medieval history—and Haskins reluctantly decided to accept.[30] "We are all in the dumps," wrote Turner. "It is like breaking up the family."[31] Haskins's replacement proved easy to find, for Haskins himself had a candidate in Dana C. Munro of the University of Pennsylvania. Munro was so doubtful that he balked at coming west for an interview, but he finally succumbed in March 1902. Two weeks later his appointment was announced, with a salary of $3000 and a reputation that the local press was already trumpeting as greater than Haskins's.[32] His arrival allowed a reshuffling of departmental offerings, with medieval history replacing ancient as the required freshman course and modern European history demanded of all sophomores.

It also encouraged Turner to undertake a major revision of the American history staff and offerings. For some time the conviction had been growing that Orin G. Libby must be sacrificed to progress; he was not an easy lecturer, was too specialized to fit well into a superior graduate department, and was lacking in tact and a cooperative spirit; too, his interest in sectionalism duplicated Turner's growing involvement in that field. Worst of all was Libby's increasing tendency to substitute bird-watching for scholarship; he organized a local Audubon Society, lectured widely on migration patterns, gave learned papers on such subjects as "The Nocturnal Flight of Migrating Birds," and spent his Saturdays leading tours for his fellow fanatics rather than working in the State Historical Society library.[33] Such a dilettante had no place in a professionalized department, and Turner did the obvious. His enthusiastic letters of recommendation, stressing Libby's desire to leave because his work was too specialized (a sentiment that Libby hardly shared), brought an offer of an assistant professorship at the University of North Dakota. Thence he departed in the summer of 1902.[34]

Here was Turner's chance not only to make a strong appointment but to create a unique department. He had already indicated its direction when announcing the establishment of the School of History; "Particular attention," this proclaimed, "is given to the study of the evolution of the various sectional groupings—social, economic, and political—in the history of the United States, and to physiographic factors in American development."[35] Now this promise could be fulfilled. Carl Russell Fish had the proper background and interest to offer a course on the "History of New England" to supplement that of Turner on the West. All that was needed was a specialist in southern history, and Turner had just the man in mind. Ulrich B. Phillips, Georgia-born and -bred, a student of William A. Dunning at Columbia, where his doctoral dissertation on "Georgia and State Rights" had captured the coveted Winsor Prize of the American Historical Association, had already attracted Turner's attention as a member of his class during a summer-school teaching stint at the University of Chicago. That brief association led to mutual admiration; Phillips was high on Turner's list of young-men-worth-watching, while Phillips found in Turner's views an inspiration for his whole thesis, as he acknowledged with lavish praise in its preface. Turner was all but committed before he began his quest, but when Dunning heaped unstinted praise on his young protégé, the decision was made. Would Phillips accept an instructorship at $800 a year?[36] Phillips accepted, and joined the faculty in the fall of 1902. He offered only introductory courses at first, but in 1903-4 he introduced his course on "The History of the South."

With his staff assembled, Turner was able to announce the curriculum of his dreams. The introductory work was shifted to his new appointees; Fish and Phillips combined to offer a year course in colonial history, while the beginning survey course (divided now at Jackson's presidency rather than 1812) was in Fish's capable hands. Both offered advanced work in diplomatic history, the economic and social history of the United States, and the usual undergraduate and graduate seminars. The heart of the curriculum, however, was in the regional courses given by the three Americanists: Turner (a westerner) on the West, Fish (a New Englander) on New England, Phillips (a southerner) on the South. Here was a unique array—a cooperative attempt to shed light on the basic forces that Turner believed had shaped the nation's past.[37] If the frontier and the section attracted the attention he believed they would, Wisconsin would be better equipped to train graduate students than any university in the United States.

These rosy dreams were never quite realized. Neither the sectional concept nor the regional studies needed to sustain it rivaled in popularity the frontier thesis, despite all of Turner's propagandizing. Instead, the trend in most universities seemed to be toward topical courses—on diplomacy, economic history, social history, and the like—or chronological courses, covering the colonial era, the Civil War period, or recent events. Eventually Wisconsin was forced to fall into line, abandoning its stress on regionalism to conform to the national pattern.

One reason for this change was the difficulty of holding the stellar performers. Carl Russell Fish was offered a Harvard instructorship as early as 1902; only an assistant professorship kept him loyal to Wisconsin. A year later Bryn Mawr sought his services, but this time Fish decided for prestige rather than more salary and again elected to remain. Phillips was also restive in 1903, for he was conscious that his $800 was less than he deserved, and he was only kept happy with a $100 increase. A double blow fell in 1907 when Fish was nominated to succeed Henry Morse Stephens at Amherst College and the University of North Carolina offered Phillips the headship of its department at $600 more than the $1400 then paid by Wisconsin. Persuasion and slight salary increases frustrated the raiders, but not for long. When Harvard in 1908 sought Fish for a temporary position that held some promise of permanence, he was so sorely tempted that only a full professorship kept him happy. Phillips was less easy to please. He was eager to return to his native South, and when Tulane University sought him as chairman of its department, he succumbed.[38] At the end of the 1907-8 academic year he packed his bags, leaving Turner's triumvirate of regionalists broken—never to be restored.

Turner made an effort to replace Phillips with another historian of the South, but when William E. Dodd of the University of Chicago showed no inclination to leave the Midway and letters of inquiry to major history departments unearthed no candidate worthy of the post, he decided to seek a colonialist and rely on occasional lecturers to enlighten students on southern history. This proved easier. The University of Pennsylvania offered a candidate in Winfred T. Root, who stood head and shoulders above others recommended, a judgment that was sustained when Turner found himself competing with Dartmouth and Princeton for the young man's services. Quick action by the administration brought Root to Madison as a $1200-a-year instructor in the fall of 1908. At the same time, Alfred H. Stone, a southern planter and self-functioning historian of the South and of race problems who had been lecturing at the University of Chicago, was imported to give a course and seminar on southern history for the second semester of the 1908-9 academic year.[39] Turner wanted to have his cake and eat it too.

European history demanded equal attention, and received it. George C. Sellery proved just as attractive to competing universities as the Americanists; Berkeley tried to hire him away in 1906 with an associate professorship at $2400, but the heartfelt pleas of Turner and Munro, a jump in salary to $1800, and the directorship of the summer school at $500 kept him in Madison. Such men could be retained in the future, Turner realized, only by lightening their teaching loads; while the university grew by one-half between 1903 and 1906, enrollment in history courses leaped two-thirds, much of it in the lower division courses, which were taught largely by Europeanists. These figures gave him an irresistible weapon, and his demand for a larger staff produced results. In 1905 he was authorized to add Alfred L. P. Dennis of the University of Chicago as a professor in European history with a salary of $2500 and generous appropriations to buy books in his period. William L. Westermann came in 1908 to teach the ancient history courses; a year later Herbert C. Bell was lured from the University of Pennsylvania, where he was completing his graduate work in French history. Wayland J. Chase also joined the department as a joint appointee with the School of Education; he taught the teaching of history.[40]

By 1910, when Turner left the University of Wisconsin, he had assembled a galaxy of historians who ranked among the finest in the nation. His own studies in frontier and sectional history had already elevated him to the pinnacle of his profession. Carl Russell Fish, although he never blossomed into the authority on New England that Turner hoped he would be, was winning fame for his published works on diplomacy and the Civil War, and for his skill as a lecturer. Winfred T. Root occupied a respectable spot in the hierarchy of colonialists, although his publications record was less than spectacular. In European history, Dana C. Munro's work on the Crusades made Madison a national center for medieval economic studies. George C. Sellery was attracting attention as a brilliant teacher in the field of Renaissance history and as co-author with Monro of a widely used book, *Medieval Civilization*. Victor Coffin, although more inclined to publish manuals and popularized narratives than learned monographs, was well known as a student of the French Revolution. Alfred L. P. Dennis published little while at Wisconsin, but he was recognized as an expert in British foreign relations. William L. Westermann had yet to make his reputation as one of the country's leading classicists, but he was becoming known through his articles on early slavery and the economic history of the Mediterranean basin. Even Wayland J. Chase, although doomed to teach the teaching of history, had scholarly inclinations and was acknowledged to be a capable scholar in the history of ancient and medieval education. The editor of the *Review of Reviews* was not overly wrong when he judged that, at Wisconsin, students "found the very best facilities to be had anywhere for advanced work in American institutional history,"[41] and that their contemporaries in European history were only slightly less favored.

Nor was there any question that Turner had wrought this miracle. True, he had had excellent advice from Munro and the hearty support of the Van Hise administration, but it was Turner who initiated all inquiries, wrote the endless letters needed to seek out the best candidates, suggested the terms needed to capture a new instructor, and made the final decisions. He was a dedicated chairman, firm in the belief that a superior department was as much an accomplishment as a superior book

—and somewhat easier to achieve. His duties were never done, whether spending hours listening to the advice of colleagues and complaints of students, or drafting the innumerable letters that were a chairman's lot, or battling the administration for the funds that would keep his charges contented. Even when he was on leave, the pace continued; during the spring of 1907, when supposedly concentrating on research in Washington, he besieged the temporary chairman, A. L. P. Dennis, with a barrage of daily suggestions and demands. "If we keep this up," wrote Dennis ruefully, "we will have a fat volume of correspondence for the records of the department."[42] Nor could Turner relinquish the helm when Dennis a short time later assumed the official title of chairman. His constant "suggestions"—"I recommend the appointment of So-and-So" (when he had already made the appointment), or "I suggest an appropriation of Such-and-Such" (when he had already made all arrangements with the administration)—left Dennis little to do but rubber-stamp decisions in which he had no part. Turner might be "King Maker" for the university, but he was "King" in his own department, with no nonsense about faculty democracy to curb his powers.

There was nothing selfish in this autocracy. Turner had only two great passions: to understand the past, and to share that understanding with mankind. His own studies were important, but no less important was the training of teachers and scholars who could preach the gospel. His crowning ambition was a department of history that would attract the cream of America's would-be historians, then equip them to carry on the crusade with the same fervor that sustained their instructors. Formal courses taught by the best teachers were needed, but more was required. Turner's desire to provide superior training for his graduate students inspired two additional steps on his part, both time-consuming. One was to direct a steady flow of guest lecturers to Madison; the other, to build a summer session for historical investigation that would lure mature students from the college and university faculties of all the West for refresher courses that would make them more effective propagandists for history.

The lecturers he provided in abundance. Not a year passed but a distinguished scholar was in residence, usually giving a course of six to eight lectures, for an attractive fee that ranged from $200 to $400. To list his guest speakers is to catalogue the eminent historians of that generation—Henry Morse Stephens, William P. Trent, J. R. Jewett, James

Harvey Robinson, Andrew C. McLaughlin, Ettore Pais of the University of Naples, Max Farrand, J. Franklin Jameson, Paul Vinogradoff, Albert Bushnell Hart. Turner chose well, and his visitors provided the graduate students with a rich and varied fare, ranging from "The Social Compact in American History" to "The Rise, Progress, and Significance of Mohammedanism."

He was even more concerned with the excellence of the summer-school offerings. One of Turner's fixed purposes was to create in Madison "a summer center for historical investigation, partly in connection with formal courses, and partly independent of them." This was essential; unless Wisconsin acted, the University of Chicago's excellent offerings would lure the best students, many of whom would stay there to complete their doctoral work. Wisconsin could compete only by improving its own program, giving more advanced work, and advertising the research opportunities offered by the State Historical Society library.[43] Turner practiced what he preached by teaching in the summer session whenever he was not attracted elsewhere; this meant devoting long hours to his courses for a pittance of a salary, when he would have preferred to concentrate on his scholarly investigations. When he could not be in Madison to fill the American history position, he saw to it that someone of comparable worth was recruited in his place: Max Farrand, Andrew C. McLaughlin, George P. Garrison, and Claude H. Van Tyne were all pressed into service. They were chosen partly because Turner saw them, correctly, as rising stars in the historical constellation, partly because their specialities were not regularly taught at Wisconsin, and would broaden the students' knowledge.

This same desire to elevate the tone of history teaching decreed that his interest in secondary education should continue unabated—and that an undue proportion of his time should be squandered on largely indifferent high school teachers. A constant stream of letters from teachers seeking advice flowed across his desk, and all were answered, often at great length. How could American history best be taught in a grammar school? One could use either the "concentric circles" approach, where the whole study was told three times in the first eight grades in varying degrees of depth, or the "cultural period" technique that encouraged the child to build an Indian wigwam or a medieval castle, as his abilities decreed. Turner preferred a combination of the two, and bolstered his judgment with a bibliography that filled page after page.

What was the best method of instruction for fourth-year American history? That question inspired six pages of sound advice, including a careful weighing of the "topical method" against the use of a standard textbook. Where did American history belong in the high school curriculum? In the senior year, because the course was primarily useful in sharpening political judgments and should be taught to mature students. Should the recent past be emphasized? By all means, for there was no better training for citizenship than understanding the elements of the past that were pertinent to the present.[44] So went the advice, in letter after letter. So often was Turner asked for the best books to be used in high school instruction that he prepared a six-page typed list of "Books for a High School Library in American History" that was broadcast wholesale.[45]

Turner's prominence also meant that he was constantly in demand by professional teachers' organizations. He regularly attended meetings of the Wisconsin State Teachers Association and the Wisconsin Teachers Institute, addressing their conventions on "The Teaching of History" or "Essentials in American History." "Advocated more time in history," wrote the secretary of one in summarizing his remarks.[46] Local associations were just as bold in pressing him into service, for talks on "American History in the Public Schools," or "Probable Results of the New Emphasis Placed on History in the High Schools." On a larger scale, he headed a committee of the Wisconsin State Teachers Association in 1903 to plan a high school curriculum that would allot adequate space to history, and for a time he served as an elected member of the six-man Madison School Board.[47] Such was Turner's recognition as an authority on secondary-school history teaching that he was asked in 1902 to lead a discussion of "The Study of History" before the national meeting of the Society for the Scientific Study of Education.[48] Faint honors, perhaps, but they underlined the fact that Turner's commitment to history teaching—on all levels of instruction—was unrivaled.

His purpose, or much of it, was to convert the University of Wisconsin into a mecca that no graduate student in history could resist, and here he succeeded admirably. In his early teaching years he had helped train a truly remarkable group of scholars, including many who were now advancing to the top of the profession, but most had entered his classes as undergraduates more by accident than design and had received their graduate training elsewhere. Now his fame, and the fame of the department, was spreading. Madison was a magnet for an ever-growing number of would-be historians from throughout the West, and even from the eastern seaboard, who came deliberately to study with Turner and his colleagues, sure that advanced degrees from such giants would lead to productive careers in research and the most advantageous academic posts. Each went forth to found his own historical colony, there to recruit still younger students for Wisconsin. Seldom has a teacher, or a department, served so many so well; by the time of World War I, Turner-taught professors or their disciples came close to dominating the profession. "Out of his seminar at Madison," wrote one, "have come almost all of the men who are today reinterpreting American history from the new viewpoint first established by this pioneering scholar."[49]

Why this popularity? What made Turner the premier graduate instructor of his generation? Partly responsible, of course, were the views that he was expounding; the frontier and sectional concepts were new and exciting, a welcome relief from the institutional studies that dominated teaching in a prior generation. Turner offered students not only challenging new trails to follow, but an interpretation of the past that had a persuasive appeal. None thought to question his basic assumptions or challenge the validity of his interpretations—that would come later. Now they joyfully embarked on their explorations, confident that their discoveries would add substance to theories that explained the American past.

Turner's ideas were alluring, but the students who sought his instruction were also attracted by tales of his skill as a teacher—tales that followed the academic grapevine to every corner of the land. He saw the function of the graduate instructor as not to encourage narrow specialization, but to deepen and broaden the student's knowledge and experience. They should be encouraged to read in every field of learning, from the arts to the sciences, and to apply what they learned to historical problems; historians should read history, he counseled only half facetiously, when they were too tired for anything else. Only in this way would their imaginations be stirred, and new vistas open before them. Turner likened the graduate school years to preparation for a voyage of discovery, where the crew learned to navigate and handle the ropes, ready to journey to undiscovered lands. They must be ready to sail boldly before the wind, alert always to hazards that might wreck their vessel, but scorning a course that was slow and safe. They were adventurers, and must find excitement in their venturing. Enthusiasm, given and received, was as much a part of graduate education as learning.[50] Turner fastened the eyes of his students on far horizons, and gave them the courage and skills needed to reach their goals.

These were the views that lured would-be historians from all the land to his seminar. This met weekly in the sumptuous new State Historical Society library on the lower campus, surrounded by the reference books needed to settle any dispute. Candidates were carefully screened to eliminate those who might slow the pace, but they were still embarrassingly numerous; twice Turner admitted twelve, although he usually was able to draw the line at nine or ten.[51] All were set to work on problems geared to Turner's current research interest: the diplomacy of the Mississippi Valley at first, then the Monroe presidency while the *Rise of the New West* was taking shape, and, after 1906, the Jackson and Van Buren administrations. Within these periods each student could select his own topic, so long as it was related to the others. One year, for example, each was assigned three states and asked to show how their internal history mirrored the national scene; again, the focus might be on the first few months of the Van Buren administration. "We spent the year getting him elected," wrote one student.[52]

Turner talked on methodology while the students' papers were being prepared, then the reports began. Each was given the time needed; one, two, or even four two-hour sessions might be allotted a student. Through them all Turner listened intently, pencil poised to jot down a note or a suggestion for improvement; members of his seminar judged the success of their papers by the number of notes that he took. This was a heady experience for the novice historian—the undivided attention of one of the nation's greatest scholars. They were suddenly important, providing Turner with new facts or fresh insights and making their contribution to the world's knowledge. Nor was this a pose on Turner's part. When asked whether he really learned from student reports, he looked surprised and answered, "Why, of course I do."[53] The dozens of pages of notes he took on such occasions (now scattered through his files) testify to the accuracy of that statement.

Turner was a master graduate teacher simply because he was not a teacher at all, but a fellow explorer whose excitement over each new discovery matched that of the discoverer. Never did he inflict his will on his students; he considered their interpretations to be as correct as his own if their methods and sources bore scrutiny. On the rare occasions when he did take exception to an interpretation, he did so gently, probing delicately until the student realized his own error. "By well-directed questions," wrote one after such a session, "he is able to make a person feel cheap for not seeing points that later seem obvious."[54] Turner could ask questions, but never would he answer one. His seminar never found out whether he thought Andrew Jackson's policies good or bad, whether he felt the states had a right to secede, whether he believed the protective tariff was right or wrong. He knew that there was no one truth, and that each student must supply his own answers. Turner treated his students as equals, even while directing their courses. Nothing could have been more flattering—or a greater incentive to be worthy of that equality.

All of this took a great deal of time. Turner himself had to prepare each topic, for he had to read almost as widely as his students did in order to be able to understand and criticize their work. Even when engaged in his own research, the needs of his students were always in mind; he did less writing than expected while at the Library of Congress in 1907, he told a friend, because he could not resist the Jackson and Van Buren manuscripts there when he thought of the seminar on Van Buren's administration he was to give that fall.[55] Each spring he spent hours in screening candidates for admission to the graduate school or for the few scholarships available. No other task took more of Turner's time, and none gave him greater satisfaction; week after week was sacrificed to the ever-growing stack of applications or to a careful reading of the essays and term papers that accompanied them. They pursued him to Washington in 1907, where hours that might have been spent on research were squandered on studying the records of the next year's applicants and writing ten letters on ten successive days—one of them ten pages long—urging his views on the department.[56]

Turner was always ready to fight for his charges. He was perennially dissatisfied that the university allowed the history department only two $400 fellowships, and that the faculty normally granted it funds for only one additional fellowship from the general fellowship funds. This might have been justified, he pointed out vehemently in 1905, if all departments attracted candidates of equal quality, but history's were superior in numbers and merit, and should have a larger share of the pie. Fourteen highly qualified persons had applied for the American history fellowship, all with at least two years of graduate training, many with publications, and most from such respectable institutions as Michigan, Texas, Cornell, and Radcliffe. The system must be changed to allot grants to departments with the best applicants, or the number of fellowships must be radically increased.[57] Turner lost that battle, but his loyalty to his students did not go unnoticed.

That loyalty paid handsome dividends in the superior candidates who earned their doctoral degrees under his direction. Simply to list a few is to underline two things: that Turner had a hand in training a sizable proportion of the historical greats of the next generation, and that he allowed them free rein in selecting their dissertation subjects. Such a list also demonstrates that most of the theses written under his supervision were good enough to publish:

> Joseph Schafer, "The Acquisition of Oregon by the United States."
> Royal B. Way, "Internal Improvements in the United States, 1817-1829."
> Carl Becker, "History of Political Parties in the Province of New York, 1760-1776."
> Charles H. Ambler, "Sectionalism in Virginia, 1787-1860."
> Amelia C. Ford, "Colonial Precedents of the National Land System."
> William V. Pooley, "The Settlement of Illinois, 1830-1850."
> Arthur C. Boggess, "Immigration to Illinois before 1831."
> William J. Trimble, "Mining Advance into the Inland Empire."
> Benjamin H. Hibbard, "The History of Agriculture in Dane County."
> Lewis H. Haney, "Congressional History of Railways."
> John L. Conger, "Nullification in South Carolina."

Such a sampling proves Turner a busy man, and a man of broad interests. An instructor who could supervise master's theses on "The Hawaiian Revolution of 1892" and "The Causes of the Transfer of Literary Supremacy from New York to New England about 1830" was certainly not riding his own hobby horse to death.

The catholicity of Turner's historical interests was nowhere better shown than in his advice to would-be doctoral candidates on suitable dissertation topics. To one he suggested a study of territorial governments revealing the social and economic forces underlying their behavior, an investigation of the reasons for emigration to the United States from one European country, the socio-economic development of any one immigrant group within this nation, some topic within the unexplored history of public lands, the role of a major railroad in encouraging and shaping westward expansion, the exploration of Populist sentiment to decide the importance of local conditions in agrarian unrest, or antislavery agitation in Nebraska, which Turner suspected was as important as that in Kansas. To another he proposed the decline of the New England Federalists after 1812, political aspects of the conflict over Church-State relations in New York or New England, the history of migration from any one New England state before the Civil War, and the history of banking or internal improvements in the Jackson administrations.[58] These were sensible suggestions, and penetrating as well.

They were also time-consuming subjects, for Turner felt that he could criticize a thesis intelligently only by familiarizing himself with the subject almost as thoroughly as its author had. Much of each spring went into that preparation as a prelude to the manuscripts that weighted his desk when the dissertations were submitted. These were read slowly, carefully, critically, each in two or three versions as it approached acceptability; each reading was followed with a long letter of criticism and advice. Then, with the thesis accepted, came the examinations: two long written papers on medieval and modern European history, one on the whole scope of American history, and an oral examination of several hours' duration, concentrating on the special field of the candidate. Those examination rooms were torture-chambers for the examiners no less than the victim, as they sat day after day asking their questions, or day-dreaming of Lake Mendota when other inquisitors took up the burden. Doctoral orals, master's orals, undergraduate honors orals—they went on in merciless procession as commencement day approached.[59]

The sense of relief that Turner must have experienced when that bedlam ended each spring was short-lived, for his obligations to his graduate students did not diminish with their doctorates. Nearly all wanted to publish their dissertations; this meant reading revised manuscripts and interceding with prospective publishers, who sometimes proved reluctant to risk printing the technical monographs that Turner sponsored. Charles H. Ambler's study of sectionalism in Virginia ran the gamut of commercial houses, from Macmillan down, before it was finally accepted, and the fate of most of them was not far different.[60] Articles drawn from theses took more of Turner's time, for each new graduate was unsure of himself and sought the advice of his mentor before risking the judgment of a journal editor. But worst of all were the efforts needed to place each new doctor in a proper academic post —and keep him there in spite of his own faults.

To re-tell the story of Turner's valiant labors in behalf of his candidates would require far more pages than anyone would care to read. He was a master at the art of letter writing, skillfully blending sufficient honesty to create an illusion of impartiality with degrees of praise that correctly mirrored the ability of the candidate. When he told a prospective employer that Charles H. Ambler showed exceptional promise and unusual ability, Ambler got the job. When he confessed to the University of Chicago that Laurence M. Larson bore "the scars of his country training" and might not fit into the urban scene, or when he admitted to the Massachusetts Institute of Technology that Benjamin H. Hibbard was insufficiently experienced in a city environment to be at home in Boston, Larson and Hibbard failed to land the posts, but Chicago and the Institute were convinced of Turner's honesty and could be counted on to take his word when he had a proper candidate for their departments.[61]

Normally such recommendations placed a student in a teaching position that he could hold until he was ready to advance a step on the academic ladder, but every professor has been burdened with some who show an uncanny ability to displease employers, and Turner was no exception. His files bulge with letters written in behalf of students who drifted from school to school (and required a dozen recommendations yearly to win each new post) or who felt themselves superior to the second-rate institution employing them (which they were not) and asked that he write again and again in their behalf. One, however, cost Turner endless hours of letter writing—and was worth it. His heroic efforts in behalf of Carl Becker saved for history one of the discipline's greatest scholars.

Becker earned his undergraduate degree at Wisconsin in 1896, and his master's two years later. Then, on Turner's recommendation, he transferred to Columbia, where he fell under the spell of Herbert L. Osgood and James Harvey Robinson. One year later financial pressures forced him to enter teaching, still without his doctorate. His appearance was against him; he was small and slight, and his country background made him ill at ease at social gatherings. Even worse, he was so retiring that he was dominated by his students. These handicaps doomed him to an almost perpetual job quest until he could prove himself intellectually. He tried first at Pennsylvania State College, then, through Turner's influence, moved to Dartmouth College, where the unruly New Englanders made his life a perpetual misery. In 1902 Becker moved again, to Kansas, after Turner tried in vain to win him a post at the University of Missouri. He did not warm to Kansas, or Kansas to him. His aloofness was interpreted by his fellow Kansans as affected superiority, and his ineptness in the classroom as a sign that he was in the wrong profession. Becker was desperately eager to move on, and Turner was willing to help, even though warning that "the best policy is to *boost* hard and make yourself indispensable by your helpfulness," rather than to nurse discontent.[62]

Becker correctly decided that his indispensability would be improved with a doctoral degree, so he returned to Madison in 1904 and completed his work there three years later. His thesis on political parties in colonial New York, published in 1908, was a landmark in historiography, and it helped convince the University of Kansas that it owned a jewel, even though a rough one. He was made a full professor, with tenure at last, but his ambition to conquer the East remained unfulfilled. Once more Turner (and Becker's own growing reputation) wrought the miracle; his move to Cornell was his last. There he ascended to the very pinnacle of the profession, justifying the faith that had inspired Turner to labor so faithfully in his behalf.

By the time Turner was ready to leave the University of Wisconsin his fame as a graduate teacher was nationwide. Four of his students— W. A. Schaper, Ulrich B. Phillips, Charles McCarthy, and Louise P. Kellogg—had won the coveted Justin Winsor prize of the American Historical Association during the first five years that it was awarded, a record unmatched by any other instructor. The local editor could be forgiven when he lamented that no prize was awarded in 1905 because he had "expected to see Wisconsin add another to her list of victories."[63] Turner's former students were everywhere: three at the University of Kansas, one at the University of Illinois, two at the University of Oregon, two more at the University of Washington, others at California, Kentucky, Indiana, Randolph Macon, Milwaukee-Downer, and the Indiana Normal School. Even more impressive were the accomplishments of those in allied disciplines he had helped train: E. R. Johnson at the University of Pennsylvania, B. H. Meyer on the Wisconsin Railroad Commission, Jesse Bullock at Harvard, E. D. Jones at Michigan, P. L. Reinsch a rising star in the field of legal history.[64] "They help explain," Turner wrote, "how the life of a teacher of graduate students checks his own historical output, but furnishes compensations."[65] So it did. He took as much pride in the roster of those attracted to Wisconsin during the 1909-10 academic year—Eugene H. Byrne, A. C. Krey, Edgar E. Robinson, William A. Robinson, Bernadotte E. Schmidt, Allen B. West, Raynor G. Wellington, Melvin J. White, and Edwin E. Witte (all destined to become well-known historians)—as he did in the articles that he published or the one book that he wrote. Wisconsin had earned a place among the top-ranking graduate schools of the nation, and Turner was a prime mover in placing it there.

XI

Undergraduate Teacher and Reformer

1901–1910

D URING his final years at the University of Wisconsin, Frederick Jackson Turner's greatness as a teacher could be measured by the graduate students trained in his seminars; few college professors of that day—or since—could boast an army of disciples of such quantity and quality. This was well, for his impact on undergraduates, which gradually diminished over his teaching career, continued to decline as his scholarly preoccupations removed him further and further from their world of interest. His reputation reached its nadir late in the decade, when he was burned in effigy on The Hill, the victim of a howling mob protesting a crusade against professionalized football that he headed. Like many college professors, he was the victim of reforming zeal that demanded sacrifices to achieve a better world; like most, he failed and suffered for his efforts.

Turner's research interests, which grew more and more specialized, doomed him to isolation from the great mass of undergraduates. The courses that he offered mirrored his own enthusiasms of the moment, rather than being geared to those of the students. The "History of the West" was offered yearly, together with his seminar, but these were the only stable items after he turned over the introductory survey of American history to Carl Russell Fish. For two years he offered a course in American diplomatic history, then a detailed examination of the period between 1819 and 1837 while he was preparing his *Rise of the New West*, then his old standby on "The Economic and Social History of the United States." Whenever possible he added instruction on the teaching of history. These were hardly designed to lure crowds to the classroom; his "History of the West" attracted between 30 and 65 students yearly, ascending once to 72 and falling to 27; his study of the 1819-27 era began with 52 students but lost much of its following in later years; and his survey of economic and social history did even less well. Once he abandoned the introductory course, Turner taught between 46 and 120 of the 5000-odd undergraduates normally enrolled in the university.[1]

Those who did attend his classes were attracted less by his reputation as a teacher than by either a genuine interest in the subject or a chance to rub elbows with a truly great scholar. He was, unquestionably, a campus showpiece; students whispered among themselves that he had published articles and books, that he had lectured at Harvard, that his writings appeared in the *Atlantic Monthly*, that he walked with the greats of the profession. They were warned that their common practice of calling him "Freddie" in private would not be welcomed in public, and were advised to attend his evening at-homes because "the tradition of the chairs elsewhere he has declined for love of his alma mater makes his nights notable."[2] Yet a popularity poll of the faculty in 1903 did not list his name; to most undergraduates he deserved to be ranked with those who were "so immersed in 'Research' or themselves, that their interest in student life has atrophied."[3]

Turner's reputation was not entirely unjustified, for the more he became immersed in his writing, the more a classroom lecture became an unwelcome interruption. He usually arrived out of breath, his arms laden with great piles of manila folders into which his notes were crammed, and always with the impression that he had been interrupted in more important labors and had grabbed a handful of lecture materials as he fled his office. These were spread on the desk in haphazard disarray as he searched one after the other, seemingly for information needed to start the lecture. As he searched he began to talk, usually with an apology: "As I hope you may remember more surely than I, at our last meeting we were discussing so-and-so." By that time he would have found what he sought—or something else that would do—and could begin. There was little in this procedure to suggest to the indifferent undergraduate that he was listening to a teacher whose concern was his education, and had prepared accordingly.

Even that indifferent student was electrified on the rare occasions when Turner laid his notes aside and lectured extemporaneously, usually during the week or so at the beginning and end of his "History of the West," when he expounded the frontier theory he knew so well. Then his vibrant voice, his radiant personality, the brilliance of his thought and expression, made all his slaves. "What a treat it was to listen to those brilliant lectures of the first three weeks," one recalled. "So well phrased, so comprehensive in their vision, so profound in their thought (at least, it seemed so to us), they practically lifted some of the students out of their seats."[4] If Turner had left his notes at the bottom of the Hill, he would have been a better lecturer.

Such was not his way, for the more he learned, the more he had to share with his classes. His lectures were increasingly crowded with data and details, far beyond the number needed to make a point or justify an interpretation. "Long lists of figures," one student wrote after seeing rows of statistics painfully copied on the blackboard, "all of which show that in spite of large growth of interior, in south, the apportionment of representation had not changed."[5] These were hardly the techniques needed to win friends among indifferent undergraduates; they wanted a clear-cut statement, not an overwhelming mass of ununderstandable proof. Turner, ever the perfectionist, could not give it to them.

To picture him, however, as one so absorbed in his studies that he failed to prepare properly for the classroom is to perpetuate a gross error. True, Turner gave his students no set speeches, believing as he did that a too-well-prepared lecture lacked the spontaneity of one delivered extemporaneously on the basis of notes recently reviewed; instead, he maintained an elaborate filing system, so that he could snatch out material for any subject, study it briefly, and speak with the enthusiasm bred of a fresh discovery. Yet no instructor could have worked harder to provide up-to-date and interesting information. He was forever badgering publishers and librarians for illustrative materials to show his classes; one form letter in 1907 requested pamphlets, maps, and pictures from a half-dozen western railroads that would show students their part in settling the West.[6] Turner's collection of "magic lantern" slides was famous; nearly all of the slides were painfully prepared by his own hand to show explorer's routes, trails westward, migration patterns, and whatever else in the expansion process that could be illustrated. Good students found them fascinating, poor students, only boring. The only notes taken by one student after a fifty-minute lecture were: "Slides: mountains and trails."[7]

Turner may not have been a spellbinder, but he had a loyal following, drawn from the ranks of the few undergraduates with a built-in enthusiasm for historical studies. To them he was the world's greatest teacher; from him they learned all that could be learned from any instructor, and in generous measure. He taught most of them few facts, despite the superabundance in his arsenal, but he did instill in them his own faith in history as the panacea for mankind's ills, a realization that the truth about the past was ever-elusive but always worth pursuing, and a conviction that such a pursuit was more rewarding and more pleasureful than any other occupation. Turner was fond of quoting the remark of Dean Basil Gildersleeve of Johns Hopkins, who called himself a radiator rather than an instructor, and insisting that he did little more than radiate enthusiasm for history. "I hope," Turner once remarked, "to propagate inquiry, not to procure disciples."[8] "Whenever I have a ten minutes' talk with Professor Turner," one student wrote, "I feel that I ought to go home, take off my coat, and get down to business."[9]

Loyalty such as this was not inspired by a man who neglected his students, or held himself aloof from their needs. Turner was constantly at the beck and call of undergraduates and graduates alike, stretching his twice-weekly office "hour" into two or three hours to accommodate the lines that queued up before his door, correcting term papers with the same loving care that he lavished on doctoral dissertations, and sharing his valuable time with anyone who needed his help. "No," his young daughter answered, when asked if she wanted to be like her father. "Everybody comes to ask him questions. I want to be like Mother, who doesn't know anything."[10] One of his students remembered with pleasure watching Turner stop to answer a question when on his way to a football game, then become so engrossed that he missed the kickoff.

He was equally concerned with providing students the study-guides needed to lead them through the chaos of his courses. His own outlines, carefully prepared with the launching of each new term, were models of masterful detail, listing the topics to be surveyed in each day's lecture and the illustrative materials to be used. Needless to say, they were seldom followed. As Turner became engrossed in explaining this point or that, all schedules were forgotten, forcing him to compress subjects to which weeks had been allotted into days instead.[11] Each year, too, a new syllabus was drafted, and usually mimeographed, for distribution to the class. This provided a detailed outline, designed to lend unity to lectures that were sometimes disorderly; an oppressively long bibliography; and a listing of current magazine articles and monographs bearing on the subject.[12]

For the more interested listeners, these signposts provided a path through the maze of his lectures that allowed them to concentrate on the flashes of insight that elevated Turner above most of his contemporaries. His interpretations, although commonplace today, were often startlingly fresh, and certainly not to be found in the printed literature. "I am unable to find," he thus told one class in 1902, "any clear evidence that the victory of George Rogers Clark had a vital influence in shaping the negotiations that closed the Revolution." This was an accurate evaluation, yet so far in advance of the times that Turner's own student, James Alton James, upheld the opposite viewpoint when he published his biography of Clark a generation later. Again, Turner anticipated today's historians by urging the study of urban growth as a means of understanding the history of the Old Northwest. "These nuclei of economic and social life," he explained, "show that life in its intensity in a peculiar and interesting way." He told his classes that Marcus Whitman's ride did not save Oregon, that much was to be said for the American cause in the Mexican War, that the Mormons were victims of a clash between streams of northern and southern emigrants no less than of religious persecution, that "Bleeding Kansas" was the battleground between two rival cultures, northern and southern, and between two different sets of social ideals. "The real significance of the slavery struggle in this period," one class was told, "is that it was a contest between expanding sections for the possession of the West." Turner predicted that the last chapter in the history of the West would see the democratic ideals of the pioneers preserved through "socialistic legislation" as the government sought to preserve equal economic opportunity for all the people.[13] Few teachers of his day were capable of such up-to-date interpretations.

Disinterested undergraduates who were unimpressed with these flashes of insight, and who saw Turner only as a research-oriented pedant, were to discover that still another Turner existed, and one even less to their liking. They were to find that a scholar could leave his dusty books to lead a crusade and be converted overnight into a reformer who wielded his sword with such devastating effect that one of the undergraduates' favorite institutions was seriously threatened. The dragon that Turner tried to destroy was college football, and he fought so masterfully that he aroused the ire of the president of the university, offended a sizable proportion of the faculty, and excited the press and the student body so violently that he was pilloried as a villain and hanged in effigy.

Football was sorely in need of reform during the early years of the twentieth century. Unsympathetic spectators saw it as little more than legalized mayhem, a "game" where brute strength was at a premium, where the awesome "flying wedge" was used to batter opponents into submission, and where players were free to cripple a sufficient number of rivals to assure victory. Athletes boasted that they were instructed by coaches to "eliminate" star performers on the enemy's side, and did so by throttling, stamping, or arm-twisting. "The players," one doctor testified, "go on the field expecting to be hurt, and are glad if they come off with nothing worse than a broken bone." Scarcely a major college game was played without at least one participant suffering a concussion or fractured arm. When the 1904 season resulted in 21 dead and more than 200 wounded, the public began to realize that changes were necessary.[14]

Equally alarming was the effect of football on the climate of college campuses throughout the land. Student enthusiasm for the game reached hysterical proportions each autumn; classes were ignored, study forgotten, the library deserted, and all talk was of next Saturday's game or last Saturday's victory. News disappeared from university papers, to be replaced by yells and songs that students were ordered to memorize, demands that they appear at rallies, and praise for the gladiators who won or laments for those who lost. With no rules governing eligibility, even the best colleges hired players openly, used them mercilessly, and sent them on their way after the Thanksgiving game. A player who performed well for a small college one week might be found on the eleven of a major university the next; one team played three others on successive weeks and faced virtually the same lineup each time. Athletes openly sought jobs in good schools, expected to be paid handsomely, and made slight pretense of attending classes. This breakdown of morality was as alarming to critics as the threat to education, the true function of a university.

Conditions on the Madison campus were little better—or worse— than on any other. Football, which began there as a minor sport with less popularity than baseball, had followed the national trend, and by the early years of the century the game was unrivaled as a generator of student enthusiasm. The university was ill-prepared to handle this situation. Its sports program was legally controlled by the "Athletic Association," a private body comprised of student representatives and a handful of faculty and alumni delegates, with the university administration having no direct voice. Such elegibility rules as existed were controlled by an "Athletic Council" selected from the faculty. The game itself was governed by the "Western Inter-Collegiate Athletic Association," or "Big Nine" as it was commonly called, composed of a "Big Four" of western football—Chicago, Michigan, Minnesota, and Wisconsin—and five "minor" schools: Iowa, Purdue, Illinois, Indiana, and Northwestern. Rules of play were established by this body, which was controlled by the athletic directors from each school. With authority divided, with the faculty having no direct voice, and with an undue power vested in student and alumni representatives on the Athletic Council, professionalized football at Wisconsin was given virtual free rein. Nor did the university administration care. President Van Hise was too concerned with weightier matters to interfere, Dean Birge was an unabashed enthusiast, willing to close his eyes to all abuses, and Professor Charles Sumner Slichter, chairman of the Athletic Council, believed that a winning team was essential to a great university.

Fortunately, a national campaign against football brutality was launched in 1904, with *The Nation* carrying the burden of protest at first, and *The New York Times* joining to demand eligibility rules and an end to mass plays. These pleas struck a responsive chord at Wisconsin. The 1903 and 1904 football seasons had been disasters; in 1904 the team lost to every major opponent, the coach resigned before the end of the season, and the graduate manager soon followed him. Virtue was a garb easily donned in such a situation; Wisconsin suffered because its purity doomed it to defeat. Or so the students proclaimed as they raised the hue and cry against professionalism in the Big Nine. "That university that can command the highest priced labor," argued the editor of the undergraduate newspaper, "can admit men of questionable standing with the least pangs of academic conscience and can finally succeed in keeping their deception from their competitors in the cleverest way is always going to win." The chorus of approval from students, faculty, and townspeople made clear that Madison was anxious to clean house—if its victorious neighbors were made to clean house, too.[15] The *Wisconsin Alumni Magazine* was less certain, but even its plea to graduates to recruit football talent was tempered by the warning that they should solicit only players who would be attracted by the "superior educational, social, and athletic advantages of the University."[16]

Turner seemed little concerned as proponents and opponents of Big Time football fought their preliminary skirmishes; during one major mass meeting to whip up sentiment for reform, he was away, addressing a far smaller group assembled to encourage the debating team on the eve of its match with Michigan.[17] Not until the autumn of 1905 did his attitude change, and then largely because a series of articles in *Collier's Weekly*, by a 1905 alumnus, Edward S. Jordan, on graft in college football, brought indisputable proof that Wisconsin's skirts were far from clean. Jordan's revelations were eye-opening: a player had threatened to desert to Michigan on the eve of an important game unless his pay was increased; another, after being expelled, was paid $500 to return; a captain was enrolled in a potpourri of easy courses, including one in football. At the root of these evils, Jordan charged, was a lack of strong leadership by President Van Hise and a faculty so indifferent that the graduate manager was the tool of a grafting athletic ring. Jordan was, predictably, denounced as a traitor to his alma mater, and the Athletic Council, just as predictably, investigated his charges and found them all false.[18]

Both town and gown, however, were left with troubled consciences, and Turner was no exception. The Congregational minister warned from his pulpit that the game must be reformed or abolished; the influential Six O'Clock Club heard a former member of the Athletic Council denounce professionalism; the local press trumpeted the decision of a national magazine not to include Wisconsin (together with Michigan and Minnesota) in its list of amateur teams of 1905, because the school had slipped into the hands of athletic grafters under the "jelly-fish" leadership of President Van Hise. Even the *Daily Cardinal*, usually a staunch supporter, pointed out that Columbia had abolished the game and that others would follow unless major reforms were begun.[19]

This was the situation when Professor Thomas S. Adams, an economist who had replaced Charles S. Slichter as the university's representative on the Western Athletic Association, returned from a meeting in December 1905, sputtering his annoyance. An attempt to change the six months' eligibility rule to a year had failed, he reported, just as had one to alter the rules to lessen brutality; nothing more significant had been accomplished than to set a top limit of fifty cents as the admission price to games. Adams would have none of such chicken-hearted reform. He ended his report to the faculty by proposing a committee of seven to review the whole place of sports in the university and to make appropriate recommendations, a resolution that was adopted after a series of amendments, designed to weight its membership with football enthusiasts, were beaten down. The committee was promptly named by the president, with Frederick Jackson Turner as a member.[20] Even the student newspaper applauded as it urged the members to restore sanity to an "athletic mad" generation.[21]

Turner's selection was indicative of the faculty's mood, for he was known as an unwavering enemy of overemphasis on college athletics. As early as 1898 he had played a leading role when two members of the team were accused of professionalism, and had helped establish their guilt. He had been openly critical of President Van Hise's namby-pamby policy of paying only lip service to reform. He was on public record as believing that football must be underemphasized to restore the intellectual life of universities.[22] So well known was his opposition that athletes shunned his classes; one who wanted to prepare a senior thesis under his direction later recalled that Turner was thoroughly discouraging. "Don't take your thesis under me," he was told, "for I have it in for all football men."[23] That those words were ever uttered may be doubted—Turner leaned over backward to be fair to his enemies—but there could be no question that at least one member of the Committee of Seven would press for drastic reforms.

Turner learned of his new assignment in December 1905, just as Albert Bushnell Hart was wielding the whip to bring him to the wire with his volume on the *Rise of the New West*, but he turned to the task with the enthusiasm of a man who had not a responsibility in the world. A stream of letters went off to friends on the Big Nine campuses: Would they agree that athletics had been overemphasized to the degree that they interfered with the serious functioning of the schools? Would they cooperate in a major reform program? Would they be willing to suspend all intercollegiate contests for two years? The replies were mildly encouraging; Andrew C. McLaughlin, now at the University of Michigan, agreed that the practice of pampering eleven sleek football players was wrong, but he doubted if abolishing sports, even for a few years, would end the evils. Others were more outspoken; Albion W. Small, at the University of Chicago, was particularly insistent that 95 per cent of the faculty felt the tail had wagged the dog too long and that most would favor suspending football.[24] All counseled that positive change could come only through the joint action of the major universities, not by any one alone. This was Turner's clue. Under Turner's prodding, President Van Hise first consulted friends at the University of Chicago; then, with their support, he asked President J. B. Angell of the University of Michigan to call together faculty representatives from the Big Nine to agree on reforms that could be recommended to the faculties of each school. They were to gather at the Beach Hotel in Chicago on January 12, 1906, with a prominent professor and an observer representing each school.[25]

While presidents and deans jockeyed to secure the right delegates, Wisconsin's Committee of Seven held three long meetings, listened to testimony on the state of the university's athletic program, and prepared a report that was submitted to the faculty on January 8, 1906. Their evidence was not too damning: one member of the 1905 team was an out-and-out professional, others were supported by a "corruption fund" illegally raised from alumni, still others were guilty of petty graft when they sold tickets to a major game. These, and other evils, could be met by instructing the university's delegate to the Chicago conference to urge resolutions protesting overemphasis on athletics, and to propose that the Big Nine abolish football for two years "to the end that rational, moral and normal relations between athletics and intellectual activities may develop in each institution." The committee's proposals were adopted by a vote of 48 to 25 after a bitter debate, and Turner was elected Wisconsin's representative to plead the case before the Chicago meeting.[26]

These actions were duly reported in the local press under the headline DOOM OF FOOTBALL NEAR AT VARSITY, TURNER REPRESENTATIVE TO

CHICAGO CONFERENCE. The reaction was predictable. A few alumni urged Turner to end "the worship of the pig skin," but the students rose almost to a man to denounce the villain who would rob them of their favorite sport. His two-year suspension proposal, rumor had it, was only a subterfuge to abolish the game altogether, and this they would have none of. "The student body," warned the *Daily Cardinal*, "demands the continuance of the game and will labor to that end."[27] Turner was painted by undergraduates as an autocrat in control of a faculty Juggernaut bent on crushing student opinion, as so prejudiced that he mistook a football player who said he needed a "pony" to finish his thesis as a cheater when the man only sought a colt to complete his assignment for a degree in agriculture, as an enemy of every form of pleasure. The faculty, an undergraduate publication warned, would soon abolish croquet because of the dangerous implements employed, ping pong because of the inverted posture necessary while hunting the ball under a piano, and marbles because of the chance it might foster gambling.[28] Facetious remarks, perhaps, but they cloaked genuine student resentment, with Turner as its target.

Gradually, the undergraduate demands focused on two points: football should be reformed, not abolished; and they should have a voice in the reforms. Above all, they wanted their representatives to share their views with Turner before he left for the conference in Chicago. This was a reasonable request with which Turner thoroughly agreed. "The professional spirit with its corruption," he told an interviewer, "and the various unhealthy features of intercollegiate athletics must be subjected to clean and effective control by student sentiment and alumni action, quite as much as by faculty representation."[29] The only problem was time, for so little remained before his departure for Chicago that there was no opportunity for the undergraduates to impress their will on the faculty.

Then the unexpected happened. The sudden death of President William R. Harper of Chicago forced postponement of the meeting until January 19, giving the students a whole week to agitate. Within hours eighteen petitions were being circulated, and within days 1500 had signed a request that the faculty hear student views. President Van Hise was sufficiently impressed to call a special meeting of the faculty for the afternoon on January 18, and to preside as student leaders read a series of carefully prepared resolutions. Turner's instructions should be changed, they asked, to urge the Big Nine to reform football rather than to suspend it for two years. The debate that followed was animated, but the decision never in doubt. "Be it . . . resolved," read the official resolution, "that the Faculty declines to modify the instructions to its delegates to the intercollegiate conference."[30] Turner and his fellow reformers had won another victory.

The students might fail to convince the Wisconsin faculty, but neither could Turner convince the Big Nine delegates during two days of heated discussion in a committee room of Chicago's Beach Hotel. When they met on the morning of January 19, he found only two other members willing to abolish football—his fellow delegate from Madison and Professor Albion W. Small of Chicago—and a solid day of persuasion failed to win the remainder completely. "I have," he reported to his wife, "had the most remarkable success in turning an adverse body into a majority of sympathizers—though Wisconsin's proposition will probably lose."[31] He proved a capable prophet. Rather than ending football, the delegates agreed to hold suspension as a threat above the member universities should the recommended reforms be rejected. Those reforms were: a full year of credit-earned residence before participation in any sport, no more than three years of play on any team, no games against high schools or academies, admission prices of no more than fifty cents, training tables to be abolished, a limit of five football games a year, no coaching save by regular members of the instructional staff whose salaries could not exceed those of others of the same faculty rank. At the same time the conference warned the Big Nine rules committee that it must alter play to end brutality. If it refused to act, and if the Big Nine schools failed to accept the recommended reforms, the conference would urge the abolition of football for a two-year period.[32] Turner had carried the day, and carried it with a vengeance.

That his victory would heighten his unpopularity with students and alumni seemed certain. So he was pleasantly surprised when he kept a long-standing engagement to speak to a meeting of the Madison alumni on January 31, on "Intercollegiate Competitive Athletics." Two hundred alumni packed Keeley's Restaurant that night, but their mood was friendly from the start. Applause, not boos, greeted him as he ticked off his points: football ended all education for two months each fall; football was a big business, carried on by professionals, and demoralizing to university ethics; football was a cruel sport that maimed or killed fine young men each year. "Brutality must go," Turner told his attentive listeners; "mercenary professionalism, immorality, deceit, and corruption of student sentiment must go." The Chicago conference had proposed changes that would substitute for organized mayhem a game that students could play, that would be subordinate to intellectual life, that would leave "no slimy trail across the campus, no stain on the fair name of our alma mater."[33] Those stirring words hit their mark. An alumnus who rose to plead that the game be let alone struck not a single spark. Before the alumni scattered that night they voted solidly that football must be reformed or abolished.

The students were woefully disappointed, no less by the turnabout of the alumni than by the acceptance of Turner's reforms by the Chicago conference. "All hail the alumni," proclaimed the *Daily Cardinal* bitterly, "who have succeeded in getting off the 'hurry-up' wagon before it reached the jail!" To them Turner was still the arch villain, bent on destroying a game that they loved. On every campus the story was the same. At Chicago, Albion W. Small reported a bad attack of the blues, while the Michigan delegate was greeted on his return to Ann Arbor as if he had been a combination of Benedict Arnold and Aaron Burr, with a tincture of James Wilkinson added.[34] The reformers had some serious opposition to beat down before their proposals would be adopted.

A more troublesome problem came up as soon as the Big Nine faculties began studying their suggestions. Did the provisions requiring coaches to be members of the instructional staff mean that professionals such as Fielding H. Yost of Michigan and Alonzo Stagg of Chicago must be replaced by amateurs recruited from the faculty? The members, after a hurried exchange of telegrams, agreed that they did not know.[35] Nor were they sure of the interpretation of a number of other clauses that had been hastily framed. Turner did his best to clarify matters when the Wisconsin faculty considered the Chicago Conference report on February 6, 1906, but he had so little success that the only action was a resolution urging a second conference to reframe its recommendations. Once again Turner was named the university's delegate, and once more he set off for Chicago to plead reform.[36] He went with heavy heart, for discouraging news was drifting in from campus after campus: Michigan had rejected the suspension of football by an overwhelming majority, other schools leaned in the same direction, all were confused by the provision that coaches must be members of the faculty and fearful that such a rule would perpetuate the reign of such power-hungry fanatics as Yost and Stagg.[37] The substantial changes recommended by the Chicago conference were ignored as debate bogged down over this one clause.

Turner might have spared himself his doubts, for when the delegates to the second "Conference of College Representatives" gathered on March 9, 1906, all went smoothly. One by one the resolutions adopted earlier were discussed and revised, usually in substantially the same form but with additional clarification. Only the section on coaches underwent major surgery. No coach, it was agreed, could be named except on recommendation of the faculty or president, and all were to be paid modest salaries.[38] With the modification of this basic ruling, the report was ready for faculty action by the Big Nine universities.

Before the report could be considered, a flurry of rumors stirred apprehension on the Wisconsin campus. Local sports writers joined those of the Chicago press in quoting the usual "informed sources" that football was doomed without professional coaches, and that the faculty really intended to abolish the game entirely after the reformed version lost its popularity. Turner was at the center of this storm, fending off interviewers almost daily with the statement that the faculty must speak for itself, but dropping a hint now and then that set the rumor mills grinding. The future of intercollegiate football was by no means assured in Madison, he told one reporter; another learned that the coach would probably be replaced by someone worthy of a faculty post who would de-emphasize the game.[39] To students fearful of the worst these words could be interpreted in only one way. Football was to be abolished!

Their fears were given substance that spring, when the track and crew coaches resigned to accept more secure posts, the baseball coach left to play with a professional team, the graduate football manager submitted his resignation, the captain of the baseball team dropped from school, and the "smashing fullback" of the 1905 eleven announced that he was transferring to the University of Pennsylvania. Those who remained caught the spirit. So few students reported for baseball practice that the season had to be canceled; members of the track team refused to compete in a meet with Michigan until assured that football would not be abolished.[40] Then came word that the Northwestern faculty had voted to suspend football for five years. This was the handwriting on the wall. Mournfully the undergraduates held a mock carnival on the lower campus to watch burly football players meet in fierce games of ping pong and marbles.[41]

An ill-advised move by Dean Birge brought matters to a head. President Van Hise was away, having left behind strict orders that the report of the Chicago Conference not be considered until his return, but Birge was apprehensive of student unrest and wanted a showdown. On March 26 he assembled the faculty members of the Athletic Council to decide between two resolutions: that the Western Conference rules be adopted, or that football be suspended for the 1906 season. They wisely refused to take a stand, deciding instead to wait for the president's return, but the harm was done. All the next day rumors flew about the campus, and that night the students acted. By 9:30 some five hundred had gathered, many carrying rifles or revolvers, to begin a march toward Frances Street shouting "Death to the faculty." Their first stop was Turner's home, which was surrounded. When he appeared on his front porch, the cry went up, "When can we have football?" "When you can have a clean game," he shouted back, "It's been so rotten for the last ten years that it is impossible to purge it." This was the red flag to the bull; for a time his life seemed endangered as Turner vainly tried to point out the evils of the game, and his words were drowned out by hisses and cries of "Put him in the lake." Eventually, the mob drifted on to the home of Dean Birge, who sang a different tune. "You want football," he told them. "I shall take pleasure in conveying your wishes to the faculty when they meet." Cheering, the students pressed on, gathering up wooden fences and board walks as they went, to build a giant bonfire on the campus. Amidst yells and cheers, three faculty members were burned in effigy. The local fire department, summoned to put out the blaze, saved only the last of these from the flames. It bore the name of "Prof. Turner."[42]

This was the troubled campus to which President Van Hise finally returned. He immediately announced that a faculty meeting would be held on April 5, and assured the students that they would be heard before it met. They assembled once more on the night of April 4, a thousand strong, but in a far different mood. Order and contrition prevailed as resolutions were adopted condemning the mob attacks on faculty members, and urging the retention of football after proper reforms improved the game. Their cooperative mood paid dividends. When the special faculty meeting assembled the next afternoon, it listened attentively to a number of petitions—one followed by thirty pages of signatures—pleading the student cause, and heard five student speakers whose sensible pleas made an excellent impression. Then came the voting. The reform suggestions of the Chicago Conference were adopted first, together with a proposal that the Athletic Association provide wholesome sports for the entire student body. The way was cleared now for the key decision: "Resolved that the Athletic Council be instructed to schedule no intercollegiate football games after 1906." The debate that followed was bitter and long, extending well into the evening after a brief adjournment for supper. Like most such issues, it could be settled only by compromise, with the magic formula devised by Professor Dana Munro. Football would continue, but games with the other Big Four schools—Michigan, Chicago, and Minnesota —would not be scheduled for the fall of 1906. For a time division on this issue threatened to continue through the night, but when Turner announced that he was in favor, it was adopted by a vote of 52 to 30.[43] Wisconsin had taken its stand, and it had to wait to see whether the other Big Nine schools fell into line.

Reaction varied with the enthusiasm of the commentator for old-fashioned football. FACULTY KILLS KING FOOTBALL, proclaimed the leading newspaper, but the *Daily Cardinal* happily announced that WISCONSIN MAY PLAY FOOTBALL, and added that "the faculty and students have won their fight for clean and legitimate football." Both were right, for the game would be played, but in a completely new garb. With the other Big Four schools agreeing to cancel all games with each other for at least a year, a "sane schedule" was arranged for the 1906 season, with North Dakota, Lawrence, Iowa, Illinois, and Purdue as opponents. Diehards might talk of "bean-bag football," or gloomily predict that Lawrence would defeat Wisconsin:[44]

> Alas! for our Badger traditions,
> That ever the time should be
> When the Lion of many a gridiron fight
> Shall be swallowed up by a Flea.

But they were to change their tune as that season progressed.

For suddenly, unaccountably, Wisconsin was winning football games, and the students were enjoying the taste of victory. The newly appointed coach had a light and inexperienced squad, but he stressed speed rather than power, with surprising success. With each win enthusiasm mounted, until two hundred rooters made the long journey to Urbana to see Illinois routed. Five victories in a row dried the tears of even the local sportswriters, who admitted that a season which began in gloom and dissatisfaction had ended by demonstrating that "reform football" was a complete success. Even those who speculated that Wisconsin might be the "Champion of the West" that year did not lament that no games were scheduled with Michigan or Minnesota to prove its claim.[45]

Such a spirit sowed the seeds of defeat for Turner's cause, for every victory stirred enthusiasm for more football and more worthy opponents. Why not a six-game schedule for 1907? Why not play at least one of the Big Four? "If we can lick Chicago," wrote a student editor, "reform football is all right." All this would be possible if Turner and his fellow-meddlers would go back to minding their own business, believing that their cause was won. "The many friends of Prof. Turner," one undergraduate declared, "are rejoicing over his recovery from his recent attack of football-phobia, which seems to have become chronic."[46] This was wishful thinking. Turner longed for the day when he could return to his uninterrupted studies, but he was too tuned to the popular mood to leave the ramparts unguarded. "I expect that we shall have to fight to hold things in this satisfactory shape," he told a friend, and fight he did.[47]

His enemies came from within and without. Turner's nemesis on the faculty was Dean Birge, a staunch friend of big-time football, and a clever manipulator of opinion to favor his cause. They clashed that winter when preparing a committee report on the university's athletic code; Birge and the majority who voted with him found it perfectly satisfactory, but Turner and one ally filed a strong dissenting statement. Faculty members on the Athletic Council, he argued, should be increased from three to four, with final authority to rule on interpretations of the code. When these two alternatives—one vesting power in the faculty, the other in the department of physical education—came before the faculty meeting of December 3, 1906, the whole theory of reform was at issue. So bitter the debate, and so even the division, that compromise was necessary. Even Turner saw this, and agreed that he was willing to yield on some points. The solution, shaped by Dean Birge and laid before the faculty on December 10, vested ultimate authority in the entire faculty, rather than in the faculty members of the Athletic Council, whenever differences of opinion developed with the physical education department. Supposedly, Turner had agreed to this settlement, but now he insisted on one amendment; faculty members on the Athletic Council would have power to enforce their interpretation of the rules pending appeal to the whole faculty.[48] He triumphed, but his triumph was short-lived. The Board of Regents, after listening to him plead his cause, reversed the decision, and lodged far more power in the physical education department than Turner thought wise.[49]

Enemies from without the campus were even more threatening. They came from the Big Four universities, where the success of reform football during the 1906 season sparked the same resurgence of enthusiasm that infected the Wisconsin student body. Even Northwestern, which had substituted intramural sports for intercollegiate games, demanded a return to conference play after the local contests revealed some surprisingly good talent. These demands surfaced in December 1906, when representatives of the Big Nine athletic departments, encouraged by the changing climate of opinion, agreed to push for a seven-game schedule providing two were with minor schools, dropped the fifty cent admission limit, and revoked the three-year limit on varsity competition for players enrolled before September 1, 1906. "It begins to look like 'Easy Street' for King Football," wrote one sports editor, with obvious satisfaction.[50]

This prophecy reckoned without Turner and his fellow reformers. Faculty approval was necessary, and at Wisconsin at least there was almost unanimous sentiment against the suggested changes. With Turner leading the attack, they were voted down one by one as students again wailed their resentment.[51] The faculty was happy, but the physical education department pointed out that a real problem remained. The Big Four schools were ready to schedule games among themselves, and some were adopting the seven-game schedule. How could relations be kept harmonious? Another conference was clearly needed, and one was promptly scheduled for Chicago, with each of the Big Nine represented by one delegate from the faculty, and one from the athletic department. Turner and C. P. Hutchins, coach and chairman of the physical education department, journeyed to Chicago together on January 12, 1907, for another day of bickering. Most of the time of this "Peace Meeting," as it was labeled by the press, went into a discussion of picayune regulations governing the treatment of visiting teams; not until late in the day, when Turner had been forced to leave, did they turn to scheduling. He would have been heartbroken at the result: Wisconsin, it was agreed, would play Minnesota in 1907, Chicago and Minnesota in 1908, Chicago and Michigan in 1909, and Michigan and Minnesota in 1910.[52] The faculty still had to give its approval, but Turner recognized the inevitable and fell into line. Instead of opposing, he presented the "Peace Meeting" proposals and personally shepherded them to passage.[53]

Turner raised no white flag with this about-face, but he did sense that support for big-time football was growing and that he could stem the tide only by making some concessions. The 1907 season was a triumphant one, and with each victory student hysteria mounted. It reached a climax on the eve of November 24, when Wisconsin was to play its last game of the season against Minnesota, the first against a Big Four opponent since reform agitation began. By this time the alumni were forming committees to press for a seven-game schedule and the return of a training table, showering letters on the president, and muttering that they would carry their case to the legislature if the faculty did not listen. Their plan was for a giant mass meeting before the big game to protest the "ping pong policy" of the university. "The faculty," read the announcements, "which is apparently composed of men who aim to tie a tin can to college sports, especially football, will be taken to task by former Wisconsin men who are now prominent."[54]

The "giant" mass meeting was not quite as large as expected, but the speeches were fiery enough to please the most avid fan. Speaker after speaker denounced the faculty as "women who wore men's pants," urged naming a full-time coach, and warned the reformers that they should resign if they did not catch the Wisconsin spirit. Resolutions adopted as the meeting drew to a close were less inflammatory, but they requested that a faculty committee of three meet with a similar alumni committee "to consider the best means of improving university athletics."[55] A day later alumni and students—and most of the faculty—watched the eleven battle mighty Minnesota to a 17 to 17 tie and voted the season a success.

The faculty, once more under Turner's leadership, took the alumni's request with proper seriousness. Meeting on December 2, 1907, they listened with approval to a series of resolutions Turner had prepared: the faculty had no intention of abolishing intercollegiate football; it felt the conference rules adequate to govern the game and did not intend to alter them locally; it encouraged the widespread participation of all students in sports programs; it was unswerving in its belief that all athletics "should be justly subordinated to the fundamental purpose of the taxpayers of Wisconsin in creating an institution for the education of youth and for the advancement of knowledge." These, the faculty agreed, would serve as instructions to the three delegates who would meet with the alumni. Turner, naturally, was named chairman of this group, and Professor James F. A. Pyre of the English department and Professor Paul S. Reinsch of political science were named as his fellow members.[56]

The meetings were amiable enough when they began at Turner's home on the night of December 14, 1907. The alumni arrived armed with a set of nonnegotiable demands: a seven-game schedule, a well-paid professional coach, alumni representation on the committees that controlled sports. One by one these points were politely refuted by Turner and his colleagues: they had no control over the coaching staff, which was hired by the president and regents; alumni representation on the Council would create the same problems of divided authority that had been responsible for past difficulties; a seven-game schedule was out of the question. These were the facts of life, and must remain the facts of life if the university was to fulfill its obligations to the state as an educational institution.[57] The alumni, bested at every turn, took refuge in a public statement in which they reiterated their demand for a seven-game schedule and urged that faculty members "known to be bitterly hostile to the declared policy of the faculty in favor of intercollegiate athletic contests" no longer be named to committees governing athletic policies.[58]

The issues were clearly drawn now, with local alumni and a majority of students favoring a seven-game schedule as the first step toward a return to big-time football, and faculty reformers grimly holding the line against them. For a time the faculty viewpoint triumphed. They won a solid victory in January 1908, when delegates from the Big Nine, meeting in Chicago to arrange schedules for that fall's games, voted five to four for a seven-game season, but with the provision that each school must approve by a two-thirds faculty vote. This was a kiss of death, as they well knew. Wisconsin, led by Turner, overwhelmingly favored five games for 1908, even though the alumni petitions had just been presented to the faculty.[59] Chicago, Illinois, Purdue, and Northwestern fell into line, assuring at least one more year for reformed football.

But only one more. That 1908 season was one of the most exciting in years, as opponent after opponent, including Minnesota, fell before the Badger eleven. Again fanaticism soared to irrational levels as the last game approached. This was with Chicago on November 21, with the mythical "Championship of the West" at stake. The campus went mad. Each night for five nights the students shouted themselves hoarse at mass meetings, the last attended by no less than five thousand cheering fans. Turner, listening to the bedlam, must have wondered how so many young men—and old alumni—could be misled into believing that the university's function was to entertain rather than to educate. Ten thousand rabid enthusiasts were on hand that Saturday afternoon to watch Chicago triumph, by a score of 18 to 12. But they were not too disappointed. Big-time football was back in Madison, despite the faculty mossbacks.

It was there to stay, for the success of the 1908 season dealt a death-blow to reform. That winter, one by one, the Big Nine universities voted to restore a seven-game schedule for 1909 and 1910, with only Wisconson doggedly clinging to five games. Turner and his supporters could not keep football reformed forever. No sooner was the 1910 season over than a motion from the Athletic Council authorizing seven games for 1911 was introduced, hurriedly debated, and passed by the faculty with 50 in favor and only 26 opposed. A few months later the regents authorized the president to name the faculty members on the Athletic Council. One by one the reforms won so painfully by Turner were whittled away.

That he won a battle and lost a war was not to his discredit, for other reformers in other days were to prove that no quantity of logic could offset the fanatical desire of youth for victories on the gridiron. Professors might argue that the function of a university was to educate, not match gladiator against gladiator; they might prove that football was a brutal sport that killed or maimed fine young men; they might demonstrate that campus hysteria brought intellectual activity to a near-standstill for two months each fall, at great expense to the taxpayers. Their arguments were irrefutable, but emotions, not logic, governed student conduct on crisp fall afternoons when the honor of the college was at stake. Turner and his fellow reformers had probably saved the necks of a few players by winning rule changes that lessened brutality, and they had certainly dampened campus hysteria for a year or two, to the benefit of a good many who took their education seriously. No other reward could be hoped. Turner had acted as his conscience dictated, but he must have wondered, as he watched the cheering crowds at Camp Randall during a do-or-die battle with Chicago, whether the career of a reformer was worth while.

XII

Leaving Wisconsin

1905-1910

URING the early years of the twentieth century, Frederick Jackson Turner squandered precious time on football reform and dedicated hours to graduate instruction instead of research. Still, almost despite himself, his reputation was skyrocketing. He contributed precious little to his own ascent; his *Rise of the New West* was a masterpiece, but it was so original that its implications escaped many traditionalist historians; his articles on early foreign policy were too specialized to stir general interest; and his speculations on the nature of sectionalism were too immature to win professional support. Even his article on "The Old West," while appealing to some, was seen by others as an exercise in local history, and of no national significance. Turner was becoming well known not through his own efforts, but because, during those years, historians had awakened to the belief that the frontier thesis was the key to understanding the nation's past, and its author the prophet whose revelation had led them to the ultimate Truth.

For this about-face in national attitude the changing times were largely responsible. As the new century dawned, America was entering its industrial age: mushrooming cities, smoke-belching factories, bitter labor conflicts, the degradation of rural values—all signaled the end of an era that gained in glamour as it receded into the past. Nostalgia for those bygone days underlay the popularity of dime novels with their cowboy fantasies, and of the works of Mark Twain and Bret Harte for readers with more elevated tastes. Historians, grasping for an interpretation more plausible than the now-discredited "Teutonic" explanation of Herbert Baxter Adams, succumbed to this atmosphere in their own way. The frontier was capturing the nation's imagination; perhaps Turner had been right in 1893 when he argued that its significance had not been appreciated.

Particularly because the thesis blended so well with the spirit of Progressivism. Democracy—political and economic—was placed on a pedestal during those years, and Turner told the historians that American democracy was a home grown product of the West. This was a comfortable theory, Jeffersonian rather than Marxist in its implications, offering a safe explanation of the conflict between eastern capitalism and western Populism, between the trusts and the people, between management and labor. Historians could side with the oppressed without tainting themselves with Marxism simply by equating democracy with rural values. Even those who refused to accept environmental determinism—and Turner was in this camp—could use Turner's tools and concepts to stage their own breaks with the past. The young Charles A. Beard was a Turnerian before he sharpened the frontier hypothesis to develop his own "economic determinism." So were Vernon Parrington, who used the thesis to substantiate his progressive interpretation of American writing, Carl Becker, who applied it to the class conflicts of the Revolutionary period, and James Harvey Robinson, who popularized the "New History." Turner might not have convinced all his colleagues that his views were valid, but all were aware that his assault on traditionalism had opened the door to fresh interpretations of the past. And all were grateful.

This acclaim from the younger "Progressive Historians" did not mean that all were swept aboard the Turner bandwagon. Older scholars, and a good many younger ones as well, distrusted the newer interpretations and were inclined to rebel against newfangled ideas that were based more on speculation than evidence. Men of this sort thought it improper to use unsubstantiated hypotheses as the bases for interpretation; they branded as "unscientific" the rewriting of history to conform to a "frontier theory" or a belief in "economic determinism" or a "New History." The stiff-backed resistance of these diehards—and the realization that they were at least partly right—inclined the Progressive historians to exaggerate claims for the validity of their own ideas. The economic factor, or the frontier factor, or the social factor, they argued, shaped *all* aspects of human behavior, not just a few. These over-statements—and Turner's followers were guilty of many of them—did much in later years to discredit the causes for which they stood. Now, however, they only helped popularize the views of the Progressives, and particularly those of Turner.

If the frontier hypothesis won acceptance because the climate was favorable, it also benefited from the proselyting of as dedicated a band of fanatics as ever preached a cause. In the van were Turner's own students, all passionately devoted to their master, all convinced that they had heard the Word and must convert the world. In the long run they did him more harm than good, for their exaggerations eventually helped discredit a theory that was basically sound; "some of my students," Turner wrote ruefully, "have apprehended only certain aspects of my work and have not always seen it in *relation*."[1] That was for the future; now those students formed a Gideon's Army, marching to rid the world of heresy. They were everywhere, for by 1910 several hundred had passed through his seminar and some two score had earned the doctorate under his direction. Albert Bushnell Hart, traveling about the Midwest at this time, found so many in colleges and universities that he accused Turner of monopolizing the field; "wherever I go," he wrote, "they seem to spring out of the ground."[2] All were winning converts and training their own students to spread the Gospel. Scores more manned the high school history departments of much of the Midwest, infecting their charges with the virus of Turnerism even before college age. Nearly all kept in touch with Turner, seeking his advice on a lecture to give or a syllabus to prepare, or enquiring about the latest findings to use in their classrooms. So conscientiously did they assign their master's writings that, when a new instructor arrived at one institution, he found the 1893 issue of the *Annual Report of the American Historical Association* and the copies of the *Atlantic Monthly* containing Turner's essays so tattered from constant wear that they could not be used.[3]

All great teachers have recruited disciples from among their students, but Turner's magnetism extended to a wider circle. He—or his theories—won as converts numerous college and high school instructors who had never entered his classes, and a sprinkling of enthusiasts from beyond the academic ranks: a New York banker who used Turner's

ideas as the basis for a book, *The New Frontier;* a political scientist
who wrote that the governmental systems of colonial America were
chiefly influenced by "an open continent, by the abundance of cheap
land, by life in a new country where social rigidity could not by the
nature of things be scrupulously maintained."⁴ Even John Bach Mc-
Master, who, in his multivolume *History of the People of the United
States,* had shown little concern with the West, devoted a major portion of his sixth volume, published in 1906, to the frontier. Max Farrand, the most devoted of Turner's admirers, accepted a post at Stanford because he wanted to learn more about the western character at
first hand, then moved to Cornell to carry the frontier campaign to the
East. So faithfully did Farrand parrot Turner's views that the Northern
California Teachers Association thanked him after three lectures on
"The West in American History" for "having presented Professor
Turner's work in such a clear and interesting manner."⁵ This he acknowledged as his due; "the fact is," he wrote Turner, "I have been
living on your ideas ever since my summer in Madison."⁶ So he had.
Farrand was more realistic than modest when he wrote on an offprint
of a *Yale Review* article: "Dear Turner, This is really your work, and
I am ashamed to send it to you."⁷ He, like many another historian of
that day, accepted the frontier thesis as the literal truth, to be neither
disputed nor questioned.

With the historical profession almost solidly in line, textbook writers awakened to the realization that they had to recast their products
to reflect the current trend. This meant a revolution. Through the
nineteenth century, high school texts either ignored the West completely or painted westerners as dissolute characters who shamed the
glorious New England heritage that had made America great. This
view was first attacked by professional historians who were abreast of
Turner's theories. John Bach McMaster's *A School History of the
United States,* published in 1897, broke the ice by devoting three chapters to the western scene; seven years later, Albert Bushnell Hart, in his
Essentials in American History urged students to read Turner's essays
and saw the West as not only "different from older communities," but
the only part of the nation "where democracy was real." With these
two eminent historians placing their stamp of approval on the frontier
thesis, its general acceptance by textbook writers was inevitable. Ros-
coe L. Ashley's *American History for Use in Secondary Schools,* pub-

lished in 1907 and destined to become one of the two most widely used texts for a generation, demonstrated this admirably. The westward movement was the one key needed to understand the past; geographic forces determined the nature of the nation's economy and social structure; the frontier was largely responsible for "the democratic and national spirit of the people."[8]

Turner himself was not sure that this emphasis on his theory was wise. He expressed himself strongly on this point when he was asked to prepare an article for an educational journal on "the value of Western history"—an article that would shift attention from political history in elementary school instruction to "the great human movement of western occupation and development." A place must be found in the curriculum for the study of the frontier, he agreed, but not at the expense of political history—a subject essential to the training of future voters and the conversion of immigrants into informed Americans.[9] His disciples showed less restraint. When the *History Teacher's Magazine* urged its subscribers to read Turner's writings and stress the westward movement as an "important phase in the national development," as it did in 1909, it mirrored the attitude of most of the profession.[10] Even political history should be sacrificed if need be to make room for the study of the frontier, the magazine stated.

Such misguided enthusiasm was to triumph over Turner's moderation, as textbook writer after textbook writer fell into line. For the next twenty years virtually all did so. David S. Muzzey, whose *An American History* first appeared in 1911 and sold millions of copies, based his book on the assumption that "the western-moving frontier was the most constant and potent force in our history." His closest rival, Willis M. West, built his *American History and Government* about the theme that the frontier, and the interaction of the frontier with the older parts of the country, explained the nation's development. These authors typified the dozens of textbook writers whose products flooded the schools through the 1920s. Even older texts were revised to meet the new standards; D. H. Montgomery's *The Student's American History*, which in its original 1897 edition listed only four references to "The West," needed 127 index entries on that topic when it was reissued twenty years later.[11] The influence of Turner's theory on textbook authors can be realized when we understand that only 2.2 per cent of the subject matter in the leading texts published between 1830 and

1870 was devoted to the West, while 93 per cent of those books printed between 1900 and 1925 stressed the frontier as a basic moulding force in the nation's history.[12] When Max Farrand advised Turner, as he did in 1909, that he must "hustle along and get your own text-book out or you will find the field already occupied," he proved an admirable prophet.[13]

Turner never wrote that book, but the dozens of authors who parroted his theories brought him fame unrivaled by any historian of his generation. Thus, early in his career, he was judged by many of his contemporaries as worthy of a place among the immortals. Writing in 1903, when the frontier theory was mushrooming in popularity, Woodrow Wilson branded him "the coming man in American history" and "already in the first class"; at that same time Henry Morse Stephens used the columns of *World's Work* to rank Turner, with Henry Adams, James Ford Rhodes, and Henry C. Lea, as one of the nation's "most important living historians."[14] J. Franklin Jameson, who knew the profession better than any man of that generation, testified before the Massachusetts Historical Society a few years later that Turner outclassed all his contemporaries in combining "accurate scholarship and large views and the power of generalization."[15] Here was high praise from his peers. So was the word from Germany: the great Professor Karl Lamprecht rated the University of Wisconsin among the country's greatest because of Turner's "model historical seminary." Even blustery Edward Channing of Harvard, who could seldom see beyond the Hudson, confided to a graduate student that "Turner and I are the only men in the country who really know the *whole* of American history. Others know it in spots, but we've got it all the way through."[16]

Such acclaim meant a succession of honors, all pleasing to Turner's ego. Prestigious societies invited him to membership: the Massachusetts Historical Society in 1904, the American Antiquarian Society in 1907, the American Academy of Arts and Sciences in 1911, Phi Beta Kappa's newly established chapter at the University of Wisconsin shortly thereafter.[17] He was given his first honorary degree in 1908, when the University of Illinois made him a Doctor of Laws, a distinction that pleased Turner especially because it came from a school whose center for the study of western history was gaining national recognition. Three years later he was awarded the honorary degree of Doctor of Philosophy by the Royal Frederick University of Christiania, Norway.[18]

The popularity of his theory also underlay his rapid rise in the councils of the American Historical Association. As usual with younger men, he began his service to that organization on hard-working committees: the program committee in 1893 and 1897; the Justin Winsor Prize committee in 1898, which gave him the dubious distinction of reading a dozen book-length manuscripts; the nominating committee in 1904, which required a heroic journey to a Chicago meeting on a train delayed fifteen hours by snow and sub-zero cold; the Executive Council in 1895 and 1898, for which he had to travel to New York two or three times a year for wearisome sessions. All this placed a heavy load on his time and pocketbook, for, while bare expenses were paid for meetings of the Council and a few committees, attendance at the association's annual conventions had to be financed from the perennially depleted Turner treasury. Some he simply could not afford; he explained to a friend that he could not attend the Philadelphia meeting in 1903 "without creating hard feelings with my numerous creditors."[19] Others he attended only by practicing rigorous economies; he normally appeared in New York after journeying from Chicago to Toledo by coach, purchasing a Pullman ticket and berth for the overnight stretch to Syracuse, then transferring back to the coach again. Time and again Turner pleaded that committee business be conducted by mail to avoid bankruptcy for members, or urged the Association to be more generous with its travel funds, lest its business be monopolized by the wealthy or those who lived along the eastern seaboard.[20]

The American Historical Association demanded sacrifices, but it also gave Turner a chance to earn a reputation as the most prolific "idea man" of his generation. He was constantly generating plans for projects that would benefit historical studies, some fanciful, but most sound enough to warrant eventual adoption. His ally was J. Franklin Jameson, a born promoter who was at his best manipulating colleagues or congressmen into action, first from his professorship at the University of Chicago, then, after 1905, as director of the historical division of the Carnegie Institution of Washington. They made an ideal pair, Turner proposing plans, Jameson cutting them down to practical size and pulling wires to win their adoption. Without them, historical studies would have lagged seriously.

The causes that they plotted together were many: governmental publication of the early records of the Old Northwest (later to blossom with the publication of the territorial papers of the United States); a national center for historical studies in Washington, where visiting scholars could live cheaply and be modestly subsidized during their sabbatical research leaves at the Library of Congress (still an objective of the American Historical Association in the 1970s); a central university, comparable to the American University of Rome, to bring together the most gifted teachers and advanced students for post-doctoral training (a perennial ambition of historians from the late eighteenth century to the present).[21] "The idea for such a thing," Jameson testified in telling a friend of the proposed historical center, "was suggested to me last year by the fruitful mind of Turner."[22] Even the historical division of the Carnegie Institution was in part Turner's brainchild, although his insistence that it be less a clearing house and more a center for the final training of graduate students got no response from the institution's trustees.[23]

The Turner-Jameson collaboration was more successful when they sought support for publication of the federal government's official records. This had long been one of Jameson's pet schemes; congressional funds and expert guidance from the American Historical Association could produce a series of documents that would provide the profession with source materials for generations to come. After several false starts, the first scent of success came when President Theodore Roosevelt expressed a lively interest. If the Association would name a distinguished committee to plan a publications program, he said, they would be given official status as the Committee on Documentary Historical Publications, with sufficient funds to pay for needed meetings. By March 1908 this blue-ribbon group was ready to operate, with Worthington C. Ford as chairman and a glittering array of members, including Turner.[24] Their assignment was obvious; each member would draft a list of documents in his own field of interest that he thought worthy of government publication.

Most had cut-and-dried tasks, but Turner's was as challenging as it was difficult; he was to select the documents needed to illustrate the social and economic history of the United States. His approach was intelligent: he first sent a letter to some two dozen economists and economic historians seeking their advice, then a more general questionnaire to a wider circle of experts on the nature of materials to be included.[25] The forty-eight tightly packed pages that he distilled from

their replies was a pioneering bibliographical survey of major importance. Materials illuminating the social and economic development of
the nation, he insisted, were more important than those in military
and diplomatic history which had been supported by Congress in the
past. Such materials had been neglected because they had to be drawn
from all forms of depositories—federal, state, and private—and because
they required editing by a number of experts specializing in the many
areas involved. To make the task easier, Turner suggested that there be
two broad categories: economic materials, including those on land,
geography, agriculture, mining and forestry, banking, currency, manufacturing, wages and prices, transportation, and industrial organization;
and social materials, divided into such topics as population, social organization, health, criminals and dependents, art and literature. For each of
these divisions Turner listed items already published—thus creating a
unique and useful bibliography—together with suggestions on the type
of sources needed for further study.[26]

This contribution to historical studies was worthy of far greater
attention than it received. True, economic materials were paid far
greater attention than social; true, too, Turner was unaware of the
many facets of social organization that were to fascinate historians of
later generations. But as a pioneering bibliographical study, it was a
remarkable achievement. A few of his contemporaries recognized its
importance. Andrew C. McLaughlin felt that Turner had opened a
whole new field of investigation into the relationships between political, social, and economic developments that would make understandable
the industrial-urban complex of modern America.[27] Congress was less
enthusiastic. The committee's report was accepted by President Roosevelt in November 1908, buried by Congress in Senate Document No.
714, and forgotten. Many years later another committee of the American Historical Association, bent on a similar quest, read it with amazement, branded it a "remarkable document," and regretted that it had
had so little effect on the profession.[28] Turner, as was often his fate,
was too far in advance of his times to make his impact felt on his own
generation.

His contributions were recognized by the intellectual elite among his
colleagues, and with that recognition came such honors as they could
award. He was, almost from the beginning of his career, welcomed
into the tight little inner circle that administered the American Histori-

cal Association, and even into the still more exclusive Nucleus Club. The operations of this tiny group were kept secret, lest members take offense at the close interrelationships of the ruling "Establishment," but occasionally word slipped out about the number of bottles of champagne consumed at their annual dinner; on one such occasion Turner left with the wrong overcoat, forcing a colleague to return to Chicago in Turner's own nine-year-old garment.[29] Associations such as these, no less than his own dedicated labors, assured Turner of the highest tribute his contemporaries could pay. This came in 1907 when he was elected to the second vice-presidency of the Association, assuring him the presidency by automatic succession two years later.

This success converted him into a valuable academic property, coveted by university presidents anxious to bolster the prestige of their faculties. To lure Turner from the University of Wisconsin was the ambition of many an administrator during those years; to stay at Wisconsin while benefiting from the bidding for his services was Turner's. With most he had no problems, for his love affair with Madison was too enduring to be disrupted except by the most tempting attractions elsewhere; offers from John Hopkins in 1902 and Amherst five years later were dismissed without a second thought. Two university presidents proved more difficult. Benjamin Ide Wheeler at the University of California and David Starr Jordan at the newly established Stanford University were persistent. Goaded on by two of Turner's best friends—Henry Morse Stephens at Berkeley and Max Farrand at Stanford—they launched a tug-of-war that cost Turner many anxious hours of decision-making and letter-writing before he finally decided against them and for yet another institution.

The negotiations that led to this unexpected result began innocently enough in 1904, when Max Farrand heard a rumor, later proven false, that Turner was considering the directorship of the historical division of the Carnegie Institution of Washington. If he could be lured from Madison by one post, he might by another. So thought President Jordan of Stanford, who was all for wiring him a direct offer, despite the lack of research facilities available at his infant institution. Turner listened with interest when Farrand told him of these aborted efforts, agreed that he must have a good library near at hand, and hinted that more research time than Wisconsin allowed him might make another university attractive. Farrand, sniffing the faint scent of opportunity, went into a huddle with President Jordan, and soon an offer was on its way: Would Turner consider a salary of $5000 yearly, and a guarantee of at least two months free of teaching to pursue his researches in libraries anywhere in the nation? He would not; the salary was not sufficiently above the $4000 paid by Wisconsin to offset moving costs and higher expenses, while the prospect of leaving his family for two months each year was hardly attractive. On the other hand he was deeply in debt and eager to get on with his studies. A whole semester free of teaching each year would certainly be attractive. Max Farrand was so delighted that he replied without consulting his president. A semester-on, semester-off arrangement would be perfectly satisfactory to Stanford. When could Turner come?[30]

Turner went—but to President Van Hise, with Farrand's letter in hand, on a June evening in 1905. He made his position clear: Wisconsin was his true love, but both his wife's health and his own research would be improved by the move. The president, faced with losing his most prestigious historian, acted predictably; if the Board of Regents would not provide the funds needed to give Turner every other semester for research, he would raise the money himself. In the meantime, Turner was to make no promises to Stanford without consulting the Wisconsin authorities. These plans proved short-lived; the regents, although properly sympathetic, showed no inclination to squander their limited funds on research leaves while private donors were impossible to find. Turner was still smarting from the rebuff when President Jordan visited Madison in the spring of 1906, bearing with him a trustee-approved contract with a salary of $5000 and two months of research leave each year. This he laid before Turner in a private conversation, sweetened with his most persuasive eloquence.[31]

Fortunately, a kindly nature intervened before Turner had to decide; no sooner had Jordan returned to California than the devastating earthquake of 1906 leveled San Francisco and laid much of the Stanford campus to waste. "LELAND STANFORD DESTROYED," Turner read in his newspaper on April 19, and he probably was relieved that he was spared an unpleasant decision. If he did so, he reckoned without President Jordan. Even before the dust had settled, Jordan was assuring Turner—in three letters written on three successive days—that the damage was slight, that all would be repaired by the fall of 1907, and

that the offer still stood. Jordan's optimism was wasted, for unbe-
knownst to him, the honors had already gone to his rival. On April 17,
the night before the earthquake, Van Hise persuaded the Wisconsin
regents to grant Turner a semester's leave each year that he might
"advantagously carry to a conclusion [Turner crossed out "carry to a
conclusion" and substituted "carry on"] the very important investigations in history upon which he has been engaged for some years."[32]
Turner was committed to Wisconsin now, apparently for the rest of
his career.

Had Turner been able to forecast his future, Stanford might have
seemed more attractive, for already forces were at work within Wisconsin that were to force him to forsake his beloved Madison. A changing political climate was responsible. Since the election of Robert M.
La Follette to the governorship in 1900, Progressive Republicanism had
dominated the state and university alike, to the growing dissatisfaction
of the business and farming interests, who spoke through the Stalwart
wing of the party. They had much to be dissatisfied with. President
Van Hise, a leading Progressive and a roommate of La Follette's in college, encouraged his faculty to favor humanistic above practical research, and to cooperate with governmental leaders in drafting progressive regulatory measures that encroached on areas traditionally sacred to
private enterprise. His noble ideals, which won him the support of his
faculties, had little appeal to the majority of Wisconsinites. A farming
people with a practical orientation, they increasingly saw Madison's
professors as dreamers who wasted tax funds on impractical investigations, fathered such heresies as the income tax and the regulation of
public utilities, spent the state's money to train graduate students from
other areas, and preached socialism or anarchism in their classrooms. A
little head-thumping to bring them to their senses was called for.

So long as Governor La Follette sat at the helm and filled the Board
of Regents with his own appointees, these anti-university sentiments
were held in check, but in 1905 La Follette was elected to the U.S.
Senate, and he relinquished his office to his lieutenant governor, James
O. Davidson. A Stalwart of moderate ability and limited education,
Davidson made no secret of his belief that the university harbored
radicals and idealists who imperiled the state and should be dismissed
as soon as possible. Gradually he packed the Board of Regents with
men who shared his views: William D. Hoard, who spoke for the dairy

industry; Granville D. Jones and Magnus Swenson, who saw Van Hise's support for conservation a threat to their electric power interests; Charles P. Cary, who feared that the university wanted to take over the school system, which he headed as State Superintendent of Public Instruction. The way was paved for a series of confrontations.

The first arose when a temporary deficit allowed the Stalwarts in the legislature to charge financial irresponsibility and name a legislative committee to investigate the university. This committee lost no time in clearing Van Hise when it met in February 1906, but its hearings sent a shudder of apprehension through the faculty. The members, instead of concentrating on finances, welcomed a parade of disgruntled students and townspeople to air their grievances: Professor Ely was away from his classroom half the time, the textbook in statistics was incomprehensible, an instructor's assignments were "too hard," a history professor knew a great deal "but he was too vague for me."[33] This was alarming, but worse was the recurring theme that the faculty spent too little time on teaching and too much on research. Turner especially read the daily reports of the testimony with growing alarm, for his new semester-on, semester-off arrangement was exactly the sort of target the attackers sought. Apparently it did not become a direct issue—Turner's own testimony was confined to a statement on the football situation and a spirited denial that he had used his research time to prepare royalty-paying textbooks—but the wave of the future was clear.[34] That he saw the shape of things to come was shown when Turner sternly told the committee: "I have preferred to investigate and lecture in a university [rather than writing textbooks]; and it seems to me that a university ought to have room, and be able to make provision, for a man with these desires, such that he can continue." Here was a scarcely veiled warning; if the university failed to appreciate humanistic research he would leave, taking with him much of its prestige.

Unfortunately, neither the committee nor the public agreed with him. The committee made its stand clear: "Investigation and research have a proper place in a university, but the training of young men and women is more important to the state than all the other activities in which a university may engage." Its sentiments were echoed—and magnified—by students and townspeople alike. The influential *Wisconsin State Journal*, a mouthpiece for the Stalwarts, harped on the theme over and over again during the next months; what was needed, it insisted, was "a sort of spiritual revival among the faculty" that would focus their energies on teaching instead of useless investigations. The *Daily Cardinal* was just as insistent, likening the faculty to medieval monks who placed themselves on pedestals and scorned ordinary mortals; "Teach," it warned them, "and teach hard." To the *Wisconsin Literary Magazine*, professors were "present day Aunt Ophelias, out of touch with their charges." The *Wisconsin Alumni Magazine* was even more vehement; graduate students were a "foreign element" that should be eliminated, research-minded faculty members were "self-deceiving dreamers who solace themselves with the idea that they are doing for the world a service by their books, while their class work goes unheeded," and administrators were misled simpletons who should see to it that all promotions were based on "good instruction rather than on research work."[35]

These were harsh words, but they could be endured so long as they were not translated into official policy by the Board of Regents. Mounting public sentiment, and the changing political complexion of the board as Governor Davidson's appointees approached a majority, meant that this day was not far distant. This was made clear in June 1908, when Stalwarts on a sub-committee of the regents felt powerful enough to make a direct attack on Turner's half-time teaching and on a similar arrangement enjoyed by Richard T. Ely. The board, it suggested, should "look forward to a discontinuance of said arrangements at as early a date as may be consistent with good faith." Progressives were still numerous enough to prevent the board from adopting such a face-slapping statement, but another that was accepted was almost as insulting: "The ability to pursue original investigation and research work, when not combined with teaching ability, should not constitute sufficient qualification for membership in the faculty of the University." Here was an ominous warning indeed, made more so by a resolution authorizing the Regents' Committee on the State of the University to launch an investigation of professors "who are not giving the proper time and attention to instructional work."[36] To Turner this was a clear indication that he was under suspicion and was to be "investigated."

Little wonder that he was seriously agitated. His state of mind was shown in a twenty-six page letter that he sent to Van Hise, chronicling the success of his students, listing the Winsor prizes they had won, showing their significance in state and nation, quoting their words of praise for his teaching. "When I regret that I have not published more books," Turner assured the president, "I take some heart from these words. . . . Some of these men, at least, are not aware of my 'lack of interest in my students.' If I had been less interested I should have published more books."[37] There was bravado in such a defense, but there was tragedy as well, that a defense should be necessary.

This was only the beginning, for during the 1908-9 academic year the Stalwarts not only won increasing support from the people, but found a leader for their cause. Regent William D. Hoard, former governor of the state, wealthy dairyman, spokesman for the farming interests, and influential publisher of *Hoard's Dairyman*, was ideally suited for this role. A thoroughly practical man, he saw no reason why state funds should be wasted on culture when more farmers were needed; his repeated tune was that money allotted the College of Letters and Science could be better spent on the College of Agriculture. Turner was particularly vulnerable to his charges; he had no shelf of completed books, as Ely did, to prove that he was not frittering away his research leaves instead of sticking to his teaching. Van Hise, anticipating an attack, sought information from Turner on his accomplishments, and was rewarded with the usual bulky documents. Turner was writing a two-volume history of the westward movement, studying the Martin Van Buren administration with his seminar preparatory to a volume on that subject, working up material for a history of the United States since 1865.[38] Yet there was precious little to show in the way of results. Once the assault came, Van Hise would be hard pressed to defend his most prestigious faculty member.

Pressure mounted steadily during the year. Stalwarts in the state legislature, emboldened by mounting public support, proposed a whole array of anti-university measures: crippling amendments to its appropriation bills, a law to admit all high school graduates regardless of qualification, another to merge the university and normal schools under one board, an investigation of fraternities as undemocratic institutions. "I don't like the tone of the thing at all," Turner confided to his wife, and he wrote to Max Farrand: "At present I have a better understanding of the horror of such Federalists as President Dwight for the *spirit* of innovation."[39] He was right, for that spring of 1909 brought the explosion. External critics touched off the fuse: an article by Lincoln Steffens in the *American Magazine*, praising Van Hise and his faculty for making the university a powerful force in the state's cultural progress; another by Edwin E. Slosson in the *Independent*, comparing Van Hise to President Eliot of Harvard as a leader in progressive education; another by Richard Lloyd Jones in *Collier's*, charging the regents with trying to trespass on purely academic ground and dictate what should be taught in the classroom. These hurt the Stalwarts, particularly Richard Lloyd Jones's article, when it was republished in the *Wisconsin Alumni Magazine.* Conservatives on the board were boiling mad as they prepared for their regular meetings in the spring of 1909.

Turner, sensitive as always, realized that an attack was coming and that he would be its principal target. He would, he knew, be blamed for Richard Lloyd Jones's muckraking revelations, for Jones was his former student, and conversations he had had with Turner during a visit to the campus a short time before the article appeared could be interpreted as deliberately planned to supply information about the regents' meddling. In his agitated state of mind Turner transplanted even innocent requests into serious threats: a form letter from the university registrar asking him to describe the allotment of his time between classroom and research became an attack on his light teaching schedule, a regents' resolution to abolish fellowships assigned particular departments an assault on the program he had won for the history department, a questioning of the value of advanced degrees a personal thrust against his role as a graduate instructor. There was only one solution. Wisconsin's future was more important than his own. As a symbol of the humanistic research and graduate instruction that was under attack, he must not give up his research leave in return for a higher salary, as his Progressive friends on the board urged; this would signal the end of pure research everywhere on the faculty. Only by resigning could he save the university from ruin. "I have been so annoyed and irritated," he told Richard T. Ely that spring, "that I would now accept any one of the six calls I have already refused, and do so by wire."[40]

Turner had made his decision, but he was too sane a man to jump without a comfortable net to assure a safe landing. Stanford and the University of California had made clear their continuing interest, and one or the other must be queried as to a permanent post. A decision was easy; Stanford was woefully lacking in the library facilities that were his life's blood, therefore he must choose Berkeley. Having made up his mind, he sent a letter off, in July 1909, to his good friend Henry Morse Stephens, hinting that all was not well at Madison. Stephens responded exactly as he was supposed to respond. "Do I not see between the lines of your letter a little dissatisfaction?" Why not teach the regents a lesson and strengthen the cause of graduate work by going elsewhere? The welcome mat was still out at California, and President Wheeler as anxious to receive him as ever. A full semester off each term might not be possible, but he could be assured a salary of $5000, a teaching load of only a lecture course and a seminar, and the historical riches of the Bancroft Library. Why not follow the star of learning westward? Johns Hopkins led, Stephens pointed out, "Harvard followed and Wisconsin took up the great cause in the history field in the West." Now the center of historical culture was ready to shift once more. Turner could hurry the move by joining the California department. Stephens's plea was seconded by President Wheeler, who dwelt glowingly on the $750,000 library under construction, the generous pension system, and the $750 that could be added to the Turner income each year by summer teaching. He would be in Chicago on September 14, contract in pocket. Could Turner meet him there prepared to sign?[41] Turner agreed, and the time of their meeting was set for three that afternoon.

The six weeks of soul-searching that followed were thoroughly unpleasant ones. From all sides came the inevitable pressures—enthusiastic letters from Berkeley ("I think my cup of happiness would run over, if you were to be my colleague here")—heartbroken pleas from President Van Hise and his Madison friends. Turner's departure would not strengthen the president's hand with the regents, he was told, nor would it aid the cause of graduate studies at Wisconsin. He must stand at Van Hise's right hand as they fought the battle together. Turner was moved by these protestations, but his mind was made up. His only concession was to agree to one more conference with Van Hise after his September 14 meeting with President Wheeler. Above all, he warned, his delay in announcing a decision did not mean that he was seeking further favors from the Wisconsin regents.[42] He was leaving, and no amount of generosity could persuade him to stay.

Turner was leaving, but fate changed his decision on a destination. A letter he wrote to his dear friend Charles Homer Haskins of the Harvard faculty, seeking advice, was responsible. Haskins was vacationing in Meadville, Pennsylvania, when this caught up with him on September 14, the very day that Turner was closeted with President Wheeler in Chicago. Only minutes were required for an urgent telegram—CAN'T YOU DELAY DECISION. IF YOU LEAVE SHOULD LIKE TO SEE WHAT CAN BE DONE ELSEWHERE—and an explanatory letter followed. Haskins and Professor Archibald Cary Coolidge had been plotting for some time to bring Turner to Harvard. An additional professorship in an already well-stocked department posed problems, but Haskins was leaving for Cambridge at once to see if those could be solved. Would Turner give him a few days' grace?

The results were spectacular. Coolidge was elected to lay the case before Harvard's newly chosen president, A. Lawrence Lowell, and he did so eloquently. A once-in-a-lifetime opportunity had risen to improve instruction in American history. Edward Channing and Albert Bushnell Hart were capable, but the number of graduate students had been declining alarmingly as Turner drained the best of the crop toward Wisconsin. Just that year one of their prize students had shifted from European to American history and forsaken Harvard for Madison. Turner might not have written much, but he was a strong man, "perhaps the strongest professor in history in the United States outside of Harvard." No one was more badly needed. President Lowell was impressed, but he was not finally persuaded until Professor Coolidge advanced an irrefutable argument. He would, he said, be willing to guarantee Turner's $5000 salary for the next five years from his own sizable income, asking only that any university funds that became available be used to reduce his payments. The chance to obtain an outstanding professor at no cost was irresistible. Lowell wired that very day; would Turner delay making a decision on California until they could talk matters over?[43]

Fortunately, a meeting between them was already arranged, for Harvard was to inaugurate President Lowell on October 6, 1909, with all the fanfare proper to such an occasion, and Turner was scheduled not only to attend as a delegate from Wisconsin, but to receive an honorary degree. He arrived at Boston's South Station on the morning of October 5, took a streetcar to Cambridge, refreshed himself at the Colonial Club, where he had a room, and made his way to the president's office. Lowell, "very cordial and broadminded," lost no time in making his formal offer, cautioning only that it could not be final until various boards had acted. Turner was still not decided, but his mind was made up during a three-hour luncheon with Henry Morse Stephens of Berkeley, who was also attending the inauguration ceremonies. Stephens was not well enough to continue to administer the California department; Turner would be expected to take charge and to recruit the faculty needed to add luster to the university. Indeed, Stephens might be forced to resign at any time. "I should," Turner explained to his wife, "then be alone with a department to *unmake* and *make*." That unpleasant prospect tipped the scales.[44] He was ready to accept the Harvard offer.

Now Turner could endure the next day's ceremonies with his mind at peace. The formal procession, with its glittering array of uniforms and academic gowns; the inaugural address; the conferring of the honorary degrees, including a Doctorate of Letters to that "pioneer in American history" who had "set forth in memorable pages the vast influence of westward expansion upon the civilization of our country"; the formal luncheon for visiting dignitaries. Only then could Turner break the news to President Van Hise (who urged him to reconsider) and Henry Morse Stephens (who was badly cut, but "took the news like a gentleman"). "So my quarter century of work at Wisconsin closes up," Turner wrote to Mae that night, ". . . They have been rich years—in experience of all things the world offers; and you have been at my side through it all. . . . We shall push on together to see the stars again, knowing that the only real joy is in the effort to fulfill what is best in us."[45]

All was over now but arranging the troublesome details. For a time matters hung in the balance when the official notification made no mention of salary, but that was soon rectified: $5000 annually, the promise of $5500 before too long, the unwelcome news that it would be paid in four quarterly installments. "This makes a long lean period for one coming here from elsewhere," Haskins warned, "but you can on the other hand recognize the arrival of your salary when it comes in such chunks."[46] While the wheels ground slowly in Cambridge, Turner was busy in Madison, placating the losers in the tug-of-war over his services. His letter of resignation, expressing the hope that President Van Hise's "wise and farsighted policy" would be supported by the regents, was graciously answered, but the regents were less courteous; they accepted Turner's resignation without a single word of regret at his leaving. To Turner's relief, President Wheeler of California was as understanding as Van Hise, recognizing that a call to Harvard could not be matched either as honor or opportunity.[47] Turner had left one university and jilted another without making a single enemy.

There was less exultation in Cambridge, and less mourning in Madison, than Turner had hoped. The Harvard Bulletin lived up to his expectations with two full columns on his career and a glowing editorial that lauded his western specialization and branded him one of the few men alive able "to combine the large view with the small one, to combine the general plan and conception with the minute examination of particulars." "You did not get as much space as the Dartmouth game," wrote Haskins as he forwarded these comments, "but you got first place."[48] Madison treated the news less well. The *Daily Cardinal* was so crowded with columns on the coming Minnesota game that it did not even mention the loss of its most distinguished scholar, while the local press found room for only two sparse paragraphs amidst its columns on the BIG GAME. "Prof. Turner," boasted the *Wisconsin State Journal*, "is one of the most scholarly and popular members of the Wisconsin faculty and Harvard has made repeated efforts to induce him to become a member of its faculty." Thus were the great mourned, with a few hurried untruths.

Fortunately, the students and alumni had better sense. No sooner did the significance of Turner's leaving sink home than a cry was raised that was heard even within the sacred cloisters of the regents' meeting-room. The student University Senate and a "Wisconsin Committee of Students" awakened belatedly to his "inspired lectures" and unanimously resolved that his resignation be refused. Newspapers, particularly in Milwaukee, discovered that he was a "rarely inspired teacher" whose loss would be irreparable. Alumni raised their voices in a chorus of protest from Seattle to the eastern seaboard, some demanding that the regents induce Turner to reconsider his resignation, others finding for the first time that he was a scholar of such repute that the university could not possibly part with his services, and all praising his years of devoted teaching. Even the *Wisconsin Alumni Magazine*, although torn between regret that a professor who had achieved so much through the state's bounty should desert, and delight that a Wisconsinite should be in such demand, eventually decided to praise rather than condemn, and hoped that the regents would persuade him to stay.[49]

If there was mourning in the university community, there was even more in the historical fraternity of the Midwest. They voiced their sorrow at the loss of their most eminent representative at a Chicago meeting of the North Central History Teachers Association. The entire program, skillfully arranged by Professor Andrew C. McLaughlin, was one long paean of praise. Turner attended, ate the fifty-cent dinner at the Hutchinson Cafe, and sat in embarrassed delight as a parade of his best friends heaped adulation on adulation, climaxed by a poem "To F. J. T.".[50]

> The frontier weeps, expansion sleeps,
> No scholar's left to learn her.
> For Eastern jeers a Niobes' tears
> Off trots our lovely Turner.

Then came the letters, some spontaneous, others inspired by James Alton James, who urged all former students to write, bound the returns in a red leather cover, and presented the lot at a touching ceremony on the eve of the Turners' departure from Madison.[51] As Turner read those tributes, ranging in praise from high to highest, he must have taken solace in knowing that his efforts had been appreciated by a good many of the region's most eminent scholars, if not by the Board of Regents.

Most of this deluge—of student resolutions, newspaper editorials, letters from friends and former pupils—touched him deeply. All were answered personally—a formidable task, for they numbered more than a hundred—and each with an intimate touch that revealed his affection. "As I read my mail," he confessed to Carl Becker, "I have felt like a ghost caught indecently in pillaging his bodily representative's obituary notices." Yet there was immense satisfaction in what he read, even (as he modestly told James Alton James) if they proved that excellent historical students could "produce very deceptive history." Best of all was the realization that he had left a plentiful crop of scholars in the West to broaden the clearing that he had begun there. "One of the satisfactions I have in changing my residence," he wrote one student, "is that I am not leaving a historical field devoid of explorers."[52] Turner could take pleasure in the indisputable fact that his mark on his native section was too indelible to be erased.

His one fear was that his move might be misinterpreted as desire for greater prestige or financial award than Madison could offer. A few letters bore out that apprehension. Wrote one former student with as little regard for the truth as for grammar: "I reallize [sic] fully that we can not expect a person to make a complete sacrifice of themselves for one's native state, when similar fields of usefulness with more attractive surroundings and better compensation call elsewhere."[53] This cut deeply, for nothing could be further from the truth. Turner would have sold his soul to stay in the Madison that he loved. "I know," he told his wife, "that I have put aside the matter of 'joy of life' for the chance to do the thing that I ought to do." Two of his students, dropping in to bid him farewell, saw him break into tears as he thought of all that he was leaving behind. Turner was not drawn to Harvard by its attractions, as too many thought. He was leaving Wisconsin only because he honestly believed that his move would benefit the university by bringing the regents to their senses. "I feel," he told a colleague, "something like a watch that has been so frequently regulated that at last it can *run*."[54] He ran, but how he hated to do so.

To the few intimates who sensed his true motive, he explained his feelings frankly. At issue was his half-time teaching arrangement. This personified the basic conflict between President Van Hise and his faculty on the one hand and the regents and public on the other. As such, it was a danger rather than a benefit to the university. "I do not," he told a friend, "feel that my research arrangement is desirable for Wisconsin or myself under existing conditions." To bow to the regents and return to full-time teaching would be an admission of defeat for the whole principle of humanistic research. Only if he subordinated his own desires to the good of the university could the regents be awakened to the dangers of their policies; only if he shocked them by leaving would they lessen their attacks on pure research, cease meddling in faculty affairs, end their insistence that the administration be subordinated to the state's school system, and reverse their attempt to elevate practical above cultural instruction. That decision reached, he had only to decide between California and Harvard. California meant "more exploring in new fields and constructing historical clearings and cabins." The time had come "to settle long enough to raise a crop."[55] Harvard offered a better climate for research, and to Harvard he went. In all his reasoning there was not a hint of self-glorification or avariciousness. He wanted to stay in Madison; he could benefit Wisconsin by leaving. His thinking was as simple and honest as that.

Turner's cause could triumph only if his resignation spurred the regents into soul-searching and change, and there seemed little chance of that as he settled to his last year of teaching at Madison. The Stalwarts on the board were as outspoken as ever that fall of 1909; W. D. Hoard was storming about the state demanding more money for the School of Agriculture—the "political Gibraltar of the University," he called it—and C. P. Cary was urging the school superintendents under his charge to rebel against training students for college when most had no interest in higher education. At the other extreme, some of Turner's less moderate friends were itching to use his resignation as a pillory for the regents who had crucified him; Richard Lloyd Jones, who had written the muckraking article in *Collier's* that helped spark the controversy, was ready to prepare a series of exposures that would reveal the board members for what they were: an "ignorant and vicious" crew whose one hope was that democratic education be "throttled and curbed and rebuked and, perhaps, set back fifty years."[56] The battle lines were still tightly drawn, and the quiet reform that Turner wanted seemed far away.

Happily, these extremists no longer ruled, for behind the scenes the moderates on both sides were working quietly toward some solution. The machinery for this was set in motion when the faculty, at the request of the regents, elected a conference committee of nine to meet with a similar committee from the board to discuss the state of the university. When this met on December 10, 1909, the faculty members seized the initiative at once, with a clear statement of their basic grievance. They were, they told the regents, uneasy and dissatisfied following Turner's resignation, and would so remain until the board ceased meddling with individual faculty members. The regents had harried Turner into leaving by first granting, then questioning, his half-time research leaves; by inquiring into his hours of work with an animus that offended him, by distracting him with false accusations until he could no longer carry on his investigations, by creating such a hostile climate that he felt he was no longer wanted. These sentiments were infectious; when a scholar of Turner's status experienced such apprehensions, his doubts were shared by every member of the staff. They had even spread beyond the campus to the point that recruiting a replacement would be difficult.

The regents on the committee listened, then asked the question they were supposed to ask: what have we done to create this atmosphere of doubt and fear? The flood-gates of faculty resentment were opened now, and complaint piled on complaint: the regents had promoted and demoted teachers without consulting the department concerned, they had refused to promote others despite departmental and administrative recommendations, they had imperiled academic freedom by trying to tell the economics department what to teach, they had threatened academic tenure by forcing resignation, they had dealt individually with members of the instructional staff, they had interfered in graduate work by attending doctoral examinations, they had withheld funds from the philosophy department and the economics department and had been unduly generous in supporting "practical" subjects, they had questioned the value of the humanistic research that was the mainstay of any great university. They had, in other words, abused their trust by intruding in the educational processes of the university.

The remedy was as obvious as the malady, and was patiently spelled out by the faculty. Regents should communicate with professors or departments only through the president, they should follow departmental and administrative recommendations on all appointments and promotions, they should bow to the will of the professors on educational matters, they should never interfere in the subject content of any course. Even if an instructor taught socialism or anarchism? asked a regent. No instructor taught socialism or anarchism, he was firmly told, but "you cannot close any field of inquiry without impairing the student's faith in the honesty of teaching." One by one these points were ticked off, until one regent asked plaintively: "What, then, becomes of the powers of the Regents? Are we merely a consulting body?" He was wrong, of course, for the statement finally agreed upon simply recognized a workable division of authority: "The Regents have no intention of interfering with the customary methods of educational administration by the Faculty; they will continue to allow the Faculty the initiative in formulating educational policies; and they desire appointments to be made through the regular channels as developed in the custom of the University."[57] Here was a clear-cut definition of policy, but here also was a crow-eating admission by the regents that they had gone beyond their powers.

Such was the climate caused by Turner's resignation that the statement was adopted without change. The faculty heard the good news at its next meeting; the regents, they were assured, had acted with the best of intentions and with no improper motives; now they agreed to conform to the bylaws of the university. The committee's report to the board, delivered by Frederick C. Thwaits, its chairman and a staunch friend of Turner, was less pussyfooting. The regents had been to blame for Turner's departure and for the campus unrest that threatened the university. They must mend their ways by adhering strictly to the school's bylaws, and by recognizing that educational policy must be determined by faculty and administration. When these recommendations were agreed upon, the battle was over.[58] The faculty had won a clear victory, and Turner was vindicated.

Leaving Wisconsin, Turner soon found, was not easy, and much of the academic year of 1909-10 was squandered on annoying tasks that divided his attention between Cambridge and Madison. Cambridge demanded hours of time. He had to arrange his Harvard courses, first of all. His "History of the West" would be offered, of course, but the seminar posed problems. Albert Bushnell Hart spelled them out: Turner could give his own, or he could participate in a general seminar on American institutions, or he could offer one with Hart. Turner had a better idea; why not a joint seminar by the department's three Americanists, Channing, Hart, and Turner? This suggestion brought an acid rejoinder from Edward Channing: "Possibly you do not know that Hart and I split a few years ago on my initiative for reasons that will be apparent to you after you have been here a year or two."[59] There would be no cooperative instruction in American history at Harvard. Turner would offer his own seminar on the Van Buren administration. The class hours he would leave to the department, but he warned that an eight o'clock class would put him out of business in short order.

Housing for the Turners also had to be found. A preliminary survey that fall indicated that unfurnished houses rented for $900 a year, furnished houses rented for $1000, and Edward Channing's rented for $1500. Such prices were too rich for the Turner bank account, but by spring they realized that they had to make a decision. Their opportunity came when a colleague, Professor Roger B. Merriman, decided to vacate his stately mansion at 175 Brattle Street because of his wife's illness. He offered to rent the house to Turner for only $1000 a year. For a time the Turners hesitated, fearful lest the house be contaminated by disease, but they were soon reassured and sealed the bargain. They would live in unaccustomed style, at least for their first year in Cambridge.

Their financial problems were somewhat eased by developments in Madison. The search for Turner's successor proved easier than anticipated; Max Farrand (the first choice) was not interested in leaving Yale to which he had just moved, but a rising young star in western history, Frederic Logan Paxson, could be lured from his professorship at the University of Michigan. Paxson proved an ideal choice for all concerned; not only did his recent book, *The Last American Frontier*, assure him a reputation that would attract graduate students, but he was willing to buy the Turner house at the asking price of $13,000—$3000 down and the balance by November 1, 1910.[60] The Turners would have a small backlog of savings to show for their years in Madison, even though most of their profits would be swallowed up by retirement of the mortgage and moving expenses.

Those troublesome matters settled, Turner settled into a busy spring of teaching and lecturing. That he taught at all was due to his own generosity, for he was due a sabbatical leave, both through his university contract and because he had accumulated credits by summer-school teaching, but he was conscious of the students' needs and offered a semester of his course on Van Buren's administration. At times he must have regretted even this much commitment to the classroom, burdened as he was by lecture engagements long agreed upon: a Phi Beta Kappa address at the University of Michigan in mid-May on "Middle Western Ideals," a paper before the Iowa City meeting of the Mississippi Valley Historical Association later that month on "The Significance of the Mississippi Valley in American History," a commencement address at Indiana University in June. These meant hours of preparation, just at a time when everyone in Madison, apparently, insisted on giving a farewell party for the Turners. They lived a gay social life that spring, climaxed by a reception at the home of Carl Russell Fish, where students and faculty gave the Turners a silver tea service, and by a departmental dinner with Reuben Gold Thwaites as host, Sellery as speechmaker, and a pair of Zeis binoculars the parting gift. Turner's delight at this homage was dampened by one glaring omission: the Board of Regents made not a single gesture to mourn his leaving. That cut deeply.[61]

Summer brought some relief from the social round, but none from the burdens of work. Turner had agreed to teach summer school—the $500 fee was essential to his budget—and he had to use every moment that could be snatched from classroom preparation on a long overdue article for the *Encyclopaedia Britannica*. His labors were magnified by Madison's excessive heat and a prolonged drought that filled the air with dust; they were magnified again when Mae and Dorothy left in early July to find a sanctuary from the hay fever that attacked early that summer, leaving him to endure the final agonies of packing alone. Books—thousands of books—had to be boxed, furniture crated, movers employed, transportation by rail arranged. A complication arose when the company that had sold the Turners their player piano announced that it could not leave the state until the final $458 due was paid, further taxing Turner's time and dwindling bank account. But at last Turner had a van trundle the household goods to the railroad yards—only to discover that the freight car assigned them was too small. A few good cigars and a modestly priced supper bribed the workmen to shift the whole lot by lantern-light, a task that was not completed until ten o'clock on the night of July 30. "I got home," he reported to Mae, "tired enough to sleep."[62]

Nor was the end yet, for Turner had to endure another week of classes before he could follow his furniture to New England. A dismal week it was, with steaming temperatures, a round of dinners with friends, lectures in an oven-like classroom, and, at night, interminable hours on the *Britannica* article. Finally, on August 10, the last task was completed, the last suitcase packed. Turner was ready to leave Madison. As a hired hack carried him along East Washington Street toward the railroad station, he could see workmen beginning to dismantle the horse market that had been a landmark since he could remember—a victim of the automobiles and paved roads that were changing the city's profile. Madison stood on the threshold of a new day when an urban swirl and a gigantic educational institution would replace the tree-shaded streets, the pleasant little college, the leisurely pace of life that Turner knew and loved. He was leaving just in time.

XIII

Harvard Years:
The Academic World

1910-1917

IF FREDERICK JACKSON TURNER had been a prudent and well-ordered man, he would have arrived in Cambridge in mid-August of 1910, ready to join his wife in her hay-fever retreat in the Berkshires and to journey with her to Hancock Point on Maine's cool coast, where she stayed with friends through September. Instead, he had to pay for his sins as a procrastinator. With him came a mountain of notes and a conscience burdened by a scandalously overdue publishing commitment. Instead of relaxing to the murmur of mountain pines, he was doomed to swelter through nights at the Colonial Club and days at the Harvard Library as he ground out page after page for a demanding editor of the *Encyclopaedia Britannica*.

Turner was hardened to the plaints of publishers, but even he admitted that this one had justice on his side. Four years had passed since he had agreed to prepare an article for the *Britannica* on the United States since 1865, with a fee of $500 as the lure. The assignment seemed simple enough at the time—twenty-five pages dealing solely with the political chronicle, to be delivered by October 1, 1907—but Turner had a knack of transforming the simplest task into a model of complexity. Here was a little-known field of marvelous fascination, scarcely touched by historians, and bursting with intriguing problems. So the deadline came and went. Periodic inquiries from the editors grew increasingly peremptory, but not until May 1910 did Turner feel that he had mastered the subject thoroughly enough to put pen to paper. By this time Turner had forgotten the 25-page space limitation, and the New York office had lost the early correspondence where it was specified. Hence they settled on any "reasonable length," which was a green light for a great deal more about the recent United States than the *Britannica* expected.[1]

Turner was at his best when working under the lash, and it was liberally applied. Letters, cables from London, pleas from the New York editors were part of his life as he labored through those hot August days. "Boston is a turkish bath," he reported. "I didn't sleep much last night, but I did get my article along aways, though it is hard travellin' for a man acclimated neither to Boston, nor to work."[2] The results were satisfactory—the first 78 pages sent on August 29, the last of the 194 three weeks later, the bibliography (1250 words longer than requested) by early October, after threats from London that the whole edition was being delayed. Turner had stretched his twenty-five page article into nearly two hundred pages, and a 750-word bibliography into 2000 words—with only the $500 agreed upon as compensation—but he had learned a great deal about a difficult period, and he had produced an article that was viewed by his generation as a major contribution.[3]

He also finished in time to spend three weeks in the Maine woods. Then, in early October, he and Mae and Dorothy moved into their elegant Brattle Street home. They were a bit overwhelmed by its magnificence; Turner was terrified by the dainty antique furniture but delighted at the prospect of keeping fit by walking about in a home that was as big as all outdoors. His friends in Madison took unabashed delight in his plight. "To have a man with your Jacksonian ideas established in a mansion on Tory Row," wrote Reuben Gold Thwaites, "came very near creating heart rupture in this neck of the woods."[4]

Turner had little time to enjoy spacious living, for he had arrived just in time to plunge into the new academic world to which he was committed. And what a fascinating world it was! Harvard, despite its eminence, was a small school by modern standards, with some 2200 students—nearly all of them haughtily indifferent to learning and content with the "Gentleman's Grade" of "C" in their courses. They were rigidly stratified on the basis of wealth and breeding, with the elite concentrated in Mt. Auburn Street's "Gold Coast," the middle group existing in shabby quarters in the "Yard," and the remainder living about Boston and commuting by trolley. Academic requirements were modest; President A. Lawrence Lowell was beginning his attack on the complete freedom of course election that had prevailed under President

Charles W. Eliot, but only gradually were his reforms accepted: "concentration" on a major subject applied first for the class of 1914, a tutorial system at about the same time, common halls for freshmen near the Charles River in 1914, an honors examination for the division of History, Government and Economics in 1917. Turner watched these changes with moderate approval, afraid that they were converting him into a combination of sausage-filling machine and private detective, as he crammed knowledge into reluctant pupils and policed them as they acquired it.[5]

The history department was more to his liking. Two of the Europeanists, his old friend Charles Homer Haskins and his new friend and benefactor Archibald Cary Coolidge, were his particular favorites. Coolidge, especially, proved a tower of strength; he could always be relied upon to convince President Lowell that this project or that of Turner's was worth supporting. His colleagues in American history were of a different stamp. One, Albert Bushnell Hart, was genuinely cordial and did his best to be friendly, but he was so absorbed in university and national politics (he was a fanatical supporter of his Harvard classmate Theodore Roosevelt) and so wrapped up in his writing and editorial chores (930 articles published during his academic years, an average of one every two weeks, and nearly one hundred books, two and one-half a year) that he had no time for companionship. The other was Edward Channing.

Turner spent his years at Harvard trying to understand Channing, and he never succeeded. A chubby dynamo of a man, short and smooth-shaven, Channing was a popular undergraduate teacher, charging his lectures with irony and wit, enlivening them with dramatic techniques, and packing them with demands on the students' time that terrorized all but the most industrious. His horizons, however, never extended west of the Hudson River and seldom beyond the Connecticut. That the frontier had been a force in American history he stubbornly refused to recognize; he only reluctantly admitted that there was a West, and the single chapter on "The Westward March" in the last volumes of his multivolume history of the United States did little more than trace the migration of a few New England families. In that work he deemed Turner's theory worthy of mention only in three footnote references. This was a deliberate slight, but Turner did his best to be charitable. "Porcupinus Angelicus," he called him (behind his back), but he was sincerely eager for a friendship that Channing would never allow. "Channing and I," he told a colleague, "had quite different conceptions of the trend of American history. . . . Nevertheless, I appreciated the scholarship of the man and his New England point of view." Channing was less charitable. "Turner is a dear fellow," he confided to a student, "but he has no idea of the value of time. He has never written any big books."[6]

There was reason for his bristly attitude. Channing, subconsciously or perhaps consciously, recognized in Turner a symbol of the futility of his own life. It was his misfortune that he was never to rise above the "scientific school" of historiography in which he had been reared; unable, or unwilling, to change with the times, he was outmoded before he reached the prime of life. Albert B. Hart offered him no reminders of this, for their views were comparable, but now a vigorous young man had come into the department to challenge his theories, lure graduate students from his seminar, and take over the major task of directing doctoral dissertations. His antagonism was deep, nurtured by his growing isolation from the local and national historical world. This the students sensed. Circulated among them was a cruel satire, purportedly a letter from Channing to the "Star Chamber," demanding that Turner be punished for destroying the sound structure of history that had reached its pinnacle "with the appearance of my fourth volume." "He treats my American history as an amoeba, capable of unlimited division," and had divided it into Old West, New West, Middle West, North West, South West, and Far West. When a copy of this document fell into Turner's hand, he scrawled on it, "Hazing me," but the rift went far deeper.[7]

On the surface, however, all was well, and Turner could begin his Harvard teaching that October with no more than the usual apprehensions. His first lecture in History 17, "The History of the West," went well enough; he found sixty-one students in his classroom, most of them New Englanders with names that spelled eastern conservatism —a Roosevelt, a Frothingham, and a Conant were enrolled—and all were utterly unversed in anything remotely resembling knowledge of the frontier. "They are engaging young rascals," he reported to a Madison friend, "and I foresee that I shall have an interesting experience in attempting to guide them over western trails."[8] Turner led them deep into the wilderness that morning: he gave them a terrifying battery of assignments first—his own essays on "The Significance of the Fron-

312 Frederick Jackson Turner

tier" and "The Problem of the West," an article in a recent *South Atlantic Quarterly* on the legacy of the pioneers, E. L. Godkin's book,
Problems of American Democracy, and Achille Loria's *The Economic
Foundations of Society*, a look at the maps in the *Census* Atlas for 1900
—then a liberal dose of frontier theory. The frontier was "a zone of
population extending between civilization and the wilderness" where
society was atomized, flying apart into individual particles; frontiersmen were altered by this unfamiliar environment, their behavior dictated by the practical problems of existence. "The course will be the
study of a PROCEDURE rather than a REGION."[9] Here was the gospel according to Turner, a gospel that was as stimulating as it was unfamiliar
to undergraduates nurtured in the belief that the alpha and omega of
American life lay in New England.

If the students found the experience pleasant, so did Turner. The
lads were alert and clever, "if not so steady at the tugs as our western
classes," and many of them were genuinely interested. Those who were
not soon fell by the wayside; the men of large means— the "Mt. Auburn
youth"—departed when they discovered that the way to salvation lay
through the library, but the football team, attracted by the promise of
a diet of cowboys and Indians, "took its medicine like men, and got
good grades."[10] The seminar raised no such problems, even though some
might feel that Turner could have selected a more lively topic than the
election of 1836 as it influenced the Van Buren administration. They
were a capable crew, led by such stellar lights as Samuel Eliot Morison
and Kenneth W. Colgrove, and they did their work so well that Turner
found them not at all inferior to his Wisconsin graduate students.
Only one, R. H. Smith, failed to appear for the second semester, while
the "History of the West" enrollment increased from 61 to 67
students.[11]

With classes under way and the family settled into its temporary
home, Turner could turn to two pressing tasks that plagued him during
his first Harvard year. One was the presidential address that he had to
deliver before the American Historical Association when it met in
Indianapolis that December. He had been increasingly aware of that
responsibility, but had delayed as usual, and when he arrived in Cambridge he was still toying with topics worthy of the occasion. No mere
rehash of his ideas on the frontier and section would do; the traditions

of the association decreed that he must select a subject significant to the entire profession, not just to his own interests. For a time he considered "Changing American Ideals," and "Perspective in American History," but eventually he settled on one more suited to his talents: "Social Forces in American History."[12]

Turner left no record of the train of thought that led him to this topic, but little imagination is needed to reconstruct his trail. As one unusually sensitive to the atmosphere of his day, he recognized that younger historians were on the point of rebellion against the traditional interpretation of the past, and that their revolt was sparked by the spirit of Progressivism that had accompanied Theodore Roosevelt into the White House. To them, no less than to the muckrakers and re-formers, social improvement was of paramount importance, so impor-tant that history must be converted into an instrument for the trans-formation of society. Change was occurring, they saw, not by the slow evolution of institutions, but through conflicts of interest and clashes between factions. Had this been the case in prior eras? Was change rather than continuity, conflict rather than consensus, the key to under-standing the past? And, if the dynamics of change and conflict could be thoroughly understood, could the lessons learned be applied to the im-provement of modern society?[13]

These were challenging questions, and as historians sought answers to them they wrought a revolution in the understanding of the past. Their spotlight was not on the European genesis of American institutions, but on the environmental pressures that adjusted those institutions to the needs of the people; not on the remote past, but on more recent events relevant to today's problems. They saw eighteenth- and nineteenth-century America not as a placid land where institutions evolved slowly, but as a country in a constant state of flux, where conflicts between contending groups underlay progress. The ultimate goal of the na-tion was not achievement of national unity, as earlier scholars had be-lieved, but social and political democracy. The historian's duty was to reveal the significance of the conflicts that led toward this goal, to show their continuity, and to demonstrate their usefulness to the social re-formers of the present.

These views had been Turner's stock-in-trade since 1891, when he prepared his paper on "The Significance of History," but they had taken root slowly through the profession and only now were ready to blossom. At the very session where Turner read his presidential address, James Harvey Robinson spoke on "The Relation of History to the Newer Sciences of Man," touching off a controversy with George Lincoln Burr and other conservatives. In that same year Carl Becker, in an *Atlantic Monthly* article on "Detachment and Writing History," launched an attack on the "objectivists" who believed in the inviolability of "facts," and Lynn Thorndike sharpened the assault by attacking "The Scientific Presentation of History," in *Popular Science Monthly*. These were the shock troops that prepared the way for James Harvey Robinson to issue his collected essays on *The New History* two years later, a volume that gave the movement its name and focus.

The "New Historians" broke sharply with the past. Their emphasis was on events relevant to the present; history they saw as an instrument for reform, not as a subject to be pursued for idle curiosity. They urged less emphasis on political chronicles and more on the social and intellectual record as a means of probing the motives of human behavior and the impact of environmental pressures; their purpose was to understand change as the product of "the underlying forces that surged beyond and behind the visible body politic" (as Turner put it). They thought of themselves as realists, shunning both "barren" empiricism and "grandiose" abstractions. They subordinated the past to the present, and searched for evidence of continuity in the contortions that periodically nudged society into progress. They urged the use of techniques borrowed from other disciplines—sociology, economics, political science, anthropology—as necessary to an understanding of the background of today's problems; the principal purpose of history was not to illuminate former eras, but to synthesize the social sciences and reveal their predictive value in solving the dilemmas of today. History, in other words, was to be broadened, enriched by borrowings from other disciplines, and used to look backward through the eyes of the present.

All this Turner recognized as he gave thought to a subject for his address. What was more logical than that he should issue a manifesto to encourage the surfacing of concepts that he had preached for a generation? Perhaps he was goaded into such a decision when he reread the 1908 presidential address of George Burton Adams, a conservative who defined history as a "science of investigation" that operated wholly independently of other disciplines to achieve a chronological arrangement of "facts." Such echoes from a bygone day had to be refuted.

Turner began his own address by recognizing that the historical fact was "not planted on the solid ground of fixed conditions." Instead, every investigator was influenced by the times in which he lived; each new generation came on the scene equipped with different insights and prejudices than its predecessors. Turner saw the pathway of history strewn with the wrecks of "known and acknowledged truths" the result of both imperfect analysis and the failure of historians to pay proper attention to the relativity and transiency of their own basis for appraisal. He took no extreme stand for relativism; while skeptical of man's ability ever to learn the exact truth about the past, he still believed that proper methodology and the use of well-formulated hypotheses allowed the truth to be approximated.

Such a methodology required liberal borrowings from other disciplines. Devoting the principal body of his address to a capsule survey of the changes in the American social order since the closing of the frontier, he drew an obvious lesson: that the transformation from a rural to an industrial-urban economy posed problems of such complexity that they could be understood only by scholars well-versed in all the social sciences. Scientists, Turner pointed out, had bridged the gap between disciplines to create electrochemistry, geophysics, astrophysics, and a host of similar cooperative fields; historians must effect alliances with economists, sociologists, political scientists, geologists, geographers, psychologists, and students of the arts if they were to be properly equipped to analyze modern society. This was a belief long preached by Turner, but new to many in his audience; he was the first president of the Association to urge an interdisciplinary approach in his presidential address.

If this was treason to the traditionalists, so were two other points that he emphasized—and that mirrored the views of the "New Historians." History, he insisted, was no mere political chronicle; its principal concern should be the subterranean social forces that determined political events, "shaping and reshaping under the conditions of a nation changing as it adjusts to its environment." Nor were the findings of the historian absolute; the function of the historian was constantly to "rework our history from the new points of view afforded by the present." These heretical views, as offensive to the orthodox as Turner's demand for an interdisciplinary approach, served as an ultimatum to the Old Guard of the profession. Turner had taken his stand for "Progressive History," and opened a new world of interpretation to his younger colleagues.[14] When Waldo G. Leland, secretary of the Association, reported that Turner's address had imposed "new duties" on scholars, he was speaking accurately. So was James Schouler, venerable spokesman for a dying generation, when he complained that history should not be re-written "to suit each new fashion of thought and interest . . . in order to please the coming age."[15] Turner had made no such suggestion, of course, but Schouler's exaggerated alarms typified the panic among the defenders of "Scientism."

James Schouler's carping, and the few echoes that it stirred among his fellow conservatives, was drowned in the chorus of approval that "Social Forces in American History" inspired. Turner was immensely pleased, but his cup of joy overflowed when the applause that greeted his address was interrupted by the arrival of a delegation of his former students, bearing with them a handsome volume with the title *Essays in American History Dedicated to Frederick Jackson Turner*. This had been long a-borning; Charles Homer Haskins made the original suggestion, Guy Stanton Ford assumed the task of extracting essays from a score of former students, and Henry Holt & Company undertook the printing on the theory that, if they could not publish a book by Turner, they would publish one for him. Turner was overjoyed. "I am as pleased as a grandfather with a new grandbaby," he told one of the contributors.[16] He was also embarrassed that his students and the publishers should suffer financially, insisting on sending a check for $8.10 for the six copies sent him—a check that was promptly returned by Henry Holt & Company. As Turner read the essays, he must have had some doubts whether his teaching had succeeded, for few of them were worthy of attention, then or since. Even Guy Stanton Ford, the editor, realized in retrospect that the volume's only virtue was to print Carl Becker's brilliant comments on "Kansas."[17] That Turner's *festschrift* was somewhat more disastrous than most was due to the catholicity of his own interests. The term "frontier" did not appear in the title of a single essay, and only two remotely touched on the subject; instead, they ranged over the whole spectrum of historical interests that Turner inspired in his pupils. Lacking emphasis on the West that the profession associated with his name, and built about no central theme, the volume was quickly—and mercifully—forgotten.

Turner returned to Cambridge from Indianapolis that December, proudly bearing his *festschrift* and with plaudits for his presidential address ringing in his ears, to plunge into a thoroughly disagreeable task that his Harvard appointment required. Even before he arrived in Cambridge, his colleagues, Edward Channing and Albert Bushnell Hart, had offered him an opportunity he could not refuse. The *Guide to the Study of American History* that they had published in 1896 was long out of date; Ginn & Company were eager for a new edition; would Turner join in the revision? He accepted, of course, and the contract was signed in December 1909: 10 per cent royalty to be divided among the three authors, $1000 for secretarial and research aid, a delivery date of January 1, 1911. Turner's assignments were sections on the West and recent history. The triumvirate almost broke up when defining "recent history"; Channing wanted to end in 1898, but Turner insisted on 1910, and he carried the day with Hart's support. So work began, slowly for Turner, whose autumn was occupied with his presidential address; predictably, he was far from done by January 1, but neither were his collaborators. By June 1911, Channing was nearing the end and Hart's portions were in galley proof, but Turner's were still in manuscript, and very rough manuscript at that. Then, too, his sections were running far beyond the word limit that had been imposed. Pressure continued through that summer and into the next school year before Hart's whip-cracking forced Turner to surrender his contributions to the publisher, but the delay was worth while. "I don't know that you have ever rendered a greater service (except your volume in the Am. Nation Series) to the sound understanding of American history," Hart assured him.[18]

These were no idle words, for Turner had made a significant contribution to the "Harvard Guide." His sections on recent history were revolutionary; topics such as "The Trust Problem," "Labor and Injunction," "Conservation," and "American Society in the Twentieth Century" were newcomers to textbooks, and helped shape the teaching of recent American history for a generation. So were the major sections on social and industrial history. His portions on "The West" were less original, largely because he had made the subject familiar to scholars, but they allowed him to garner an unearned increment. A list of the more important books and articles that he had surveyed were brought together in a guide for his students, published in 1911: *List of References in History 17: History of the West.* This modest work of 89 pages was incomplete and was, in Turner's later judgment, an "obvious atrocity,"[19] but it was the progenitor of a whole succession of editions of *List of References* that would be purchased by generations of Harvard students and that would influence the teaching of the subject nationally.

More to Turner's liking was a final assignment inflicted on him by the energetic Albert Bushnell Hart. Would he prepare three articles— "The Frontier in American Development," "Sectionalism in the United States," and "The West as a Factor in American Politics"—for the *Cyclopedia of American Government* that Hart and Andrew C. McLaughlin were editing? The honorarium was generous and the subjects so dear to Turner's heart that he could not refuse, even though he shuddered at the prospect of another deadline. Well he might. The date agreed upon—December 1911—came and went with work scarcely under way; six months later, Hart was warning that the whole volume was ready to go to press and that he must turn elsewhere unless the articles were delivered by June 17, 1912. Turner tried, but he was so deluged by proof on the *Harvard Guide* that not until the end of the month could he write his daughter: "Tonight I start on the race to finish the articles."[20] "Race" was hardly the word; they were not ready for delivery until mid-September and then they were not in publishable form; the 2000 words allotted to the frontier had grown to 2600, the 2000 on sectionalism to 3900, and the 2500 on the West in American politics to 5400. Back they went to him for another month of work before Hart was satisfied.[21] They made but scant contribution, for Turner had said the same things before, but they did compress most of his frontier and sectional theories into a relatively brief space.

The succession of deadlines that kept Turner's nose to the grindstone during his first year in Cambridge meant that his social life was restricted, but with the last galley of proof on the *Harvard Guide* read, and the last encyclopedia article delivered to Hart's office, he could settle into the comfortable routine that was to last until World War I toppled his world into chaos. He and Mae fitted moderately well into Harvard's unfamiliar society and they enjoyed themselves—but again in moderation. The luxurious home of Professor Merriman proved so comfortable that after a year there they moved into a nearby house at 153 Brattle Street that was only slightly less elegant and not at all cheaper; again in 1914 they shifted to a somewhat more modest property at 7 Phillips Place, where the annual rental was only $800. There they lived for the next decade. "We are," Turner reported to a friend in Madison, "well and comfortably housed in our second quarters since the main migration. But it is among other peoples' books and pictures and among other friends and it is not entirely natural yet."[22] Each of these establishments required more care than tiny Mae could give; at least one "Nellie" or "Lizzie" was always in residence and usually two, along with the stenographer Turner needed to drive him to his writing.

These extraordinary expenses doomed him to a constant struggle against bank overdrafts. The $13,000 paid by Paxson for their Madison home was spent before the summer of 1910 was over—$5000 to pay off the mortgage note held by his sister, $4466 to retire miscellaneous debts, a few modest investments—and Turner reached Cambridge with only $300 in the bank and the prospect of borrowing before the first Harvard paycheck came, on December 1. This paltry sum, five shares of American Telephone and Telegraph worth $712 and five of Great Northern Railroad worth $630, a pianola that had cost $950 in 1908 and would sell for less now, a Remington rifle, a Columbia bicycle, a canoe, and a considerable number of books—these were Turner's principal assets after two decades of service to the historical profession. He had also contracted for $17,000 in life insurance that cost him heavily in premiums and was used less as a cushion against the future than as collateral for frequent bank loans.[23] That was all he had. His salary—$5000 a year to 1915 and $5500 thereafter—was adequate for its day, but hardly generous, while other sources of income were almost nonexistent. Royalties on the *Harvard Guide* did not begin until 1920, when he received a check for $13.82, and they never exceeded $35 a year thereafter.[24]

The one bright spot in the Turners' financial future was a speculative stock on which they pinned their hopes for a comfortable old age. President Van Hise was responsible. Hearing rumors of iron deposits in the wilds of Brazil, that eminent geologist made a personal investigation in 1910 that revealed resources as rich as those of Minnesota's

Mesabi Range. Options were taken out, the Brazilian Iron and Steel Company formed, and a few friends allowed to buy stock in a venture that was a gamble, but that promised fabulous returns. Turner contracted for thirty shares, using $500 from the sale of his house as a down payment, and scraping together the remaining $2500 over the next years. His faith in that nest egg was almost pathetic; over and over again he cautioned his family never to sell the "Brazil" stock save as a last resort, assuring them that it would soon pay them $4000 yearly. Alas for such pipe dreams. Every effort to raise the capital needed to develop the properties failed, then the company collapsed completely as Europe plunged into the 1914 war. Turner's hopes of a bountiful retirement and security for Dorothy vanished with his small investment.[25]

The Turners lived always on the brink of debt, but most of their professorial friends were in the same plight, and they saw no reason to complain. They settled into the social life of Cambridge and Boston, as the usual round of dinners, teas, and receptions widened their circle of acquaintances. Friends—the close friends they had known in Madison—were few; Charles Homer Haskins was their sole intimate until his marriage in 1912 added his bride to the little group. Both of the Turners missed the easy give-and-take they had known with the Van Hises and Slaughters on Frances Street, but both were properly respectful of the fashionable events that Bostonians understood so well: stately dinners at the home of James Ford Rhodes, affairs at the Algonquin Club, an evening with Josiah Royce, who was "very bright and interesting," another where Mrs. William James so overawed Turner that he could do no more than admire her conversation "in brilliant spells of silence."[26] "Interesting" experiences, Turner would have labeled them, but hardly the old-shoe friendships that he so enjoyed in the past.

His clubs were also more invigorating than relaxing. Two welcomed him to membership: the Shop-Club, where he matched wits with such lights as Frank W. Taussig, Edwin F. Gay, and Ephraim Emerton in monthly evening meetings where papers were read and discussed; and the Thursday Club, whose members met over an elaborate dinner, plentiful wines, and light conversation before listening to the inevitable essay by one of the members on a topic dear to his research interests. There Turner rubbed elbows with such giants as William James, Harlow Shapley, John Livingston Lowes, and Zachariah Chafee, and there he heard discussions that ranged from "The Old Testament as a German Type" to color blindness in fish (he was delighted to find that they could see the lures that he tied to attract them).[27] There, too, he tried out his own essays; many written during his Harvard years were specifically prepared for this club or that. Historical societies also afforded some relaxation; soon after he arrived, the Cambridge Historical Society enlisted him for a paper on "History and the Local History Society" (spent largely in describing the glories of the State Historical Society in Wisconsin),[28] and over the next years he regularly attended meetings of the American Antiquarian Society in Worcester, where he mingled with such headliners as President Taft and Lord Bryce; the Massachusetts Historical Society, where he advocated enough additions to the list of reference books to bankrupt the organization; and the Colonial Society of Massachusetts, which he served as president in 1914. In a moment of misguided patriotism, Turner even accepted membership in the Bunker Hill Monument Association, only to be called upon as a frequent speaker at their meetings.

These ventures into New England clubland were pleasant enough, but there, too, Turner lacked the intimate comradeship that Madison had provided. So it was that he welcomed the friendship of a lady who seemed utterly unsuited to the role, but who offered him the sympathetic companionship that he needed. Mrs. Alice Forbes Perkins Hooper, wife of "Squire" William Hooper of Boston's elite North Shore, and herself the well-to-do daughter of Charles Elliott Perkins, entered his life shortly after he arrived in Cambridge. She and her husband were having an intimate dinner for President and Mrs. William Howard Taft, and one of her guests had failed her. Could Turner fill in? "I dare say you are old friends." Those arrangements fell through, but Turner and Mrs. Hooper lunched in a less formal setting a week later, and there she unfolded a plan dear to her heart. She wanted to establish a living memorial to her departed father, who had done so much to develop the West by building the Burlington Railroad. A fund to buy books in western history for Harvard's Library had occurred to her. Would Turner approve? Turner did, with enthusiasm, and over the next months they nurtured the plans that culminated in the Harvard Commission on Western History, with Mrs. Hooper its generous angel and Turner its guiding spirit.[29]

The years spent guiding this Commission to its successes in book collecting—and its failure when Harvard officials declined to provide the support it had to have in the inflationary years following World War I —cemented a friendship that was one of Turner's most treasured possessions. They saw each other often, usually over a waffle lunch at Mrs. Hooper's extravagant home, "Elsinaes," in Manchester-by-the-Sea, to talk endlessly of history, of world affairs, of the whole spectrum of art and literature. Mrs. Hooper was a fascinating woman, exceedingly large, crippled to such a degree that she often used crutches, but with a vitality that lured to her home a constant procession of diplomats, college professors, authors, actors, musicians, and unclassifiable characters, all of whom graced her board and refurbished her vast supply of anecdotes and information. "Elsie's house," her mother once declared, "was the only *salon* in Massachusetts." Turner thoroughly enjoyed her remarkable mind, her breezy lack of orthodoxy, her professions of loyalty to the Midwest, where she had spent part of her girlhood. "I really think," he told her once, "I should explode if I couldn't talk out a common point of view with you occasionally. Frankly you are the best thing I have discovered in New England."[30] Mrs. Hooper filled a gap in his life that Madison and his close friends there had provided.

Yet now, as in Wisconsin, Turner found his principal pleasures not in clubs or historical societies or friends, but in the bosom of his own family. He and Mae were inseparable as she watched over his comfort, guarded his health, and ran the household so efficiently that he was free to concentrate on his work. Dorothy, their lone child, was just as adored and just as adoring. Blessed with her mother's petite beauty and her father's wit and charm, she had grown into an irresistible young lady, capable of scattering broken hearts behind her as she moved through circles of Madison and Cambridge. Such a combination meant that she would soon leave them. That day came when she succumbed to the attentions of John S. Main, an old friend of the family, during a visit to Madison in the spring of 1913. Nothing would do but that he visit the Turners that summer to win their approval; they were to be at Kennebago Lake in Maine, and Turner's letter of invitation sounded more like a summons to a fisherman's convention than to the home of the intended's parents. John arrived without the assortment of rods, reels, and flies he had been advised to bring, and with the shameful confession that he fished with worms, but Turner forgave him when he saw the adoration in his daughter's eyes.

That fall the parental consent was formally asked. Turner lectured his would-be son-in-law on the dangers and duties of marriage—"we want you both to be reasonably sure that you have talked out your tastes, your habits, your convictions far enough to be sure that you can both bear and forbear on the matters of divergence; that you love each other well enough to make mutual adjustments; that you do not love an image but the real man and woman"—then wired his consent before his letter could reach Madison. The engagement was announced in November 1913, and in the spring of 1914 they were married. Turner was as happy as his daughter was with the addition to his family. "His only substantial limitation," he told Dorothy, "is that he doesn't know how to fish with a fly. But he seems able to land his trout, and that's something, isn't it?"[31]

That marriage was to bring the Turners sorrow and joy over the next years. Sorrow first in the early spring of 1915, when the first baby was due and Mae hurried to Wisconsin to take charge. Turner, keeping bachelor quarters in Cambridge, was alone when he opened a black-bordered telegram; the child had been born dead. "Your pathetic letter almost broke my heart when I read of our little girl's wonder if she had wanted her baby hard enough," he wrote that night. The tiny body was buried beside the graves of the Turners' own lost children, opening wounds that had never completely healed. Not until a year and a half later were their sorrows swept away with word of the arrival of a handsome grandson on August 8, 1917.[32] Jackson Turner Main, Dorothy named him—a prophetic gesture, for that child was destined to become an eminent American historian.

Turner's joy at the arrival of Jackson Turner Main was touched with pathos, for he was increasingly aware of his own deteriorating health. He made periodic attempts to check the decline; giving up tobacco provided a yearly exercise in willpower that he always lost, while the diets that he inflicted on himself at irregular intervals were either so unrealistic or so temporary that they did little good. Severe colds, influenza, and painful sore throats were Turner's usual winter lot, compounded always by a stubbornly high blood pressure. A worse blow to his ego followed shortly after his fiftieth birthday, when his eyes gave out, requiring that he be permanently dressed in glasses. "By the time you return," he reported to Dorothy, "I shall have false teeth and a long grey beard and a shrill treble voice and a cane and shall need you to help me rise from my easy chair in the corner."[33]

Turner joked about his ailments, but they were no laughing matter. Recurring bouts with illnesses taught him that. In January 1914, a painful carbuncle required lancing under ether and ten days in bed for recovery. A year later a boil in the inner ear erupted into excruciating agony with a fever that shot to 104 degrees, then gave way to erysipelas that began on the face and spread over the body. For a fortnight Turner suffered such torment that his mind wandered as Boston specialists were summoned to save his life. "It was a distinctly rocky road, and I am still more or less shaken up by the journey," he told a friend.[34] Again, in the spring of 1917, he went under the knife for a hernia operation that left him bedridden for three weeks and a walking shadow of himself for a year thereafter.[35] Increasingly slow recovery, no less than the illnesses themselves, showed that Turner was far from the robust person he appeared to his friends.

He believed, with some justification, that his deteriorating health was a by-product of mental strain; whenever he immersed himself too deeply in a problem or grappled overlong with a historical enigma, he ended in bed. His prescription for a cure was based on long experience; a summer in the north woods or the mountains would not only rejuvenate his health but immunize him against illness for the next academic year. Turner saw holidays not as vacations, but as medical necessities; hence he continued the practice, begun at Wisconsin, of accepting summer-school assignments in the West, where he could exchange a few weeks of teaching for an equal time in the Rockies or Sierras.

The universities of Washington and Oregon lured him westward in 1914 with a joint appointment that was hard to resist: fifteen lectures at each on "Phases of the Western Influence in American History," with a total salary of $1200 and time to unwind amidst the rugged beauty of the Cascade Mountains. The cherry on the pudding was an additional payment of all his expenses if he would deliver the commencement address at Washington. Turner did so, very badly he felt, for he had been too busy ending the Harvard year and marrying Dorothy to John S. Main to prepare a proper address on "The West and

American Ideals."[36] The rest of the summer was more satisfactory. Students at Oregon and Washington may not have heard, as their catalogue promised them, "an inspiring lecturer combining in his attitude of mind the qualities of the philosopher, the poet and the statesman,"[37] but they were treated to a first-rate series by a very competent scholar. Turner was happy with the results and with the "good stuff" in his classes.

He was far happier with the weekend expeditions into the Cascades and the ventures he made to nearby trout streams almost every afternoon. His friend and former student, Professor Edmond S. Meany, was his knowledgeable guide, and together they spent so much time in the wilderness that the local press reported that Turner enjoyed fishing more than American history, while a group of like-minded fanatics in Seattle pressed his candidacy for the presidency of the university so seriously that he came dangerously near election before withdrawing. One memorable Fourth of July weekend that Turner called "unextinguishable" ended when he and Meany sat far into the night before a "friendship fire" at the foot of the Olympic Mountains—an event that impressed Meany so deeply that he immortalized it in verse:[38]

> But, O, the throb of ling'ring joy!
> New faith on tiny flames aspire;
> When on the sand from sea-cleansed wood
> We build our sacred friendship fire.

Better still was the escape into the rugged mountains of southern Oregon after the last summer-school class was over, and the weeks spent "beyond the edge of civilization" in the Bitterroot Mountains of Montana, where the Turners lived in sleeping bags, tramped trails blazed by the Nez Percé Indians, caught trout "to suffocation," and absorbed enough of nature's tonic to last through another school year.

They were back again in 1915, this time to Berkeley, where a midsummer meeting of the American Historical Association was scheduled to commemorate San Francisco's Panama Pacific International Exposition. Turner's friend Henry Morse Stephens made the arrangements; six of the nation's most eminent historians were invited to give six lectures each to the California summer school, with an honorarium of $250 each to offset expenses. J. Franklin Jameson, Max Farrand, and

Turner were the choices in American history, with Turner to lecture on the "Study and Sources of the History of the Westward Movement in America." If his usual tendency toward procrastination had not piled duty on duty that spring, and if illness had not again laid him low, Turner might have added a new dimension to his scholarship in those lectures. The last two, he planned, would deal with "The Pacific Coast in the Westward Movement" and "The Significance of the Great Plains, the Rocky Mountains, and the Deserts in American History." They would involve a great deal of work, for he had shamefully neglected the Far Western frontier, but they would lead to papers that Turner saw as equivalents of his essays on the significance of the Ohio Valley, the Mississippi Valley, and the Midwest in American history.[39] If he gave those lectures, as presumably he did, they were so inadequately prepared that he had no urge to publish them; his views on the Far West remain today as obscure as they were during his lifetime.

However successful his course, Turner had a splendid time in California, enjoying the "highjinks" of the famed Bohemian Club in its redwood grove, mingling with old friends at the Association meetings, spending two weeks with a Sierra Club pack train in the High Sierra behind Yosemite Valley, returning strong and healthy and looking very much the woodsman in his bacon-stained khaki trousers, grey flannel shirt, red bandana handkerchief, and much abused sombrero hat. This was happiness. So were the weeks at the end of the summer which he spent with Mae, camping and fishing at Glen Alpine in the High Sierra near Lake Tahoe. A year later the Turners were back again, after the excessive heat of Madison convinced him that he should not spend the summer in research at the State Historical Society as he had planned. Instead, they fled civilization entirely to spend a month in the wilds near Glacier National Park, traveling with three pack horses, led by a delightful guide who wore a Blackfoot hunting shirt. They looked for all the world (as Turner noted) like a caravan out of the Oregon Trail. "I shot the shoots down long rapids on my unhappy back," he reported gleefully to Max Farrand, "fell off wobbly logs, lay down in the Big Badger with a three pound trout at the end of my rod (and kept him from taking the slack he was entitled to) and did all kinds of silly tenderfoot things un-restrained and unmindful of history."[40] The purgatory of Cambridge was endurable for another year after that glimpse of heaven.

To say that Turner saw his return to Harvard each fall as a descent into the inferno would be a slight exaggeration. He was never passionately fond of teaching, but he thoroughly enjoyed contacts with the students and the intellectual challenge that they offered. His duty, as a conscientious instructor, was to teach to the very best of his ability, even though that meant revising and re-revising his lectures in a never-ending effort to make them more appealing and informative. "This lecture work," he told a student, "if adequately done, would engage all of my own energies except such as involved in consultation and advice."[41] Turner practiced what he preached. His lectures were never repeated; all were recast every year with new materials crammed in and older materials revised. His own copy of his *List of References on the History of the West* he filled with suggestions for improvements: "Interpolate a section on Western Constitution Making and Ideals, 1840-1851," and, "Add section on Am. Agricultural competition in Europe and its results." Particular stress was placed on recent events; yearly he re-planned his lectures to include discussion of "Combines," "Progressives," or "Western Ideals" in the period after 1900.[42] Turner believed that past and present merged in the historical process, and he did his best to make this clear, although he was usually so pressed for time that the last two weeks of his course became a jumble of briefly mentioned topics.

If Turner gave a great deal of himself to his students, he expected a great deal in return. His assignments were somewhat stiffer than they had been at Wisconsin: he required 120 pages of reading weekly, a classroom quiz every fortnight, midterm and final examinations, a thesis of at least twenty-five pages each semester. The students' reactions varied with the degree of their enthusiasm for history, just as they had at Madison. A few found his lectures the most inspirational ever delivered. "It is not too much to say," wrote one, "that Turner's class in the History of the West opened to me a new heaven and a new earth"; "he has discovered a new continent for us to conquer," added another.[43] Those not hopelessly infected with a love of the subject were less ecstatic. "Fine course," wrote one at the end of his lecture notes. "Fair lecturer who points out the 'whyfor' of many modern movements."[44] That Turner was no more a modern pied piper at Harvard than he had been at Wisconsin was shown by the declining enrollment in the History of the West: 96 in 1910, 117 a year later, 84 in 1912, 46 in 1913, 38 in 1914, and only 30 in 1915.⁴⁵ From that time on, it varied between 35 and 50, and never could be ranked among the popular undergraduate courses.

When, for a brief period between 1914 and 1916, Turner was forced to lecture in the second semester of the American history survey course, "History 32b," he found the audience more receptive. The period, "The History of the United States from 1830," was much to his liking, for his hours of labor on the *Encyclopaedia Britannica* article left him better prepared on recent history than most of his generation was. Building on this solid foundation, supplemented with the additional research that his sense of perfection demanded, he began preparing a set of lectures, each dictated fully, which he hoped to convert into a textbook on "The United States since 1865." As usual, his ambitious program collapsed within a few weeks; he lectured from then on from hastily prepared outlines, and dreams of the book went glimmering. Now, however, the lectures struck a spark. The broad topics that had to be covered did not lend themselves to the statistical illustrations that deadened undergraduates in his frontier course, while Turner's ability to use the past to illuminate the present gave his subject a timeliness that was irresistible, even to dullards. Then, too, he responded to the larger audience by being deliberately appealing; he spiced his descriptions with well-turned phrases, painted personalities with deft strokes, and ventured broad interpretations that endowed the past with new meaning for his listeners.⁴⁶

Here was Turner at his best as an undergraduate lecturer, and the students responded with enthusiasm. Enrollment, a normal 122 the first time Turner lectured, leaped to 186 a year later, when he gave the course for the last time.⁴⁷ The students attended regularly, too, and applauded when applause was due. His last lecture brought their approval to a fitting climax. "I've always wanted to carry one course down to date," he began, then deftly described the Federal Reserve and Clayton acts, analyzed recent foreign policy, and appraised Woodrow Wilson's virtues and faults as President. There remained time to glance back over the last quarter-century in quest of a generalization that would give it meaning to the students. "An old order has changed," Turner told them. "Is the United States in the twenty-five years that are to follow to be assimilated into Europe or is a new American democracy to be worked out? And that, I think, is the logical conclusion to this course." Then a word of apology: "I have been somewhat confusing in this course, but I didn't try to be explicit. I tried confusion so that you would have to think out your own conclusions. As Mr. Dooley says, I haven't felt it necessary to do the thinking for your father's sons. And I thank you." Then the class stamped and clapped and cheered as Turner grinned, held out his hand, said "Someone will think I'm a candidate for office," and left the room amidst laughter and applause.[48] Turner had shown in History 32b that he could rival the spellbinders when he forsook details for generalizations and interpretation.

Yet his popularity among Harvard undergraduates never rivaled the acclaim that he received from his graduate students there—and with good reason. To Turner, who passionately believed that a nation could plot its course into the future only if it thoroughly understood its past, every doctoral candidate was a prospective missionary in the cause of national survival. These were men and women worth training, and worth training well. No task was too time-consuming, no duty too unpleasant, if spent in aiding a student who would add his mite to the nation's understanding of itself. When Turner resigned from the Executive Council of the American Historical Association in 1914 so that he could have time to talk to young historians and listen to their papers, he revealed his belief in the importance of historical studies no less than his love of mankind.[49] He revealed that belief again, almost daily, as he neglected his own investigations to read patiently through voluminous dissertations ("I have two big theses on my desk to read and it does look as though I was booked for a long sentence"), or to advise former students on organizing their courses, or to read the manuscripts of their books and articles, or to serve as a brokerage agency as they sought their first jobs or advancement to more prestigious institutions. Nor were these courtesies reserved for his own students. Dixon Ryan Fox, then a beginning instructor, expected only a two-line acknowledgment when he sent an offprint of his first article to Turner, but was delighted to receive a half-dozen pages of mixed praise and criticism in reply.[50]

Turner's appeal to his students stemmed partly from this dedication, partly from the fertility of his mind and warmth of his personality, but more from his humble belief that he and they were equals, working together to discover the truth about the past. A man of lesser breadth might have expected his eminence in the profession to demand respect and obedience from lesser souls, but not Turner. His graduate students were simply fellow investigators, deserving of respect and comradeship. With them he shared board and sometimes bed, feeding the lost souls stranded in Cambridge over the Thanksgiving and Christmas holidays, welcoming them into his home for social occasions, listening to their problems with all the sympathy of a kindly father. Their accomplishments he treasured even more than his own; every printed program of the American Historical Association or Mississippi Valley Historical Association was checked to identify his students, who sometimes numbered a third of those reading papers.[51]

Graduate students responded by flocking into his seminars and vying for the privilege of securing Turner as a thesis director. He gave them virtually a free rein for their intellectual interests: a seminar on the Van Buren administration was abandoned after a year for one on "Selected Topics in the History of the West," and that, in turn, after two years, for "Selected Topics in American History." Turner tried to concentrate on one period each year, sometimes the decade of the 1830s or the fifteen years after 1880, but his usual course was to indicate that topics should be chosen within the 1830-60 span. Within these broad limits, students could select subjects that appealed to their particular interests. In one typical seminar, papers were read on education during the 1850s, the German influence on politics in the years just before the Civil War, the settlement of Wisconsin, Illinois politics of 1850-60, the extension of railroads into northern New England, Mormon institutions, the evolution of New York newspapers, and the emergence of transportation facilities in the South Central states.[52]

This freedom was balanced with sound instruction. Each seminar began with a review of the period to be covered, where Turner spoke informally and the students read widely, as the basis for a two- or three-page table of contents for a history of the United States during those years. Those who intended to map election returns were shown proper techniques and supplied with outline maps ordered from Washington. In the meantime, topics were assigned and research begun. Reports followed after two or three weeks, usually an hour-long presentation of the problems involved, materials available, and progress to that time. Two written papers were required at the end of the term, one covering the topic generally, the other treating a narrow aspect in depth. As these were read, Turner listened, pencil poised to jot down a new idea or bit of information, always ready to offer advice, reprove careless work, or throw out suggestions for fresh approaches or interpretations. "Turner," one student remarked to another as they walked out of such a session, "is as full of ideas as a dog is of fleas."[53] Always his criticism was tempered with an encouraging word of kindness; "you show a subject *opened*, but not conquered," he told one hapless candidate, then added, "you could carry it further by more time and less pressure of other duties, I imagine."[54]

The many who prepared doctoral dissertations under his direction were treated with the same blend of strict discipline and gentle encouragement. Each chose his own topic, for Turner realized that enthusiasm for historical studies multiplied when a student pursued a subject within his own areas of interest. If pressed for suggestions, he normally proposed a subject already familiar to the student; one from Ohio, for example, might be encouraged to write on "Politics of Ohio, 1850-60, with Emphasis on Underlying Social Forces," one from Alabama, on that state's altered political behavior during the 1880s. Turner's function, as he saw it, was to plant the seeds, then shape the plant as it matured. This usually meant drastic pruning; when E. E. Dale wanted to write a history of Oklahoma, Turner gradually narrowed the topic to a study of the range cattle industry there. He insisted on only two qualifications: the subject must be manageable, and it must make a contribution to knowledge. The contribution could be of two sorts, either a "keener criticism and analysis than has been made, or new material handled in an original way."[55] These were sound suggestions, and they saved many a candidate from floundering in an unworkable dissertation subject.

The students responded by producing a series of outstanding theses that helped launch their authors on the road to professional eminence. The subjects ranged over the whole spectrum of American history, just as did Turner's own interests. Some theses were on the West—Solon J. Buck's "The Granger Movement," George M. Stephenson's "The Political History of the Public Lands from 1840 to 1862," Edward E. Dale's "The History of the Range Cattle Industry in Oklahoma," James B. Hedges's "The Development of Transportation in the Pacific Northwest, 1860-1893," Arthur P. Whitaker's "The Old South-

west, 1783-1796." Others explored unknown aspects of the colonial
era—Kenneth W. Colgrove's "The Early History of State Instruction
to Members of Congress," Daniel H. Bacot's "The Progress of South
Carolina during the Confederation and Federalist Periods," Arthur H.
Buffinton's "The Policy of the Northern British Colonies toward
the French in the Treaty of Utrecht"—or the middle period—Thomas
P. Abernethy's "The Formative Period in Alabama, 1815-1828," Arthur B. Darling's "Jacksonian Democracy in Massachusetts," Elwyn C.
Gage's "The National Election of 1824." The Civil War era offered
subjects for Frederick Merk, "The Economic History of Wisconsin
during the Civil War Decade," and H. Donaldson Jordan, "England and
the War of Secession." Equally typical of Turner's catholic tastes were
the dissertations that he supervised in social history—Colin B. Goodykoontz's "The Home Missionary Movement and the West," Marcus
L. Hansen's "Emigration from Continental Europe"—and in diplomatic
history—Samuel F. Bemis's "The History and Diplomacy of the Jay
Treaty," Thomas P. Martin's "The Influence of Trade in Cotton and
Wheat in Anglo-American Relations from 1829 to 1846," and Reginald F. Arragon's "The Panama Congress of 1826."[56] Surely no other
instructor of that day allowed his students to range so widely, kept
pace with their researches so thoroughly, and directed such a distinguished galaxy of historians as Turner.

Equally remarkable was the disproportionate number of Turner-
directed dissertations that blossomed into books. This was no accident.
The sound advice given during the selection of a topic (always with
publication in mind), the careful supervision during the preparation
of the thesis, and the encouragement and help offered as soon as the
degree was won all contributed, but particularly the last. Turner had
an uncanny ability to diagnose the weakness of a manuscript, and to
offer exactly the right advice on improvement. All authors were advised to let the thesis lie fallow for several months; this allowed them
to gain perspective and ponder how the subject could be broadened
to fit into the pattern of American history. "*Think* about the meaning
of it all," he told Thomas P. Abernethy. Then, on re-reading, they
would recognize the highlights that deserved greater emphasis, the
extraneous materials that should be discarded, the interpretations that
had been obscured during the hurry of meeting a degree deadline. They
should also keep the needs of the general reader in mind when revising,

condensing quotations, eliminating unessential footnotes, sharpening the style, lessening the length.[57] Only in this way could they produce the mature books that would benefit them and the world of scholarship.

If Turner was a master at wet-nursing his doctoral students through the ordeal of the thesis, he was also remarkable in the way he guided them through their final examinations with a minimum of disaster. His instructions were specific: re-read the multi-volume histories by James Ford Rhodes and Edward Channing, be thoroughly abreast of recent monographic literature, know all important articles in the leading journals, be familiar with the bibliographical guides and collections of documentary sources. Those who followed this advice should have had no difficulties, but the few who did flounder by the wayside were always sure of a helping hand. Rarely could Turner convince himself that a candidate should be failed, no matter how superficial his knowledge or how deficient his reasoning powers. One who was unable to name a single important case decided by the Supreme Court was passed; so was one who did not know how to locate materials essential to the study of economic history.[58] Surely, Turner argued with his colleagues, even such men must have some redeeming features and should be saved for the profession.

Turner's kindness indicated no lowering of standards, but only his tendency to associate himself with his students as fellow laborers in historical research. They had worked together, usually for some years by the time the degree was in sight, in class and seminar, and always on a problem that excited the instructor as much as the student. Each was a friend, not a pupil, and deserved to be treated as such. So Turner, remembering always his own miserable performance on his final examinations at Johns Hopkins, was a lion at their sides, hoping for the best, but unwilling to recognize the worst. If even the shakiest candidate could be salvaged, a human being had been aided and another recruit added to the army carrying on the assault against ignorance of history.

His coddling of two students in particular revealed the depths of his compassion. One was Kenneth W. Colgrove, later a prominent political scientist. Colgrove was burdened with a sense of inferiority that was not improved when he did badly on his preliminary doctoral examinations. His thesis satisfied neither him nor Turner when it was submitted in first draft; it was badly written, focused more on background than the topic, and included whole chapters of extraneous materials. Instead of sending it back for complete revision, Turner persuaded the committee that it be accepted and then revised. Then, with the author's self-esteem restored, he suggested the changes needed: drastic reduction of the first chapters with emphasis on essentials, illustrations to relieve the dry narrative, more stress on personalities and human interest, an expansion of the sections at the heart of the study. Colgrove took these criticisms like a man and capably performed the complete rewriting that was necessary.[59] If the thesis had been rejected initially, he would probably have fled the profession. Turner had saved a man, and a good man, for historical studies.

He faced a far more difficult problem with Arthur H. Buffinton. A capable if not overly energetic young man who had earned his master's degree at Harvard in 1909 and was an instructor at Williams College, Buffinton was the first graduate student to see Turner in the fall of 1910. They met in the library stacks on October 4, 1910, to agree upon a thesis topic on the New York frontier in the eighteenth century. For a time all went well, although Buffinton was burdened with a heavy teaching load and showed an obvious inclination to spend more time in the classroom than in the library. By the end of the summer of 1913 he had read all printed documents and secondary works, written 265 pages in rough draft, and had only some newspapers and manuscripts to read. Turner had every hope of seeing the completed dissertation by the spring of 1914, but not a line appeared. Instead, Buffinton sent him letters—telling of a sick colleague whose teaching had to be assumed, or of a new course to be prepared, or of the demands of students on his time. But he would start arranging his notes soon and might get some writing done that summer or fall.

By this time Turner was beginning to recognize the magnitude of the problem on his hands. Buffinton was obviously cast in his own image; he was a perfectionist who found writing difficult and would do anything to avoid putting pen to paper. Theirs was to be a battle of wills, with Turner committed to extracting a thesis, and Buffinton congenitally incapable of submitting one unless driven to do so. Turner could wield the whip better personally than by letter, and he urged his reluctant pupil to spend summers, and even a year's leave of absence, in Cambridge. Buffinton did spend the summer of 1914 at Harvard, but did nothing more than add 66 more pages to his first chapter and make some discoveries ("By discovery I mean that it was new to me, not necessarily to historians").[60] Nor did the next year produce much more, even though he was on leave and under his master's supervision. Chapters were submitted, true, but they were overly long, crammed with unnecessary detail, and so woefully lacking in interpretation that their contributions were lost on the reader. The degree seemed as far away when he returned to Williams that fall of 1915 as it had been five years before.

Nor was there progress as the months—and years—slipped by. Turner urged, demanded, cajoled, appealed, but to no avail. His reluctant charge was as adept with alibis as Turner was with arguments; a new course demanded his attention, a sick colleague had to be replaced, a family situation disrupted his schedule, a bout with illness ended all work. Worst of all, Buffinton discovered that the materials he had already gathered lent themselves to publication, and he began writing articles instead of chapters. They enjoyed only moderate success at first, the *American Historical Review* rejected the first, but it was accepted by *The Historical Outlook*, subjecting him to another Turner lecture on learning to write before he appeared in public. These "Polonius-like dicta," as Turner called them, went unheeded. Buffinton spent the next few years preparing articles, some of them excellent, while the thesis gathered dust in his desk drawer.

As Buffinton's publications multiplied, and as Turner's years at Harvard drew to a close, Turner had an inspiration. If Buffinton would put his printed articles together, write an introduction and some transitional passages, and submit them as his thesis the degree could be granted. Once more Turner reckoned without his pupil's fatal perfectionism; only two of the publications were of high enough quality to please the faculty, Buffinton insisted, and he would be ashamed to let the remainder be seen. That was that, but some good had been done. During the 1922-23 academic year Buffinton did settle into the harness, goaded by regular letters from Cambridge urging him on. As chapters began arriving for Turner's scrutiny, a new problem arose; each of his suggestions for slight revision sent Buffinton to the library for further investigation. "Draw your conclusions now from what you *have*," Turner urged. "If they need verification by further study, do that later."[61] Again, his sound advice went unheeded. Turner learned to keep his suggested changes to a minimum, lest each send his pupil on a time-consuming quest, and to make them in soft pencil on the manuscript so they could be easily erased.

So progress was made as the pile of completed chapters mounted through the summer of 1923 and into the 1923-24 academic year, Turner's last before his retirement. The thesis had to be in his hands by April 1 to assure Buffinton a degree that year, and both were confident; Turner even made arrangements for its reception at the graduate school office and drafted a carefully selected committee of readers to assure its acceptance. April 1 came and went, and no bulky package arrived from Williamstown, but there was still a last chance. Turner would be about Cambridge late that summer and would be glad to help, even though he could not sit on the jury that made the final decision. Miraculously, Buffinton succeeded. Turner had to rewrite much of his summary chapter and do major surgery on a good many other sections, but the result he found acceptable. Before leaving the East that fall of 1924, he saw to it that the proper forms were signed, the committee briefed, and all in readiness for the final act in the drama. "So endeth the *last* lesson," he wrote Buffinton as he told him of these preparations, "and may the Lord have mercy on your soul."[62] That prayer was answered. A few months later Buffinton wrote Turner triumphantly that he had met his committee and they were his. He might have added that under any system of justice that doctorate should have been awarded to Frederick Jackson Turner rather than to Arthur H. Buffinton.

The heroic efforts that won Colgrove and Buffinton their degrees were not typical, of course, but they demonstrate in exaggerated form Turner's dedication to his students and his unshakable determination to see them succeed. He was, by all standards, an outstanding graduate teacher, not solely because his methods were more helpful or his techniques more advanced or his mind more fertile than those of other instructors, but because he saw his students as mirror images of himself and treated them accordingly. If he had maintained a master-slave relationship he would have trained capable investigators; by accepting his students as equals in their joint journeys of exploration into the past he elevated them a step higher, and made them the devoted disciples they proved to be.

XIV

Harvard Years:
Conflict—Academic and International

1915-1920

F REDERICK JACKSON TURNER hoped that after a few years of adjustment to the Harvard scene he would have time to resume his long-neglected study of sectionalism. So he might, had not the orderly world of his dreams been shattered by two conflicts in which he became hopelessly involved. One, the titanic struggle between the Allies and Germany that began in Europe in 1914 and entangled the United States three years later, made such demands on his time and emotions that for two years research was unthinkable. The other, a teapot tempest within the American Historical Association that reached a climax in 1915, was no less fatal to Turner's ambitions.

He had, from the beginning of his professional career, given of himself freely to the association, recognizing this as one of the many time-consuming obligations expected of successful academicians. His years of apprenticeship on burdensome committees meant gradual ascent to the little clique that was in control, with membership on the Executive Council of the association, a post that was his for life after his presidency, and on the Board of Editors of the *American Historical Review*, where he served for two six-year terms. There he joined a tightly knit group of eminent historians who were, in their own eyes, selfless servants of the profession, giving generously of their time and energy to provide leadership and maintain standards. They had, however, drifted into an "Establishment" philosophy and an "Establishment" system of management that operated through a series of interlocking director-ships: all officers were named by a nominating committee which was itself appointed by the Executive Council; the second vice-president automatically ascended to the presidency and then to lifetime membership on the Council; the six-man editorial board of the *Review* was self-perpetuating, for it suggested replacements for its retiring members to the Executive Council, which always approved. In effect, some 2800 members of the association were governed by two or three dozen professors from a half-dozen prestigious universities, most of them well advanced in years. A rebellion against such undemocratic procedures was inevitable, particularly in an era of political progressivism when all interlocking directorships, even those operated by staid historians, were fair game for crusaders.

The leaders of the insurgent faction that rose to meet this challenge were an unlikely crew, bound together only by a belief that the "Eastern Establishment" had denied them the acclaim they deserved. At their head was Frederic Bancroft, librarian of the state department, professional gadfly, and a newly elected member of the association's Council; his principal lieutenants were Dunbar Rowland, director of Mississippi's Department of Archives and History, and Professor John H. Latané of the Johns Hopkins history department. Their followers varied in numbers with their changing fortunes, but were recruited largely from the South and West, where resentment against New England's domination of the profession was strongest. To drive the "ring" from power, these rebels believed, they first had to oust J. Franklin Jameson from his editorship of the *Review* and secretaryship of the association. This meant removing ownership of that journal from the Board of Editors, where it had rested since 1895, and vesting it in the association; so long as Jameson operated his own show he was safe from attack. As Jameson's closest associate, Turner could be expected to defend his friend most effectively. Hence, Turner must go.

This decision brought into focus the basic divisions within the association. All agreed that reform was necessary; they differed on the means. Turner was the principal spokesman for the vast majority of members, who were confident that democratization could come from within; they pinned their hopes on a Committee of Nine, headed by Professor Andrew C. McLaughlin of the University of Chicago, which had been created by the Executive Council in November 1914, to propose changes in the governmental structure that would allow greater participation by the membership. The insurgents, on the other hand, were sure that McLaughlin was a tool of the Establishment, and that the Committee of Nine would only whitewash its actions. He and his ilk must be discredited. Bancroft set out to do so; an examination of the association's financial records disclosed that members of the Establishment had been reimbursed for their travel expenses to Council and Board meetings, and that they had even charged an occasional luncheon to the association! These "revelations" he unfolded in a scurrilous pamphlet, published in July 1915. *Why the American Historical Association Needs Thorough Reorganization* was no more sensational than its title; it repeated charges that an inner "ring" controlled the association, maintained that they used funds extravagantly, and argued that the Committee of Nine was rigged by "political hocus-pocus" to vindicate the Establishment. The official nominee for the presidency, George Lincoln Burr of Cornell, must be defeated and a complete slate of reformers elected to the Council.

So long as Bancroft confined his attacks to the Executive Council, he was guilty of nothing but bad taste, for he was a member of the Council and was entitled to examine its records, even though he misused the results. His next assault on the Board of Editors of the *American Historical Review* posed more problems, for he had no official connection with that body and any catering to his demands might be interpreted as tacit admission that the association owned the *Review*—a point that was still in dispute. Yet Bancroft had to attack, for he wanted Jameson's scalp and was convinced that the association would back him when its members found that the editorial board had used expense-account funds for extravagant living. Hence, he had to examine the account books of the Board of Editors. In October 1915 two peremptory letters were sent to Turner, one demanding access to the board's minutes, the other demanding a record of all its financial transactions. Turner was adamant on the minutes; they dealt largely with discussions of articles that had been submitted to the *Review* and making them public would embarrass would-be authors. "I would," he wrote, "as soon open the doors of my house to a fire bug."[1] The financial accounts contained no such confidential information and Turner saw no harm in showing them to Bancroft, although he hesitated lest this be interpreted as truckling to his demands. Jameson had a better idea. Why

Captions for the following four pages

1. Frederick Jackson Turner (right) with his younger brother, Will.

2. Andrew Jackson Turner, father of Frederick Jackson Turner.

3. Turner at the time of his graduation from the University of Wisconsin in 1884.

4. Professor William Francis Allen, Turner's principal mentor at the University of Wisconsin.

5. The University of Wisconsin in 1884, when Turner was a student.

6. Turner (right) and Charles Homer Haskins, a fellow Johns Hopkins student and boarder at Miss Ashton's, who was to become Turner's closest friend and colleague.

7. The Johns Hopkins University seminar room. These students worked for their doctoral degrees with Turner in 1890. Left to right: Charles Homer Haskins, James Albert Woodburn, John H. McPherson, Professor John M. Vincent, Professor Herbert Baxter Adams, Andrew Stephenson (who failed to complete his degree), and Toyokichi Iyenaga.

8. Frederick Jackson Turner in 1893, when he read his paper on "The Significance of the Frontier in American History." Reproduced from the *Badger for 1893*, the University of Wisconsin yearbook, through the kindness of F. Frank Cook, Director of the University Archives.

9. Mae Turner in 1893, with the two oldest children, Jackson Allen Turner and Dorothy Kinsey Turner.

10. Mae Turner about 1905.

11. Frederick Jackson Turner in 1905, as he completed work on his first book, *The Rise of the New West*.

2

1

3

4

5

8 9
10 11

12

13

14

15

16

17

18

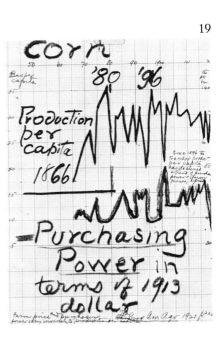

19

Captions for the preceding four pages

12. Turner hanged in effigy by the Wisconsin students for opposing "Big Time" football, as seen by a cartoonist for the *Wisconsin State Journal,* March 31, 1906.

13. The Turners' home at 629 Frances Street, Madison, with Lake Mendota in the foreground.

14. Turner's seminar meeting in the Library of the State Historical Society of Wisconsin in June 1894. Left to right (standing): Emma Hawley (Library staff), W. B. Overson, Orin G. Libby, E. F. Dithmar, Joseph Schafer, C. L. Baldwin, and Florence Baker (Library staff); (seated): Estelle Hayden, Kate Bucknam, Ada Taylor, Annie Pellow, Dena Lindley, Sadie Bold, Flora Barnes, Professor Turner, and Catherine Cleveland. Reproduced from the collections of the State Historical Society of Wisconsin.

15. Mae Turner with their daughter, Dorothy Turner Main, in the early 1920's.

16. The cottage at 2214 Van Hise Avenue, Madison, built by the Turners in 1924 for their retirement years.

17. Turner on a camping trip during the early 1920's.

18. One of the many maps Turner prepared for his studies on sectionalism. This one correlated election returns with illiteracy in 1848.

19. One of the hundreds of charts Turner drew and used in his classes. This one related corn production to population growth.

20. Turner at the door of the Huntington Library, about 1928.

21. The Huntington Library in 1927, when Turner joined the staff. This copy was presented by Turner to his devoted secretary, Merrill H. Crissey.

not send copies to *all* members of the Executive Council and the Committee of Nine?[2] Here was a sensible procedure that was adopted at once.

Copying the records took time, however, and Bancroft was in no mood to take delay lightly. Scarcely a day had passed before a telegram to Turner warned of what was to come:

> UNLESS BEFORE 6 P.M. MONDAY NEXT I AM GIVEN PERMISSION TO IN-
> SPECT AND COPY CONTRACTS AND NAMES OF FOUNDERS AND GUARANTORS
> I SHALL PUBLICLY EXPOSE YOU AND THE BOARD'S ATTITUDE.

Those records, Turner explained patiently, were being prepared for distribution and would be in the mail shortly. This kept the peace for only a short time. Then Turner received another telegram:

> WHERE ARE COPIES OF CONTRACTS SUPPOSEDLY IN MAIL TWENTY-FOUTH
> INST?

More telegrams, more accusations, more demands by Bancroft until the missing documents finally reached him. They were, he exulted, just what he wanted. They showed the editors had no financial liability, and hence did not legally own the *Review*.[3] He would expose their perfidy when the Executive Council met on November 26, 1915. This was the prospect that awaited Turner and his colleagues when they journeyed to New York to begin their meetings.

The Board of Editors met first, heard Turner describe his correspondence with Bancroft, and, with blood pressure properly elevated, adopted a series of resolutions denying Bancroft access to the minutes and everything else he demanded. This done, they listened approvingly as Edward P. Cheyney, their secretary, read a report that he proposed be distributed to the association's membership. Cheyney recited the whole sad story of the controversy with Bancroft, denied that the board ever dabbled in association politics, and made it clear that the members never abused the expense-account privileges to which they were entitled. When this was presented to the Executive Council the next day, it was overwhelmingly adopted. The Council, the resolution of adoption read, expressed "its full confidence in the efficiency and unselfish manner in which the board of editors has conducted the affairs of the *Review* since its foundation."[4] Bancroft had suffered a thumping defeat, but such were his illusions that he believed his stand would be vindicated in the association's business meeting, which was to be held a month later. "The rule of Jameson, Turner, McLaughlin and Burr should end this year," he predicted gleefully.[5]

First he had to convince the membership. Using Cheyney's report as a basis, he prepared two pamphlets, which were distributed throughout the association in late November and early December. *The Attempt to Seize the American Historical Review,* and *Misrepresentations and Concealments in Opposition to Reform in the American Historical Association* were typically Bancroft, rambling through page after page of unsubstantiated charges and misleading quarter-proofs. Columns of figures revealed the "exorbitant" sums collected by the "ring" for travel to board meetings; still larger sums, he hinted, had doubtless been used "for purposes both unauthorized and unknown either to the Council or the Association." Turner was Bancroft's particular target now, for he had refused access to the editorial board's minutes. Why had he had concealed those documents unless he had something to hide? Why had he been elected president of the association only after coming to Harvard? Here was proof that the "ring" manipulated its puppets for its own benefit.[6] "Isn't this," wrote Jameson as he finished the last page, "great business for an immortal soul in A.D. 1915, when the whole world is on fire and civilization is going to pieces."[7]

Both sides were prepared when the American Historical Association met at Washington's New Willard Hotel on December 28, 1915. Bancroft and his insurgents were not only housed together at the nearby Albany Hotel, where they could plot their strategy, but they had held a dinner meeting at the Metropolitan Club the night before and assigned each man his role. The Establishment made fewer plans. Some talked of an agreed-upon candidate to defeat Bancroft's bid for reelection to the Executive Council, but Turner ended their plotting by pointing out that this decision was for the membership to make, not the governing clique.[8] The "ring" was willing to let democracy operate at the business meeting, confident that its stand would be upheld.

And it was. Turner was not there when five hundred members crowded into the hotel's ballroom—he had been called to the bedside of his brother, who was critically ill—but he was not needed. The report of the Committee of Nine saw to that, for its recommendations were those long advocated by Turner and other moderate reformers. The members, realizing that democracy could be achieved without adopting the Bancroftians as bedfellows, were in a mood to praise, not bury, the Establishment. They showed their hand when Cheyney opened the meeting by reporting for the Board of Editors. Every mention of Turner or Jameson brought applause, just as did Jameson's own remarks when he rose to underline Cheyney's statement that the board would happily surrender the *Review* whenever the association was ready to assume its financial obligations. The cheers that followed Jameson to his seat brought Claude H. Van Tune to his feet with a ringing resolution; attacks made on the character and motives of certain honored individuals within the past year, he proposed, "meet with our entire disapproval," and "we hereby express our full confidence in the men whose motive and conduct has been thus impugned." The shout of approval was almost unanimous; Bancroft had left the hall and his followers dared not buck the tide.[9]

There was no question of the fate of the Committee of Nine's report now. One by one its recommendations to democratize the association were adopted: there were to be eight, rather than six, elected members of the Executive Council, former presidents were to serve only three years, the powers of the business meeting over the Council were to be enlarged; the nominating committee was to be elected by the business meeting, rather than appointed by the Council; additional nominees were to appear on the ballot when supported by a petition signed by twenty members. The last recommendation was most controversial of all—that proposing ownership of the *Review* by the association—but this too was adopted after a series of crippling amendments were voted down. When, late in the meeting, Frederic Bancroft withdrew his name as a candidate for the Executive Council, he was simply acknowledging that he and his followers had been devastatingly defeated.[10]

Reform from within, cleverly manipulated by Turner, had triumphed over attack from without. Congratulations were in order among the Establishment now, and they flew thick and fast. "I have never doubted the outcome," wrote Turner, "but I confess I had not expected the Three Misquoters to make such an inglorious comic end."[11] Yet scars remained. Turner showed the deepness of his hurt when Charles H. Ambler, one of his former students who had served as a Bancroft lieutenant, attempted to make his peace. His protestations that he had infiltrated the insurgents' ranks solely to urge restraint were brushed aside as hypocritical nonsense. "Let us," Turner told him after an exchange of letters, "not continue the correspondence."[12] Ambler and his fellow conspirators had forever lost the respect of Turner, and of most of the profession.

Despite the pain he had suffered, and despite a year of such total immersion in associational affairs that all research was shelved, Turner was to benefit from the Bancroft rebellion. Now, with victory assured, he could quietly withdraw from the irksome professional duties that had become increasingly burdensome in recent years. This would fulfill a mounting ambition; for some time he had chafed under the endless chores imposed on the editorial board of the *Review,* and he believed that a younger man should take his place. So he welcomed the expiration of his second term, just as he did the recommendation of the Committee of Nine that ex-presidents resign from the Executive Council after three years of service. "For myself," he wrote Jameson, "I have done all that I can, probably, for the Association." He would devote the future to the research he had neglected for so long.[13]

The prospect was doubly alluring, for, as the Bancroft affair neared its climax, negotiations were under way for a full year away from the classroom—a full year to read and think and write. J. Franklin Jameson was responsible, and the Department of Historical Research of the Carnegie Institution which he administered gave the means. Almost from the day Jameson assumed the directorship, in 1905, he had wanted to bring Turner to the Institution, turn him loose on his own researches in the Library of Congress, and have him constantly on tap for discussions on how to revitalize historical studies. Turner was the only man in the United States, Jameson assured the Institution's officers in 1913, who could "wake me and the Department up."[14] Now his chance had come, for Turner was in a mood to leave Harvard for a time, and funds were available. In March 1915 the official invitation arrived, just as the Bancroft rebellion was moving toward its climax. Would Turner be interested in spending six months of the sabbatical year due him in 1916-17 in Washington? The salary would be $600 a month, the duties light, and ample time allowed for research in the Library of Congress.

Turner was delighted. The Carnegie money would let him stretch his scheduled half-year of leave at full pay into a full year at half pay —a whole year to pursue his investigations. When Harvard offered no objections, he accepted eagerly, and in November he received from the president of the Carnegie Institution, Robert S. Woodward, a formal invitation to spend six months in Washington, beginning November 20, 1916. That day Turner noted in his diary "3,600 + 2750 half salary from Harvard = 6350."[15] His Carnegie year promised to be profitable in more ways than one. Jameson was just as elated. "The presence of Professor Frederick J. Turner, of Harvard University, as Research Associate," he wrote in his annual report, "will stimulate all the work of the Department."[16] Turner was able to endure the burdens of Harvard teaching as he buried himself in his many duties during the spring of 1916, dreaming of the fall when his time would be all his own.

Those duties were plentiful, for endless arrangements had to be made. The Cambridge house was to be sublet to a clergyman (though Turner insisted that he would rather fish with a worm than rent to a cleric) who was attracted by the presence of two churches and a theological school nearby, not to mention a front-yard fence built by the Reverend Thomas Hooker in 1632 and an apple tree that was originally in the Garden of Eden. Or so Turner told his daughter. A modest flat or rooming house at no more than $50 a month had to be located in Washington; they settled on a small apartment in the Brighton Hotel, which they rented for nearly $100.[17] Term papers and bluebooks had to be read, oral examinations conducted, theses criticized, and grades reported to the registrar. Then the "Star Chamber Trial"—modified for the occasion—was held. Every professor going on leave, Turner was told, had to be tried by the graduate students and formally expelled from the Yard. In his case a vigilante committee would be substituted for the chamber. He would appear before that august body and accept his fate. He did appear—to be stuffed with soup and shad roe and steak and frozen pudding, then solemnly tried, and banished for a year, although he was allowed to make a statement before his sentence began. Turner enjoyed himself hugely; the students long remembered his booming laugh and beaming face.[18]

The Turners fled Cambridge then, first to Madison, where a personal investigation proved there were no trout in nearby streams, and where the summer's heat drove them westward for a Montana vacation. Such work as was done during those months went into the preparation of five lectures to be delivered at Western Reserve University in late October. Those completed, the Turners settled into their Washington apartment on November 1, 1916, for six months of uninterrupted research. They followed a pleasant routine; each morning Turner and J. Franklin Jameson walked to work together ("thereby," Jameson told a friend, "benefitting the physical health of both, and my mental condition"),[19] then separated as Turner sought out his desk at the Library of Congress and the pile of manuscripts or newspaper file that waited him.

How he reveled in those intellectual treasures as he probed ever deeper into the story of sectionalism in the 1830s and 1840s! But only for a short time, for Turner was emotionally incapable of long periods of sustained work, and temptations were abundant. Scarcely a day passed but he was persuaded to settle down with Jameson and his staff for long discussions of historical problems and the role of the Institution in solving them. Each week he lectured to the department on the economic and social development of the Middle West, a pleasant assignment, but one that required constant preparation.[20] Occasionally he was seduced into delivering other lectures; one he gave before the Harvard Club of Washington in February allowed him to extoll the virtues of the Harvard Commission on Western History. Congress demanded his attention now and then, with a day in the Senate or House gallery, and the conclusion that there was no such thing as a first-class politician; "it is," he reported, "a painful thing to watch."[21] Those were happy months in Washington for Turner, even though they did not produce the great stack of research notes that he had hoped.

He can be excused for not sticking to his last, for the winter of 1916-17 was a poor one for scholarship everywhere. What did the past matter when the whole western world was going up in flames? World War I began in Europe in August 1914, and, although President Woodrow Wilson urged Americans to remain "impartial in thought as well as action," the sinking of the *Lusitania* in May 1915, the *Arabic* crisis a few months later, and the torpedoing of an unarmed French passenger ship, the *Sussex*, in the English Channel in March 1916, drove the United States slowly along the road to war. Passions were heightened by the "rape of Belgium," when German troops overran that small country, and by an effective Allied propaganda that painted the Central Powers as enemies of democracy and civilization. President Wilson's peace efforts, climaxed by his announcement of terms for a "just peace" in January 1917, were answered by Germany's announcement that it was resuming unrestricted submarine warfare against all merchant ships bound for the British Isles. Wilson broke off diplomatic relations at once, at the same time asking Congress for authority to arm American vessels. A filibuster led by Senator Robert M. La Follette defeated that measure, but evidence piled on evidence that the Central Powers would be satisfied with nothing less than total victory, and the President only mirrored majority opinion when he led the nation into war on April 6, 1917.

All of these stirring events Turner watched from his grandstand seat in Washington. As he did so, his views on the global role of the United States were revolutionized. His sympathies, from the very beginning of the war, lay with the Allies; Germany was a monstrous threat to self-rule in Europe, and a German victory would mean a triumph for militarism and autocracy. The Allies had to save civilization and the democratic values that had been bred into Americans by their frontier experience. Turner was so annoyed with Senator La Follette's pro-German stand that he canceled his subscription to *La Follette's Magazine* in the spring of 1916; at the same time he commended Wisconsin's other senator, Paul O. Husting, for the support he rendered England and France.[22] Only an early Allied victory, Turner believed, would check the Balkanization of the United States, as each new crisis drove a new wedge between Irish-Americans and German-Americans and Italian-Americans. This ethnic atomization had to be checked, for America must revitalize postwar Europe by providing a shining example of a successful democracy that unified people from many backgrounds. Not only national survival, but the future peace of all the world, hung in the balance.[23]

Reasoning in this fashion, Turner assumed a strong anti-interventionist stance during the early years of the war. He expressed his views in February 1916, when he spoke at Trinity College on "Why Did Not the United States become Another Europe?" His answer was predictable; Americans had succeeded, as Europeans had not, in perfecting a system of adjustment and compromise that allowed the differing sections to live together peacefully. They had also proven that the oppressed from all the globe could be welcomed and absorbed. This was an example too valuable to be destroyed in any war. The United States had to remain aloof from Europe's holocaust; it had to persist as a bastion of democracy that would serve as a model when reconstruction began. Pressures for intervention were steadily increasing, Turner admitted, but it did not follow that "we should be carried into that maelstrom, and particularly not on European terms. Washington's warnings against entangling alliances still have validity and they gain new force from the awful tragedy which meets our gaze whenever we look across the Atlantic."[24]

There spoke Turner, the Jackson Man, for no backwoods champion of the Hero of New Orleans could have believed more fervently that America's frontier-rooted democracy underlay a governmental system that all the world should—and would—imitate. His were noble dreams, but they were sadly outmoded by the realities of a Europe at war. Not the future, but immediate survival, was the concern of the United States, and as Turner watched events unfold from his Washington vantage point his views changed. By February 1917, two months before war was declared, he believed that "it is time to assert ourselves or bear the stigma of servitude"; a month later he wrote that unless we "strengthen our sinews and harden our tissues and learn our national lesson," Americans would fall before the juggernaut of Kaiserism.[25] To a man with these violent views, the sectionalism of the 1830s was remote and unimportant. "I am finding it difficult to write my historical stint," he confessed. "I want to enlist in spite of my aged imperfections." So strongly did Turner feel that he offered his services for any type of clerical work in the government that would be useful to the army.[26] By the time war was declared, he was ready to make any sacrifices for the holy crusade that was making the world safe for democracy.

Others in Washington shared Turner's views, and through the early days of April the historians among them debated the role they could play in the struggle that had just begun. Jameson, as usual, spearheaded these discussions, and, as usual, Turner bubbled with ideas that his friend could implement. The result was an invitation to a large group of historians to meet in Washington on April 28, 1917, to form an organization that would place the "competence and patriotic good will" of the profession in the service of the government. Two days of discussion gave birth to the National Board for Historical Services, with

James T. Shotwell of Columbia its chairman and Turner among its nine members. Its purposes would be threefold: to channel historical activities throughout the nation into support for the war, to supply the public with trustworthy information on the background and purpose of the conflict, and to father regional or state committees that would organize lecturers and authors to spread information.[27]

From the first, this program raised eyebrows throughout the profession. Would the National Board adhere to canons of objectivity, or would it be simply another propaganda machine for the government? In Turner's mind there was no question that the members were on the side of the angels, and that the use of history to further "present action" was justified. Yet he was haunted by doubts, and protested so vehemently in his campaign to convert the doubters that he revealed his own apprehensions. The Board, he insisted, had a "trust to keep as ministers of historic truth," and this would not be violated. Instead it would only keep alive traditional values and ideals—values and ideals that were often forgotten amid the passions of war. Certainly the truth would not be sullied if the Board emphasized episodes from the past that would illuminate present problems and aid the achievement of a just peace.[28] Turner satisfied his own conscience by such arguments, but converts among his friends were few. Well they might be, for he was arguing that history should be warped to suit the national purpose, even though still wearing the garb of objectivity.

In actual practice, the National Board for Historical Services was neither the propaganda agency feared by its enemies nor the model of impartiality envisaged by its friends. It did perform valuable services by circulating an annotated edition of the President's War Message, placing articles in popular magazines, supplying speakers for numerous occasions, and flooding the news media with historical information needed to make current events meaningful. Yet the profession remained skeptical. Turner's own enthusiasms cooled rapidly; he tried to resign when he returned to Cambridge in May 1917, and even though he was dissuaded from doing so, he played a relatively small role from then on. The atmosphere at Harvard did nothing to rekindle his enthusiasm. Only Edward Channing was outspokenly opposed to the National Board, on the grounds that past precedents did not apply to the present situation—"He explained at some length to me that the submarine had so modified the art of war that the naval and military lessons of the Revolution and Civil War were inapplicable"—but the rest of his colleagues were so cool that efforts to press them into service were soon abandoned.[29] Turner's deep-seated faith in his native land had warped his judgment momentarily, and blinded him to the importance of unvarnished truth, even in periods of national crisis.

That same faith condemned him to some thoroughly unpleasant hours of teaching during the wartime years. Harvard's attitude was very much Turner's own; President Lowell made it clear from the beginning that his sympathies were with the Allies and that the university would do everything possible to speed their victory. By the time Turner returned, in May 1917, the Yard resembled an armed camp, with most of the student body in a Reserve Officers Training Corps and the banks of near-by Fresh Pond so scarred with trenches that pedestrians were unsafe there. Here was an atmosphere to Turner's liking, and he responded predictably. He was too old for military service himself, but he could scrimp to buy Liberty Bonds—and did to the extent of $6000 during the war years—and he could preach that total victory was essential to the survival of mankind. "The world," he wrote in the autumn of 1917, "will not be worth occupying with the kind of Germany that has been revealed at the head of civilization." Anyone who did not make every sacrifice to head off that catastrophe would be judged narrow and selfish in the "Book of Judgment" of history.[30] Turner was determined that he would pass the test.

His own contribution had to be made in the classroom. Regular classes dwindled during the 1917-18 school year; the History of the West shrank to a handful of the halt and the lame, and the seminar disappeared entirely. Rather than mark time, Turner volunteered to serve as instructor in the modified edition of the European history survey that was being peddled to the Student Army Training Corps as "Problems and Issues of the War." This meant that he had to take a major refresher course in a field he had long forgotten; it also meant that he had to read 150 blue books weekly, conduct quiz sections for indifferent students who wanted to be off to the trenches, and grade outline maps for freshmen who located Bohemia in France, Lombardy near Berlin, and Moscow in Italy. He had his finger in the pie, even though he complained that "a pie of 150 papers a week is rather plump."[31]

When peace came in November 1918, it brought a lessening of

frenzy on the Harvard Yard, but it also brought new classroom duties that were only slightly less arduous than those of the war years. These stemmed from a laudable desire of the history faculty to explain America's role in the reconstruction of the world to the returning students. A new course, on the "History of Liberty," was given, starting in the 1919-20 academic year, with a staff of six from the history and government departments. Turner's task was to deliver seven lectures describing and appraising the history of liberty in the United States as revealed in the colonial and Revolutionary eras, the framing of the Constitution, Jacksonian democracy, the period of slavery and reconstruction, the "New Nationalism," and the "safe world" that was beginning with the defeat of Germany.[32] This was a challenging assignment; he would be indoctrinating a considerable proportion of Harvard's students as they prepared themselves for the national stage. No slipshod lectures would do.

Because Turner did take his duty seriously, and continuously revised his offerings, he was forced to do more thinking about the impact of the frontier than he had since the 1890s. When he began, his thoughts were those of 1893, with institutions moulded largely by environmental forces as they took shape in the American wilderness. American liberty, his students were told, was based not alone on Magna Carta or Plymouth Rock or Jamestown. "What is *American* in it is the result of the interaction of the wilderness—vacant land—with the men and institutions." The colonists brought with them a body of habits, traditions, and customs. Some were abandoned, some continued virtually unchanged, and still others thrived as they had not in the less congenial soil of the Old World. These last institutions, developed and transformed by the greater opportunity for the individual existing on the frontier, were those that gave liberty in the United States its unique dimension.

Underlying this greater opportunity were the free arable land and unexploited resources in the zone just west of the settled area, a zone that receded constantly as society was reborn with each fresh advance into the wilderness. This successive rebirth allowed men and their institutions to change as they responded to the environment. "Old institutions were modified, new ones created, new ways of looking upon the world were evolved. The advance was a continuous process of creation, of Americanization, of differentiation from the European type.

The frontier was a gate of escape from custom, class restraints, economic and social burdens." So long as the frontier moved westward, the social order would remain plastic, capable of rapid adaptation. "Crystallization was impossible while the West stood at the border. Society refused to jell."

Of the changes that stemmed from this process, none was more important than the reshaping of the theory and practice of democracy. The West was a land of social equality, where refugees from oppression could begin life afresh. Class lines were less firmly drawn along the frontier, where all could occupy self-sufficient farms, than in the East; attacks on privilege were more common where society was fluid and innovation a daily necessity. Hence the great documents that were mileposts along the road to liberty—the Bill of Rights, the Declaration of Independence, the statutes of civil and religious liberty—could be translated from theory into practice in the newer regions of the West. Had settlement been confined east of the Appalachians, "a modified European type of class rule" would have emerged there; instead, eastern stability was upset and restraints there lessened. The frontier prevented land monopolization, diminished social and class distinctions, and fostered an extended franchise, the disestablishment of churches, free speech, and a free press.

This being the case, what was the prospect for American liberty as the era of free lands drew to a close? Turner had no pat answer to that troublesome question. The people, he noted, were turning increasingly to government for protection from exploitation by business interests, now that escape to free land was impossible. The result was that the state imposed restrictions on the free use of private property as the needs of society took precedence over the interests of the individual. Turner held out no hope for the unrestrained economic liberty of pioneer days. In its place, he predicted, must come an "adjusted liberty" as governmental controls were extended in the interest of society as a whole.

Turner was too wise a man to abide by theories that did not stand careful scrutiny. As he worked and re-worked his History of Liberty lectures, he began to realize that his earlier explanations explained less than he would have liked. The frontier did play a part in the evolution of American liberties, but it was by no means solely responsible. Turner perfected no new hypothesis, but by 1922, when he gave his lectures for the last time, he seemed increasingly aware of the complexity of his subject, and of the danger of oversimplified explanations.

Americans, he taught at that time, generally accepted three forms of liberty to a greater degree than Europeans. First, liberty in the United States was based on the belief that the European balance-of-power system had protected them from aggression and was, in part, the shield behind which their democratic practices had evolved. Second, it rested on a sense of free government, built on a written constitution that employed a system of checks and balances to prevent the concentration of excessive power in any one branch. Third, American liberty exaggerated freedom for the individual, which had been derived partly from English legal concepts of the common law. On this rested the belief that one man was as good as another before the law, that equality of opportunity should be enjoyed by all without social prejudice, and that conditions of bargaining should assure that neither party in a prospective contract be at the mercy of the other. To Turner, at this stage of his thinking, economic opportunity meant not simply an absence of restraint, but a positive complex of conditions resting on law and custom that assured the greatest number of people the greatest opportunity to develop their abilities.[33] He realized, as he had not in 1893, or in 1919, that the frontier had been a significant moulding force, but that its impact was understandable only if other comparable forces were thoroughly understood.

If Turner's frontier theories helped him explain the postwar world to Harvard's undergraduates, his sectional concepts underlay his own thinking on the international problems that plagued the United States between 1918 and 1920. Like most Americans, he viewed with mounting alarm the social ferment that kept Europe in turmoil as reconstruction began; Russia's "Bolsheviki" he saw as heralds of a disorderly future, potentially more dangerous than German "imperialism." Unlike his fellow countrymen, however, he was wise enough to realize that this was social revolution that would eventually culminate in a better world for the masses of people. "A new society must be born in the Old and New World," he predicted.[34] Turner was also alarmed by the curbs on freedom of speech that accompanied the Great Red Scare in the United States, feeling that it was "better to let steam escape than to try to keep it sealed up. . . . The way to make radical revolutionaries is to shut off men who do not think conventionally, from the ordinary avenues of expression." Moreover, what was "wild and dangerous" today might be considered "wise and good" in the future. Yet Turner was shocked by the rapidity of change and the constant threat of violence. The world would be a better place if it could recapture the spirit of the old frontier cabin-raising days—"construction by mutual efforts, toleration and good humor"—even when he knew that those happy days would never return.[35]

His first reaction was a brief escape into isolationism. Better for the United States to retreat into its shell than to risk tainting its democratic institutions by contact with less favored nations. "It would be a pity," Turner wrote early in 1918, "if the United States lost her isolation from Europe so that we could no longer preserve this continent from the struggles for power incident to the application of Old World rivalries to the western hemisphere." A league to enforce peace would plunge the United States into European politics. If Europeans wanted to modify their systems, "let them come to us and follow our practices and system rather than that we should take the burden of the inheritance of the sad old world habits and experiences."[36] Turner, like the pioneers he admired, could dream of an isolated America, just as he could of frontier cooperation, as a panacea for modern problems.

But Turner was a sensible man, and soon discarded such fantasies. The world was shrinking, like it or not; the United States had to learn to live with its neighbors, and this required an effective world organization powerful enough to block future wars. Long before January 1918, when President Wilson proposed an "association of nations" to Congress, Turner was speculating on the basic problem certain to confront such an organization: how to transcend the nationalistic loyalties that were so strongly rooted in European tradition. As early as the spring of 1915 he had found one answer, based, as usual, on the American experience. Any central authority, Turner wrote, must operate directly on individuals, not on nations, and must have control of transportation, business intercourse, tariffs, currency, and banking. This concentration of economic power in the super-government would encourage the formation of political parties across national lines, for the common interests of class groups in England and Germany would be greater than their distinctive interests as Englishmen or Germans. The parties would serve as perpetual bonds of union, as they did in the

United States, where they bound the sections together.[37] These were brave thoughts in a war-torn world where nationalism raged uncontrolled.

These speculations took on new meaning when the President sought to rebuild the world on the foundation of an organization of nations. Turner realized that his views should be shared with the statesmen entrusted with this awesome task, for familiarity with the American experience would help them erect an enduring international body. His public duty was clear. Two remarkable documents resulted. One, filling twenty-three pages in his own hand, and entitled "Syllabus of Considerations on the Proposed League of Nations," was obviously a worksheet for his eyes alone. The other, labeled "International Political Parties in a Durable League of Nations," condensed into seven pages the highlights of his thinking, and was intended for the diplomats then preparing to remake the map of Europe.

In both papers Turner stressed the parallels between the American sections under the federal Constitution and the European nations under a league of states. What, he asked, had held the sections of the United States together? There were many answers—joint ownership of the public domain, fear of outside nations, interstate commerce, the effectiveness of the federal system—but no cohesive force was as strong as political parties. As national organizations, parties forced statesmen to fashion policies beneficial to the entire nation rather than to any one region; they also helped arrange the compromises and concessions that allowed the sections to cooperate together. Hence, party conventions were comparable to international congresses, and agreements that reconciled regional jealousies were similar to treaties. The basis for Europe's political parties had already been laid, with the International Socialists, Industrial Workers of the World, and Bolsheviki on one side, the business combinations and middle-class workers on the other. Some might object to letting the Russian serpent into the Garden of Eden, but it was certain to enter eventually and would be less dangerous if welcomed openly rather than allowed to strike in the dark. Political parties shaped by class interests would emerge only if Wilson's proposed League of Nations operated through a legislative body endowed with real but limited power over fiscal and economic matters. Only this would assure permanence for the League.[38]

These conclusions, Turner firmly believed, might alter the course of history if they could reach the President before the peace conferences began at Versailles. Two emissaries were entrusted with this task. One, Harvard's George Grafton Wilson, carried a copy to Washington in late November 1918, in the hope of handing it to Wilson just before the delegation sailed for France, but apparently he was unsuccessful. Charles Homer Haskins had better luck with the second. As a member of the delegation himself, he was able to slip Turner's memorandum to one of the President's secretaries three days before the party reached Europe.[39] Wilson probably was shown the document, but the tragic events at Versailles gave him no chance to build the effective international organization that he and Turner envisioned. The impotent League of Nations that emerged as a monument to the nationalism and selfishness of the Allied leaders who fashioned the Treaty of Versailles made no provision for a legislative body representative of the people, let alone for the political parties that would assure its permanence.

Yet even this sad shadow of the powerful organization that Turner wanted was too idealistic for the Washington politicians. They were waiting to pounce when President Wilson laid his plans for a League of Nations before them. Turner watched with mounting indignation as they first emasculated, then rejected, the League that he felt would alone assure world peace. The arch-villain in his eyes was Henry Cabot Lodge, a man, "little and spiteful," who played great issues as pawns in a game to satisfy his own wounded vanity and glorify the Republican party. For Turner, alert as always to the forces shaping political decision-making, was utterly convinced by this time that American ideals could best be secured "by cooperative council and concert in the world," not by a head-in-the-sand retreat from responsibility. "Much as we rightfully distrust European diplomats," he wrote late in 1919, "the path of safety may be in forming an international fire service."[40] Yet there was little that he could do save sputter his discontent and vote for Democratic pro-League candidates, even though this meant charges of insanity from his Boston friends. He voted a solid Democratic ticket in 1918 for the first time in his life, and in 1920 was passionately opposed to Warren G. Harding—a "marionette president" who danced at the end of strings pulled by selfish interests.[41] Turner believed that "Henry Cabot Lodge and the good Lord will have an unpleasant half hour if he ever climbs up for the interview."[42]

His complete about-face is nowhere better illustrated than in two Washington's Birthday addresses, delivered seven years apart. In 1916 he could caution that "Washington's warnings against entangling alliances still have validity and they gain new force from the awful tragedy that meets our gaze whenever we look across the Atlantic." But by 1923 Turner was arguing that the first President spoke only for the needs of his day and would not want the judgment of 1796 to control the nation in 1923. Then the United States was weak and isolated; now it was strong, and was faced with the need to survive in a shrinking world. "We have found that when Europe is aflame we cannot find isolation or security. The embers of that volcano fall on our own houses. . . . The world is one, and we cannot escape its misfortunes."[43] Here was a new Turner speaking. The realities of World War I and its aftermath had converted him from a Jackson Man into a Wilson Man.

Yet Turner could never quite fall into step with postwar America. He identified himself so completely with his frontier and frontiersmen that he believed their way of life held the key to happiness; if pioneer ideals could be projected into the present, the nation—and the world—would be better places. When reason governed, as it did most of the time, he spoke as he did in his 1923 Washington's Birthday address; when nostalgia ruled, he looked over his shoulder into a dead past and yearned for it to come alive again. The League of Nations might be a step toward peace, but the real basis for a perfect world was "mutual understanding and good will and 'give' as well as 'take'—the old pioneer custom of the neighborly 'house raising.'"[44] Noble sentiments, those, but totally unrealistic, as Turner well knew. He had to live in the twentieth century, and he was able to enjoy life there more than most of his generation. The League of Nations might be a feeble shadow of the powerful international organization that he sought, social change might be too rapid for his taste, the nation might be less perfect than it had been in pioneer times, mankind might be askew as new wars and rivalries flamed in Europe. But there was work to be done, problems to be solved, a past to be investigated. Turner's interest in politics did not fade with his disillusionment, but his crusading zeal was gone. History would monopolize his energy for the remainder of his days.

The wartime years brought trial and disillusionment to Turner, but they also provided him with a by-product that was one of his proud-

est possessions—the second (and last) book published during his lifetime. This had been long a-borning. For a dozen years his friends—and
a good many strangers—had urged him to collect his scattered essays
into one volume, where they could be used by students; copies of the
original journals in which they appeared were long out of print, while
those in libraries were so worn by generations of use that they were
almost unreadable. "I have," one professor reported, "spent a small fortune (for a professor) and eighteen months trying to get two copies
of each article for my alcove and the end is as far off—as peace."[45]
These complaints were based on real need, not flattery; dozens of
courses on the History of the West lacked the reading materials necessary for the proper interpretation of their subject matter.

This was recognized by a number of authors and publishers, and
they set out to remedy the situation in their own way. If Turner would
not republish his essays, they would—and at no profit to him. Scarcely
a month passed but a request arrived to reprint this article or that—the
McKinley Publishing Company planned a series on "American History
in American Schools" and wanted to include "The Significance of the
Frontier in American History"; Norman Foerster felt that his forthcoming collection on *American Ideals* would not be complete without
"Contributions of the West to American Democracy"; the American
Book Company sought permission to use that same essay in a book on
"Americanism"; two instructors at Annapolis also wanted it for their
volume on *Contemporary Issues and Ideals;* historians galore asked the
right to reprint one or the other in collections of documents they were
editing. So it went, as Turner's brainchildren appeared in every possible medium, ranging from *Readings in Agricultural History* to *Essays
for College English.* One of his former students, Solon J. Buck, had the
audacity to announce that he planned to combine a number of Turner's
essays and chapters from his *Rise of the New West* into a book of readings for college courses, and that a publisher had assured him that it
would have a large market.[46] Turner clearly had to stir himself into
action, or he would watch royalties disappear into other pockets.

His opportunity was provided, strangely enough, by the National
Board for Historical Services. A bibliography on problems of the
peace, prepared by that wartime agency and published in *The Historical Outlook*, listed a number of Turner's articles, praised them as essential to an understanding of the national character, and noted that they
"ought to be brought together in a single convenient collection."[47] This

sensible suggestion attracted the attention of Edward N. Bristol, the patient Henry Holt & Company editor who had been trying to pry a book from Turner since 1897. Here was his chance. "I wonder," he wrote, "how these essays would comport themselves in one volume? Do they contain duplications?" If not, and if they could be prepared for the press "without any preliminary attention from you to speak of," Holt would be very much interested.[48]

Turner was delighted. He had long contemplated revising his essays into a book on *The Significance of the Frontier*, but, as usual, ambition outweighed accomplishment, and he had done nothing. Now the publishers, fully aware that once he started rewriting he would go on forever, specified that he give them no "preliminary attention" but print them as they originally appeared. This posed problems. On the one hand, he would not be able to eliminate duplicating passages, incorporate modern scholarship, and weld the separate articles into a unified statement of his views on the frontier. On the other, to undertake a complete revision would mean a major delay in publication, and might subject him to charges that he had borrowed too heavily from his own disciples. For once, Turner made the right decision. "I decided," he wrote a friend, "to let them stand much as originally printed with some omission of duplicate passages, and with such indication of time of original publication as would clear up questions of priority."[49] The die was cast. He would have another book, even though an imperfect one.

That decision was reached in record time; Edward Bristol's invitation presumably reached him on the morning of April 24, 1919 (it was mailed from New York the day before), and before the morning was out his reply was on its way. Yes, he agreed that the essays would have some value if published unchanged; to do so would be to mirror the self-consciousness of the American people in successive years and to demonstrate the impact of his ideas on the interpretation of the nation's past. He would be glad to have them published if Mr. Bristol felt they did not duplicate each other too greatly. Copies of the eleven that he planned to include would be sent that afternoon. They must be carefully guarded, for Turner had no others.[50] He was on his way to a new book, he told friends, with publication less than a year away.

His dreams of a handsome volume miraculously produced without his lifting a finger were soon scattered, for even assembling essays for a publisher demanded a fair amount of labor. What about duplication? The Holt editors had no apprehension on that score; a competent historian who had read the collection at their request reported that overlapping passages were few and unimportant. But not to Turner, the perfectionist. Detailed instructions bombarded New York: omit six lines after "Gallatin" in such and such an essay, discard the last two paragraphs on page 23 of another, delete three sentences from still another. Corrections had to be made: substitute Virginia for South Carolina on the last line of page 247. Decisions had to be reached on the order in which the essays would appear. Publisher and author had to stage the usual debate on the number of footnotes to be included. Fugitive essays had to be located; Turner was ready to omit a speech on "Middle Western Pioneer Democracy," which he had given before the Minnesota Historical Society, because he could not find a copy, but one appeared at the last moment. Above all, permissions had to be secured to republish copyrighted items; particularly troublesome was the quest for a vanished former editor of the *International Monthly*, who was only brought to bay just before the volume appeared.[51] There was, Turner decided, no such thing as an instant book. But there were rewards, too, in the form of a contract dated June 10, 1920, promising a fat 15 per cent royalty on all copies sold.[52]

He was to earn his royalties, for in that day of small, efficient publishing houses, there was little rest for the author. Three days after the contract was signed, and just as Turner was to leave for a summer in Maine, the first bundle of galley proofs arrived. He carried them northward in his suitcase, grumbling that he must manipulate a pencil rather than a fishing rod during the next weeks, and settled to his task. A major task it was; Holt was so eager to have a book by Turner on its lists that it made no attempt to standardize footnotes in the manuscript, assuring him that he could care for that slight matter when reading proof. Yet all went so well that just one month and three days after the first galleys were received, the bulky page proofs were delivered at his door. A month later printing began, even though Turner was still discovering corrections that had to be made. *The Frontier in American History* was published on October 6, 1920, less than four months after the manuscript was received and the contract signed.[53]

Doubts beset Turner as he thumbed through his second-born. He liked the dust jacket and found the smooth blue cloth binding attractive, but the quality of the paper was less to his taste, a victim of post-war scarcities and the high cost of living. He was even more apprehensive as he skimmed the contents. "Does it not strike you as frightfully dull and full of repetitions?" he asked a friend. "Honest! I hesitated long over publication because of this doubt."[54] Turner might have been doubtful, but he showed no hesitancy in asking the publishers to send no less than forty-four free copies to former students, friends, and prominent historians. Holt & Company balked at such a wholesale distribution, pointing out that they customarily provided only a few complimentary copies, but they did send him eleven, and he agreed to purchase twenty more at half price.[55] Those went off to a diverse list that ranged from Woodrow Wilson and Lord Bryce, on the one extreme, to his erstwhile student and Bancroftian enemy, Charles H. Ambler, on the other.

The response was worth the effort. True, President Wilson, responded only in a stiff note written by his secretary, an affront that hurt deeply, but Turner had no cause for complaint in the general reaction. From Lord Bryce came four pages of pure flattery, and others were even less restrained—"the most significant contribution of this generation to United States history"; "a new era in American historical interpretation"; "the greatest real contribution that has been made"; "epoch-making essays"; "ideas which changed the trend of historical interpretation in this country"; "conclusions that must influence historians years and decades after you and I are gone"; "I have met no more illuminating discussion of American civilization"[56]—these were the phrases that gladdened Turner as he read his mail during the next weeks. Newspaper commentators were just as flattering: "an historical study of compelling interest"; "the most important single contribution to the subject made in our generation"; "a notable collection of studies."[57] Even the staid Boston press discovered the prophet in its midst. "Professor Turner," announced the *Transcript*, "has pointed the way to a new, and more truly national school of historical research." Little wonder that he chuckled his delight at being found by Boston after living for some years in successful concealment there.[58]

Magazine critics were no less restrained, with emphasis now on the enduring contributions that Turner had made to the study and teaching of American history. "No other teacher of American history," declared the *Review of Reviews*, "has done more to direct the thinking of students and to mark out fields of research than Professor Turner"; *The Nation* agreed that "in giving direction to the methods of investigation in American history and in furnishing new light for its interpretation, the share of Mr. Turner has been the most profound and abiding of this generation." To the *Yale Review*, Turner was responsible for "the most pregnant thinking on American history in the past generation"; to the *Atlantic Monthly*, his book was "a great achievement." Turner clipped all of these heartwarming comments, mounted them on heavy paper, underlined them to call attention to the most favorable passages, adorned them with marginal arrows opposite the very highest praise, and pasted them in a scrapbook, to be re-read when his ego needed rejuvenation. "I am liable," he confessed, "to take myself seriously if my friends and reviewers aren't careful."[59] Yet he loved every word that he read.

Charles A. Beard intruded the one harsh note into this chorus of acclaim. Writing in the *New Republic*, Beard readily agreed that the 1893 essay had "an immense and salutary" influence on historical writing, but he found on re-reading it that Turner's thesis was riddled with overstatements and faulty interpretations. One by one he ticked these off: the existence of an area of free land did not "explain" American development any more than a dozen other factors, including industrialism and the southern plantation system, did; national legislative measures dealing with tariffs and land disposal were "conditioned" no more by the frontier than they were by forces that Turner failed to mention; the "loose construction" of the Constitution was furthered by easterners such as Thomas Jefferson as much as it was by western influences; the thesis paid too little attention to conflicts between capital and labor. Nor was it convincing, for it was built on speculation rather than documentation.[60]

Turner was stung by this attack, as well he might be. "I find myself," he told a friend, "like a great grandfather in reference to the essay on *The Frontier*, quite ready to see its imperfections myself, but disposed to pick up the cudgels when someone else finds flaws in its features."[61] A strong letter answered Beard's points one by one: in the *early* history of the United States free land exerted a greater influence on legislation than slavery or industry did; the West, as the most concerned section, conditioned land legislation far more effectively than the East did; westerners were loose constructionists because this was the expedient position for them to adopt; the frontier served as an effective instrument for Americanization by converting all newcomers into small farmers. He would not compromise with Beard's basic position. "The capital and labor side has an importance which I think emphasizes the importance of the *ending* of the frontier," Turner explained to his daughter, "while he thinks the movement was all along more important than the frontier. The truth is both were related."[62]

Beard was willing to dispute the points made by Turner, but he refused to come to grips with the fundamental issue: to what degree did the frontier and to what extent did economic divisions shape American civilization?[63] This was an insoluble problem, and Beard had no desire to begin an impossible debate with a man he admired as much as he did Turner. He had, he feared, gone too far as it was; for years he regretted that his review had hurt rather than enlightened. "It was," he confessed, "sharper than I should have made it in view of the great service he had rendered to American history."[64] Beard could not know that he had struck the first blow in the assault on Turner's theories, an assault that would crest in the 1930s and 1940s and concern historians for generations to come.

Turner might be annoyed by Beard's criticism, but he was right when he predicted that it would do no harm. Sales were surprisingly good for such a specialized work, reaching 1076 in 1920 and 1345 in 1921, before slipping back to seven or eight hundred yearly.[65] This was not only gratifying, it also allowed Turner to fulfill a long-standing ambition. Since 1905 his conscience had periodically reminded him that he had accepted an advance of $500 from Henry Holt & Company for a textbook in American history that was still unwritten. The publishers were not concerned; as they surveyed sales figures for *The Frontier in American History* in the spring of 1921, they sent back the note he had signed with the word CANCELLED written across the front. Turner would have none of this; the note was promptly returned with CANCELLATION REFUSED added. Nor would he give the Holt editors peace until they allowed him to retire his debt with his first two royalty checks. He received a cash return of only $8.88 on the year of sales that they covered, but he enjoyed far more receiving the much-traveled note with "Paid in full by royalties earned on The Frontier in American History" scrawled across its face.[66] Turner failed his publishers as a profitable textbook writer, but he did set a precedent for honesty that few of his successors were to follow.

His gesture provided a happy climax to the not-too-pleasant experiences he had endured during the years of World War I and its aftermath. Turner had wasted more days than he liked to remember on activities that had contributed to the national welfare but that had not advanced his own researches one whit. Now, with peace restored to the nation, with his affairs in order, and with his Harvard routine established, he could turn eagerly to the investigations into sectionalism that were to occupy his last years as a teacher—and speed his retirement.

XV

Harvard Years:
The World of Scholarship

1917-1924

T O FREDERICK JACKSON TURNER—and to a good many college professors from his day to the present—the duties that occupied most of his waking hours were roadblocks in the path of his principal objective: to broaden the scope of knowledge by research and publication. He moved to Harvard in 1910 partly to escape the commitments that multiplied with the passing years at Wisconsin, but at Harvard he found himself so involved with his teaching, forming the Harvard Commission on Western History, and protecting his reputation against the allegations of Frederic Bancroft, that for some years he scarcely put pen to paper. With the ending of World War I his prospects brightened. Now, Turner resolved, nothing would stand in the way of his ambitious publication program.

This was already outlined in his mind—he would pile proof on proof to convince his fellow craftsmen that sectionalism was no less significant than the frontier in moulding the American past—but his interests were too catholic, his enthusiasms too mercurial, to let him follow any one intellectual path exclusively. He was, quite naturally, besieged with invitations to speak on a spectrum of subjects tangential to his main interests, and while he had the good sense to refuse many—including four lectures at the University of London, twelve at the New School for Social Research (with a $1000 fee), and one before the Montreal Women's Canadian Club on the current Balkan situation[1]—his resistance collapsed now and then, with time-consuming results. His fellow historians were particularly hard to deny: Turner was persuaded to address the annual dinner of the Mississippi Valley Historical Association in 1920 on his early flirtations with western history (and was dismayed when 250 people appeared, instead of the thirty or so for whom he had prepared informal remarks), and the Agricultural History Society, two years later, on "Agricultural History as a Field for Research." The latter assignment pleased him particularly, partly because it gave him an opportunity to catalogue dozens of topics crying for investigation, more because he suddenly realized that he was viewed as the patron saint of that discipline.[2] "It's funny," he confessed to a friend. "I know too little of agriculture to distinguish barley from wheat; but I have started a lot of these men off in historical study of agriculture so they asked me to share myself."[3] These were events pleasing to the ego, but Turner's extracurricular interests led him principally into two bypaths, one focused on the very early period of American history, the other on the very recent.

His excursions into the colonial era began when he was asked to speak before the New England Historic Genealogical Society, in June 1911, on "The Colonial Frontier about 1700." He did so, not very well, he thought, but his tentative explorations into the documents awakened a new interest. Such proof as could be advanced for the frontier thesis he had drawn largely from his midwestern experience; why not dig deeply enough to show that the seventeenth century demonstrated that his theories were valid, just as did the mid-nineteenth? Here was a quest to his liking; Turner spent months searching colonial records for evidence of the frontier's significance, with surprisingly rich results. His findings, delivered before the Colonial Society of Massachusetts, in 1914, as "The First Official Frontier of the Massachusetts Bay," revealed the same reversion to wilderness barbarism, the same succession of frontier types, the same tendency of the newer settlements to serve as a "safety valve" for the old, the same drift toward greater democracy, the same rising spirit of independence, that Turner had observed in his own Wisconsin.[4] His audience was less impressed with the revelations than was Turner—he was not sure that many among those staid Bostonians "understood or enjoyed," and he was conscious that a goodly number listened with stern disapproval as he described their ancestors as wild frontiersmen—but serious-minded historians recognized that he had opened a new vista on the study of the colonial past. Charles McLean Andrews, Samuel Eliot Morison, and Winfred T. Root all testified that they had to recast their thinking to fit the frontier thesis into their interpretations.[5]

Turner was sufficiently gratified to take up the cudgels for the frontier interpretation whenever one of his converts threatened to defect. He did so with a vengeance in 1918, when Charles McLean Andrews was asked by the Massachusetts Historical Society to explain the views of the "Imperial School" that he headed. The colonies, Andrews argued, could be understood only if viewed from the vantage point of London instead of Boston or Williamsburg, and the total pattern of imperial trade and regulation made part of the story. Turner struck back at the next meeting. The "Imperial School" had corrected past distortions, but was guilty of even more when it ignored the "purely American aspects of the subject." The adjustment of the colonists to their new environment could not be ignored. "Was not the more important thing the play of the new influences, the grappling with unaccustomed conditions in surroundings, economic life, the breaking of old customs, the creation of new institutions, the modification of the type?" Boston had a wilderness at its back door no less than an ocean at its front, and each formed part of the equation. Why not view the colonial past from both west and east, from the frontier as well as from the center of empire?[6] Turner may not have swayed his New England audience, but he seriously influenced the study and teaching of colonial history for a generation by these remarks; a "frontier school" not less than an "imperial school" and a "nationalistic school" were to thrive until the 1930s.[7]

He was scarcely less influential when he focused his spotlight on the recent past, as he did frequently during the 1920s. His interest in these later years was natural. During the era of post-World War I disillusionment, the nation turned more and more within itself as it licked its wounds and sought to solve its own problems instead of those of Europe. One of the most serious of those problems was adjustment to a frontierless existence, now that the era of cheap lands was drawing to a close; how to live in a closed-space world, how to feed increasing multitudes with the public domain no longer open, how to apportion the dwindling natural resources equitably—these were questions that plagued solid scientists no less than the sensation-seeking hacks whose lurid tales in magazines and newspapers predicted the imminent starvation of all mankind. Turner, with his proprietary interest in the frontier, listened with special attention to these cries of doom, and he spent far more time than he should reading and speculating on the nation's fate as its people learned to live with fixed borders.

Twice he shared his conclusions with the community, once in 1916, when he addressed social science students of the University of Chicago on "The Last Quarter-Century," again in 1923, when he delivered the Founder's Day address at Clark University on "Since the Foundation." Both required an inordinate amount of preparation—Turner filled folders with notes, clippings, sample pages, and outlines before those two lectures were written to his satisfaction[8]—and for both he had to grapple with some problems that were so difficult that they defied solution. His basic question was readily defined: what would happen now that American society was no longer "undergoing the transformations due to creative interaction with fresh supplies of free land, and natural resources, fresh fields for political and social institutions?" The years since 1890 provided a partial answer; they had witnessed higher living costs, conservation, immigration restriction, and a declining birth rate, as the physical adjustment to a closed-space existence began. But they had witnessed also the rise of monopoly as giant trusts absorbed the remaining natural resources, a tightening of class lines, and an increase in governmental regulation of private enterprise. During those years the nation lost much of its optimistic faith in the future, much of its belief in its mission to remake the world in its own image. These were debits in the balance sheet, but there were credits as well: the mechanical inventions and technological innovations that went with industrialization, the revolutions in transportation that shrank the planet to a quarter its former size, the cultural renaissance that accompanied urbanization, the democratization of politics during the Progressive era. Turner drew no conclusions at the time (he was to speculate far more on the subject in later years), but his message was still clear: the era of expansion had passed and with it one form of life and living; Americans had to adjust to the twentieth century, no matter how deep their nostalgia for the nineteenth.[9]

Turner was safer, and happier, when he stuck to his own last, rather than venturing along the fascinating detour that led him to the present. There his duty, and purpose, were clear—and had been since his *Rise of the New West* was published in 1906. "I am," he wrote as early as 1907, "beginning to see increasingly a great opportunity for a work to fill in between *1815-1850* and I want to do it in the course of a few years."[10] Such a book would not only fill a major gap in American historiography, but provide an opportunity to examine the interplay of sectionalizing and nationalizing forces, to observe the interaction of sections as they bargained and compromised while shaping national legislative programs, to reveal the regional pressures on cultural expression. Gradually the shape of the book formed in his mind—a volume that would describe each of the nation's sections as it existed in 1830 (a more realistic date than 1815), then trace their relationships as revealed in political, economic, and cultural history during the next two decades. Thus was born the image of the book—THE BOOK, his friends were soon calling it—that was to be Turner's *magnum opus*.

This was a major assignment—a volume that analyzed *all* aspects of American culture—and Turner did not approach the task lightly. Much of the needed preparation was already behind him; he had learned a great deal about physical geography while preparing his *Rise of the New West*, and he had done a major amount of thinking about the nature of sectionalism. All that he had learned, however, only proved that he knew too little to draw any conclusions. He had to do more investigation, and a great deal more research, before he could begin to understand the changing sectional pattern in the 1830-50 period, the role of sub-sections within the larger regions, and the correlation between political, cultural, and economic behavior in their relationship with physiographic and ethnic pressures.

Turner spent such time as he could snatch from his many other duties on these investigations, but progress was slow. He had to immerse himself in the literature of a dozen disciplines, from literary history to statistics, with geography the most important; in 1914 he joined the Association of American Geographers, and a short time later he was made a fellow of the American Geographical Society. He had to gather data from an infinity of sources, on everything from county politics to literary productivity; his files grew remarkably during these years as he added folder after folder crammed with notes and charts. As he did so, another stumbling block arose, for the eight- by five-inch sheets on which he recorded his reading notes proved too small to hold the voluminous data he was accumulating, requiring a shift to the larger, typewriter-paper, size. That, in turn, meant that he had to paste his older notes—notes that he had been accumulating since about 1890—on the new sheets, two to a sheet. Even modern newspaper stories that shed light on sectional patterns were grist for his mill; Turner regularly clipped items from the New York, Boston, and Chicago press to be added to his file drawers.[11] This early, he was being overwhelmed by the sheer volume of the research materials he was accumulating.

How to distill meaning from these masses of data? Statistical charts, graphs, and tables of figures were inadequate to reveal the correlations that interested him; maps were the only answer. All his information must be mapped, using the county as the basic unit, for no larger division would reveal the sub-sections formed within sections by environmental and ethnic pressures. Turner was constantly alert to the work of other scholars who might have transcribed some of the information that he sought; letters went off regularly to confirm a rumor that Indiana had available maps showing religious preferences and illiteracy by counties, or that Tennessee had published county maps of the elections of 1824 and 1832, or that an historical atlas being prepared at the Carnegie Institution would contain mappings of the 1850 congressional votes.[12] When he had the good fortune to find a map already prepared (as he seldom did), it filled only a tiny portion of his needs. Most had to be painstakingly constructed from the oceans of information that he culled from newspapers, almanacs, state and local census returns, travel accounts, and a bewildering variety of sources.

They required infinite patience and time, for three types of maps had to be prepared to reveal classifications of data. One group had to show physical conditions—topography, soil structure, economic activities, and ethnic composition; another, cultural factors—denominational preponderance, percentages of illiteracy, numbers of grade school and high school graduates in proportion to the population, newspaper distribution, literary productivity, and the prevalence of libraries; a third, political behavior in each election between 1830 and 1850—which counties were normally Whig or Democratic, and which swung between the major parties. These maps completed, Turner began his correlations, hoping to determine whether the voting patterns resulted from physiographic, ethnic, or economic forces, or whether other social forces were responsible. Did a group of counties in the South that consistently voted Whig vary from that region's traditional Democratic pattern because better soils produced more abundant crops? Or because they were settled from Tidewater Virginia rather than backwoods Tennessee? Or because the percentage of illiterates was low? Or because a majority were Episcopalians rather than Baptist? These were the questions that Turner hoped his maps would answer. Dozens of those maps crowded his files, most crudely drawn, and many designed to shed light on such unlikely subjects as the political sophistication of states with legislative reference libraries as contrasted with those without, and the effect of local-option prohibition on county politics.[13] Hours, days, months of toil went into their preparation, but all seemed worthwhile, for Turner sincerely believed that they would unlock secrets that had eluded historians.

By 1914 Turner was convinced that they had done so, and that he was ready to share his findings with his colleagues. One group, the professional geographers, responded as he hoped they might when he addressed a joint meeting of the Association of American Geographers and the American Geographical Society that spring on "Geographic Influences in American History," showing them some sixty lantern slides of election returns counterposed against maps of soil differences and comparable economic determinants.[14] They were entranced, for here was a whole new field of scholarship that fitted well with the prevailing belief in environmental determinism. "So many problems were opened up by the maps and your explanation of them," one told Turner, "that we could well have spent the remainder of the session in discussing them."[15]

His fellow historians were less impressed when he appeared before them a few months later. The occasion lent itself to drama; the American Historical Association met in Chicago that December, with its evening sessions scheduled for the Art Institute. In that same building, just twenty-one years before, Turner had read a paper on the significance of the frontier that had altered the course of historical studies. Now he would read another on "The Significance of Sectionalism in American History," and again remake the interpretation of the nation's past.

How tragic the difference. Turner argued his cause earnestly; sectionalism, one of the "most characteristic features of all American history," underlay violent eruptions (the Hartford Convention and the Civil War), but it was also a governing force in presidential elections, legislative contests, congressional votes, and the manners, customs, and social traits of the people. All were products of "the reaction between stock and environment," and all demanded further study before the true political history of the United States could be told. Thus, between 1856 and 1908, the lake counties of Illinois, Indiana, and Ohio voted consistently Republican, while the southern portions of those states went Democratic; this did not mean that there was a direct relationship between "hard rocks and Democracy, or glacial lobes and Republicanism," but it did mean that certain types of immigrants were attracted by certain physiographic conditions, and that the combination of geographic and ethnic factors created political attitudes. These were not determined solely by either stock or environment; wealthy property holders within each of the sections or sub-sections tended to unite with comparable property holders in other sections. Political parties mirrored these class divisions just as they did regional groupings; hence, the parties served as bonds holding the union together.[16]

If Turner's paper on "The Significance of Sections" was confused and confusing, so was Turner himself. He had, he realized, attempted too broad a generalization on too scant evidence. Many more elections must be plotted, many more maps drawn, many more examples of ethnic or environmental pressures analyzed before the nature of sectionalism became clear. Were the conflicts that he had described based on regional or class antagonisms? Turner was not sure; his own hesitant suggestion that class lines blurred sectional divisions suggested the doubts that beset him. He was sure, however, that neither his paper before the geographers nor his essay on "The Significance of Sections" deserved publication. The editor of the *Annals of the Association of American Geographers* virtually demanded the former, but Turner could never find the time for revision, and the whole matter was soon forgotten. J. Franklin Jameson, editor of the *American Historical Review*, was even more insistent, embarrassing Turner with letters and telegrams urging the immediate printing of his essay on the significance of sections, even without the revisions the author hoped to make. Instead of leaping at the opportunity to share his theories with the profession, Turner let weeks and months slip by with only an occasional plea for more time to make needed changes. Three years later, Jameson was still pleading and Turner was doing his best to forget the whole matter.[17] He realized, perhaps unconsciously, that mere revision was not enough. He had to do a great deal more work before the complexities of sectionalism could be explained.

In order to do so, he undertook a more searching analysis of the section most familiar to him—the Midwest—over the next few years. His progress was marked by occasional lectures that showed his deepening knowledge—five at Western Reserve University under the McBridge Lectureship in the fall of 1916, when he talked to a dwindling audience on "The Development of the Middle West"; a paper on "The Significance of the Middle West, 1830-1850," delivered before the annual meeting of the American Historical Association a year later; a dedicatory address on "Middle Western Pioneer Democracy," given in 1918, which celebrated the opening of the Minnesota Historical Society's new headquarters.[18] Those lectures also showed, however, that he suffered from a fatal misconception. Turner, despite his protestations to the contrary, still thought in terms of geographic determinism, and he sought explanations for political and social behavior in physiographic pressures, rather than in the many forces responsible. When he could speak, as he did before the American Historical Association, of ethnic streams being "fused in this great geographic melting pot while society was still plastic," or when he told his Minnesota audience that bowie-knife southerners, cow-milking Yankees, beer-drinking Germans, and wild Irishmen were merged into "a new type, which was neither the sum of all its elements, nor a complete fusion in a melting pot" by impact with an unfamiliar environment, Turner was admitting a bias that blocked his understanding of sectionalism. So long as he thought of geographic forces that were strong enough to transcend ethnic differences and that created in each section a standardized community where all lived and voted and thought alike, he was far from his mark.

Turner realized this now and then, and asked himself some very pertinent questions. Tucked among the pages of the paper he gave before the American Historical Association was a single sheet that dramatically revealed his dilemma. "Why," he wrote, "does Indiana not show the same facts in regard to glacial influences as her neighbors on either side?" Why was illiteracy so widespread there? Why did voting patterns there fail to correspond to glacial moraines, as they did in Illinois? Turner had the key to many of his questions when he wrote those words; later investigations showed that Indiana's settlers came primarily from the upland South and did not bow to environmental forces as the environmentalists believed they should. But Turner closed his eyes to this ethnic factor. "Are there," he asked himself, as he sought to answer his own queries, "concealed geographic influences?"[19] He was too wedded to environmentalism as a basic factor, if not as a determinative one, to recognize that the puppets on his stage were responding to pulls from a dozen strings, not just one.

This same prejudice permeated the series of talks that best reveal Turner's views on sectionalism at this stage of his development—the Lowell Institute Lectures delivered in Boston during the early spring of 1918. Turner was delighted when the invitation to participate in this prestigious event arrived, and well he might be; preparing eight lectures on "The United States and Its Sections, 1830–1850" would force him to write most of THE BOOK that would culminate his life's work—the book destined to be published three years after his death as *The United States, 1830-1850: The Nation and Its Sections.* So he spent the next eight months—between June 1917, when the invitation arrived, and February 26, 1918, when he walked on the stage at Huntington Hall— in a desperate effort to produce something worthy of the occasion— and on time. All that summer the fishing rod was forgotten as maps were drawn and re-drawn, pages written and re-written, lectures reproduced. All that autumn every moment that could be snatched from classes and graduate students went into the final polishing that Turner's sense of perfection demanded. Six days before the first lecture was to be delivered, he was still at work. "They are," he reported, "taking every ounce of energy which I can find or borrow." In the end the lectures were completed, and in a form that pleased the select audience that tradition, if not the subject, attracted. "To the cold witness of charts, maps, and statistics," reported the *Boston Transcript*, "he has added the warm color of his own deft and humanly vivid descriptions, moving through the whole with a quiet charm very personal to him."[20] Turner's Lowell Lectures created no sensation in Back Bay society, but they were accepted well.

This was their due, for Turner lavished a great deal of thought as well as time on their preparation, and they revealed exactly the views on sectionalism held at that time. Turner made clear the importance of his findings at the outset; "the frontier and the section lie at the foundations of what is distinctive in American history." No understanding of nineteenth-century politics, or life, or culture was possible without familiarity with sectional interplay. For the sections—and the environmental forces that shaped each—were influential, even if not determinative, in controlling the political, economic, and cultural behavior of the settlers. Ethnic differences, Turner readily admitted, influenced behavioral patterns, but this was largely because geographic conditions attracted differing racial stocks to any region; differences in background might be reflected in voting, but factors of land and climate concentrating different "stocks" at certain places were ultimately responsible.

Hence, American history could be understood only by studying sectional conflicts, and the resolution of those conflicts by adjustment, compromise, bargaining, and, in one case, war. "These relations between sections," Turner told his audience, "are to the United States what international relations are to Europe; the section is in fact a denatured nation." The sections had been held together over the centuries by the Constitution, operating as it did on individuals rather than regions or states, and by the cohesive force of political parties, which ran across sectional borders. Whenever party and sectional lines became practically identical, as they did in the case of New England Federalism and proslavery Democracy, the United States faced a situation comparable to that constantly faced by Europe. This meant war rather than peaceful adjustment.

Turner readily admitted that he was asking questions rather than providing answers; sectionalism offered historians a laboratory for the study of the relationship between history and geography and a test tube for the analysis of the relative influence of ethnic and physiographic pressures. Such studies, if made without the taint of "sectional provincialism," would for the first time fully explain the nineteenth century and shed some light on the twentieth. They should be made soon, for at this stage of his thinking, Turner believed that sectional influences were succumbing to nationalizing forces. "The forces of sectional disunion were culled out by the very fact of growth in nationalism, were, in fact, the vain resistance of minority areas to the powerful stream of national tendency." With the passing of the sections, much would go from American life; the richness, the variety, the contradictions of society were, in large measure, the products of regional provincialism. "The sections have saved the nation from deadening uniformity, from unchecked waves of passion, and from the tyranny of a continental majority." The nation would be a poorer land with their passing.[21] This Turner sought to prove to his audience by first capturing the atmosphere of the four sections that existed in 1830—the Northwest,

South, Middle West, and Far West—then describing their clashes and compromises as the political history of the next two decades unfolded.

Even the most enthusiastic among his audience were less excited about Turner's performance than a New York editor was when he read the sketchy accounts that appeared in the press. To Edward N. Bristol of Henry Holt & Company, the Lowell Lectures were a heavensent opportunity: Turner would *have* to write a book. Long before the first was delivered, Bristol had hurried a contract northward—delivery of the manuscript within one year, royalties of 15 per cent of the retail price —and great was the rejoicing when it was returned to New York with that familiar signature.[22] After waiting in vain since 1897, Holt & Company were assured an actual volume from Frederick Jackson Turner, and a very important volume at that.

The publishers cheered too soon, for there was many a slip between a contract and the delivery of a manuscript, as they were to discover again, to their sorrow. Their awakening began in April 1918, shortly after the last lecture was delivered, when they made polite inquiry as to his progress; they wanted to list the volume in their fall catalogue and needed the manuscript soon. It was not quite ready, Turner confessed. Lectures were lectures, and a book was a book; he had to recast them into publishable form. This meant removing some extraneous items designed to be heard rather than read, and adding others calculated to please the eye rather than the ear.[23] If Edward Bristol and his fellow editors had been realists, they would have given up hope then and there. Turner had not written the book they wanted, and he never would; his Lowell Lectures were an artist's preliminary sketch, fresh and radiant, but only an outline; completing the portrait, with all its subtlety and refinement of organization and interpretation, was simply beyond him. Because there were few details in the lectures, they could be completed; because there must be many details in a book, he could go on forever and never finish the writing. At that moment *The United States, 1830-1850* was doomed.

More, the strain of writing and delivering the Lowell Lectures left Turner a sick and tired man. Broken veins in his eyes warned of high blood pressure and weakening arteries; he had to enter on a career of vegetating at once or risk the consequences. "I would," he told Edward Bristol, "give an eye for a worth-while book, or even consent with some serenity to being suddenly snuffed out, but I wouldn't wish to smoke out like a sputtering candle."[24] He was so worn and lethargic that work was impossible. A thorough medical examination showed why; overstrain had reached a point where any effort might prove fatal; even reading and writing could turn an "explosive eye" into a painful carbuncle. The only remedy was to forsake all mental effort for months—perhaps forever. Turner was over the hill and could only hope not to "make too much of a mess of the remainder of the descent."[25]

Only one sanctuary beckoned for that summer of recovery, and that was the snug cottage on Hancock Point, in Maine, which the Turners had visited periodically since 1912. Here was a spot well-suited to his needs, low enough in altitude that his heart would not suffer, as it might in mountain excursions, but primitive enough to satisfy any woodsman. Hancock Point was a tiny backwoods community on Frenchman's Bay, with the usual frame two-story summer hotel, the usual two or three stores, and a dozen or so cottages for escaping Bostonians. Their rented house—"The Moorings," they called it—was a modest cottage, weathered by the salt air, with a hand-painted mantel, a fearsome Baptist clock with painted mottoes, and a broad porch where a sick man could gaze out at the fog-shrouded harbor or read in peace. There were tempting activities, too, that kept a man busy: daily picnics with the neighbors, fishing expeditions on near-by streams, walks along lanes through groves of birch and balsam between banks of wild roses and fireweed and meadow rue, dips in the icy Atlantic waters. There was work to be done of a sort: wood to be chopped, flounder to be caught in the bay, clams to be dug on the tidal flats, lobsters to be purchased for a few pennies from the fishermen. But mostly one could loaf about in old clothes and slouch hat, and call the down easters "Asa" and "Ed," and be called "Fred" in return. Turner loved every minute of life at Hancock Point, so much so that eventually, in 1919, he and Mae sank most of their life savings into purchasing "The Moorings" for $5000, and its furnishings for another $600.[26]

There the Turners went that summer of 1919 for the rest that he badly needed, laden with ice chests and sterillizers and baby carriages and pack sacks stuffed with history notes and trunks and fishing rods and thermos bottles and a baby bed, for Dorothy Main and their grandson were to spend some months with them. Turner's health began to return with his first dip in the frigid ocean (contrary to doctors' orders), but not enough to incline him to work; that summer was spent in unprofitable fishing expeditions, paddling about the bay in a canoe named "Mumps" (because of its bulging sides), and playing with little Jackson Turner Main, who constantly studied his grandfather with "a judicial but penetrating inquiry" that made him "regret the things I have done and left undone."[27] By September Turner was ready to return to the traces, but he still had no more energy than needed to meet his classes and confer with his graduate students.

Nothing was done on THE BOOK in the 1918-19 academic year save a rare scribbled page of suggestions to himself, or a note of statistics to be analyzed later.[28] Nor was the summer of 1919 at Hancock Point any more fruitful, for again Dorothy Main and her son were with the Turners, and again picnics and fishing and loafing and a two-week camping trip to Mount Katahdin monopolized his time. "I didn't find myself able to do any mental work," he reported that fall, "—not having the necessary machine to do it with."[29] The academic year of 1919-20 was little better; that summer Turner once more journeyed to Maine with two packs filled with history manuscript, and once more they were scarcely opened.

The truth of the matter was that Turner had discovered the only recipe for existence that would keep him alive. His sin was neither laziness nor an unconquerable love of the out-of-doors. By this time, his health was so precarious that he ended his teaching each spring totally exhausted and capable of nothing save vegetating. Every fall his first business on returning to civilization was to visit a whole array of doctors—"the ear specialist, who spoke disrespectfully of my hearing; the eye specialist, who discussed the ravages of time; the dentist, who buzzed away at the same theme."[30] Most discouraging of all was the heart specialist, who reported that improvement was too slight to be noticed. Writing on THE BOOK was simply impossible. "Whenever I try to go ahead under full steam," Turner wrote to his publishers, "and that is the way I write most effectively . . . I have landed in the hospital."[31] He might joke of the Hancock Point handyman who always disappeared when most needed, and explained his absence by saying, "B'Gorry, I went fishin'," but vacationing to Turner was a grim necessity—he needed it to stay alive.

Maine's elixir refreshed his body, but as the months passed with no progress on THE BOOK, he grew increasingly despondent, burdened by a sense of failure and oppressed by the realization that his historical findings would never be shared with his profession. So deep was his melancholy that by the spring of 1920 his Harvard friends became concerned lest his emotional problems overbalance his physical. Those problems would continue so long as teaching so sapped Turner's strength that the summer was needed for recovery; his writing could go on only if he escaped from the classroom. A word to President Lowell was sufficient. In April 1920, Turner was told that he would be granted leave for the second half of the 1920-21 academic year without diminution of salary "to enable him to complete for publication one or more books on American history, on which he has been engaged."[32] This time he made no attempt to change the wording of his pardon from "complete for publication" to "carry on," as he had in 1906 under similar circumstances; Turner sincerely believed that with six months of freedom THE BOOK would be ready for the publishers.

How wrong he was. He made his first fatal mistake in February 1921, when his leave began; he would use his freedom not to make the few changes necessary to put his Lowell Lectures in shape for publication, but to convert them into a major book of at least 100,000 words. "This would be difficult," he wrote in a memorandum to himself, "but worth while if possible." Worthwhile, perhaps, but utterly impossible, for the problems that had to be solved for such a thorough study would occupy him forever: sectional rivalries in commerce, the influence of regionalism on literature, the economic impact of the plantation as opposed to the factory, the philosophy of humanitarianism as it varied from region to region. Turner took one look at the questions he had to answer and turned to less burdensome pursuits. He began his leave not by making progress, but by bothering the publishers with useless questions: could they provide an octavo format? would a 120,000-word manuscript be acceptable? how many maps would they allow? would "The United States, 1830-1850" or "The Development of the United States, 1830-1850" be the better title? Better not to settle on the name of the child until it is weaned, they suggested politely.[33] Why not write the book first?

That sensible suggestion did produce an excellent outline—a chapter on the United States in 1830, six more on the six regions that he would analyze, four on the sectional interplay in successive periods between 1830 and 1850—but hardly a word to flesh out the skeleton. Instead,

Turner had to lay the foundation for his interpretations by drawing county-by-county maps to show political behavior, social conditions, and economic activities, then correlate these with maps of natural conditions to show the relationship between physiographic pressures, ethnic forces, and economic pursuits. That took care of the spring. By the time the Turners were ready to leave for Hancock Point in the summer of 1921, he had drawn eight complicated maps that showed such things as the distribution of ethnic groups, political party concentrations, degrees of white illiteracy, the value of farm lands and improvements, and crop specialization. Still to come were ten more that would reveal the presidential vote by counties between 1832 and 1856, as well as other political data.[34] Eight maps—less than half of those needed before analysis could begin—to show for a sabbatical half-year. THE BOOK was still a long way from publication.

Progress ground to a halt during that summer at Hancock Point. "I took a long rest this summer," he reported as he prepared to return to Cambridge, "and feel just now that I know more about trout, canoes, and Fords than I do about maps."[35] Nor was much done during the next two school years, for Turner had found a new plaything and was so fascinated with it that there was little time for serious pursuits. He discovered, during that autumn of 1921, that he had something to tell his friends that they wanted to hear. Not the oft-repeated story of sectionalism in the 1830s—"I am interested in the results myself, but I find when I try it on a class or club that they do not get very excited over it"[36]—but the story of sectionalism in the 1920s. Here was an apt subject: papers were filled with tales of battles between the western "Farm Bloc" and eastern bankers, between advocates of the St. Lawrence Seaway from the Midwest and their opponents from New England, between high-tariff congressmen from the East and low-tariff congressmen from the West. These were matters that Turner understood and could interpret to a wider audience. So he forgot his larger studies as he clipped newspaper items, drew maps showing congressional divisions, prepared correlations to show that the Republican wing of the Farm Bloc was strongest in regions with the greatest number of cars per capita, and drafted talks for his mens' clubs on "Geography of Political Parties," or "Recent American Sectionalism."[37]

These were not completely wasted efforts—save in the eyes of his publishers—for they forced Turner to do a deal of thinking about the nature of sectionalism, and they prepared him to produce one of his most influential, if not one of his most enduring, publications. His speculations led to an about-face in his beliefs. For some time he had been convinced that sectional influences were succumbing to the forces of nationalism, as his Lowell Lectures made clear, but the more he studied modern trends, the less sure he was. By December 1921, he had persuaded himself that sectional conflicts were intensifying, and would continue to divide the nation—that they would, indeed, displace the class struggle as the most divisive force for the forseeable future, for workers would tend to concentrate in certain regions, farmers in others, capitalists in still others, to deepen the antagonisms already created by geographic separatism. Turner envisaged the day when New England, New York, and Pennsylvania would merge into a unit dominated by vested interests and ally itself with the North Central states, when the West would raise the banner of agararian rebellion against the domination of these two regions, and when the South would walk alone as it defended its attitude toward the Negro. As frontier mobility declined, lines between the sections would be ever more tightly drawn, for geographic forces operated more persistently on a stable population than on a migratory one.[38] America's future, he predicted, was one of steadily mounting conflict.

These conclusions were too important to be buried in filing cases. Turner resurrected them in the spring of 1922, first for Phi Beta Kappa addresses at the universities of Michigan and Chicago, then for the commencement address at the University of New Hampshire in June, and finally for an article which he considered his most important contribution since the appearance of *The Frontier in American History*.[39] This last version, Turner felt, was worthy of publication, and in the summer of 1922 a copy of a manuscript called "Sections and Nation" went off to the *Atlantic Monthly*, only to be rejected as unsuited to the publications program of that elite journal. He was hurt by this (his wife immediately canceled their subscription), but he tried again, this time with greater success. The *Yale Review* was delighted to give "Sections and Nation" the place of honor in its October 1922 issue, and there it appeared, on schedule.[40] "I regard it," wrote Wilbur Cross, the editor, "as one of the very best things I have ever published."[41]

There was some truth in these words, for nowhere did Turner better argue the case for twentieth-century sectionalism. He described the regions of the United States first—New England, Middle States, Southeast, Southwest, Middle West, Great Plains, Mountain States, Pacific Coast—each with its geographical peculiarities, each with its unique economic capacities, each with its rival interests, all "partly determined by geographic forces." The gulf between them was not as large as that between European countries, for the regions were not divided by language barriers or memories of historic wars, but they still were shadowy nations that could coexist only by compromise and adjustment, and because they were united by political parties. "Like an elastic band the common national feeling and party ties draw sections together, but at the same time yield in some measure to sectional interests when these are gravely threatened." Congress was comparable to a diplomatic assemblage, arranging ententes and seeking to preserve the balance of power. "We in America are in reality a federation of sections rather than of states. State sovereignty was never influential except as a constitutional shield for the section." Here was Turner's key point, and he used page after page of illustrations from the nation's history to drive it home.

But sectionalism was more than political. A "sectionalism of material interests" could be identified, marked by different types of economic enterprise, as could a "sectionalism of culture" that stamped the people of each region with distinctive traits and interests. Each had its own ideals, New Englanders defending economic conservatism and the protective tariff, midwesterners, the policies favored by the Farm Bloc, southerners, low tariffs and Negro separatism. These ideological divisions, no less than political differences, doomed the nation to a future of conflict, intensifying steadily as the modifying influence of intersectional migration lessened. "The sections are settling down into definite form, and, as they mature, as their physiognomy and character are formed, their differences and even their antagonisms, will become more marked." The nation could survive only if its people ceased to follow an ostrich policy by burying their heads in the sands of the region where they lived. "There must be sympathetic understanding, sacrifices, concessions, and adjustments."[42]

Here was the gospel of sectionalism according to Turner, and an opinion-stirring gospel it was. Nothing that he wrote, and few essays from the pens of historians of his day, excited such comment as did "Sections and Nation." Newspaper editorial writers, ranging from *The*

New York Times to the *Fresno Republican*, joined in a chorus of praise: a "memorable article," "a most absorbing study of political movements," "one of the most striking and valuable articles that has been published in any magazine," a study that would "revolutionize thought on the future development of the United States politically and economically"—these were the phrases that Turner read, clipped, underlined in red, and filed away. He was delighted even with the few dissenting voices. The *Boston Transcript* haughtily insisted that New England was universally loved instead of viewed with suspicion, as Turner implied, while a letter-writer to that same journal thought that his prediction of a future federation of sections "comes pretty close to treason."[43] "By one clipping," he reported delightedly to his daughter, "you will see that I am at least regarded as a proper subject for arrest by the federal and state authorities both. So far I am at large."[44] He was equally pleased by praise from friends and strangers, and especially by enthusiastic comment from such public figures as Walter Lippmann, Senator Irvine L. Lenroot, and the Austrian publicist Josef Redlich.[45]

All of this was very satisfying, but Turner was aware of the fact that essays on modern sectionalism did not bring THE BOOK nearer to completion. It was inching along, particularly during those rare periods when he could find an efficient stenographer. Then he wrote as he liked to write, sitting at a desk buried with notes and charts and maps that he consulted constantly, dictating an overlong and often poorly written text packed with facts and interpretations. This was slow work. "Dictation is hard for me," he confessed to Mae after one day when little progress was made, "and I am rather discouraged to find how much there is to do before the book can be said to be ready. I think I was cut out for a farmer after all."[46] He felt that way even more strongly when he began compressing the gargantuan first chapter to usable size and found the task excruciatingly difficult. At times such as these THE BOOK seemed as far from completion as it had been a decade before, and melancholy gripped Turner. "I don't see how I can do it," he wrote Mae as he prepared to leave for Hancock Point in the spring of 1922. "If I bring up another big lot of notes and take them back again as last year, I might as well confess failure and go out. . . ."[47] Then a burst of progress, when the words flowed and the interpretations fell into logical pattern, would make him happy. Those days, alas, were few.

Still, slowly, almost miraculously, a manuscript took shape. The springs were free now, for Harvard granted him additional half-year leaves from teaching in 1922 and 1923, and the results could be measured in a mounting pile of completed pages. By March 1922, an outline and a rough draft—a very rough draft—of an overlong "Introduction" went to join the previous year's eight maps in the publisher's vault—an "Introduction" that explained Turner's methodology and views on sectionalism.[48] That summer his latest stenographer journeyed to Hancock Point with Turner, to add to the confusion of a household already overcrowded with their daughter and two grandchildren (Jackson was a lively five-year-old now and his sister Betsy was two), the children's nurse, the family cook, and the Turners themselves. Turner insisted on going fishing once a week, much to the disgust of his stenographer—and young Jackson, who wandered in each day to ask politely how many books he and the secretary had written—but dictation was a daily event and the pile of rough-draft pages mounted steadily.[49] Too steadily, for by summer's end Turner awakened to the fact that he had given so little thought to space restrictions that he had enough for several books. "I can see," he admitted to the publishers, "that I have a frightful job of condensation before me," but he would apply the hydraulic press that fall and squeeze it into usable form.[50] He returned to Cambridge in 1922 well-satisfied with the summer's work.

So euphoric was his mood, indeed, that he was bubbling with pipe dreams of a manuscript completed by December—or perhaps November. If the publishers had the whole book by then, could they assure him that proof could be read before his spring leave began? He had plans to do some traveling to celebrate. They could, of course, but the editor who made this solemn assurance must have known that Turner was indulging in fantasy.[51] He discovered this himself when he returned to the classroom and the hours of homework that teaching required; "the crop of theses has been gathering on my table," he wrote a friend, "some 75 of them in all, and I fear the only 'book' will be blue books for the present."[52] The skies brightened with his spring leave of absence (at half pay, this time, but worth it to finish THE BOOK); once more daily sessions with the stenographer were the order of business, and once more the summer at Hancock Point was as profitable as it was busy.

The results were impressive, if not spectacular. Turner was still dwelling in a dream world that April of 1923, when he promised the Holt Company six chapters by the end of May and the remainder by September 1, but during May the first batches of manuscript reached New York. Others followed at regular intervals, until by the end of August three completed chapters were in the publisher's hands. The fourth followed more slowly, but it was virtually finished by October. In all, this burst of energy produced 155 pages of text, after being typed in the Holt office, and very good text it was. Too long, perhaps, but the editors felt that only a few passages needed to be eliminated. They would be happy to have a 200,000-word book, instead of the 100,000 that Turner had planned. "What we want," they assured him, "is the book as you feel it *ought* to be written."[53] This was heady news, and Turner was elated. "The Book will be out sometime within the year," he assured a friend."[54]

That was the high-water mark of progress. Whenever Turner worked too hard, his system rebelled, and so it was now. In May 1923, just as he was settling down with his stenographer at Hancock Point, a siege of influenza and recurring bilious attacks laid him low for a month and drove him back to Cambridge for medical advice. "So far this summer I have been worthless," he confessed at the end of June, and even when his health was restored he was forced to work at a slower pace.[55] Again in December fatigue and a weakened system not only ended all effort but forced the physicians to put him on a comfortless regime. "I am," he told a friend, "still cigaretteless, and pipeless, and cigarless, and even chewless—and cheerless too!"[56] Turner was slowing down, and THE BOOK had to wait.

Worse, he was succumbing once more to the near-fatal disease of perfectionism. Much of his energy during the spring and summer of 1923 went not into writing new chapters, but in revising old ones. The "Introduction" was completely rewritten into sixty-one pages of manuscript—and even this he considered tentative. Chapters I through III were torn apart in a major recasting; through them he sprinkled marginal notes reminding himself to move this paragraph into the sectional surveys and that one into the analysis of the 1830s. Even more fatal was his decision that the maps drawn three years before were in need of updating; would the publishers please return them to be redrawn? The publishers, reluctantly, did so, and he set to work to redo the map on "Distribution of Population" completely and to incorporate fresh material into the others.[57] Once Turner began rebuilding the very foundations of THE BOOK he could go on forever. By November 1923, progress was at a complete standstill.

Even before this breakdown he had come to the conclusion that he had to forsake the classroom to complete his magnum opus. This was not a difficult decision, for Turner was dedicated neither to undergraduate teaching nor to Harvard. Few, save among his closest friends, realized this; those who knew him only casually believed him the most enthusiastic of teachers and the most loyal of Harvardians. The students he found indifferent: "Harvard undergraduates," he once told a friend, "aren't interested in Western history," while the graduate students were no better than those he had taught in Madison.[58] Nor did Turner ever feel really at home in Cambridge. Max Farrand, who was closer to him than any other man save Charles H. Haskins, knew why. "Turner," he once said, "was *recognized* rather than appreciated."[59] Harvard provided him little of the warm companionship, the easy informality, the ego-satisfying adulation that was so abundant in Wisconsin. The East, too, was less to his liking than he would usually admit. "I love my Middle West," he told Carl Becker, and sometimes he wondered why he had ever left there. "I am," Turner confessed, "still a Western man in all but my residence."[60]

True, Turner had twice refused invitations to return to that land of his first love. Both opportunities came in 1913, when he was still under the spell of Harvard's eminence, and neither was of the sort that he could accept. One was provided by the State Historical Society of Wisconsin, when it sought a replacement for Reuben Gold Thwaites; he could return to Madison as superintendent of the society and professor of history at the university with a salary matching that he earned in Cambridge. Turner realized full well that he had neither the talent nor inclination to administer a large library, yet he hesitated so long before refusing that the Madison papers proclaimed his return and the *Boston Transcript* mourned his departure.[61] He listened to the siren call again a few months later, when the University of Chicago offered him its most attractive professorship, with only graduate students to teach and ample time for research. Turner was sufficiently interested to let it be known that he might be persuaded if a suitable salary could be arranged, but negotiations ended when Chicago could offer no more than $5000; Turner's joint Harvard-Radcliffe earnings were $6100.[62] His decision was no indication of his loyalty to Harvard; he might well have returned to the Midwest if the salary had been tempting.

So now, in 1923, his conscience bothered him not at all as he laid plans to escape the classroom forever. One obstacle stood in his way: how could he live on the meager pension that would be his after retirement? As he laid his plans during 1923, his bible was the manual on annuity systems issued by the newly established Carnegie Foundation for the Advancement of Teaching. Every line was read and reread, every margin filled with notes, every blank page crowded with columns of figures, as he tried to balance possible income against probable outgo. The results were not too encouraging. He could count on a pension of $3208.33, royalties of roughly $275 a year from *The Frontier in American History*, $750 from his wife's investments in the Madison Store Company and a few stocks, and $300 from rental of the cottage at Hancock Point, if that became necessary. If worse came to worst, rigid economies could be made. "The Moorings" was worth a good $6000 and could be sold; his life insurance policies, which totalled $22,000 and cost $800 a year in premiums, could be reduced to $9000 on a paid-up basis; in an extreme emergency the $3000 in Brazil stock could be sold at $160 a share and the money reinvested, although this would be done only as a last resort. Turner could also add a bit to the family coffers by lecturing, which was allowed under his retirement plan. All in all, they could count on from $5000 to $5200 a year. That was far less than the $8000 salary paid him by Harvard since 1922, but the Turners could probably afford a small flat in Madison or possibly a tiny house there.[63] Cambridge was out of the question; it was far too expensive.

So the decision was made. "I shall at least not die in the class room," Turner told a friend, "an act for which I have always had a dislike— too spectacular, even if it isn't messy."[64] In April 1923, he submitted his resignation, to take effect on September 1, 1924, a few weeks before his sixty-third birthday.[65] Turner could resign knowing that his shoes were to be well filled. Frederick Merk, a fellow-Wisconsinite who had proven himself a brilliant student when he earned his doctorate at Harvard in 1920, had taught "The History of the West" admirably during the spring terms that his master had been on leave, and he would now take over. His junior rank allowed the department to name another senior professor, and, due partly to Turner's insistence, the post was offered to Arthur Meier Schlesinger of the University of Iowa, a pioneer in the study of social and intellectual history. Schlesinger came to Harvard rather than Columbia, which also sought his services, largely because of Turner's urging.[66]

These matters settled, Turner could begin his last year of teaching confident that a brighter future lay ahead. His conscience decreed that he had to dedicate that year to the classroom rather than THE BOOK, even though materials unearthed in hours of preparation would never be used again. No yellowing notes were used for the first semester of the History of the West, presented at Harvard to fifty-six more-or-less eager students, and at Radcliffe to nine; instead, each lecture was carefully re-prepared, with new information added and old refurbished. "Yesterday," he told a former student, "in preparing a class lecture on the French-English contest for the interior, I had occasion to re-read your Albany, Crane's Southwest in Queen Anne's War, and Volwiler's papers on George Croghan."[67] His seminar was as time-consuming as always, for the eleven enrolled (including such future greats of the profession as John D. Barnhart, James Phinney Baxter III, and R. L. Morrow) roamed widely, forcing Turner to read on such diverse topics as the relation between banking and politics in New England, 1889-96, the southern iron industry, interstate migration into Indiana, and Appalachia politics.[68]

His dedication to his students was again proven during the second half-year. A prudent man would have continued teaching "The History of the West," which was already adequately prepared, but Merk had given that before and was ready to give it again. So it was that THE BOOK was shelved once more, while Turner presented a completely new course on "The History of the United States, 1880-1920." He revealed a great deal about his own enthusiasm for the past when he explained his purpose to the twenty-nine undergraduates who assembled for his first lecture. The modern period, he said, was particularly challenging, bringing into bold relief the problems faced by historians in analyzing any era. Recent events were clouded with the prejudices of class, section, and party; they had to be understood without access to the manuscript records that would allow a view from the inside; they were unbelievably complex and could be comprehended only by destroying the watertight compartments into which knowledge was divided. The students—and Turner—would learn much of economics, even though this was not a course in economics, much of political science, though it was not a course in political science, much of sociology, though it did not deal directly with that subject. "I give the course," Turner confessed, "because I know too little of the period. Want to know more."[69]

So the days and weeks of the 1923-24 academic year slipped away as lectures were prepared, theses graded, doctoral dissertations read and read again. Turner was also to find that retirement involved rituals too traditional to be forsaken, even though his wish was to step across the line unnoticed. He had to talk to the Harvard History Club, and did, in a gay little speech that stressed trivial influences of his boyhood that had stirred his interest in western history. "I enjoyed shocking them," he gloated. "Already I seem to be shedding the academic robe and hood and using my mortar board for a football."[70] He had to sit for a crayon portrait by a gifted portraitist, Alexander James, because his seminar insisted that Harvard should have a perpetual reminder of his services, even though Turner sputtered that the money could be better used to buy books on the frontier.[71] And, above all, he must be the guest of honor at a dinner, where the portrait was presented and proper tribute paid to his years as a teacher.

A gala dinner it was. On May 24 dozens of his friends and former students gathered at the Harvard Club, where the walls of the banquet hall had been decorated with maps and charts showing the migration of Plymouth Rock chickens ("males in blue, females in red, all others in green"), the spread of jackrabbits, the influence of flat feet on the Populist vote, and similar statistical information. They seated themselves at a U shaped table, before place cards on which each was caricatured, with Turner in the middle and two of his dearest friends, Max Farrand and Charles Homer Haskins, on either side. They ate magnificently. Then not one portrait, but two, were presented, that of Turner by Alexander James to the history department, another a cartoon by Julius Klein, a former colleague, to Turner, bearing the title "Westward the Course (History 17) of Empire takes Its Way." Turner's laughter rang out as he studied the details: peaks and prairies from Hoboken to San Francisco staked out with his preemption notices, a caravan of prairie schooners laden with his slides and maps, buffaloes pawing the plains and coyotes saying "woof woof," "open spaces" made by cutting holes in the paper, and his ear, well to the front, labeled the "Frontear in American History."[72]

Then came the speeches. Turner had wanted none, but not even he could overrule tradition. So they rose to speak—Theodore Clark Smith and Verner W. Crane, representing the graduate students of Wisconsin and Harvard; Frederick Merk, to read letters and telegrams from the many who were unable to attend; Max Farrand, in behalf of friends outside the university; Allyn A. Young of the economics department, to present tributes from the non-historians of Harvard. The praise lavished on Turner that night was unrestrained. "Your interpretation of American history," Farrand told him, ". . . has been the determining influence . . . for many years." So it had, but Allyn Young came nearer to portraying the inner Turner than any other speaker—a man passionately interested in the economic, political, and social life of his own generation and of his own country, a man who made large contributions to American history because he asked new and significant questions, a man who used words as an artist would designs to convince his colleagues of theories that revolutionized historical studies.[73] Turner's response to this avalanche of adulation was typical; he deserved less credit than Professor William Francis Allen, who had taught him all he knew, and the students, who had worked with him to unlock the vaults of the past. He had done nothing more than place the keys in their hands. As he seated himself amidst thunders of applause Turner was thoroughly happy. "We had a jolly time," he told a friend, "a real wake with the corpse participating."[74]

Over the next weeks tributes continued to descend on Cambridge, from friends and strangers. The *Harvard Crimson*, which in those days found football more worthy of space than it did professors, awarded him "an enviable niche in the hall of America's great historians." Former students in distant parts kept the telegraph wires humming; six in Minneapolis assured him that he might withdraw from teaching but never from an "abiding place in our esteem and affection"; while Joseph Schafer wired from Madison that his many friends there "are with you in spirits [sic]." Charles Homer Hockett found prose inadequate to express his feelings, and he contributed a page of verse:

> Tense drama of the woods and plain!
> 'Twas but chaotic, meaningless and vain
> Until a Seer arose! To him, All hail, again.

William E. Dodd confided that few men of their generation could retire with the consciousness of so much work so ably done, while Claude H. Van Tyne would "rather have written your comparatively limited number of pages than all the reams of pages of some of the other historical brethren who awe the average student of history." Even the Twin Cities History Club of Minneapolis sent its best wishes.[75] Those were sweet words, and Turner relished them all.

But at long last the tumult and the shouting died, and the Turners could turn to dismantling their house, engaging packers and movers, investigating freight rates, hiring vans, and packing crate after crate with the books that Turner had accumulated in his years at Cambridge. They also had to endure the interminable round of farewell dinners —including a very stiff affair given by the A. Lawrence Lowells—and farewell luncheons and farewell teas. But at last the final goodbyes were said, the furniture loaded, Mae bundled onto a train for Hancock Point, and Turner was alone for a last day of packing. At 2:10 on the afternoon of June 1, 1924, he swung aboard the Boston and Albany's crack "Wolverine," bound for Chicago and Madison, to begin life anew. "It's a good deal like starting life over as a pioneer in a new clearing," he wrote his daughter.[76] His first crop, he confidently believed, would be THE BOOK.

XVI

The Twilight Years

1924-1932

$\mathfrak{F}$REDERICK JACKSON TURNER left Boston that June day burdened with many problems, but two of the most pressing had been solved—his immediate financial burdens were to be eased by a lucrative summer-school post in Utah, and his future home was to be a small house in Madison, rather than the apartment he had dreaded. He had reached these decisions amidst the turmoil of departure and was well-satisfied with both, but he was particularly pleased at the prospect of a home of his own near his grandchildren and old friends.

A sensible suggestion from his daughter prompted that move. She had found that the lot next to the elegant home that she and her husband were building on Van Hise Street was for sale for $1400. Land that near the university was always in demand; too, the small house needed by the Turners would be easily rentable to visiting faculty while they were summering at Hancock Point. Here was a prospect too tempting to be denied, and within a week John Main had his instructions: buy at once, with a $200 payment to bind the deal. By April 21 the lot was theirs and house-planning under way. Dorothy Main was instructed to find a good builder who could promise a Nantucket-like cottage, similar to the one illustrated in the latest issue of *House Beautiful*, for no more than $6500. (Frank Riley would do if reminded that the Turners would be more prompt in their payments than they had been when they rented from him the first year of their marriage.) Turner wanted the house to have a basement, for he remembered the cold floors of Portage, but needed no such fancy frills as a sunken

391

bathtub or a tiled bathroom.[1] He would raise the money somehow if construction could begin soon and be completed by November.

Turner was able to assure Dorothy that needed funds could be raised because his last months at Harvard had been brightened by two unexpected windfalls. One could not be collected until the autumn; he was to give five lectures before the Dowse Institute of Cambridge in November, for a healthy fee of $500. The other was more immediately available, for when Turner left Cambridge he was bound for Logan, Utah, and an unbelievably profitable three weeks of teaching. Such an assignment had been farthest from his mind when he laid his retirement plans—his whole purpose was to put the finishing touches on THE BOOK—but he reckoned without the persuasive skills of Elmer G. Peterson, president of the Agricultural College of Utah. Peterson's dream was a "National Summer School" at Logan, staffed by a dozen eminent scholars attracted by the beauty of the Cache Valley and by exceptional financial inducements, and attracting, in turn, at least a thousand students from all over the country. Turner was the one historian who could add the greatest luster to his galaxy of stars, and no price was too high to pay for him.[2]

When negotiations began, in the fall of 1923, Turner had the good sense to refuse a regular six-week appointment at a salary not spectacularly higher than those usually offered, but President Peterson would not surrender. He had mentioned a fee of one-sixth the regular Harvard salary for the full session. How about half that sum for only three weeks of teaching? Turner sharpened his pencils and went to work: one-sixth of $8000 would be $1333, one-half of that, about $666. Add the $300 expense fund that Peterson had mentioned and the figure was $966—or very near $1000. That was too tempting to resist. He would come for that round sum, and would offer two three-week courses, one on "Aspects of the Westward Movement," the other on "The United States, 1830-1850: A Study of Sections."[3] His replacement for the remainder of the six-weeks session, he suggested, might be Frederick Merk, who had taken his place at Harvard. Turner planned to use his three weeks for profit rather than pleasure; he would come west on a special excursion rate that cost only $118.16 for the round trip, live in a dormitory at $35 a month, and eat in a dining room operated by the Home Economics Department at $14 a week. A sizable nestegg would be his reward for that last stint in the classroom.

Turner returned from his three weeks in Logan with a wealth of happy memories, as well as some $700 in savings. He and his colleagues were treated like the lions that they were—"the most eminent faculty ever assembled in the West or indeed, in the nation for summer school courses" according to the college catalogue[4]—and he had a thoroughly good time. His was an instant love-affair with the mountain-rimmed Cache Valley, the orderly community, the neat campus, the kindly people. An earthly paradise, he assured his wife—adding quickly "lacking my particular Eve."[5] Scarcely a day passed but he was entertained or feted, whether by the local Kiwanians, who cheered his talk on "Men with Gifted Feet," or by the Mormon stake, or by the resident faculty, who arranged almost daily tours to scenic spots, or by the town's best fisherman, who served as his guide on the opening day of the season—with no results. Turner was charmed. "I am a Mormon in everything but *revelation*," he reported to Mae after a few days of such treatment. "It is a most lovable, sincere, sound, clean population, and I love them."[6]

Best of all were the classes. Nearly three hundred undergraduates crowded into his two courses to hang eagerly on every word and applaud each lecture. Here was an audience that knew and loved the West as he did and could appreciate him as he wanted to be appreciated. His students refused to let him leave until they had presented him with a handwoven Navajo blanket, along with extravagant praise; the undergraduate newspaper echoed their sentiments when it bade him farewell in an editorial telling how he had "won the hearts and minds of his students here by his patience, sympathy and keenness of suggestion."[7] Turner was overwhelmed; he received more acclaim in three weeks in Logan than he had in fourteen years at Harvard. "Everybody is *too* kindly appreciative of my course," he wrote. "I am utterly spoiled."[8] (President Peterson was wise enough to capitalize on this sense of satisfaction by inviting Turner back for the summer of 1925, this time for one six-week course at a handsome salary of $1500. Mae came with him that year and enjoyed the land and its people as much as he did.)[9]

Much as Turner loved Utah, he was willing to catch the eastbound train, for almost daily bulletins from Dorothy on the progress of the new Madison home had his curiosity at fever pitch. The structure was rising rapidly, she reported, and so were the costs, to the point where they might reach $8000 instead of the $6500 agreed upon. Also, the

builder wanted half his payment when the building was half done. Turner arrived in Madison in early July to find the roof nearly on, the
outside shingling almost completed, and a sheaf of bills awaiting his
attention. High finance occupied his next weeks: an American Telephone and Telegraph Company bond was sold for $1026.79, a share in
the Edison Electric Illuminating Company for $964.58, a Northern
States Power Company bond for $1000.53, odd shares of stock in three
copper companies for $964.58. These modest sums, added to the nearly
$700 that he had managed to save from his Utah salary, allowed him to
pay the contractor half the final price of $7105.50 on July 19. A like
amount had to be raised by October, together with money for moving
expenses, furnishings, and a $1000 assessment for street improvements.
Turner borrowed $5800 against his life insurance policies at first, then,
realizing that his reduced income would never allow him to meet the
interest and principal charges on this sum, he reluctantly sold the
policies during the summer, keeping only one worth $5000 as a cushion
for Mae, should he die suddenly.[10] Turner retired from a lifetime of
teaching with a home worth less than $10,000, a cottage in Maine,
stock in the Sullivan Machinery Company that paid $220 yearly, roy-
alties of less than $200, and one $5000 insurance policy—these were the
total assets of one of the nation's most eminent teachers.

He was ready to recuperate from his financial exercises when he
joined Mae at Hancock Point for the last weeks of that 1924 summer,
but retiring was a never-ending job and it left little time for the trout
streams. Instructions had to be sent to Dorothy on decorations for the
house, two van-loads of furniture had to be removed from the Cambridge home before their lease expired on September 1, nearly two
tons of books had to be boxed and shipped to Madison—and almost as
many to Hancock Point—the five lectures that were to be given in
November before the Dowse Institute had to be prepared. As usual,
the lecture preparation was left until last, and, as usual, an unexpected
cold snap froze the pipes and converted Turner from a scholar into a
hewer of wood for the fireplaces and drawer of water for the kitchen
sink.[11] He arrived in Boston on November 1 very badly prepared and
nursing a severe cold that attacked his vocal cords whenever he used his
voice. Turner endured those five evenings but took no pride in his
performance; during the first he could scarcely speak above a whisper,
in the middle of the second a siege of coughing almost drove him from

the platform, and he was able to talk at all during his final appearance because the maid at the Kenmore Hotel prescribed a mixture of egg whites and lemon juice. "It has been a test of my fortitude," he reported, "and of the audience's as well."[12] Turner was utterly exhausted when he left for Madison in mid-November to begin his retirement.

A lively retirement it was. He fell in love with his new home at 2214 Van Hise Avenue on sight. "The Chimney Corner," he named it (after rejecting "The Shack" as discouraging to renters and "The Fisherman's Cottage" as too *House-Beautiful*-like). Small and cozy (Turner's bedroom was so tiny that he considered sleeping with his feet out of the window), and modeled after a Nantucket cottage, it was roomier than its neat shingled exterior suggested, with a great chimney of local limestone, an ample fireplace, and a book-lined study on the southwest side, where it could catch the afternoon sun. "It's like living in a ship's cabin," he reported.[13] But it was vastly superior to any apartment they could have found.

Madison proved a disappointment to the Turners after their high expectations. It had changed in fourteen years, from a friendly college town into an unattractive city peopled by strangers. "New and interesting as a strange land," he found it, and felt himself rubbing his eyes at times—"a later Rip Van Winkle!"[14] So they were content to live their own lives, finding in their family and the little world about them the joys that companions had formerly provided. Turner never tired of watching the antics of the chickadees, nuthatches, brown creepers, woodpeckers, and jays who crowded his windowsill feeding station during the winter, or providing robins with lengths of string for their nests in the spring, or listening to the songs of the meadowlarks on summer evenings. When the sun was warm he enjoyed puttering about the yard, spraying the shingles with a salt solution to imitate the soft grey of the seashore (he never succeeded) or trying to transform sun-baked clay into a green lawn. But the Turners found their greatest joy in their daily meetings with Dorothy and John, who lived next door, and in the grandchildren—Jackson, a studious lad of seven, and Betsy, a carefree four. They were in and out of the Turner cottage all day long, to listen wide-eyed to Puff Puff's stories (so named because he was always puffing on a pipe or cigar) or to gaze enraptured as he fashioned outlandish animals with paper and scissors for "Turner's World Menagerie and Circus," or to watch in awe as those animals were transformed into terrifying creatures with the aid of a magic lantern. Simple pleasures, but they added up to happiness. "Such little things make up our life," Turner told a friend.[15]

That life would have been pleasant, indeed, save for two recurring problems: how to supplement the pittance of an annuity on which they had to live, and how to keep well in Madison's frigid winters. Turner was increasingly concerned with the inadequacy of their income in that day of skyrocketing inflation. Mae did her best to help out, doing without a maid or cook for the first time since their marriage, and finding to her surprise that washing dishes and sweeping the living room rug was not unpleasant; "as thrilling as pioneering," she reported to a friend, then added that it was very elegant pioneering indeed with a centrally heated house, a gas water heater, a water softener, an electric range, a telephone, and electric lights.[16] Even this sacrifice was not enough, and Turner was faced with the uncomfortable realization that he had to add to the family coffers by the only means he knew: teaching, lecturing, and writing.

During the next three years he did far more than he should of all three, but lecturing proved a particular burden. Some of the many invitations that came his way were welcome for the financial returns they promised, some because they encouraged him to explore new subjects, but none was more eagerly received than the first that he accepted on his arrival in Madison. Would he celebrate his return to active membership in the State Historical Society of Wisconsin by delivering the principal address at their annual meeting, in January 1925? Turner would, eagerly. He was well aware that some thirty years before he had revealed the significance of the frontier to an annual meeting of that society. Now he would prepare an equally momentous address on the significance of the section. "I have always tried to have what an astronomical friend of mine calls a 'bright idea' when I have addressed that organization," Turner assured the director. "I should like to do something worth while."[17]

He did his best, but the result was a sad anticlimax. "The significance in American history of the advance of the frontier and of its disappearance is now generally recognized," he began boldly. "This evening I wish to consider with you another fundamental factor in American history—namely, the Section." Then came the usual history of the sectional conflicts of the nineteenth century, the usual predictions that sectional antagonisms would deepen as mobility lessened, the usual plea for governmental policies that would keep friction to a minimum. Turner dwelt more fully now than before on the sub-sections within the sections, whose interests often opposed those of the section itself; he saw them as among the cohesive forces that held the United States together by serving as "a limitation upon the larger section in case it attempts a drastic and subversive policy toward other sections."[18] Yet he had little to add to a story that was already well known to historians and was by no means convincing. The address, printed in the *Wisconsin Magazine of History* and circulated widely throughout the profession, stirred none of the excitement of his frontier thesis. Turner's old Harvard friend, Frank W. Taussig, spoke for most when he complimented Turner on "carrying your old lines of analysis to a further stage."[19] This was an embarrassingly accurate judgment. Turner had little to add to the "old lines" save complicating qualifications that made his argument even less convincing. Yet he was doggedly insistent that his critics were wrong. "I am possessed with the idea," he told a friend, "that twenty years or so from now my Sections paper will travel along with my frontier as interpretations."[20]

The confidence that underlay that statement was further shaken in the spring of 1925, when he was invited to deliver a course of seven lectures at the University of Wisconsin. The chance to serve again as a "special lecturer" in his old department, and the honorarium of $500, were both too tempting to be refused, even though days of preparation were needed. When Turner trudged up the Hill toward Bascom Hall on the afternoon of April 15, carrying his box of slides and numerous notes, his expectations were high: he was sure he would find eager students and faculty swept into conviction by the abundance of proof that he would use to bolster his sectional theories. What he said that day, and on subsequent days, was in his best tradition; again, he traced the history of sectional conflicts, appraised the role of sub-sections, predicted the deepening of regional antagonisms as nationalizing forces weakened the power of the states, and urged governmental policies to maintain national unity.[21] But somehow his listeners failed to catch fire as they did when he talked of the frontier. "His audience dwindled day by day," wrote a former student sadly, "the spark was gone."[22]

Turner might have endured—even enjoyed—the time-consuming

preparation and physically debilitating effort required by lecturing if he had swept his audiences into his own enthusiasm for sectionalism, but, when he could not, each appearance became a greater burden. Yet they had to go on, for fees of the sort he could command were irresistible. So Turner traveled that spring through Illinois, speaking at Knox and Decatur and the University of Illinois on sectionalism, meeting with students, conducting seminars, talking to Harvard and Wisconsin clubs, attending the luncheons and dinners and smokers that were the bane of all intellectual lions. "Bread-and-buttering," he called that swing around the circuit, but cruelly hard work it was, too, when audiences did not respond as they should and diminished day after day. "I shall swear off all talking I think after this," Turner wrote his wife.[23]

That was the last of his moneymaking speaking tours, but by no means the last of the side-excursions that kept him from settling to work on THE BOOK. One that gave him particular satisfaction was a paper he read before the Association of American Geographers, when that body met in Madison in December 1925. Turner prepared his remarks carefully, knowing that his audience would be sympathetic to any discussion of "Geographic Sectionalism in American History"; he would win converts among the geographers if he could not among historians. "I hope," he told a friend at the time, "to awaken the brethren to the intimate relationship between regional geography and American history. Judging from my experience in getting the Frontier idea a hearing, this will take twenty years, and I shall have to lean over the battlements to hear it spoken of as a trite conception."[24] The response was gratifying, for this was one of Turner's most persuasive arguments, and it was greeted warmly. Even his fellow historians showed a spark of interest when the printed version was distributed; Merle Curti felt the same thrill that he had experienced when he read the "Significance of the Frontier," Arthur M. Schlesinger believed that the sectional thesis was now indisputably proven, and Norman Foerster experienced a blinding revelation as the full importance of the sectional hypothesis burst upon him.[25] This was music in Turner's ears, and some compensation for the days of labor that had been stolen from THE BOOK.

Retirement meant a chance to lecture, but it also meant a chance to write—on a variety of topics that promised some financial return or that gave him an excuse not to struggle with the masses of data accumulated for his magnum opus. Two major efforts occupied far too much of his time, one inspired by curiosity, the other by a promise of a $300 fee for what seemed to be a cut-and-dried article that could be written in a few days. The editor of *World's Work* was the tempter; could Turner prepare 5000 words on the changes that had altered the West during the past fifty years? Turner did, but only after using twenty times that number in his early drafts; in his perfectionist mind even such a simple task required reading every scrap of information about the trans-Mississippi country—census returns, state reports, travel accounts, books and magazine articles—and recording what he had learned on hundreds upon hundreds of pages.[26] All of this was compressed into a draft double the size wanted by the editors, then painfully squeezed into the allotted space by casting aside all but the statistics. Turner was not happy with "The West—1876 and 1926" when he finally released it to the mails (he thought it "arid" and too condensed to be readable), but he had performed a remarkable feat of compression; every significant change—in agriculture, industry, politics, social life, and culture— was chronicled in detail.[27] Yet the editors were more than satisfied, as a check for $400 rather than the agreed-upon $300 testified, and Turner had managed to avoid work on THE BOOK for another few months.

He squandered still more time on a paper that could do nothing save satisfy his intellectual curiosity. Ever since 1891, when he had read an article by Henry Cabot Lodge in the *Century Magazine,* arguing that frontier barbarism and materialism stifled the creative spirit in the West, Turner had itched to set the record straight. He could not dispute the basic conclusion, for Lodge's findings were based on an analysis of the 14,243 persons listed in *Appleton's Encyclopedia of American Biography* and were probably correct, but Turner could show that the second generation of frontiersmen contributed as much to the nation's culture as did New Englanders, and at the same time he could demonstrate the relationship between human ability and the geographic environment.[28] He had gathered data casually since at least 1917; now he had the leisure and the excuse to make a thorough investigation. The excuse this time was not even an editor's check, but an invitation to deliver a paper before the Madison Literary Club at its November meeting in 1925. Turner agreed to speak on "The Children of the Pioneers."

He had doomed himself to a major task. Days stretched into weeks,

and weeks into months, as he searched through biographical diction-
aries, newspapers, magazines and books, carefully copying the name
and record of every westerner who had made his contribution to
American life.[29] Eventually his results crammed a whole filing drawer
—all gathered for one presentation before a few friends in a town-and-
gown society. Not a very successful presentation, either. Turner
thought his thirty-three-page manuscript too "listy" and only "toler-
ated by the friendly gathering."[30] It was crammed with the names of
westerners who had succeeded in business, government, and the arts
but Turner was too good a historian not to distill some meaning from
his columns; his westerners, he believed, gained Lincolnesque stature by
their dedication to the interests of the ordinary people, inventing or
writing or worshipping or painting to glorify and instruct the common
man. Here was a finding worth sharing; "The Children of the Pioneers"
was accepted by the *Yale Review*, if enough names could be squeezed
out to bring it down to 8000 words. It appeared in the July 1926 issue,
enriching Turner by $100 and providing him slight justification for
having indulged his passion for learning while THE BOOK languished.

There was reason for this neglect, for he was finding that retirement
provided no panacea for the illness that laid him low whenever he
became too involved in a major task. Now his health was further imperiled by Madison's frigid winters. Turner's first year in his new home
was divided between attacks of influenza and the lectures that he had
contracted, as progress on his book came to a standstill. When he did
emerge from his bouts with influenza he was so plagued by colds and
so weak that he was afraid to venture outside, lest his staggering give
the neighborhood a bad reputation—or so he reported.[31] Mae was little
better off, particularly during the raw spring of 1925, when recurring
sore throats plagued both the Turners. There could be no relief, the
doctors decreed, until their tonsils were removed. Both were operated
on in Chicago in mid-May, Mae successfully, Turner less so when his
stitches loosened and he was forced to have them replaced, this time
with no anaesthetic. "I don't like to be stitched in the throat without
dope," he told a friend, with masterful understatement.[32]

Better times were around the corner. Turner was greatly cheered
when an unexpected bonanza came his way that spring. Word arrived
that he was one of the first group to be benefitted by Harvard's newly

established Milton Fund—he was to have a grant of $2500 "to complete a History of the United States for the period from 1830 to 1850," with no strings attached save that the money be used to further scholarship.[33] Now a secretary could be hired, a map-maker employed, and necessary office equipment purchased for his cubbyhole in the State Historical Society library. With that nest egg to be drawn upon, and the doctors' assurance of better health with the loss of his tonsils, Turner was ready to begin work on THE BOOK in earnest after his 1925 summer-school stint in Logan. At that time, three chapters and part of the fourth were in Henry Holt & Company's New York vault, together with half-a-dozen manuscript maps; the remainder of Chapter IV and parts of Chapter V were in rough draft. He settled to his task as soon as he proved that all trout had vanished from the streams near Hancock Point. His first move was inauspicious; he asked the publishers to return two of the early chapters for revision! They did so reluctantly, fearing they would never see them again, but by the end of that summer they were revised to Turner's satisfaction and could be returned with the assurance that more had been accomplished on Chapter IV and that Chapter V was virtually done. Turner was confident now that the whole book would be completed by the spring of 1926, and could be announced for fall publication. "You are," he added with a rare touch of realism, "too well aware, however, of my imperfections, to be safe in announcing anything at present."[34]

That warning was as justified as it was unnecessary, for illness and research on "The Children of the Pioneers" monopolized the next winter, with progress on THE BOOK at a dead halt. Summer brought better health, however, and Turner left Madison for Hancock Point in May 1926 confident that the next months would produce an abundance of finished chapters. His dreams were short lived. While in Boston, where he and Mae stopped to see friends, he suffered a painful disturbance of the middle ear, with dizziness and nausea so intense that he was hurried into the Stillman Infirmary for a two-week stay. There he improved until he could walk without staggering, but the deafness remained, to persist for the rest of his days. That summer went not into writing, but into a round of visits to doctors in a vain quest for better hearing, and into the rest he needed to regain his strength. "I haven't," he confessed as they prepared to return home in October, "been able to write a line—or wet a line, except once, with no results."[35]

Winter came early that fall of 1926, as it did often in Madison, with biting cold that kept Turner huddled before an open fire rather than dictating in his office at the Historical Society. As day after day passed with nothing done, he sank into a deepening depression, one that worried Mae and his friends. Clearly, escape to a warmer climate was called for, even though the below-zero state of the Turner bank balance made such a dream unrealistic. Then came a stroke of good fortune. When his sister, Breese De Moe, visited Madison that Christmas, she recognized the problem and the cure; nothing would do but that Mae accept a present of sufficient funds to take the Turners to Florida or Arizona or California. They accepted gratefully, and by mid-January of 1927 they were in New Orleans, basking in the warm sun and stuffing themselves on oysters and fish at Antoine's. The French Quarter was expensive, however, and after a week they were on their way westward, stopping at San Antonio and Tucson, taking life-restoring side-trips under the warm desert skies, and having the time of their lives. Eventually they reached Claremont, California, where they found delightful quarters at 1111 Harvard Street, with a view of the snow-clad mountains from their patio, oranges and lemons on their own trees, and plentiful friends to guide them on tours of the flower-bright countryside.[36] Here was the Eden they had been seeking. Turner sent for the trunkful of notes he had packed and prepared to settle down until summer.

Fate, in the person of Max Farrand, was to prolong that brief visit into a lifetime stay. Farrand, one of Turner's oldest and dearest friends, had just at that time accepted the directorship of the Huntington Library and Art Gallery, the magnificent benefaction near Pasadena bequeathed to the world of scholarship by Henry E. Huntington.[37] Farrand was in the East at the time, but no sooner did he hear of Turner's presence in California than he sent word to George Ellery Hale, a member of the library's board of trustees and an eminent astronomer. Turner was the one person in the world who could be most helpful in transforming Mr. Huntington's rare books and manuscripts into a research library—an ambition dear to both Hale and Farrand. Could the trustees seek him out and convince him to stay on as a senior research associate at $500 a month? Such an appointment would establish a standard that would attract the attention of the entire academic world. Hale acted with an enthusiasm that matched Farrand's own; by March

5 Turner had been brought to Pasadena, persuaded to spend the next
month there as consultant, and offered a permanent post as associate
for the following winter—a position that he promised to take if all
went well. Farrand was delighted. "Congratulate Mr. Huntington and
trustees," he wired, "and kiss Turner for me."[38] Turner could not know
that he stood on the threshold of some of the happiest—and most tragic
—years of his life.

Certainly the month spent at the library that spring was heaven itself. The Turners moved to a small rented bungalow at the "Court
of the Oak" in Pasadena on March 15. Each day thereafter he wandered among the books and manuscripts, a sheaf of papers in hand to
take notes on the marvels that he saw. Each new box opened sparked
his enthusiasm. Materials for his own study were so numerous that he
would have to spend a year reading them all. Rare items on the colonial
period would allow scholars for the first time to understand the forces
underlying political events. The story of the westward movement between the Appalachians and the Rockies would have to be completely
rewritten. Such were the riches of the Huntington that it seemed certain to become "a new center of civilization in the United States."[39]
As he admired, Turner offered a great deal of sound advice on the library's future. It should build to its strengths when collecting rare
items, specializing on the colonial era and the West, but with greater
stress on the Midwest and on the recent Far West; the function of history was to explain the present, and modern materials were needed for
this. It should collect economic, social, literary, and religious books
as well as those in the social sciences; "we need allied workers and allied
books, just as the astronomer needs the co-operation of chemist, physicist, geologist, etc. etc., in his work of deciphering the meaning of the
heavens." Most of all, the Huntington library required the reference
works that were the tools of all scholars; not to buy them on the
ground that they were available in other Los Angeles libraries would
be equivalent to asking a factory worker to travel ten miles each time
he needed a hammer or wrench. The trustees should buy the large sets
and the historical journals and the monographs and the government
documents (even though they had to build a new wing to house them),
and buy them at once. "The nuggets are mined; what is needed is the
machinery and the material for treating this gold."[40]

This was sound advice, and much to the library's future benefit. It convinced Farrand and the trustees that Turner was too valuable an asset to be relinquished, just as Turner's months at the Huntington persuaded him that he could be happier in Pasadena than in Madison. His health was better than it had been for years; Mae felt that he had undergone a miraculous resurrection, and he agreed that his weeks at the library had been "a real rebirth of enthusiasm for me."[41] Turner was not so enthusiastic that he forgot to bargain when the trustees offered him a permanent post as senior research associate; he wanted assurance that his principal efforts could be directed toward THE BOOK and that he be allowed to spend his summers in Maine. These terms were thoroughly acceptable and were written into the contract that was signed that summer. Turner was to join the library staff on October 15, 1927, as senior research associate, guaranteeing to spend at least the next six months in Pasadena in return for a salary of $5000 to offset his travel and living costs.[42] The trustees were glad to provide space for his own books and to arrange for the use of a car and driver to transport him between his home and the library if he so desired. On June 28 the local press announced that one of the world's greatest historians would soon add luster to Pasadena's cultural life.

The Turners spent that summer in Maine—a cold, rainy summer that kept Turner before the fire or in bed and confirmed their realization that California was their valhalla—then fled back to Madison in September to rent their home and pack clothes and books and notes for the journey westward. There they found a modest small house at 23 Oak Knoll Gardens for $100 monthly rental, complete with a spreading walnut tree, a sleeping porch, a next-door airedale who trotted in at all hours, and sufficient grackles and mocking birds and milkmen to make alarm clocks unnecessary. Each day Max Farrand called for Turner at nine, drove him to the library, and deposited him at his desk among the riches that he loved. Each noon they munched sandwiches together in Farrand's Gothic office, talking library business as they did so; occasionally Turner broke this routine to join the male staff members in a basement room where they brewed coffee, lunched from paper bags, and talked endlessly of books and history and fishing. "The Huntington Library," he reported happily, "is quite a paradise." He helped make it so. All who worked there fell victim to his gentle charm, his modesty, his patience, his outgoing affection for those about him. Turner contributed a great deal to the library that year—

sound advice, lists of reference works to be purchased, hundreds of his own books that the institution lacked—but his greatest contribution was a practical demonstration of the needs and methods of a research scholar. This was enlightening to the staff, who had been training under Mr. Huntington to care for a collector's library only. Turner gave them advice, gently and with understanding, but he also gave them a lesson in scholarship that was far more meaningful than any amount of counsel. Had he not been in residence, the conversion of the Huntington library into a magnificent research institution would have been far slower and more difficult.[43]

All this Turner greatly enjoyed, just as he enjoyed his new life in California. Friends, new and old, were almost as numerous as in Madison or Cambridge, and sometimes embarrassingly persistent in their attention; every time he started to write, someone dropped in with an invitation to drive to Ojai or Claremont or La Jolla, or a suggestion that they dine at the La Ramada or the La Solano or some other restaurant with a Spanish name and Boston clam chowder at the head of the menu. By the time the Turners started for Hancock Point in May 1928, they had been permanently weaned from the East. That spring they rented their Madison house unfurnished and packed the furniture and books to be sent westward; that summer neither particularly enjoyed the rain and humidity at Hancock Point. Both were happy to reach Pasadena again in early October, there to settle into a larger rented house at 16 Oak Knoll Gardens, where there was room to move about, even though the house next door was so close that, as Turner put it, "we can hear our neighbors change their minds."[44] They were becoming Californians.

Best of all was the sense of financial security that came with the library salary. Turner was forced to surrender his annuity from the Carnegie Corporation, but Harvard continued to pay him $598.32 yearly, the rental of their Madison house added another thousand, royalties brought in a few hundred, and the $5000 yearly from the Huntington relieved them of financial burdens. Turner insisted that his library salary be cut to $3500 after 1929, arguing that he was worth no more at his age and that they could live comfortably on the lesser sum. The soaring prosperity of the late 1920s added to their affluence; in February 1929 an aging relative in the East surprised them with a gift of $2000, while at about the same time they sold their Madison house to their son-in-law for $10,000, with a $5000 down payment and the remainder on a 6 per cent mortgage. These windfalls went into investments, as did most surplus money in that day of a skyrocketing stock market; some to the business ventures of John Main, some into such stocks as Drug Incorporated or the International Match Corporation, some into bank deposits. Their dividends in 1928 reached $1500 and their total income $7915.86—a satisfactory sum for a man who had expected to live on a pittance after his retirement.[45] Mae could even afford a maid now to help her with the work.

Life was good for Turner, but it would have been far better if he had had the willpower to refuse the invitations to write and speak and consult that were the lot of all new lions in a community. Lecture invitations poured in: from the Lincoln Centennial Commission of Illinois, who wanted an address on their hero; from the University of Texas, which would listen to anything he had to say on any subject; from Knox College, which needed a distinguished speaker for its Founder's Day; from DePauw University, where the officials were so impressed with his *The Last Frontier* [sic] that they thought he should deliver the Horizon Lecture Series; from the Pasadena Kiwanis Club which sought a free entertainer for its Washington's Birthday luncheon.[46] These Turner managed to refuse, but he was too neighborly to reject invitations from his new-found friends in Pasadena. His appearances there cost him a great deal of time; during his first two years in California he spoke before students of the University of California at Los Angeles on sectionalism, before the Pasadena Library Club on the value of bibliographies to historians, before the Harvard Club and the Pacific Coast Branch of the American Historical Association on the virtues of the Huntington library, and, in February 1928, in the prestigious Pasadena Lecture Series on Current Topics on "Sectionalism in American Politics."[47] That was the end; from that time on Turner parried all invitations by pleading ill health or the pressures of writing.

The end, that is, until an invitation arrived that could not be refused. The California Institute of Technology had recently added the distinguished political scientist William B. Munro to its faculty. What was more logical than that he cooperate with the two other scholars of equal distinction in the area, Turner and Max Farrand, in a course on history and historical methodology for the culturally deprived engineers? Arrangements were quickly made; for a $500 fee Turner would offer a second-term course on "The Jackson Era, 1828-1838," to be preceded by a term on "The Constitutional Era," with Max Farrand in charge, and followed by another under Munro on "From Cleveland to Wilson." Turner accepted partly because he convinced himself that preparing lectures would force him to get on with THE BOOK, but he was sadly mistaken. Most of that winter term of the 1928-29 academic year went into drafting syllabi, compiling reading lists, selecting source materials for analysis, grading examinations, and enduring ten two-hour sessions with eleven bored undergraduates who were so indifferent that four accepted incompletes and five earned only the grade of "C."[48] Turner could say no more of his last stint in the classroom than that it was "an interesting if fatiguing experience"—and he vowed never to do it again.[49]

Those students he could escape; his doctoral candidates and near-candidates from his Harvard and Wisconsin days he could not. They required constant nursemaiding and were never reluctant to ask for favors. Would Turner support so-and-so for a Guggenheim Fellowship, or for a post in such-and-such college? Would he recommend the best possible man in western history to this university or that? Would he help a worried board of trustees by suggesting an ideal president for the University of Washington—or Indiana, or Iowa? "I feel like a bureau," he confessed after a whole day of such letters.[50] Even those who did not feel themselves worthy of better positions added to his burden by asking him to criticize their articles and lectures and books and to aid them in convincing a publisher of the worth of their products. Turner took such duties seriously, reading each manuscript carefully, taking extensive notes, and writing voluminous criticisms, always leavened with enough praise to encourage the author to greater heights. These were the unsung contributions of the professor—whether retired or not—and were cheerfully rendered without thought of personal gain. Turner differed from his colleagues only in the number and quality of his students, and the greater burdens that they imposed.

But there were dividends to be paid by those students as well, and Turner profited handsomely. He had reached the point of distinction now that tributes were his due, and they came in abundance, largely from those who had been awakened to the excitement of history under his direction. Some dedicated their books to Turner; he was gratified with each recognition and kept careful lists of those who honored him in this way. Others painted flattering pen portraits of their old friend and master; Harold J. Laski, a former Harvard colleague many years Turner's junior, pictured him for the *Century Magazine* as one of the nation's greatest teachers, while Joseph Schafer, in an article on "The Author of the Frontier Thesis" for the *Wisconsin Magazine of History*, sketched him in such glowing colors that Turner was not sure he was the man described. "I look back on that young man," he confessed to Schafer, "with a perhaps pardonable indulgence and a sense of detachment that enables me to read your words without the blushing confusion that would be normal."[51] Of these many tributes, however, Turner was particularly pleased by those from two of his outstanding students, Carl Becker and Merle Curti.

Both wrote with a purpose in mind, Becker to describe his teacher, in a volume on *American Masters of Social Science*, which appeared in 1927, Curti to appraise Turner's methodology in a learned work, *Methods in Social Science, A Case Book*, which was sponsored by the Social Science Research Council and published in 1931. Each made full use of Turner's memory, plying him with questions on the origins of his theories, his philosophy of history, and the techniques that he employed. Turner responded generously with twenty- and thirty-page letters that not only answered his questioners but supplied them with invaluable information on his work, his accomplishments, and his students.[52] Both Becker and Curti used this mine of information wisely, producing model essays that gave Turner his due as a pioneer theorist and trailblazer in the realm of interdisciplinary studies. He was unabashedly delighted. "A premature obituary," he labeled Becker's masterpiece, but confessed that "I have reached the age where that sort of thing from a former student gives me real pleasure."[53] Curti's brilliant appraisal of his historical techniques was just as pleasing. "I would like to have my contributions as a whole seen as you present them," he assured the author, at the same time telling friends that the essay "has set forth my ideas and aims very well."[54] The important thing to Turner was to have his ideas presented so lucidly to an audience of social scientists, but he would have been less than human had he not glowed with pride at such recognition. He must have felt, as he read those two essays, that his life had not been wasted.

Turner must also have been haunted by doubts, for he was sadly aware of the fact that work on THE BOOK was lagging far behind his self-imposed schedules. He had settled in Pasadena in the fall of 1927 glowing with confidence that not only his study of sectionalism in the 1830-50 era would be completed within a few months, but that a whole five-foot-shelf of books would follow: a general volume on sectionalism in American history, another on the struggle between rural and industrial elements, a third on the relations of capital and labor in their class consciousness, and, if possible, "an interpretative general survey of American history coordinating frontier, regional geography, sections, population factors (including immigration), and such religious and art and literary history as needed to explain the other things."[55] THE BOOK had to be finished first, but he thought that would take only a few months. Turner drew up a time schedule that year: April 9 to 30 to revise the introduction and the first two chapters on New England and the Middle States, the four weeks in May for the four remaining chapters describing the major regions, June 1 to July 15 to complete the four chapters surveying the political impact of sectionalism between 1828 and 1844, July 16 to August 15 for the final two chapters carrying the story to 1850.[56] Turner's optimism was irrepressible.

Nor was it diminished by the prospect of a secretary of such terrifying efficiency that Turner would not dare let THE BOOK languish. Merrill H. Crissey had been one of the prods that made the *Rise of the New West* possible when he had worked for Turner as an undergraduate in 1905; the two had drifted apart since Crissey's graduation in 1906, but now he was available again and free to start work on January 1, 1928. He had read of Turner's appointment at the Huntington and would be willing to endure a financial sacrifice to renew their old relationship. Turner pointed out that those sacrifices might be considerable, for he could pay no more than $175 a month from the funds left in his Milton grant and could guarantee employment for no more than six months yearly. Not even these uncertainties could dissuade Crissey. He would arrive on schedule and would be happy to receive any salary that seemed suitable. Turner was assured not only excellent secretarial help, but an adoring slave driver who would be at his side for the rest of his days.

He dusted off his notes and manuscripts in November 1927, confident (as he told a friend) that he would "be able to complete the book within the year."[57] The three chapters and portions of the fourth in the Henry Holt & Company vault had to come back first, together with the half-dozen maps he had sent them some years before, so that he could refresh his memory and make a few changes. The manuscript was returned promptly, with appropriate words of encouragement, but the request for the maps brought an embarrassing admission: both they and the correspondence concerning them had disappeared. This was disaster, even though Turner had photostat copies of all but two. All had to be redrawn before interpretation could go on.[58] By the beginning of 1928 that hurdle was cleared, and work was resumed under the efficient prodding of Merrill Crissey. Their procedures were soon perfected: Turner sat in his pleasant office at the Huntington library, his notes about him, filling page after page with his bold hand; as each was finished, it was copied in triplicate by Crissey on the typewriter, with two of the copies set aside for Turner's corrections. These were many. Scarcely an hour passed but progress halted while Turner searched back through the typed pages to rewrite a paragraph or add a tidbit of information or alter an interpretation. "Though they were presumably copy for the publisher," Crissey wrote sadly as he saw his neatly typed pages torn apart, "the refining process continued, for whenever they were re-read there were further alterations."[59] Often these were time-consuming, requiring a search for confirming evidence, sometimes obtainable only in a distant library. So meticulous was Turner that he once halted progress for days while obtaining data on the 1843 census in Southport, Wisconsin, because his own figures did not jibe with those in an article he had read.

These delays were bad enough, but worse were those that occurred while Turner stopped to dig more deeply into problems that he constantly encountered. Two of those problems were particularly irksome. Turner found that the sections he was analyzing concealed a number of smaller sub-sections that differed politically from the region in which they were located; each of these had to be carefully analyzed and its behavior explained in terms of geographic or ethnic factors—an endless task. He discovered also that most of the secondary books he had counted on to supply incidental information were too inaccurate to be trusted, and that only by digging out every fact himself could he avoid mistakes. This was a fatal realization, for now he had an excuse to bury himself in the riches of the Huntington, his writing forgotten. "The library is as delightful a workshop as ever," he reported late in 1928, "but the book moves more slowly than I want it to."[60] Yet it did move; by October 1928 all but the last of the "sectional" chapters—that describing the Far West—were "finished." His rash predictions of a book in 1929 seemed within the range of possibility.

That burst of activity took its toll, for sustained intellectual effort was fatal to Turner's weakening system. "I have never learned to work moderately when I get interested in a problem," he told a friend that winter, and now he had to pay the piper.[61] The first setback came in February 1929, when he suffered a severe attack of vertigo when leaving the library and stopped himself from falling only by grabbing a "No Admittance" sign. Tension, high blood pressure, and a weakening heart was the official verdict; Turner was sentenced to bed for two weeks and warned that he must do no work the rest of that spring. He followed his spartan regime to the letter, but when he failed to improve, the doctors agreed that an infection in his bladder was poisoning his system. Two operations were needed, one to insert drainage tubes, the other to probe the bladder itself. The first was performed in late April, the second on May 15, both so successfully that by the end of May he could be wheeled into the flowering gardens of the Pasadena Hospital, eat squab for lunch, and resume smoking like an incinerator.[62]

Those gains were deceptive, for no sooner was he out of the hospital than the spells of dizziness began again, accompanied with acute nausea. The doctors allowed him to visit Hancock Point that summer of 1929, partly so that he could consult specialists in Madison and Boston. They could do nothing; a major attack of vertigo in August sent him to his bed for ten days. "I am not worth much," he reported sadly to a friend.[63] Worse was the doctors' prognosis for the future. Turner's attacks stemmed from a malfunctioning heart that was beyond cure. He might be able to lead a normal life for a brief time, but he would never be well, and the end could not be far distant. He returned to Pasadena that September a very sick man; friends noticed his heightened color, his increasing frailty, the dullness of his eyes, his lack of zest for work.

California's wonders worked their magic, however, and by November progress on THE BOOK was resumed, with 485 manuscript pages completed and far more to be done. Procedures had to be changed now, for Turner was too weak to visit the library and dictated to Crissey from a couch in his home. Crissey played a heroic role. Each morning he gathered notes for the day's dictation, transcribed the most essential onto slips of paper, and carried them to the cottage at 23 Oak Knoll Gardens. There Turner examined them and gave his instructions: more information must be found on this subject in such-and-such documents; this book or that must be consulted on the next point to be covered. When Crissey had located all the needed materials and made the necessary notes in his precise hand, he returned to Turner's home, where the notes were filed in proper order with guide-cards of colored cardboard at intervals to indicate dates or topics. With these before him, Turner began his dictation, selecting cards on various subjects to be correlated with others. Progress was slow, for he could work no more than an hour or two before fatigue forced a halt. Crissey then returned to the library to type the day's dictation into a triple-spaced manuscript (with ample room for the inevitable deletions, interpolations, and changes), and to begin research on material for the next day's effort.[64]

So the work inched on, month after month, with no improvement on Turner's part. "The book is moving like molasses," he reported sadly in February 1930.[65] There were interruptions, too, when weakness forced a halt to all writing for weeks at a time, or when friends who had been asked to read chapters sent in their criticism, and revision replaced writing. More than a month went into selecting and polishing a chapter to be published in the first issue of the *Huntington Library Bulletin;* Turner wanted his treatment of the Jackson administration to be used, because he thought it particularly original, but Farrand chose that on New England as the only chapter short enough not to fill a whole issue.[66] Still the pile of "completed" manuscript grew; by the end of March 1930, a "preliminary draft" of all the "sectional" chapters had been typed, rough drafts of those covering the Jackson and Van Buren administrations had been completed, and that on the Tyler administration begun. Only the last three chapters, on Polk, Taylor, and the state of the nation in 1850, were still to be written in their entirety. THE BOOK might yet appear in 1931, if Turner's health held up.

Instead it steadily worsened. Late in March the doctors broke the news to Max Farrand; Turner's heart was growing weaker and might stop at any time. There was no immediate cause for alarm, but his family should be informed, and above all he should not strain himself by visiting Hancock Point that summer. Dorothy responded with her usual good sense; she would tell her father that she was tired of Hancock Point and would like to visit a Pacific coastal resort that summer. This would keep him from traveling without letting him know his true condition. Dorothy might have saved herself the trouble. No doctor's warning was needed to tell Turner that his days were numbered. Painstakingly during those months he was scattering guideposts through his notes for those who might have to complete THE BOOK in his stead; "In case the chapters dealing with the subjects ennumerated on the attached sheet should not be completed . . . ," one began, with instructions following on the treatment he had intended. All were to be placed in the hands of Dr. Farrand, who would find more instructions at the back of a drawer.[67]

The Turners spent that summer of 1930 in a rented house at La Jolla, with Merrill Crissey on hand to continue dictation and Dorothy and her three children—little Lois had been born in December 1928, to complete the Main household—present to add joy and distractions. Turner disliked La Jolla, with its sultry air and well-manicured lawns, but he was convinced that further trips east were too expensive and too tiring to be practical. Then, too, the depression was deepening and the family income shrinking as stocks and bonds abandoned dividends; it declined to $4772 in 1930 and $4312 a year later.[68] Common sense decreed that they should sell their cottage at Hancock Point and buy a modest home in Pasadena rather than pay high rental. That fall they moved into an attractive house at 26 Oak Knoll, with an option to buy at $8500. Buying this proved easier than selling "The Moorings"; Turner made the purchase early in 1931 for $8000—with a $3500 mortgage attached—but a series of prospective customers for the Hancock Point cottage changed their minds as economic conditions worsened. That treasured possession remained in the family to be enjoyed by Dorothy's children and her children's children. Turner managed to sell only his canoe and paddle—for forty dollars.

With the easing of his financial problems came better health; by the end of November 1930, Turner was able to visit the library for a few hours daily, there to dictate from a couch in his office or direct Merrill Crissey's expeditions into the stacks for needed information. By the end of June some 250,000 words had been written, with at least another 150,000 to go, and Turner was inquiring anxiously whether the publishers would accept two volumes. He might have spared his fears. Crissey could not be with him when the Turners established themselves at the Highlands Inn in Carmel for the summer of 1931—a happy one it was, amidst the rocky shores and pine forests and cold fog that reminded them of Maine—leaving Turner nothing to do but resume his eternal revising. Revise he did, so thoroughly that, when Crissey attempted to convert the much-penciled manuscript into legibility that fall, he found 675 pages with passages crossed out or rewritten, whole sections reorganized, and marginal notes in abundance telling him to consult newly published studies or to incorporate fresh information; "add material from Huntington on coal-land prices and coal mining derived from D. Green and Rockwell papers," read one such reminder.[69] Turner even found time to restudy maps and footnotes and propose numerous changes. The "Carmel Revisions," as they came to be known, kept Crissey so busy that fall that there was little time for the main task, yet even then Turner could not accept them as the last word. When the rewritten pages were filed away he marked the folder: "Revised (final?) to page 676." Max Farrand was right when he remarked that THE BOOK would have remained unfinished if Turner had lived forever.

Turner was not to live forever. In October a painful phlebitis of the leg forced him into bed, where he spent most of the next two months, too weak even to dictate. Then, to the surprise of the doctors, his health gradually improved until, in February 1932, he could resume daily visits to the library. These proved to be a mistake, for now he could pursue his researches once more, writing forgotten. One problem intrigued him particularly and must be solved before he dictated the section on the Compromise of 1850: what were John C. Calhoun's motives in swinging to an aggressively proslavery stand? Turner's older interpretation had been upset by manuscripts he had discovered at the Huntington; now he had to re-read the documents and re-formulate his conclusions. By March 14 he had the answer and was able to dictate a memorandum on his findings: "The correspondence with Calhoun in the summer and fall of 1847 shows that he was being pushed to leadership and advice with regard to protecting the South, and that he was not merely initiating a movement of revolt."[70] Noon was at hand by the time Crissey's pothooks recorded this new interpretation, but Turner had one more short letter he wanted to dictate. Marion Sheldon, a former Radcliffe student, had asked him for advice on materials dealing with Silas Wright, a politician whose sketch she was preparing for the *Dictionary of American Biography*. He had replied at length a few days earlier, but now he remembered an additional source she would find useful; "*Niles' Register* (Vol. LXXXII, p. 6, Sept. 4, 1847)" contained a reprint of an editorial from the *Union* on Wright, a biographical sketch from the *Democratic Review*, and other important information. "On the chance that you may not have seen this, I venture to send it on."[71] Those were the last words written by Turner. Typically, they were to a student engaged in a worthy historical task.

He had been in unusually good health and spirits that morning, so there was no premonition of danger when he returned home to lunch with Mae and lie down for a short rest. Yet when she returned from a short walk she found him still in bed, and complaining of a pain about the heart. The physician who was called gave him an injection and assured them both that he would be fine. Turner stirred himself to answer. "I know this is the end," he said. Mae remonstrated, reminding him that small attacks such as this were common, but he repeated: "I know this is the end. Tell Max I am sorry that I haven't finished my book." Then, after a few joking words with the doctor, he slipped into unconsciousness. At 7:30 that night of March 14, 1932, Frederick Jackson Turner died. His heart, too often abused, was unable to overcome the clot that stopped its beating.[72]

Turner was dead, but he had left behind a great deal of unfinished business to be completed by his friends. First, they mourned and paid their tributes. The funeral, held on March 19 in the spacious living room of Max Farrand's home, was a simple Episcopalian service attended by some sixty close friends. Avery Craven, a young historian from the University of Chicago studying at the library that year, prepared the tribute which Farrand read—a moving memorial to a teacher and scholar and friend. Craven, who had studied briefly with Turner at Harvard, harked back to those days: "No man of our day has been more 'borrowed from' and more 'imposed upon' by those who 'get' but give little"—a teacher who inspired his students to his own standards of perfectionism—a scholar who gave of himself freely. "I will never be certain about anything, but never satisfied with anything as long as I am uncertain," said Craven. "That was what Turner did for me."[73] These were words that Turner would have liked.

He would have liked even more the chorus of tribute that rose from friends and strangers. Letters came by the score—so many that eighty-five of the most precious were bound into a book for preservation—nearly all expressing the deep personal loss felt with the passing of a close friend. Editorials appeared in most of the nation's leading journals, venerating the scholar who had opened a new page in American history, and bemoaning the fact that one of such importance should be so little known to the public. Resolutions and memorials were voted by the institutions that he had aided—the State Historical Society of Wisconsin, the American Historical Association, the Huntington, the faculties of the universities where Turner had taught, a dozen more. "The most distinguished Americanist of his generation," they called him, who had "made necessary a reappraisal of the forces of American history" and imbued his students with "the imperative need of integrating the historical with other social sciences."[74] High praise indeed, but revealing of the esteem in which Turner was held by those of his generation who knew him best.

They could not know, those who wrote these words, that Turner was to erect still more monuments to his own memory, for the twist of fate decreed that a man who had been able to publish only two books during seventy-one years on earth would publish two more within little more than three years of his death. The first—a volume of essays similar to *The Frontier in American History* but with sectionalism as its theme—was conceived by Turner in the months before his death; when Merrill Crissey searched his files he found several memoranda listing the eleven articles that might be included and even suggesting a title: "Significance of Sections in American History."[75] Such a command from the grave could not be ignored; on April 6, at a conference of the Huntington library research staff, Max Farrand was instructed to seek a publisher, while Crissey prepared copies of the eleven essays with Turner's corrections. The publisher posed no problems; Henry Holt & Company had waited a generation for a book by Turner and would sign a contract gladly. Preparing the manuscript was less easy, for permissions had to be obtained and a decision made whether to incorporate the often-confusing changes that Turner had noted in his copies of the papers. In the end only factual corrections were made, and in this form *The Significance of Sections in American History* appeared in January 1933.[76]

The volume stirred far less interest than its predecessor of thirteen years before. Such popular journals as thought it worthy of mention were generally favorable, but the tone of the reviewers suggested that they were praising a beloved historian rather than bestowing their benediction on his latest product; of Turner's greatness there can be no question, they seemed to say, but of the book's there was. Fortunately, this opinion was not shared by one of Turner's old Harvard acquaintances, Mark A. DeWolfe Howe, a member of the committee that would select the Pulitzer Prize winner for that year. Turner's book was called to Howe's attention by Allan Nevins when they lunched together just after its appearance; Howe sought it out at once, read it, agreed with Nevins that it was far and away the most significant work in history eligible for the prize. When the award was announced, in May 1933, the book world was astounded; one critic who had never heard of the volume accused Henry Holt & Company of publishing it "almost secretly." Yet Turner's friends were delighted, and Turner's widow enriched by the award of $2000 and the royalty on 700 extra copies sold in the next six weeks.[77]

His friends were to celebrate again, for scarcely was Turner in his grave than the publishers demanded the manuscript of THE BOOK; Turner had assured them only a few weeks before, they said, that it was almost completed. So he had, but he had exaggerated shamefully, as usual. The final three chapters consisted only of outlines, scattered fragments, and a series of memoranda listing subjects to be discussed, while even the "completed" portions were so crowded with penciled changes, marginal suggestions, and scribbled additions that they were almost indecipherable. Months, even years, of patient effort would be necessary to transform this mass into a publishable book, but Avery Craven and Merrill Crissey selflessly assumed that task. Few men have worked harder. They agreed that the volume should be Turner's, not theirs, and that they would make no attempt to include later findings or to complete the unfinished chapters. Yet they had to sort and arrange the fragments that would form the later sections, test every statement for accuracy, check each footnote and add others when they were lacking, choose illustrations, decide which of the marginal suggestions to include, and recast the whole manuscript stylistically.[78] These were herculean labors, done with no thought of reward. Yet they were performed so efficiently that in mid-March of 1934 the 930 pages of text and thirty maps that were to make up *The United States, 1830-1850: The Nation and Its Sections* were in the hands of Henry Holt & Company. The book was officially published on March 28, 1935, just three years and two weeks after its author's death.

To all but the most dedicated Turnerians, it seemed a sad anticlimax to a distinguished career. Its theme was already familiar, while the fine refinements of sectional theory that Turner had intended to develop were either yet to be added or discernible to only a handful of experts. Too, the book showed unmistakable signs of its troubled background; it was often poorly written, marred by a lack of transitions, and lacking in the sense of drama that it might have possessed if brought to the intended conclusion. Throughout were evidences of hasty preparation, needed corrections, out-of-date conclusions, and inadequate analysis. An earlier generation of historians might have accepted these inadequacies for what they were, but those living in 1935 would not. By this time the deepening Great Depression had focused historical interest on new problems; the rural past seemed insignificant in a day when industrial-urban disorganization demanded attention, and the sectional antagonisms of the nineteenth century were inconsequential to men who were dealing with the capitalist-labor conflicts of the twentieth. *The United States, 1830-1850* was a non-functional book at a time when the world was concerned with the malfunctions of capitalism and crying for blueprints for social reform. Such luxuries were out of place in the shattered world of the 1930s.

This did not mean that the reception was universally hostile; Turner was too venerated, and his disciples too numerous, to permit an abrupt about-face in his popularity. Yet such was the spirit of the time that some among the reviewers, at least, were emboldened to say that the great god had nodded. The tone of criticism was set by the *Saturday Review of Literature* when it labeled the volume "disappointing," not simply because of the author's death, but because the sectional thesis did not explain American politics as Turner thought that it did; the reviewer found the chapters on politics hackneyed and the whole book suffering from a midwestern bias. These were harsh words—perhaps harsher than justified—but they only slightly exaggerated the reception that *The United States, 1830-1850* received from all but the most fanatical of Turner's disciples.

These judgments were only a final footnote in the life of a historian who had contributed more to the understanding of the American past than any scholar of his generation. Turner the man was dead, but Turner the speculative historian lived on. His theories on the frontier and section were to influence more students, generate more controversy, and excite more writing after his death than they had when he lived. Turner's legacy was not simply the thin shelf of books and articles produced during his lifetime, but the vitality that he breathed into historical studies, the concepts that brought historians nearer the truth, and the lessons that he taught the men of a younger generation as they attacked the bastions of ignorance with the multidisciplined weapons that he had placed in their hands.

XVII

Frederick Jackson Turner: A Portrait of the Man

HEN the mortal remains of Frederick Jackson Turner were laid to rest in a Madison cemetery beside the bodies of his two small children, there seemed every reason to believe that he and his theories would soon be forgotten. His sectional concepts had failed to strike a spark and the book that would have given them vitality would never be published. His frontier hypothesis was out of tune with the times, outmoded by a Great Depression that fastened the attention of historians on the urban-industrial world of the present. Many a young scholar labeled Turner a false prophet during those years and rode to fame by proving his theories wrong and his expression of those theories misleading. The frontier thesis, so venerated by Turner's own generation, seemed fated to complete rejection by the next. Turner himself, so respected in his own time, appeared certain to be forgotten.

Yet today Turner lives in the memories of American historians as do none of his contemporaries. More of his books—in paperback editions—are sold now than were published during his lifetime. More articles about him have been written in the past decade than about any former historian, even including Charles A. Beard. Only the papers of Henry David Thoreau attract more scholars to the Henry E. Huntington Library than do the papers of Frederick Jackson Turner. The University of Wisconsin boasts a Frederick Jackson Turner residence hall and a Frederick Jackson Turner professorship. The Organization of American Historians awards its most prestigious prize in his name. When the American Historical Association asked its Executive Council to name the six greatest historians in the nation's history, Turner was the only academic scholar to be ranked first by every member. When the Republic of Mexico invited the United States to select its two most important historians, Turner and Francis Parkman were the nominees; their portraits hang side by side in the hall of the History Commission at the University of Mexico.[1] No fanatical Turner cult exists today as it did in his time, but neither has he been forgotten—as seemed probable in 1932.

Why this about-face? How can one account for the fact that Turner and his concepts are more respected in the 1970s than they were in the 1930s? The persistence of his theories is basically responsible, of course; latter-day students have sought to test his frontier and sectional hypotheses objectively, with neither the blind adulation of his own generation nor the irrational rejection of the next, and have found aspects of them useful in understanding the nation's past. Yet Turner's own image has helped perpetuate his influence, an image preserved by his students and friends to become a permanent part of the folklore of historiography. Turner can be visualized by most Americanists today: a vital man of medium build with penetrating eyes and vibrant voice, radiant with good health, his tanned face and tweedy clothes testifying to his passion for the out-of-doors, fascinating students with his lecturing skills and winning friends with the warmth of his personality—a good man, excessively modest in manner but sparkling with ideas that altered the interpretation of American history. This is the image. How closely does it resemble the Frederick Jackson Turner who lived and thought during the dying years of the nineteenth century and the first decades of the twentieth?

Those who have pictured him for later generations were correct when they stressed the immense charm that won him friends and disciples. Few among his contemporaries combined to such a rare degree the qualities of the scholar with those of a warm, outgoing, fallible, human being. In that era of academic posturing, when the professor was inevitably stuffed-shirtish and disdainful of ordinary mortals, Turner radiated friendship and good fellowship, not just to his peers, but to all about him. His students found him a companion no less than an instructor, always ready to step from the pedestal to become one of them. So did the fishermen and caretakers and ferry-boat operators at his summer home in Hancock Point. Turner was a down-to-earth, old-shoe type of mortal, not through affectation, but because he cast himself in the role of the historical character he most admired: the Jackson Man. His social attitudes were governed by his belief in the goodness and common sense of those about him, whatever their walks in life. Turner was the living embodiment of the frontier egalitarianism that he venerated.

Turner loved the world, and the world loved Turner. Those who met him first were struck by the grey-blue eyes that lighted his face when he smiled, and by the rich timbre of his voice, whether in the low musical pitch of ordinary conversation or the hearty resonance of the lecture platform. Those who came to know him better were impressed by his sympathetic understanding, his eagerness to please, his utter lack of pretense or animosity. Insatiably curious, and thoroughly read on a variety of subjects, Turner was always an interested listener, ready to flatter by the close attention that he paid to any conversation. "His understanding and appreciation of people," one of his friends observed, "must have been one of the secrets of his insight into people in history."[2]

There was no pomposity, no cant, in Frederick Jackson Turner. His happiest moments were spent with guides or lobster fishermen who called him "Fred" rather than "Dr. Turner" and accepted him as their equal. Many letters from distinguished persons were in his files—letters from Theodore Roosevelt, Woodrow Wilson, Lord Bryce, Josef Redlich, and many others—but none was more treasured than a simple note from the caretaker and coach-driver at Hancock Point:

> Dear Friend Turner: Glad to hear from you. Was up at Molasses Pond Saturday after salmon and caught 1 2½ pounder. It did show a great fight. I see one caught weighing 7½.

Details, then, about the cottage, and: "Say Turner when you get here the salmon will still be biting."[3] The "H. W. Johnson" who signed that letter was his sort of a person. Turner was born to live in old clothes, in a remote cabin far from the bustle and tensions of twentieth-century America, amidst the H. W. Johnsons of the world.

To him, all men were equal and all men were good. Few historians of his day enjoyed a wider or more cordial relationship with others in his profession—a profession not without its jealousies and malicious back-biting. All were Turner's friends, none his enemies. Even those who opposed his views directed none of their animosity toward him. Frederic Bancroft attacked Turner for his membership in the "ring" that controlled the American Historical Association, but he had only kind words for Turner the man. In return, Turner saw only good in his enemies; even when he was the victim of Bancroft's most vicious attacks he could muster no more than a tone of annoyance in his letters. Only once was his patience strained. When a very mediocre former student addressed a letter to him as "My Dear Turner"—a form of intimacy reserved in those days for one's closest friends—Turner was sufficiently annoyed to begin his reply "Dear MR. Gochenour," then crossed that out to write "Dear Professor Gochenour." Even this gentle reproof was lost on Mr. Gochenour, who began his answer: "Dear Turner."[4]

His supply of modesty was bountiful—or so the world believed. To those about him, he was the most self-effacing of men, disclaiming glory, abhoring praise, shunning all pomp and ceremony, and shying from the limelight. When elected president of the Colonial Society of Massachusetts, he stirred a palace revolution by refusing to allow the "LL.D." to which he was entitled to be listed after his name, forcing the director of publications to drop the honorary degrees of all past presidents.[5] Yet this façade hid a vast yearning for recognition and a life-size inferiority complex. Scattered through his files are evidences of his need: lists of books dedicated to him, others chronicling the accomplishments of his students, favorable book reviews (and only favorable book reviews) with the most flattering passages underlined in red or identified by a hand-drawn arrow, newspaper columns and editorials that glorified his contributions, also heavily underlined. When historiographical books mentioned his work, each was purchased and the favorable passages identified. In some Turner even added to the index the list of pages where his name appeared that had been missed by a careless indexer. And everywhere he signed his name—a flowing "Frederick J. Turner"—on file covers, pamphlets, blue books, boxes, slips of paper, newspaper clippings, anything with a writable surface. One battered box in which he kept notes he signed no less than a dozen times.

His friends loved him for his modesty, however false it might have been, and they loved him also for the cheerful optimism that was his stock-in-trade. Almost never did he give way to doubt or despair, and then only when progress on THE BOOK had slowed to a standstill. Such moods soon passed, to be replaced with a cheerful belief in the future that was one of his greatest charms—and weaknesses. When Turner wrote his friends, as he did over and over again, that THE BOOK would be out in a year, he was deceiving himself more than he was deceiving them. Like the frontiersmen he so much admired, Turner saw things not as they were, but as they should be. THE BOOK would be finished, the textbook that he longed to write completed, the half-dozen other volumes that he planned speedily written. His reason told him now and then that these were pipe dreams, but reason was brushed aside as too unpleasant a companion. Turner saw the world through rose-tinted glasses, and a happy world it was.

Friends were warmed by Turner's optimism, and they were captivated by his enjoyment of life. He was a contented man who shared his happiness with those about him. His contentment he found in the quiet of his home and the love of his wife, Caroline Mae Sherwood Turner. The Turners were deeply, devotedly, perpetually in love. "Darling Little Mae," as he addressed her in his letters, was his Eve, wherever she was, his Eden. The one unforgettable blot on his happiness was the death of their two small children; the one great joy of his declining years his daughter Dorothy Turner Main and her three offspring. Turner was in the best sense of the word a family man, content with the simple pleasures of home and fireside.

Mae Turner was not an academic helpmate in the traditional sense; she did not type his manuscripts or check his references or read his proofs. She could not even provide Turner with the intellectual companionship that he often required; he found this in his colleagues, his men's clubs, and in his friend Mrs. William Hooper, whose conversations and letters he treasured for their mind-tingling stimulation. But Mae gave him something he needed far more: her devoted attention and a well-run home that left him free for his own studies. This Turner knew, and he was never backward in expressing his appreciation. Mae, in turn, took quiet pride in her husband's happiness and accomplishments. "I know that Fred loved our quiet fireside," she told Max Farrand shortly after his death, "and the logs never smoked. They were dry wood and carefully selected."[6]

On only one point did the Turners differ, and here a mutual truce kept the peace. Mae was ardently religious; Turner felt no need for spiritual comfort. His rebellion against orthodoxy had begun when he rejected the "nonsense" forced on him by a Portage Sunday School teacher; it continued through his college years as he searched for a creed that placed less stress on the supernatural and more on the goodness of man. "If men would simply teach the beauty of right action," he complained at the time, "they would do some good. But they don't—and so myself and a good part of the world, too, drift into paganism."[7] Not paganism, but Unitarianism, eventually attracted Turner and held his interest for the half-dozen years he was in college and graduate school. "My creed," he wrote, "is summed up in the commandment which enjoins love to God, and to man."[8] Even the humanism of the Unitarian Church failed to satisfy his needs; he eventually drifted away, and, through most of his adult life, he worshipped not at all. Mae was distressed, but she was sensible enough to let her husband go his way while she went hers. Their religious differences placed no strain on their love.

Instead, they grew ever closer with the passing years, bound by their affection for their one surviving child as she grew into attractive womanhood, married, and blessed them with three grandchildren. These were the apples of their grandfather's eye. Jackson Turner Main, born in 1917, was a talented lad who inherited a passion for reading and history that rivaled Turner's own. As early as his fifth year Jack rebelled against the naps that interfered with more important pastimes ("I don't go to sleep, you know, I only lie in bed and suffer"); when he was nine he buried himself so deeply in Turner's books while summering at Hancock Point that a dangerous eye inflammation required his hospitalization; by the time he was fourteen he had written a learned paper analyzing the effect of the age of senators on their attitude toward war. Turner was delighted. "I think it fine," he told Jack, "that you should be thinking of the causes that lay behind historical events."[9] He would have been even more delighted if he could have peered into the future to see his grandson a distinguished historian of colonial America and a pioneer in the use of statistical techniques that shed light on "the causes that lay behind historical events."

For his two granddaughters Turner had equal affection, even though they did not share his love of history. Betsy, born in 1920, and Lois, eight years her junior, never knew when the postman would deliver a special letter addressed to them, often with an original poem:

> I love you good, I love you *bad*;
> I love you happy, I love you sad.

Or when their grandfather would welcome them into his study, push his writing aside, and draw a fantastic picture of himself as a fish with a pipe in his mouth. Or charm them with an illustrated verse about the boll weevil:

> He's not the Jabberwock, but he is very evil;
> He never learned to talk; they call him Old Boll Weevil.[10]

Other grandfathers of that day were as devoted as Turner, but few could have been more so. In his expanding family he found happiness, and that happiness made him even more appealing to his friends.

To picture Turner as a devoted grandfather, amusing his grandchildren with pictures and doggerel, is to recognize that he was no inner-regulated scholar who dwelt in the world of the abstract. He was not. Turner lived and wrote with the undisciplined impetuosity of the poet rather than with the restrained exactness of the scientist. Latter-day critics were to bemoan his lack of definitions and quarrel with his imprecise terminology, but neither Turner nor his contemporaries were aware of the fact that he was violating the canons of scholarship. He knew, and they knew, what he meant, even though he varied the meaning of the word "frontier" three times within a single essay. This was the prerogative of the artist, and Turner was as much an artist as he was a historian. His pen-pictures convinced scholars, not through the process of reason, but in exactly the same way that a fine novel or beautiful painting was "convincing." His writings were built on values, not on mechanics, and if no two readers found the same message, no two viewers saw the same thing when they admired a great picture. When Merle Curti accused Turner of being as much an artist as he was teacher or scholar or thinker, Turner was admittedly pleased. "I always wanted to be an artist," he told Curti, "tho' a truthful one."[11] Words were his passion, words that sang, words that set the reader tingling with excitement—these were the words that appealed to Turner, even though they might cloud the exactness of his meaning.

Because he did love words, he played with them, just as would any poet. Phrases that pleased him were borrowed, with proper credit, for his own works; he was particularly fond of Ralph Waldo Emerson's "the nervous, rocky West," and of the lines from Tennyson's "Ulysses" that caught the spirit of pioneering:

> for my purpose holds
> To sail beyond the sunset, and the baths
> Of all the western stars, until I die.

Rudyard Kipling's "Explorer," who fronted death to find the unknown, "lost behind the ranges," was a Turner favorite, as was that author's "The Foreloper":

> He shall desire loneliness, and his desire shall bring
> Hard on his heels a thousand wheels, a people and a king. . . .
> For he must blaze a nation's way, with hatchet and with brand,
> Till on his last-won wilderness an empire's bulwarks stand.

Many a Turner class in the "History of the West" heard the stirring words from Robinson Jeffers's "Californians":

> They rose, and trekked westward the wilderness.
> Now I, the latest in this solitude
> Invoke thee from the verge extreme, and shoal
> Of sand that ends the west. O long pursued
> Where wilt thou lead us now? [12]

Turner believed that the image-charged phrases of a poet could tell something about the frontier that ordinary language could not. He was constantly on the look-out for striking metaphors that would convey the spirit of the westward movement to his readers. The frontier, to Turner, "leaped" over the Alleghenies, "skipped" westward, "passed in successive waves," or "stretched" like a "cord of union" across the backcountry; the California gold rush sent a "sudden tide" of adventurers westward. Once when complimented for calling the mountain folk of the Appalachians "fossil remains of an earlier age," he confessed to rather liking the image himself.[13] Students recalled that phrases such as "we are all poor creatures," or "tickled pink," or "like the breaking up of a hard winter" were used over and over again in his lectures. On Turner's desk when he died was a note correlating features of the American landscape with historical figures:

Washington: the waves of the Atlantic
Jackson: the forest and the Indian
Lincoln: the prairies (waving grass and flowers) . . .
Roosevelt: the Great Plains and the Grand Canyon

None but a man with the soul of a poet could seek such analogies, and seek them so successfully.[14]

Turner did have the soul of a poet and the urge to create beauty with words, whether verse or cadenced prose. His love affair with Mae inspired a dozen poems, all hidden from the world in his Commonplace Books:

And the lake lies all transfigured
Silver glories, all its dross
Every wavelet flashing silver
Laughing dancing filled with life
Such the face of my beloved—
Moonlit waters, dimpling silver
Dancing eye-eaves when she smiles.[15]

Turner wrote verse, as he wrote his essays, with the passionate convictions of the poet rather than the cold impersonality of the exact scientist.

In his more mature years his enthusiasm for poetry was restrained to reading and memorizing the works of others, but when he did venture into rhyming the result was usually light and gay, as befitting a grown man who must keep his emotions in check. Once, when picnicking with good friends, he jotted down a few lines that revealed a surprising taste for Morris chairs and tasty beverages, rather than the joys of the wilderness:

Who would break his neck a-rowing
Raise a thirst and burn his nose
When the fragrant mint is blowing
And the whiskey gently flows?

Picnic weather's always nasty;
Radiators are the thing;
Better is a flask of Asti
Than pale water from a spring.[16]

Again in 1907, when walking across a Washington park at dusk, the song of a thrush animated his pen:

> I like little thrushes,
> The song haunts me yet;
> I like little thrushes,
> But mostly *en brochette*.

This success inspired a second attempt:

> I like little crabbies,
> Their gait is so queer;
> But would they be quiet
> If broiled, served with beer?

Thereupon, he wrote his wife, he decided to find out, went to Harvey's Restaurant, and did find out.[17]

Love and laughter inspired most of Turner's attempts at versifying, but once he wrote under a more tragic impulse. The scene that he described was real; during the summer of 1904, when camping in the High Sierra, the Turners stumbled into Desolation Valley, near Lake Tahoe—a vast granite basin swept clean by glaciers and dotted only by a few small lakes or clumps of trees. Mae broke down and wept hysterically; for hours Turner sat beside her to offer comfort before he could lead her away. Both were visibly shaken, for the grim sight brought memories flooding back of their two children who had died so tragically five years before. That winter he tried to capture on paper the emotions that surged through him as he looked:

> Across life's garden, where the flowers grow gay and wanton
> Where high aspiring pines raised up their heads toward God,
> Where tender blossoms dipped their faces in warm mirroring pools,
> Came the grim glacial flood and filled this cup of joy;
> Swept all things clean away—the passions and the pride of life,
> The vital glowing crimsons and the ardent greens of flower-starred
>   meads,
> Swept all things clean and graved the smiles
> To a Medusa face, of calm immobile ash-grey rock.
> And yet, deep opalescent lakes with mystic isles are set within.[18]

None but a man of sorrow, none but a sensitive human being touched with the wand of the poet, could have written those lines. Turner's cheerful, bluff exterior hid a wealth of tragedy and a deep emotionalism that the world seldom saw.

To picture him as a head-in-the-clouds aesthete, however, is to fracture the truth, for Turner was no lofty demigod addicted to Rationalism, Virtue, and Proper Conduct. Name a weakness that distinguished the Imperfect Man from the Perfect, and he had it. His persistent inability to resist temptation was one of his most appealing characteristics. Turner was a feet-of-clay mortal, a hedonist in a Victorian world, a Babylonian in Puritanland, bent on satisfying his appetite for pleasure whatever the consequences. True, he lived a very proper and very respectable life, unmarred by overindulgence save on very rare occasions, and presented a façade of righteousness to his friends. Turner could always be counted on to do the "proper" thing. But never the "right" thing.

He showed this in his appetite for food and drink. Turner was no glutton, but neither could he adhere to a diet, despite constant apprehension about his weight. On one of his several unsuccessful attempts he prepared a menu that provided such bountiful breakfasts and lunches —two slices of bread, oranges, coffee with sugar, and a doughnut in the morning; bread, vegetables, meat, a potato, salad, and pie at noon—that he was left with only 300 of his 1600 allotted calories for dinner and a bedtime snack.[19] Neither was Turner tempted to alcoholic overindulgence—he was defeated for the presidency of the Madison University Club when he ran on a prohibition ticket—but he was always ready for a stimulating cup or three on the proper occasion, despite Mae's disapproval. "The man who drinks champaign [*sic*] pretty regularly," he advised one student, "gets along surprisingly well compared with the man who doesn't."[20]

Turner was a very moderate drinker, but he was a thoroughly immoderate smoker who resisted all attempts at reform with a tenacity that was Mae's despair and his doctor's concern. Cigars, cigarettes, pipes—he used them all with passionate delight. Like Mark Twain, he found that he could stop easily when his wife's pleading became too insistent—he stopped often. And always with the best of intentions. "I should not be greatly astonished," he told Mae on one such occasion, "if I became virtuous and ceased to use the charming but wicked weed altogether. Think of the spring bonnets that would mean for you and Dorothy." That thought suggested a more appealing possibility. If he only smoked expensive cigars he could save even more money by stopping. Therefore he would indulge in very costly ones for a few months before swearing off on the right financial basis. That was the end of that attempt at reform. Turner never did succeed in abandoning tobacco for more than a few days at a time, and he smoked to his dying day with unashamed enjoyment.

His highly stretchable moral fibre decreed that he could never adhere to a budget, manage his finances sensibly, or save money regularly. Who could dislike a man who could begin his married life, as Turner did in the fall of 1889, by buying a paperbound notebook, labeling it "Expense Account, 1890," writing on the first page "In State Bank 78.65. Cash 2.00"—and then leaving the rest of the book blank? That was the story of Turner's life. He was well paid by the standards of the academic world of his day—up to $4000 a year at Wisconsin before 1910 and $8000 at Harvard by the time of his retirement—but he possessed a magician's ability to make money disappear more rapidly than it accumulated. Turner spent his life in an effort to satisfy creditors while balancing a budget, but he never did succeed.

Much of their income went for living expenses, for the Turners believed that life should be enjoyed, not endured. Their homes were comfortable, if not extravagant. Almost always the household ménage included one maid, and often two; sometimes a nurse or cook was added, or a secretary to shame Turner into the writing that he abhorred. At intervals between maids they seldom ate at home, for Mae preferred restaurants to mastering the mysteries of cooking, even when they could scarcely afford such a luxury. Their dinner parties, although infrequent, were usually elaborate. On one occasion seven guests were served soup, a fish course of smelts in tartar sauce, roast chicken with chestnut dressing, beans, browned potatoes, hot rolls, a lettuce and tomato salad, cheese with wafers, a bombe, walnut cake, nuts and candies. On another, Mae's instructions to the serving maids suggested unusual gastronomic delights—and the cultural barbarism inflicted on civilization by Prohibition:

I

Clear soup with egg balls. Crouton sticks. Pass olives.

II

Fillet flounder—sauce tartar. Graham sandwiches. Cucumber
and tomato in French dressing. Pour White Rock.

III

Fillet beef—mushroom sauce. Spinach. Potatoes, currant
jelly. Warm rolls. Pour orange soda.

IV

Lettuce and cellery [*sic*] salad in French dressing
Cheese straws.

V

Ice cream—chocolate cake. Sponge cakes. Coffee after.[21]

That was a lavish dinner to be served by the wife of a professor, even of
a professor at Harvard, and helps explain why Turner spent a good
many hours struggling to keep income and outgo on an even balance.

His problem was confounded by the utter inability of both Turners
to resist the buying urge. His extravagances were fishing apparatus and
books, the latter especially; thousands upon thousands of volumes filled
the Turner homes from basement to attic, many of them multivolume
files of magazines, newspapers, and government documents.[22] His book-
ish tastes were matched by Mae's love of fine clothes—a passion that her
husband thoroughly approved, save at bill-paying time. A gown made to
order for $71.50, a hat for $23.25, another for 25.50, a pair of shoes for
$14.40, a coat for $79.50—costly items for a family with an income of
slightly more than $5000. Each month the bills that poured in from
Boston's department stores threatened to exhaust the bank account completely—and sometimes did: $68.85 due at Stearns, $92.95 at Filene's,
$151.41 at S. S. Pierce's gourmet grocery store.[23] Turner's occasional
attempts to bring the family's expenditures into line were futile, for
every budget that he devised was so unrealistic that it was soon
discarded.

Instead, he was doomed to a constant flirtation with near-bankruptcy.
On many an occasion he paid only half his bills each month, alternating
creditors to keep all more or less satisfied. Even this devious device was
insufficient, and Turner was regularly forced to borrow to pay his
bills—a $200 loan for one month, $1500 for nine more, $700 from the
bank to tide them over until payday—always in the hope of better times

ahead. His letters to Mae when on one of his necessary trips contained regular warnings in oft-used phrases: "Remember the bank account is low," "Ascertain balance if you draw checks," or "Give me a margin of safety if you conveniently can. . . . I am down to about $40."[24] Turner waged his battle with the bills through most of his lifetime, yet he was far too human to change his ways.

He was also human enough to live in a constant state of rebellion against the tension-laden urban life of twentieth-century America. For Turner, life began when he fled civilization; everything about him, from the tweedy clothes that he affected to his tales of the four-pound trout that got away, stamped him as an outdoorsman who could find happiness only in field and stream. So he was, and by necessity, for Turner was both physically and emotionally incapable of living long amidst the bustle of the city. Emotionally, the backwoods offered a haven from a modern industrial society that he neither liked nor understood. "I sometimes am in doubt about 'civilization,'" he once confessed. "Perhaps that is because I like to go trout fishing."[25] Physically, Turner required wilderness life as a tonic to rejuvenate a jaded system worn by the pressures of teaching and writing. Only a few months of either and his whole nature rebelled. Those who knew him best recognized the symptoms—a nervous irritability, a far-away look in his eyes —that meant he *must* find solace in the forest or risk serious disorders. When he wrote, as he once did, that he was "tired of thinking and should like to be a cabbage for a century or two," Turner was not succumbing to indolence.[26] His body and spirit could not endure without periodic refurbishing by the wilderness.

Turner's instincts told him when escape into the forest was necessary; his reason convinced him that the forest should contain a well-stocked trout stream to do the greatest good. He had been, since his earliest youth, a fanatical fisherman who would (as he once said) rather catch three trout on a single leader than study American history—and that, to Turner, was the ultimate comparison. Even as a young man he could write his fiancée that "of all the beautiful things a gleaming, gold and crimson trout throwing himself out of water after a fly is the most beautiful"—then remembered to whom he was writing and added, "almost."[27] As a mature scholar he saved his greatest scorn not for the critics of his theories, but for those misguided souls who thought that the object of fishing was to catch a fish; "it's the getting him with the right thrill—otherwise why not turn Prussian and dynamite him, or kill him with laughing gas, or dam up the brook and shovel him out?"[28] Turner's idea of Heaven, he once confessed, was a good fishing camp in some remote part of Paradise where the work of creation was not too far advanced.[29]

So long as he taught at Wisconsin, escape was easy, for his Old Town canoe was stored on the porch of his Frances Street home, Lake Mendota was at his doorstep, and the familiar streams around Portage were not too distant. But Harvard and Cambridge offered a greater challenge. His canoe went with him (he placed it first, and his Corona typewriter last, on a list of his insured possessions—a fair indication of his scale of values), but the Charles River was a sad substitute for Lake Mendota. Turner did his best. During the summer he slept in a tent on the back porch of his Brattle Street house, "lulled by the lapping of the automobiles and the murmer of the neighbor's maids, and awakened in the early morning by the tinkle of the milkman's bottles."[30] "It seems like a vacation from about 11 P.M. to 7 A.M.," he wrote wistfully.[31] Winters were made endurable by long hours spent discussing the art of dry fly casting with fellow fanatics at the Boston Fishing Club, or reading a new volume on *American Trout Stream Insects*, or, on a mild day, journeying a few miles to make a few casts in a brook that *might* hide a few trout, but never did. Once, when the first hint of spring was in the air, he walked all the way to the Boston aquarium to gaze at a tank of live trout. "I bought a book on dry fly fishing," he reported on a warm March day in 1915, "and the woods and lakes all came back like a healing vision. . . . But I utterly forgot that I was to preside over a meeting of the Colonial Society of Massachusetts."[32] Of all the presents received on his fifty-fifth birthday, the most treasured was a handkerchief from his daughter embroidered with a fishhook monogram. Any reminder of a trout stream was food for Turner's soul.

Summers made life endurable, whether spent in the Rockies or Sierras after a stint of teaching in the West to pay expenses, or at his summer home in the Maine woods. Usually a packsack of notes went with him to Hancock Point, and he always took along a stern ambition to make progress on the lagging book, but his good resolutions faded once he scented a balsam forest or glimpsed a woodland stream. "No, your paper didn't go astray," he confessed to a student whose thesis waited reading. "I did. I wandered off into lobster harbors, and stray islands, and thrush-haunted woods, and rose-lined lanes, and lost myself in the icy waters of the Maine coast, and strayed into the back yard and chopped wood."³³ Turner loved it all—the riotous banks of firewood and meadow rue, the groves of birch and pine, the melodious chant of the hermit thrush at evening. He delighted in defying his doctor's orders by swimming in the frigid waters of the North Atlantic, in digging clams, in chatting endlessly with the down east folk who made him one of themselves. This was Heaven; the classroom was a purgatory to be endured until the next summer. "Opening up Harvard has been something of a job," he wrote one autumn, "and a rather sharp contrast with life by the Hancock Point tides watching time's ceaseless progress to eternity without caring how fast he progged."³⁴ Turner, like the frontiersmen he studied, could not resist when nature beckoned. His human frailties, no less than his historical theories, endeared him to his generation.

If Turner's love affair with the wilderness stamped him as a spiritual son of the pioneers, so did his views of society and government. Within him were embodied the best—and worst—features of the Jackson Man. He was, to his credit, utterly democratic socially and politically, but he was also inclined toward a myopic nationalism that blinded him to the virtues of other peoples, highly individualistic in an age when the industrial-urban complex outmoded individualism, and prejudiced toward minorities who threatened the traditional "Americanism" that he venerated. All of these traits stemmed from Turner's inherent distrust of the factory and city, both of which threatened the rural values that he deemed essential to the welfare of the Republic. Enemies of those pioneer values were his enemies, whether immigrants threatening established institutions, agrarian radicals endangering the private enterprise system, or reformers preaching the need of a government strong enough to control the marketplace. Turner was as inconsistent in his views as the frontiersmen he emulated; he vacillated between a conviction that the individual should be unrestrained and a belief that government should act forcibly to guard the welfare of the many. Yet he was consistently conservative, living proof of his own thesis that the westerner might favor innovation and democracy, but was basically dedicated to maintaining the status quo.

His love of the United States and of his own Midwest was unshakable. Turner was a fair example of the Jackson Man in his staunch patriotism, his passionate faith in the nation and its freedoms. This did not mean that he was a flag-waving super-patriot; at one time he refused to do a book that would have appeared in a "100% series," and never did he associate himself with the head-in-the-sand isolationists who sought to protect Americans from all contact with other countries. Instead, Turner, as one of his French friends observed, had tried so hard to understand and explain his native land that he had reached a plane of moral nobility somewhat higher than that of his fellow men.[35] With understanding went respect, for the nation and for the midwestern heartland that he believed to epitomize national values. In the Midwest Turner found the free-and-easy social intercourse, the willingness to accept newcomers at face value instead of on the basis of ancestral reputation, that he associated with America's greatness. Easterners were never quite to be trusted; "there is," he wrote, "a love of the whimsical, of the clever thrust, the ironic and cynical, in your unadulterated Boston Yankee" that was almost un-American.[36] Pioneer values, exaggerated though they might be in the West, made that region the symbol of all that was best about the United States.

And of much that was worst, for when Turner borrowed western idealism as the basis of his political philosophy he borrowed prejudice and bigotry as well. Just as the Jackson Man was stirred to nativistic outbursts against the Germans and Irish flooding America's shores in the early nineteenth century, so Turner saw the New Immigrants of the late nineteenth and early twentieth centuries as a menace to traditional values and institutions. They would, he feared, upset the balance between capital and labor that free land had sustained, presaging a destructive class war. In the same way, minority groups of alien race or color must be restrained lest they alter the dominant "American" social order. Turner gave little heed to what he would have called the "Negro Problem," but twice he was asked whether the Fifteenth Amendment's guarantee of the franchise to all was wise, and twice he answered that it was not.[37] His judgment was partly based on his belief that political rights should be granted by state and local governments rather than national, but lurking in the back of his mind was a fear that Negroes and aliens were not quite equal to Yankees.

Turner also shared the prejudices of his day in his attitude toward Jews, bolstered, in his case, by a frontier-like distrust of all aliens whose life-patterns differed from what he considered the norm. His first encounter with their Old World culture came in 1887, when he visited the East and wandered into the Boston ghetto. The very strangeness of the sight was shocking—a street "filled with big Jew men—long bearded and carrying a staff as you see in a picture, and with Jew youths and maidens—some of the latter pretty—as you sometimes see a lily in the green muddy slime."[38] There spoke rural America, with all its prejudices. It spoke again when Turner assured his fiancée that "however you shatter the Jewish jar, the scent of the roses of Israel will cling to it still, and socially I can't say that I ever found one I could be contented with."[39] These were harsh words, but they came from a young man who reflected the bigotry of the times as much as his own prejudice. Certainly he moved a notch or two toward greater tolerance in his later years; in 1922 he disapproved President Lowell's "rather drastic treatment" of the subject when the Harvard faculty debated means of limiting the university's Jewish population, and a few years later he applauded a former student for resigning from the Daughters of the American Revolution to protest that society's anti-Negro bias.[40] Yet his prejudices remained; he might disapprove President Lowell's anti-Semitism, but he also disliked the prospect "of Harvard a New Jerusalem and Boston already a New Cork." "Rejoice in your Maine Yankee neighbors," he wrote his wife at Hancock Point.[41]

Turner's attitude toward minorities was unfortunately consistent, but such could not be said of his political beliefs, which vacillated considerably during the late nineteenth and early twentieth century. Two problems underlay this vacillation. One was his inherited conservatism. Reared in a family that was unimpeachably Republican politically, Turner as a youth found himself torn between the dictates of his heritage and the instincts of a basically liberal young man. The other was the need to fit the pioneer values that he so much admired to the needs of an industrial-urban society. How could the individualism of the frontier—the right of every man to help himself to nature's bounties—be reconciled with the democracy so venerated in the West, now that those bounties were no longer abundant? If the individualistic rights of the few were maintained, the nation's productive resources would be monopolized by industry to the disadvantage of the many; if the welfare of the people was given first priority, individualism must be circumscribed. Which of these frontier values must be sacrificed?

That was Turner's dilemma, and in his effort to solve it he shifted his party allegiance to conform to the ideal that seemed most essential at the time.

His first political experiences were governed more by tradition than reason. He was reared in a household where Republican politics bulked large in the dinner-table conversation, where Republican funds helped pay the grocery bill, and where Satan's disciples—the Democrats—were equated with treason and anarchy. Turner learned his lessons so well that as a senior at the University of Wisconsin he helped form a Young Men's Marching Club to support James G. Blaine in the election of 1884, addressed its members on the virtues of Republicanism, and presumably cast his first ballot against Grover Cleveland. His graduate training changed that; Turner was in full rebellion against parental tradition by 1888, when he voted the Democratic ticket, but his deflection from orthodoxy was brief. During the 1890s alarm over the strident demands of trade unionists and Populists brought his basic conservatism to the fore. In his eyes, the financial chaos threatened by free silver imperiled traditional values no less than the "socialistic" programs of the Pullman strikers or Coxey's Army did. When Turner wrote, as he did in his 1893 essay, that "a primitive society can hardly be expected to show the intelligent appreciation of the complexity of business interests in a developed society" he was offering a text for the times, no less than a judgment on the past. He voted for William McKinley in 1896 —and probably in 1900—as a protest against the monetary "heresies" of the Democrats, and not as an endorsement of conservative Republicanism.[42]

His stay in the anti-Democratic camp was brief, for by the turn of the century a more dangerous enemy threatened frontier values. Turner saw trusts and corporations, symbolized by the giant United States Steel Corporation, which was formed in 1901, as more menacing to democracy and individualism than the Populists were. With this awakening, his opinion of agrarian reformers underwent a remarkable transformation. They became not dangerous agitators, but heralds of an overdue social revolution that would win economic equality for all people; tubthumpers for the Omaha Platform who had seemed dangerously radical in 1892 were now legatees of the Levellers who rose with Cromwell against Stuart tyranny and of the frontier farmers who spoke for liberty in 1776.[43] The business corporation not only posed a greater danger to the individual's freedom of decision than had the agrarians, but threatened to divide the nation into haves and have-nots by wiping out the middle class, where frontier values were best preserved. Turner saw the outcome of unrestrained corporate growth to be a world torn between trust magnates on the one hand and socialist agitators on the other. Neither group was to his taste. "The socialism regime in the hands of its present friends," he wrote a friend, "would be somewhat irksome, and while J. P. Morgan and Carnegie and Rockefeller might make a gilded cage for learning and art, it would be a cage after all."[44] Somewhere between the two extremes lay the course the nation should follow.

Turner found the ideal navigator in Theodore Roosevelt; Roosevelt and his insurgent friends might reap a whirlwind but a worse whirlwind would grow from a Hanna-McKinley planting.[45] Yet even now he could not embrace the President's goals completely, for he realized that trust-busting ran counter to the trends of history and economic efficiency. Turner's political philosophy during the Progressive era was the solution offered by his good friend Charles R. Van Hise, in his influential volume, *Concentration and Control: A Solution to the Trust Problem in the United States*, published in 1911. Regulation, not fragmentation, was Van Hise's plan; he would allow the large corporation to exist, but only under federal controls, thus achieving the economies of large-scale production while protecting the worker and consumer. Embracing such a platform meant a major shift in Turner's thinking. In doing so he was sacrificing the "rugged individualism" of the frontier for the welfare of the consuming and working masses. Popular democracy was given precedence over the right of the individual to use natural resources and laborers as he wished. Turner could vote for Theodore Roosevelt in 1904 and William Jennings Bryan in 1908 with a clear conscience, confident that he was acting in the national good, even though one of his treasured frontier traits had been sacrificed.[46]

This decision placed him squarely in the Democratic camp, for during the next years the Republican party fell increasingly into the hands of the business-oriented conservative wing led by William Howard Taft. Turner did waver during the election of 1912, a contest that fascinated him with its sectional implications. Theodore Roosevelt was nominated first by the Republican Insurgents, and Turner was delighted; as a staunch admirer of the former President and of Robert M. La Follette, his principal supporter, he would cast his ballot for Roosevelt without a second thought. So ardent was Turner's enthusiasm that he shed the cloak of political anonymity that he had always worn on the campus and spoke before the Harvard La Follette Club.[47] When Woodrow Wilson entered the race, however, Turner was less sure. He was pleased with the prospect of a three-way battle—"a prehistoric conflict," he called it, between a mastodon, a bull moose, and a Democratic donkey in a scholar's skin—but now he had to decide between two good friends, both of whom he greatly admired.[48] For a time he debated voting for both Wilson and Roosevelt, with a favorable mention of La Follette, so sympathetic was he to all of their views.[49] Instead, he took up his pen to draw a balance sheet, weighing the merits and demerits of each. His appraisal displayed both his skill as a political analyst and his faith in frontier values.

Taft he eliminated immediately; the election of that paragon of conservative Republicanism would mean control of the economy by the trusts, "tempered by the danger of revolution." As for Wilson, Turner liked him personally but disapproved of his faith in local governments and his willingness to leave trust control to the states. He was fearful, too, that Wilson's political philosophy was outmoded, and he was afraid that the southern Democrats who would ascend to power with him would be so prejudiced by their experiences with slavery and Negroes that they would not respond properly to humanitarian demands for bettering the lot of workers. On the other hand, Theodore Roosevelt's "Square Deal" suggested some sort of "deal" with the captains of industry, while the high tariffs advocated by many of his supporters would imperil the economy.[50] "I shall vote against Taft and Prosperity," Turner told his wife a few weeks before the election, "but aside from voting the Mass[achusetts] state progressive ticket, and the democratic congressional ticket, I'm still undecided."[51] Not until November 2 did he make up his mind, and then because he convinced himself that any Republican victory—even of Republican Insurgents—would mean higher tariffs. Turner voted for Woodrow Wilson and the state Progressive party that year, and was delighted when his candidate entered the White House.

Wilson's progressive domestic program and the lofty idealism that dictated his foreign policy won Turner's heart completely and decided his votes not only during the dying years of Progressivism, but well into the 1920s. He voted a straight Democratic ticket in 1916 for the first time in his life, and in 1920 he favored James M. Cox when party affiliation, affection for the martyred Woodrow Wilson, and a firm belief that Warren G. Harding would ruin the nation dictated his choice. Harding, particularly, stirred Turner's resentment; he would not, he told his daughter, vote for a marionette until he knew who pulled the strings.[52] By 1924 the political apathy that deadened the nation during the "Era of Normalcy" had dampened Turner's enthusiasm for reform. So slight was his faith in any of the candidates in 1924 (including Robert M. La Follette, who ran as a Progressive) that for a time he thought of voting "the straight IWW ticket"—if, that is, he could find anything straight about it—but in the end habit and a somewhat more liberal Democratic platform won his support for John W. Davis.[53] Gone now from letters to friends were spirited discussions of candidates and issues; they were filled instead with delighted comments on the manner in which this congressional vote or that confirmed his views on sectionalism. "The congressional margin is close enough," he gloated after the elections of 1926, "to furnish new material for my (posthumous) magnum opus on Sectionalism in American Politics."[54] Turner, like the nation, had been lulled into indifference by the mediocrities who misgoverned the country during the 1920s.

In this mood his political philosophy underwent a complete about-face. Throughout the Progressive era, whenever he debated which of the frontier values that he treasured—individualism or democracy—must be sacrificed in an industrial world, he had decided that the individual's right to exploitation must be restricted for the benefit of society as a whole—that the ideal of individualism must be subordinated to the ideal of democracy. Now, with prosperity calling the tune, with the masses willing to surrender control to hack politicians who danced on the strings pulled by Big Business, with the democratic ideal buried by popular indifference, such a decision was less easy to maintain. Was democracy the final goal? Or should the industrial barons who seemed able to put two chickens in every pot and two cars in every garage be given a free hand to do as they pleased? Should the frontier goal of individualism take precedence over the pioneer ideal of democracy?

Turner's answer was governed partly by the rise of a new hero who seemed to personify the best of the frontier values that he held so dear. Herbert Hoover had been one of his favorites since the days of the Belgium Relief Program after World War I; Turner deeply admired Hoover's precise mind, his skill as an executive, and his honest expression of principles. That admiration deepened when Hoover responded to a gift of *The Frontier in American History* (a book that he read "with very deep interest") by sending Turner a copy of his own little volume, *American Individualism.*[55] Here was a message that the new Turner could appreciate. "It is," he assured the author, "the platform on which all genuine Americans can stand, a noble statement of the fruits of our past and the promise of our future."[56] Turner was a complete Hoover convert now; with the approach of the election of 1928 he saw his new friend as "a promising sign in the heavens" who would have his vote should the Republicans have the good sense to nominate him.[57]

Turner did cast his ballot for Hoover that year, and when he did so he climaxed the completion of a full cycle in his political thinking. Hoover spoke, and spoke eloquently, for the unrestrained individualism of the frontier past, an individualism free of all governmental interference, an individualism based on faith in the working of natural economic laws under complete freedom in the marketplace. The Turner who embraced these views was not the Turner who applauded the "New Nationalism" of Theodore Roosevelt and the "New Freedom" of Woodrow Wilson, or who built his political edifice on Charles R. Van Hise's platform of governmental control of Big Business. He had realized that his two pioneer ideals—of the economic democracy preached by the Progressives and the rugged individualism favored by Hoover—were irreconcilable in a post-frontier world. So long as the democratic ideal seemed obtainable, as it did during the Progressive era, he could cast his lot with reform, but the negative do-nothingism of the 1920s dimmed his hopes and elevated individualism above democracy in his scale of values. Turner, like the frontiersmen he emulated, made inconsistency a virtue; he was ready, as they had been, to choose the theory that seemed best fitted to the needs of the moment.

One might speculate that if Turner had lived into the 1930s the spirit of reform generated by the New Deal would have rekindled his faith in democracy and reversed his political thinking once more. Perhaps, but probably not, for he could neither have understood nor enjoyed the era that was dawning as he went to his grave. In the largest sense, the world of Frederick Jackson Turner died with him. He knew, and loved, a land where a moving frontier altered men and institutions as it swept westward, where sectional conflicts helped shape congressional legislation and altered the political profile. That nation died when the Great Depression brought into focus the giant social upheaval that had been shaping for a generation. The new America that emerged was adjusted to a closed-space existence, its governmental philosophy was built on the belief that men must be protected from corporate exploitation now that escape to the West was no longer possible, its political processes were reconstructed on the basis of the nationalizing forces that healed sectional divisions. Turner would have felt a stranger in that post-depression world. When he died in 1932, the curtain was already falling on the America that he loved so deeply.

XVIII

The Persistence of a Theory:
the Frontier and Sectional
Hypotheses

REDERICK JACKSON TURNER was known during his lifetime, and has been known since, primarily as the progenitor of two ideas, one holding that the frontiering experience helped shape the character of the American people and their institutions, the other that sectional conflicts underlay much of the political decision-making of the nineteenth century. Turner himself strongly resented this image. His concern was with the broad panorama of the nation's history, and his emphasis on frontier and section was only a means of completing the total picture as seen by historians. "It is all one country, acting and reacting," he wrote at one time, "and it is the scholar's duty to see it nationally as well as sectionally."[1] He, more than most men of his day, recognized that the pageant of the past was understandable only through the interrelation of human ideals, economic interests, and cultural ambitions, and that all were so intertwined as to be inseparable. But the fact remains that he did spend most of his lifetime analyzing frontier and sectional phenomena, and that his contemporaries and successors equated him with those interests.

Were those two theories sufficiently meritorious to justify the acclaim they won Turner during his lifetime and the criticism they have engendered since? Certainly no historian rivaled his impact on the profession during the 1910s and 1920s. Americanists almost to a man set out to rewrite the history of the United States within Turnerian guidelines; they discovered that western forces underlay the Revolution, touched off the War of 1812 and the Mexican War, shaped the nature of the

Kansas-Nebraska Act, and brought the slavery issue to a bloody climax in Civil War. The *Mississippi Valley Historical Review*, established in 1907, published so many articles exploring frontier themes that it might better have been named the *Journal of Frontier History*. Southern historians, long absorbed in constitutional history, awakened to the fact that geographic forces were determinant and poured forth books and articles describing economic groupings in the plantation South, exploring conflicts between coast and interior, and analyzing conflict and change in terms of hostility to the planter class. Textbook writers leaped on the van; every text published between 1926 and 1930 made the frontier the focal point of American history, and of the twenty-four most widely used, sixteen cited Turner by name and nineteen accepted the principle of geographic determinism as unassailable.[2] When the *History Teacher's Magazine* published an article on "How to Teach the History of the West in American History" in 1916, the author felt no need to plead his cause and devoted himself entirely to techniques.[3]

Americanists succumbed most completely, but other historians, and men in other disciplines, were not far behind. Medievalists, led by James Westfall Thompson of the University of Chicago, rewrote the story of the Middle Ages in Turnerian language, tracing the expansion of Germany eastward over Slavonic lands in the twelfth and thirteenth centuries, glorifying free land as the causal force underlying migrations, and isolating the same stages of social evolution discernible in the American West. His purpose, Thompson told Turner, was "to interpret the history of the frontier of medieval Germany somewhat as you have interpreted that of the United States"; he succeeded so remarkably that one of his fellow medievalists cried out in protest in 1923 that "while American history is our first business, it is not our sole business."[4] Economists succumbed to the contagion; John R. Commons explained the principal characteristics of the nation's labor movements as products of the frontier, while Selig Perlman built his whole economic theory on the premise that free land produced a working class that was job-conscious rather than class-conscious. Sociologists sprinkled their books with Turner's theories and reproduced his essays in their collections of readings. "I should," wrote Franklin H. Giddings in 1928, "find it hard to think of a scholar who has in my judgment made more significant contributions to the study of those processes of mass activity and organization which go back to frontier environment and experiences."[5] Students of American literature, rebelling against the genteel traditions of their craft, responded with irrational enthusiasm when Norman Foerster in 1926 urged them to recognize the "frontier spirit" as a determinative force in their studies, and they set to work on such books as *The Literature of the Middle Western Frontier*, *The Rediscovery of the Frontier*, and *The Frontier in American Literature*.[6] The whole scholarly world was at Turner's feet by the close of the 1920s.

Nor was the scholarly world alone. Increasingly, the frontier and sectional theories touched the public pulse, the latter especially lending itself to the needs of policy-makers. Publicists and senators praised Turner's views or sought his advice; Walter Lippmann and Charles Merz borrowed his ideas for their widely publicized comments, Newton D. Baker found them essential in the conflict over the St. Lawrence Seaway, Senator Arthur Capper urged them on his constituents, Felix Frankfurter testified to their usefulness even before he ascended to the Supreme Court, and newspapers from *The New York Times* to the *Los Angeles Times* parroted his words in their editorials, approvingly or disapprovingly as their prejudices dictated.[7] When Philip La Follette was inaugurated as Wisconsin's governor in 1931, his inaugural address praised Turner, summarized his views, and concluded that, with the passing of the frontier, "we must find our freedom and make our opportunity through wise and courageous readjustments of the political and economic order of State and Nation to the changed needs and changed conditions of our time."[8] Like it or not (and he liked it a great deal), Turner was a public figure by the time of his death, and his theories the stock-in-trade of politicians and public opinion makers throughout the land.

They made their most impressive impact during the debate over Franklin D. Roosevelt's New Deal. Proponents found them a perfect weapon; so long as free lands existed, laissez faire in government and rugged individualism in business could shape national policy, but with escape to the frontier impossible, the federal government had to provide the security and opportunity that had been found in the West. "Our last frontier has long since been reached," Roosevelt told a Commonwealth Club audience in 1932. "There is no safety valve in the form of a Western Prairie. . . . Our task now is not discovery or exploitation of natural resources. . . . It is the less dramatic business of administering resources and plants already in hand . . . of distributing wealth and products equitably."[9] Opponents of the New Deal found the frontier hypothesis as useful as its proponents did. Governmental meddling in the marketplace, they argued, would undermine the frontier-bred individualism and self-reliance that was the nation's principal strength. Regimentation was no substitute for expansion. The force and sinew of the United States could be preserved only by perpetuating the freedoms of pioneer days.[10] Probably most who debated the merits of New Dealism had never heard of Turner, but his theories were so deeply planted in the public mind that they could be used by all.

Such was their impact, too, on statesmen who argued the course of America's foreign policy. Since the turn of the century, imperialists and anti-imperialists had bent the frontier thesis to their own purposes; the passing of free lands at home, said the former, required the acquisition of new territories and new markets abroad to satisfy the expansionist urge and the needs of the business community; overseas colonies, argued the latter, would undermine the democratic ideals bred of pioneering and rob the Americans of their treasured freedoms. This conflict was updated when President Franklin D. Roosevelt voiced the view that the nation's frontier was the world and urged the American people to join in ending nineteenth-century colonialism everywhere. By the 1930s, Turner's frontier could be used as a basis for a new manifest destiny of the United States beyond the seas.[11]

All of this recognition—by fellow historians, by patrons of other disciplines, by politicians and statesmen—was balm to Turner's soul during his last years. "One of the major satisfactions of Professor Turner's life," wrote his secretary at that time, "must have been the spontaneous evidences of profound appreciation of him . . . that came in a veritable flood during the years of his association with the Huntington Library."[12] Yet the adulation was not without its dangers, for it courted an inevitable reaction. Turner had not, as he freely admitted, advanced an infallible formula for interpreting American history; he had simply proposed an untested hypothesis, to be accepted or rejected after proper research. When a bibliographer suggested listing his 1893 essay as a "Research Paper," he objected, pointing out that "it was really an attempt at interpretation, rather than a piece of formal research."[13] Unfortunately, few of his disciples exercised such caution. To the Turnerian generation the frontier thesis was no hypothesis, but Holy Writ —the Bible and the Declaration of Independence and the Constitution rolled into one—to be literally expounded as Divine Truth.

Nor did Turner help his cause by his own tendency to advance untested generalizations. These appeared largely in the many articles and lectures forced upon him during his prime years by editors and college administrators who demanded that he write and speak about the frontier at a time when his own research was focused on the section. Because Turner had nothing new to say, he was inclined to substitute extravagant rhetoric for investigation, poetic imagery for facts, and elaborate metaphors for soundly based theories. In much of his later writing and speaking he *assumed* that pioneers acted in a certain way, even though he had no proof that they did so. These assumptions, often false, were recorded as established facts, sanctified by his approval.

One example will show how Turner helped dig his own grave. In October 1913, he agreed to give the commencement address at the University of Washington the following June on "The West and American Ideals"—a title that permitted wide-ranging generalizations. Turner hoped to prepare his remarks that winter, but, as usual, he procrastinated, and by spring not a line had been written. The avalanche of end-of-the-year bluebooks and doctoral dissertations, a move from his Brattle Street home to 7 Phillips Place, and preparations for his daughter's marriage doomed all hope of progress before he started west on June 4. There was still a chance during the week scheduled in Madison, but friends and a round of parties decreed that work be forgotten. The Turners reached Seattle on June 15 or 16 with his address still untouched—and commencement only a day or two away. To make matters worse, he had mislaid the package of notes on which it was to be built.[14]

That commencement address, hastily written in a hotel room, was to embarrass Turner when he was alive and give fuel to his critics after his death. Into it he crowded many of the unproven clichés of frontier history. The pioneer "knew not where he was going but he was on his way, cheerful, optimistic, busy and buoyant." He was "an opportunist rather than a dealer in general ideas," but blessed with "a courageous determination to break new paths." American democracy "was born of no theorist's dream; it was not carried in the *Sarah Constant* to Virginia, nor in the *Mayflower* to Plymouth. It came out of the

American forest, and it gained new strength each time it touched a new frontier." In that one inadequately prepared address Turner provided his future critics with enough unsubstantiated generalizations to keep them busy for years.

To his credit, it must be said that he was far from happy with his performance. "I am," he confessed two days later, "still moving by reflex action after my poor commencement address," adding that he felt like a man who relaxed in the electric chair after the first shock. His one solace was that crying babies in the audience of 2500 drowned out most of his words. "Always," he advised a friend, "take along a supply of babies when you preach."[15] These bantering words hid genuine humiliation. At first he refused to allow his paper to be published —"it was written to be spoken," he explained—but when the editor of the *Washington Historical Quarterly* persisted he finally succumbed. Only when he saw his words in print did he realize how seriously he had tortured the truth. His first impulse was to pull out his red pencil to correct factual errors, add marginal qualifications, and scrawl beside one of the most flamboyant statements "TOO STRONG."[16] Not all of Turner's latter-day essays on the frontier were laden with such distortions—his studies of New England, the Old West, and the Midwest were admirably structured on the basis of solid research—but he was far too ready to mouth unsustainable extravagances. He, no less than his overzealous disciples, paved the way for the inevitable reaction against the man and his theories that blossomed during the 1930s.

The Great Depression sparked that assault. In a world beset by a bewildering economic cataclysm, historians began to question the study of a remote agrarian past that bore little relation to the pressing problems of the present. In a world where governmental planning was essential to salvation, a theory that preached the virtues of individualism seemed dangerously outdated. In a world that could be saved from totalitarianism only by international cooperation, the nationalism glorified by Turner appeared more a menace than a blessing. Did a thesis that was so grossly inadequate to the modern day have any validity for the past? Had the United States ever been the land that it seemed to Turner, or had industry and urbanization and immigration and class conflict played a major role that his teachings obscured? The time was ripe for a complete reorientation of historical studies, with the goal now comprehension of the urban-industrial complex that had gone askew in 1929. This was the mood of American historians by the mid-1930s, but it had been building toward its climax for a decade. As early as 1925 Turner himself predicted that the pessimistic reaction against World War I would generate a sympathetic reaction against pioneer ideals and the rural past, with a new focus on the European experience and the class struggle. "There seems likely to be," he prophesied, "an urban reinterpretation of our history."[17] So there was, and he was its sacrificial lamb.

Fortunately for Turner, death spared him the bulk of the criticism directed against him, but he did live to read the work of two of his attackers. In 1925, John A. Almack, a professor of education at Stanford University, led the way with a discursive article on "The Shibboleth of the Frontier" in *The Historical Outlook*. Turner's theory, Almack argued, combined diluted Marxism and geographic determinism; it was "simply not in accord with the facts" when it preached that the best of the American tradition stemmed from the frontier. Instead, pioneering slowed cultural progress, which was generated instead in factories and cities. Turner's friends hurried to assure him that his critic was an uninformed educationalist who had set up a straw man to knock it down—a man so eager to be a second David that he had constructed a Goliath to fit his stone.[18] Yet Turner was deeply hurt, not at the attack, but because his own essays were subject to such misinterpretation. He held no brief for the frontier hypothesis as sacrosanct and unalterable, and expected it to be criticized. "But the job could have been better done. The idea that I was attributing all that was good in American civilization to the frontier and the backwoodsman in his cabin and that a statistical demonstration that education and ability existed in the east was needed by a Stanford man gives me pain as it shows me how ineffective my mode of statement must be."[19] But he would not reply; those who knew his essays would realize that Almack was tilting at windmills, and those who did not might be curious enough to read them and learn the truth.

He was cut even more deeply by a second criticism, this an article by Benjamin F. Wright, Jr., of Harvard's political science faculty, on "American Democracy and the Frontier," which was printed in the *Yale Review* late in 1930. Aiming his guns at Turner's statement that American democracy originated in the forests of the New World, and ignoring the fact that he had been speaking only of *American* democratic theory and practice, Wright paraded statistics and arguments to demonstrate that democracy had emerged in the Old World and had generally moved from east to west, rather than vice versa. Once more Turner's friends leaped to his support, and once more he assured them that his essays had been misread—"I think Mr. Wright fails to realize that what I was dealing with was, in the first place, the *American* character of democracy as compared with that of Europe or of European philosophers; and that, secondly, whatever may be said regarding the writings and activity of coastal men in promoting it, they had as a background the American western experience and were influenced thereby"—but that he had no intention of replying. If Wright was correct in his strictures, a good many able men had been misled and were capable of taking up the cudgels in Turner's behalf.[20] Besides criticism was healthy, and there was sure to be more of it.

There was more, in mounting crescendo over the next two decades. Critics made their assult on three fronts: they questioned Turner's *statement* of the frontier hypothesis and damned him for inexact usage and failure to define his terms; they challenged a methodology that failed to explain *how* pioneering altered the American character; and they criticized his judgment in overstressing the frontier as a moulding influence, rather than emphasizing eastern-based forces such as capital accumulation, the expansion of domestic and foreign markets, industrialization, urbanization, and class conflicts.[21] The validity of these criticisms calls into question the whole significance of Frederick Jackson Turner in American historiography. Was he as grossly in error as his attackers charged, and, if so, does he deserve the fame accorded him by his contemporaries and later generations? Turner could not answer directly, but he left an abundance of evidence in his letters and unpublished writings to show that his rebuttals would have been generally effective. To reconstruct his replies is to recognize that the frontier thesis, as he understood it, was by no means error-proof, but that it was far less vulnerable than his assailants realized.

True, he did not offer the precise definition of terms that a later generation of scientific historians demanded; Turner defined the "frontier" in his published essays as everything from "the hither edge of free land" to a "graphic line which records the expansive energies of the people behind it." Twice he was forced to grapple with the problem—once in 1894, when he prepared an article on the subject for *Johnson's Universal Encyclopedia*, and again in 1914, when he accepted a similar assignment from the *Cyclopedia of American Government*. Neither was completely satisfactory. That of 1894 was particularly unsuccessful: "those outlying regions which at different stages of the country's development have been but imperfectly settled, and have constituted the meeting-ground between savagery and civilization." His second attempt, made twenty years later, was only a slight improvement: "the temporary boundary of an expanding society at the edge of substantially free lands . . . that zone of settlement nearest the wilderness, wherein society and government are loosely or incompletely organized." Turner had yet to devise a satisfactory definition. "I have never," he admitted in 1926, "published an adequate discussion of this phase of the 'frontier,' with the result that some readers of my first essay seem to think that I imagined all that is significant in American life as having been born on the extreme edge of things."[22]

He did not think that, of course, and increasingly in his later years he groped toward a definition that would convey his true meaning. As he did so, he stressed more and more the concept of a broad, westward-moving zone, rather than a line, a belt in which the stages of civilization were being reenacted from primitive to complex forms. "A zone of population extending between civilization and wilderness," was Turner's description to a Harvard class; a few years later the frontier had become in his mind "a migratory section, rather a stage of society than an area."[23] These definitions made good sense, particularly because they stressed two points on which Turner was emphatic. He had not, he insisted, ever intended to suggest that the "raw outer edge" of the geographical frontier played an important role in American civilization; those who accused him of believing that mental ability or cultural progress moved from the outer edge of society eastward completely misunderstood him. He had, on the contrary, always maintained that "what went on behind the frontier" was of broader significance than what went on on the frontier; national developments in industry, thought, and politics were "deeply influenced by the fact that there was a frontier of settlement which continually opened up new fields for social development."[24] Turner anticipated many modern restatements of his hypothesis when he made those observations.

Whatever his success in shaping his own beliefs on the nature of the frontier, Turner had no trouble communicating with his own generation. To assign three meanings to the word "frontier"—as place, population, and process—was no crime, for the English language bristles with words burdened by a number of meanings. Any reader of his essays knew perfectly well what he meant when a term was placed in context, and saw no contradiction when that term was used in a different context a few paragraphs later. Turner wrote with exemplary clarity for those not seeking a semantic quarrel with him. His real achievement was to make this single word the key to so much of American history, and so meaningful in its separate usages. When he remarked that this aspect of the past could be understood only if "sharp definitions" were sacrificed for "elastic" usages, he was perfectly right.

He enjoyed less success when grappling with the problem of *how* expansion altered American character and institutions. This was basic to his whole theory, and repeatedly asserted: "the settlers transformed the wilderness but in the very process they were themselves transformed," he wrote, or "American character has been formed by this expansion of the social organism."[25] But what wrought this change? Here Turner, in his published writings, was more prone to bald statements than to a search for correct answers. Merely crossing the Appalachians, he suggested on occasion, aroused new ambitions and new social ideals, even though he must have known that conditions west of the range were identical with those on the east. More often he ascribed the alterations to the reversion to primitivism that occurred in pioneer communities: settlers cast off their cultural baggage when they went west, then, as they rebuilt civilization, they adopted practices and concepts adjusted to the new environment. "American social development," he wrote in 1916, "was continually beginning over on the frontier."[26] To accept this simple explanation, however, was to subscribe to the doctrine of environmental determinism, and Turner was too wise to succumb to that doctrine—or at least he did not do so as completely as most of the geographers of his generation did. Frontier culture, he realized early in his career, was the product of three forces: "the European germs, the native races, and the physiography of the new continent."[27] Turner spent much of his life attempting to weigh the exact influence of each.

The "native races"—the Indians—received far too little of his attention; he saw them only as retarding the advance of civilization and
"compelling society to organize and consolidate in order to hold the
frontier."[28] The relative importance to be assigned "European germs"
and the "physiography of the new continent" was at the heart of his
problem, and a major problem it was. In his more extravagant moods,
as when composing a popular lecture or article, he was inclined to refer
grandly to the West as a "huge geographic mould for a new society,"
and to speak of the manner in which nature "pressed into her mould the
plastic pioneer life." These unfortunate exaggerations were not typical,
for Turner was constantly aware that people responded in varying
ways to an identical environment, or even failed to respond at all. "The
different ways in which these different peoples reacted to the same
scene interests me," he wrote in 1923. Solving this equation occupied
most of his lifetime. He failed, but his speculations brought him surprisingly near a correct answer. He ruled out complete environmentalism at once; "I haven't quite gotten sure of what I think myself on the
degree of *control* by geographic factors," he wrote a friend in 1908,
but of one thing he was sure: "I think it clear that those who believe in
geographic determinism go too far."[29] As proof Turner could, and did,
cite case after case in which the invading stock resisted change: Yankees and southern uplanders who clung to their own civilizations even
when living side by side in the Mississippi Valley, New England Mormons who transported their ways of life to the arid Great Basin, German farmers in the Great Valley of the Appalachians whose agricultural techniques varied little from those of the Old World, Indian-hating
Puritans with an urge for self-government and Indian-loving French-
men content with royal absolutism who both occupied comparable
geographic regions. "I have the impression," he wrote a former student,
"that the provincialism of Oregon rural regions, and in part of Port-
land, is in some degree a survival of the special type that pioneered that
region."[30] The geographic "moulds" that Turner described in his flamboyant moods simply did not operate. There were, he believed, "inherited ideas and customs to consider, and personal leadership too. It is
a complex with which we have to deal."[31]

In the end he isolated at least three explanations of the manner in
which frontiering changed men and their institutions, all of them
based on good sense and ample evidence. First, the mere fact of migra-

tion, he believed, affected migrants; it "gave a shock to old conventions, usages, attitudes of mind, fundamental assumptions."[32] Second, migrating stocks tended to seek a physical environment comparable to that left behind, thus allowing the use of skills suited to the area. This accentuated sectional differences and gave the impression of stronger geographic forces than actually existed.[33] Finally, Turner saw that the *social* environment of frontier regions was a major influence in altering traits and institutions, even though the physical environment was not. Men living amidst the relatively greater opportunity provided by "free land" and a fluid social order would develop characteristics and institutions different from those of the cramped East, where a stabilized society and limited economic opportunity firmed class distinctions. "Environment," Turner wrote in 1928, "includes both geographical and social forces, and the physical environment is changed by changing economic forces and interests."[34] Moreover, the resulting changes would influence subsequent generations; children reared in the atmosphere of change and speculation common to frontier communities would view life differently than those raised in settled regions where stability and thrift were the rule. "The ideals of the frontier," he told a Harvard class in 1911, "were handed down to each succeeding generation."[35]

As Turner visualized the frontier process, immigrants reached each new frontier bearing with them traditions, habits, and institutions which transplanted to the new region much of the life and thought of the area they had departed. They also carried with them the seeds of ideals and institutions that had failed to thrive in the East, but that grew rapidly when unfettered by tradition. Even more important, pioneers found in frontier opportunity "occasions for the development of new institutions, the transformation of old institutions, and the greater freedom of the individual man."[36] Turner's emphasis, then, was on change through altered social environments. This would always vary from place to place, for ethnic stocks entering each region would never be identical and physical conditions would differ in degree. Rejecting, as he did, the belief that the physical environment cast all into a common mould, Turner expected that the similarities between frontier areas would be greater than differences, but that in all those areas the cultural traditions carried westward by pioneers would be slightly altered.

Turner came to a surprisingly correct conclusion concerning the frontier process, even though he lacked the statistical tools to determine the relative influence of "stocks" and environment—physical and social —in the resulting equation. His instincts also led him to a reasonably accurate understanding of the nature of the westward movement, and of its significance in American history. He did not, unlike some of his followers, ascribe it undue credit as a moulding force. Only a few months before his death he complained that a critic "incorrectly thinks that I had made the frontier phenomenon the one key to American history." He had not, of course. "It *was* a key, and a neglected one."[37] Turner, by his stress on the West, only tried to achieve a balance that was badly needed. In the same way he avoided the trap of localism into which so many frontier historians have fallen. "The real significance of Western history," he told the American Historical Association in 1896, " is that it is national history." Turner believed, correctly, that "there was no region, class or interest which did not feel the reactions due to this moving frontier. It was not a local phenomenon. It was a national experience."[38] The West's impact on the East was more important than what happened in the West itself. When, late in his career, he read an economist's judgment that "a considerable part of the significance of the frontier lies behind the frontier" Turner added a marginal note: "Perhaps it would be correct to say *most* of its significance."[39] He was no victim of localitis; the broad pattern of American civilization as influenced by westering—and dozens of other factors—was his concern.

Nor was he as guilty of overemphasizing one frontier area, as many of his latter-day critics complained. True, Turner drew most of his examples from the forested upper Mississippi Valley, but he also made serious investigations of the New England frontier, the Old West, the Ohio Valley, and the Mississippi Valley, and was genuinely concerned with the story of expansion into the Far West. He did not, he once assured Herbert Eugene Bolton, fail to recognize the importance of that area, even though he never had occasion to preach about it in an essay. During his late years, particularly, Turner recognized that the Great Plains and Rocky Mountain country had been slighted, and he urged that the oversight be corrected. In 1928, when he was unable to attend a conference on the subject, he sent instead a four-page, single-space list of topics crying for research. "A neglected region (so far as synthesis goes especially)," he called it, "in American cultural, social and economic history."[40] Neglected it might be, but Turner's own reading notes on the Far West, scattered through two file drawers and numbering into the thousands, showed that he was better informed than even his admirers thought possible. So did his occasional speculations. Life in the land of the "league-long furrow," he once observed, required different standards of measurement than life in the Midwest. Then, too, it deserved particular study because the conflict of cultures there—Spanish and English—provided a laboratory to measure the relative influence of hereditary and environmental forces.[41]

Turner made no investigations of the Southwest along the lines he suggested, but he did base revisionist conclusions on two important phases of the migration process on solid research. One concerned the validity of the "safety valve." In his early days Turner accepted this universally held belief—that the West drained excess workers from American factories and thus served as a deterrent to labor radicalism —and incorporated it unthinkingly in his essays. "In Europe," he told a class in 1904, "labor said, raise wages or we will fight. In the United States labor said, raise wages or we will go west."[42] His first serious investigation into the subject apparently began during his research for the *Rise of the New West*, and with it came his first doubts. Could an eastern laborer save enough from his pittance of a salary to migrate? "Compare the cost of taking a Virginia farm in mid-17th century," he noted as a reminder to himself, "an Indiana farm about 1820, an Iowa or Wisconsin farm 1850, a Dakota farm 1890, a Canadian farm 1906." Turner followed his own advice. A folder an inch thick, filled with notes on farm-making costs in the 1850s, allowed him to reach the conclusion he voiced in *The United States, 1830-1850*: that the $1000 necessary to buy and stock a farm in the Midwest was beyond the reach of factory workers and that "direct access to cheap Western lands was not open to the poorer people of the Northeastern states and of Europe."[43] Turner concluded that the frontier was not a direct safety valve a dozen years before economists branded him a false prophet for saying that it was.

He also revised his views on the stages of frontier society that he had learned from Richard T. Ely and had parroted in his early writings. His first doubts arose in 1906, when he was asked to comment on a paper by Edwin F. Gay, read before the American Historical Association, which questioned the whole concept of natural laws in human behavior. Turner refused, pleading inadequate time to assemble the masses of data needed, but his curiosity was piqued and he spent months reading and taking notes. As he read, he recognized that what he had learned on the sequence of frontier types—trapper, cattleman, miner, pioneer farmer, equipped farmer, and town dweller—had to be modified in two ways. First, the stages were not immutable, but were governed by economic needs and opportunities. "Where social pressure or demand from a higher stage exists," he wrote in a note to himself, "there will be an incentive to omit a whole stage (eg in Mountains that bear minerals—or on the great plains when once the RR reaches them)." Second, the steps from stage to stage were taken by intelligent human beings, and hence were determined not by a grand design that shaped the evolution of society, but by the laws of supply and demand. "The 'obvious' stages of 'hunting,' 'pasturage,' and so forth," Turner concluded, "will doubtless go chiming down the ages as the Mother Goose philosophy of history."[44] Those were bold conclusions, challenging as they did a basic belief of historians and political economists of that day.

His curiosity satisfied, Turner turned to more pressing matters, but work on THE BOOK demanded that he again consider the stages of society that unfolded during the 1840s and 1850s. To do so meant further modifications of his theories to include a number of hitherto unrecognized frontier types as investigation revealed the complexity of the settlement process. Land speculators, missionaries, soldiers, gristmill operators, and a dozen more deserved a place with trappers and ranchers and pioneer farmers; land speculators particularly intrigued Turner and inspired bundles of research notes that could have resulted in several ground-breaking articles if he had been so inclined.[45] He also saw that these frontier types advanced westward in no set sequence. "Often," he wrote in 1925, "the economic stages represented by these waves of advancing population were blended or intermixed." This was the case because westward expansion was governed by a variety of factors, including the state of the grain market, transportation facilities, credit, the availability of capital, interest rates, and other man-made influences.[46] Turner was coming to conclusions that were not based on speculation, but on hard research. And they were, like most opinions built on such a foundation, thoroughly accurate.

Unfortunately, he never found time to investigate one aspect of

frontier theory that fascinated him. Did the experience of other frontiering peoples substantiate his findings about the Americans? Were the
peasants who advanced eastward across Siberia, the grain-farmers who
conquered the prairie provinces of Canada, the gauchos who led the
way into the interior of Argentina, the Portuguese who peopled the
sertao of Brazil, and the squatters who drove their sheep through gaps
in the Blue Mountains into the "backs" of Australia altered, as were
Americans, by contact with frontier opportunity? Or did such changes
as took place in their traits and institutions show that ethnic traditions were more important than environmental pressures in governing
human conduct? These questions vastly intrigued Turner, even though
his investigations did not lead in that direction. Others, he hoped, would
carry on the quest, and he particularly urged his own students to do so.
"Russia ought to have its frontier interpretations," he told one; "South
America should be a rich field," he suggested to another. Indeed, the
next and most needed step in frontier studies might well be "the comparison and correlation with the land experiences of other peoples."[47]
Insatiably curious, Turner was an eager student of comparative frontiers, even though he made no contribution of his own.

To summarize his views on the frontier process is to recognize that
they would be accepted by most historians today. He was aware that
environmental forces were not determinant, and that men of differing
races and backgrounds reacted in differing ways to the same geographic
setting. He found in the social environment a far more effective instrument for change than the physical. He viewed the westward movement
as principally significant for its impact on the East, and hence an important national phenomenon. He was emphatic in believing that it was
only one of many influences moulding the nation's civilization. He was
aware that the West was not a direct safety valve luring displaced
factory workers, and that expansion proceeded in no well-defined and
immutable stages. He recognized that the impact of the American
frontier could never be accurately appraised without a study of comparative frontiers. Turner had, in other words, reached conclusions
that were sufficiently accurate to be accepted today.

If Turner stands acquitted, on the basis of his scholarly articles and
privately expressed views, of the lack of understanding of the frontier
process that his critics claimed, did he have a similar understanding

of the impact of westering on traits and institutions? Were his latter-day detractors correct when they argued that democracy did not originate in the forests of the West, but in the cities of the East? Did they err when they charged that not the frontier, but forces stemming from the Revolution produced the intense nationalism of the United States? Were they accurate when they insisted that cooperation was the rule in pioneer areas—with community enterprise underlying everything from cabin-raisings to law enforcement—rather than the individualism that Turner postulated? What in Turner's own theories, voiced in speeches and letters and unpublished essays, can exonerate him of these accusations?

That Turner did exaggerate the role of the frontier as a breeding ground for democratic theory and practice cannot be denied, but neither can his views be understood without a new look at the type of democracy he was discussing. When he wrote, as he did in 1894, and 1896, and 1906, and, finally, in 1914, that American democracy "came from no theorist's dream" but rose "stark and strong and full of life, from the American forest," he was in effect advancing a completely new definition for the benefit of his historical brethren.[48] He was saying, first of all, that *American* democracy (as distinguished from its European ancestor) was unique, and a product of the Jacksonian-egalitarian-Populist faith in the common man, originating not in the days of Thomas Jefferson, but in the era of Andrew Jackson. As such, his "democracy" shared little with the European-Neo-Federalist concept of the same term, which accepted a rigid class structure, refused to treat all men as equals, and retained other relics of an aristocratic past. Turner saw the frontier as an enemy of this brand of democracy; there, where "free land" and untapped natural resources opened opportunities for the enterprising, the society (as he put it) was one of "expectant capitalists"—a social order based on the principle of a fair chance for all, rather than arbitrary leveling by external decree or law.[49] American democracy, unlike European, was "the rise of the people to economic and consequently to political power and self-consciousness." This was what Turner meant when he wrote that *American* democracy emerged from the forest, or that it was due to the existence of "free lands."[50]

Viewed in this light, many of his most extravagant statements take on a more logical meaning. Turner never denied that democracy originated in Europe and that many of its theories and practices migrated from east to west. "It was," he told a Harvard audience, "based not alone on Magna Charta, nor Plymouth Rock, nor Jamestown. What is *American* in it is the result of the interaction of the wilderness—vacant land—with the men and institutions."[51] Rule by all the people as a right, not a concession, was its basic ingredient. This, in turn, underlay two basic changes, uniquely important to the functioning of government in the United States. One was a shift in power from national to local units; frontiersmen believed their problems so different as to require local solutions, and they demanded the right of self-rule, from the days of the Mayflower Compact and Watauga Association down to the end of the nineteenth century. The other was a transfer of authority from an elite group to *all* the people; greater opportunity for self-advancement in the West bred a faith in "King Numbers," whatever the educational or cultural deficiencies of the decision-makers. Turner was fond of quoting a backcountry petition for statehood, arguing that "a fool can sometimes put on his coat better than a wise man can do it for him."[52] Here, in the simple language of the pioneers, was a definition that said a great deal. *American* democracy did differ from the European democracy in which it had originated, and the differences were traceable in part to the frontiering experience.

So did the nationalism that Turner insisted was intensified in the West. This was one of his fundamental beliefs; his essays listed over and over again the factors in pioneer life that heightened loyalty to the central government at the expense of the states: the need for defense and a generous land-disposal system, the lessening of sectional loyalties as men from differing backgrounds met and mingled, the necessity of expanding the constitutional powers of Congress to deal with unanticipated problems originating in the borderlands. When he wrote, as he did early in his career, that "the different sectional colorings were mixed in the palette of the West into a common national hue," he was voicing a sentiment from which he never wavered during his lifetime.[53] Not long before his death, Turner jotted down several reasons for the West's role: the public domain was a common source of revenue, a region to be defended by national armies, an area to be disposed of by the national government, a territory to be governed, a birthplace of new states.[54] Frontiering in his mind was a principal adhesive force creating a strong nation and generating loyalties among its people.

If this were true, how could the frontier generate both nationalism and the localism that was, in his view, a principal by-product of American democracy? Turner never could answer that question satisfactorily, although it plagued him for many years. He tried often enough; the central government "was too remote to lay much restraint upon daily life; and at the same time it was able to furnish them the backing for their designs of building up the region into which the nation was expanding."[55] Such explanations were logical; westward expansion did enhance a nationalistic spirit by diverting attention from Europe to the interior, by deflecting commerce from the sea to the land, by weakening state loyalties, and by enhancing the patriotism of westerners who looked to the central government for protection, aid, and largess. Many a traveler during the nineteenth century commented on the excessive patriotic zeal of the people of the interior as contrasted with the temperate attitude of those who lived on the seaboard. Yet the fact remained that expansion bred sections, and that sections challenged national loyalties. Turner was well aware of this, but he was unable to reconcile the two attitudes. Nor could later scholars; man's unpredictable behavior is seldom based on logic.

Turner faced another dilemma when he stated that individualism was a trait fostered by the frontiering experience. He was perfectly aware of the fact that in all pioneer communities cooperation, rather than freedom for the individual, was necessary for survival; community efforts underlay defense, road and school building, the first governmental structures, and such neighborhood activities as cabin-raisings and logrollings. There was, often, greater restraint on freedom of action in the West than in the East. How could a spirit of individualism emerge from such a setting? Turner defined the term in a peculiarly American way, just as he had democracy. On the frontier, individualism meant only two things: participation in the decision-making process in which regulatory measures were enacted, and freedom from interference in economic affairs by an external government. The pioneer was willing to burden himself with regulatory measures if he knew them to be for the common good, but he did not want a distant congress to limit his money-making capacity in the interest of national welfare. This seemed fair enough in a land where untapped natural resources appeared limitless. "Population was scarce," Turner told one audience, "and there was no multitude of jostling interests, such as accompanied dense settlement and required a complicated system of government."[56] So long as expansion went on, individuals should be free to monopolize the richest bottom land, the finest timber plot, the most valuable mill site, and the most promising ore beds—for just ahead lay other bottom land, other timber plots, other mill sites, other ore beds. They could be sought out by the enterprising without harm to society. This Turner called the "squatter ideal."

That ideal could prevail so long as the westward movement prevailed, but what of the new closed-space world of the twentieth century, where the best of the nation's resources were already in private hands? Had the closing of the frontier burst the bubble of individualistic opportunity? Turner gave a great deal of thought to that question, particularly during the 1920s, when publicists and social scientists awakened to the problems of a frontierless world.[57] How, he asked himself, could the "squatter ideal" be reconciled with the pioneer "ideal of democracy"? If the "squatter ideal" persisted, wealthy individuals and corporations would monopolize the remaining resources at the expense of the general welfare. If the "democratic ideal" endured and the public good was elevated above private interests, the treasured right of the individual to economic freedom would be sacrificed. Which of these ideals must go for the greatest public good? "Time has revealed," Turner told the American Historical Association in his presidential address, "that these two ideals of pioneer democracy had elements of mutual hostility and contained the seeds of dissolution."[58]

He struggled long and hard with this question, filling sheet after sheet with lists of alternatives: on the one side, freedom of action, giving rise to combinations, discrimination, cut-throat competition, and monopoly; on the other, restraint of economic freedom, fostering investigative commissions, legislative controls, and assaults on private property.[59] Which would better perpetuate the pioneer values that gave America its greatness? For a time Turner clung to the hope that business would require no regulation; "in a sense," he told a class in 1902, "a corporation is a socialistic device; Rockefeller, Carnegie, etc. may prove to be pioneers in the direction of social activity."[60] When that hope was shattered, Turner placed his faith in voluntary organization, finding in corporate cooperation, farm associations, and "better business" bureaus the same spirit that motivated the barn-raisings and logrollings in pioneer times, and forseeing the day when they would serve as self-regulating devices for corporations. This dream also proved illusory, as monopolistic trusts continued to place profits above the general welfare. Reluctantly, Turner came to the conclusion that pioneer democracy must take precedent over pioneer individualism, and be preserved by positive government action. Only this could protect the freedom of opportunity formerly provided by free land.[61]

This was a tragic decision for Turner, for it symbolized the passing of the frontier America that he knew so well and loved so much. His values and his ideals were those of the pioneers he studied; the world would never be quite so attractive now that they were outmoded. For Turner had been largely accurate in defining the frontier's influence and isolating the traits and institutional changes traceable to its impact. He had erred in detail, of course, and had been guilty of overstatement in his popular speeches and essays. His tendency to exaggerate, to sacrifice accuracy for a rhetorical flourish, and to generalize on the basis of inadequate evidence cost him heavily in credibility, as his critics of the 1930s and 1940s demonstrated so effectively. But, basically, Turner was right; modern scholars agree that the interpretations embodied in his research papers are for the most part sustainable.

Whatever the detractions of Turner's critics, the fact remains that generations of travelers from abroad have found Americans different from their cousins in Europe or Asia or Africa. Social scientists, using techniques far more sophisticated than those available to Turner, have demonstrated that some, at least, of these differences were exactly those that he ascribed to frontiering. Scholarship since the 1950s has swung more and more to his side, not irrationally, as during his lifetime, but because careful testing has shown him to have been correct. The frontier was an important force—among many—in helping shape the nation's course during the eighteenth and nineteenth centuries. Its passing has created problems that baffled Turner, and that continue to challenge statesmen and politicians as the world seeks to adjust itself to a closed-space existence.

Yet all the scholarship that has been squandered arguing the merits of Turner's frontier thesis—a body of learning that forms a fitting monument to the impact of his theories—only provides a footnote to something that Turner and his generation knew instinctively. Modern Americans living in urban-industrial complexes, to whom the rural past is only a near-forgotten memory, are inclined to forget that somehow the continent was settled, and that this settlement generated social stresses certain to influence those enduring them. No nation could spill a sizable portion of its population into a wilderness for two centuries without being affected by the experience. No people who realized that opportunity for self-advancement beckoned beyond the western horizon could escape changes in mental attitudes and social traits. Such experiences defy historical analysis, but their significance cannot be ignored. One of Turner's students, E. E. Dale, sputtered his indignation at the myopia of his master's critics. Had they seen the territory of Oklahoma grow in seventeen years from a population of a few hundred cowboys and Indian agents to 400,000? Had they seen, as Dale had, 100,000 homesteaders rush into the Cherokee Outlet—to people a region as large as New England within twenty hours? Did they realize that in two decades the population of the Dakotas rose from 14,000 to 719,000, that of Nebraska from 120,000 to a million, that of Kansas from 340,000 to a million and a half?[62] Mass movements of that magnitude made their impact on people and government, even though the extent of that impact defied measurement. Turner knew this, and he was perfectly right in thinking it worth remembering.

He died in 1932, confident that his frontier thesis had bettered man's understanding of the past, and that it would continue as a significant interpretation into the future. This does not mean that he felt it inviolate; Turner was well aware of the inadequacies of his theory. Once, when criticized for overstressing the frontier's influence and for failing to test some of his generalizations, he replied sharply that he was well aware that other forces were just as important, and that he knew the limitations of some of his interpretations better than most of his detractors.[63] But he also knew that his basic premise was correct, and would never be completely invalidated. When he remarked, as he did on one occasion, that his interpretations would become "airy nothings as time goes on," he was being more self-effacing than honest.[64] Only a few months before his death, when reminiscing with his secretary, he stated firmly that the frontier hypothesis, although doubtless calling for reconsideration in detail, was essentially sound.[65] So it was.

The same can be said, although with considerably less assurance, about Turner's second major contribution to historiography: his sectional hypothesis. That he introduced an important concept into American historiography cannot be disputed. Until his day scholars wrote only of the North-South division that had culminated in civil war, closing their eyes to the more numerous regions that clashed and bargained to shape the history of the nineteenth century. For this Turner substituted an understanding of the United States as a "kind of checkerboard of differing environments," from six to ten in number, interacting each with the others much as did European nations. Like European nations, too, they differed not only in political behavior, but in economic structure, psychological attitudes, religious climate, and cultural outpourings. All had to be investigated and understood if one was to appreciate the role they played in the nation's past.[66]

Central to Turner's theory was the concept of conflict, based not on sectional self-seeking, but on the deep-seated belief of each that its culture and economy were superior, and worthy of national adoption. The sections did not fly asunder, however, for two forces held them together. Political parties served as one bond of union, stretching like elastic bands to meet each new crisis, but seldom breaking. "It is not too much to say," Turner wrote in a draft of his last book, "that but for party loyalty, operating as a check on sectional loyalty, this league of sections called the United States might have followed the fortunes of European leagues and alliances."[67] The other unifying force was the existence within each section of sub-sections, or "regions," as Turner called them, which held views antagonistic to the section itself. Often a "region" found more in common with similar "regions" lying outside its section than with its parent section. This complex of cross-lines prevented any major combination of sections from dominating the remainder. The sub-sections, with the political parties, served as a deterrent to separatism. Thus, the history of the United States could never be understood until it was retold in terms of sectional conflict, adjustment, and compromise. "American society," Turner believed, "is the outcome of the interaction of the various sections."[68]

As this belief deepened, the principal passion of Turner's life became the proof of his hypothesis. Here, in his eyes, was a searchlight into the past that had been ignored by his fellow craftsmen. They must be enlightened and converted. His plea was for a common assault on this area of darkness—by historians, geographers, economists, students of literature and the arts, even linguists—for the problems to be solved were too many and too complex for any one investigator.[69] Some few responded to his urging. Many among them had been his students— Charles H. Ambler, Joseph Schafer, Homer C. Hockett, Edgar E. Robinson, and Raynor G. Wellington contributed important findings. Others were younger scholars who were convinced that here was a fruitful field for exploration—Lois K. Mathews, Ulrich B. Phillips, Avery O. Craven, and William E. Dodd accepted Turner's invitation and acknowledged their use of his theories. But in truth the converts were few, and the sum of their findings added up to no very significant reinterpretation of American history. They, like their guide, simply failed to find in the sectional thesis the convincing insights furnished by the frontier hypothesis.

Three obstacles stood in their way, each virtually insurmountable. One was the indisputable fact that the more deeply Turner or his disciples investigated sectional phenomena, the more diffuse and uncertain their findings became. Sections refused to remain well-defined; instead, the more they were studied, the more they overlapped, subdivided, and blurred. Voters failed to respond to environmental or economic pressures as they were expected to, showing a stubborn inclination to cast their ballots for reasons that had no connection with their habitats or means of making a living. This Turner freely admitted. "Generalizations which make physical geography or economic interests alone the compelling explanation of political groupings," he wrote in 1925, "are mistaken. There are also the factors of ideals and psychology, the inherited intellectual habits, derived from the stock from which the voters sprang."[70] In other words, the forces responsible for sectional groupings were not sufficiently consistent to be trustworthy. This being the case, the whole sectional concept was discredited. If geographic or economic influences failed to explain the behavior of some groups, how could they explain others? Why did Mississippians illustrate the hypothesis while North Carolinians did not? Could it be that Turner was wrong, and the sectional thesis was inadequate to the tasks assigned it?

This Turner never admitted publicly, but he was sometimes beset by doubts as his months of research ended in negative or inconclusive results. Wealthy planters with a high literacy rate living in rich-soil regions of the pre-Civil War South *should* have voted Whig; small farmers with low incomes and a low scale of literacy who occupied inferior lands were *supposed* to favor the Democratic Party. Too often they did not. So many factors entered into political decision-making that the sectional tests simply did not apply. Turner recorded some of these in notes that he jotted as he went along. "Impossibility of saying purely economic determinism," he wrote at one time, "e.g. classification of votes by agricultural areas when the thing may be areas of stock." "Voting *habit* and the spiritual element," he noted again. On still another occasion he went on record that "men will vote at times for patriotic, or religious, or moral motives against their personal interests."[71] Strong leaders, or politicians who deliberately confused issues to win votes, also distorted the picture, as did political inertia. "The investigator," Turner confessed to a friend, "must apply the 'multiple hypothesis' and note the coexistence of more than one influence."[72] Perfectly true. But to do so meant that the sectional hypothesis failed to provide an adequate explanation. Emotions, paternal loyalties, ideals, moral issues, patriotism, and the host of other motives governing human behavior simply were not measurable in sectional terms. Turner was honest enough to admit the deficiencies of his thesis, but he would never agree that they were fatal.

He was unable to prove otherwise, however, because of a second handicap that doomed his hopes of a sectional reinterpretation of the nation's history. The maps over which he labored were simply incapable of revealing correlations between geographic and economic conditions, on the one hand, and political behavior, on the other. This Turner recognized, and during his investigations he listed at least five reasons for their inadequacy. First, the county units with which he worked were too large to show the exact relationship between social factors and vote-distribution; on the other hand, use of a smaller unit, such as a precinct, posed practical problems that were insurmountable. Second, the maps created a false impression by making a large county with a sparse population seem more important than a small county with a large population. Third, they concealed minorities almost as large as the majorities that they depicted, and this was a near-fatal weakness. Using Turner's techniques, a region that was 51 per cent Whig and 49 per cent Democrat would appear to be all Whig; a county that barely voted for one party in one election could cast 100 per cent of its votes for that party in the next without altering the map in the least; a populous city in one corner of a county might carry the whole county into the Democratic column, when all the rest of that county was Whig. The one way out of the difficulty—to show the size of the plurality by percentage—was virtually impossible to do on a map. The fourth defect listed in Turner's self-criticism was equally serious. In many elections, he noted, candidates deliberately subordinated economic or social issues and appealed to voters through their personalities, thus upsetting all correlations. Finally, strong leaders led voters along paths that defied logic; they often persuaded voters to vote against their own sectional or economic interests, thus removing the counties they led from their natural groupings. Even when the leader correctly mirrored the views of his constituents, his influence was enough to cast doubts on many of Turner's results.[73]

These were grave deficiencies, but they were compounded by the inadequate technique Turner used in his analysis. His elaborate maps failed to reveal the correlations that he sought. No matter how carefully drawn or how small the unit employed, maps were unsuited to the type of statistical investigation he had undertaken, yet he was so wedded to their use that he closed his eyes to more practical methods. Neither he nor his students showed any awareness of the tools available in the early twentieth century; sampling methods, correlation devices, time-series trending, and punch cards for storing and sorting data were all in use at the time, and they were far more suitable to the type of data analysis that interested Turner. Instead, he crowded fact on fact until his maps became undecipherable jumbles of colors and symbols. Even when the maps were kept simple, the visual correlation of two or more to identify patterns of association was almost impossible, unless the degree was so high that it was unmistakable.[74] Turner, using inadequate tools, was unable to demonstrate to fellow historians that the sectional hypothesis was valid enough to justify their attention.

His tragedy was his failure to recognize this. Turner went to his grave convinced that he had altered the profile of American history by the findings his maps revealed, and that the alteration would accelerate as improved cartographic devices were developed. After all, he had demonstrated (at least to his own satisfaction) the direct correlation between illiteracy and poor soil, the close relationship between literacy and glaciated areas, the tendency of counties with dense slave populations to vote Whig, the preponderance of Democratic strength in the barrens of the upland South, and a good many other things that shed light on the past. "I think my studies of 1830-1850," he told a friend just before his death, "will prove that there is a real relation between these areas of party preponderance and areas of physical geography, soils, illiteracy, industries, even literature and religion."[75]

Turner's sectional hypothesis, discredited by the inadequacy of his statistical techniques and by his inability to prove a relationship between geography and political behavior, was cast still deeper into the shadows by the inaccuracy of some of his own predictions. Had he been content to confine his analysis to the pre-Civil War era, where his main interest lay, he would have remained on safe ground, but the present fascinated him no less than the past, and the atmosphere of the 1920s was of a sort to whet that fascination. That was a day of raw regional conflict, with New England and the Midwest snarling over the projected St. Lawrence Seaway, with South and North at arms over the racial issue, with a farm bloc demanding legislation to lift agriculture from its doldrums. To Turner this was sure proof that sectionalism was on the ascent, and that divisions would deepen almost to the point of regional warfare. He watched with excited interest, clipping items from newspapers and magazines, mapping congressional votes, and jamming his files with evidence that would prove his thesis.[76] Every new bit of evidence was proof that sectional divisions held the key to the present no less than to the past.

This was all very well, but when Turner went on to insist that sectional divisions would continue to deepen, he was flying in the face of common sense. True, his reasons were logical. Regional loyalties would intensify as the population stabilized with the closing of the frontier. They would be heightened as mounting population density made each section more aware of the need to guard its own resources and enhanced its political power to do so. Even class and ethnic conflicts, certain to increase with continued industrialization, would add tinder to the flames, for workers and immigrants in one section would be arrayed against farmers and Yankees in another. He summed up his conclusions in 1925: "The significant fact is that sectional self-consciousness and sensitiveness is likely to be increased as time goes on and crystallized sections feel the full influence of their geographical peculiarities, their special interests, and their developed ideals, in a closed and static nation."[77]

Few even among his most ardent supporters could agree with such a prediction. They knew that the very forces Turner isolated as responsible—the closing of the frontier, denser populations, improved transportation and communication facilities, the radio and airplane, industrialization and urbanization—would operate instead as nationalizing pressures that would dampen sectional loyalties. They were right. As regional loyalties gave way to dependence on the national government during the Great Depression of the 1930s and the World War of the 1940s, the sectionalism that had bulked so large a generation before was forgotten. As it passed from the scene, historians turned their attention elsewhere: to the biographical studies popular in the late 1920s, to the economic analysis and investigations of the class structure that captured their interest in the 1930s, to the "consensus" history that dominated the profession during the 1940s and 1950s. In none was there room for Turner's sectionalism. The consensus school, particularly, relegated it to oblivion by glorifying national unity at the expense of all forms of conflict, whether of section, class, group, or ideology. Turner's sectional thesis was as discredited by the end of the 1950s as his frontier hypothesis had been at the close of the 1930s.

Its fate should not be interpreted to mean that the hypothesis lacked some significance or that it will not regain respectability among future historians. Turner exaggerated when he wrote, in 1927, that "the sectional (regional-geographic) factor is as important—for the future, at least—as the frontier doctrine,"[78] but it was a theory that helped explain certain aspects of the past and had to be taken into account in any interpretation of the nineteenth century. Modern historians, equipped now with computers and sophisticated statistical techniques, and substituting tables and equations for maps, have again begun to probe the sectional phenomenon, although with inconclusive results. The day will never come, as Turner hoped it would, when "my Sections paper will travel with my frontier as interpretations,"[79] but neither will the theory be totally forgotten. His was a dual legacy to mankind and the historical profession.

XIX

The Significance of
Frederick Jackson Turner
in American History

ET US indulge in a very unhistorical speculation. Let us assume that
Frederick Jackson Turner's offer to relinquish his place on the
1893 program of the American Historical Association to his student,
Orin G. Libby, was accepted by the committee. Let us imagine that he
then turned to other investigations, leaving his essay on "The Significance of the Frontier in American History" unfinished. If, as he believed, the intellectual climate was ripe for the announcement of the
frontier hypothesis, some other historian would have produced a comparable essay within a few years, and he would have been acclaimed as
the father of a thesis that would revolutionize historical studies. Assuming that all of these improbable events had taken place, would
Turner's impact on his own generation have lessened? Would he be acclaimed today as one of the half-dozen historians most influential in
shaping the study of the nation's past?

Probably not, for the world usually honors the spectacular rather
than the enduring, and the frontier thesis captured both professional
and popular attention as have few others. Yet a perfectly plausible
argument can be made that Turner would have been just as venerated
by his colleagues and successors if he had never advanced his famed
hypothesis. That hypothesis, and the controversy it aroused, has obscured his many other contributions to historical studies, some of them
of broader significance than his theories on both the frontier and section. His proper place in American historiography can never be appreciated until those contributions are known and understood.

To his friends, Turner's appeal lay not only in his unwritten books and scintillating essays, but also in the originality of his ideas as he roamed across the whole field of American history. His mind was a veritable grab bag of fresh viewpoints, constantly replenished by his omnivorous reading and research, and open to all to use as they wished. "I should want," J. Franklin Jameson told his superiors when he assumed direction of the historical division of the Carnegie Institution, "a man overflowing with ideas, . . . who in daily talks would wake me and the Department up, and make suggestions affecting our plans and our thinking. One man in America would fill that bill perfectly, and that is Frederick Jackson Turner."[1] Few of those ideas appeared over his own name; instead, they were seized upon by others and nursed into articles and monographs that probed the borders of knowledge. The dozen books dedicated to him, and the dozens more that acknowledged his help in their prefaces, testified to the fertility of his mind and the breadth of his influence on historical writing in his day.

Two trivial episodes illustrate the freshness of his thought. One occurred when he and Max Farrand visited Independence Hall in Philadelphia. As Turner viewed that historic shrine, a brilliant idea flashed before him; the very shape of the room, he excitedly told Farrand, allowed George Washington to dominate the proceedings as the Constitution was being drafted. Farrand was so impressed that for the next years he taught and lectured that the nation's constitutional structure was determined by the size and shape of the room where its basic document was written. Then came the letdown. "I have just obtained unmistakable evidence," he wrote Turner delightedly, "that the convention *met upstairs.*"[2] So much for that theory.

Turner's logic was just as sound—and his conclusions more valid—on a second occasion, when he was called upon to help settle the controversy over the Kensington Rune Stone. His involvement began when the stone's staunchest defender, Hjalmar R. Holand, spoke in Madison in 1910, then entered into a spirited argument with Turner who was in the audience. Fortunately, the local newspaper reporter leaped to the completely false conclusion that Turner was in agreement with Holand, and so stated in his account of the affair. Turner's indignant letter to the editor set the matter straight; "I desire," he wrote emphatically, "to disclaim the utterances attributed to me."[3] This exchange came to the attention of a commission named by the Minnesota

Historical Society to determine the stone's authenticity, and Turner's advice was solicited. His reply, filling four tightly reasoned pages, asked a number of questions so adroitly phrased that the paper is still considered a classic in rune methodology. Did the weathering of the runes and the remainder of the stone reveal age differences? Could the carving have been done while the stone was locked beneath the tree where it was found? Had a stonecutter capable of such neat lettering lived near by? Was there any teacher or minister familiar enough with runes to frame the text who was a friend of the farmer who made the discovery? Were books available on runes? Had a member of the community visited a Minneapolis library where such books could be consulted? So Turner went on, for page after page, urging the use of stonecutters, jewelers, scholars, and skilled lawyers to ferret out the answers. If the investigating commission had followed his advice the Kensington Rune Stone would have been proven a hoax at that time, rather than inviting controversy for another half-century.[4]

These were hardly earthshaking accomplishments, but they demonstrated Turner's ability to summon fresh explanations and apply traditional techniques to unusual problems. He was equally appreciated by his contemporaries for his campaigns to supply researchers with new tools. One effort went toward creating a historical center in Washington where visiting scholars could live comfortably, be supported while carrying on their investigations, and enjoy the stimulating company of a core of permanent senior research associates. J. Franklin Jameson, who was always ready to work for goals inspired by what he called "the fruitful mind of Turner," labored in vain for the enormous sums needed for such a center; not until the 1960s and 1970s did the American Historical Association revive the plan as one of its principal objectives.[5] More successful was Turner's program for an up-to-date atlas of American history, mapping election returns and social data; he made the initial suggestion for such a work to the Carnegie Institution in 1903, converted Jameson to the plan when that energetic promoter became director in 1905, and helped shape the volume when an editor was finally appointed in 1913.[6] Charles O. Paullin's *Atlas of the Historical Geography of the United States*, published finally in 1932, was a monument to Jameson's dogged determination, but it was also a monument to Turner's insistence that such a volume would benefit historical studies.

Far more important was Turner's campaign to provide the profession with a multi-volume biographical dictionary of Americans, comparable to the British *Dictionary of National Biography*. Many had dreamed of such a publication, but the suggestion that led to its completion was made by Turner to the first meeting of the American Council of Learned Societies, in January 1920. They listened with interest, but no one was ready to solicit the enormous sum needed; Turner preached his message annually for two more years before Jameson could be persuaded to head a committee that agreed to try. The first step was to plan a salable product; Jameson, realizing this, extracted enough money from his business friends to call the committee together for a planning session in Washington in April 1923. That was Turner's show. He came with a bulky memorandum which the committee did little more than endorse: the dictionary would include men from all walks of life as well as statesmen; it would be written by scholars and assembled by a staff working under an editor in chief named by the American Council of Learned Societies; it would fill twenty-five volumes of 750 pages each and would cost some $600,000, with more than half that sum going to contributors, who would be paid $20 for each 1000 words. Ultimate authority, Turner suggested, and the committee agreed, would be vested in two groups: a Board of Trustees, made up of prominent business leaders, who would be entrusted with the task of raising money, and a Board of Editors, drawn from the ranks of historians, economists, political scientists, and other social scientists, who would determine editorial policies.[7]

These guidelines established, Jameson, with Turner's assistance and advice, set about finding an angel with the half-million dollars needed. This proved understandably difficult, until the promoters hit on the idea of interesting a prominent newspaper to play the role that the London *Times* had played in financing the *Encyclopaedia Britannica*. *The New York Times* was an obvious target; through the winter of 1923-24 Jameson cultivated the publisher, Adolph S. Ochs, and his right-hand man, John Finley, so persuasively that they agreed to meet with the entire planning committee on April 18, 1924. Plans were laid carefully; authors known to Ochs were persuaded to write the biographies of some of his former friends, every member was instructed to be present and well-informed lest any lack of interest discourage the sponsors, John Finley was even considered as editor but rejected lest this seem too blatant favor-seeking. These tactics triumphed. When Turner and his fellow committeemen left the meeting, they carried a contract in which *The Times* agreed to advance $50,000 a year for ten years to publish a twenty-volume *Dictionary of American Biography.* "I introduced the resolution proposing the undertaking," Turner proudly wrote a friend, "so it gratifies me that a donor has been found."[8] He could not attend the dinner that celebrated the publication of the first volume two years later, but his leading role was not forgotten, as letters from the celebrants testified.[9]

Turner might reveal his commitment to historical studies by sparking such diverse projects as an atlas and a biographical dictionary, but those who would measure the impact of his contributions must turn to the concepts that he popularized to realize the debt due him by the profession. When he began his career, historians believed that a single motivating force dominated each period of the past, whether the urge for democracy in the early years of the Republic or the slavery controversy in later years; attention was focused on the distant past, rather than the near-present; "scientists" believed that they could discover the absolute truth; and all were concerned with politics, to the exclusion of the social forces shaping behavior. When he ended his career, historical studies had come of age, with most of the concepts popular today generally accepted. Neither he nor any other historian was solely responsible for this revolution, but none was more influential than Turner in setting the wheels of change in motion. He, more than any scholar of his generation, helped popularize the basic beliefs that underlie today's interpretation of the past: presentism, relativism, multiple causation, and recognition of the subsurface social and economic pressures determining political behavior.

That Turner should have made his most significant contributions in the realm of the philosophy of history was ironic, for throughout his lifetime he repeatedly professed that he had no philosophy. He told a friend in 1928, "I have never formulated a philosophy of history, or of historical research."[10] Turner protested too much. Actually he was well-versed in the works of the leading authors, past and present, who speculated in that realm; his library contained well-thumbed volumes by R. Rochell, *Die Philosophie der Geschichte* (1878), Johann Gustav Droysen, *Outlines of the Principles of History* (1893), Frederick Harrison, *The Meaning of History* (1896), Charles V. Langlois and Charles Seignobis, *Introduction aux études historiques* (1898), Antonio Labriola, *Essays on the Materialistic Conception of History* (1904), Karl Lamprecht, *Moderne Geschtswissenschaft* (1905), Frederick J. Teggart, *Prolegomena to History* (1916), and a good many more. Turner was more concerned with the nature and purpose of historical studies than he was willing to admit.

His speculations, no less than his own researches, led him to two unshakable beliefs: that multiple causal forces determined each event of the past, and that society could be understood not through studying its institutional or political behavior, but by understanding the subterranean forces governing that behavior. His faith in multiple causation, borrowed early in his career from the writings of his geologist friend T. C. Chamberlin, was fundamental. "In truth," he told an audience in 1908, "there is no single key to American history. In history, as in science, we are learning that a complex result is the outcome of the interplay of many forces. Simple explanations fail to meet the case."[11] If he did not practice what he preached when he overemphasized the significance of the frontier and section, he used overemphasis as a necessary corrective, not because he believed these forces were more influential than others. "The truth is," he confessed in 1922, "that I have found it necessary to hammer pretty hard and steadily on the frontier idea to 'get it in,' as a corrective to the kind of thinking I found some thirty years ago and less."[12] This Turner regretted; in his later years he resented the association of his name with frontiering and sectionalism, and loved to dwell on the contributions he had made to other fields of history. If he had one keystone belief to sustain his historical philosophy, it was a belief in multiple causation.

From this belief stemmed another that was equally alien to the profession when he began his studies. Turner was among the first to recognize that no "fact" cited by historians was immutable, and that all varied through changing interpretation. "Each age," he wrote in his first published essay in 1891, "writes the history of the past anew with reference to the conditions uppermost in its own time." He realized, too, before most of his generation did, that "facts" were altered not only by changing intellectual climates, but by different interpreters; objectivity was a goal beyond the reach of any historian. Each was a man, "played upon by prepossessions, affected by his own experience and his own ideals, dominated—try however he may to resist them—by the influence of his nationality, by the class in which his lot is cast, by the age in which he lives."[13] This was as it should be. Because no two scholars viewed the past through the same eyes, the way was left open for their successors to correct and reconstruct—and be reconstructed. Turner was perfectly right in that judgment; not a theory or factual finding advanced in the past half century but has been revised, and re-revised—including his own.

He was no less committed to the belief that past and present were inseparably linked, the one significant only as a prelude to the other. History was important not as a device for escape into a remote age, but as an essential ingredient in man's understanding of himself and his times. Turner quoted no phrase more often than Droysen's: "History is the self-consciousness of humanity." In his eyes, historical studies underlay the informed citizenship necessary for statesmanlike public decisions, civic responsibility, and cultural progress. They were guideposts along the path to social evolution, counterbalancing revolutionary tendencies, yet pointing the way to constructive change. "The past," he told an audience in 1904, "is so stubborn a thing that much of it flows back in the old channels. History is the minister of conservative reform."[14] Turner saw society, like the cathedrals of medieval Europe, as in continuous construction by successive generations, "still in process of completion."[15] History was the architect, serving as a brake on excessive change, yet encouraging growth and alterations essential to a sound and usable structure.

Because the past's principal importance lay in its illumination of the present, historical studies should concentrate on the portions of mankind's experience that shed greatest light on current problems. Turner held no brief for eliminating the study of remote eras; even the most distant happenings of classical antiquity had some bearing on today. Yet overemphasis on earlier ages was a luxury that the world could no longer afford; conditions in former ages were so different that "lessons derived from anything but the most recent history are apt to be misleading."[16] He regretted that historians played an undue role in reconstructing the world after World War I, when economists and business leaders were better equipped to grapple with the complexities of that troubled era. This was Turner's creed, enshrined in his essays, preached over and over again to his classes. In a day when the usual

American history course ended with the close of Reconstruction, Turner brought his down to yesterday. "It is the contact with the present," he told one of his students, "which gives vitality to undergraduate instruction."[17]

His faith in the usability of the past led him to another realization: that historians had to probe the underlying social and economic forces governing mankind's behavior, not simply the political manifestations of those forces. Turner's concern was the hidden bulk of the iceberg of civilization, not the tiny portion above the surface. He saw social progress as a product of the thoughts and aspirations of the common people, acting in a commonplace way. The historian's duty was to study these ordinary folk, to investigate why they behaved as they did, and to advance approximate explanations; only then would he know how civilization marched, how it altered with the passing of the centuries, how and why governments manifested those alterations. The United States was an ideal laboratory for such an investigation, for he believed, with Achille Loria, that its brief history compressed the evolution of all society. To understand the progress of the common man in America was to understand the emergence of civilization. This, to Turner, was the essence of his chosen subject.

His life was dedicated to the search for such understanding. When he told a publisher in 1897 that the textbook he proposed to write "should give a clear elucidation of the more important lines of development of economic life, political institutions, and social ideals," he was outlining the research program that would occupy the rest of his days—as well as giving a warning that the textbook would never be written.[18] From that time on, he took every opportunity to drive home the message. In classroom lectures, in public addresses, and in essays and books, he preached the doctrine that history was not only past politics, but past economics, past sociology, past literature, past art. History, to Turner, was "the study of all the lines of human activity and social institutions in their development."[19] Understand the life of John and Jane Doe, know their thoughts and aspirations and activities, realize how and why they behaved as they did, and you will unlock the secrets of all past civilizations. That was Turner's credo.

Woe unto those who failed to join his crusade. His cruelest barbs were reserved for authors who skimmed the political surface without examining the subsurface strata, or who oversimplified the past by stressing one causal influence at the expense of others. When Turner condemned one of his contemporaries in 1897 for using only political sources, while neglecting "the vast social transformations by immigration, interstate migration, industrial development, revolution of the transportation system, and all the forces of change involved in Westward expansion," he was arguing for a broader historical perspective, not simply propagandizing for his own frontier thesis. He was doing the same thing when he castigated James Ford Rhodes[20] for overemphasizing slavery at the expense of economic growth, immigration, industrial change, and the evolution of transportation systems; all these, Turner believed, would be accorded a larger place than the slavery issue when future historians appraised mid-nineteenth century development.[21] Nor did he overstress the significance of economic forces at the expense of social ones. "The occupation of the vacant spaces of the vast interior," Turner told a class in 1915, "the economic struggles of conflicting sectional and class interests, the proposals of social reorganization, the humanitarian movements, the profound modification of American stock by new tides of European immigration, the increasing entanglement in world politics brought about by modifications in transportation, communication and commercial connections, in short, the economic and social problems of a Democratic society compelling the possession of its own land, and finding itself involved in the fortunes of Europe and of Asia—these facts may well seem to the future American historian the dominant facts of the second half of the century."[22] So they did.

His stress on underlying social and economic forces did not blind him to the realization that orderly evolutionary patterns could be upset at any time by catastrophic events or the rise of strong leaders. Personality and accident played a part in history, Turner felt, although their influence had been exaggerated by historians and biographers. Yet even here he was quick to point out that something caused the accident, and some social pressures shaped the character of the leader. The more he studied, he wrote in 1928, the more he became convinced that "much of what was regarded as 'sheer accident,' or 'fortuitous circumstances' and 'personality' was really dependent upon preparatory conditions, deep laid tendencies released by the special circumstance on man, rather than the extemporized work of accident or individual." The leader's environment, the society in which he lived, the lesser men whose support he needed, were more important than the traits with which he had been endowed.[23] Turner was too wedded to a belief in social evolution to do more than pay lip service to accident as a causal force in historical determination.

These views doomed Turner to a lifetime of research, with few visible products to show for his efforts. All the relics of mankind must be investigated—not only government documents, but church records, newspapers, magazines, novels, paintings, labor union documents, industrial reports—anything that recorded the hopes or activities of past generations. He saw the materials of history as "a great heap of fragments which must be made into a mosaic." The scholar could not examine every fragment, but he must seek out "the essential, the really typical, the vital, in the mass that lies before him."[24] In theory, this could be accomplished by intelligent sampling; Turner described his own method as one of digging deeply in spots, testing other diggings, and then trying to envisage the historical landscape without being compelled to sink wells every few inches.[25] This was a perfectly feasible technique, but for one fatal defect: he was too much of a perfectionist to stop his posthole digging until every bit of the terrain had been investigated. Turner was a glutton for data; he was even suspicious of ancient and medieval studies because they dealt with such scant materials. Once, after reading two lengthy monographs on the settlement of Missouri and Illinois, he wrote that "when we get similar studies of all the western states" the evolution of societies and institutions there would be better understood.[26] Turner's standards were so high, his sense of perfectionism so demanding, that he never could write history as he knew it must be written.

Despite his own inadequacies, he did prod the profession into a far more sophisticated technique of historical analysis than it had known before his day. He also helped revitalize the study of local history. Properly performed, he believed, investigations on the town, county, and state level would provide historians with the many stones needed to fashion the mosaic of the past. Turner saw the fragments of information dredged out by antiquarians as comparable to the tiny rocks from which geologists deduced important generalizations; as the rocks revealed the evolutionary forces that created the earth, so local records revealed the social forces that shaped society. An item of local history was to Turner a specimen that told its own story, and fitted into the larger picture as well.[27]

Important as such information was, it was only a prelude to the next and most important step the historian must take: the analysis and interpretation that was the essence of history. Turner thoroughly respected narration; he was an ardent admirer of Francis Parkman, whose works he read and regularly assigned to his students. Yet he recognized his own deficiencies as a narrative historian and believed that he, and others less gifted than Parkman, could make their greatest contribution by distilling meaning from the data gathered by researchers. This was the message he preached to his students; "take courage and go ahead," he told one, "seeking the goal of interpretation as well as the facts."[28] Turner followed his own advice. His books and more serious essays, although based on excessive accumulations of data, were also sparked with fresh explanations, most of them commonplace today, but new in their time. "That is the difference between you and me," Max Farrand told him on one occasion. "You have to get your larger and more original point of view. I am content to do what is within my more limited powers."[29]

Gifted as he was in extracting meaning from the past, Turner carefully guarded himself against the cardinal sin of his profession in those days—the danger of over-generalization. This was a tempting bypath; historians thought of themselves as exact scientists and saw no reason why they should not postulate laws of human behavior, just as physical scientists were laying down laws that explained the behavior of the universe. To his credit, Turner refused to succumb to this temptation, for he was wise enough to realize that human conduct was too erratic to sustain predictions. "The human soul is too complex," he told an audience in 1904, "human society too full of vital energy and incessant change, to enable us to pluck out the heart of its mystery—to reduce it to the lines of an exact science or to state human development in terms of an equation."[30] This was good sense. Turner was prone to reckless generalizations when he spoke to popular audiences on the frontier thesis, but when he donned the cloak of the scholar he set a worthy example for his generation.

To sum up his historical beliefs is to realize that he could rub elbows with historians of today without feeling more than slightly outdated.

They would honor him for nursing into reality such useful tools as the *Atlas of the Historical Geography of the United States* and the *Dictionary of American Biography*. They would applaud his belief in multiple causation and his faith in the doctrine of relativism. They would agree with him that the past should be studied to illuminate the present, and that those aspects most useful in understanding modern society deserved greatest emphasis. They would accept his dictum that history was far more than past politics and could be understood only by comprehending the subsurface social and economic currents that shaped political events. They would acknowledge him correct when he cautioned against postulating laws of human behavior. Turner, clearly, outdistanced most of his contemporaries in embracing views considered modern by today's professional fraternity. As a pioneer in popularizing those views, he performed a service respected in his day, but largely forgotten since. Viewed in this light, rather than solely as the father of the sectional and frontier interpretations, Frederick Jackson Turner's significance in American historiography is far greater than his successors have generally realized.

He earned this position because he was one of the few scholars who preached what he practiced. Turner was no narrow specialist, absorbed exclusively in the history of frontier and section. Most of his published essays, it is true, were built on those themes, but he spoke the truth when he pointed out to a friend that "my studies for my college classes and in general have taken a wider scope."[31] Turner's interest was in *all* American history, not any one part. He read constantly, widely, voluminously. Late in his career, when asked to evaluate some fifty books on history that had appeared during the preceding two decades, he reported that he was familiar with all but three, and proved his point by summarizing the merits and defects of each. Again in 1923, when he was called on for a list of the most important recent books on the American past, he was able to name two dozen that he had purchased and read, including such diverse fare as Arthur M. Schlesinger's *New Viewpoints in American History*, James Truslow Adams's *Founding of New England*, John S. Bassett's *Andrew Jackson*, Frederic L. Paxson's *Recent History of the United States*, and James Harvey Robinson's *Mind in the Making*.[32] Turner was interested in *everything* about the past, not in any small segment.

Thumbing the thirty-four commodious file drawers of reading notes that he accumulated before his death makes that clear. Here was no evidence of specialization; every phase of the past, from Christopher Columbus to Herbert Hoover, excited his interest and inspired pages of notes, ending with a sheet or two filled with his conclusions and interpretations. He read on the origins of New England towns, and the Great Awakening, and the laws of trade and navigation, and the military campaigns of the Revolution, and the causes of the War of 1812, and the Mexican War, and Reconstruction, and the Free Silver issue, and Progressivism, and the Venezuela Affair, and the diplomatic background of the Washington Conference of 1922. When Turner spent three class periods proving to the Harvard students in History 17 that Justin H. Smith's conclusions on the origins of the Mexican War were largely wrong, he was simply demonstrating the breadth, not the depth, of his learning.[33] He could have discussed most topics in his nation's history with as much knowledge and good sense as he displayed on that occasion.

Nor was Turner's study of the past dictated by idle curiosity alone. His students, he felt, deserved not textbook pabulum, but the sophisticated treatment that only intense study could provide. And, more important, he found all aspects of the past so fascinating that the urge to investigate each in detail was irresistible. At the height of his career he had irons in so many fires that his colleagues chided him with being a "historical trust magnate" who would leave them nothing to do when he published the results of all his investigations. This Turner cheerfully admitted. "My craft goes tramping about so many ports that I feel unable to chart out a sailing route," he confessed to Max Farrand in 1909. Yet he was unwilling to relinquish any of his staked claims. "Until my studies go farther I can't be sure that it would be wise for me to eliminate any period into which I may need to go in the development of my bent."[34] Nor did that urge for universal knowledge abate. "I sometimes wonder," he told Carl Becker, late in his life, "if after all I have not been simply, rather blindly, trying to explain American history to myself instead of writing history!"[35] That was the story of Turner's life.

Nowhere was his catholicity of interest better shown than in the topics studied by his graduate students. Not one of the dozens he trained produced a dissertation that included the word "frontier" in its title; instead, they investigated economic, social, political, cultural, and diplomatic problems in bewildering variety. Their subjects ranged, chronologically, from the study of primitive Indian tribes to the efforts of post-World War I governments to solve labor problems; geographically from the Atlantic to the Pacific and into Latin America. Once, in a reminiscent mood, Turner jotted down the names of those who specialized in agricultural history (fifteen students), the history of public lands (seven), the history of transportation (six), commerce and internal trade (two), literature and thought (two), religion (three), political history (seventeen), diplomacy (ten), and the history of immigration (seven).[36] "They help explain," he wrote, "how the life of the teacher of graduate students checks his own historical output, but furnishes compensations."[37]

Not only his students', but his own writings and speculations added significantly to knowledge in a number of fields not usually associated with his name. In several he served as a pioneer, plowing new ground and suggesting to his colleagues that here was a field worth cultivating. In all, his germinal ideas stimulated progress, even though his own contribution was slight. Those who reaped the harvest recognized this and acknowledged his leadership; during his lifetime he was glorified by agricultural historians, social historians, urban historians, diplomatic historians, and economic historians as the pioneer who had led them into new areas worthy of exploitation. To understand Turner's significance in American history, one must appraise his impact on these varied fields of learning.

His venture into diplomatic history, early in his career, was a by-product of his frontier studies; while investigating the peopling of the Southwest during the late eighteenth century he awakened to the superficiality of the books dealing with English–French–American relations. They were inadequate, he realized, because they failed to weigh the forces shaping diplomatic decision-making, particularly those generated along the southern frontier. "I found it necessary," he later remembered, "to go behind the diplomat and the treaties of annexation to the frontier forces and sectional interests."[38] Here was a new approach to diplomatic history—built on the sensible realization that negotiations could not be understood without understanding the forces operating on the negotiators—that was to revolutionize investigation in that field. Just as innovative was Turner's use of documents from

French, Spanish, and British archives; Henry Adams had pioneered in emphasizing foreign sources, but Turner added further proof that they could not be ignored. "It necessitates the rewriting of the diplomatic history of that period," wrote a prominent historian, after reading one of his articles.[39]

That was a fair judgment by a peer. Turner was, to his contemporaries, a diplomatic historian, worthy of all the honors their profession could bestow. In 1903 he was invited to deliver the annual lectures on diplomatic history before the Naval War College at Newport, and did so with success. Twice, in 1906 and 1907, he was asked to give the prestigious Albert Shaw Lectures in Diplomatic History at the Johns Hopkins University, a series that attracted the most eminent students of foreign affairs. Turner refused, despite the lure of a $250 fee for ten lectures, because he felt that he had strayed far from the field and "hardly dare to trust myself to get into the fascinating web again," but the invitations suggest the high esteem in which he was held.[40] So does a proposal made by Samuel F. Bemis, many years later, that Turner prepare the biographical sketches of James Monroe and Daniel Webster for the multi-volume series on the secretaries of state that he was editing. Again Turner declined, but once more the invitation indicates his reputation as a diplomatic historian among those who knew him best.[41]

His contributions to the study of immigration history were only slightly less significant. When he began his investigations at the turn of the century, no subject was less understood; its students were a handful of sociologists who confined themselves to cataloging the evil results of immigration and compiling statistics on the increase in crime, intemperance, and poverty in areas tainted by the newcomers. Turner did not erase that picture, but he did pioneer a more reasonable—and more accurate—understanding of the contributions of immigrants to the national culture. This was a viewpoint that emerged slowly, and largely as a result of his studies. In his early writings, he was inclined to view westward expansion as a product of Anglo-American superiority and to pay little attention to the impact made by later arrivals on the economy and culture. The series of essays on immigration that Turner wrote for the *Chicago Record-Herald* in 1901—"pot-boilers," he called them—mirrored the racial prejudice of that day and gave newcomers a negative mark when weighed against Anglo-Americans. At this stage of his career he was less bigoted than most of his contemporaries, although he still had much to learn.

Yet even at this time he broke with traditionalism, and the gulf steadily widened. His 1901 essays laid down guidelines for future immigration historians: they should investigate the origins of migration in Europe, the impact on European nations of the exodus, the interaction between environmental and ethnic factors in the process of acculturation, the varying abilities of racial types to achieve integration into American society. These were valuable hints, and they helped shape the course of immigration studies. So was Turner's calm analysis of the "extravagant apprehensions" of nativists, who feared the submersion of native stocks beneath the immigrant tide. By the 1910s he was convinced that American democracy and culture were not solely a product of the Anglo-Saxon heritage, but had been enriched by the mingling of peoples from differing backgrounds. "The reaction of these various stocks," Turner wrote in his last book, "with their different habits, morals and religious doctrines, and ideals, upon one another, led to cross-fertilization and the evolution of a profoundly modified society."[42]

As was usual, however, Turner's most significant contribution to immigration history was made not in his own sparse writings on the subject, but through the students he led into the field. His first doctoral candidate, Kate A. Everest, blazed the trail with her study of German migration to Wisconsin, and blazed it so successfully that Turner repeatedly tried to convince others to follow. "The field of immigration offers an excellent opportunity," he told one student as early as 1902, pointing out that it would be necessary to study in Italy or eastern Europe, to understand the forces inducing emigration, and in the United States, to trace the social, economic, and political progress of the newcomers. Twenty years later Turner was still proselytizing: "there is," he assured a student in 1926, "an opportunity to make a national, indeed international, reputation in the history of immigration to the United States."[43] These were tempting inducements, but the expense of foreign travel and the lack of academic interest in immigration history discouraged all but the most dedicated. In the end, Turner trained only three doctoral students in the subject: Kate A. Everest, George M. Stephenson, and Marcus Lee Hansen.

Miss Everest's contributions were minimal, and those of George Stephenson more traditional than inspirational, but in Marcus Hansen

Turner found a disciple worthy of the master. Hansen's doctoral thesis, presented in 1924, mirrored Turner's own views in its skillful handling of "Emigration from Continental Europe, 1815–1860, with Special Reference to the United States." That emigration, the author argued in the best Turnerian fashion, was simply a continuation of the exodus that had begun in the sixteenth century, and could be understood only in terms of the expelling forces operating on the Continent. Too much had been made of differences between the "Old Immigration," from northern and western Europe, and the "New Immigration," from southern and eastern; both were part of a centuries-old migration pattern that had peopled the United States, bolstered its economy, and enriched its culture. Hansen's findings only footnoted conclusions long held by Turner, but they were revolutionary for that day. So Turner recognized as he set to work to win his young disciple a fellowship for a year's study in Europe before converting his dissertation into a book.[44]

If Hansen had had his way, he would have hoarded his findings until they could be used in the several books that he planned to write. Fortunately, Turner had other ideas. He insisted that Hansen prepare an essay at once on "Immigration History as a Field for Research," to waken the profession to the possibilities of immigration studies. Hansen was less sure. Why should he attract others into a field that he found so profitable? That dog-in-the-manger attitude Turner would not tolerate. "The college instructor," he lectured, "finds a part of his pleasure in letting down the bars, in this revelation of what is behind them; and in these indications of how to get at the grass." Moreover, there was room for any number of researchers in immigration history, and such a paper would clarify its author's own thinking, let him survey his materials as a whole, and allow him to develop new hypotheses.[45] Turner was right. The article, published in the *American Historical Review* early in 1927, launched the modern study of immigration history and won its author distinction as a pioneer in a new era of historical research.

It did not, however, win him a job, for Hansen and Turner were to find that few universities shared their enthusiasm for the study of migration. This Turner was determined to change, even though he foresaw the difficulties. "If Chicago, or Illinois, or Minnesota, or Iowa or Wisconsin could only realize the opportunities in such a field," he wrote, "it would be a great thing—but institutions do not as a rule have the constructive imagination."[46] His best chance was to convert one of the midwestern universities, which he felt to be less tradition-bound than those in the East, and long after his retirement he labored to convince his friends there of the merits of immigration history and Marcus Lee Hansen. Even the Huntington was asked to add Hansen to its staff as a research associate; "there is opportunity here," Turner told the director, "for opening a valuable field on the composition of the American people."[47] Eventually a post was located at the University of Illinois, and there Hansen spent the few years until his untimely death, in 1938, as the nation's premier instructor in immigration history. The lusty growth of that discipline during the next decades obscured his pioneering efforts, but the fact remains that the serious study of migration began with this disciple of Turner, under Turner's guidance and inspiration.

Turner also had a slight claim—less valid, perhaps—to the designation of pioneer in the larger field of economic history. Here he was free to admit that his interest in the rural past prejudiced him against the urban-industrial studies that were gaining in popularity in the twentieth century. "One whose activity has been more continuously in an urban environment," Turner wrote in 1922, "would no doubt lay more stress than I have in my published essays on the importance of the economic revolution substantively."[48] This was too modest a self-appraisal. Turner's search for causal forces led him inevitably into investigation of the economic influences that underlay political behavior, at the same time awakening him to awareness of their importance. As early as 1892 he warned his fellow craftsmen that "very often, the cause of great political events, and great social movements, is economic, and has hitherto been undetected."[49] This was Turner's own discovery; he borrowed little from English and German theorists, although he did rely on the works of J. T. T. Rogers, a British pioneer. Instead, he was one of a little group of social scientists at the University of Wisconsin —among them Lester Ward, Richard T. Ely, and John R. Commons— who were the first to recognize that society rested on an economic base and to redirect attention from surface political manifestations to materialistic causes and motives. Of this group, Turner and Commons went further than the others in integrating economics with history.

The results were less than spectacular in Turner's case, for few of his theories were translated into the written essays that would influence his contemporaries. Yet they recognized that something unusual was happening in Madison, and that students trained in Turner's seminars were better versed in economic theory and more aware of the role of economics in shaping public policies than those trained elsewhere. When Charles A. Beard, later to be credited with originating the economic interpretation of American history, wrote, as he did in 1913, that "almost the only work in economic interpretation which has been done in the United States seems to have been inspired at the University of Wisconsin by Professor Turner," he was simply recognizing something known to his generation, but forgotten since.[50] Turner was not the first to realize the significance of economic forces, but he was among the first in America to do so. Beard was perfectly right when he wrote in 1928 that "Mr. Turner deserves everlasting credit for his services as the leader in restoring the consideration of economic facts to historical writing in America."[51]

Nor was Turner, as his latter-day critics often charged, blind to the importance of a Marxian type of class struggle in American history. Turner read widely on the subject and was familiar with the Marxian interpretation; one of the most heavily underlined books in his library was Antonio Labriola's *Essays on the Materialistic Conceptions of History*, published in 1904 to plead the socialist cause. He realized, however, that class conflicts in the United States were a by-product of industrialization, and played a lesser role than sectional divisions in the rural era that was his concern. In 1908 Turner spoke of the "steady stratification of our society by the development of contesting social classes," but he also pointed out that only in very recent times was it possible "to use the words proletariat and capitalistic classes in reference to American conditions."[52] Turner's detractors, with their ex-post-facto approach to industrialism, failed to appreciate this. They also were unaware of the fact that his students were told that the contest between "the capitalist and the democratic pioneer" was a fundamental fact of the nation's past from early colonial days onward. By both recognizing the role of class conflict in history and refusing to exaggerate its importance, Turner came nearer the truth than some of his critics. He was also correct when he reiterated, as he did time and time again in his letters, that he was not an "economic determinist." With an unshakable belief in multiple causation, Turner scorned overemphasis on any one causal force, even one as persuasive as economics. "I tried," he confessed in 1928, "to keep the relations steadily in mind; but it isn't an easy job, and the effort is sometimes conducive to unwritten books."[53] Turner, to his credit, did "keep the relations steadily in mind," and he refused to succumb to the belief that any one force, whether geographic or idealistic or economic, was deterministic.

If his concern with subsurface influences on political behavior made Turner a pioneer among economic historians, it also assured him a place as a trailblazer in the field of social and intellectual history. To him man was the product of social forces, no less than economic, governed always by ideals, cultural aspirations, and relationships with his fellow-men. Turner awakened to that viewpoint with the beginning of his investigations, but not until he prepared the section on social history for the American Historical Association's Committee on Documentary Historical Publication in 1908 did he realize the woeful lack of publication in that field. "One of the most serious gaps in American historical writing," he wrote that year, "is that of accounts of the social thought of the country." This, he was convinced, would be the next important field of investigation cultivated by scholars. "Thank God," he told a friend, "there will be something left for the next generation of historical seekers!"[54]

That "next generation" showed little inclination to leap on the social history bandwagon; not until a quarter-century later did Arthur Meier Schlesinger and Merle Curti (both ardent admirers of Turner) pioneer that new discipline. Turner filled those years with persistent tub-thumping for the subject. More and more social history materials were larded into his lectures; when one of his former students introduced a course in social history at the University of Illinois, he confessed to Turner, "you might initiate some sort of action, if you knew how heavily I was drawing on your writings and suggestions for the back-bone of the course."[55] Every occasion was used to urge investigation into social and intellectual problems. In 1919, when he was asked to suggest programs that might be supported by the Commonwealth Fund, Turner proposed not only "The Formation of Classes and Class Contests" and "The Natural History of Political Parties," but also "American Ideals as Expressed in Literature, Periodicals, Newspapers," "The Study of Common and Higher Education," "The Church Studied as an Expanding Social Institution," and "The Role of the Oriental, Negro, and Indian in American Society." "American history and American literature cannot be understood apart from each other," he wrote in 1923, adding, a year later, that "a valuable study might be made of the pioneer woman and her place in history."[56] One article, published in 1931, contained such an abundance of social history that a friend believed it would convince the profession that "there is little indeed that is new in the gospel of social intellectual history" then being trumpeted by younger scholars.[57]

Turner's concern with social history was a natural by-product of his own probing into the subsurface forces influencing political behavior. His interest in urban history was less clearly related to his own investigations. Yet, throughout his academic lifetime, Turner saw the city as a major force in American life and worthy of far more attention than it was receiving from historians. As early as 1895, when he addressed the graduating seniors of the Madison High School on "The High School and the City," he could picture the center of national power and culture shifting from the country to cities with the passing of the frontier, and urge his young listeners to change their interest from the rural past to the urban future. "As wealth accumulates as Americans cease their feverish rush for exploiting the country," Turner predicted, "and begin looking for means of life as well as means of livelihood, they will more and more combine their activities to make the city a worthier place."[58] These were strange words for a nineteenth-century historian. They forecast an interest in a phase of history that was not even to be defined for a half-century.

Unfortunately, his reading and speculation on urban history was confined to satisfying his own curiosity or enlightening his classes. Turner's focus, naturally, was on the emergence of western cities and their role in the expansion process. On this subject he read widely, filling a thick folder with enough research notes to prepare a respectable book on western urbanization. Perhaps Turner planned such a book at one time; tucked away in his files was an outline on "The Significance of Western Cities, 1820-1830," that listed such topics to be treated as "Nuclei of Regions," "Centers of Dispersion and Collection," "Markets, Local and Internal Commerce," "Infant Industries and Home Market," and "Intellectual, etc. Influence."[59] That book was never written, but Turner's classes heard a great deal about the importance of western cities. "Study the way in which these cities grew," he urged his students in 1902, "what economic force particularly worked upon them; how they became the metropolis of the particular region in which each of them was located, and how they reacted, in turn, upon the area." Such studies would illuminate not only the story of expansion but the entire history of the United States.[60] This was a bold message for the turn of the century.

Nor was Turner's concern only with western cities. In his later years, particularly, he recognized that future historians would find in urban history the same fascination that his own generation had found in frontier history: "there seems likely to be," he wrote in 1925, "an urban reinterpretation of our history."[61] Once, when progress on THE BOOK was discouragingly slow, Turner went so far as to begin an essay on "The Significance of the City in American History." Typically, this progressed no further than a scant outline and notes, but even those fragments suggest the direction of his thinking: "When and how and why did cities become densely populated. . . . How did urban (including alien) ideas, interests and ideals react on frontier and section. . . . Extent to which the cities were built up by movement from interior rural areas to city. . . . Include editors, teachers, preachers, etc. . . . Its counter influence in modifying frontier and sectional traits."[62] That essay, if it ever had been written, might have set the pattern for urban studies, just as his 1893 essay laid down the guidelines for frontier studies.

Turner's interest in urban history—and social history and economic history and diplomatic history and every other kind of history—was unusual, but not surprising. Once he formulated the basic premise of his historical philosophy—that the past could be understood only by analyzing the social and economic forces that shaped political behavior—he was committed to investigating *every* form of human thought and activity. Turner saw man as a puppet, manipulated by a complex of strings, each representing one of the hundreds of forces—social, economic, idealistic, political, religious, cultural—that operated in combination to control his thought and action. His goal was to understand each of those strings and its relation to all the others. That goal was unobtainable, as Turner found when he tried in THE BOOK to interpret even the two decades between 1830 and 1850, but his striving gave him the breadth of knowledge and the universality of historical experience that won him the respect of his peers.

It also decreed him fame as the historical profession's pioneering crusader for interdisciplinary studies. This, too, was the inevitable result of his view of history. Anyone who sought to master the totality of the human experience had to use not one, but a whole trunkful of tools, borrowed from economists, political scientists, sociologists, demographers, anthropologists, geographers, statisticians, psychologists, and all the rest. Turner used them all, many for the first time, so effectively that his friends in the profession sometimes wondered whether he had deserted them entirely. This made no difference to Turner. He was delighted when he overheard a Harvard undergraduate remark that what Turner was doing in the classroom "might be all right, but it wasn't history." He would willingly be branded a sociologist or an economist or a geographer, as he was on occasion, if that label helped him understand the past. "It is the subject that I am interested in," he told a friend, "and I don't particularly care what name I bear." Nor did he. "I am," he wrote in an undelivered lecture, "one of those who believes in breaking line fences, even at the risk of arrest for trespass, or disclosure of being an amateur, or something worse, breaking into the professional's game."[63]

This was the message that Turner preached to his students and colleagues. Underlying his faith in an interdisciplinary methodology were two basic assumptions. One was his recognition that history was the core subject of the social sciences, and hence the most essential of all to understanding human behavior. Others, such as political science and sociology, had splintered from it, but history would always remain the sum total of the parts into which it had divided. The historical scholar, Turner told the Wisconsin Graduate Club in 1897, must draw his data and techniques from these branches, just as from the main stem.[64] Turner's other basic assumption was that, while history was a complex of social sciences, all the social sciences were one, all part of the whole.[65] "The conception of the One-ness of the thing," as he put it to Carl Becker, was forever in his mind. "I have always," he wrote in 1928, "regarded the interdependence of all the social sciences as fundamentally important and, while I realize that there must be also a division of labor, I think that the division has been so sharply made in the past that there has been a loss to students . . . from the water-tight compartments in which the social sciences have previously been divided."[66] Turner saw history as the mother of the social sciences, and he believed that history's destiny was to unite the scattered family for the benefit of all.

He must, then, convince his fellow craftsmen that this was their duty, and his sermons on the value of the interdisciplinary approach were delivered often. His 1904 address at the St. Louis Exposition, on "Problems in American History," laid down the ground rules more specifically than had his 1892 paper under the same title: "data drawn from studies of literature and art, politics, economics, sociology, psychology, biology, and physiography, all must be used. . . . Without the combined effort of allied sciences we shall reach no such results in the study of social development as have been achieved in the physical world by the attack on problems of natural science by the combined forces of physics, chemistry, and mathematics."[67] Again, in his presidential address before the American Historical Association, Turner returned to the theme—the first president of the Association to do so. One of his last professional acts when joining the Huntington library staff in 1927 was to urge the director to buy books in all the social sciences. "We need allied workers, and allied books," Turner pleaded, "just as the astronomer needs the co-operation of chemist, physicist, geologist, in his work in deciphering the meaning of the universe."[68]

Dedicated evangelist that he was, Turner saw to it that his own researches utilized every possible tool, whatever its label. The nature of those investigations meant that he would lower the barriers between history and geography and history and statistics, particularly the former. This he did so successfully with his use of physiographic data and map-drawing techniques that he was hailed by geographers as one of their own. Turner's occasional addresses before geographic societies were notable affairs; when he spoke before a joint meeting of two of the leading associations in 1914, his talk was hailed as the hit of the session and one of the most stimulating ever presented. "Your work," he was assured, "is so sympathetic with respect to geographic factors that it is a pity we do not see more of you and hear a paper every year."[69] He was made a member of the Association of American Geographers—an honor restricted to about one hundred of the most significant contributors to the field—and a Fellow of the American Geographical Society. His passing was mourned by them as sincerely as by historians. "Professor Turner," recorded the *Geographical Review*, "was a rare combination of historical originality with geographical insight. His death is a loss no less severe to American geography than to the study of American history."

He was only slightly less successful in trampling the line fence separating history and statistics. His sectional studies, requiring as they did the analysis of voting patterns, forced Turner to pioneer the empirical investigation of human behavior on the basis of mass data; he was the first historian to attempt a quantitative study of political motivation. He was also the first to employ statistical techniques to establish correlations between economic activity and politics; thus his figures demonstrated the relationship between support for high tariffs and the concentration of wool production in certain areas. The tables and charts used to authenticate his conclusions seem overly simple to today's statisticians, just as the maps that he used to establish correlations between physiographic conditions, economic activity, and political preferences seem overly complex, yet to his own generation they were marvels of ingenuity. Statisticians glorified him, just as geographers did. When the American Statistical Society sought a speaker to celebrate its seventy-fifth anniversary in 1913, Turner was the one selected—"No one," the president assured him, "is better qualified to speak on this subject from the point of view of the historian than you are." When, a decade later, a book was planned on the inter-relationship of the social sciences, Turner was the logical choice for the essay on the connections between history and statistics.[70] He declined both invitations, but the fact remains that contemporaries in both camps saw him as the premier historical expert in the use of statistical techniques.

Geography and statistics might have been most useful to Turner, but political science and sociology were also appropriated for his toolbag, and in both disciplines he won respect and imitators. Political scientists were so impressed with his systems of election analysis that they paid him the tribute of adopting them for their own use; such distinguished students of government as Frederick Ogg, Paul Reinsch, Arthur Holcombe, and Wilfred Binkley acknowledged that the techniques that won them their reputations were borrowed from Turner. Sociologists were always eager to welcome Turner to their meetings and applaud his findings. "Without so describing himself," wrote the dean of that discipline, Franklin H. Giddings, "he is a sound sociologist, and a ground breaking one of first rate importance."[71] Turner was that rare being who ranged so far beyond his own specialty that he could rub elbows with geographers, cartographers, statisticians, political scientists, economists, and sociologists, and feel as much at home among them as he would at a gathering of the American Historical Association.

Therein lay the measure of his greatness. It has been his misfortune to be labeled by later generations as a monocausationist, riding his hobby-horses of frontier and section, and ignoring the broader historical currents that emerged from the industrial-urban world of the twentieth century. No judgment could be more false. Turner, more than any scholar of his generation, recognized the complexity of the historical process and the need of employing every tool available to understand its every facet. He emphasized—even overemphasized—his own special fields of interest, but his fertile mind illuminated every phase of the past, and his research techniques provided colleagues with the methodology that would bring them closer to the truth. The boldness of his imagination gave his fellow craftsmen stately new edifices to build, and the tools with which to build them. Avery Craven, his friend and admirer, summed up the judgment of Turner's contemporaries when he told the mourners who had gathered to memorialize their friend's departure: "He is claimed by the historians, the sociologists and the geographers and yet he was more than any of these. He was a student of the whole field of social sciences and more than any other man I have ever come in touch with, saw the field as one and was able to integrate it."[72] Turner would have loved that epitaph.

NOTES

Chapter I
From Boyhood to Manhood
1861-1884

1. *Turner Family Magazine*, I (Jan. 1916), and *Turner Genealogy, 1628-1919* (n.p., n.d.), 1-7, Frederick Jackson Turner Papers, Henry E. Huntington Library and Art Gallery, TU Box 62 (hereafter cited as HEH TU). See also HEH TU Box K.

2. For Andrew Jackson Turner's reminiscences of his boyhood and early life, see *Portage Daily Register*, July 11, 1891, and letter to his son, Aug. 21, 1878 (HEH TU Box A). For a brief biographical sketch, see *Wisconsin State Register*, Sept. 25, 1880. More complete is Donald J. Berthrong, "Andrew Jackson Turner, Workhorse of the Republican Party," *Wisconsin Magazine of History*, XXXVIII (Winter 1954), 77-86.

3. Turner to Constance L. Skinner, March 15, 1922, HEH TU Box 31; "Notes for Talk to Harvard History Club, April 24, 1924," HEH TU Box 56.

4. Census Office, *Population of the United States in 1860; Compiled from the Original Returns of the Eighth Census* (Washington, D.C., 1864), 527; James S. Ritchie, *Wisconsin and Its Resources* (3rd ed., Chicago, 1858), 132.

5. For a historical sketch of Portage, see *Portage Democrat*, Aug. 31, 1894. See also John W. Hunt, *Wisconsin Gazeteer* (Madison, 1853), 177-78, and *A History of Columbia County* (Chicago, 1880). Items in *Wisconsin State Register* and *Portage Democrat*, too numerous to be cited, provide information on life in the city.

6. *Wisconsin State Register*, Nov. 23, 1861.

7. Mary O. Turner to "Dear Sister Martha," Jan. 22, 1862, HEH TU Box A; F. J. Turner to Caroline Mae Sherwood (hereafter "Mae Sherwood," the name used by Turner), May 9, 1888, HEH TU Box C.

8. This picture of life in Portage reconstructed from files of *Wisconsin State Register*, 1861-80.

499

9. Ibid. Nov. 22, Dec. 9, 1873. The paper listed forty members of the "Young Fogies," including "Fred Turner."

10. *Portage Democrat,* Oct. 26, 1877.

11. Scrapbook, HEH TU Box 62. Columns in *Wisconsin State Register,* Jan.–Feb. 1878.

12. Loa K. Mausolff to Turner, Nov. 10, 1929, HEH TU Box 42. The *Wisconsin State Register* regularly published high school records.

13. *Wisconsin State Register,* June 22, July 6, 1878.

14. *Wisconsin State Register,* May 23, 1868.

15. Turner to Mae Sherwood, June 15, 1887, HEH TU Box A.

16. *Wisconsin State Register,* June 5, 1875.

17. An appraisal of A. J. Turner's legislative career, taken from the *Milwaukee Journal,* was reprinted in *Wisconsin State Register,* Dec. 26, 1885.

18. Ibid.

19. Ibid. March 11, Aug. 12, 1871; March 16, 23, 1872; Aug. 24, 1899. Berthrong, "Andrew Jackson Turner," 85-86. Turner, "A Talk to a Local Woman's Club," HEH TU Box IV, is on the history of Portage.

20. Turner to Constance L. Skinner, March 15, 1922, HEH TU Box 31.

21. Turner to Mae Sherwood, Sept. 7, 1888, HEH TU Box C.

22. Turner to Joseph Schafer, Oct. 13, 1931. Joseph Schafer Papers, State Historical Society of Wisconsin, MSS IL (hereafter cited as SHSW, Schafer Papers).

23. Turner to F. J. Turner, Feb. 6, 1887, HEH TU Box A.

24. A. J. Turner, letter to *Wisconsin State Register,* June 15, 1867. That journal, Aug. 26, 1865, printed a two-column account by A. J. Turner of "A Trip to the Trout Brooks."

25. Ibid. July 3, 1884; Turner to Mae Sherwood, May 20, 1888, HEH TU Box C.

26. *Wisconsin State Register,* Sept. 18, 25, Oct. 2, 1869.

27. In 1877, and again in 1879, A. J. Turner visited the pineries in connection with land speculations, taking young Fred along. For his printed accounts of these expeditions, see *Wisconsin State Register,* July 28, 1877, July 5, 1879.

28. The *Wisconsin State Register* for 1873 describes in detail the removal of the Indians. See James E. Jones, *A History of Columbia County, Wisconsin* (2 vols., Chicago, 1914), I, 29-31.

29. Turner to Carl Becker, Dec. 16, 1925, HEH TU Box 34A.

30. Ibid. For statistics on ethnic groups in Columbia County, see Census Office, *Statistics of the Population of the United States at the Tenth Census (June 1, 1880). Vol. I* (Washington, D.C., 1883), 446, 534-35.

31. Turner to Mae Sherwood, Sept. 5, 1887, HEH TU Box B.

32. A. J. Turner to Turner, Aug. 21, 1878, HEH TU Box B. In his later years F. J. Turner attached a note to this letter, telling something of his father's boyhood, and adding: "a beautiful example of a tactful parting admonition to a son about to go to college."

33. Frederick Jackson Turner Transcript, University of Wisconsin, University of Wisconsin Archives, Frederick Jackson Turner Miscellaneous File (hereafter cited as U. of Wis. Arch., Turner Misc. File).

34. See *Wisconsin State Register,* Aug. 1879–May 1880.

35. Turner, Commonplace Book, 1881, HEH TU Vol. III (1).

36. *Wisconsin State Register,* April 30, 1881; *University Press,* April 30, 1881.

37. President Bascom's speech is in *The Campus,* Oct. 6, 1881, 6. For the state of college education at the time, see Lawrence R. Veysey, *The Emergence of the American University* (Chicago, 1966), 23-30.

38. *The Badger,* Dec. 7, 1882; Sept. 8, 1883; *University Press,* Jan. 5, 1884.

39. *Wisconsin State Journal,* Sept. 10, Dec. 3, 1881, Jan. 23, 1882. At the back of his Commonplace Book, 1881, Turner listed the concerts, plays, and lectures he enjoyed during the year [HEH TU Vol. III (1)]. *The Badger,* Feb. 23, 1882, 8, notes his trip to Chicago to see a play. For a program of *Othello* which Turner attended in Milwaukee, March 26, 1883, see HEH TU Box 59.

40. *University Press,* Sept. 16, 1882, 5, and *The Badger,* Sept. 30, 1882, 5, describe Turner's election to the Board.

41. Turner, Commonplace Book, 1881, HEH TU Vol. III (1).

42. Turner's speech, *Wisconsin State Journal,* Dec. 1, 1882.

43. *The Campus,* Oct. 6, 13, 1881; *The Badger,* June 23, 1883. For Turner's undergraduate journalistic career, see Fulmer Mood, "Frederick Jackson Turner and the Milwaukee *Sentinel,* 1884," *Wisconsin Magazine of History,* XXXIV (Autumn 1950), 21-28.

44. *University Press,* Nov. 11, 1880.

45. For a history of the university's literary societies, see *Trochos* (April 1884), 72-89; *The Badger,* Jan. 12, May 10, June 15, 1883.

46. For origins of this oration, see Turner, Commonplace Book, 1881, HEH TU Vol. III (1).

47. Turner, oration text, *Wisconsin State Journal,* May 19, 1883; *University Press,* May 26, 1883; *The Badger,* May 24, 1883.

48. Turner listed the books he read in 1881 and 1882 [Commonplace Book, 1881, HEH TU Vol. III (1)].

49. The university recognized three types of "special students": those with inadequate background, those who wished to enter a professional course and needed preparatory training, and those who could not keep up with their regular classes. Turner fitted only the first of these categories (*University Press,* Dec. 27, 1878, *The Aegis,* Sept. 23, 1887).

50. "Frederick Jackson Turner Transcript, University of Wisconsin," U. of Wis. Arch., Turner Misc. File.

51. Turner to Carl Becker, Oct. 26, 1920, HEH TU Box 30.

52. For Allen's teaching methods, see Allen to Herbert B. Adams, Aug. 8, 1886, W. Stull Holt (ed.), *Historical Scholarship in the United States, 1876-1901: as Revealed in the Correspondence of Herbert B. Adams* (Baltimore, 1938), 88; Allen, *University Press,* Feb. 10, 1883; Allen, "Gradation and Topical Method of Historical Study," in G. Stanley Hall (ed.), *Methods of Teaching History* (Boston, 1884), 251-56. Owen G. Stearns, "William Francis Allen: Wisconsin's First Historian," M.A. Thesis (unpubl.), Univ. of Wisconsin, 1955, has been kindly loaned me by the author.

53. Quoted in David B. Frankenburger biographical sketch, William F. Allen, *Essays and Monographs by William Francis Allen: Memorial Volume* (Boston, 1890), 13. For Allen's views on history, see his "The Study of History," *University Press,* Feb. 17, March 2, 16, April 1, 16, May 1, 1874.

54. Allen, "The Study of History," *University Press,* Feb. 17, 1874.

55. *Catalogue of the University of Wisconsin for 1881-1882* (Madison, 1882), 49.

56. Turner, notebooks on Allen's lectures, Frederick Jackson Turner Papers, State Historical Society of Wisconsin (hereafter cited as SHSW, Turner Papers); quotations from Sept. 6, 1882 entry notebook labeled "Ancient Institutions."

57. Notebook, "Medieval Institutions," Oct. 20, 1883, ibid.

58. Allen, "American History Notebook," William Francis Allen Papers, State Historical Society of Wisconsin (hereafter cited as SHSW, Allen Papers).

59. Allen, *History Topics for the Use of High Schools and Colleges* (Boston, 1883); Allen "List of Books for Reference on the History of the United States," *The Badger*, Feb. 15, 1883.

60. John A. Doyle, *History of the United States* (New York, 1876), 7.

61. Herbert B. Adams to W. F. Allen, April 6, 1882; Allen to Adams, April 16, 1882, quoted in Stearns, "William Francis Allen," 241-42.

62. At his son's request, A. J. Turner wrote the son-in-law of Augustin Grignon, April 16, 1883, asking for information [State Historical Society of Wisconsin, Green Bay and Prairie de Chien Papers, Vol. XXVII, 56 (Wis. MSS C)]. For a sound appraisal of Turner's scholarship, see Fulmer Mood and Everett E. Edwards (eds.), "Frederick Jackson Turner's History of the Grignon Tract on the Portage of the Fox and Wisconsin Rivers," *Agricultural History*, XVII (April 1943), 113-14. The essay, reprinted there, originally appeared in the *Wisconsin State Register*, June 23, 1883.

63. Turner, Commonplace Book for 1883, HEH TU Vol. III (2).

64. Ibid.

65. Turner to Carl Becker, Dec. 16, 1925, HEH TU Box 34A.

66. Turner copied many of Bascom's remarks into his Commonplace Book for 1883 [HEH TU Vol. III (2)].

67. For Turner's courses and grades, see "Frederick Jackson Turner Transcript, University of Wisconsin," U. of Wis. Arch., Turner Misc. File, and William F. Allen, "Class Record Books, 1882-1883 and 1883-1884," SHSW, Allen Papers. One of Turner's papers, "Why did Cromwell Fail," is in HEH TU Box 54.

68. "Class Album. University of Wisconsin. Class of 1884," U. of Wis. Arch., IWXF+1884.

69. For Class Day and Commencement ceremonies, see *Wisconsin State Journal*, June 16, 17, 18, 1884, *University Press*, June 21, 1884, and *Wisconsin State Register*, June 21, 1884. His address is in June 21 issue of the last. Ideas and phrases later incorporated in it are in Turner, Commonplace Book for 1883, HEH TU Vol. III (2).

Chapter II
The Making of a Historian: Wisconsin
1884-1888

1. J. Franklin Jameson, "Early Days of the American Historical Association, 1884-1895," *American Historical Review*, XL (Oct., 1934), 2.

2. Frederick J. Turner, *Reuben Gold Thwaites; a Memorial Address* (Madison, 1914), 38. The *Wisconsin State Journal*, June 19, 1884, and *University Press*, June 21, 1884, reported the offer of an assistant instructorship in rhetoric, and his refusal.

3. Quotation, *Wisconsin State Journal*, April 17, 1884. For Turner's activity on the *Milwaukee Sentinel*, see Fulmer Mood, "Frederick Jackson Turner and the Milwaukee *Sentinel*, 1884," *Wisconsin Magazine of History*, XXXIV (Autumn 1950), 21-28.

4. The *Wisconsin State Register*, Feb. 7, 1885, began a column of Madison news signed "F." For Turner's career on the *Inter-Ocean*, see Fulmer Mood, "Frederick Jackson Turner and the Chicago *Inter-Ocean*, 1885," *Wisconsin Magazine of History*, XXXV (Spring 1952), 188-94, 210-18.

5. *Wisconsin State Journal*, April 11, 1885.

6. *Catalogue of the University of Wisconsin for the Academic Year 1885-1886* (Madison, 1885), 9, 64.

7. *Wisconsin State Journal*, May 29, 1886; *University Press*, June 4, 1886.

8. Turner to Mae Sherwood, Aug. 8, 21, 1886, HEH TU Box A.

9. University of Wisconsin, Instructional Report, Fall Term, 1886. Each instructor filed a report each quarter listing courses, hours of instruction, and number of students (U. of Wis. Arch.).

10. *The Aegis*, April 13, May 4, 1887. This was apparently a voluntary extra course, listed in neither the catalogue nor the quarterly "Instructional Reports."

11. *Catalogue of the University of Wisconsin for the Academic Year 1886-1887* (Madison, 1886), 16.

12. Turner to Andrew J. Turner, Sept. 23, 1885, HEH TU Box A.

13. Turner to Mae Sherwood, May 22, 1887, HEH TU Box A.

14. Turner to Mae Sherwood, June 27, 1886, ibid.

15. Turner to Mae Sherwood (n.d.), ibid.

16. Turner to Mae Sherwood, [June 16, 1887], HEH TU Box B.

17. Turner's letters to his mother, father, and sister describing his adventures are in HEH TU Box B; also published in Ray A. Billington (ed.), "Frederick Jackson Turner Visits New England: 1887," *New England Quarterly*, XLI (Sept., 1968), 409-36.

18. Turner to Mae Sherwood, July 25, 1888, HEH TU Box B.

19. Ibid. Aug. 24, 1887.

20. Ibid. Nov. 12, 1887.

21. Ibid. March 10, 1888, HEH TU Box C.

22. Ibid. Oct. 23, 1887, HEH TU Box B.

23. Ibid Jan. 14, 1888, HEH TU Box C. The *Wisconsin State Journal*, Jan. 23, 1888, reported that Turner had assumed the teaching of Allen's classes. For statistics on teaching hours and number of pupils, see Turner, Instructional Report, Winter Term, 1887-1888, U. of Wis. Arch.

24. Turner to Mae Sherwood, Oct. 4, 1887, HEH TU Box B.

25. Ibid. Sept. 11, 1887.

26. Turner, American History Notebooks, 1887-88, HEH, Vol. XIV (1), (2); Vol. XV (1), (2).

27. Turner to Mae Sherwood, Oct. 16, 1887, HEH TU Box B. For a description of the library, see *Wisconsin State Journal*, Feb. 2, 1885. Clifford

Lord and Carl Ubbelohde, *Clio's Servant: A History of the State Historical Society of Wisconsin* (Madison, 1967), is a full history.

28. Turner to Mae Sherwood, Sept. 5, 1887, HEH TU Box B.

29. Ibid. March 25, 1888, HEH TU Box C.

30. Ibid.

31. Turner, Commonplace Book [1886], HEH TU Vol. III (3).

32. Turner to William F. Allen, July 11, 1888, SHSW, Turner Papers, Box II.

33. Turner to Mae Sherwood, [Aug. 21], 1887, HEH TU Box B.

34. Turner, "Review of Edward E. Hale and Edward E. Hale, Jr., *Franklin in France* (Boston, 1887)," *The Dial*, VIII (May 1887), 7-10; "Review of Edward E. Hale and Edward E. Hale, Jr., *Franklin in France*, Part II (Boston, 1888)," ibid. IX (Dec. 1888), 204-6. Copies of reviews, HEH TU Box 54. Turner's careful preparation is revealed in notes summarizing every book or article on the subject then in print (HEH TU File Drawer 4C, Folder: Peace Treaty).

35. Turner, "Review of Gilmore, *John Sevier*," *The Nation*, Oct. 6, 1887, 278.

36. Turner to Mae Sherwood, March 21, 1888, HEH TU Box C.

37. Turner, "Wisconsin," *Encyclopaedia Britannica* (9th ed., New York, 1888), XXIV, 616-19. Reprinted, with editorial notes and introduction, in Fulmer Mood (ed.), "Little Known Fragments of Turner's Writings," *Wisconsin Magazine of History*, XXIII (March 1940), 328-38.

38. Turner described his struggle to finish the work on time in letters to Mae Sherwood, Jan. 22, July 30, Aug. 8, 1888. On its publication, the *Wisconsin State Journal* (Sept. 20, 1888), noted: "He is a very able and industrious young man, and a thorough student. His many friends feel confident that the world will yet hear from him."

39. Turner, *Outline Studies in the History of the Northwest* (Chicago, 1888). A rough draft of what is apparently an early version, labeled "The Development of the Great West," is attached to Turner to William F. Allen, Oct. 31, 1888, HEH TU Box 1.

40. Turner expressed his views on religion in a letter to his mother, Mary O. Turner, July 15, 1887, and in letters to Mae Sherwood, Dec. 12, 1886, Jan. 22, 1888 (HEH TU Boxes A, B, and C).

41. *The Aegis*, April 8, 1887, 10. The Channing Club was described in *Trochos*, III (1888), 161. Turner was also active in the Shakespeare Club (Turner to Mae Sherwood, Dec. 2, 1887, Feb. [9], 1888, HEH TU Boxes B, C).

42. Turner to Mae Sherwood, Sept. 15, 1887, HEH TU Box B.

43. For discussion on von Holst's history, see *Wisconsin State Journal*, Nov. 11, 1886; for Henry George's lecture, ibid. March 23, 30, 1887. Discussion of George's thesis, ibid. April 28, 1887, and Turner to Mae Sherwood, May 11, 1887, HEH TU Box A.

44. *Wisconsin State Journal*, Dec. 31, 1887, Jan. 16, 31, 1888, described the series.

45. Turner to Mae Sherwood, Jan. 7, Feb. 9, 28, March 3, 1888, HEH TU Box C.

46. Draft of Turner's address, HEH TU File Drawer 14A, Folder: Ordinance of 1787.

47. For extended summary of lecture, see *Wisconsin State Journal,* March 10, 1888.
48. Turner to Mae Sherwood, March 10, 1888, HEH TU Box C.
49. *Wisconsin State Journal,* March 27, 1888.
50. Turner to Mae Sherwood, Sept. 4, Oct. 16, 23, Dec. 4, 1887; April 22, 1888, HEH TU Boxes B and C.
51. Ibid. Oct. 16, 1887, HEH TU Box B. See *Wisconsin State Journal,* Nov. 15, 1887, for Turner's talk, "The Fur Trade of Wisconsin."
52. Turner to Mae Sherwood, May 2, 8, 1888, HEH TU Box C.
53. Ibid. May 2, 1888, HEH TU Box C.
54. Ibid. May 12, 1888.
55. For report of meeting and summary of Turner's paper, see *Wisconsin State Journal,* May 15, 1888, *Wisconsin State Register,* May 26, 1888. See also MS, "Journal of the Madison Literary Club, 1877-1903," MSS Division, State Historical Society of Wisconsin.
56. Turner to Mae Sherwood, May 14, 1888, HEH TU Box C.
57. Turner, "The Character and Influence of the Fur Trade in Wisconsin," *State Historical Society of Wisconsin Proceedings,* XXXVI (Madison, 1889), 52-98. Quotation, pp. 97-98. Notes on the geography of the region, probably from reading done at this time, are in HEH TU File Drawer 15, Folder: Physical Geography U.S.
58. Turner to Mae Sherwood, April 13, 1888, HEH TU Box C.
59. *Wisconsin State Journal,* June 20, 1888. Turner described his negotiations with President Chamberlin (Turner to Mae Sherwood, April 13, 19, 22, 1888, HEH TU Box C). By the time he applied to Johns Hopkins the deadline for scholarship applications had passed (ibid. May 23, 1888).
60. *Wisconsin State Journal,* June 8, 1888.
61. Turner to Mae Sherwood, June 15, Aug. 8, 18, 1888, HEH TU Box C.

Chapter III
The Making of a Historian: Johns Hopkins
1888-1889

1. Turner to Mae Sherwood, Sept. 16, 1888, HEH TU Box C.
2. Ibid. Sept. 5, 1888.
3. Ibid. Sept. 26, 1888.
4. Ibid. Sept. 29, Oct. 2, 1888, Jan. 21, 1889, HEH TU Boxes C and D; Turner to Mary O. Turner, Oct. 6, 1888, HEH TU Box D.
5. *Johns Hopkins University Circulars,* VIII, No. 68 (Nov. 1888), 6, listed the students in each class. Turner was the only graduate student in the introductory mathematics class. See also "Transcript of Graduate Record of Frederick Jackson Turner," office of University Registrar, Johns Hopkins. A copy was supplied to the Huntington Library by Irene M. Davis and Ellen G. Klages of that office.
6. Turner, "The West as a Field for the Scholar," apparently a lecture to a Johns Hopkins alumni group (HEH TU File Drawer 15A, Folder: The West as a Field).
7. *The Aegis,* Dec. 14, 1888, 8. For a description of instructional methods at Johns Hopkins, see Hugh Hawkins, *Pioneer: A History of the Johns*

Hopkins University, 1874-1889 (Ithaca, 1960), 220-29; and A. S. Eisenstadt, *Charles McLean Andrews* (New York, 1956), 5-7. Andrews was Turner's contemporary at Johns Hopkins.

8. Herbert B. Adams, *The Study of History in American Colleges and Universities* (Washington, D.C., 1887), 173-92 (quotation, p. 192), describes the seminar.

9. For history teaching at that time see Frederick Rudolph, *The American College and University* (New York, 1962), 334-96. For the origins of the American Historical Association, see David D. Van Tassel, *Recording America's Past. An Interpretation of the Development of Historical Studies in America, 1607-1884* (Chicago, 1960), 171-79.

10. Excellent on American historiography at that time is John Higham *et al., History* (Englewood Cliffs, N.J., 1965), 92-97, 158-60, and two works by Edward N. Saveth, "A Science of American History," *Diogenes,* XXVI (Summer 1959), 107-22, and "Scientific History in America: Eclipse of an Idea," Donald Sheehan and Harold C. Syrett (eds.), *Essays in American Historiography* (New York, 1960), 1-19.

11. Herbert B. Adams, *The Germanic Origins of New England Towns* (Baltimore, 1882), 1. Brief accounts of Adams' career are in Hawkins, *Pioneer: A History of the Johns Hopkins University,* 169-186, and in *Herbert Baxter Adams, Tributes of His Friends* (Baltimore, 1902), 9-49. The best account of the Teutonic school in America is Jurgen Herbst, *The German Historical School in American Scholarship* (Ithaca, 1965).

12. Turner to Mae Sherwood, Oct. 5, 6, 1888, HEH TU Box D. Charles McLean Andrews was a member of this seminar, and he described the meetings in weekly letters to his mother [Charles McLean Andrews Papers, Historical Manuscripts Division, Yale University Library (hereafter cited as Yale, Andrews Papers)]. The seminar's secretary's reports are: Johns Hopkins University, "Seminar Records," Archives of Johns Hopkins University (microfilm copies in Huntington Library).

13. Turner to Mary O. Turner, Oct. 7, 1888; Turner to Mae Sherwood, Oct. 12, 1888, HEH TU Box D.

14. Turner, "Notes for Talks to Graduate Club, University of Wisconsin, December 19, 1908." HEH TU Box 55. For Allen's advice, see William F. Allen to Turner, Oct. 14, 1888; Turner to Allen, Oct. 31, 1888, HEH TU Box 1.

15. Turner to Mae Sherwood, Feb. 3, March 16, 1889, HEH TU Box D.

16. Ibid. Dec. 27, 30, 1888.

17. Ibid. May 14, 1889. The *Wisconsin State Journal,* Jan. 4, 1889, described the reading of the paper. Parkman to Turner, May 2, 1889, HEH TU Box 1.

18. Johns Hopkins University, "Seminar Records, 1888-1889," 420-21. These records are in Wendell H. Stephenson (ed.), "The Influence of Woodrow Wilson on Frederick Jackson Turner," *Agricultural History,* XIX (Oct. 1945), 252 n. 11. The remark praising the paper was made by Woodrow Wilson (Turner to William E. Dodd, Oct. 7, 1917, HEH TU Box 29).

19. Turner to Mary O. Turner, Oct. 6, 1888, ibid. Box D. Turner also described the first seminar in letters to William F. Allen, Oct. 6, 1888, and

Mae Sherwood, Oct. 7, 1888 (HEH TU Boxes 1 and D). John M. Vincent, "Herbert B. Adams," Howard W. Odum (ed.), *American Masters of Social Science* (New York, 1927), 99-127, explains Adams' interest in adult education.

20. Turner to Mae Sherwood, March 29, 1889, HEH TU Box D. A printed program and outline of the lecture is enclosed in this letter. He described his apprehension in letters to Mae Sherwood, Jan. 13, Feb. 8, 13, 1889, HEH TU Box D.

21. Turner to Mae Sherwood, Feb. 13, 1889, ibid.

22. Ibid. Feb. 28, 1889.

23. Turner to Mae Sherwood, Feb. 3, 8, 22, April [?], 1889, ibid. Box D.

24. *Johns Hopkins University Circular*, VIII, No. 71 (March 1889), 54.

25. Turner to Mary O. Turner, Oct. 6, 1888; Turner to Mae Sherwood, [Feb.-March, 1889], HEH TU Box D.

26. Turner to Mae Sherwood, March 30, April [?], 1889, ibid.

27. Ibid. April 14, 1889.

28. The effect of Johns Hopkins on Turner can be realized by comparing the two versions of his thesis, that printed as "The Character and influence of the Fur Trade in Wisconsin," *Wisconsin State Historical Society Proceedings*, XXXVI (Madison, 1889), 52-98, and the doctoral version, "The Character and Influence of the Indian Trade in Wisconsin, A Study of the Trading Post as an Institution," *Johns Hopkins University Studies in Historical and Political Science*, 9th Series (Baltimore, 1891). The quotations are from the latter.

29. Ibid. 89, 104, 168-69, 172.

30. Turner to Mae Sherwood, March 16, April 18, 1889, HEH TU Box D.

31. Turner to Richard T. Ely, Jan. 28, 1902, Richard T. Ely Papers, Manuscripts Section, State Historical Society of Wisconsin, Wis. MSS. MK (hereafter cited as SHSW, Ely Papers).

32. Herbert B. Adams, "Special Methods of Historical Study as Pursued at the Johns Hopkins University and at Smith College," *Johns Hopkins University Studies in Historical and Political Science*, 2nd Ser. (Baltimore, 1884), 15.

33. Turner to William F. Allen, Oct. 31, 1888, HEH TU Box 1.

34. Turner to Helen Solliday, May 27, 1920, HEH TU Box 44.

35. Turner's notes on Small's course, HEH TU File Drawer 15A, Folder: Notes on A. W. Small (18 pp.).

36. Turner's notes on Wilson's course, HEH TU File Drawer 1A, Folder: Mass. Town Lands, "Wilson Lectures at JHU" (6 pp.). Wilson incorporated many of his lectures in *The State: Elements of Historical and Practical Politics* (Boston, 1889).

37. Turner to William E. Dodd, Oct. 7, 1919, HEH TU Box 29.

38. The standard treatment of Ely is Benjamin G. Rader, *The Academic Mind and Reform: The Influence of Richard T. Ely in American Life* (Lexington, Ky., 1966), which deals more with Ely's reform activities than with his economic theories. Ely is also pictured in Oliver E. Baker to Henry G. Taylor, Feb. 19, 1944, SHSW, Ely Papers.

39. Turner copied the list of books assigned by Ely and pasted it in his copy of John Stuart Mill, *Principles of Political Economy* (London, 1886),

Huntington Library, Accession No. 211882. Ely at this time was lecturing from the manuscript of a book: *An Introduction to Political Economy* (New York, 1889); the views that he expressed in his lectures, and probably much of the language, may thus be determined.

40. Note in Simon N. Patten, *The Premises of Political Economy* (Philadelphia, 1885), 69. Turner's copy of the book, with this and other marginal notations, is in the Huntington Library (Call No. HB 171 P 3).

41. Mill, *Principles of Political Economy*, 17, 109, 110, 261.

42. Francis A. Walker, *Land and Its Rent* (Boston, 1883), 21, 25-26, 45-47; Patten, *Premises of Political Economy*, 11-12. Turner underlined a passage in Patten's book stating that intruding lower classes with lesser living standards normally displaced higher classes because they consumed less and hence could sell a larger proportion of their produce. He later used this quotation in a letter to Professor W. F. Allen (Dec. 31, 1888, HEH TU Box 1), discussing the changes in the Wisconsin countryside resulting from the German migrations.

43. Ibid.

44. Turner assumed that he would return to Madison; all through the winter he discussed course offerings with Professor Allen (Turner to William F. Allen, Oct. 31, Dec. 31, 1888, ibid). He told of his campaign among friends in a letter to Mae Sherwood (Feb. 3, 1889, ibid. Box D).

45. *Wisconsin State Register*, Jan. 12, 1889; *Wisconsin State Journal*, Feb. 9, 1889.

46. Thomas C. Chamberlin to Turner, April 10, 1889, enclosed in Turner to Mae Sherwood, April 15, 1889, HEH TU Boxes 1 and D. Chamberlin's final offer to Turner is in Chamberlin to Turner, Feb. 27, 1889, ibid. Box 1.

47. Turner to Mae Sherwood, Feb. 28, 1889, ibid. Box D. Official letter of appointment from Board of Regents, July 8, 1889, ibid. Box 1.

48. Turner left no description of his examination, but the scene can be reconstructed from the account written by Charles M. Andrews to his mother, April 22, 1889 (Yale, Andrews Papers). Turner was informed of his success in Richard T. Ely to Turner, June 27, 1889 (pasted in Turner's copy of Mill, *Principles of Political Economy*, [HEH Accession No. 211882]).

Chapter IV
Teaching—and the Emerging Frontier Thesis
1889-1892

1. Turner to Mae Sherwood, July 4, 1889, HEH TU Box D.

2. Ibid.

3. Ibid. Aug. 2, 1889, HEH TU Box E.

4. Oscar D. Brandenburg to Turner, April 20, 1889, HEH TU Box 1. Professor Brandenburg estimated $240 a year for a house, $130 for a servant, $75 for fuel and light, and $480 for food and drink.

5. Turner, "Theodore Roosevelt, *The Winning of the West* (G. P. Putnam's Sons)," *The Dial*, X (Aug. 1889), 71-73.

6. Turner to Constance L. Skinner, March 15, 1922, HEH TU Box 31.

7. Turner to Mae Sherwood, Sept. 8, 1889, HEH TU Box E.

8. Ibid. Sept. 15, 1889. All universities were increasing rapidly in size at this time. See Lawrence R. Veysey, *The Emergence of the American University* (Chicago, 1966), 264-66.

9. Turner to William F. Allen, Jan. 16, March 14, 1889, HEH TU Box 1.

10. University of Wisconsin, "Instructional Report, Fall Term, 1889-1890." U. of Wis. Arch.

11. Turner to Mae Sherwood, Nov. 19, 1889, HEH TU Box E. They discussed preparations for the wedding in letters of Oct. 21, 25, Nov. 5, 14, 15, 1889, ibid.

12. *Chicago Tribune,* quoted in *Wisconsin State Journal,* Nov. 29, 1889.

13. *Wisconsin State Register,* Nov. 30, 1889.

14. Ibid. Dec. 22, 1889; *Wisconsin State Journal,* Jan. 25, 1890; Turner to Mae Turner, Jan. 25, 30, 1890, HEH TU Box E.

15. William F. Allen, *A Short History of the Roman People* (Boston, 1890), v.

16. Turner to Herbert B. Adams, Jan. 11, 1890, HEH TU Box 1; Univ. of Wis., "Instructional Reports, Fall, Spring Terms, 1889-1890," Univ. of Wis. Arch.

17. Turner left no description of his doctoral examinations, but they probably duplicated those taken by Charles McLean Andrews in May 1889, which Andrews described to his mother in a letter, May 19, 1889 (Yale, Andrews Papers).

18. Turner to Lois K. Mathews, March 21, 1906; Turner to Thomas P. Abernethy, March 12, 1926, HEH TU Boxes 6, 35.

19. Turner delayed publication while he sought permission to add, at his own expense, maps locating Indian tribes and illustrating boundary disputes (Turner to Herbert B. Adams, May 7, Oct. 19, 1891, HEH TU Box 1).

20. *The Aegis,* Jan. 15, 1892, and *Wisconsin State Journal,* Dec. 14, 1891, commented favorably on the book and noted the "charm of an excellent literary style."

21. Turner to Woodrow Wilson, Jan. 23, 1890, HEH TU Box 1.

22. Turner to Mae Turner, Sept. 30, 1891; Oct. 15, 1892, ibid. Box E.

23. Mae Turner prepared two baby books for her children, describing their growth and illnesses (HEH TU Vol. X). See also *Portage Daily Register,* March 17, 19, 26, 28, April 16, 1891.

24. *Wisconsin State Journal,* Jan. 3, 1890, Jan. 16, May 28, June 1, 10, Dec. 8, 1891; Feb. 3, Sept. 26, 1892.

25. Ibid. March 5, 1890.

26. Turner to Richard T. Ely, Jan. 25, 29, 1892, SHSW, Ely Papers, Box 8.

27. Ibid. Feb. 1, 1892.

28. *Wisconsin State Journal,* Feb. 15, April 8, 1892. For a scrapbook containing printed notices of the new school, see SHSW, Ely Papers, Box 8 (16 pp.). The founding of the school is described in Benjamin G. Rader, *The Academic Mind and Reform: The Influence of Richard T. Ely in American Life* (Lexington, Ky., 1966), 106-11.

29. *The Aegis,* April 8, 1892, 447-50 (this was reprinted as a circular and 15,000 copies circulated). *Daily Cardinal,* April 13, 1892.

30. *Daily Cardinal,* Nov. 16, 1892; *Wisconsin State Journal,* Nov. 16, 1892.
31. Univ. of Wis., "Instructional Reports, 1891-1892," U. of Wis. Arch.
32. *The Badger for 1891* (Madison, 1890), 174; *The Badger for 1893* (Madison, 1892), 76-77.
33. Syllabi, HEH TU File Drawer 4D, Folder: Constitutional History Syllabus. Scattered fragments of lectures in HEH TU File Drawer 2C, Folder: Colonial Central Government; File Drawer 3A, Folder: Local Government; File Drawer 12B, Folder: Sovereignty; and File Drawer 15B, Folder: Puritanism, English.
34. *The Aegis,* May 8, 1891, *Wisconsin State Journal,* May 9, June 13, 1891; *Portage Daily Register,* May 11, 1891, described the course and the reaction to it.
35. See HEH TU Box 54.
36. Turner to Merle Curti, Aug. 8, 1928, HEH TU Box 39.
37. *The Aegis,* Oct. 10, 1890.
38. Turner to Herbert B. Adams, Oct. 19, 1891, HEH TU Box 1. *The Aegis,* Oct. 2, 1891, reported the seminar would stress the 1830-40 period. Its operation described, ibid. May 27, 1892.
39. Ibid. May 27, 1892; *Daily Cardinal,* Dec. 13, 1892.
40. Notes, HEH TU File Drawer 6B, Folder: Wisconsin Milwaukee Area. Old Settlers. Turner's early graduate students are described in Fulmer Mood, "The Development of Frederick Jackson Turner as a Historical Thinker," *Colonial Society of Massachusetts Transactions, 1937-1942,* XXXIV (Boston, 1943), 328-31.
41. Turner to Herbert B. Adams, Dec. 8, 1890, HEH TU Box 1.
42. *The Aegis,* Feb. 6, 1891. Address published, *Proceedings of the State Historical Society of Wisconsin,* XXXVIII (Madison, 1891), 93-99.
43. *Wisconsin State Journal,* Aug. 27, 1890; *Wisconsin Journal of Education,* XXI (Oct. 1891), 230-34, (Nov. 1891), 253-56.
44. Turner described his extension experiences in "The Extension Work of the University of Wisconsin," *University Extension,* I (April 1892), 311-24, and George F. Ames (ed.), *Handbook of University Extension* (2nd ed., Philadelphia, 1893). Local newspapers also reported his speaking engagements (see esp. *Wisconsin State Journal,* Jan. 24, Sept. 16, Oct. 22, Nov. 6, 10, 13, 1891).
45. Turner to Herbert B. Adams, Jan. 18, 1892, HEH TU Box 1.
46. Indications of the books Turner read may be gained from a sheet listing books on "Colonization in General," as well as from the syllabi in which he listed readings (HEH TU File Drawer 15D, Folder: Colonization Bibliography). In this same folder are three pages of his reading notes, with the observations quoted above.
47. John A. Doyle, *English Colonies in America. Virginia, Maryland, and the Carolinas* (New York, 1882), 1-2.
48. See HEH TU File Drawer 5D, Folder: Extension Lecture.
49. Frederick J. Turner, *The Colonization of North America* (n.p., n.d. [1891?]); *Syllabus of a University Extension Course of Six Lectures on the Colonization of North America* (Madison, n.d. [1892?]); *The Colonization of North America from the Earliest Times to 1763* (Madison, 1893), HEH TU Vol. VI (1) (2) (3).

50. For Turner's colonization lectures, see HEH TU File Drawer 1E, Folder: Colonization Lecture; File Drawer 15A, Folder: Norsemen as Colonizers; File Drawer 15C, Folder: Spain as Colonizer; File Drawer 15D, Folder: Spain as Colonizer c. 1905-1910; File Drawer 15D, Folder: France as Colonizer; File Drawer 15D, Folder: Colonization Modern England; File Drawer 2D, Folder: Virginia Colonization; File Drawer 15D, Folder: Colonization: Oriental, Roman, Teutonic.

51. This lecture (33 pp.), typed, is in HEH TU File Drawer 15A, Folder: Lecture. American Colonization. Turner notes on the cover that it was delivered February 9, 1891, but prepared in January 1891.

52. *The Aegis*, Oct. 9, 1891.

53. Ibid. Nov. 4, 1892. Turner put a copy of this issue in a manila folder, on which he wrote: "Contains first form of my doctrine of frontier. Prior to my paper in AHA 1893 I had not read Ratzel, or Godkin, or other writer who deals with this problem" (HEH TU Box 54). Also preserved is a copy of the essay on which Turner wrote: "This with the Fur Trade thesis constitute the beginning of my writings on the frontier as a symbol of the western movement & its reactions on the East and the Old World" (HEH Accession Order No. 126772). The essay was reprinted in *The Early Writings of Frederick Jackson Turner* (Madison, 1938), as was his "The Significance of History."

54. Turner to Max Farrand, Oct. 13, 1916, HEH TU Box 26.

55. Simon N. Patten to Turner, Nov. 14, 1892; Francis N. Thorpe to Turner, Dec. 11, 1892; Emory R. Johnson to Turner, Nov. 14, 1892; Charles M. Andrews to Turner, Nov. 29, 1892; Herbert B. Adams to Turner, Nov. 28, 1892, HEH TU Box 1.

Chapter V
The Genesis of the Frontier Thesis
1892-1893

1. The topics covered in this chapter are developed in Ray A. Billington, *The Genesis of the Frontier Thesis: A Study in Historical Creativity* (San Marino, Calif., 1971).

2. Edwin L. Godkin, "Aristocratic Opinions of Democracy," *North American Review*, CCVI (Jan. 1865), 194-232. American writers who speculated on the frontier's influence before Turner are described in Herman C. Nixon, "Precursors of Turner in the Interpretation of the American Frontier," *South Atlantic Quarterly* XXVIII (Jan. 1929), 83-93; English writers are discussed in William M. Tuttle, Jr., "Forerunners of Frederick Jackson Turner: Nineteenth-Century British Conservatives and the Frontier Thesis," *Agricultural History*, XLI (July 1967), 219-27. Ernest Marchand, "Emerson and the Frontier," *American Literature*, III (May 1931), 149-74, cautiously explores Ralph Waldo Emerson's views on the impact of frontiering. Turner was probably unfamiliar with most of his precursors; he first saw Godkin's essay in 1896, read it, chuckled, and said, "Godkin has stolen my thunder."

3. The social background of Turner's essay is admirably described in Lee Benson, "The Historical Background of Turner's Frontier Essay," *Agricultural History*, XXV (April 1951), 59-82.

4. Josiah Strong, *Our Country* (New York, 1885), 160-61. For the relationship between the closing of the frontier and the immigration restriction movement see John Higham, *Strangers in the Land* (New Brunswick, N.J., 1955), 133-41.

5. Benson, "Historical Background of Turner's Frontier Essay," *loc. cit.* 70-76, summarizes these arguments.

6. Newspaper clippings and outlines for the immigration sequence, HEH TU File Drawer 16D, Folder: Immigration Syllabus. The undergraduate thesis on "The Effect of the Settlement of the Public Domain on Immigration" was prepared in 1894 by Court W. Lamoreux.

7. Edward Channing, "Genesis of the Massachusetts Town," *Proceedings of the Massachusetts Historical Society*, 2nd Ser., VII (1891-92), 388-89; Charles M. Andrews, "Some Recent Aspects of Institutional History," *Yale Review*, I (Feb. 1893), 381-410. Andrews' rebellion is described in A. S. Eisenstadt, *Charles McLean Andrews* (New York, 1956), 12-25, 37-60, 79-105. The best general account of this period is John Higham, *History* (Englewood Cliffs, N.J., 1965), 162-70; a special aspect is explored by Robert E. Lerner, "Turner and the Revolt Against E. A. Freeman," *Arizona and the West*, V (Summer 1963), 101-8.

8. This point is well made in Richard Hofstadter, *The Progressive Historians. Turner, Beard, Parrington* (New York, 1968), 49-50.

9. Turner to William E. Dodd, Oct. 7, 1919, HEH TU Box 29.

10. Roland B. Nixon, "Notes on Anthropology," *Bulletin of the American Geographical Society*, XXXI (1899), No. 1, 60. A valuable account of environmentalism among geographers at that time is G. Tatham, "Environmentalism and Possibilism," Griffith Taylor (ed.), *Geography in the Twentieth Century* (London, 1951), 128-62. William Coleman, "Science and Symbol in the Turner Frontier Hypothesis," *American Historical Review*, LXXII (Oct. 1966), 22-49, describes the manner in which Turner was influenced by findings in geography and biology.

11. James D. Dana, *Manual of Geology* (4th ed., New York, 1896), 1034.

12. Justin Winsor, *The Mississippi Basin* (Boston, 1895), dedication; B. A. Hinsdale, *How To Study and Teach History* (New York, 1894), 110-26.

13. Henry F. Osborn, "The Present Problem of Heredity," *Atlantic Monthly*, LXVII (March 1891), 354. *See also* Harland E. Allen, "Hugo de Vries and the Reception of the 'Mutation Theory,'" *Journal of the History of Biology*, II (Spring 1969), 55-65; Edward J. Pfeifer, "The Genesis of American Neo-Lamarckism," *Isis*, LVI (Summer 1965), 156-61, and George W. Stocking, Jr., "Lamarckianism in American Social Science," *Journal of the History of Ideas*, XXIII (April-June 1962), 239-56.

14. Turner joined the Academy as a graduate student in 1887 and was a frequent contributor to its programs thereafter.

15. "Review of: 'Statistical Atlas of the United States. Part II.–Population, Social and Industrial Statistics. Part III.–Vital Statistics,'" *The International Review*, II (Jan. 1875), 131. For the influence of statistical cartography on Turner, see Fulmer Mood, "The Rise of Official Statistical Cartography in Austria, Prussia, and the United States, 1855-1872," *Agricultural History*, XX (Oct. 1946), 209-25, and "The Development of Frederick Jackson Turner as a Historical Thinker," *Transactions of the Colonial Society of Massachusetts, 1937-1942*, XXXIV (Boston, 1943), 283-352.

16. Francis A. Walker, *Statistical Atlas of the United States Based on the Results of the Ninth Census* (n.p., 1874), 1-4.

17. A note jotted by Turner about 1891 reads: "Walker puts body of continuous settlement thus: 1790–83° W. Long. 1810–88°30′, 1830–95°; 1850–99°; 1870–99°45′″ (HEH TU 3 × 5 Drawer 1, Section: Frontier).

18. Francis A. Walker, "Growth and Distribution of Population," *The First Century of the Republic: A Review of American Progress* (New York, 1876), 211.

19. Henry Gannett, "The Settled Areas and the Density of Our Population," *The International Review*, XII (Jan. 1882), 70.

20. Fletcher W. Hewes and Henry Gannett, *Scribner's Statistical Atlas of the United States Showing by Graphic Methods Their Present Condition and Their Political, Social and Industrial Development* (New York, 1883), copy acquired by State Historical Society of Wisconsin in 1887. Turner, in 1887-88, listed "Scribner's Statistical Atlas" among works assigned his students [HEH TU Vol. XIV (1), American History I].

21. For Turner's copy of this bulletin, published in 1891, see HEH TU Black Box No. 9 (160-68), Item 164.

22. *Observations on the North-American Land-Company, Lately Instituted in Philadelphia* (London, 1796), 113; Henry L. Nelson, "The Growth of Federal Power," *Harper's New Monthly Magazine*, LXXXV (July 1892), 245. Turner's notes indicate that he read these works and all others mentioned below.

23. Francis J. Grund, *The Americans, in their Moral, Social, and Political Relations* (Boston, 1873), 211; "Western Prairies," *American Whig Review*, XI (May 1850), 526.

24. Robert Baird, *View of the Valley of the Mississippi, or the Emigrant's and Traveller's Guide to the West* (Philadelphia, 1834), 101-3.

25. Emile Boutmy, *Studies in Constitutional Law. France-England-United States* (London, 1891), 127-28. Turner copied several passages of this volume into his notes (HEH TU File Drawer 15, Folder: Boutmy). Churillon's essay is on p. 488.

26. Henry George, *Progress and Poverty* (n.p., 1882), 350. This was the note that Turner reminded himself to copy. His copy of the book is heavily underlined in spots (HEH Accession No. 152218).

27. Walter Bagehot, *Physics and Politics: An Application of the Principles of Natural Selection and Heredity to Political Society* (Humboldt Library of Popular Science, New York, 1880), 146. Turner's notes, HEH TU 3 × 5 Drawer No. 1.

28. Bagehot, *Physics and Politics*, 147, 150. Turner's notes, HEH TU 3 × 5 Drawer No. 1.

29. Francis A. Walker, "The Growth of the Nation," *Providence Journal*, June 19, 1889. Turner clipped this address from the paper, pasted it on cardboard, and underlined it heavily (HEH TU File Drawer 15B, Folder: F. A. Walker, PBK 1889).

30. Achille Loria, *Analisa della Proprietà Capitalista* (2 vols., Torino, 1889). An ingenuous argument to show that Turner borrowed most of his thesis from Loria is Lee Benson, "Achille Loria's Influence on American Economic Thought: Including His Contributions to the Frontier Hypothesis," *Agricultural History*, XXIV (Oct. 1950), 182-99.

31. Richard T. Ely, *Outlines of Economics* (New York, 1893), 5, tells of Powers' aid and thanks Turner and Haskins for reading portions of his manuscript.

32. Turner's notes (6 pp.) cover the material on pp. 46-55, Vol. II, of the *Analisa* (HEH TU File Drawer 15A, Folder: Notes on A. Loria).

33. Clarence W. Bowen to William F. Poole, April 14, 1892, William F. Poole Papers, Newberry Library, Chicago, Box: Jan.-April, 1892 (hereafter cited as Newberry, Poole Papers). Bowen was treasurer of the American Historical Association.

34. William F. Poole to C. W. Bowen, Nov. 28, 1892; Herbert B. Adams to Bowen, Dec. 9, 1892. American Historical Association Papers, Division of Manuscripts, Library of Congress, Box 213, Folder: Treasurer's File, 1892 (hereafter cited as LC, AHA Papers).

35. Herbert B. Adams to C. W. Bowen, Dec. 30, 1892, ibid.

36. Herbert B. Adams to C. W. Bowen, March 4, 1893, ibid. Box 213, Folder: Treasurer's File, 1893.

37. Turner to Charles K. Adams, Feb. 23, 1893, SHSW, Turner Papers.

38. Justin Winsor to Herbert B. Adams, March 22, 1893, W. Stull Holt (ed.), *Historical Scholarship in the United States, 1876-1901: as Revealed in the Correspondence of Herbert B. Adams* (Baltimore, 1938), 199.

39. Herbert B. Adams to C. W. Bowen, June 3, 1893, LC, AHA Papers, Box 213, Folder: Treasurer's File, 1893.

40. Turner to W. F. Poole, May 10, 1893, Newberry, Poole Papers, Box: April-June, 1893. This letter, with explanatory remarks, is in W. L. Williamson, "A Sidelight on the Frontier Thesis: A New Turner Letter," *Newberry Library Bulletin*, III (April 1953), 46-49.

41. *Wisconsin State Journal*, May 16, 1893.

42. Turner to Woodrow Wilson, July 16, 1893, HEH TU Box 1. Turner wrote to Wilson four days after delivering his paper, apologizing for not writing sooner because he had been in the final agonies of getting out his paper.

43. "The Auxiliary Congresses," *The Dial*, XV (Aug. 1, 1893), 60. This unsigned article was written by William F. Poole. The congresses are described in *Chicago Tribune*, July 10, 11, and 12, *The New York Times*, July 12, p. 8, and Johnson Rossiter, *A History of the World's Columbian Exposition* (4 vols., Chicago, 1894), IV, 169-73.

44. That he did not read the full paper is suggested by the "Report of the Proceedings of the Ninth Annual Meeting of the American Historical Association," *Annual Report of the American Historical Association for 1893* (Washington, D.C., 1894), 6. This summary omits many points made by Turner in the later published version.

45. Turner, "The Significance of the Frontier in American History," *The Frontier in American History* (New York, 1920), 1-38.

46. This was the impression of Andrew C. McLaughlin, who, many years later, described the scene to Avery Craven, his colleague at the University of Chicago. Craven to author, Jan. 8, 1970.

47. *Chicago Tribune*, July 13, 1893, 3. The letter of thanks to Poole was from Mrs. Ellen H. Walworth of Saratoga, who read a paper, "The Value of National Archives." Mrs. Walworth to Poole, July 26, 1893, Newberry, Poole Papers, Box: April-July, 1893.

48. Charles K. Adams to A. J. Johnson of *Johnson's Universal Cyclopaedia*, July 17, 1893, University of Wisconsin Archives, Presidential Papers 4/8/1, Charles K. Adams, General Correspondence, 1891-1901, Box 5 (hereafter cited as U. of Wis. Arch. Pres. Corr.); Andrew J. Turner to Helen M. Turner, July 23, 1893; HEH TU Box E; *The Aegis*, Nov. 3, 1893.
49. Letters, HEH TU Box 1.
50. John Fiske to Turner, Feb. 6, 1894; Talcott Williams to Turner (n.d.), ibid. Ratzel's comments were in a review quoted in Murray Kane, "Some Considerations on the Frontier Concept of Frederick Jackson Turner," *Mississippi Valley Historical Review*, XXVII (Dec. 1940), 398-99. Ratzel incorporated much of Turner's thesis in one of his own essays. Copy, underlined by Turner to indicate references to himself, HEH TU File Drawer 21C, Folder: Miscellany.

Chapter VI
The Busy World of the Professor
1893–1901

1. Turner wrote these figures on the back pages of a paper notebook, "Expense Account, 1890" (HEH TU Box 61). His home was modest by faculty standards, paying taxes of $71.97 in 1897 and $110.17 in 1899. Other professor's homes were taxed at from $115.80 to $167.30 in the latter year (*Wisconsin State Journal*, May 19, 1897, Feb. 18, 1899).
2. A branch of the society was organized in Madison in December 1897, with E. A. Birge president and Mrs. Turner one of the directors (ibid. Dec. 9, 1897).
3. Turner to Charles H. Haskins, July 16, 1895, Charles Homer Haskins Papers, Firestone Library, Princeton University (hereafter cited as Princeton, Haskins Papers).
4. Mae Turner to Lucinda A. W. Sherwood, Oct. 23, 1897 (HEH TU Box F).
5. Libby's thesis, with an introduction by Turner, was published in 1894. When asked, some years later, whether Turner had suggested the map technique that he used so successfully, Libby escaped into generalizations, replying that "my map on the geographical distribution of the vote on the Constitution was the first effort along that line that I have been familiar with" (Orin G. Libby to Merle Curti, Aug. 24, 1928, HEH TU Box 39).
6. For Libby's later career at Wisconsin, see Fulmer Mood, "The Development of Frederick Jackson Turner as a Historical Thinker," *Transactions of the Colonial Society of Massachusetts, 1937-1942*, XXXIV (Boston, 1943), 331-35.
7. *Catalogue of the University of Wisconsin for 1895-1896* (Madison, 1896), 140.
8. *Wisconsin State Journal*, Nov. 22, 1895.
9. Course announcement, ibid. Feb. 10, 1896. Trent's lectures were later published as *Statesmen of the Old Regime* (New York, 1897).
10. The first quotation is from Frederick J. Turner, *The Colonization of North America. University Extension Department. Instruction by Correspondence* (Madison, [1897]), 1-2; the second from Frederick J. Turner,

American Development, 1789-1829. University Extension Department (Madison, 1895), 12; Turner also prepared a syllabus, *The Colonization of North America from the Earliest Times to 1763.* University Extension Department *Syllabus No. 23* (Madison, 1894) (HEH TU Vol. VI). The work of the extension speakers was described in *Wisconsin State Journal,* Nov. 30, 1895.

11. For notes Turner used in preparing this course in 1898, see HEH TU File Drawer 1D, Folder: English History. Summer School 1898.

12. Turner to Carl Becker, Nov. 7, 1898, HEH TU Box 2.

13. HEH TU File Drawer 1C.

14. See 3 × 5 file cards, "Program" or "Program Spring," on which Turner listed the lectures to be given each term (HEH TU Box 54). These show that the lectures varied greatly each year.

15. Louise P. Kellogg, "The Passing of a Great Teacher," *Historical Outlook,* XXIII (Oct. 1932), 271. For Turner's thesis topics and examinations during this period, see HEH TU Box 54 and File Drawer 15D, Folder: Notes for Organization of a Class, 1895-1896.

16. Laurence M. Larson to James A. James, May 22, 1910, HEH TU Vol. I, Red Book. This book contains numerous letters written by former students in 1910, when Turner left Wisconsin for Harvard.

17. Carl Becker, "Frederick Jackson Turner," Howard W. Odum (ed.), *American Masters of Social Science* (New York, 1927), 273-318; Joseph Schafer, "The Author of the Frontier Hypothesis," *Wisconsin Magazine of History,* XV (Sept. 1931), 86-103; Kellogg, "The Passing of a Great Teacher," loc. cit., 270-72; Wilbur R. Jacobs (ed.), "Turner As I Remember Him, by Herbert Eugene Bolton," *Mid-America,* XXXVI (Jan. 1964), 54-61. See also Wilbur R. Jacobs, "Frederick Jackson Turner—Master Teacher," *Pacific Historical Review,* XXIII (Feb. 1954), 49-58.

18. Quotations from Carl Becker, "Tribute to Frederick Jackson Turner," HEH TU Vol. I, Red Book.

19. This picture of Turner emerges particularly in reminiscences of Guy Stanton Ford, Oral History Research Office of Columbia University, pp. 76-79, 91-92. Ford's less-than-favorable impressions contrast with the remarks he made in his tribute to Turner in 1910 (HEH TU Vol. I, Red Book).

20. University of Wisconsin, Instructional Reports, 1893-1900, U. of Wis. Arch.

21. *The Sphynx,* I (April 13, May 11, 1900), 151, 169; *The Badger for 1894* (Madison, 1893), 252; *The Badger for 1895* (Madison, 1894), 277.

22. The titles of honor's theses were listed in the catalogues of the university.

23. Turner to Carl Becker, Nov. 7, 1898, HEH TU Box 2.

24. Titles of all master's theses were listed in the catalogues of the university.

25. *Daily Cardinal,* March 10, 1897, March 8, 1898. On May 8, 1898, the paper reported that Turner would not meet his classes for a week owing to his absence while inspecting secondary schools.

26. Turner's views on this subject were admirably expressed in Turner to James A. James, Jan. 21, 1894, HEH TU Box 1. Reference to his work on the committee to standardize history teaching is in Mrs. W. A. Noyes to Turner, Aug. 15, 1928, HEH TU Box 39.

27. These lectures were noted in the *Daily Cardinal,* Dec. 11, 1894, Jan. 6, 1897, Jan. 12, 1898; *Wisconsin State Journal,* Oct. 11, Nov. 30, 1901.

28. See MS (28 half-pp.), HEH TU Box 54, and *Wisconsin State Journal,* June 14, 15, 1895.

29. Text of address, *Portage Weekly Democrat,* Jan. 3, 1896, reprinted in Fulmer Mood (ed.), "Frederick Jackson Turner's Address on Education in the United States Without Free Lands," *Agricultural History,* XXIII (Oct. 1949), 254–59. Mood shows that Turner anticipated many of the views on education later popularized by John Dewey.

30. Plan described, *Wisconsin State Journal,* Nov. 23, 1901. Pamphlet, *Free Traveling Library, Series G. Contains a Group of Books Relating to the Revolution. Sent by Wisconsin Free Library Commission* (Madison, n.d.), copy, HEH TU File Drawer 15E, Folder: Wisconsin Library Commission.

31. *Wisconsin State Journal,* July 31, 1894. The controversy is fully described in Benjamin G. Rader, *The Academic Mind and Reform: The Influence of Richard T. Ely in American Life,* 130–58. Turner's efforts in Ely's defense noted in *Wisconsin State Journal,* Aug. 7, 9, 21, 22, 24, Sept. 18, 1894. In his testimony Turner quoted Adam Smith, John Stuart Mill, and other *laissez faire* economists to show they could be accused of statements far more radical than those ascribed to Ely.

32. *Daily Cardinal,* Feb. 20, 1900.

33. Turner represented Wisconsin at the inauguration of the chancellor of the University of Kansas in 1902, and he spoke to alumni groups there (*Daily Cardinal,* Nov. 3, 1902; May 20, 23, 1905).

34. The final volume of this eight-volume history was published in 1902. Turner's notes for his review are in HEH TU 3 × 5 Drawer No. 1. The manuscript of his address of January 23, 1894, is in HEH TU, File Drawer 15A, Folder: Essay on History of US by Von Holst. The meeting was reported in the *Wisconsin State Journal,* Jan. 23, 24, 1894; *Daily Cardinal,* Jan. 23, 24, 1894.

35. When Turner visited Chicago a month later he was told that Von Holst's colleagues were trying to prevent him from seeing the issue of the *Daily Cardinal* in which the essay was summarized. Turner to Mae Turner, Feb. 23, 1894, HEH TU Box F. William P. Trent in 1896 sought to publish the essay in the *Sewanee Review,* which he edited, but Turner refused. It was first published in Wilbur R. Jacobs (ed.), *Frederick Jackson Turner's Legacy: Unpublished Writings in American History* (San Marino, Calif., 1965), 85-104.

36. Turner, talk to Graduate Club early in 1897, "What Is History," *Daily Cardinal,* Feb. 18, 1897.

37. Turner to Alumni Dinner, June 1897, "The University of the Future," summarized in *The Aegis,* Sept. 1897, 10. The notes he used are in HEH TU File Drawer 15B, Folder: The University of the Future.

38. *Wisconsin State Journal,* Feb. 9, June 7, 9, 1897, June 9, 16, 1898.

39. Reports of Turner's lectures, Contemporary Club and Madison Literary Club, *Wisconsin State Journal,* May 17, Sept. 11, Nov. 13, 1894; Oct. 19, 1895; May 9, 11, 1896; Jan. 11, 12, 1897; *Daily Cardinal,* Nov. 13, 1894; Oct. 19, 1895; May 11, 1896; Jan. 12, 1897.

40. *Wisconsin State Journal,* Oct. 15, 1896. Turner's notes for this talk

(16 half-pp.), HEH TU File Drawer 15C, Folder: Talk before Madison Women's Club 1896.

41. Turner not only read widely on early Virginia history, but purchased copies of documents totaling 20,000 words. Address, "The Colonization of the James," HEH TU File Drawer 1D, Folder: Colonization of the James.

42. Correspondence between Wilson and Turner, Nov. 5–27, 1896, Frederick Jackson Turner Papers, Houghton Library, Harvard University (hereafter cited as Houghton, Turner Papers), Library of Congress, Woodrow Wilson Papers, Box 8 (hereafter cited as LC, Wilson Papers). Letters summarized in George C. Osborn, "Woodrow Wilson and Frederick Jackson Turner," *Proceedings of the New Jersey Historical Society*, LXXIV (July 1956), 219–27. The negotiations are described in Wilbur R. Jacobs, "Wilson's First Battle at Princeton: The Chair for Turner," *Harvard Library Bulletin*, VIII (Winter 1954), 74–87.

43. Wilson to Turner, March 31, 1897. Houghton, Turner Papers; Henry W. Bragdon, *Woodrow Wilson: The Academic Years* (Cambridge, 1967), 226, which quotes from Wilson's diary.

44. Charles K. Adams to Turner, May 12, 1897, HEH TU Box 2.

45. John B. McMaster to Turner, April 12, 1897; Simon N. Patten to Turner, May 8, 1897; James Harvey Robinson to Turner, April 12, 1897; Charles C. Harrison to Turner, May 7, 1897; HEH TU Box 2. In December 1897, he was asked by the president of Western Reserve University if he would be interested in moving, and told him that he would not (HEH TU Box 2).

46. *Wisconsin State Journal*, Feb. 11, 20, Oct. 23, 1899; *Daily Cardinal*, Oct. 17, 20, 23, 1899; *Madison Democrat*, Oct. 24, 1899.

47. Turner to Carl Becker, Nov. 17, 1899, HEH TU Box 2.

48. Charles McCarthy to J. Franklin Jameson, March 10, 1900, Elizabeth Donnan and F. L. Stock (eds.), "Letters: Charles McCarthy to J. Franklin Jameson," *Wisconsin Magazine of History*, XXXIII (Sept. 1949), 72.

49. Turner to Woodrow Wilson, March 12, 1900, LC, Wilson Papers, Box 10.

50. Note in Turner's hand, filed with newspaper clippings on children's deaths, HEH TU Vol. X.

51. William R. Harper to Turner, Feb. 14, 1900, HEH TU Box 3. A note attached reads: "March 10, 1900. Pres. Harper in personal interview invited me to accept head professorship in place of von Holst, salary 4000 first 2 years and 5000 thereafter."

52. Charles K. Adams to Board of Regents, March 16, 1900, enclosed in Adams to Turner, March 22, 1900, HEH TU Box 3.

53. Harper to Turner, April 6, 1900, HEH TU Box 3. Haskins had already informed Turner that he was not tempted by a $3000 salary, but that he would move if Turner decided to go. Haskins to Turner, April 4, 7, 8, 1900, HEH TU Box 3.

54. Harvey Pratt Judson to Turner, April 19, 1900, HEH TU Box 3. Turner to Dean E. A. Birge, April 14, 1900, setting forth the terms under which he would stay, U. of Wis. Arch., Pres. corr. Charles K. Adams, Box 6. Rough draft in Turner's hand, HEH TU Box 3.

55. *Daily Cardinal*, April 21, 1900. For a fuller account, Ray A. Billington,

"Frederick Jackson Turner Comes to Harvard," *Proceedings of the Massachusetts Historical Society*, LXXIV (1962), 55-59.

56. Turner to Edward L. Hardy, Feb. 15, 1902, University of Wisconsin Archives, College of Letters and Science, Department of History, Turner Correspondence, 1902-5 (hereafter cited as U. of Wis. Arch., L and S, Hist., Turner Corr.), Box 1, Folder H.

57. Turner to Charles H. Haskins, Aug. 7, 1900. Princeton, Haskins Papers; notebook, HEH TU Box 62.

58. Turner described the family's travels in letters to his mother, father, and sister, Sept. 9, 1900, to March 7, 1901 (HEH TU Box F). Quotation, Turner to "Dear Father," Sept. 17, 1900.

59. Turner to Mae Turner, April 30, 1901, HEH TU Box F.

60. *Daily Cardinal*, April 24, May 3, 1901.

Chapter VII
Broadening Historical Horizons
1893-1910

1. Turner to Charles H. Haskins, July 15, 1896, Princeton, Haskins Papers.

2. T. C. Chamberlin, "The Method of Multiple Working Hypotheses," *Journal of Geology*, V (Nov.-Dec., 1897), 837-48. Paper, Society of Western Naturalists, 1889, reported in *Science*, XV (Feb. 7, 1890), 92-96. *See also* Wilbur R. Jacobs, "Turner's Methodology: Multiple Working Hypothesis or Ruling Theory?" *Journal of American History*, LIV (March 1968), 853-63.

3. For Turner's notes, see HEH TU File Drawer 1A, Folder: New England Towns. He also prepared a brief essay on the subject (HEH TU File Drawer 3D, Folder: New England Towns).

4. Turner to J. Franklin Jameson, June 9, 1895, HEH TU Box 2. Jameson met Turner at the New Haven meeting of the American Historical Association in 1898 (Jameson to Mae Turner, March 17, 1932, HEH TU Vol. V).

5. Extended correpondence between Turner and Jameson, August 16–Sept. 6, 1895, HEH TU Box 2.

6. As the first installment was being printed, Turner was still gathering information for the second (Herbert L. Osgood to Turner, Sept. 19, 1896, HEH TU Box 2; *see also* Notes in HEH TU File Drawers 4B and 4C). At about this time Turner published "The Rise and Fall of New France," *Chautauquan*, XXIV (Oct. 1896), 31-34, (Dec. 1896), 295-300, reprinted in Fulmer Mood (ed.), "An Unfamiliar Essay of Frederick J. Turner," *Minnesota History*, XVIII (Dec. 1937), 381-98.

7. See Waldo G. Leland, "J. Franklin Jameson and the Origin of the National Historical Publications Commission," Ruth A. Fisher and William L. Fox (eds), *J. Franklin Jameson: A Tribute* (Washington, D.C., 1965), 27-36. Minutes of first meeting, J. Franklin Jameson Papers, Library of Congress, Manuscripts Division, Box 7 (hereafter cited as LC, Jameson Papers).

8. Turner to Woodrow Wilson, Dec. 27, 1896, LC, Wilson Papers, Box 8.

9. Many years later Turner told a class that his interest in diplomatic his-

tory had begun when he was reviewing the fourth volume of Theodore Roosevelt's *The Winning of the West* for the *American Historical Review* in 1896. He disbelieved Roosevelt's statement that President Jefferson was personally involved in the intrigues of Citizen Genêt and decided to make his own investigation of the episode (*Kansas City Star*, Jan. 20, 1923; HEH TU File Drawer 15D, Folder: Frontier in American History. Reviews).

10. Notes taken by Turner for his editorial duties, HEH TU File Drawers 5B and 6D. All articles and documents were published in the *American Historical Review* or the *Annual Report of the American Historical Association* between 1897 and 1903.

11. Turner to W. C. Ford, Feb. 19, 1902, U. of Wis. Arch., L. and S., Hist., Turner Corr., Box 1, Folder F. For other letters from Turner to Ford, completing arrangements for publishing the documents, see HEH TU Boxes 3 and 4.

12. Turner to Edward G. Bourne, Feb. 27, Sept. 30, 1903, Jan. 29, Nov. 9, 1904, HEH TU Box 4. Bourne to Turner, March 8, 14, May 1, Sept. 30, Oct. 3, 1903, Jan. 26, Nov. 14, 1904. U. of Wis. Arch., L. and S., Hist., Turner Corr., Box 3, Folder B.

13. Turner to J. Franklin Jameson, Oct. 3, 1905. LC, Jameson Papers, Box 6.

14. *Wisconsin State Journal*, Jan. 14, 1902; *Daily Cardinal*, March 10, 1902. Turner's Notes, HEH TU File Drawer 5C, Folder: Louisiana Purchase.

15. Lecture, stenographic report, HEH TU File Drawer 14C, Folder: After Dinner Speech. Notes used in speaking, HEH TU File Drawer 15D, Folder: Historical Significance of Louisiana Purchase. Draft of article, HEH TU File Drawer 15C, Folder: Early Form of Policy of France.

16. Turner to Max Farrand, April 15, 1905, HEH TU Box 5.

17. Turner to John M. Vincent, March 10, 1907, HEH TU Box 7.

18. Turner discussed the Russo-Japanese War before the Six-O'clock Club of Madison (*Wisconsin State Journal*, Dec. 7, 1904).

19. Turner to Mae Turner, [Sept. 1, 1901, incorrectly dated 1903], describes his long hours of work while preparing these articles (HEH TU Box F). Invitation to prepare the articles, C. H. Dennis, *Chicago Daily News*, to Turner, July 17, 1901, HEH TU Box 1. Extensive file on Irish immigration, HEH TU File Drawer 5A, Unmarked folder. Notes and map on German immigration, HEH TU File Drawer 2C, Folder: Germans to Penn; manuscript of a portion of this article, HEH TU File Drawer 8D, Folder: Germans in West.

20. The articles in *Chicago Record-Herald*, Aug. 28, Sept. 4, 11, 18, 25, Oct. 16, 1901, were clipped by Turner, pasted, and bound (HEH, Rare book Accession No. 126565). Merrill H. Crissey to Fulmer Mood, Jan. 7, 1938, HEH TU Box 52, is a discussion by Turner's secretary of the immigration articles.

21. F. J. Turner, "Recent Studies in American History," *Atlantic Monthly*, LXXVII (June 1896), 837. Turner was invited to review a number of books in ten pages of the magazine, at $8 per page. Horace E. Scudder to Turner, Feb. 7, 14, June 5, 1896, Houghton, Turner Papers.

22. Turner's review of Burgess, *The Middle Period, 1817–1858*, appeared in the *Educational Review*, XIV (Nov. 1897), 390-95, and his review of James Ford Rhodes, *History of the United States from the Compromise of*

1850, Vol. III, in the *Political Science Quarterly*, XI (March 1896), 167-70.

23. Turner reviewed Winsor, *The Westward Movement*, in the *American Historical Review*, III (April 1898), 556-61; Elliott Coues, *History of the Expedition under the Command of Lewis and Clark*, in *The Dial*, XVI (Feb. 1, 1894), 80-82; Alexander Brown, *English Politics in Early Virginia History*, in the *American Historical Review*, VII (Oct. 1901), 159-63; and Reuben G. Thwaites, *Early Western Travels*, in *The Dial*, XXXVII (Nov. 16, 1904), 298-302, XLI (July 1, 1906), 6-10.

24. Review of Mrs. Neville and Miss Martin, *Historical Green Bay, 1634-1840*, *The Aegis*, VIII (April 24, 1894); Turner to J. Franklin Jameson, June 9, 1895, HEH TU Box 2.

25. F. J. Turner, "Francis Parkman and His Works," *The Dial*, XXV (Dec. 16, 1898), 451-53.

26. Turner to Woodrow Wilson, Dec. 24, 1896, LC, Wilson Papers, Box 7.

27. *American Historical Review*, VIII (July 1903), 762-65.

28. Years later Turner told his secretary that "the severance of the warm friendship of many years between Woodrow Wilson and him was caused by adverse comments in his review" (HEH TU Box 35, Folder: Merrill H. Crissey, Drafts of Biographical Data). Turner did review H. M. Chittenden, *History of Early Steamboat Navigation on the Missouri River*, and the latter volumes of Thwaites, *Early Western Travels*, in 1906. He also reviewed J. B. Winslow, *The Story of the Great Court: Being a Sketch of the Supreme Court of Wisconsin*, *American Historical Review*, XVII (July 1912), 859-60.

29. Wilson to Mrs. Wilson, April 27, 1903, copy in HEH TU Box 4.

30. Guy Stanton Ford, "Reminiscences of Guy Stanton Ford," Oral History Research Office, Columbia Univ.

31. So he told his secretary (HEH TU Box 35, Folder: Merrill H. Crissey, Drafts of Biographical Data).

32. Turner's reviews of the last two volumes of Roosevelt, *Winning of the West*, appeared in *The Nation*, LX (March 28, 1895), 240-42, LXIII (Oct. 8, 1896), 277, and in the *American Historical Review*, II (Oct. 1896), 171-76. Roosevelt initiated the correspondence (April 2, 1895). He wrote Turner again April 10, 26, 1895, Nov. 4, and Dec. 15, 1896 (Houghton, Turner Papers).

33. Turner's review of Channing, *A Student's History of the United States*, was published in the *Educational Review*, XVIII (Oct. 1899), 301-4.

34. F. J. Turner, "The Development of American Society," *The [Illinois] Alumni Quarterly*, II (July 1908), 120. He gave a prior version of this talk as the Phi Beta Kappa address at the University of Nebraska, June 10, 1907. MS of lecture, "Social Forces in American History," HEH TU Box 55.

35. Turner owned copies of Droysen, *Grundriss der Historik* (Leipzig, 1882), and *Outline of the Principles of History* (Boston, 1893). Both are underlined and contain his marginalia (HEH Accession Nos. 124357, 124480).

36. F. J. Turner, "The Historical Library in the University," Brown University, John Carter Brown Library, *The Dedication of the Library Building, May the Seventeenth, A. D. MDCCCCIIII. With the Addresses by*

William Vail Kellen, LL.D., and Frederick Jackson Turner, Ph.D. (Providence, 1905), 57.

37. Turner, "Social Forces in American History," HEH TU Box 55.
38. Turner, "Historical Library in the University," *loc. cit.* 50-51.
39. Turner, "Development of American Society," *loc. cit.* 120-21.
40. For correspondence with speakers for the 1904 historical congress in St. Louis, see Albion W. Small Papers, Univ. of Chicago Library, Special Collections Dept., Box I, Folder 9 (hereafter cited as Chicago, Small Papers).
41. This address, bearing a notation that it was delivered in Madison, is in HEH TU File Drawer 14A, Folder: Madison 1901 October 16. A comparison with the 1904 paper shows that the second was re-written from the 1901 version, with more mature insights and interpretations.
42. Turner to Mae Turner, Sept. 17, 21, 23, 25, 1901, HEH TU Box F. Turner discussed the publication of the paper with Albion W. Small, hoping to have it appear in a national journal of prominence. Turner to Small, Oct. 31, 1904; Small to Turner, Nov. 2, 1904. U. of Wis. Arch., L. and S., Hist., Turner Corr., Box 5, Folder S.
43. Turner, "Problems in American History," Howard J. Rogers (ed.), *International Congress of Arts and Science, Universal Exposition, St. Louis, 1904* (Boston, 1906), II, 183-94, reprinted in Turner, *The Significance of Sections in American History* (New York, 1932), 3-21.

Chapter VIII
Popularizing the Frontier Thesis
1893-1910

1. See Lee Benson, "The Historian as Mythmaker: Turner and the Closed Frontier," David M. Ellis (ed.), *The Frontier in American Development. Essays in Honor of Paul Wallace Gates* (Ithaca, 1969), 15-19.
2. See Peter J. Schmitt, *Back to Nature: The Arcadian Myth in Urban America* (New York, 1969); for a more interpretative account see Roderick Nash, *Wilderness and the American Mind* (New Haven, 1967). On the relationships between the closing of the frontier and American foreign policy, see Walter LaFeber, *The New Empire: An Interpretation of American Expansion, 1860-1898* (Ithaca, 1963), 62-72.
3. Woodrow Wilson, "Mr. Goldwin Smith's 'Views' on Our Political History," *The Forum*, XVI (Dec. 1893), 495-97. After reading this review, William E. Dodd asked Wilson whether he had developed the frontier thesis before Turner. He was told that Turner was entirely responsible, and that Wilson's materials were supplied by him (Dodd to Turner, Oct. 3, 1919, HEH TU Box 29). For correspondence, Ray A. Billington, *The Genesis of the Frontier Thesis: A Study in Historical Creativity* (San Marino, Calif., 1971), 181-201. Wendell H. Stephenson (ed.), "The Influence of Woodrow Wilson on Frederick Jackson Turner," *Agricultural History*, XIX (Oct. 1945), 249-53, had earlier reproduced some of the letters.
4. Turner to Wilson, Dec. 30, 1893, LC, Wilson Papers, Box 6.
5. Quotations from Woodrow Wilson, "The Proper Perspective in Amer-

ican History," *The Forum*, XIX (July 1895), 544-59, and "The Course of American History" Wilson, *Mere Literature and Other Essays* (Boston, 1896), 231-32. John Fiske also popularized the thesis. He wrote (March 15, 1895) that he had addressed the Missouri Historical Society on "The Influence of the Frontier upon American Life" [Ethel F. Fiske, *The Letters of John F. Fiske* (New York, 1940), 639].

6. Charles A. McMurray (ed.), *Fifth Yearbook of the National Hebart Society* (Chicago, 1899), 7-41. The different versions of the essay printed at this time are compared by Fulmer Mood in Turner, *The Early Writings of Frederick Jackson Turner* (Madison, 1938), 275-92.

7. A. M. Simons to Turner, Oct. 21, 26, 1905; Turner to Simons, March 30, 1903. Simons first asked permission to reprint the essay in 1903, then again in 1905. U. of Wis. Arch., L. and S., Hist. Turner Corr. Box 5, Folder S. Turner's copy, *International Socialist Review*, VI (Dec. 1905), 321-46, HEH Accession No. 126776.

8. Jesse C. Bullock, *Select Readings in Economics* (Boston, 1907), 23-59.

9. H. Morse Stephens to Turner, Aug. 19, 1895; Turner to Stephens, May 29, 1896. Henry Morse Stephens Papers, University of California at Berkeley (hereafter cited as Calif., Stephens Papers).

10. Turner to Stephens, Dec. 22, 1896, ibid.

11. For Turner's paper and comments that it inspired, see *Annual Report of the American Historical Association for 1896* (Washington, D.C., 1897), I, 281-96.

12. C. K. Adams to W. E. Appleton, July 17, 1893, U. of Wis. Arch., Pres. Corr., C. K. Adams General Corr., Box 5, is Adams's letter of recommendation [Published in *Johnson's Universal Cyclopaedia* (New York, 1894), III, 606-7; reprinted in Fulmer Mood (ed.), "Little Known Fragments of Turner's Writings," *Wisconsin Magazine of History*, XXIII (March 1940), 338-41].

13. Notes, HEH TU File Drawer 15C, Folder: Old Northwest. Notes and Drafts. 1896. The letter of rejection, suggesting other topics on which Turner might write, is Horace E. Scudder to Turner, April 10, 1896, Houghton, Turner Papers.

14. Walter Hines Page to Turner, May 29, July 14, 24, 29, Aug. 6, 1896, ibid. A portion of Turner's manuscript, incorrectly labeled as an early draft of the 1893 essay, is in HEH TU File Drawer 15, Folder: Draft of Turner's 1893 Essay.

15. Page to Turner, Aug. 22, 1896, Houghton, Turner Papers. Turner suggested and was paid a fee of $75.

16. *Chicago Tribune*, Aug. 30, 1896; *Boston Herald*, Aug. 22, 1896. Newspaper clippings, reviews and comment, HEH TU Box 54, Folder: Reviews of Turner's 'The Problem of the West.'

17. Page to Turner, Aug. 22, Sept. 4, Oct. 8, 1896; Turner to Page, Aug. 30, 1896, Houghton, Turner Papers. The *Wisconsin State Journal*, Dec. 3, 1896, printed an advertisement of the series.

18. Page to Turner, Feb. 25, March 26, June 11, July 2, Sept. 9, 1896, Houghton, Turner Papers.

19. Turner, "The Middle West," reprinted in Turner, *The Frontier in American History*, 147-48.

20. Turner, "Contributions of the West to American Democracy," ibid. 268. The *International Monthly* requested another article on "The Comparison of Social Conditions of the East and West" which Turner agreed to do but never submitted. Frederick A. Richardson to Turner, Jan. 3, 10, 1902; Turner to Richardson, Jan. 7, 1902. U. of Wis. Arch., L. and S., Hist., Turner Corr., Box 1, Folder R. Correspondence concerning the *World's Work* article, HEH TU Box 4 and File Drawer 15B, Folder: Jottings on the State University of the Midwest; correspondence with W. C. Cunliff of *World's Work*, U. of Wis. Arch., L. and S., Hist., Turner Corr., Box 3, Folder C.

21. *Evanston Index,* Jan. 31, 1903.

22. This sampling of a few of the speeches given by Turner has been compiled from notices in the *Wisconsin State Journal, Daily Cardinal,* and other newspapers, and from Turner's own notes and correspondence. Typical are: "Notes for Speech 30 Minutes on Frontier Soldier" (HEH TU File Drawer 2E, unmarked Folder); "The Old Forts of Green Bay" (File Drawer 15C, Folder: Address at Green Bay, Wis.); and "George Washington" (File Drawer 15B, Folder: A Talk: Three Pioneers).

23. Correspondence concerning these lectures is in HEH TU Boxes 13 and 14. Turner's honorarium, normally $50, was $150 for the Indiana commencement address. An early draft of the lecture, in which he removed references to Kansas history, is in U. of Wis. Arch., Misc. File: Frederick Jackson Turner.

24. The address was first printed in the *Indiana University Bulletin,* VIII (June 15, 1910), 6-29, and reprinted in Turner, *The Frontier in American History,* 269-89.

25. Turner to Mae Turner, Dec. 1, 2, 3, 1903, HEH TU Box F; April 17, 18, 19, 21, 24, 26, 29, 1910, ibid. Box G. He was paid $500 for the Pennsylvania series.

26. The lectures were published in the professional journals of the sponsoring organizations at the time (reprinted in Turner, *The Frontier in American History,* 157-76, 177-204, quotations, pp. 170, 203).

27. Henry Holt & Co. to Turner, Feb. 14, March 6, 1895, HEH TU Box 63; Turner to Holt, Feb. 26, 1895. Henry Holt & Co. Archives, Dept. of Rare Books and Special Collections, Princeton Univ. Library (hereafter cited as Princeton, Holt Arch.).

28. Holt to Turner, Nov. 16, 1895, Jan. 9, 28, 1895, HEH TU Box 63; Turner to Holt, Jan. 16, Oct. 2, 1896, Princeton, Holt Arch.

29. W. P. Trent to George P. Brett, March 14, 1896, Macmillan Co. Records, New York. Letters, supplied to the Huntington Library by the Macmillan Co. (HEH TU Box 2).

30. George P. Brett, Macmillan Co., to Turner, March 18, April 4, 1896; Turner to Brett, March 28, 1896; William P. Trent to Turner, April 6, 1896, HEH TU Box 2.

31. Kate Stephens to Turner, June 3, 16, Oct. 8, 1897, HEH TU Box 2. In refusing the Putnam invitation, Turner held the door open. He wrote on the last letter, "If details with others not satisfactory will accept offer to make proposals." G. P. Putnam's Sons to Turner, March 27, April 7, Sept. 23, Oct. 10, 1897, HEH TU Box 2.

32. Holt & Co. to Turner, May 27, June 17, July 28, Aug. 19, 1897, HEH

TU Box 63; Turner to Holt, June 11, July 21, Aug. 15, 1897, Princeton, Holt Arch.

33. Macmillan Co. to Turner, Sept. 13, 18, Oct. 14, 1897, HEH TU Box 2.

34. A memorandum (October 18, 1897) filed with his correspondence describes the interview with Bristol. The contract for the college textbook was sent to him on November 3, 1897, that for the high school text (HEH TU Box 63), on September 5, 1900. In the latter contract, he agreed to produce a 200,000 to 250,000-word manuscript within fourteen months.

35. Macmillan Co. to Turner, Nov. 3, 1897, HEH TU Box 2.

36. Reference to the contract with Ginn and Co. is in Ginn and Co. to Turner, Dec. 9, 1901, May 8, 1906, U. of Wis. Arch., L. and S., Hist., Turner Corr., Box 1, Folder G, and Ginn and Co. to Turner, May 8, 1906, HEH TU Box 7. The company archives were destroyed a generation ago, and no copy of the contract has been preserved. Negotiations concerning the "Western State-Making" book are in F. F. Browne to Turner, Nov. 12, Dec. 2, 1901, U. of Wis. Arch., L. and S., Hist., Turner Corr., Box 1, Folder B.

37. Walter H. Page to Turner, Oct. 8, 1897, March 7, 1898, Aug. 18, Oct. 30, 1899, Houghton, Turner Papers.

38. Houghton, Mifflin and Co. to Turner, Feb. 26, May 2, Aug. 5, 1901, U. of Wis. Arch., L. and S. Hist., Turner Corr., Box 1, Folder H.

39. To Turner's credit, he rejected almost as many offers from publishers as he accepted—including the editing of historical works for L. B. Lippincott and Co. and Arthur H. Clark Co.; an updating of Woodrow Wilson's *Division and Reunion* for Longman's, Green and Co.; a history of Wisconsin for Houghton, Mifflin and Co.; a biography of Cyrus Hall McCormick, suggested by his son; a volume on the teaching of American history, suggested by John Dewey for Appleton and Co.; a section on the United States from 1789 to 1850 for the *Cambridge Modern History;* and a volume in the collaborative economic history of the United States, sponsored by the Carnegie Institution of Washington. In rejecting the last, Turner wrote J. Franklin Jameson, "I am already a bankrupt in promises, and have determined not to add to my liabilities this year" (Turner to Jameson, Sept. 28, 1904, ibid., Box 5, Folder J).

40. Turner to Houghton, Mifflin, January 21, 1902, HEH TU Box 3.

41. Houghton, Mifflin to Turner, Sept. 19, Nov. 20, 1902; Turner to Houghton, Mifflin, Nov. 12, Dec. 4, 1902, June 9, Oct. 9, 1903, U. of Wis. Arch., L. and S., Hist., Turner Corr., Boxes 2 and 3, Folder H.

42. Notes, HEH TU File Drawer 13.

43. Houghton, Mifflin to Turner, June 15, Nov. 4, 1904, March 10, 1905, Aug. 21, 1908, May 26, 1924; Turner to Houghton, Mifflin, March 17, 1905. The letters of 1904 and 1905 are in U. of Wis. Arch., L. and S., Hist., Turner Corr., Box 5, Folder H; the letters of 1908 and 1924 are in HEH TU Boxes 11 and 33.

44. Turner to Frank O. Lowden, Jan. 6, 1904. U. of Wis. Arch., L. and S., Hist., Turner Corr., Box 4, Folder L. Turner expressed the same views in an interview (*Wisconsin State Journal,* Oct. 28, 1903).

45. Max Farrand to Turner, Oct. 3, 1905, ibid. Box 5, Folder F.

46. Turner to Max Farrand, Jan. 3, 1905, HEH TU Box 5.

Chapter IX
The Genesis of the Sectional Concept
1893-1910

1. Turner to Constance L. Skinner, March 15, 1922, HEH TU Box 31.

2. Quotation from fragment of lecture prepared about 1922, HEH TU File Drawer 15A, Folder: Piece on Sectionalism.

3. G. Tatham, "Geography in the Nineteenth Century," Griffith Taylor (ed.), *Geography in the Twentieth Century* (London, 1951), 64-65.

4. R. J. Harrison Church, "The French School of Geography," ibid. 75-76; Thomas W. Freeman, *A Hundred Years of Geography* (Chicago, 1962), 82-84. An extreme statement of this point of view, with which Turner was certainly familiar, was James Bryce, "The Relations of History and Geography," *Contemporary Review*, XLIX (March 1886), 426-43. Using English counties as examples, Bryce argued that the economy, and hence political behavior, was the product of geographic conditions. He urged historians to apply this principle to a complete re-study of the past.

5. E. W. Hilgard, "A Report on the Relation of Soil to Climate," U.S. Dept. of Agriculture, *Weather Bureau Bulletion No. 3* (Washington, D.C., 1892), 1-59.

6. Advances in statistical cartography are described in Richard Jensen, "American Election Analysis: A Case History of Methodological Innovation and Diffusion," Seymour M. Lipset (ed.), *Politics and the Social Sciences* (New York, 1969). Turner almost certainly heard Henry Gannett when he delivered two lectures in Madison in 1896, on "Topographical Methods of the Great National Survey" (reported, *Wisconsin State Journal*, April 29, 1896).

7. Turner to William E. Dodd, Oct. 7, 1919, HEH TU Box 29. The influence of Jedidiah Morse and other early geographers on Turner is appraised in Fulmer Mood, "The Origin, Evolution, and Application of the Sectional Concept, 1750-1900," Merrill Jensen (ed.), *Regionalism in America* (Madison, 1951), 5-98.

8. Memorandum, HEH TU File Drawer 15D, Folder: Sectionalism and Nationalism.

9. Turner's offprint, published originally in *Transactions of the Wisconsin Academy of Sciences, Arts and Letters* (Madison, 1888-91), VIII, 7, is in HEH TU File Drawer 14B, Folder: Sectional Feature in American Politics.

10. Quotation from John I. Hare, *American Constitutional Law* (Boston, 1889), I, 13, copied by Turner, along with other quotations and a list of books mentioning sectionalism, on cover of Desmond article (note 9, above).

11. Turner's copy of Powell's essay, 1895 version, underlined and annotated, HEH TU File Drawer L2, Folder: Powell. Before Powell's maps appeared Turner had drawn his own showing sectional divisions, based on contour maps of the U.S. Geological Survey (described in Turner to Woodrow Wilson, Dec. 24, 1894, LC, Wilson Papers, Box 7).

12. Turner discussed this subject in a twenty-one page letter to Walter Hines Page, Aug. 30, 1896, Houghton, Turner Papers (printed in Mood, "Origin, Evolution, and Application of the Sectional Concept," loc. cit. 91-96).

13. Turner to Merle Curti, Aug. 8, 1928, HEH TU Box 39.

14. Josiah Royce, *Provincialism. An Address to the Phi Beta Kappa Society of the State University of Iowa* (Iowa City, 1902), 5. Turner's copy, HEH TU File Drawer L2, Folder: 0501.

15. Turner's notes of Van Hise's lectures, Oct., Nov. 1898, are in HEH File Drawer 12C, Folder: Van Hise Course; 14D, Folder: Lecture Physical Geography; and 15A, Folder: Notes on Van Hise's Lectures. The course was described by the *Daily Cardinal*, Oct. 4, 1898.

16. *Daily Cardinal*, May 15, 1895; *The Aegis*, June 7, 1897.

17. A typescript of the 1901 thesis by William F. Dickinson, "The Personnel of the Wisconsin State Legislature for the Years 1850, 1860, and 1870," is in the State Historical Society of Wisconsin Library. Jesse Macy and Turner discussed some of his student assignments (Macy to Turner, Jan. 28, 1903, Turner to Macy, Feb. 10, 1903, U. of Wis. Arch., L. and S., Hist., Turner Corr., Box 3, Folder M).

18. Undated portion of lecture labeled "History of the West," summer 1902, from lecture notes kept by a student, Homer C. Hockett. Copies of these lectures are scattered through HEH TU.

19. Lecture on "The Upland South: The Colonization of a Province," HEH TU File Drawer 3A, Folder: Formation of the Upland South. Turner in a lecture to the Chicago Geographical Society about this time, postulated the different course of American history if the land had been flat and had had an unvarying climate (HEH TU File Drawer 14A, Folder: Influence of Geography upon the Settlement of the United States).

20. These changes are analyzed in Fulmer Mood, "A Comparison of Differing Versions of 'The Significance of the Frontier,'" Turner, *The Early Writings of Frederick Jackson Turner* (Madison, 1938), 275-92. For a statement of Turner's views on sectionalism at this time, see his review of Ellen C. Semple and Albert P. Brigham, "Geographical Interpretations of History," *The Journal of Geography*, IV (Jan. 1905), 34-37.

21. Turner to J. Franklin Jameson, Jan. 10, 1900, HEH TU Box 3.

22. Albert B. Hart to Turner, Jan. 2, 10, 1902; Turner to Hart, Jan. 7, 1902, U. of Wis. Arch., L. and S., Hist., Turner Corr., Box 1, Folder H.

23. Turner to Jameson, Feb. 4, 1902, ibid. Box 1, Folder J.

24. Turner to Charles R. Van Hise, Dec. 14, 1904, ibid. Box 5; Folder V. Hart to Turner, Feb. 13, March 12, 1902; Turner to Hart, March 8, 12, 1902, ibid., Box 1, Folder H.

25. Courses described in university catalogues for 1904-7. Two half-sheets in Turner's hand, "Program, 1905-1906. 1st Semester. History 14 US 1816-37," HEH TU File Drawer 15B, Folder: Program, U. S. 1816-1837, reveal the schedule of lectures. The last line was prophetic: "Possibly get to 1837."

26. Turner kept most of the materials prepared by his students (HEH TU File Drawer 9B, Folder: Seminary, History 58, 1904; HEH TU Collection of Student Papers, Boxes 1-5).

27. Turner's reading notes, HEH TU Box 55, and File Drawers 5C, 9A, and 9C. The two outlines, Oct. 1, 1904, and Nov. 17, 1905, HEH TU File Drawer 7E, Folder: Table of Contents, 1819-29.

28. These lectures were summarized in the *University of Michigan News-Letter*, Feb. 20, 1905, and the *Daily Cardinal*, March 4, 1905.

29. Hart to Turner, June 3, 9, 24, 1905, HEH TU Box 5. Correspondence on the maps for the period May 11 to July 23, ibid.

30. Reminiscences of Merrill H. Crissey, HEH TU Box 57, Folder: Merrill H. Crissey, Drafts of Biographical Data. Crissey continued to work with Turner until the fall of 1906, when he left to take a position with his uncle in the South.

31. Turner to Hart, Aug. 3, 1905; Hart to Turner, Aug. 16, 1905, U. of Wis. Arch., L. and S., Hist., Turner Corr., Box 5, Folder H.

32. Hart to Turner, Aug. 23, 28, 1905, HEH TU Box 5.

33. Hart to Turner, Oct. 12, 21, 24, 25, 1905, HEH TU Box 5. Turner to Hart, Sept. 29, 1905, U. of Wis. Arch., L. and S., Hist., Turner Corr., Box 5, Folder H. The Nucleus Club was an informal organization of the inner circle that controlled the American Historical Association. The members usually met for a gala dinner after the annual convention (Turner to Mae Turner, Dec. 7, 1905, HEH TU Box G). Turner was asked at this time to allow the *American Historical Review* to print portions of the book before it was published. He and the editor eventually agreed on the chapter on the South, and extracts from the chapters on the West and the Far West. They were printed in January and April, 1906. Correspondence between Turner and J. Franklin Jameson, leading to their publication, is in U. of Wis. Arch., L. and S., Hist., Turner Corr., Box 5, Folder J.

34. Hart to Turner, Dec. 9, 11, 13, 14, 1905, HEH TU Box 5.

35. Hart to Turner, Jan. 10, 16, Feb. 8, 23, 24, March 1, 12, 13, 14, 1906, HEH TU Box 6.

36. Turner to Max Farrand, Dec. 29, 1905; Hart to Farrand, June 2, 1933, HEH TU Boxes 5 and 50A.

37. Turner, *Rise of the New West, 1819–1829* (New York, 1906), xvii.

38. Copies of these reviews and others, HEH TU Box 55.

39. James Ford Rhodes to Turner, July 11, 1908; Charles R. Van Hise to Turner, Oct. 5, 1906, HEH TU Boxes 11 and 7. Sales justified a second printing in 1907, giving Turner a chance to correct some twenty-five minor errors (Turner to Harper & Brothers, Jan. 22, 1907, HEH TU Box 8).

40. Memorandum attached to letter from Holt & Co., May 25, 1905, summarizing letters he had written making these suggestions. Negotiations continued: Holt & Co. to Turner, May 5, 25, June 12, 1905; Turner to Holt & Co., May 25, 1905 (HEH TU Box 63); Ginn and Co., to Turner, May 8, July 27, 1905 (HEH TU Box 7).

41. Turner to Holt & Co., Aug. 10, 1905; Holt & Co. to Turner, Oct. 7, 14, 1905, HEH TU Box 63. Turner insisted on giving the company his personal note, promising to repay the $500 within two years if the book had not appeared (described in handwritten addition to letter received Oct. 14, 1905). His optimistic estimate of his completion date, Turner to Max Farrand, Oct. 13, 1905, U. of Wis. Arch., L. and S., Hist., Turner Corr., Box 5, Folder F.

42. Holt & Co. to Turner, Oct. 26, 1905, HEH TU Box 63. Proof of an announcement of the book was sent to Charles Homer Haskins, editor of the American Historical Series in which it was to appear (proof in Edward N. Bristol to Haskins, May 16, 1907, Princeton, Haskins Papers).

43. Notes and schedules, HEH TU File Drawer 15C, Folder: College History of the US.

44. Drafts of chapters, ibid. The quotation is from the Introduction.
45. William S. Robinson to Turner, Jan. 28, 1907; William R. Shepherd to Turner, Nov. 17, 1911; Homer C. Hockett to Turner, Sept. 27, 1913, HEH TU Boxes 8, 16, 20.
46. Holt & Co. to Turner, Jan. 24, 1911, HEH TU Box 63; Holt & Co. to Turner, Dec. 6, 1915, Princeton, Holt Arch.
47. Turner to Mae Turner, Dec. 30, 1908, March 11, 1915, HEH TU Boxes G and I.
48. Turner to Charles R. Van Hise, March 1, 14, 1907, describe his life in Washington (U. of Wis. Arch., Pres. Corr., C. R. Van Hise Gen. Corr., Box 16, Folder: F. J. Turner). Lectures described in *Daily Cardinal*, April 9, 1907, and arrangements for Johns Hopkins visit discussed in Turner to John M. Vincent, March 19, April 2, 1907, HEH TU Boxes 8 and 9.
49. Turner to Mae Turner, May 4, 13, 1907, HEH TU Box G.
50. Turner to Ellen C. Semple, Sept. 24, Oct. 21, 1907; Turner to C. H. Haskins, Sept. 24, 28, 1907, HEH TU Box 9A.
51. Turner to George L. Burr, Nov. 9, 1907; Burr to Turner, Nov. 13, 1907, George Lincoln Burr Papers, Division of Regional History and Archives, Cornell University (hereafter cited as Cornell, Burr Papers). Turner's report of this discussion, addressed to William A. Dunning, is in HEH TU Box 10 [printed in *Annual Report of the American Historical Association for 1907* (Washington, D.C., 1908), I, 45–47]. For a discussion of the meeting, see H. Roy Merrens, "Historical Geography and Early American History," *William and Mary Quarterly*, XXII (Oct. 1965), 538.
52. Turner to Claude H. Van Tyne, April 25, 1908. Claude H. Van Tyne Papers, Clements Library, University of Michigan (hereafter cited as Clements, Van Tyne Papers). Another session relating geography to history, at the 1908 meeting of the Association, was no more successful. Again, George Lincoln Burr voiced his strong objections to geographical determinism. Turner, who served as discussant, did little more than urge an analysis of "the various divisions of America to see of what economic sections they are composed." He was far from happy with the results (Turner to Mae Turner, Dec. 30, 1908, HEH TU Box G).
53. A copy of this article from the *Yale Review*, Nov. 1906, was sent Turner by Johnson; he followed his usual practice of underlining and adding marginal notations (HEH TU File Drawer L2, Folder: 0090).
54. Typed version, HEH TU File Drawer L3, Folder: 0524; printed in *American Journal of Sociology*, XIII (March 1908), 661–75.
55. Turner in talk to Thursday Club (Cambridge, Dec. 15, 1921, HEH TU File Drawer 14A, Folder: Draft, Revised, Recent American Sectionalism). Discussion summarized, *American Journal of Sociology*, XIII (May 1908).
56. The essay was printed in the *Proceedings of the State Historical Society of Wisconsin for 1908* (Madison, 1908), 184–233. Turner's copy, heavily annotated and with the comment (p. 15), "Add a special paragraph on democracy," HEH Accession No. 126665.
57. Charles M. Andrews to Turner, March 27, 1909; Albion W. Small to Turner, March 22, 1909; Carl Becker to Turner, March 19, 1909; Max Farrand to Turner, March 18, 1909; Edward Channing to Turner, March 19,

1909, HEH TU Box 12. In replying to Farrand, Turner urged colonialists to investigate the eighteenth-century settlement of interior New England— "its relation to land pressure, and to social and economic factors such as the development of proprietary control of town land as a possession instead of a trust" (Turner to Farrand, March 21, 1909, HEH TU Box 12).

Chapter X
Teacher and Administrator
1901-1910

1. Max Farrand to Mae Turner, April 4, 1906, recalled these scenes as Farrand saw them during a two-week visit to the Turner home (HEH TU Box 7).
2. *Daily Cardinal*, March 4, 1910, Jan. 23, 1903. Turner later denied that he ever played tennis as a young man, but his memory was obviously faulty (Turner to Joseph Schafer, Oct. 14, 1931, SHSW, Schafer Papers).
3. Details of Turner's financial arrangements discussed with his brother shortly after his father's death in 1905 (Turner to Will Turner, Oct. 1, 1905, HEH TU Box G).
4. Turner to Mae Turner, June 26, 1908, HEH TU Box G. Entries in his pocket diary (March 11, 1907, Jan. 6, 10, Feb. 10, 1910, numerous other dates) tell of borrowing money to meet immediate needs (HEH TU Box 62).
5. Turner to Mae Turner, April 25, 1909. HEH TU Box G. Entries in his pocket diary (Dec. 15, 1908, Feb. 16, 1910) tell of financial problems related to the purchase (HEH TU Box 62).
6. Accounts of the family finances, Turner to Will Turner, Oct. 1, 1905, Turner to Mae Turner, May 9, 1907, HEH TU Box G. He also listed his assets and liabilities on the flyleaf of his pocket diary for 1908-12 (HEH TU Box 62).
7. Turner to Max Farrand, Nov. 14, 1907. HEH TU Box 9A.
8. The first canoe trip lasted from August 22 to September 4, 1907, the second from mid-July to mid-August 1908. Turner kept a record of the first in day-by-day entries in his pocket diary (HEH TU Box 62). Mae Turner recorded the second in a handwritten diary (HEH TU Vol. XI). He drew $400 from the bank to finance the 1908 journey.
9. The correspondence between Turner and William J. Truesdale, director of the summer school, was extensive, and much of it on Turner's part highly indignant at the treatment he received (U. of Wis. Arch., L. and S., Hist., Turner Corr., Box 1, Folder T). Attached to Turner to Truesdale, March 26, 1902, is a schedule of the sixteen lectures he planned to give.
10. Turner to Max Farrand, Oct. 1, 1902, ibid. Box 2, Folder F; Turner to J. F. Jameson, Aug. 24, 1902, HEH TU Box 3.
11. Turner to Max Farrand, Oct. 17, 1903, ibid. Box 4.
12. *Wisconsin State Journal*, Oct. 24, 1903.
13. Correspondence between President Charles W. Eliot and Turner regarding the position (Dec. 12, 1902–March 10, 1903) is in U. of Wis. Arch., L. and S., Hist., Turner Corr., Boxes 3 and 4, Folder E. Turner's ruffled feelings, arising from the $1500 salary offered, were smoothed by Charles H.

Haskins, who was on the Harvard faculty. He assured Turner that $1500 was the usual compensation for two courses, and that Eliot was astounded to learn that anyone at Wisconsin earned more than this (Haskins to Turner, March 10, 1903, ibid. Box 3, Folder H).

14. Turner to A. Lawrence Lowell, Feb. 19, 1903, ibid. Box 3, Folder F. Official notice of the appointment, April 1, 1903, naming Turner a "Lecturer in History," HEH TU Box 53.

15. Turner to Mae Turner, May 25, 1904. Guests included Edward E. Hale, Josiah Royce, Bliss Perry, Davis R. Dewey, Albert B. Hart, and Frederick P. Vinton. All signed Turner's menu (HEH TU Box 59). Turner described living in Boston in Turner to Reuben G. Thwaites (Feb. 29, 1904, WSHS, Thwaites Papers).

16. Albert G. Waite, "Frederick J. Turner Lecture Notes in History 10b, Harvard University, spring term, 1903-1904" (Harvard University Archives, Call No. HUC 8903.338.10.92). Some of Turner's own notes suggesting the scope of the course are in HEH TU File Drawer 12, Folder: Harvard Lectures.

17. Turner to Mae Turner, May 23, 1904, HEH TU Box F. Mae returned home in mid-May, and Turner spent the rest of his stay in the Colonial Club.

18. Edward Channing to Turner, May 16, 1905, HEH TU Box 5. Turner described the events of that spring in letters to Mae (May 28, 31, 1904, HEH TU Box F). He found Peterboro, New Hampshire, so quiet that when a horse and a bicycle went by he heard a farmer say: "It does beat all what a commotion there is in town tonight."

19. Turner to Edmond S. Meany, April 6, 1904, Roy Lokken (ed.), "Frederick Jackson Turner's Letters to Edmond S. Meany," *Pacific Northwest Quarterly*, XLIV (Jan. 1953), 32-33.

20. Turner to President B. I. Wheeler, Oct. 9, 1903; Turner to H. Morse Stephens, Oct. 22, 1903. U. of Wis. Arch., L. and S., Hist., Turner Corr., Box 4, Folders S and W. Turner to Richard T. Ely, Aug. 30, 1904, SHSW, Ely Papers.

21. Turner to B. I. Wheeler, March 7, 1906, has a note attached, describing the courses Turner planned to give (HEH TU Box 6). Turner described his experiences in letters to Richard R. Van Hise (June 15, Aug. 3, 1906, U. of Wis. Arch., Pres. Corr., C. R. Van Hise, Gen. Corr., Box 16, Folder: F. J. Turner). Turner kept a record of his wilderness experiences in his pocket notebook, May 6 to Sept. 12, 1906 (HEH TU Box 62).

22. Turner to Mae Turner, Sept. 22, 1906, HEH TU Box G.

23. George E. Fellows to Turner, Oct. 26, 1901, U. of Wis. Arch., L. and S., Hist., Turner Corr., Box 1, Folder F. Turner may have remembered a letter received from Birge in August 1901; Birge quoted a student who said that anyone could pass Turner's course by attending his lectures without doing outside reading, and demanded to know if this were true. Such distrust of a faculty member was bound to rankle (U. of Wis. Arch., Pres. Corr., E. A. Birge, General Corr., 1901-3, Series 4/8/1, Box 7).

24. Van Hise's election is described in Merle Curti and Vernon Carstensen, *The University of Wisconsin, 1848-1925* (Madison, 1949), II, 11-13, and Maurice M. Vance, *Charles Richard Van Hise: Scientist Progressive* (Madison, 1960), 70-75.

25. Emil Baensch to Turner, Feb. 7, 1902; John C. Kerwin to Turner, June 6, 10, 19, 1902; Turner to Kerwin, June 11, 1902; Arthur J. Puls to Turner, March 24, 26, 1903, HEH TU Boxes 3 and 4; U. of Wis. Arch., L. and S., Hist., Turner Corr., Box 2, Folder K. In Turner to Puls, March 26, 1903, ibid., is a six-page memorandum, in Turner's hand, on the proper qualifications of a Wisconsin president.

26. *Wisconsin State Journal*, May 28, 1902, April 20, 22, 1903; *Milwaukee Sentinel*, Aug. 13, 14, 1902.

27. Turner's address, *Wisconsin State Journal*, June 7, 1904, Van Hise's address, *Jubilee of the University of Wisconsin* (Madison, 1909), 121–23.

28. J. Franklin Jameson to Turner, May 12, 1900, HEH TU Box 3; Turner to C. K. Adams, May 8, 23, 1900, U. of Wis. Arch., Pres. Corr., C. K. Adams, General Corr., Box 6; Turner to George C. Sellery, May 28, 1901, HEH TU Box 3.

29. *The Sphynx*, III (March 15, 1902), 97.

30. Haskins to President Eliot, Dec. 21, 1901; Haskins to E. A. Birge, Feb. 21, 1902, Princeton, Haskins Papers.

31. Turner to Carl Becker, Jan. 7, 1902, HEH TU Box 3.

32. Turner to Dana C. Munro, March 8, 18, 1902, U. of Wis. Arch., L. and S., Hist., Turner Corr., Box 1, Folder M; *Daily Cardinal*, April 3, 1902.

33. The *Daily Cardinal* printed regular notices of bird walks organized by Libby. He spent the summer of 1899 not in research, but in helping friends dig up the bones of those who helped John Brown at Harper's Ferry, then reburying them at North Elba, beside their leader (ibid. Nov. 13, 1899).

34. Turner to President Webster Merrifield, Feb. 5, 1902, U. of Wis. Arch., L. and S., Hist., Turner Corr., Box 1, Folder M.

35. *Catalogue of the University of Wisconsin for 1900-1901* (Madison, 1901), 175.

36. Turner to William A. Dunning, April 17, 1902; Turner to Ulrich B. Phillips, April 17, May 13, 1902; Phillips to Turner, April 21, May 13, 1902, U. of Wis. Arch., L. and S., Hist., Turner Corr., Box 2, Folder P.

37. One applicant who sought a position and was rejected by Turner was Charles A. Beard (Beard to Turner, April 8, 24, 1903; Turner to Beard, April 22, 1903, ibid. Box 5, Folder B). Turner discussed departmental offerings in letters to Dana C. Munro (April 18, May 6, 1902, ibid. Box 2, Folder M); and in a report on the first two years of the School of History to acting President E. A. Birge (ibid. Box 6, Folder: History Department).

38. Turner sought to forestall these raids by generous salary increases, advancing Fish from $1400 to $1600, Sellery from $1200 to $1500, and Phillips from $1300 to $1400 in 1905, even without outside offers (Turner to E. A. Birge, April 25, 1905, U. of Wis. Arch., L. and S., Dean's Files, Birge Corr., Box 1, Folder T-Z).

39. William E. Dodd to Turner, July 1, 3, 1908, HEH TU Box 11. Herman V. Ames to Turner, May 7, 11, 1908; Turner to Winfred T. Root, May 11, 1908; Root to Turner, May 14, 1908, U. of Wis., Dept. of Hist, Turner Papers.

40. These changes were described in the *Wisconsin Alumni Magazine*, XI (Nov. 1909), 78, and noted in the yearly editions of the university catalogue.

41. Quoted in *Wisconsin State Journal*, June 9, 1904.

42. A. L. P. Dennis to Turner, March 14, 1907, U. of Wis., Dept. of Hist., Turner Papers.

43. Turner set forth his views on the role of the summer session in an undated memorandum (Univ. of Wis. Arch., Summer School File). It is quoted at length in S. H. Goodnight, *The Story of the Origins and Growth of the Summer School and the Summer Session, 1885-1940* (Madison, 1940), 41-45.

44. Turner advanced his views in letters to Ernst Greverus, June 26, Dec. 19, 1901, Mary Peckham, Feb. 14, 1903, and F. O. Holt, Jan. 22, 1909. These, and others like them, are scattered through the files that Turner kept as chairman of the department (U. of Wis. Arch., L. and S., Hist., Turner Corr., Boxes 1-6).

45. Copy, ibid. Box 5, Miscellaneous.

46. Elizabeth Waters to Turner, Jan. 2, 1903; Turner to Elizabeth Waters, Jan. 2, 1903, ibid. Box 3, Folder W. Notices of Turner's lectures to these groups appeared regularly in the *Daily Cardinal* and *Wisconsin State Journal*.

47. Turner resigned in February 1904, when he left Madison to teach a term at Harvard (*Wisconsin State Journal*, Feb. 10, 13, 1904).

48. Nicholas Murray Butler to Turner, Jan. 24, 1902; Turner to Butler, Jan. 30, 1902, U. of Wis. Arch., L. and S., Hist., Turner Corr., Box 1, Folder B.

49. Clarence W. Alvord, "Review of *The Frontier in American History*," *Mississippi Valley Historical Review*, VII (March 1921), 404.

50. Turner, notes for "Talk to Graduate History Club, December 19, 1908," HEH TU Box 55.

51. "Instructional Reports," U. of Wis. Arch.

52. A. C. Krey, "My Reminiscences of Frederick Jackson Turner," *Arizona and the West*, III (Winter 1961), 379. Turner's seminar topics were listed in the university catalogues, those for the 1909 seminar are in a note in his hand (HEH TU Box 55).

53. "Reminiscences of Guy Stanton Ford," Oral History Research Office, Columbia University, 141.

54. Edwin Witte, "Diary, 1909-1910," Feb. 25, 1910 manuscript, MSS Division, State Historical Society of Wisconsin.

55. Turner to Max Farrand, May 15, 1907, HEH TU Box 9.

56. Turner to Carl R. Fish, March 29, April 3, 1907, HEH TU Box 9.

57. Turner to C. R. Van Hise, May 11, 1905, U. of Wis. Arch., L. and S., Hist., Turner Corr., Box 1, Folder T-Z.

58. Turner to L. E. Aylsworth, Aug. 2, 1902, to W. C. Rice, Nov. 18, 1903, and to J. L. Conger, July 24, 1905, ibid. Box 2, Folder A, Box 4, Folder R, and Box 5, Folder C.

59. Turner described graduate requirements in letters to Carl Becker, Jan. 9, 1904, Judson G. Rosebush, March 2, 1906, and Homer C. Hockett, March 5, 1906, HEH TU Box 6.

60. Charles H. Ambler to Turner, Jan. 13, 1909; Turner to Macmillan Co., Jan. 19, 1909, HEH TU Box 12.

61. Turner to president of the University of West Virginia, June 15, 1907; Turner to J. F. Jameson, July 19, 1902, HEH TU Boxes 9 and 3. Turner to D. R. Dewey, July 23, 1902, U. of Wis. Arch., L. and S., Hist., Turner Corr., Box 2, Folder D.

62. Turner to Carl Becker, April 13, 1907, HEH TU Box 8.
63. *Daily Cardinal,* Jan. 4, 1906.
64. Turner listed some of these accomplishments in a letter to C. R. Van Hise, June 19, 1908 (HEH TU Box 11). The *Daily Cardinal,* Oct. 15, 1908, also catalogued Turner students who were teaching throughout the nation.
65. Turner to Constance L. Skinner, March 15, 1922, HEH TU Box 31.

Chapter XI
Undergraduate Teacher and Reformer
1901-1910

1. Frederick J. Turner, "Instructional Reports," 1901-9, U. of Wis. Arch.
2. *The Sphynx,* III (May 7, 1902), 122; *Wisconsin State Journal,* Sept. 29, 1905.
3. Ibid., May 9, 1903; *The Sphynx,* VI (July 15, 1905), 152.
4. A. C. Krey, "My Reminiscences of Frederick Jackson Turner," *Arizona and the West,* III (Winter 1961), 379. Valuable on Turner as a teacher is Ulrich B. Phillips, "The Traits and Contributions of Frederick Jackson Turner," *Agricultural History,* XIX (Jan. 1945), 21-23.
5. Albert G. Waite, "Frederick J. Turner Lecture Notes in History 10b, Harvard University, spring term, 1903-1904," Harvard Univ. Archives, HUC 8903.338.10.92.
6. Turner to Passenger Traffic Agent, Chicago and North Western Railroad, July 6, 1907, HEH TU Box 9A. Other letters to railroads are in this box, and in Box V, Folder: Transportation, of the Harvard Commission on Western History Papers, Correspondence Ser., Harvard Univ. Archives, Call No. UA III 50 29.12.2.5. (hereafter cited as Harvard Arch., HC on WH Corr.).
7. Waite, "Frederick J. Turner Lecture Notes," Lecture of May 25. Hundreds of slides prepared by Turner are among his papers at the Huntington Library.
8. Quoted in Phillips, "Traits and Contributions of Frederick Jackson Turner," *loc. cit.* 23.
9. Carl Becker, "Frederick Jackson Turner," *Wisconsin Alumni Magazine,* XI (Jan. 1910), 144. This excellent appraisal, written at the time Turner left Wisconsin for Harvard, sheds light on his teaching techniques.
10. Krey, "My Reminiscences of Frederick Jackson Turner," *loc. cit.* 380.
11. One such outline is in HEH TU File Drawer 15D, Folder: Notes for Ec. and Soc. Hist. US, 1815-1850.
12. Mimeographed syllabus, "History of the West, 1909," HEH TU Vol. VI (3) Syllabus of Lectures. History of the West. A shorter syllabus, apparently used about 1904, is also in this folder.
13. Of several sets of lecture notes taken by students in the "History of the West" during these years, the most complete was that of Homer C. Hockett, made during the summer of 1902. Hockett took shorthand well, and he recorded the lectures stenographically. Copies given to Turner are scattered through his notes under the topics covered (HEH TU File Drawer 2E, Folder: Piedmont and Great Valley; Drawer 3A, Folder: Unmarked;

Drawer 3B, Folder: Interior vs. Coast; Drawer 4A, Folder: West in Revolution; Drawer 4A, Folder: Lecture Notes Summer 1902; Drawer 12A, Folder: West. Frontier in N. Eng.; Drawer 15B, Folder: Hockett, Filling in the Southwest; Drawer 15C, Folder: History of West 1902).

14. *The Nation* LXXXI (Nov. 30, 1905), 437-38. This, and other clippings on the football controversy, were pasted by Turner on 5×8 slips of paper, labeled, dated, and filed. U. of Wis. Arch., University Faculty, Athletic Board. Frederick J. Turner File: Football Reform Movement, 1906. Series 5/21/5, Box 1). They provide an excellent history of the subject. The national crusade against professionalized football is described in John H. Moore, "Football's Ugly Decades, 1893-1913," *Smithsonian Journal of History*, II (Fall 1967), 49-68, the local contest in Merle Curti and Vernon Carstensen, *The University of Wisconsin, 1848-1925* (Madison, 1949), II, 536-42.

15. *Daily Cardinal*, Dec. 1, 3, 1904.

16. *Wisconsin Alumni Magazine*, IV (Feb. 1903), 201.

17. *Daily Cardinal*, March 29, 31, 1905; *Wisconsin State Journal*, March 29, 1905. Minutes of the Meeting of the University Faculty, Dec. 12, 1904. Univ. of Wis. Arch. (hereafter cited as U. of Wis. Arch., Minutes, University Faculty).

18. *Daily Cardinal*, Nov. 5, 24, 1905.

19. Ibid. Dec. 7, 1905; *Wisconsin State Journal*, Dec. 5, 11, 23, 1905.

20. U. of Wis. Arch., Minutes, University Faculty, Dec. 4, 1905.

21. *Daily Cardinal*, Dec. 8, 14, 1905.

22. Turner's views on Van Hise, one of his best friends, are in Turner to Mae Turner, May 31, 1904, HEH TU Box F, and on the overemphasis of football, in Turner to Frederick Whitton, Nov. 18, 1904, U. of Wis. Arch., L. and S., Hist., Turner Corr., Box 5, Folder W. Whitton was an official of the Alumni Club of Chicago.

23. Harvey Holmes to Turner, June 23, 1925, HEH TU Box 34. Holmes, a football player, recalled this conversation—but so many years later that its authenticity may be doubted.

24. Turner's letters have not been preserved, but their nature can be inferred from some of the answers he received. See esp. Andrew C. McLaughlin to Turner, Dec. 15, 1905, and Albion W. Small to Turner, [Jan. 1906], HEH TU Boxes 5 and 6.

25. For arrangements for this conference, see Harry Pratt Judson to Van Hise, Dec. 28, 1905; Van Hise to Judson, Dec. 25, 1905; Van Hise to James B. Angell, Dec. 26, 1905, Jan. 3, 1906; Angell to Van Hise, Jan. 1, 5, 1906, HEH TU Boxes 5 and 6.

26. A typed copy of this report is in University of Wisconsin Archives, University Faculty, Sec. of the Faculty. Faculty Minutes, Documents, etc. Ser. 5/2/2, Box 2, Folder: 253-70 (hereafter cited as U. of Wis. Arch., University Faculty, Sec. of Faculty). Action on the report is given in U. of Wis. Arch., Minutes, University Faculty, Jan. 8, 9, 1906.

27. *Daily Cardinal*, Jan. 9, 1906. Student unrest was heightened by newspaper reports, later proven false, that Harvard had abolished football.

28. *The Sphynx*, II (April 7, 1906), 125; *The Badger for 1907* (Madison, 1906), 505.

29. *Daily Cardinal,* Jan. 10, 1906.

30. U. of Wis. Arch., Minutes, University Faculty, Jan. 18, 1906.

31. Turner to Mae Turner, January 20, 1906, HEH TU Box G.

32. Printed minutes of conference (13 pp., untitled), U. of Wis. Arch., University Faculty, Athletic Board, Turner File, Box 1, page 10. Although the members were pledged to secrecy, the *Daily Cardinal* and the *Wisconsin State Journal,* Jan. 22, 1906, published fairly accurate accounts.

33. A typed copy of this Turner speech is in U. of Wis. Arch., University Faculty, Athletic Board, Turner File, Box 1, Folder: Madison Alumni Address. At the bottom, in Turner's hand, are the words: "Passed by an overwhelming majority." The speech was reported in the *Wisconsin State Journal,* Feb. 1, 1906.

34. *Daily Cardinal,* Feb. 1, 2, 1906; Albion W. Small to Turner, Jan. 22, 1906; Andrew C. McLaughlin to Turner, Jan. 26, 1906, HEH TU Box 6.

35. A. H. Pattengill to Turner, Jan. 23, Feb. 3, 1906; Turner to Pattengill, Jan. 26, 1906, HEH TU Box 6.

36. U. of Wis. Arch., Minutes, University Faculty, Feb. 6, 1906.

37. A. H. Pattengill to Turner, Feb. 9, 1906; Andrew C. McLaughlin to Turner, Feb. 10, 19, 1906, HEH TU Box 6. Northwestern, however, voted overwhelmingly against a seven-game schedule. James A. James to Turner, Feb. 19, 1906, ibid.

38. "Report of the Second Conference of Collegiate Representatives," Chicago, March 9, 1906 (5-pp. report, signed by H. J. Barton, secretary). Copy, U. of Wis. Arch., University Faculty, Athletic Board, Turner File, Box 1.

39. *Wisconsin State Journal,* March 13, 15, 1906; *Daily Cardinal,* March 13, 1906. One of the interviewers later recalled that he went to Turner's home expecting to meet a football-devouring ogre, but instead found a sympathetic and rational man who had the best interests of the university at heart (R. D. Hetzel to Joseph Schafer, Aug. 6, 1932, SHSW, Schafer Papers, MSS II). Hetzel was president of Pennsylvania State College.

40. *Daily Cardinal,* March 16, 17, 21, 1906; *Wisconsin State Journal,* March 17, 1906.

41. *Wisconsin State Journal,* March 26, 1906.

42. Ibid. March 28, 1906; *Daily Cardinal,* March 28, 1906.

43. *Daily Cardinal,* April 3, 5, 1906; U. of Wis. Arch., Minutes, University Faculty, April 5, 1906.

44. *The Sphynx,* VIII (Oct. 13, 1906), 21.

45. *Wisconsin State Journal,* Nov. 13, 1906.

46. *The Sphynx,* VIII (March 15, 1907), 133.

47. Turner to James A. James, Dec. 5, 1906, HEH TU Box 7.

48. U. of Wis. Arch., University Faculty, Sec. of Faculty, Faculty Minutes, Documents, etc. Box 2, Folder: 253-70; U. of Wis. Arch., Minutes, University Faculty, Dec. 3, 1906; Turner to E. A. Birge, Dec. 7, 1906. U. of Wis. Arch., College of Letters and Science, Administration. Dean's Files, Box 4, File T (hereafter cited as U. of Wis. Arch., L. and S., Dean's Files).

49. Board of Regents, Minutes. University of Wisconsin Archives, Ser. 1/1/1, Box 6, pp. 517-19 (hereafter cited as U. of Wis. Arch., Regents' Minutes).

50. *Wisconsin State Journal,* Dec. 4, 1906.

51. U. of Wis. Arch., Minutes, University Faculty, Dec. 11, 1906.
52. "Resolutions of the Conference between Representatives of Chicago, Michigan, Minnesota, and Wisconsin" (n.d.), SHSW, Turner Papers, Box II. The new schedules were announced in the *Wisconsin State Journal,* Jan. 28, 1907.
53. Turner had stated in an interview, "I am heartily in favor of the movement, and will speak in favor of it at the faculty meeting." *Daily Cardinal,* Jan. 28, 1907. He did so (U. of Wis. Arch., Minutes, University Faculty, Feb. 4, 1907).
54. *Wisconsin State Journal,* Nov. 19, 1907.
55. Ibid. Nov. 25, 1907; *Daily Cardinal,* Nov. 25, 1907.
56. U. of Wis. Arch., Minutes, University Faculty, Dec. 2, 1907; University Faculty, Sec. of Faculty, Faculty Minutes, Documents, etc., Box 3, Folder: 1-25. A press release, headed "Faculty Favor Athletics," describing the action is in HEH TU Box 55.
57. Manuscript minutes, U. of Wis. Arch., University Faculty, Sec. of Faculty, Faculty Minutes, Documents, etc., Box 2, Folder: 253-70. Attached is a "Supplementary Report" to the faculty in Turner's hand, much underlined and corrected, reiterating his views on de-emphasizing football.
58. *Daily Cardinal,* Jan. 11, 1908; *Wisconsin State Journal,* Jan. 10, 1908. Stephen S. Gregory, chairman of the alumni committee, and Turner exchanged sentiments of mutual gratification after the meeting, although they still differed sharply on naming an alumnus to the Athletic Council (Gregory to Turner, Dec. 16, 1907; Turner to Gregory, Dec. 19, 1907, U. of Wis. Arch., University Faculty, Sec. of Faculty, Faculty Minutes, Documents, etc., Box 2, Folder: 253-70).
59. *Daily Cardinal,* Dec. 2, 1907, Jan. 6, 14, Feb. 25, 1908; U. of Wis. Arch., Minutes, University Faculty, Jan. 13, 1908.
60. Ibid. Jan. 17, June 6, Dec. 5, 1910.

Chapter XII
Leaving Wisconsin
1905-1910

1. Turner to Carl Becker, Dec. 1, 1925, HEH TU Box 34.
2. A. B. Hart to Turner, March 29, 1912, HEH TU Box 17.
3. Edgar E. Robinson to Turner, Aug. 2, 1911, HEH TU Box 16.
4. Guy Emerson, *The New Frontier. A Study of the American Liberal Spirit, Its Frontier Origin, and Its Application to Modern Problems* (New York, 1920); Andrew C. McLaughlin, *Steps in the Development of American Democracy* (New York, 1920), 96-97. Emerson, a Harvard graduate, was a correspondent of Turner's.
5. Max Farrand to Turner, Feb. 23, 1905, HEH TU Box 5.
6. Max Farrand to Turner, Oct. 24, 1903. U. of Wis. Arch., L. and S., Hist., Turner Corr., Box 4, Folder: F.
7. Turner's copy of Farrand, "The West and the Principles of the American Revolution," *Yale Review,* o.s., XVII (May 1908), 44-58, HEH TU File Drawer L2, Folder: 0112.

8. The spread of the Turner thesis in textbooks is described in Henry M. Littlefield, "Textbooks, Determinism and Turner: The Westward Movement in Secondary School History and Geography Textbooks, 1830-1960," Ph.D. thesis (unpubl.), Columbia Univ., 1967. The author has generously allowed me to use his findings. Valuable also is Ruth M. Elson, *Guardians of Tradition: American Schoolbooks in the Nineteenth Century* (Lincoln, Nebr., 1964), based on an examination of about a thousand books used before 1900.

9. Genevieve Melody to Turner, Nov. 5, 1906; Turner to Genevieve Melody, Nov. 21, 1906, HEH TU Box 7.

10. Clarence W. Alvord, "The Study of Western History in Our Schools," *The History Teacher's Magazine*, I (Oct. 1909), 28.

11. Willis M. West, *American History and Government* (Boston, 1913). West apologized for incorporating so many of Turner's ideas, and justified himself only because "yours has been so long delayed" (West to Turner, Nov. 4, 1911, HEH TU Box 16).

12. Irene T. Blythe, "The Textbooks and the New Discoveries, Emphases and Viewpoints in American History," *Historical Outlook*, XXIII (Dec. 1932), 398-99.

13. Farrand to Turner, May 24, 1909, HEH TU Box 12.

14. Woodrow Wilson to editor of *New York Critic*, printed in *Wisconsin Magazine of History*, XXVI (June 1943), 471; Henry Morse Stephens, "Some Living American Historians," *World's Work*, IV (July 1902), 2316-27. Turner wrote Stephens: "I felt rather lonesome in my full-page illustration among the men who have done something. Seriously, however, it is very well worth having friends who believe in you" (Turner to Stephens, March 31, 1902, U. of Wis. Arch., L. and S., Hist., Turner Corr., Box 1, Folder W).

15. J. F. Jameson to Charles Francis Adams, Sept. 12, 1907, Elizabeth Donnan and Leo F. Stock (eds.), *An Historian's World: Selections from the Correspondence of John Franklin Jameson* (Philadelphia, 1956), 108.

16. Lamprecht's opinion quoted in *Wisconsin State Journal*, Feb. 7, 1905, Channing's in Lois K. Mathews to Turner, March 9, 1906, HEH TU Box 6.

17. Turner's diplomas and certificates of election to honorary societies are in HEH TU Box 53.

18. The president, on conferring the degree, noted Turner's battle against the football interests by stressing his "high minded work for the promotion of lofty university ideals" (Edmund J. James to Turner, June 15, 1908, HEH TU Box 11).

19. Turner to Charles H. Haskins, Dec. 16, 1903, U. of Wis. Arch., L. and S., Hist., Turner Corr., Box 3, Folder H.

20. Such a trip is described in Jameson to Turner, Nov. 18, 1902, ibid. Box 3, Folder J.

21. Jameson described Turner's plan to publish the territorial papers in his diary, printed in Donnan and Stock (eds.), *An Historian's World*, 98-99. Their correspondence concerning a historical center includes Jameson to Turner, April 12, 1902; Turner to Jameson, April 29, Nov. 1, 1902, U. of Wis. Arch., L. and S., Hist., Turner Corr., Box 2, Folder J.

22. Jameson to Clarence W. Bowen, Oct. 15, 1901, Donnan and Stock (eds.), *An Historian's World*, 78.

23. Jameson to Turner, April 18, 1905; Turner to Jameson, May 11, 1905, U. of Wis. Arch., L. and S., Hist., Turner Corr., Box 5, Folder J.

24. A brief history of the commission is in Donnan and Stock (eds.), *An Historian's World*, 11-12.

25. A letter typical of the many mailed to historians is Turner to Claude H. Van Tyne, April 21, 1908, Clements, Van Tyne Papers. An example of his second mailing, addressed to "My Dear Professor," is in SHSW, Turner Papers, together with a number of the replies.

26. Turner's draft, with many corrections, HEH TU File Drawer 15C, Folder: Report, Draft by Turner on Social and Economic Documents. Final version (48 pp.), May 9, 1908, ibid. File Drawer 15A, Folder: Report on Documents Economic and Social; published, 60th Cong., 2nd sess., *Senate Document No. 714* (Washington, D.C., 1909), 1-45.

27. A. C. McLaughlin to Turner, Nov. 23, 1908, HEH TU Box 11. Mc-Laughlin urged Turner to address the University of Chicago's social science group, on research in social history.

28. *Annual Report of the American Historical Association for 1917* (Washington, D.C., 1920), 73-74.

29. Turner to Max Farrand, Jan. 3, 1905, HEH TU Box 5.

30. Farrand to Turner, Dec. 4, 1904, June 6, July 2, 1905; Turner to Farrand, Jan. 3, June 23, 1905, HEH TU Box 5.

31. Memorandum (July 1905) attached to Farrand to Turner, June 6, 1905, HEH TU Box 5.

32. Jordan to Turner, April 18, 19, 20, 1906, HEH TU Box 7. Notice from Board of Regents, April 20, 1906, confirming Turner's research leaves, ibid.

33. *Wisconsin State Journal*, Feb. 15, 21, March 7, 1906. Printed *Report of the Joint Legislative Committee on the Affairs of the University* (n.p., n.d.), 1-24, U. of Wis. Arch., Pres. Corr., C. R. Van Hise General Corr., Box 14, Folder: Legislative Investigating Committee.

34. Turner to Senator Wylie, Feb. 22, 1906, HEH TU Box 6. That Turner's leave of absence arrangements were mentioned before the committee is suggested in D. MacGregor to Van Hise, April 16, 1906, ibid. Box 7.

35. *Wisconsin State Journal*, Sept. 24, Oct. 19, 1907; *Daily Cardinal*, March 3, 24, 1906; *Wisconsin Literary Magazine*, V (Dec. 1907), 135-36; *Wisconsin Alumni Magazine*, VIII (Jan. 1907), 145-46.

36. U. of Wis. Arch., Regents' Minutes, Vol. 7, 199, 200. Report of committee, Board of Regents Executive Committee, 1888-1939, Box 11, Folder: Executive Committee Minutes, June 29-July 6, 1908.

37. Turner to Van Hise, June 19, 1908, HEH TU Box 11. Several copies of the letter, one marked "not sent," are in this box. Van Hise replied wryly that he was glad to have Turner's "brief statement," and that it would be useful to him (Van Hise to Turner, June 20, 1908, HEH TU Box 11).

38. Turner to Van Hise, Oct. 12, 1908, ibid.

39. Turner to Mae Turner, May 1, 1909; Turner to Max Farrand, March 21, 1909, HEH TU Boxes G and 12.

40. Richard T. Ely, *Ground Under Our Feet. An Autobiography* (New York, 1938), 196-97. In notes on a draft of his letter to Van Hise of Oct. 12, 1908, Turner wrote that his support for Van Hise's presidency occasioned many of the attacks on him, and that three of his friends on the Board of

Regents had urged him to take a higher salary in lieu of research leaves (HEH TU Box 11).

41. Turner's letters to Stephens have not been preserved, but their tenor can be inferred from Stephens's replies, July 25, Aug. 15, 1909, HEH TU Box 12. The Chicago meeting was suggested in Benjamin I. Wheeler to Turner, Aug. 17, Sept. 3, 1909, ibid.

42. Turner to Van Hise, Sept. 11, 19, 1909; Van Hise to Turner, Sept. 15, 1909, U. of Wis. Arch., Pres. Corr., C. R. Van Hise, General Corr., Box 23, Folder: Executive Committee, Regents.

43. C. H. Haskins to Turner, Sept. 14, 16, 25, 1909, HEH TU Box 12; Archibald C. Coolidge to A. Lawrence Lowell, Sept. 28, 1909; Lowell to Turner, Sept. 30, 1909, A. Lawrence Lowell Correspondence, Harvard University Archives, UA I 5 160, Folder: 881 (hereafter cited as Harvard Arch., Lowell Corr.).

44. Turner to Mae Turner, Oct. 6, 1909, HEH TU Box G.

45. Ibid. Oct. 7, 1909. Copies of printed program for inauguration, and menu and seating list for dinner, HEH TU File Drawer 15E, Folder: Harvard University Inauguration. Diploma given Turner, HEH TU Box 53. Events described, *Harvard Bulletin,* Nov. 17, 1909.

46. C. H. Haskins to Turner, Oct. 21, 1909, HEH TU Box 13.

47. Turner to Van Hise, Nov. 15, 1909, HEH TU Box 13; Van Hise to Turner, Nov. 16, 1909, ibid. Turner was informed that "your resignation as professor of American history was accepted, to take effect at the end of the current college year," with never a word of regret or praise (Board of Regents to Turner, Jan. 21, 1910, HEH TU Box 13).

48. *Harvard Bulletin,* Nov. 17, 1909; Charles H. Haskins to Turner, Nov. 20, 1909. Harvard had just defeated Dartmouth in football, 12 to 3.

49. *Daily Cardinal,* Dec. 16, 1909; Wisconsin Committee of Students to Turner, Dec. 22, 1909, HEH TU Box 13; *Milwaukee Sentinel,* Nov. 28, 1909; *Wisconsin Alumni Magazine,* XI (Dec. 1909), 108-9, 121-25; (Jan. 1910), 142-44, 166-68.

50. A. C. McLaughlin to Turner, Feb. 4, 14, 16, 1910; Edwin E. Sparks to Turner, April 1, 1910, HEH TU Box 14. Copy of printed program, HEH TU Box 59.

51. James A. James to Merrill H. Crissey, July 13, 1934, HEH TU Box 51.

52. Turner to Carl Becker, Jan. 15, 1910; Turner to James Alton James, Jan. 24, 1910, HEH TU Box 15.

53. Charles H. Ambler to Turner, Oct. 26, 1909, HEH TU Box 13.

54. Turner to Charles S. Slichter, Nov. 14, 1909, Charles S. Slichter Papers, U. of Wis. Arch. Turner to Mae Turner, Oct. 7, 1909, HEH TU Box G; A. C. Krey to Max Farrand, June 8, 1932, HEH TU Box 48. Krey recalled visiting Turner and seeing his tears as he thought of leaving Madison. A few students realized the reason for Turner's resignation. One wrote that "the reactionary attitude of the regents" was the only thing that could separate Turner from the library of the State Historical Society (Edwin E. Witte, "Diary, 1909-1910," Nov. 19, 1909, MSS Division, State Historical Society of Wisconsin).

55. Turner to Matthew B. Hammond, Nov. 21, 1909; Turner to Max Farrand, Oct. 28, 1909; Turner to Carl Becker, Dec. 5, 1909, HEH TU Box 13.

For a discussion of Turner's departure for Harvard, see Ray A. Billington, "Frederick Jackson Turner Comes to Harvard," *Proceedings of the Massachusetts Historical Society*, LXXIV (1962), 51-83.

56. Richard Lloyd Jones to Turner, Nov. 15, 24, Dec. 11, 1909, HEH TU Box 13.

57. Two accounts of the meeting were preserved. Paul Reinsch of the faculty kept virtually a stenographic record ("Minutes of the Joint Meeting of the Conference Committee of the Regents and Faculty of the University of Wisconsin," U. of Wis. Arch., Regents, Sec. Papers, Meetings of Board of Regents, 1849-1939. Box 23, Folder: Board of Regents Meeting, Jan. 19, 1910). A briefer account was kept by the regent who served as chairman (Fred C. Thwaits, "Report by the Chairman of the Meeting of the Conference Committees of the Regents and Faculty, held on the afternoon and evening of Friday, December 10, 1909," copy, U. of Wis. Arch., Misc. File, F. J. Turner).

58. U. of Wis. Arch., Regents' Minutes, Vol. 7, 435.

59. Edward Channing to Turner, Dec. 19, 1909, HEH TU Box 13.

60. Frederic L. Paxson to Turner, March 30, 1910, HEH TU Box 14. Paxson paid $100 down, $3000 on June 1, and the balance on November 1, 1910. Turner invested the surplus in American Telephone and Telegraph stock at $142 a share, and in Great Northern Railroad at $126, after paying off his mortgage and other debts (pocket diary, 1908-12, April 12, Nov. 1, 5, and 10, 1910, HEH TU Box 62).

61. Turner to Mae Turner, Aug. 5, 1910, HEH TU Box G.

62. Ibid. Aug. 7, 1910.

Chapter XIII
Harvard Years: The Academic World
1910-1917

1. Charles C. Whinery (*Encyclopaedia Britannica*) to Turner, Aug. 23, 1910, HEH TU Box 14. Correspondence concerning this article is scattered through Boxes 7 to 14, esp. the latter.

2. Turner to Mae Turner, Aug. 26, 1910, HEH TU Box G.

3. Turner's draft of this article, much corrected, is in HEH TU File Drawer 15E, Folder: Encyclopaedia Britannica Article; the manuscript of the bibliography is in HEH TU Vol. VII.

4. Reuben G. Thwaites to Turner, Oct. 10, 1910, HEH TU Box 5.

5. Turner to Frederick Merk, Feb. 17, 1927, Houghton, Turner Papers.

6. Turner to Frederick Merk, March 26, 1931, HEH TU Box 45; E. E. Dale, "Memories of Frederick Jackson Turner," *Mississippi Valley Historical Review*, XXX (Dec. 1943), 347-48.

7. This letter, titled "The Star Chamber, Am. House, Boston," is in HEH TU Box 20. It was written about 1913.

8. Turner to Joseph Jastrow, Oct. 5, 1910, HEH TU Box 15. Data on Turner's classes are drawn from the Harvard University Course Lists (Harvard Univ. Arch., First Half-Year, 1910). These list all students in each course taught at Harvard.

9. Horace J. Smith, Lecture Notes: History of the West. Harvard University, 1910-1911, HEH TU Vol. XXIII.

10. Turner to Homer C. Hockett, Oct. 19, 1910; Turner to August C. Krey, Feb. 6, 1911, HEH TU Boxes 15 and 16.

11. Copies of reports prepared in this seminar by W. C. Hunter and H. R. Townsend, HEH TU File Drawer B3, Folder: Election of 1836.

12. On August 27, 1910, Turner wrote in his pocket diary: " 'Changing Am. Ideals' as subject for Pres. Address. Or 'Perspectives in Am. History.' " HEH TU Box 62.

13. This discussion of Progressive history relies heavily on John Higham, History (Englewood Cliffs, N.J., 1965); Edward N. Saveth, "A Science of American History," Diogenes, XXVI (Summer 1959), 107-22; Charles Crowe, "The Emergence of Progressive History," Journal of the History of Ideas, XXVII (Jan.-March 1966), 109-24; and John H. Randall, Jr., and George Haines IV, "Controlling Assumptions in the Practice of American Historians," Theory and Practice in Historical Study: A Report of the Committee on Historiography (New York, 1946), 43-50.

14. Turner, "Social Forces in American History," American Historical Review, XVI (Jan. 1911), 217-33.

15. James Schouler to Turner, May 25, 1911, HEH TU Box 16.

16. Turner to Homer C. Hockett, Jan. 3, 1911, HEH TU Box 16.

17. Guy Stanton Ford, "Reminiscences of Guy Stanton Ford," Oral History Research Office, Columbia Univ., p. 269. For Turner's effort to pay for his copies, see Turner to Holt & Co., Jan. 23, 1911; Holt to Turner, Jan. 24, 1911. Princeton, Holt Arch.

18. Albert B. Hart to Turner, May 21, 1912, HEH TU Box 17. Contract with Ginn and Co., Dec. 10, 1909, HEH TU Box 55.

19. Turner to Max Farrand, Oct. 3, 1916, HEH TU Box 26.

20. Turner to Dorothy Turner, June 28, 1912, HEH TU Box H. Hart was a masterful persuader. "Don't spend any more time reading this letter," he wrote on May 21, "for you need it all to finish up your Cyclopedia articles so that I can get them next week" (HEH TU Box 18).

21. Manuscript drafts, corrected by Turner and Hart, HEH TU File Drawer 14C, Folder: Sect. in Am. Hist. MSS, and File Drawer 15E, Folders: West as a Factor in American Politics, and Frontier in American Development. At this time Turner also prepared an article, "The Territorial Development of the United States," for the Harvard Classics University Extension Course [published in William A. Neilson (ed.), The Harvard Classics University Extension Course, I History (Cambridge, 1913), 35-40].

22. Turner to George C. Sellery, Dec. 22, 1911, HEH TU Box 16.

23. Pocket diary, June 1, July 8, 1911, and flyleaves of two other diaries for the 1910-11 period, HEH TU Box 62. Details of insurance policies, Phoenix Insurance Co. to Turner, Feb. 17, 1914, HEH TU Box 21.

24. Royalty statements from Ginn and Co. are in HEH TU Box 28.

25. Purchases of Brazil stock listed in pocket diaries, March 25, 1911, March 8, 1913, June 10, 1914, HEH TU Box 62. Turner's optimism that the stock would provide for the family's future is shown in Turner to Mae Turner, July 1, 1912, Jan. 1, 1914, HEH TU Boxes H and I.

26. Turner to Dorothy Turner, Nov. 19, 1912, Nov. 21, 1913; Turner to

Mae Turner, Nov. 16, 1912, HEH TU Box H. Turner recalled Rhodes' generous hospitality in Turner to M. A. DeWolfe Howe, Jan. 9, 1928, HEH TU Box 38.

27. Programs for the 1918, 1923, and 1924 meetings of these clubs, with lists of members, HEH TU Box 59. Turner described meetings to his wife, Jan. 5, 1918, April 16, 1920, HEH TU Box I.

28. Rough notes for this talk, and recommendations to the Massachusetts Historical Society, labeled "Report of the Committee of the Library and the Cabinet," HEH TU Box 56.

29. Turner's relations with Mrs. Hooper and the Harvard Commission on Western History are described in Ray A. Billington (ed.), *Dear Lady. The Letters of Frederick Jackson Turner and Alice Forbes Perkins Hooper* (San Marino, Calif. 1970), 13-74.

30. Turner to Mrs. Hooper, Nov. 5, 1918, HEH TU-H Box 4.

31. Turner to John S. Main, Oct. 24, 1913, HEH TU Box H. Four days later he wrote in his pocket diary: "Wired Dorothy approval of her engagement to John Main," HEH TU Box 62. Turner deplored John's lack of fishing skills in a letter to Dorothy, Nov. 21, 1913, HEH TU Box H.

32. Turner to Mae Turner, March 8, 1915; Turner to Dorothy Turner Main, Dec. 12, 1917, HEH TU Box I.

33. Turner to Dorothy Turner, Nov. 30, 1912, HEH TU Box H. Dieting menu inserted in pocket diary for 1911-12. Blood pressure, recorded yearly since 1918, listed Aug. 30, 1923, HEH TU Box 62.

34. Turner to Mrs. Hooper, June 1, 1915. HEH TU-H Box 3; Mae Turner to Clarence W. Alvord, May 24, 1915, Clarence W. Alvord Papers, Illinois Historical Survey of the University of Illinois, Lincoln Hall, Urbana (hereafter cited as Hist. Survey Univ. of Ill., Alvord Papers).

35. Turner to Dorothy Turner Main, June 13, 1917, HEH TU Box 1, and Mrs. Hooper, June 10, 1917, HEH TU-H Box 3.

36. Turner to Charles H. Haskins, June 18, 1914, Princeton, Haskins Papers.

37. *University of Oregon Bulletin*, XI (March 1914), 14-15, copy, HEH TU Box 56. Turner's outline of lectures that he intended to give, HEH File Drawer 15D, Folder: Lecture Plan. University of Washington.

38. Edmond S. Meany to Max Farrand, Dec. 28, 1932, HEH TU Box 49. Clipping from *Seattle Star*, June 13, 1914, discussing Turner's love of fishing, HEH TU File Drawer 21C, Folder: Miscellany.

39. Turner to Henry M. Stephens, May 14, 1915, Herbert E. Bolton Papers, Bancroft Library, University of California, Berkeley (hereafter cited as Bancroft, Bolton Papers).

40. Turner to Max Farrand, Oct. 13, 1916, HEH TU Box 26; Turner's description of trip above Yosemite Valley, Turner to Mrs. Hooper, Aug. 6, 1915, HEH TU-H Box 3; Turner to Dorothy Turner Main, Aug. 12, 1915, HEH TU Box I.

41. Turner to Thomas P. Martin, Sept. 29, 1916, H.C. on W.H., Corr., Box V, Folder: Extracts from Personal Files.

42. Turner and Merk, *List of References on the History of the West, 2nd Half-Year, 1919-1920*. Turner's heavily annotated copy, with pages inserted on which he has written suggestions, HEH TU Vol. XX (1).

43. Edward E. Dale, "Turner—the Man and Teacher," *University of Kansas City Review*, XVIII (Autumn 1951), 25-26; Lewis D. Stilwell to Turner, April 26, 1924, "Blue Book," HEH TU Vol. II.

44. Horace J. Smith, "Lecture Notes, History of the West, 1910-1911," HEH TU Vol. XXIII.

45. Harvard University Course Lists, 1910-24, record students in each course, and are complete save for the period of World War I. Harvard Univ. Arch.

46. Turner's lectures, varying from finished copies marked "Dictated" to very rough notes, are scattered through a number of folders in HEH TU File Drawer 22A. Reading lists are in File Drawer 22B, Folder: Notes and Other Material 1880-1920.

47. Harvard University Course Lists, Second Half Year, 1914-15, 1915-16, Harvard Univ. Arch.

48. Lecture notes, K. M. Elish, 1915-16, Harvard Univ. Arch., Call No. HUC 8915.338.32.

49. J. F. Jameson to Turner, Jan. 26, 1915, HEH TU Box 23.

50. Dixon Ryan Fox to Max Farrand, Jan. 25, 1933, HEH TU Box 50.

51. Programs scattered through HEH TU Boxes 59 and 60.

52. Turner to Oscar C. Stine, Jan. 17, 1920, HEH TU Box 30. Student papers, some from his Harvard seminar, are in HEH TU Student's Papers (1)-(5). Others are in HEH TU File Drawer B4, Folder: Election of 1836, and F4, Folder: Germans.

53. Frederick Merk to Turner, July 4, 1927, HEH TU Box 37.

54. Turner to Fulmer Mood, Feb. 1922, is a five-page criticism of Mood's seminar paper (HEH TU Box 31).

55. Turner to Arthur P. Whitaker, July 21, 1921, HEH TU Box 31.

56. List compiled from *Doctors of Philosophy and Doctors of Science who have Received their Degree in Course from Harvard University, 1873-1926 with the Titles of their Theses* (Cambridge, 1926), 86-96.

57. Turner to Thomas P. Abernethy, July 16, 1920, Abernethy to Turner, Nov. 29, 1919, HEH TU Box 29; Turner to George M. Stephenson, Feb. 11, 1917, HEH TU Box 27.

58. Turner to Abernethy, Nov. 17, 1921, HEH TU Box 31. For special pleading for students who had written unsatisfactory examinations, see Turner to C. J. Bullock, May 10, 1915, Turner to William S. Ferguson, Dec. 30, 1918, HEH TU Boxes 24 and 28.

59. Kenneth W. Colgrove to Turner, March 29, 1915, Turner to Colgrove, Jan. 5, April 3, June 1, 1915, HEH TU Box 23 and 25.

60. Buffinton to Turner, June 21, 1914, HEH TU Box 21.

61. Turner to Buffinton, Dec. 21, 1922, Feb. 5, Nov. 23, 1923, HEH TU Box 32.

62. Turner to Buffinton, Dec. 12, 1924, HEH TU Box 33. From that time on Turner took puckish pleasure in addressing his student as "Dr. Buffinton."

Chapter XIV
Harvard Years: Conflict—Academic and International
1915-1920

1. Turner to A. C. McLaughlin, Oct. 6, 1915, HEH TU Box 25. Bancroft's letters to Turner, Oct. 5, 1915, ibid. Turner sought Jameson's advice in two letters written on the same day, Oct. 9, 1915 (LC, AHA Papers, Box 283, Folder: T).

2. Jameson to Turner, Oct. 15, 16, 18, 20, 23, 24, 1915, HEH TU Box 25; Turner to Jameson, Oct. 15, 1915. LC, AHA Papers, Box 283, Folder: F.

3. Bancroft to Turner, Oct. 23, 28, Nov. 3, 1915; Turner to Bancroft, Oct. 24, 28, 1915, HEH TU Box 25; Jameson to Turner, Oct. 23, 1915; Turner to Jameson, Oct. 23, 1915. LC, AHA Papers, Box 283, Folder: T.

4. Described in Jameson to H. Morse Stephens, Dec. 1, 1915, ibid. Box 31, Folder: S. The printed minutes are in the Annual Report of the American Historical Association for 1915 (Washington, D.C., 1917), 75-79.

5. Bancroft to Edgar A. Bancroft, Nov. 29, 1915, Frederick Bancroft Papers, Department of Special Collections, Columbia Univ. Library, Box 1 (hereafter cited as Columbia, Bancroft Papers).

6. Bancroft to William K. Boyd, Dec. 8, 1915, ibid.

7. Jameson to A. C. McLaughlin, Nov. 18, 1915, in Elizabeth Donnan and Leo F. Stock (eds.), An Historian's World: Selections from the Correspondence of John Franklin Jameson (Philadelphia, 1956), 186.

8. E. B. Greene to Turner, Dec. 15, 1915; Dana C. Munro to Turner, Dec. 18, 1915; E. P. Cheyney to Turner, Dec. 22, 1915; Turner to G. L. Burr, Dec. 20, 1915, HEH TU Box 25.

9. Printed minutes, Annual Report of the American Historical Association for 1915, 49-51. The meeting described by Sidney B. Fay in The Nation, CII (Jan. 6, 1916), 22-23, and in Jameson to A. C. McLaughlin, Jan. 4, 1916, in Donnan and Stock (eds.), An Historian's World, 189-90.

10. Minutes, second session of business meeting, Annual Report of the American Historical Association for 1915, 51-54; report of Committee of Nine, ibid. 69-75. Printed ballot of the nominating committee, committee's report, other papers, HEH TU Box 59.

11. Turner to G. L. Burr, Jan. 8, 1916, Cornell, Burr Papers.

12. Ambler to Turner, Jan. 16, 22, 23, Feb. 5, 1916; Turner to Ambler, Feb. 9, 1916, HEH TU Box 26.

13. Turner to Jameson, Dec. 25, 1915. LC, AHA Papers, Box 283, Folder: T.

14. Jameson to Robert S. Woodward, July 3, 1913, in Donnan and Stock (eds.), An Historian's World, 158.

15. Jameson to Turner, March 13, 1915; Turner to Jameson, April 3, 1915, HEH TU Box 23 and LC, Jameson Papers. Robert S. Woodward to Turner, Nov. 15, 24, 1915; Turner to Woodward, Nov. 20, 1915, HEH TU Box 25. Pocket diary entry, Nov. 20, 1915, HEH TU Box 62.

16. Carnegie Institution of Washington, Year Book No. 15 (Washington, D.C., 1917), 169.

17. Turner to Dorothy Turner Main, April 15, 1916, HEH TU Box I.

18. Place card (rough paper with picture of a coffin pierced by a dagger), together with menu, presented by Professor Emeritus Robert H. George of Brown University to Huntington Library, 1968.

19. Jameson to A. C. McLaughlin, Nov. 20, 1916, in Donnan and Stock (eds.), *An Historian's World*, 202.

20. Carnegie Institution of Washington, *Year Book No. 16* (Washington, D.C., 1918), 151. Syllabus for lecture series, HEH TU File Drawer 15B, Folder: Outline of Talk on North Central States; lecture on "The Middle West, 1830-1850: The Formation of a New Society," TU File Drawer F, Folder: Chap. VII North Central States.

21. Turner to Mrs. William Hooper, March 21, 1917, HEH TU-H Box 3.

22. Turner to Dorothy Turner Main, March 26, 1916; Senator Paul O. Husting to Turner, April 29, 1916, HEH TU Boxes I and 26.

23. Turner to John S. Main, March 31, 1916, HEH TU Box I.

24. Address of Feb. 22, 1916, HEH TU File Drawer 15A, Folder: Trinity College Lecture. Turner expressed many of the same views in a letter to A. C. McLaughlin (March 26, 1916, HEH TU Box 26).

25. Turner to Mrs. Hooper, Feb. 2, 5, 1917, HEH TU-H Box 3.

26. Turner to Mae Turner, July 9, 1917; Turner to Mrs. Hooper, March 21, 1917; Turner to Dorothy Turner Main, April 18, 1917, HEH TU Box I, TU-H Box 3.

27. For history of the National Board for Historical Services, see George T. Blakey, *Historians on the Homefront: American Propagandists for the Great War* (Lexington, Ky., 1970), and James M. Mock and Fredric Larson, *Words that Won the War: The Story of the Committee on Public Information, 1917-1919* (Princeton, 1939), 158-86.

28. Turner to Carl Becker, May 11, 1917; Turner to Max Farrand, May 5, 1917, HEH TU Box 27.

29. Turner to Jameson, May 20, 1917, in Donnan and Stock (eds.), *An Historian's World*, 207-8.

30. Turner to C. H. Van Tyne, Nov. 2, 1917, HC on WH Corr., Box VIII, Folder: TUV. Liberty Bond purchases listed in pocket diary for 1918, HEH TU Box 62.

31. Turner to Mrs. Hooper, Nov. 5, 1918, HEH TU-H Box 4.

32. Many "History of Liberty" lectures, with outlines, reading lists, and revisions, HEH TU File Drawers 10A and 10B. The lecture notes of a student, Frederick Merk, in TU Student's Papers (4), Folder: Merk: History of Liberty Notes.

33. Quotations drawn largely from lecture, "History A. Liberty. Introduction," HEH TU File Drawer 10B, Folder: Liberty, Introduction.

34. Turner to Mrs. Hooper, Oct. 9, 1919; Turner to William E. Dodd, May 26, 1920. HEH TU-H Box 4, TU Box 30.

35. Turner to Mrs. Hooper, Oct. 13, 1917, Oct. 19, 1919; Turner to Dorothy Turner Main, Jan. 26, 1917, HEH TU-H, Box 4, TU Box I.

36. Observations, probably written early in 1918, HEH TU File Drawer 15A, Folder: It Would be a Pity if the United States Lost.

37. Turner to Richard H. Dana, May 3, 1915, Richard Henry Dana Papers, Massachusetts Historical Society, Boston.

38. Turner's rough-draft "Syllabus," HEH TU File Drawer 14A, Folder: Syllabus of Considerations; reading notes, TU File Drawer 14A, Folder: Draft on League of Nations, 1918; versions of final paper, "International Political Parties," ibid. File Drawer 14B, Folder: International Political Parties in a Durable League of Nations," original, LC, Wilson Papers, File II,

Box 157. This copy, interlined and with marginal notes indicating it was carefully read, published in William Diamond (ed.), "Turner's American Sectionalism and World Organization," *American Historical Review*, XLVII (April 1942), 545-51.

39. C. H. Haskins to Turner, Dec. 13, 1918, HEH TU Box 28. Mae Turner to Guy Stanton Ford, April 5, 1942, HEH TU Box 52, and Turner to Mrs. Hooper, May 6, 1920, HEH TU-H Box 5, describe efforts to put the paper in Wilson's hands.

40. Turner to Mrs. Hooper, Oct. 9, Nov. 23, 1919, HEH TU-H Box 4.

41. Turner to Mrs. Hooper, Nov. 5, 1918; Turner to Dorothy Turner Main, Oct. 30, 1920, HEH TU-H, Box 4, TU Box I.

42. Turner to Mrs. Hooper, Jan. 16, 1920, HEH TU-H Box 5.

43. Turner, "Notes for an Address on Washington's Birthday, February 22, 1923," HEH TU File Drawer 15A, Folder: Notes for an Address on Washington's Birthday. He spoke before the Massachusetts Society of the Sons of the American Revolution.

44. Turner to Mrs. Hooper, Feb. 10, 1922, HEH TU-H, Box 5.

45. Archer B. Hulbert to Turner, Jan. 5, 1915, HC on WH Corr., Box 3, Folder: Hulbert, Archer B.

46. Solon J. Buck to Turner, Feb. 26, 1920, HEH TU Box 63.

47. National Board for Historical Service, "Peace and Reconstruction: Preliminary Bibliography," *The Historical Outlook*, X (March 1919), 156.

48. Edward N. Bristol, Holt & Co., to Turner, April 23, 1919, HEH TU Box 63.

49. Turner to Guy Stanton Ford, Nov. 27, 1920, SHSW, Turner Papers, Box II.

50. Turner to E. N. Bristol, April 24, 1919, Princeton, Holt Arch.

51. Letters concerning permission to reprint, HEH TU Box 63. Turner described his efforts in Turner to Lincoln MacVeagh, Feb. 26, March 9, 1920, Princeton: Holt Arch.

52. Two copies of the contract were sent on June 10 and returned same day (Holt & Co. to Turner, June 10, 19, 1920). One copy is in HEH TU Box 63.

53. Turner to Holt & Co., May 19, June 13, 23, 24, 1920, ibid; Holt & Co. to Turner, June 9, 23, 24, July 16, Aug. 14, 30, Oct. 6, 1920, HEH TU Box 63.

54. Turner to Edgar E. Robinson, Dec. 4, 1920, HEH TU Box 30.

55. Lincoln MacVeagh to Turner, Oct. 9, 14, 1920, HEH TU Box 63. Turner's list, TU Box 56.

56. Herbert E. Bolton to Turner, Oct. 23, 1920; Max Farrand to Turner, Nov. 8, 1920; C. H. Van Tyne to Turner, Nov. 14, 1920; U. B. Phillips to Turner, Dec. 16, 1920; Thomas M. Marshall to Turner, Dec. 21, 1920; William E. Dodd to Turner, Feb. 15, 1921; Harold J. Laski to Turner, Jan. 27, 1921, HEH TU Boxes 30 and 31.

57. *Milwaukee Sentinel*, Jan. 30, 1921; *Minneapolis Journal*, March 12, 17, 1921; *Boston Herald*, Nov. 15, 1920. HEH TU File Drawer 15D, Folder: Frontier in American History. Reviews.

58. *Boston Transcript*, Nov. 19, 1920; Turner to Edgar E. Robinson, Dec. 4, 1920.

59. Turner to Mrs. Hooper, Jan. 20, 1921, HEH TU-H, Box 5.

60. Charles A. Beard, "The Frontier in American History," *New Republic*, XXV (Feb. 16, 1921), 349-50.

61. Turner to Mrs. Hooper, Feb. 13, 1921, HEH TU-H, Box 5.

62. Turner to Dorothy Turner Main, Feb. 18, 1921, HEH TU Box I. No copy of Turner's letter seems to have survived, but its contents can be surmised from Beard's reply.

63. Charles A. Beard to Turner, May 14, 1921, HEH TU Box 31.

64. Beard to Merle Curti, Aug. 9, 1928, HEH TU Box 39.

65. Royalty statements, 1921-30, HEH TU Box 56.

66. Canceled note, HEH TU Box 63.

Chapter XV
Harvard Years: The World of Scholarship
1917-1924

1. P. J. Hartog, Univ. of London, to Turner, Dec. 19, 1919, Feb. 2, 1920; Charles A. Beard to Turner, March 13, 1919; James Harvey Robinson to Turner, March 15, May 7, 1919, HEH TU Boxes 29 and 30.

2. HEH TU File Drawer 14A, Folder: Address Agricultural History, 1922; printed in Wilbur R. Jacobs (ed.) "Research in Agricultural History; Frederick Jackson Turner's View in 1922," *Agricultural History*, XLII (Jan. 1968), 15-22.

3. Turner to Mrs. William Hooper, Dec. 19, 1922, HEH TU-H Box 5.

4. A portion of this manuscript comparing conditions in Virginia and Massachusetts, not included in the published version, is in HEH TU File Drawer 3A. The essay, "The First Official Frontier of the Massachusetts Bay," was published in the *Publications of the Colonial Society of Massachusetts*, XVII (Boston, 1915), 250-71.

5. Root to Turner, June 14, 1914; Andrews to Turner, June 15, 1914, HEH TU Box 21. Morison followed one of Turner's suggestions, presenting his findings to the Colonial Society a year later. Henry H. Edes to Turner, Feb. 2, 1915, HEH TU Box 23.

6. Manuscript notes, HEH TU File Drawer 14A, Folder: Turner, What is Colonial History.

7. Turner's influence in fathering the "frontier school" of colonial history is discussed in Wilbur R. Jacobs, "Colonial Origins of the United States: The Turnerian View," *Pacific Historical Review*, XL (Feb. 1971), 21-38.

8. Notes and MS for University of Chicago lecture, HEH TU File Drawer 15A, Folder: Lecture University of Chicago, 1916; for Clark University address, ibid. File Drawer 15E, Folders: Address Clark University, Notes, and Since the Foundation, 1924. The Clark address was printed in *Clark University Library Publications*, VII (Feb. 1924), 9-29.

9. The editor of *The Historical Outlook* sought permission to republish the paper (Albert E. McKinley to Turner, June 30, 1924, HEH TU Box 33). It was printed in *The Historical Outlook*, XV (Nov. 1924), 335-42, under the title, "Since the Foundation of Clark University, 1889-1924."

10. Turner to Max Farrand, May 15, 1907, HEH TU Box 9.

11. For clippings and pasted items on sectionalism see HEH TU File Drawers 16, 17, and 18, esp. File Drawers 14B and 14C.

12. Turner to Logan Esarey, Nov. 24, 1917; Turner to J. Franklin Jameson, Nov. 24, 1917; Turner to George Hempl, Nov. 24, 1917, HC on WH Corr., Box VIII, Folders B, EF, and HIJ.

13. An excellent set of maps prepared at this time is in HEH TU File Drawer 17C, Folder: Sections 1908.

14. No manuscript of this paper has been preserved, but an abstract was published in the *Bulletin of the American Geographical Society*, XLVI (Aug. 1914), 591-95.

15. Isaiah Bowman to Turner, April 7, 1914, HEH TU Box 21.

16. Four manuscript drafts, holograph and partially typed, in HEH TU File Drawer 14A, Folder: Significance of Sections, 1914. A fifth, much rewritten, is in HEH File Drawer 14C, Folder: Sections. AHA Chicago Meeting, 1914.

17. Turner to Isaiah Bowman, May 26, 1914, HEH TU Box 21. Turner to J. F. Jameson, Jan. 27, April 15, 30, May 2, 5, 1915; Jameson to Turner, Feb. 2, April 14, 17, 28, May 3, 1915, Feb. 15, 1918. LC, AHA Papers, Box 283, Folder T.

18. Turner to Mae Turner, Oct. 25, 28, 1916 (HEH TU Box I), describe his disappointment at his reception at Western Reserve University. Two drafts of Minnesota Historical Society paper, HEH TU File Drawer 15E, Folder: Significance of the Middle West.

19. Sheet of paper, inserted, ibid.

20. A. Lawrence Lowell to Turner, June 26, 1917, contains the invitation to deliver the lectures (HEH TU Box 27). Turner's remark about the energy required to produce the lectures, Turner to J. F. Jameson, Feb. 20, 1918, HC on WH Corr., Box VIII, Folder HIJ. The *Boston Transcript*, March 23, 1918, contained the favorable remark about them.

21. "The First Lowell Lecture," MS, HEH TU File Drawer E1, Folder: Lowell Lectures, 1918.

22. Holt & Co. to Turner, Sept. 8, 1917; Turner to Holt & Co., Sept. 13, 1917, Princeton, Holt Arch. Contract, HEH TU Box 63.

23. E. N. Bristol to Turner, April 9, 1918, HEH TU Box 63.

24. Turner to Bristol, May 8, 1918, Princeton, Holt Arch.

25. Turner to Mrs. William Hooper, Oct. 9, 1918; Turner to Moses S. Slaughter, Oct. 12, 1918, HEH TU-H, Box 4 and TU Box 28.

26. A description of the Moorings, with a record of the purchase and upkeep, is in a scrapbook in which Turner pasted bills, letters, and receipts (HEH TU Vol. XXI).

27. Turner to Mrs. Hooper, June 19, 1918, HEH TU-H, Box 4.

28. HEH TU File Drawer 11B, Folder: North Atlantic, 1830-1850. Shifting of Population.

29. Turner to Mrs. Hooper, Oct. 9, 1919, HEH TU-H, Box 4.

30. Ibid. Oct. 12, 1920, HEH TU-H, Box 5.

31. Turner to Lincoln MacVeagh, April 5, 1921, Princeton, Holt Arch.

32. Notice of leave of absence, HEH TU Box 56. Turner wrote his wife, "the requirement is *merely* (!) to write a book" (Turner to Mae Turner, April 25, 1920, HEH TU Box I).

33. Turner memorandum, HEH TU File Drawer 10A, Folder: U.S. 1830-1850. New England Politics; letters from Holt & Co. (Lincoln MacVeagh)

to Turner, Feb. 3, March 26, April 4, 8, 1921, HEH TU Box 63.

34. Turner to Holt & Co., May 30, Oct. 10, 1921. Princeton, Holt Arch. Holt & Co. to Turner, May 31, Oct. 4, 1921, July 25, Oct. 31, 1922, HEH TU Box 63.

35. Turner to Merle Curti, Oct. 12, 1921, HEH TU Box 31.

36. Turner to Claude H. Van Tyne, Nov. 1, 1924, Clements, Van Tyne Papers.

37. Turner's notes and drafts, HEH TU File Drawer 12A, Folder: Sectionalism. Harding Administration; 14A, Folder: Draft Recent American Sectionalism; 14B, Folder: Recent American Sectionalism, and 15A, Folder: Talk at Thursday Club.

38. Talk on "Recent American Sectionalism," MS, HEH TU File Drawer 14A, Folder: Draft Recent American Sectionalism.

39. Draft of lecture at Chicago and Michigan, HEH TU File Drawer 14A, Unmarked Folder; drafts of commencement address at Univ. of New Hampshire, HEH TU 14C, Unmarked Folder.

40. Turner to Wilbur L. Cross, July 5, 29, 1922, Yale Review Papers, Beinecke Library, Yale Univ., Folder: F. J. Turner (hereafter cited as Beinecke, Yale Review Papers); Cross to Turner, July 9, 29, 1922, HEH TU Box 31. Sections of MS, much rewritten, HEH TU File Drawer 14A, Folder: Essay on Sectionalism 1920s.

41. Wilbur L. Cross to Turner, Sept. 1, 1922, HEH TU Box 31.

42. Turner, "Sections and Nation," *Yale Review*, XII (Oct. 1922), 1-21.

43. Clippings, HEH TU File Drawer 14B, Folder: Sections and Nation.

44. Turner to Dorothy Turner Main, Oct. 12, 1922, HEH TU Box I.

45. Walter Lippmann to Turner, Feb. 16, 1923; Irvine L. Lenroot to Turner, Dec. 23, 1923; Josef Redlich to Wilbur L. Cross, Nov. 10, 1922, HEH TU Box 31.

46. Turner to Mae Turner, May 20, 1922, HEH TU Box J.

47. Turner to Mae Turner, [May or June 1922], HEH TU Box J. Someone, probably Mrs. Turner, destroyed the last portion of this letter.

48. Copies of "Introduction," HEH TU File Drawer A1, Folder: The United States and Its Sections, and File Drawer A1, Folder: Introduction.

49. For summer's activities, see HEH TU Vol. XXI, The Moorings; Turner to Mrs. Hooper, Aug. 12, 1922, HEH TU-H Box 5.

50. Turner to Lincoln MacVeagh, Aug. 12, 1922, HEH TU Box 63.

51. MacVeagh to Turner, July 25, Aug. 8, 1922; Turner to MacVeagh, July 11, 29, 1922, HEH TU Box 63.

52. Turner to Mrs. Hooper, Dec. 19, 1922, HEH TU-H Box 5.

53. Receipts for insured mail show that Turner sent manuscript on May 3, 5, and 8, August 13, 23, and 30, September 7, 8, 10, 15, and 29, and October 16 and 23, 1923. His illness in June and July accounted for the lack of production at that time (HEH TU Box 63). Holt's reaction to the manuscript is in Lincoln MacVeagh to Turner, May 8, July 12, 18, Aug. 16, 31, Sept. 7, 8, 17, 23, 25, Oct. 18, 26, 1923. Quotation, MacVeagh to Turner, May 4, 1923, HEH TU Box 63.

54. Turner to John M. Gaus, May 9, 1923, HEH TU Box 32.

55. Turner to J. Franklin Jameson, June 26, 1923, LC, Jameson Papers.

56. Turner to Mrs. Hooper, Dec. 8, 1923, HEH TU-H, Box 5.

57. Typical notes, HEH TU File Drawer A1, Folder: US 1830-1850, Folder: Introduction. *See also* Holt & Co. to Turner, Jan. 21, 30, 1924, HEH TU Box 63.

58. Guy Stanton Ford, "Reminiscences of Guy Stanton Ford," Oral History Research Office, Columbia Univ., p. 364.

59. Max Farrand to Mae Turner, [1932], HEH TU Box 49.

60. Turner to Carl Becker, March 10, 1916, HEH TU Box 26; Turner to James W. Thompson, Dec. 29, 1913, University of Chicago Archives, Department of History Papers, Box VIII, Folder 1 (hereafter cited as U. of Chi. Arch., Dept. of Hist. Papers).

61. Turner delivered the memorial address for Reuben Gold Thwaites, who died October 22, 1913. It was printed as *Reuben Gold Thwaites: A Memorial Address* (Madison, 1914). Five days after Thwaites died, Turner was offered the position by President Charles R. Van Hise (C. R. Van Hise to Turner, Oct. 29, Nov. 4, 1913, HEH TU Box 20A). Turner described his reaction in letters to Mae Turner, Nov. 13, 18, 22, 1913, HEH TU Box H.

62. James W. Thompson to Turner, Dec. 18, 1913; Turner to Thompson, Dec. 29, 1913, HEH TU Box 20A; Turner to Andrew C. McLaughlin, Jan. 15, 1914; McLaughlin to Turner, Feb. 10, June 1, Sept. 1, 1914. U. of Chi. Arch., Dept. of Hist. Papers, Box VIII, Folder 1.

63. Turner's copy of Carnegie Foundation for the Advancement of Teaching, *Act of Incorporation, By-laws for the Admission of Institutions and for the Granting of Retirement Allowances* (New York, 1920), 1-25, contains information used in this paragraph (HEH TU Vol. XIX). Additional information is in Turner to Dorothy Turner Main, Jan. 26, 1923 (HEH TU Box J), and Turner's income tax returns for 1924 and 1925 (HEH TU Box 56). His income in 1924 was $8,997.44, on which he paid a tax of $116.88.

64. Turner to Edgar E. Robinson, Nov. 22, 1923, HEH TU Box 32.

65. Harvard Univ. to Turner, May 11, 1923; Turner to A. Lawrence Lowell, April 27, 1923, HEH TU Vol. XIX.

66. Arthur M. Schlesinger, "Reminiscences of Arthur M. Schlesinger," Oral History Research Office, Columbia Univ., pp. 83, 85-86.

67. Turner to Arthur H. Buffinton, Nov. 6, 1923, HEH TU Box 32.

68. Students in Turner's last classes, with the grades assigned them, are listed in Turner and Merk, *List of References on the History of the West* (Cambridge, Mass., 1922), HEH TU Vol. XX (2).

69. "Opening Remarks for First Lecture, History of the US 1880-1920," HEH TU Box 56.

70. Turner to Mrs. Hooper, May 1, 1924, HEH TU-H Box 5. Turner's notes, HEH TU Box 56.

71. Turner to Mrs. Hooper, May 1, 1924 (HEH TU-H Box 5) describes Turner's pleasure at sitting for his portrait. Frederick Merk to "Dear Sir," June 16, 1924, soliciting funds to pay for the drawing, Houghton, Turner Papers.

72. Seating chart for banquet, HEH TU Box 33. He described the evening in letters to Mrs. Hooper, May 1, 1924, and Dorothy Turner Main, April 30, 1924 (HEH TU-H Box 5 and TU Vol. XXII).

73. The speeches were not recorded, but Allyn A. Young later recalled his remarks for Carl Becker (Young to Becker, Oct. 9, 1925, HEH TU Box

34A). The banquet was described in the *Boston Herald,* May 25, 1924, and the *Christian Science Monitor,* May 26, 1924.

74. Turner to Mrs. Hooper, May 1, 1924, HEH TU-H Box 5.

75. *Harvard Crimson,* May 24, 1924. Most of the letters and telegrams were bound into a "Blue Book," comparable to the "Red Book" compiled when Turner left Madison (HEH TU Vol. II Blue Book). Letters from Dodd and Van Tyne, May 24 and June 3, 1924, HEH TU Box 33.

76. Turner to Dorothy Turner Main, May 28, 1924, HEH TU Vol. XXII.

Chapter XVI
The Twilight Years
1924-1932

1. Details of the house planning and financing, Turner to Dorothy Turner Main, April 6, 9, 30, 1924; Dorothy Turner Main to Turner, April 6, 21, 1924; Turner to John Main, April 22, 1924, HEH TU Vol. XXII.

2. Turner's teaching at Logan in 1924 and 1925 is described in Ray A. Billington, "Frederick Jackson Turner and Logan's 'National Summer School,'" *Utah Historical Quarterly,* XXXVII (Summer 1969), 307-36.

3. Elmer G. Peterson to Turner, Oct. 8, Nov. 2, 1923; Turner to Peterson, Nov. 6, 1923, HEH TU Box 32. Turner's calculations were made on the back of one of President Peterson's letters.

4. Agricultural College of Utah, *Bulletin. Summer Catalogue, 1924* (Logan, March 1924), 7.

5. Turner to Mae Turner, June 17, 1924, HEH TU Box J.

6. Ibid. June 29, 1924.

7. *Student Life,* June 23, 1924.

8. Turner to Mae Turner, [July 1924], HEH TU Box J.

9. Elmer G. Peterson to Turner, June 20, Aug. 2, Sept. 20, 1924; Turner to Peterson, Oct. 2, 6, 1924, HEH TU Box 33.

10. Memoranda, "Financing 2214 Van Hise Ave." and "Income Budget, Oct. 1924–Oct. 1925," HEH TU Vol. XXII. Turner discussed finances in Turner to Mae Turner, July 4, 1924, HEH TU Box J.

11. Turner to John Main, Oct. 25, 1924, HEH TU Box J; Turner to Mrs. William Hooper, Oct. 30, 1924. HEH TU-H Box 5.

12. Turner to Mae Turner, Nov. 15, 1924, HEH TU Box J.

13. Turner to Frederick Merk, Dec. 7, 1924, Houghton, Turner Papers.

14. Mae Turner to Mrs. Hooper, March 29, 1925, HEH TU-H Box 6; Turner to Samuel E. Morison, July 30, 1926, HEH TU Box 35A.

15. Turner to Mrs. Hooper, Dec. 23, 1925, HEH TU-H Box 6. Pictures and cut-out animals prepared by Turner to amuse his grandchildren, HEH TU Box 62.

16. Mae Turner to Mrs. Hooper, March 29, 1925, HEH TU Box 6.

17. Turner to Joseph Schafer, March 26, April 5, 1924, HEH TU Box 33.

18. "The Significance of the Section in American History," *Wisconsin Magazine of History,* VIII (March 1925), 255-80.

19. Frank W. Taussig to Turner, April 16, 1925, HEH TU Box 34.

20. Turner to Arthur M. Schlesinger, May 5, 1925, ibid.

21. Several drafts of the lectures given in this series are in HEH TU File Drawers 14C and 15B, Folder: University of Wisconsin Lectures, 1925, and Lecture on Sectionalism.

22. A. C. Krey, "My Reminiscences of Frederick Jackson Turner," *Arizona and the West*, III (Winter 1961), 381.

23. Turner to Mae Turner, March 20, 21, 1925, HEH TU Box J.

24. Rough draft and typed final version, HEH TU File Drawer 14D, Folder: MSS Geographic Sectionalism in American History; published, *Annals of the Association of American Geographers* XVI (June 1926), 85-93. Turner expressed his ambition in Turner to Homer C. Hockett, Jan. 21, 1926, HEH TU Box 35.

25. Merle Curti to Turner, Oct. 6, 1926; Norman Foerester to Turner, Aug. 4, 1926; Arthur M. Schlesinger to Turner, Sept. 8, 1926, HEH TU Box 35A.

26. Hundreds of notes taken by Turner are in HEH TU File Drawer 14D, Folder: World's Work Article.

27. Two drafts, with many corrections, HEH TU File Drawer 15E, Folder: Draft and Final MSS, 1876-1926 Essay.

28. Henry Cabot Lodge, "The Distribution of Ability in the United States," *Century Magazine*, XLII (Sept. 1891), 687-94.

29. Notes taken by Turner fill HEH TU 3×5 File Drawer 8. Two drafts, HEH TU File Drawer 15C, Folder: Turner's Children of the Pioneers, and Folder: Revised Children of the Pioneers.

30. Turner to Prof. Reed, Nov. 11, 1925, Beinecke, Yale Review Papers.

31. Turner to Mrs. Hooper, March 7, 1925, HEH TU-H Box 6.

32. Ibid. April 11, May 16, 1925.

33. President and Fellows of Harvard University to Turner, Feb. 24, 1925, HEH TU File Drawer A1, Folder: Milton Fund. The fund had been established a short time before by William F. Milton with an endowment that provided $50,000 a year for research (*Boston Evening Transcript*, March 5, 1925).

34. Turner, memorandum to Holt & Co., May 28, 1925, HEH TU Box 63.

35. Turner to Mrs. Hooper, Aug. 1, 1926, HEH TU-H Box 6. That summer's events described in "The Moorings," HEH TU Vol. XXI, and Turner to Mrs. Hooper, May 28, July 7, Aug. 1, 29, Sept. 28, 1926, HEH TU-H Box 6.

36. Turner to Dorothy Turner Main, Jan. 23, 27, Feb. 6, 24, March 2, 1927, HEH TU Box K.

37. For the transition of the Huntington Library to a research library, see Ray A. Billington, "The Genesis of the Research Institution," *Huntington Library Quarterly*, XXXII (Aug. 1969), 351-72.

38. Max Farrand to George Ellery Hale, March 7, 1927, HEH TU Box 36. Correspondence between Hale and Farrand, George Ellery Hale Papers, California Institute of Technology, Box 22.

39. Turner to Joseph Schafer, April 24, 1927, SHSW, Schafer Papers. Turner's notes and impressions, HEH TU File Drawer 15A, Folder: Memo by Turner on Research Materials.

40. Turner, "Memoranda" to Farrand, ibid. Many have been published in Wilbur R. Jacobs (ed.), "Frederick Jackson Turner's Notes on the West-

ward Movement, California, and the Far West," *Southern California Quarterly*, XLVI (June 1964), 161-68.

41. Turner to Mrs. Hooper, Easter, April 20, 1927, HEH TU-H Box 7.

42. Turner to Max Farrand, March 8, 19, 1927; Farrand to Turner, March 11, 24, 27, 1927, HEH TU Box 36.

43. Robert O. Schad, "An Impression of FJT at the Huntington Library," HEH TU Box 57, and Mary Esther Jackson, "Reminiscences of Turner at the Huntington Library," Huntington Library Trustees' Files. Lists of books given the library by Turner, HEH TU Boxes 39 and 57.

44. Turner to Dorothy Turner Main, Oct. 3, 28, 1928, HEH TU Box K.

45. Income tax returns, 1927, 1928, and 1930, and list of holdings, March 25, 1929, HEH TU Box 61. He discussed financial affairs in letters to John Main, Jan. 12, March 6, 1929, HEH TU Box K.

46. One folder in HEH TU Box 37 is filled with lecture invitations.

47. For lecture at the University of California at Los Angeles, see HEH TU File Drawer 15A, Folder: Turner's talk at UCLA; for the talk to the Harvard Club, Box 57; for remarks to Pacific Coast Branch, File Drawer 15A, Folder: Talk to Pacific Coast Branch; for lecture, Pasadena Lecture Series, File Drawer 14B, Folder: Sectionalism in American Politics.

48. Mimeographed syllabus, HEH TU Box 57; Turner's lecture notes, HEH TU File Drawer 14B, Folder: Cal Tech Lectures; class lists, HEH TU Box 57.

49. Turner to Mrs. Hooper, Jan. 21, 1929, HEH TU-H Box 7.

50. Turner to Frederick Merk, Jan. 15, 1927, Houghton, Turner Papers. Letters written in behalf of former students fill much of HEH TU Boxes 38 and 39.

51. Turner to Joseph Schafer, [Sept. 1931], HEH TU Box 46.

52. Letters to and from Becker and Curti, HEH TU Boxes 34A, 35, 39, and 40. All reproduced in Ray A. Billington, *The Genesis of the Frontier Thesis: A Study in Historical Creativity* (San Marino, 1971), 221-85.

53. Turner to Dorothy Turner Main, April 25, 1927, HEH TU Box K; Turner to Carl Becker, May 14, 1927, Cornell, Becker Papers.

54. Turner to Merle Curti, Jan. 5, 1931; Turner to Max Farrand, Jan. 5, 1931, HEH TU Box 45.

55. Turner to Max Farrand, March 8, 1927, HEH TU Box 36.

56. HEH TU File Drawer 15B, Folder: Schedule of Writing Deadlines.

57. Turner to President and Fellows of Harvard University, Nov. 22, 1927, HEH TU File Drawer A1, Folder: Milton Fund.

58. Turner to Holt & Co., Nov. 21, 1927, Jan. 9, 1928, Princeton, Holt Arch.; Charles A. Madison, Holt & Co., to Turner, Oct. 24, Nov. 21, 1927, Feb. 3, 1928, HEH TU Box 63.

59. Merrill H. Crissey, "Memorandum on Professor Turner's Writing of His Book," HEH TU Box 49.

60. Turner to Mrs. Hooper, Dec. 27, 1928, HEH TU-H Box 6.

61. Turner to Dorothy Turner Main, March 6, 1926, HEH TU Box K.

62. Ibid. April 25, May 7, 14, 28, 1929, HEH TU Box K.

63. Turner to Merle Curti, Aug. 16, 1929, HEH TU Box 42.

64. Crissey, "Memorandum on Professor Turner's Writing of His Book," HEH TU Box 49.

65. Turner to Joseph Schafer, Feb. 18, 1930, HEH TU Box 43.
66. Turner to Max Farrand, Feb. 4, April 21, 1930; Farrand to Turner, April 18, 1930, HEH TU Box 44.
67. HEH TU File Drawer A1, Folder: Suggestions by Turner for Dedication and Preface, and File Drawer D4, Folder: Turner's Plan for Another to Complete His Book.
68. Income tax forms, 1930, 1931, HEH TU Box 61.
69. Proposed changes for Chapter II, HEH TU File Drawer A1, Folder: Ch. II US 1830-50; for Chapter IV, File Drawer A2, Folder: The Middle States; for Chapter VII, File Drawer A3, Folder: VII North Central States. Memorandum on map revision, HEH TU File Drawer A5, Folder: U.S. 1830-50.
70. Folder "Wilmot Proviso Notes," containing copies of documents that puzzled him, on his desk at the time he died (HEH TU File Drawer D4, Folder: Wilmot Proviso Notes). Last dictated memorandum (Drawer D4 also), labeled: Turner's Last Dictation and Comments by Crissey.
71. Turner to Marion C. Sheldon, March 14, 1932, HEH TU Box 47.
72. Max Farrand to Arthur M. Schlesinger, March 18, 1932, HEH TU Box 47.
73. Max Farrand to John Main, March 19, 1932; *Pasadena Star-News*, March 19, 1932; Avery Craven, "Appreciation of FJT," HEH TU Box 57.
74. Letters of condolence, HEH TU Vol. V; newspaper clippings, HEH TU Box 57; extracts from resolutions, HEH TU Box 60.
75. Memoranda, HEH TU File Drawer L2, Folder: Possible Volume of Essays on Sectionalism, File Drawer 14A, Folder: Possible Volume of Essays.
76. Correspondence, Max Farrand and Holt & Co., concerning publication, HEH TU File Drawer 14C, Folder: Farrand-Holt Correspondence, File Drawer L2, Folder: Correspondence with Henry Holt & Co.
77. Richard H. Thornton to Mrs. Turner, May 18, 1933, HEH TU Box 50A.
78. The labors performed by Crissey and Craven can be realized by comparing the original manuscripts with the published version. See esp. carbons of Chapter IV, HEH TU File Drawer A2, Folder: IV The Middle States.

Chapter XVII
Frederick Jackson Turner: Portrait of the Man

1. W. Paul Resop to Mrs. Turner, July 7, 1940; Paul Knaplund to Howard K. Beale, Merle Curti, and Fulmer Mood, March 8, 1949, HEH TU Box 52.
2. Curtis Nettels to Mrs. Turner, Feb. 8, 1941, ibid.
3. H. W. Johnson to Turner, May 29, 1918, HEH TU Box 28. Mrs. Turner wrote on this letter: "We think this rather nice in that it shows the friendly spirit on both sides."
4. M. L. Gochenour to Turner, June 12, 1912; Turner to Gochenour, July 7, 1912, HEH TU Box 18.
5. Albert Matthews to Turner, Dec. 14, 1915, HEH TU Box 23.
6. Mae Turner to Max Farrand, May 17, 1932, HEH TU Box 48.
7. Turner to Mae Sherwood, Dec. 12, 1886, HEH TU Box A.

8. Turner to Woodrow Wilson, Feb. 5, 1890. LC, Wilson Papers, Box 3.

9. Turner to Jackson Turner Main, Jan. 14, 1932, HEH TU Box K.

10. Turner to Betsy Main, May 16, 1922, Feb. 14, 1923, HEH TU Box J ("Betsy" was the nickname of Elizabeth W. Main).

11. Turner to Merle Curti, June 30, 1927, HEH TU Box 36.

12. Copies pasted by Turner in his copy of *List of References on the History of the West* (Cambridge, Mass., 1922), obviously to be read to the class, HEH TU Vol. III (3).

13. Merrill H. Crissey, "Reminiscences of Frederick J. Turner," HEH TU Box 57, Folder: Biographical and Autobiographical Data. Turner's style is explored by students of literature in Harold P. Simonson, "Frederick Jackson Turner: Frontier History as Art," *Antioch Review*, XXIV (Summer 1964), 201-11, and Merrill E. Lewis, "The Art of Frederick Jackson Turner: the Histories," *Huntington Library Quarterly*, XXXV (May 1972), 241-55.

14. Card, HEH TU Box 47.

15. Commonplace Book for 1886, HEH TU Vol. III (3).

16. Cards, probably written in 1904 during picnic with the Moses S. Slaughters, HEH TU Box 55.

17. Turner to Mae Turner, May 5, 1907, HEH TU Box G.

18. Max Farrand, who was with the Turners, described the scene in a memorandum, May 5, 1932. Memorandum and several versions of the poem, HEH TU Box 55.

19. Menu in pocket diary for 1911-1912, HEH TU Box 62.

20. Turner to Edgar E. Robinson, Oct. 29, 1912, HEH TU Box 18.

21. Household Account Book, 1921-22, HEH TU Vol. XII.

22. Inventory of books at 7 Phillips Place, SHSW, Turner Papers; another of books at Hancock Point, "The Moorings," HEH TU Vol. XXI.

23. Turner, "Miscellaneous Personal Accounts," HEH TU Box H; "Personal and Household Accounts," HEH TU Box G; "Household Account Book," HEH TU Vol. XII.

24. Turner to Mae Turner, August 7, 1913, July 20, 1917, HEH TU Boxes H and I; entries in pocket diary for July 10 and 13, 1911, HEH TU Box 62.

25. Turner to Edward T. Hartman, Jan. 11, 1926, SHSW, Turner Papers.

26. Turner to Mrs. William Hooper, June 19, 1916, HEH TU-H Box 4.

27. Turner to Mae Sherwood, Aug. 8, 1886, HEH TU Box A.

28. Turner to Dorothy Turner Main, April 15, 1916, HEH TU Box I.

29. Turner to Mrs. Hooper, July 13, 1919, HEH TU-H Box 4.

30. Ibid. July 16, 1913, HEH TU-H Box 2.

31. Turner to Dorothy Turner, Sept. 20, 1912, HEH TU Box H.

32. Turner to Mae Turner, March 25, 1915, HEH TU Box I.

33. Turner to Edgar E. Robinson, Oct. 29, 1912, HEH TU Box 18.

34. Turner to Dorothy Turner, Sept. 30, 1912, HEH TU Box H.

35. Bernard Fay, "An Invitation to American Historians," *Harper's Magazine*, CLXVI (Dec. 1932), 30.

36. Turner to Edmond S. Meany, Jan. 11, 1919, HEH TU Box 29.

37. W. E. Green to Turner, Jan. 27, 1902; Turner to Green, Jan. 28, 1902; Turner to R. S. Whitelaw. U. of Wis. Arch., L. and S., Hist., Turner Corr., Box 1, Folder G; Box 3, Folder W.

38. Turner to Ellen Breese Turner, June 30, 1887, HEH TU Box B.
39. Turner to Mae Sherwood, April 19, 1888, HEH TU Box C.
40. Turner to Lois C. M. Rosenberry, April 28, 1930, HEH TU Box 44.
41. Turner to Mae Turner, May 23, 1922, HEH TU Box J.
42. Turner's activities in 1884 were reported in *Wisconsin State Journal,* Aug. 26, 29, Sept. 3, 1884; his vote in 1888, Turner to Mae Sherwood, May 9, 1888, HEH TU Box C. He later recalled that he had voted for McKinley in 1896, but his name is not among those of faculty members supporting the Republican candidate (*Wisconsin State Journal,* Oct. 17, 1896).
43. Turner expressed these views in "Dominant Forces in Western Life," "The Middle West," and "Pioneer Ideals and the State University," published in 1897, 1901, and 1910 [reprinted in Turner, *The Frontier in American History* (New York, 1920), 240, 155, and 281].
44. Turner to Max Farrand, Nov. 24, 1907, HEH TU Box 9A.
45. Turner to Charles S. Slichter, March 16, 1907, U. of Wis. Arch., Misc. File: F. J. Turner.
46. Turner to William E. Dodd, Oct. 9, 1908, HEH TU Box 11.
47. Turner to Mrs. Hooper, June 2, 1912, HEH TU-H Box 1.
48. Ibid. Aug. 8, 1912.
49. Turner to Dorothy Turner, Oct. 11, 1912, HEH TU Box H.
50. Turner to Mae Turner, Oct. 18, 1912, ibid.
51. Ibid. Oct. 22, 1912.
52. Turner to Dorothy Turner Main, Oct. 30, 1920, ibid., HEH TU Box I.
53. Turner to Mrs. Hooper, March 16, Nov. 16, 1924, HEH TU-H Box 5.
54. Ibid. Dec. 14, 1926, HEH TU-H Box 6.
55. Richard S. Emmet (secretary to Herbert Hoover) to Turner, Jan. 15, 27, 1923, HEH TU Box 32.
56. Turner to Herbert Hoover, [Jan. 1923]; a copy of this letter, now in the Herbert Hoover Presidential Library, West Branch, Iowa, has been furnished the Huntington Library by Thomas T. Thalken, director.
57. Turner to Charles S. Slichter, Feb. 14, 1923. U. of Wis. Arch., Misc. File: F. J. Turner; Turner to Mrs. Hooper, May 27, 1928, HEH TU-H Box 6; Turner to Dorothy Turner Main, Nov. 16, 1928, HEH TU Box K.

Chapter XVIII
The Persistence of a Theory: The Frontier
And Sectional Hypotheses

1. Turner to Laurence M. Larson, June 24, 1910, HEH TU Box 15.
2. Irene T. Blythe, "The Textbooks and the New Discoveries. Emphasis and Viewpoints in American History," *The Historical Outlook,* XXIII (Dec. 1932), 398-99; Henry M. Littlefield, "Textbooks, Determinism and Turner: The Westward Movement in Secondary School History and Geography Textbooks, 1830-1960," Ph.D. thesis (unpubl.), Columbia Univ., 1967.
3. Howard W. Caldwell, "How to Teach the History of the West in American History," *The History Teacher's Magazine,* VII (April 1916), 125.

4. Charles H. Haskins, "European History and American Scholarship," *American Historical Review*, XXVIII (Jan. 1923), 215. Thompson's views are expressed in his "Profitable Fields for Investigation in Medieval History," *American Historical Review*, XVIII (April 1913), 490-504, and in his popular textbook, *An Economic and Social History of the Middle Ages, 300-1300* (New York, 1928), 518.

5. Franklin H. Giddings to Merle Curti, Aug. 20, 1928, HEH TU Box 39.

6. Norman Foerster, "American Literature," *Saturday Review of Literature*, II (April 3, 1926), 677-79. For relationship of these books to Turner thesis, see Ray A. Billington, *America's Frontier Heritage* (New York, 1966), 14.

7. Newton D. Baker to Turner, Oct. 8, 1926; Charles Merz to Turner, May 25, 1925; Arthur Capper to Turner, Aug. 4, 1926; Felix Frankfurter to Turner, Dec. 17, 1925, HEH TU Boxes 34, 35, 35A.

8. *Madison Capital Times*, Jan. 15, 1931.

9. *New York Times*, Sept. 24, 1932. For Turner's impact on Roosevelt and the New Deal, see Curtis Nettels, "Frederick Jackson Turner and the New Deal," *Wisconsin Magazine of History*, XVII (March 1934), 257-65, and Steven Kesselman, "The Frontier Thesis and the Great Depression," *Journal of the History of Ideas*, XXIX (April-June 1968), 253-68.

10. James T. Adams, "Rugged Individualism Analyzed," *New York Times Magazine*, March 8, 1934, 1-2, 11.

11. For impact of Turner's thesis on foreign policy, see William A. Williams, "The Frontier Thesis and American Foreign Policy," *Pacific Historical Review*, XXIV (Nov. 1955), 379-95, and Lawrence S. Kaplan, "Frederick Jackson Turner and Imperialism," *Social Science*, XXVII (Jan. 1952), 12-16. Williams, *The Roots of the Modern American Empire* (New York, 1970), uses momentum of expansion created by the frontier to explain much of modern foreign policy.

12. Merrill H. Crissey, "Professor Turner's Last Years," HEH TU Box 57, Folder: Merrill H. Crissey. Drafts of Biographical Data.

13. Turner to Maurice G. Fulton, Oct. 12, 1931, HEH TU Box 46.

14. Turner to Max Farrand, Oct. 26, 1914, HEH TU Box X. Memorandum giving Turner's schedule for summer, HC on WH Corr., Box 5, Folder: Turner, F. J.

15. Turner to Charles H. Haskins, June 18, 1914, Princeton, Haskins Papers.

16. Copy of article, with Turner's notations, HEH TU File Drawer 15B, Folder: Commencement Address University of Washington.

17. Turner to Arthur M. Schlesinger, May 5, 1925, HEH TU Box 34.

18. Arthur M. Schlesinger to Turner, May 2, 1925; Frederick Merk to Turner, May 18, 1925, HEH TU Box 34.

19. Turner to Schlesinger, May 5, 1925; Turner to Merk, May 6, 1925, HEH TU Box 34.

20. Turner to Merk, Jan. 9, 1931, HEH TU Box 45.

21. For the attack on Turner, see Ray A. Billington, *The American Frontier Thesis: Attack and Defense* (Washington, D.C., 1971), and Billington, *America's Frontier Heritage* (1966).

22. Turner to John C. Parish, April 14, 1926, HEH TU Box 35.

23. George W. Bell, "Lecture Notes. History of the West. Harvard University, 1910-1911, and T. C. Smith, "Lecture Notes: The History of the West. Harvard University, 1910-1911," first lecture, HEH TU File Drawer 14C, Folder: Notes on Professor Turner's History of the West.

24. Turner to Luther L. Bernard, Nov. 24, 1928, HEH TU Box 40.

25. "Sectionalism in American History, January 1, 1926," HEH TU File Drawer 14D, Folder: MSS. Geographical Sectionalism in American History; and "Some Sociological Aspects of American History, April 13, 1895," HEH TU File Drawer 15A, Folder: Some Sociological Aspects.

26. Turner, "The Last Quarter Century, 1890-1916," HEH TU File Drawer 15A, Folder: Lecture Univ. of Chicago, 1916.

27. Turner, "Some Sociological Aspects of American History, April 13, 1895," HEH TU File Drawer 15A, Folder: Some Sociological Aspects.

28. Turner, "Summary Hist. 17 1st Half," HEH TU File Drawer 13C, Folder: Turner, Frederick Jackson. Summary of First Term's Work.

29. Turner to Claude H. Van Tyne, April 25, 1908, Clements, Van Tyne Papers; Turner to Arthur H. Buffinton, Oct. 20, 1926, HEH TU Box 35A.

30. Turner to Reginald F. Arragon, July 31, 1924, HEH TU Box 33.

31. Turner to Arthur H. Buffinton, Oct. 20, 1926, HEH TU BOX 35A.

32. Turner, "The Middle West, 1830-1850: The Formation of a New Society," Carnegie Institution Lecture, HEH TU File Drawer F, Folder: U.S. Chap. VII North Central States.

33. Turner to Dorothy A. Dundore, July 22, 1924, HEH TU Box 33.

34. Turner to Merle Curti, Aug. 27, 1928, HEH TU Box 39.

35. George P. Ettingheim, "Notes on Lectures in Turner's 'History of the West Course,' Harvard University, 1911-1912," SHSW, MSS Division.

36. Turner, "Lecture in History of Liberty Series," HEH TU File Drawer 10B, Folder: History of Liberty. Colonial Period.

37. Turner to Isaiah Bowman, Dec. 24, 1931, HEH TU Box 46.

38. Turner, "Lowell Lectures, 1918," First lecture, HEH TU File Drawer E1, Folder: Lowell Lectures, 1918.

39. Notation made while reading Norman Ware, *The Industrial Worker, 1840-1860* (Boston, 1924), HEH TU File Drawer 14C, Unmarked folder.

40. Turner to Colin Goodykoontz, June 21, 1927, Western History Collections, University of Colorado, Boulder. Turner to James F. Willard, Dec. 23, 1929, lists suggested research topics (HEH TU Box 42).

41. Fragment of a lecture on "The Far West, 1830-1850," HEH TU File Drawer K1, Folder: V The Far West; "Memorandum on the Huntington Library," HEH TU File Drawer 15A, Folder: Memo. Turner on Research Materials.

42. Albert G. Waite, "Frederick J. Turner Lecture Notes in History 10b, Harvard University, spring term, 1903-1904," Harvard Univ. Arch., Call No. HUC 8903.338.10.92, Lecture for May 11, 1904.

43. Turner's note, HEH TU File Drawer 7B, Folder: Western Classes; folder with materials on farm-making costs, HEH TU File Drawer F5, Folder: Cost of Moving. Turner's conclusions coincided almost exactly with those of one of his later critics, Clarence H. Danhoff, "Farm-Making Costs and the 'Safety Valve': 1850-1860," *Journal of Political Economy*, XLIX (June 1941), 317-59.

44. Notes, HEH TU File Drawer 7B, Folder: Western Classes.

45. Notes on land speculation, HEH TU File Drawer 3A, Folder: Speculative Land Companies in Virginia, and 7A, Folders: N.Y. Speculation.

46. Lectures on sectionalism for Univ. of Wisconsin, April 1925, notes, HEH TU File Drawer 14C, Folder: University of Wisconsin Lectures.

47. Turner to Arthur H. Buffinton, Oct. 27, 1922; Turner to Frederick Merk, Feb. 17, 1927; Turner to Frank W. Fetter, Oct. 25, 1927, HEH TU Boxes 31 and 37.

48. This phrase, with slightly different wording, was used by Turner in his lecture on Hermann von Holst delivered in 1894, in his "Problems on the West" in the *Atlantic Monthly* in 1896, in his *The Rise of the New West* in 1906, and in his commencement address at the University of Washington in 1914 on "The West and American Ideals." The last is the best-known version.

49. Statement in Turner's first Lowell lecture, 1918, HEH TU File Drawer E1, Folder: Lowell Lectures, 1918. For his interpretation of American democracy, see Irving Kristol, "American Historians and the Democratic Idea," *American Scholar*, XXXIX (Winter 1969-70), 97-99.

50. Turner used the first phrase in his "Essay on von Holst's History," pp. 35-36 (HEH TU File Drawer 15A, Folder: Essay on History of U.S. by von Holst); the second in his Lowell lecture on "The Middle West" (HEH TU File Drawer E1, Folder: Lowell Lectures).

51. Turner, "History of Liberty Lectures," HEH TU File Drawer 10B, Folder: History of Liberty. Introduction.

52. Turner, "Lowell Lectures, 1918. First Lecture," HEH TU File Drawer E1, Folder: Lowell Lectures, 1918; Turner, "Sectionalism in American Politics. Lecture at Pasadena Feb. 20, 1928," HEH TU File Drawer 14D, Folder: Sectionalism in American Politics, 1928.

53. Turner, "Some Sociological Aspects of American History," HEH TU File Drawer 15A, Folder: Some Sociological Aspects of American History.

54. Single sheet of paper, HEH TU File Drawer 5C, Folder: Land Claims and Cessions.

55. Turner, "Lowell Lectures, 1918. First Lecture," HEH TU File Drawer E1, Folder: Lowell Lectures, 1918.

56. Ibid.

57. For Turner's reaction to the closing of the frontier, see Ray A. Billington, "Frederick Jackson Turner and the Closing of the Frontier," Roger Daniels (ed.), *Essays in Western History in Honor of T. A. Larson* (Laramie, Wyo., 1971), 45-56.

58. Turner, "Social Forces in American History," *The Frontier in American History* (New York, 1920), 320.

59. Two half-sheets, HEH TU File Drawer 17B, Folder: US 1890-1909. Bryan-Roosevelt Era.

60. Homer C. Hockett, "Lecture Notes in the History of the West," Lecture of August 6, 1902, HEH TU File Drawer 15C, Folder: Lecture, History of the West, 1902.

61. Lecture notes, HEH TU File Drawer L1, Folder: Sequence to End of Frontier. During the 1920s Turner reversed his position again, to embrace

the "rugged individualism" preached by Herbert Hoover (see above, pp. 441–42).

62. E. E. Dale, "Turner—The Man and Teacher," *University of Kansas City Review,* XVIII (Autumn 1951), 27.

63. Charles O. Paullin to Max Farrand, Oct. 11, 1932, HEH TU Box 49.

64. Turner to Max Farrand, March 23, 1911, HEH TU Box 16.

65. Merrill H. Crissey, "Notes on Frederick Jackson Turner," HEH TU Box 57, Folder: Merrill H. Crissey. Drafts of Biographical Data.

66. Turner's printed articles on sectionalism, with his annotations and corrections, HEH TU File Drawer L1, Folder: Sections. Printed Articles.

67. Handwritten section labeled "Incorporate this in preface or concluding chapter," HEH TU File Drawer A1, Folder: Introduction.

68. Fragment of lecture on "The Upland South: the Colonization of a Province," HEH TU File Drawer 3A, Folder: Formation of Upland South.

69. Talk to Association of American Geographers, 1926. Abstract printed as "Geographic Sectionalism in American History," *Annals of the Association of American Geographers,* XVI (June 1926), 205-6.

70. Turner, "The Significance of the Section in American History," in Turner, *The Significance of Sections in American History* (New York, 1925), 48-49.

71. Turner to Dixon Ryan Fox, March 27, 1919, HEH TU Box 29. Turner's notes on sectionalism, from which these quotations were taken, are in HEH TU File Drawer 18D, Folder: Sectionalism, 1926. With them are numerous clippings on the subject.

72. Turner to Dixon Ryan Fox, March 27, 1919, HEH TU Box 29.

73. Notes listing faults of maps in revealing data, HEH TU File Drawer 10A, Folder: US 1830-1850. New England Politics.

74. An excellent analysis of Turner's problems is in a manuscript article by Richard Jensen, "The Development of Quantitative Historiography in America," which he was kind enough to let me read.

75. Turner to Merle Curti, Sept. 8, 1930, HEH TU Box 44.

76. Merrill H. Crissey, "Notes on Frederick Jackson Turner," HEH TU Box 57, Folder: Merrill H. Crissey. Drafts of Biographical Data.

77. Turner, "Significance of Sections in American History," *loc. cit.* 45.

78. Turner to Norman Foerster, Aug. 6, 1926, HEH TU Box 35A.

79. Turner to A. M. Schlesinger, May 5, 1925, HEH TU Box 34.

Chapter XIX
The Significance of Frederick Jackson Turner
in American History

1. J. F. Jameson to Robert S. Woodward, July 3, 1913, in Elizabeth Donnan and Leo F. Stock (eds.), *A Historian's World: Selections from the Correspondence of John Franklin Jameson* (Philadelphia, 1956), 158.

2. Max Farrand to Turner, Feb. 24, 1908, HEH TU Box 10.

3. *Wisconsin State Journal,* Feb. 3, 7, 8, 10, 1910.

4. Gisle Bothne to Turner, Feb. 4, 1910; Turner to Bothne, Feb. 10, 1910, HEH TU Box 14. Turner's letter has been printed in Theodore C. Blegen

(ed.), "Frederick Jackson Turner and the Kensington Puzzle," *Minnesota History*, XXXIX (Winter 1964), 133-40.

5. J. F. Jameson to Clarence W. Bowen, Oct. 15, 1901, Donnan and Stock (eds.), *An Historian's World*, 78.

6. Turner to J. F. Jameson, Oct. 13, 1905. LC, Jameson Papers. For history of this project, see John K. Wright, Jr., "J. Franklin Jameson and the Atlas of the Historical Geography of the United States," Ruth A. Fisher and William L. Fox (eds.), *J. Franklin Jameson: A Tribute* (Washington, D.C., 1965), 66-79.

7. Turner's "Prior Notes for Meeting of April 6, 1923," and "Minutes of Meeting of Committee on American Biography, April 6-7," are bound with correspondence on the genesis of the *Dictionary of American Biography* in HEH TU Vol. VIII. A history of the enterprise is Dumas Malone, "J. Franklin Jameson and the Dictionary of American Biography," in Fisher and Fox (eds.), *J. Franklin Jameson*, 80-84.

8. Turner to Mrs. William Hooper, Nov. 16, 1924, HEH TU-H Box 5. Committee reports, letters, and copy of agreement, HEH TU Vol. VIII.

9. Jameson to Turner, April 28, 1924, ibid. Waldo G. Leland to Turner, Dec. 15, 1928, tipped into Turner's copy of J. F. Finley, *Dictionary of American Biography* (New York, 1928), HEH, Accession No. 126689.

10. Turner to Merle Curti, Aug. 8, 1928, HEH TU Box 39.

11. Frederick J. Turner, The Development of American Society," *The [Illinois] Alumni Quarterly*, II (July 1908), 120-21.

12. Turner to Arthur M. Schlesinger, April 18, 1922, HEH TU Box 31.

13. Turner, Phi Beta Kappa lecture, Univ. of Nebraska, June 10, 1907, HEH TU Box 55.

14. Frederick J. Turner, "The Historical Library in the University," in John Carter Brown Library, *The Dedication of the Library Building, May the Seventeenth, A. D. MDCCCCIIII. With the Addresses of William Vail Kellen, LL.D., and Frederick Jackson Turner, Ph.D.* (Providence, 1905), 57.

15. Turner, Phi Beta Kappa lecture, Univ. of Nebraska, June 10, 1907, HEH TU Box 55.

16. Turner to Richard H. Dana, May 3, 1915, HEH TU Box 24.

17. Turner to Kenneth W. Colgrove, July 21, 1919, HEH TU Box 29.

18. Turner to Edward N. Bristol, June 11, 1897, Princeton, Holt Arch.

19. Turner, "Historical Library in the University," *loc. cit.* 48-49.

20. Turner, Review of J. W. Burgess, *The Middle Period, 1817-1858*, *The Educational Review*, XIV (Nov. 1897), 390-91.

21. Turner, "Recent Studies in American History," *Atlantic Monthly*, LXXVII (June 1896), 841.

22. Turner, "Lecture for History 32b," April 12, 1915, HEH TU File Drawer 22B, Folder: Class Lectures. Period 1865-1887.

23. Turner to Merle Curti, Aug. 8, 27, 1928, HEH TU Box 39.

24. Turner, Phi Beta Kappa lecture, Univ. of Nebraska, June 10, 1907, HEH TU Box 55.

25. Turner to Marcus L. Hansen, Jan. 7, 1926, HEH TU Box 35.

26. Turner to E. M. Violette, Jan. 18, 1907, HEH TU Box 8.

27. Turner, "Outline for Address on History and the Local Historical Society," HEH TU Box 56.

28. Turner to T. P. Abernethy, March 12, 1926, HEH TU Box 35.
29. Max Farrand to Turner, Oct. 23, 1909, HEH TU Box 13.
30. Turner, "Historical Library in the University," *loc. cit.* 52-53.
31. Turner to John E. Iglehart, Jan. 14, 1930, HEH TU Box 43.
32. "Answer of Professor Turner," Hist. Survey, Univ. of Ill.: Alvord Papers; Turner to Mr. Holzbog, Nov. 2, 1923, HEH TU Box 32.
33. Note by Fulmer Mood inserted in HEH TU File Drawer D2, Folder: Justice of the Mexican War.
34. Turner to Max Farrand, Oct. 19, 1909, HEH TU Box 13.
35. Turner to Carl Becker, Feb. 13, 1926, HEH TU Box 35.
36. Turner listed his students who had entered various fields (HEH TU Box 56).
37. Turner to Constance L. Skinner, March 15, 1922, HEH TU Box 22.
38. Ibid.
39. Max Farrand to Turner, Feb. 23, 1905, HEH TU Box 5.
40. Turner to Mae Turner, July 14, [1903], HEH TU Box F. Arrangements for the Johns Hopkins lectures are discussed in John M. Vincent to Turner, April 16, 1906, Feb. 25, 1907; Turner to Vincent, May 14, 1906, March 10, 19, 1907, HEH TU Boxes 7 and 8.
41. Samuel F. Bemis to Turner, July 21, 1925; Turner to Bemis, Aug. 13, 1925, HEH TU Box 34A.
42. Frederick J. Turner, *The United States, 1830-1850: the Nation and Its Sections* (New York, 1935), 286. Turner's influence on immigration studies is appraised in Edwin Mims, Jr., *American History and Immigration* (Bronxville, N.Y., 1950).
43. Turner to L. E. Aylesworth, Aug. 4, 1902, SHSW, Turner Papers; Turner to Marcus L. Hansen, June 20, 1926, HEH TU Box 35.
44. Allan H. Spear, "Marcus Lee Hansen and the Historiography of Immigration," *Wisconsin Magazine of History*, XLIV (Summer 1961), 258-68, is brief biography. Carlton C. Qualey, "Marcus Lee Hansen," *Midcontinent American Studies Journal*, VIII (Fall 1967), 18-25, is less flattering.
45. Turner to Marcus L. Hansen, June 20, July 11, 1926, HEH TU Boxes 35 and 35A.
46. Turner to Marcus L. Hansen, Dec. 21, 1926, HEH TU Box 35A.
47. Turner to Marcus L. Hansen, July 22, 1927, HEH TU Box 37.
48. Turner to Arthur M. Schlesinger, April 18, 1922, HEH TU Box 31.
49. *The Aegis*, VI (April 8, 1892), 448.
50. Charles A. Beard, *An Economic Interpretation of the Constitution of the United States* (New York, 1913), 5-6.
51. Charles A. Beard to Merle Curti, Aug. 9, [1928], HEH TU Box 39.
52. Turner, "Development of American Society," *loc. cit.* 133-34.
53. Turner to Merle Curti, Aug. 15, 1928, HEH TU Box 39.
54. Turner to John R. Commons, Nov. 30, 1908; Turner to Carl Becker, March 25, 1909, HEH TU Boxes 11 and 12.
55. Marcus L. Hansen to Turner, Nov. 27, 1929, HEH TU Box 42.
56. Turner to Max Farrand, Feb. 13, 1919; Turner to Dorothy A. Dundore, May 23, 1923; Turner to E. E. Robinson, March 3, 1924, HEH TU Boxes 29, 32, and 33.
57. Merle Curti to Turner, Aug. 18, 1931, HEH TU Box 46.

58. Turner, "The High School and the City," HEH TU Box 54.

59. Notes on western cities, HEH TU File Drawer 6A, Folder: Cities, 1790-1800; "Outline of a possible book," File Drawer 8D, Folder: West Cities, 1820-1830.

60. Homer C. Hockett, "Classroom Lecture Notes, History of the West, August 6, 1902," HEH TU File Drawer 15C, Folder: Lecture History of the West 1902.

61. Quoted in Arthur M. Schlesinger, "The City in American History," *Mississippi Valley Historical Review*, XXVII (June 1940), 43.

62. HEH TU File Drawer 14A, Folder: City, Frontier and Section.

63. Turner to Merle Curti, Aug. 8, 1928; Turner to Luther L. Bernard, Nov. 24, 1928; HEH TU Boxes 39 and 40. Last quotation from pages marked "Omit from lecture on sectionalism" (HEH TU File Drawer 14A, Folder: Talk on Sectionalism, April 1922).

64. *Daily Cardinal*, Feb. 18, 1897.

65. Turner to Carl Becker, Dec. 1, 1925, HEH TU Box 34A.

66. Turner to Luther L. Bernard, Nov. 24, 1928, HEH TU Box 40.

67. Frederick J. Turner, "Problems in American History," reprinted in Turner, *The Significance of Sections in American History* (New York, 1932), 20-21.

68. Turner, "Memorandum to Max Farrand, 1927," HEH TU Box 36; Turner to Max Farrand, March 8, 1927, HEH TU Box 36.

69. Isaiah Bowman to Turner, Feb. 17, March 13, April 7, 1914, HEH TU Box 21.

70. John Koren to Turner, Nov. 18, 1913; William F. Ogburn to Turner, Dec. 15, 1924, HEH TU Boxes 20A and 33.

71. Franklin H. Giddings to Merle Curti, Aug. 20, 1928, HEH TU Box 39.

72. Avery Craven's remarks, delivered by Max Farrand at Turner's funeral service, are in HEH TU File Drawer 57.

BIBLIOGRAPHICAL NOTE

The following bibliographical note makes no attempt to list or appraise the voluminous literature dealing with Frederick Jackson Turner's frontier and sectional hypotheses. This is described in Ray A. Billington, *The American Frontier Thesis: Attack and Defense* (American Historical Association Pamphlet No. 101, Washington, D.C., 1971), and analyzed in Billington, *America's Frontier Heritage* (New York, 1966). Some of the principal articles attacking or defending the frontier thesis have been gathered in George R. Taylor (ed.), *The Turner Thesis Concerning the Role of the Frontier in American History* (Boston, 1949, and later editions); Lawrence Burnette, Jr. (ed.), *Wisconsin Witness to Frederick Jackson Turner: A Collection of Essays on the Historian and the Thesis* (Madison, 1961); Ray A. Billington, *The Frontier Thesis: Valid Interpretation of American History?* (New York, 1966); and Richard Hofstadter and Seymour M. Lipset, *Turner and the Sociology of the Frontier* (New York, 1968).

A largely complete bibliography of Turner's essays, reviews, and other publications, compiled by Everett E. Edwards, is in Frederick J. Turner, *The Early Writings of Frederick Jackson Turner* (Madison, 1938), 233-72. Edwards, however, failed to locate a few items in geographical journals, the most important being a review article, "Geographical Interpretations of American History," *Journal of Geography*, IV (January 1905), 34-37. Turner's essays have been collected and published in Turner, *The Early Writings*, mentioned just above, Turner, *The Frontier in American History* (New York, 1920), and Turner, *The Significance of Sections in American History* (New York, 1932). The most useful articles from these three volumes have been assembled in Ray A. Billington (ed.), *Frontier and Section: Selected Essays of Frederick Jackson Turner* (Englewood Cliffs, N.J., 1961). Other essays, unpublished during Turner's lifetime, have been edited by Wilbur R. Jacobs, *Frederick Jackson Turner's Legacy: Unpublished Writings in American History* (San Marino, Calif., 1965), reprinted in paperback as *America's Great Frontiers and Sections: Frederick Jackson Turner's Unpublished Essays* (Lincoln, Neb., 1969). In addition to his essays, Turner completed two books, *The Rise of the New West, 1819-1829* (New York, 1906; paperback edition, New York, 1962); and *The United States, 1830-1850: the Nation and Its Sections* (New York, 1935).

Since Turner's death in 1932, several of his lesser writings have been edited for publication by Fulmer Mood and Wilbur R. Jacobs. Mood prepared "Little Known Fragments of Turner's Writings," *Wisconsin Magazine of History*, XXIII (March 1940), 328-41; "Frederick Jackson Turner's History of the Grignon Tract on the Portage of the Fox and Wisconsin Rivers," *Agricultural History* XVII (April 1943), 113-20; and "Frederick Jackson Turner's Address on Education in the United States Without Free Lands," *Agricultural History*, XXIII (Oct. 1949), 254-59. Jacobs edited "Frederick Jackson Turner's Notes on the Westward Movement, California, and the Far West," *Southern California Quarterly*, XLVI (June 1964), 161-68; "Research in Agricultural History: Frederick Jackson Turner's View in 1922," *Agricultural History*, XLII (Jan. 1968), 15-22; "*Wider Frontiers*—Questions of War and Conflict in American History: The Strange Solution of Frederick Jackson Turner," *California Historical Society Quarterly*, XLVII (Sept. 1968), 219-36; and "Frederick Jackson Turner's Views on International Politics, War and Peace," *Australian National University Historical Journal*, VI (Nov. 1969), 10-15.

Two volumes of Turner's letters have appeared in recent years: Wilbur R. Jacobs (ed.), *The Historical World of Frederick Jackson Turner. With Selections from His Correspondence* (New Haven, 1968), and Ray A. Billington (ed.), with the collaboration of Walter Muir Whitehill, *"Dear Lady": The Letters of Frederick Jackson Turner and Alice Forbes Perkins Hooper, 1910-1932* (San Marino, Calif., 1970).

A few brief biographical sketches of Turner have been written. Of these the best is Merle Curti, *Frederick Jackson Turner* (Mexico, D.F., 1949). Less comprehensive are Wilbur R. Jacobs, "Frederick Jackson Turner," *The American West*, I (Winter 1964), 32-35, 78-79, reprinted in slightly extended form in Wilbur R. Jacobs, John W. Caughey, and Joe B. Frantz, *Turner, Bolton, and Webb. Three Historians of the American Frontier* (Seattle, 1965); Richard Hofstadter, *The Progressive Historians. Turner, Beard and Parrington* (New York, 1968), which deals largely with Turner's ideas; and Howard R. Lamar, "Frederick Jackson Turner," in Marcus Cunliffe and Robin W. Winks (eds.), *Pastmasters: Some Essays on American Historians* (New York, 1969), 74-109.

Other articles have explored aspects of Turner's life. The most comprehensive of these is Fulmer Mood, "The Development of Frederick Jackson Turner as a Historical Thinker," *Transactions of the Colonial Society of Massachusetts, 1937-1942*, XXXIV (Boston, 1943), 283-352, a germinal study. Less valuable is the same author's "Turner's Formative Period," in Turner, *The Early Writings of Frederick Jackson Turner*, 3-39. Both deal with his education and early teaching career as it influenced his thought. Other periods are described in Ray A. Billington, "Young Fred Turner," *Wisconsin Magazine of History*, XLVI (Autumn 1962), 38-48; Fulmer Mood, "Frederick Jackson Turner and the Milwaukee *Sentinel*, 1884," *Wisconsin Magazine of History*, XXXIV (Autumn 1950), 21-28; Fulmer Mood, "Frederick Jackson Turner and the Chicago *Inter-Ocean*, 1885," *Wisconsin Magazine of History*, XXXV (Spring 1952), 188-94, 210-18; Ray A. Billington, "Frederick Jackson Turner Visits New England: 1887," *New England Quarterly*, XLI (Sept. 1968), 409-36; Wilbur R. Jacobs, "Wilson's First Battle at Princeton: The Chair for Turner," *Harvard Library Bulletin*, VIII (Winter 1954), 74-87; George C. Osborn, "Woodrow Wilson and Frederick Jackson Turner," *Proceedings of the New Jersey Historical Society*, LXXIV (July 1956), 208-29; Ray A. Billington, "Frederick Jackson Turner Comes to Harvard," *Massachusetts Historical Society Proceedings*, LXXIV (1962), 51-83; Ray A. Billington, "Frederick Jackson Turner and Logan's 'National Summer School,' 1924," *Utah Historical Quarterly*, XXXVII (Summer 1969), 307-36; and Max Farrand, "Frederick Jackson Turner at the Huntington Library," *Huntington Library Bulletin*, III (Feb. 1933), 157-64.

A number of Turner's friends and former students recorded their reminiscences, some of which shed a great deal of light on his character and thought. The best of these include: Joseph Schafer, "The Author of the Frontier Hypothesis," *Wisconsin Magazine of History*, XV (Sept. 1931), 86-103; Louise P. Kellogg, "The Passing of a Great Teacher," *Historical Outlook*, XXIII (Oct. 1932), 270-72; Grace L. Nute, "Frederick Jackson Turner," *Minnesota History*, XIII (June 1932), 159-61; Frederick Merk, "Frederick Jackson Turner," *American Historical Review*, XXXVII (July 1932), 823-24; Max Farrand, "Frederick Jackson Turner: A Memoir," *Massachusetts Historical Society Proceedings*, LXV (May 1935), 432-40; Avery Craven, "Frederick Jackson Turner, Historian," *Wisconsin Magazine of History*, XXV (June 1942), 408-24; Avery Craven, "Some Historians I Have Known," *The Maryland Historian*, I (Spring 1970), 1-11; Avery Craven, "A History Still Unwritten," *Western Historical Quarterly*, II (Oct. 1971), 377-83; Edward E. Dale, "Memories of Frederick Jackson Turner," *Mississippi Valley Historical Review*, XXX (Dec. 1943), 339-58; Edward E. Dale, "Turner—The Man and Teacher," *University of Kansas City Review*, XVIII (Autumn 1951), 18-28; Ulrich B. Phillips, "The Traits and Contributions of Frederick Jackson Turner," *Agricultural History*, XIX (Jan. 1945), 21-23; Wilbur R. Jacobs (ed.), " 'Turner As I Remember Him,' by Herbert Eugene Bolton," *Mid-America*, XXXVI (Jan. 1954), 54-61; and A. C. Krey, "My Reminiscences of Frederick Jackson Turner," *Arizona and the West*, III (Winter 1961), 377-81.

Three of Turner's friends recorded their recollections of him for the Oral History Research Office of Columbia University: "The Reminiscences of Frank Maloy Anderson," an important document in the story of the Frederick Bancroft rebellion against the American Historical Association in 1915; "The Reminiscences of Guy Stanton Ford," which contain an excellent account of Turner as a teacher; and "The Reminiscences of Arthur M. Schlesinger."

Any study of Turner's historical and methodological concepts should begin with articles by two of his most gifted students: Carl Becker, "Frederick Jackson Turner," in Howard W. Odum (ed.), *American Masters of Social Science* (New York, 1927), 273-318, a warm portrait of the man and teacher; and Merle Curti, "The Section and the Frontier in American History; The Methodological Concepts of Frederick Jackson Turner," in Stuart A. Rice (ed.), *Methods in Social Science. A Case Book* (Chicago, 1931),

353-67, a brilliant analysis. Rudolf Freund, "Turner's Theory of Social Evolution," *Agricultural History*, XIX (April 1945), 78-87, and George D. Blackwood, "Frederick Jackson Turner and John Rogers Commons—Contemporary Thinkers," *Mississippi Valley Historical Review*, XLI (Dec. 1954), 471-89, deal with Turner's status as a social scientist, and his borrowings and contributions to the social sciences.

Aspects of Turner's background, education, training, and teaching that helped him formulate the frontier hypothesis are investigated in Ray A. Billington, *The Genesis of the Frontier Thesis: A Study in Historical Creativity* (San Marino, Calif., 1971). This volume includes letters written by Turner in his later years in which he speculated on the origins of his thesis; one of these, written to Constance L. Skinner, was earlier published as "Turner's Autobiographical Letter," *Wisconsin Magazine of History*, XIX (Sept. 1935), 91-103. Three important articles on the intellectual climate at the time the thesis was developed are: Gilman M. Ostrander, "Turner and the Germ Theory," *Agricultural History*, XXXII (Oct. 1958), 258-61; which shows that Turner relied more on the germ theory than he would have admitted; Robert E. Lerner, "Turner and the Revolt Against E. A. Freeman," *Arizona and the West*, V (Summer 1963), 101-8, demonstrating that English scholars were rebelling against the overemphasis on political history; and William Coleman, "Science and Symbol in the Turner Frontier Hypothesis," *American Historical Review*, LXXII (Oct. 1966), 22-49, a brilliant analysis of developments in biology and geography as they influenced Turner's thought.

In recent years historians have become aware that Turner's contributions extended far beyond his frontier and sectional theories. Two articles that explore his multitudinous interests in general terms are: Wilbur R. Jacobs, "The Many-Sided Frederick Jackson Turner," *Western Historical Quarterly*, I (Oct. 1970), 363-72, and Ray A. Billington, "Frederick Jackson Turner: Non-Western Historian," *Transactions of the Wisconsin Academy of Sciences, Arts and Letters*, LIX (1971), 7-21. In "Turner's Methodology: Multiple Working Hypothesis or Ruling Theory?" *Journal of American History*, LIV (March 1968), 853-63, Wilbur R. Jacobs argues that Turner was guilty of treating his frontier and sectional concepts as ruling theories, not as hypotheses to be tested, while in "Colonial Origins of the United States: The Turnerian View," *Pacific Historical Review*, XL (Feb. 1971), 21-38, he demonstrates Turner's contributions to the study of the colonial era. Jack Anderson, "Frederick Jackson Turner and Urbanization," *Journal of Popular Culture*, II (Fall 1968), 292-98, examines Turner's published works to show that he was fully aware of the significance of the city in American development. A stimulating analysis of Turner's social thought is Paul M. Maginnis, "The Social Philosophy of Frederick Jackson Turner," an unpublished Ph.D. dissertation submitted at the University of Arizona in 1969.

Wilbur R. Jacobs, "Frederick Jackson Turner—Master Teacher," *Pacific Historical Review*, XXIII (Feb. 1954), 49-58, was prepared before the author had access to the Frederick Jackson Turner papers, and hence needs revision. Turner's inability to write major books is the theme of Ray A. Billington, "Why Some Historians Rarely Write History: A Case Study of Frederick

Jackson Turner," *Mississippi Valley Historical Review*, L (June 1963), 3-27. Indicative of a growing interest in Turner's writings by students of non-historical disciplines are Harold P. Simonson, "Frederick Jackson Turner: Frontier History as Art," *Antioch Review*, XXIV (Summer 1964), 201-11, Merrill E. Lewis, "The Art of Frederick Jackson Turner: the Histories," *Huntington Library Quarterly*, XXXV (May 1972), 241-55; Goodwin F. Berquist, "The Rhetorical Heritage of Frederick Jackson Turner," *Transactions of the Wisconsin Academy of Sciences, Arts and Letters*, LIX (1971), 23-32, and Ronald H. Carpenter, "The Rhetorical Genesis of Style in the 'Frontier Hypothesis' of Frederick Jackson Turner," *Southern Speech Communication Journal*, XXXVII (Spring 1972), 233-48, the first two by professors of English, the last two by professors of speech. Turner's views on one subject are explored in Ray A. Billington, "Frederick Jackson Turner and the Closing of the Frontier," in Roger Daniels (ed.), *Essays in Western History in Honor of T. A. Larson* (Laramie, Wyo., 1971), 45-56.

Revealing as these secondary works are, the basic story of Frederick Jackson Turner's life must be extracted from the manuscript collections in which his letters and documents have been preserved. They have been the principal source used in preparing this book. The "Turner Papers" themselves are deposited in four libraries; in addition, other materials pertinent to his career are in numerous other manuscript collections. In the listing that follows, the "Turner Papers" are first described, then the additional depositories that have been used. In each instance, the italicized phrase in parentheses following each designation is the abbreviation employed in the notes to this volume.

I. Frederick Jackson Turner Papers, Henry E. Huntington Library and Art Gallery, San Marino, Calif. On his death in 1932 Turner willed the Huntington Library all of his letters and documents, as well as his books. Since that time the collection has been greatly increased by gifts of additional correspondence and manuscripts from former students, friends, and especially his daughter, Mrs. John S. Main. Moreover, duplicates have been obtained of the more important Turner letters from other depositories, as well as newspapers, magazines, and other published works essential to the study of Turner's career. These manuscripts, supplemented by Turner's own books with their annotations and marginal comments, make the Huntington Library essential to any serious study of Turner. His papers have been opened to qualified scholars since January 1960, and they have been much used. They fall into several categories:

A Correspondence, Manuscripts and Documents

1. General Correspondence (*HEH TU Box 1 ff.*) Seventy-two flat boxes of letters and related documents, each in a separate folder, chronologically arranged. Boxes 1 through 52 contain letters to and from Turner, Boxes 53 through 57 manuscripts of his speeches and similar items, and Boxes 58 through 62 ephemera, business papers, pages from his pocket diaries, and photographs. Box 63 holds his correspondence with Henry Holt & Co., his principal publisher, much of it photocopied from the Holt & Co. Archives, Firestone Library, Princeton University.

2. Turner-Hooper Correspondence (*HEH TU-H Box 1 ff.*) Alice Forbes Perkins Hooper, daughter of Charles Elliott Perkins and husband of William Hooper of Manchester, Massachusetts, began a correspondence with Turner in 1910 that lasted until his death. This is the only sustained body of letters left by Turner. It is housed in ten boxes, the last two containing typed versions of the manuscripts. The best of these letters have been published in Ray A. Billington (ed.), *"Dear Lady": The Letters of Frederick Jackson Turner and Alice Forbes Perkins Hooper, 1910-1932* (San Marino, Calif., 1970).

3. Family Letters (*HEH TU Box A ff.*) Letters between Turner and members of his family fill eleven boxes, designated A through K. Most important are letters written by Turner to his fiancé between 1887 and 1889, when he was in graduate school.

B   Reading and Research Notes

1. Reading Notes and Lectures (*HEH TU File Drawer 1A ff.*) Turner left the Huntington Library twenty-two file drawers filled with his notes, clippings, manuscripts, lectures, and assorted materials. These are now housed in cardboard boxes, five boxes to each original drawer, designated as File Drawer 1A, 1B, etc. File Drawers 14 and 15 contain many of Turner's speeches and drafts of articles, some unpublished.

2. Notes on Sectionalism (*HEH TU File Drawer A1 ff.*) Twelve file drawers left by Turner were filled with notes on sectionalism which he used in preparing his last book, *The United States, 1830-1850: The Nation and Its Sections* (New York, 1935). They also contain drafts of speeches and other materials essential to understanding his views on the sections. The materials are contained in cardboard boxes, five to each original file drawer, designated as File Drawer A1, A2, etc.

3. Three-by-five file drawers (*HEH TU 3×5 File Drawer 1 ff.*). Nineteen metal 3×5 inch file drawers hold the thousands of brief notes kept by Turner. These include bibliographical cards, research notes, lecture notes, and the like. Drawers 1 and 2 were apparently begun during the 1890s and contain materials important to his early teaching career and the origins of his frontier thesis. Drawers 13 through 19 house the notes used in dictating his last volume.

4. Manuscript volumes (*HEH TU Vol. 1 ff.*) Twenty volumes of albums, scrapbooks, manuscripts, and the like were compiled (and usually bound) by Turner to be shelved separately from his other collections. These include the Commonplace Books he kept as a graduate student, his early syllabi, and the Red Book and Blue Book presented on his leaving Wisconsin in 1910 and Harvard in 1924.

C   Miscellaneous Documents

1. Newspaper and Magazine Clippings (*HEH TU Black Box 1 ff.*). Nineteen black boxes kept by Turner are filled with clippings, pamphlets, magazine articles, and other printed materials, all catalogued and filed by number. In them are some of the census bulletins that influenced his thought on the frontier.

2. Maps (*HEH TU Maps 1 ff.*) Two large boxes hold the many maps drawn by Turner in connection with his studies of sectionalism.

3. Lantern Slides (*HEH TU Lantern Slides 1 ff.*). Lantern slides made under Turner's supervision and used in his lectures fill nine boxes.

II. Frederick Jackson Turner Papers, The Houghton Library, Harvard University, Cambridge, Mass. (*Houghton: Turner Papers*). One box contains letters given to Harvard University by Turner at the time of his retirement. This holds three folders: (1) seven letters from Woodrow Wilson to Turner, 1889-1902, and two from William E. Dodd concerning Wilson's views on the frontier thesis, (2) seven letters from Theodore Roosevelt to Turner, 1894-98, and (3) Letters from Walter Hines Page and other editors of the *Atlantic Monthly*, 1896-99.

III. Frederick Jackson Turner Papers, State Historical Society of Wisconsin, Madison, Wis. (*SHSW: Turner Papers*). Turner presented to the library of the State Historical Society three boxes of papers, most of them related to the state's history. Box 1 contains items associated with Turner's father, Andrew Jackson Turner; Box 2 a few letters and many manuscripts dealing with his teaching at the university, and Box 3 notes taken by Turner while a student, as well as some of the classroom notes used by his professor, William F. Allen.

IV. Frederick Jackson Turner Papers, Archives of the University of Wisconsin, The Memorial Library, University of Wisconsin, Madison, Wis. (*U. of Wis. Arch., L&S, Hist., Turner Corr., Box 1 ff.*). Six boxes of Turner's papers, kept largely when he was chairman of the department of history, are officially catalogued as "College of Letters and Science. Department of History. Turner Correspondence, 1901-1905. Series N 7/16/2. Boxes 1-6." The first five boxes contain letters to and from Turner dealing with departmental and university affairs, but scattered through them are others having to do with his publishing and scholarly activities. Box 6 has one folder of correspondence, but is filled largely with reports and items on the administration of the School of History. In addition to these six boxes, the Archivist maintains a small file of miscellaneous Turner material in his outer office, filed in a desk drawer. This has been referred to as *U. of Wis. Arch., Misc. File: Frederick Jackson Turner.*

While the bulk of the most useful Frederick Jackson Turner materials are included in the four collections described above, other important letters and documents may be found in numerous other collections. The most important of these are:

Charles Kendall Adams Papers, State Historical Society of Wisconsin, Madison, Wisconsin. (*SHSW: Adams Papers*). A sparse collection filling only one box, and covering the years 1872-1902. Many more of President Adams's letters are in the University of Wisconsin Archives, President's File, listed below.

William Francis Allen Papers, State Historical Society of Wisconsin, Madison, Wisconsin (*SHSW: Allen Papers*). One box of papers, covering the period from March 1848 to December 1889, and consisting largely of Allen's diplomas, transcripts, and articles. Included, however, are some of his class record books with notations about Turner and his work.

Clarence W. Alvord Papers, Illinois Historical Survey of the University of Illinois, 418 Lincoln Hall, Urbana, Ill. (*Hist. Survey Univ. of Ill.: Alvord Papers*). This collection contains some thirty letters exchanged between Alvord and Turner between 1908 and 1931. Copies have been supplied the Huntington Library through the kindness of Mrs. Marguerite J. Pease, Director.

American Historical Association Papers, Manuscripts Division, Library of Congress, Washington, D.C. (*LC: AHA Papers*). The Association's papers fill 211 linear feet of shelf space, and contain more than 155,000 items. Materials for the 1892-93 period when Turner was preparing and presenting his frontier thesis are disappointingly few. They are plentiful, however, for the years when Turner was active in the Association, and especially for the 1914-15 era, when Frederic Bancroft staged his rebellion against the establishment. Particularly useful are Boxes 27-31 (Secretary File for 1915), Boxes 243-49 (Executive Council Secretary File), Boxes 255-56 (Minutes of Council Meetings), Boxes 257-85 (Editorial Correspondence, *American Historical Review*), and Box 370, which contains only materials related to the Bancroft affair.

Charles McLean Andrews Papers, Historical Manuscripts Division, Yale University Library, New Haven, Conn. (*Yale: Andrews Papers*). Andrews was a student with Turner at Johns Hopkins University; his letters for the 1888-89 academic year describe the life that Turner knew, although they do not mention Turner.

Frederic Bancroft Papers, Special Collections, Columbia University Library, New York, N.Y. (*Columbia: Bancroft Papers*). Four boxes in this voluminous collection contain letters and documents essential to an understanding of Frederic Bancroft's rebellion against the "ring" that operated the American Historical Association. A microfilm copy of the contents of these boxes has been supplied the Huntington Library through the courtesy of the Columbia University Library.

Carl Becker Papers, Collection of Regional History and University Archives, Albert R. Mann Library, Cornell University, Ithaca, N.Y. (*Cornell: Becker Papers*). Letters to and from Turner and Becker for the years 1896 to 1932 provide one of the richest sources on Turner's historical beliefs. Some of the most important of these, exchanged while Becker was preparing his article on Turner (listed above), have been printed in Ray A. Billington, *The Genesis of the Frontier Thesis: A Study in Historical Creativity* (San Marino, Calif., 1971).

Edward A. Birge Papers, State Historical Society of Wisconsin, Madison, Wis. (*SHSW: Birge Papers*). Birge, a professor of biology, dean, and president of the University of Wisconsin, was not one of Turner's intimate friends, but they shared many common problems during their years together in Madison. The papers fill fifteen boxes, covering the period 1897 to 1948.

Herbert Eugene Bolton Papers, The Bancroft Library of the University of California, Berkeley, Calif. (*Bancroft: Bolton Papers*). Included in this large collection are sixty-six letters exchanged between Bolton and Turner during the years 1909-28. Copies of these have been deposited in the Turner Papers at the Huntington Library through the initiative of Professor Wilbur R. Jacobs.

George Lincoln Burr Papers, Division of Regional History and Archives, Cornell University Library, Ithaca, N.Y. (*Cornell: Burr Papers*). Burr was active with Turner in the American Historical Association, and he was deeply involved in the Frederic Bancroft rebellion. Thirty-eight letters in the collection touch on this episode, including many exchanged with Turner.

Thomas C. Chamberlin Papers, Department of Special Collections, University of Chicago Library, Chicago, Ill. (*Chicago: Chamberlin Papers*). Seven boxes of papers largely dealing with Chamberlin's scientific projects, conservation, and the like. Little on his activities at the University of Wisconsin, when as president he dealt much with Turner.

University of Chicago Archives, Department of Special Collections, University of Chicago Library, Chicago, Ill. (*U. of Chi. Arch.: Dept. of Hist. Papers*). Eight Turner letters have been preserved, two in the President's Papers, written to President William Raney Harper, and six in the Department of History Papers for the period 1912-16.

Richard T. Ely Papers, State Historical Society of Wisconsin, Madison, Wis. (*SHSW: Ely Papers*). This collection of 279 boxes of letters and manuscripts contains more than fifty letters between Ely and Turner, largely for the period 1892 to 1894, when Turner was arranging Ely's transfer to the University of Wisconsin. A "Turner Index" is available on cards, but it is incomplete.

Carl Russell Fish Papers, State Historical Society of Wisconsin, Madison, Wis. (*SHSW: Fish Papers*). This comprises seventeen boxes covering the period from 1891 to 1932. Most of the letters deal with the period after 1910, when Turner left Wisconsin, but some touch on his activities in Madison.

Ginn and Company Papers, Boston, Mass. (*Boston: Ginn and Co.*). Turner's correspondence with this company, dealing largely with the textbook he contracted to prepare for them, was destroyed when the firm moved some twenty years ago. Only one contract, that of 1910 for the volume he prepared with Edward Channing and Albert Bushnell Hart, remains. I am indebted for this information to Mr. Henry M. Halvorson of Ginn and Company.

George Ellery Hale Papers, University Archives, California Institute of Technology, Pasadena, Calif. (*Cal. Tech.: Hale Papers*). Hale, a well-known astronomer and promoter of scientific projects, was influential in bringing Turner to the Huntington Library in 1927. His correspondence, arranged alphabetically under the names of individuals and institutions, contains a great deal of information on the appointment. It is filed under Henry E. Huntington, Max Farrand, Henry M. Robinson, H. M. Goodwin, and Elihu Root.

Harvard Commission on Western History Papers, Harvard University Archives, Widener Library, Harvard University, Cambridge, Mass. (*Widener: HC on WH Corr.*). Twelve boxes of letters deal with the formation of the commission and its operation to 1920; the collection also contains card indexes, lists of acquisitions, and other items. Many of Turner's letters that are included deal with non-commission matters, and were apparently filed by mistake when he was active in the commission.

Harvard University Archives, Class Lists (*Harvard Arch.: Class Lists*). Large scrapbooks in which are pasted printed or mimeographed lists of students enrolled in each class for each term. Some for the World War I period are missing. An important source of information on Turner's teaching at Harvard.

Charles Homer Haskins Papers, The Firestone Library, Princeton University, Princeton, N.J. (*Princeton: Haskins Papers*). This collection contains a number of letters from Turner, largely for the period before 1910. It is, however, disappointing, for Haskins and Turner were intimate friends and wrote often and confidentially. If Haskins had saved more of the many letters he received, the collection would be extremely valuable.

Henry Holt & Co. Archives, Firestone Library, Princeton University, Princeton, N.J. (*Princeton: Holt Archives*). Included are some fifty letters from Turner, largely for the periods about 1897, 1920, and the late 1920s, when he was corresponding regularly concerning his last book. They admirably supplement the letters from Holt & Co. in his own correspondence at the Huntington Library.

Henry E. Huntington Library and Art Gallery, Huntington Biographical File, San Marino, Calif. (*Huntington: Biographical File*). This extensive documentary collection on the history of the Library contains a number of letters from Turner dealing with his appointment and research at the Library. Also included are three volumes of Minute Books of the Board of Trustees for 1919-23, the "Trustees' Files," and the "Hale Letters," having much on Turner's career in Pasadena.

John Franklin Jameson Papers, Manuscripts Division, Library of Congress, Washington, D.C. (*LC: Jameson Papers*). Filling 181 boxes, this is an essential collection in the study of any topic in American historiography for the period between the 1890s and 1921. It includes numerous letters to and from Turner, together with fragmentary information on his 1893 paper, the latter contained in Box 7.

Johns Hopkins University Seminar Records, Johns Hopkins University Archives, The Library, Johns Hopkins University, Baltimore, Md. (*JHU: Seminar Records*). These records, kept by an appointed secretary from within the class, are in two versions, one the handwritten copy taken by the secretary, the other the final typed form. The records of the latter for the 1888-89 year when Turner was in attendance fill pages 387-449 of the minutes book. A microfilm copy is in the Henry E. Huntington Library.

Charles A. Krey Papers, University Archives, University of Minnesota Library, Minneapolis, Minn. (*Minnesota: Krey Papers*). This collection of 278 folders contains several letters from Turner, written to Krey, his former student.

Victor H. Lane Papers, Michigan Historical Collections, Rackham Building, University of Michigan, Ann Arbor, Mich. (*Mich. Hist. Coll.: Lane Papers*). Judge Lane was one of the University of Michigan representatives dealing with the athletic controversy that involved Turner in 1905 and 1906. Several letters from and to Turner shed light on the conflict.

Orin G. Libby Papers, State Historical Society of North Dakota, Bismarck, N.D. (*SHSND: Libby Papers*). Libby, Turner's student and colleague, exchanged many letters with his teacher, but failed to keep a single one. His papers are valuable only for the light that they shed on his own career, of which Turner was particularly proud.

A. Lawrence Lowell Papers, Harvard University Archives, Widener Library, Harvard University, Cambridge, Mass. (*Harvard Arch.: Lowell Papers*). This collection contains a number of letters concerning Turner's appointment to the Harvard faculty and concerning the operations of the Harvard Commission on Western History. I have been allowed access through special action of the Harvard authorities, and particularly through the courtesy of Clifford K. Shipton, university archivist.

Andrew C. McLaughlin Papers, Department of Special Collections, University of Chicago Library, Chicago, Ill. (*Chicago: McLaughlin Papers*). A small collection covering the period 1899-1938, filling only eight boxes. The first three boxes hold letters to and from Professor McLaughlin, some of them from Turner.

The Macmillan Company Archives, New York, N.Y. (*New York: Macmillan Company*). Only three of Turner's letters to George P. Brett concerning a contract for a textbook have survived. Copies of those have been supplied the Huntington Library by Mr. Harry H. Cloudman of the Macmillan Company.

William F. Poole Papers, The Newberry Library, Chicago, Ill. (*Newberry: Poole Papers*). Twenty-six boxes of letter, chronologically arranged, cover the period from 1858 to 1894. Many have to do with Poole's role as chairman of the committee arranging the session in Chicago in 1893 where Turner read his paper on "The Significance of the Frontier."

Dunbar Rowland Papers, Mississippi Department of Archives and History, Jackson, Miss. (*Miss. Arch.: Rowland Papers*). Among the 6000 pieces housed in this collection are some thirty letters to or from Rowland having to do with the 1914–15 rebellion in the American Historical Association.

Joseph Schafer Papers, State Historical Society of Wisconsin, Madison, Wis. (*SHSW: Schafer Papers*). Schafer, as Turner's most loyal student, preserved all letters received from his teacher. These are scattered through the extensive collection of his papers. All to or from Turner have been photostated, and copies added to the Turner Papers at the Huntington Library.

Albion W. Small Papers, Department of Special Collections, University of Chicago, Chicago, Ill. (*Chicago: Small Papers*). Box I of this small collection deals with the Congress of Arts and Sciences at the 1904 St. Louis Exposition where Turner spoke; Small was vice president in charge of arrangements.

Henry Morse Stephens Papers, University of California Archives, University of California Library, Berkeley, Calif. (*Calif.: Stephens Papers*). Several letters from Turner are included, but none dealing with the 1908-9 period when the University of California history department, with Stephens at the helm, was trying to lure Turner to its faculty.

Reuben Gold Thwaites Papers, State Historical Society of Wisconsin, Madison, Wis. (*SHSW: Thwaites Papers*). A number of letters to and from Turner were preserved by Thwaites during his period as superintendent of the State Historical Society of Wisconsin.

Charles R. Van Hise Papers, State Historical Society of Wisconsin, Madison, Wis. (*SHSW: Van Hise Papers*). Most of Van Hise's papers as president of the University are in the university archives, presidential papers (see below), but this collection of nine boxes of correspondence contains some information on Turner.

Claude H. Van Tyne Papers, Clements Library, University of Michigan, Ann Arbor, Mich. (*Clements: Van Tyne Papers*). Of the nine boxes in this collection, four contain correspondence for the period 1901 to 1930, arranged chronologically. Several letters from Turner are included.

Woodrow Wilson Papers, Manuscripts Division, Library of Congress, Washington, D.C. (*LC: Wilson Papers*). A voluminous collection, including a number of letters from Turner during the years 1889-1902. All will eventually appear in the definitive set being edited by Arthur Link, *The Papers of Woodrow Wilson* (Princeton, 1966 ff.).

University of Wisconsin Archives. Included in this invaluable depository are a number of groups of papers essential to the telling of Turner's story. These are:

Board of Regents Executive Committee, 1888-1939 (*U. of Wis. Arch.: Regents Exec. Comm.*). A series of committee reports and documents originating in or submitted to the executive committee of the Board of Regents of the university. Series 1/1/2, Box 1 ff.

Board of Regents Minutes (*U. of Wis. Arch.: Regents Minutes*). Large volumes, handwritten, and with two or three volumes to the year. Paged. Series 1/1/1, Vol. 1 ff.

Class of 1884 Minutes (*U. of Wis. Arch.: 1884 Minutes*). A single paperbound notebook kept by the secretaries of the class of 1884 during the four years the class was in the university. But few mentions of Turner, who was apparently not active in class affairs. Series: IWXF 1884 X.

College of Letters and Science. Administration. Dean's Files (*U. of Wis. Arch.: L and S, Dean's Files*). Included are numerous letters from Turner concerning departmental and university affairs. The correspondence is largely with Dean Birge. Series 7/1/12-2 and 7/1/2-1.

Instructional Reports, Fall 1886 to Spring 1910. (*U. of Wis. Arch.: Instructional Reports*). Each term instructors reported the courses taught, the hours of instruction, the number of students enrolled, and the like. Those prepared by Turner shed light on his teaching. They are filed in a series of boxes in the university archives.

Minutes of the Meetings of the University Faculty, September 1900–July 1961 (*U. of Wis. Arch.; Minutes of Univ. Faculty*). Volumes 5–7 cover the period when Turner was a member of the faculty. Disappointingly brief, but essential especially for the story of Turner's battle against professional football.

Presidents of the University. General Correspondence (*U. of Wis. Arch.: Pres. Corr.*). Included are 142 boxes of general correspondence to and from the presidents of the university, arranged chronologically with letters filed alphabetically within chronological periods. A number of important Turner letters can be easily located. Numbered as follows: Chamberlin Series 4/7/1; Adams Series 4/8/1; Van Hise Series 4/9/1.

University Faculty. Athletic Board. Frederick Jackson Turner (*U. of*

Wis. Arch.: Athletic Board). A single box filled with clippings and reports concerning the athletic controversy of 1905-7. Obviously prepared by Turner, with annotations in his hand. Series 5/21/5.

University Faculty. Secretary of the Faculty. Faculty Minutes, Documents, etc. (*U. of Wis. Arch.: Faculty Sec.*). Committee reports and other documents submitted to the faculty, arranged chronologically by meetings. Series 5/2/2.

Yale Review Papers, The Beinecke Library, Yale University, New Haven, Conn. (*Beinecke: Yale Review Papers*). A folder labeled "F. J. Turner" contains a dozen or more letters, most of them dealing with the publication of his articles in the *Yale Review*.

Among the manuscript sources used in preparing this book were several sets of student lecture notes taken in Turner's classes, and one student diary. Those that proved most useful were:

K. M. Elish, "Frederick J. Turner Lecture Notes in History 32b, Harvard University, 1915-1916," Harvard University Archives, Call No. HUC 8915.338.32. An excellent set of notes, taken by a student who apparently knew some shorthand, with a number of direct quotations.

George P. Ettenheim, "Notes on Lectures in Turner's 'History of the West' Course," Harvard University, 1911-1912. This full set of notes is owned by the library of Washington State University, Pullman, Wash. A set on microfilm has been supplied the Huntington Library. Full notes, including tables and maps.

Homer C. Hockett, "Lecture Notes, 'History of the West,' " University of Wisconsin, Summer 1902. These notes are scattered through the File Drawers of the Turner Papers at the Huntington Library, filed according to topic. Hockett took shorthand; the notes are full and informative.

Horace J. Smith, "Lecture Notes: History of the West," Harvard University, 1910-11. The author kept full notes, which are bound into a volume with examination questions, the syllabus, and blue books. The notes are in HEH TU Vol. XXIII.

Theodore C. Smith, "Lecture Notes: The History of the West," Harvard University, 1910-11. Careful notes by a good student, in handwritten and typed version, covering the entire year of the course. They are in HEH, TU File Drawer 14C, Folder: Smith, T. C., Student Notes.

Albert G. Waite, "Frederick J. Turner Lecture Notes in History 10b, Harvard University, Spring Term, 1903-1904," Harvard University Archives, Call No. 8903.338.10.92. Some 200 pages of notes on the semester course given by Turner when he visited Harvard University during the 1903-4 academic year. The entire westward movement is covered in one half-year.

Edwin E. Witte, "Diary." Witte was a student at the University of Wisconsin in 1909-10 and kept a full diary, recording his impressions of Turner's seminar and of his resignation from the faculty. The diary is in the possession of the Manuscripts Division, State Historical Society of Wisconsin.

Newspapers

Essential as manuscript sources have proven in preparing this book, many events could not be dated and many others would have escaped notice without a careful reading of the newspapers associated with each phase of Turner's life. The following have proved valuable.

At Portage, Wisconsin, for the period 1861 through 1894:

Wisconsin State Register. This weekly newspaper began publication on March 16, 1861, and a month later Andrew Jackson Turner, Frederick J. Turner's father, became one of the publishers. In February, 1878, he sold his interests to John T. Clark, but the paper continued through the 1890s.

The Portage Democrat. A weekly paper launched on April 13, 1877, to offset the strong Republican bias of the *Register.* Less local news was published and more attention given to political causes. Read through 1894.

Portage Daily Register. The first issue appeared on March 1, 1886, published by the firm then publishing the *Wisconsin State Register.* It contained six columns on four to eight sheets daily. Issues between 1886 and 1894 have been read for this study.

At Madison, Wisconsin, for the period 1881 to 1910:

Wisconsin State Journal. This was Madison's leading paper, rivaled only by a smaller Democratic paper. It was published daily, in from four to twelve pages, and contained a regular column of "University News" as well as coverage of all town events. Numerous speeches and activities of Turner are recorded. Read for the period 1881 through 1910.

At the University of Wisconsin, for the period 1878 to 1910:

The University Press. The first undergraduate newspaper and literary magazine at the University, published by a private group representing the literary societies between 1871 and 1885 as a semi-monthly or weekly journal. Volumes VII through XVIII, covering the period from 1876 to 1886, have been read for this biography.

The Campus. A weekly undergraduate newspaper, started in October 1881 by students who resented the private control of *The University Press,* and published through December of that year. One literary article a week was published in its twelve pages, together with notes, campus news, and editorials.

The Badger. Weekly undergraduate newspaper, successor to *The Campus,* and published by the same group between January 1882 and June 1885. It contained in its eight to twelve pages a "Local" column, news items, editorials, and other features. In September 1885 it merged with *The University Press.*

The Aegis. Published between September 1886 and June 1900, this weekly paper displaced *The University Press* as the official student newspaper of the University of Wisconsin. In 1892, with the establishment of a rival daily paper, it became a bi-weekly publication with greater stress on literary articles, and in October 1895, a monthly literary magazine.

The Daily Cardinal. Published first on April 4, 1892, this daily undergraduate newspaper represented the student body during the remainder of Turner's years at Wisconsin. Issues from the first through 1910 have been read. Although woefully inadequate in reporting local news, it is an essential source for Turner's activities. Copies of this, and of all other university publications, are in the Archives of the University of Wisconsin; microfilm copies have been supplied the Huntington Library.

Magazines at the University of Wisconsin:

The Trochos. A class yearbook containing information on class activities, the faculty, and university affairs. Published between April 1884 and February 1887.

The Badger. A successor to *The Trochos,* published as a yearbook each year by the junior class after February 1888. Read for the period 1888 through 1910.

The Sphynx. The campus humor magazine began publication in September 1899, with the usual jokes, verse, cartoons, and stories. Published every other week, it contained a number of quips involving Turner and one brief item by him. Read for the period 1899 through 1910.

The Wisconsin Literary Magazine. The usual collection of stories, verse, and articles by undergraduates. Published monthly after December 1903. Surprisingly little on Turner or the intellectual atmosphere on the campus. Read through 1911.

Newspaper at Harvard University

The *Boston Evening Transcript.* A daily Boston paper with a great deal of emphasis on Harvard events. Read for specific periods between 1910 and 1924.

INDEX

Abernethy, Thomas P., as FJT's student, 332

A. C. McClurg Company, plans book by FJT, 204

Adams, Charles K.: ignores "significance of the Frontier," 129; as president of Wisconsin, 132; seeks to keep FJT at Wisconsin, 155-56; enlists FJT as writer, 190; resigns from Wisconsin, 240

Adams, George Burton, presidential address, 314-15

Adams, Herbert Baxter: suggests study of land systems, 29; FJT's courses with, 60; as founder of AHA, 63-64; as advocate of "germ" theory, 65-66; organizes extension program, 69-71; plans textbook, 72; influence on FJT, 74-75; wants FJT at Johns Hopkins, 80; examines FJT, 87; supports FJT for professorship, 88; named to Johns Hopkins professorship, 91; aids extension program at Wisconsin, 97-98; praises FJT essay, 106; arranges 1893 AHA meeting, 124-26; views on New England towns, 162-63; theories discredited, 282

Adams, James Truslow, works read by FJT, 483

Adams, Thomas S., in football controversy, 267

Adelphian Society: FJT helps form, 19-20; FJT as member, 23-24

Aegis, The, FJT's "Problems" essay in, 104-5

Agricultural College of Utah, FJT at summer school, 392-93

Agricultural history, FJT as pioneer in, 365

Agricultural History Society, FJT addresses, 365

Aikman, Robert K., as Johns Hopkins student, 59

Albert Shaw Lectures, FJT invited to deliver, 170, 486

Alden, George H., as FJT's student, 144

Allen, William Francis: introduces FJT to historical studies, 25-26; views on nature of history, 26; teaching methods, 26-31; FJT's tributes to, 31, 389; takes leave from teaching, 36; employs FJT as assistant, 37; as FJT's graduate director, 38; illness, 43; influence on FJT, 47; arranges book reviewing for FJT, 48; asks FJT to prepare outline on West, 49-50; organizes lecture series, 51-53; supervises FJT's masters thesis, 54-56; use of maps by, 62; FJT reads paper for, 68; views on institutions, 75; FJT explains frontier views to, 79; death, 86-87; views on sectionalism, 213

Almack, John A., attacks FJT's frontier thesis, 450

Ambler, Charles H.: as graduate student, 254; FJT aids publication of book by, 256; recommended by FJT, 256; supports rebellion against AHA leadership, 342-43; FJT sends book to, 360; writes on sectionalism, 467

Hale, Edward Everett: book reviewed by Turner, 48; on 1893 AHA program, 125; comments on "Significance of the Frontier," 130

Hale, George Ellery, lures FJT to Huntington Library, 402-3

Hancock Point, Me., Turners vacation at, 237, 308; FJT buys house, 376; summers at, 376-77; 379; 382, 383, 384, 394, 401, 404-5, 411; efforts to sell house, 413; FJT's love of, 434-35

Haney, Lewis H., as FJT's graduate student, 254

Hanford, Samuel, as FJT's ancestor, 4

Hanford, Thomas, as FJT's ancestor, 4-5

Hansen, Marcus L., as FJT's student, 332, 487-89

Harding, Warren G.: FJT opposes views, 355; FJT distrusts, 441

Harper, William Rainey, offers FJT professorship, 154-56; death, 269

Harper & Brothers, publishes *Rise of the New West*, 217-23

Harrison, Frederick, works read by Turner, 476-77

Hart, Albert B.: edits *Rise of the New West*, 217-23; teaches seminar with FJT, 237; entertains FJT, 238; recommends C. R. Fish to Wisconsin, 243; as lecturer at Wisconsin, 249; quoted 283; uses frontier thesis in textbook, 284; arranges courses with FJT, 305; as Harvard colleague, 310-11, prepares *Guide to American History*, 317-18; publishes FJT's articles, 318

Harvard Bulletin, welcomes FJT, 300

Harvard Commission on Western History, FJT forms, 321-22

Harvard Crimson, praises FJT, 389

Harvard *Guide to American History*: prepared by Channing, Hart, and FJT, 317-18; royalties from, 319

Harvard History Club, FJT speaks to, 388

Harvard La Follette Club, FJT speaks to, 440

Harvard University: FJT teaches at, 237-39; offers C. R. Fish position, 245; offers FJT professorship, 297-300; awards FJT honorary degree, 299; FJT moves to, 305-7; state of education, 309-10; history department, 310-12; undergraduate teaching, 327-29; graduate teaching, 329-36; in World War I, 349-52; FJT resigns from, 385-90

Haskins, Charles Homer, as Johns Hopkins student, 59, 66, 70-71; accepts Wisconsin instructorship, 88; made professor, 92; offers seminar with FJT, 95-96; accompanies FJT to 1893 AHA meeting, 126; names new faculty members, 134; assistant provided for, 153; declines Chicago professorship, 155; accompanies FJT to 1904 St. Louis fair, 180; edits historical series for Henry Holt & Company, 201; vacations with FJT, 227; accepts Harvard professorship, 243; attracts FJT to Harvard, 297; as Harvard colleague, 310; proposes FJT *festschrift*, 316; as family friend, 320; delivers FJT paper to Wilson, 355; at retirement dinner, 388

Hedges, James B., as FJT's student, 331

Hendrickson, C. L., accompanies FJT to historical meeting, 126

Henry, William W., on 1893 AHA program, 125

Henry Holt & Company, contracts for FJT textbook, 201-4; efforts to secure textbook, 223-26; publishes *Frontier in American History*, 358-60; cancels FJT's note, 362-63; signs contract for Lowell Lectures, 375; seeks to secure manuscript of *The United States, 1830-1850*, 383-84, 401; loses maps, 410; publishes last FJT books, 416-18

Herbertson, A. J., contributes to sectional studies, 211

Hewes, Fletcher W.: as statistical cartographer, 116-17; contributes to sectional studies, 212

Hibbard, Benjamin H.: as FJT's student, 254; recommended by FJT, 256

Hilgard, E. W., contributes to sectional studies, 211

Hinsdale, B. A., comments on "Significance of the Frontier," 130

Historical and Economic Club, FJT forms, 148

Historical and Political Science Association, formed at Madison, 92-93

Historical Outlook, urges publication of FJT essays, 357-58

History: A. J. Turner's interest in local, 18; at Wisconsin, 25-31; in 1884, 34; FJT's first teaching, 36-38; FJT begins graduate work, 38-39; teaching of, 43-44; at Johns Hopkins, 60-62; in

{ but there was only one, in 1910